MANUAL OF

HERBACEOUS
ORNAMENTAL PLANTS

FOURTH EDITION

by

DR. STEVEN M. STILL

Department of Horticulture

The Ohio State University

FIRST PRINTING

ISBN 0-87563-433-8

Published by
STIPES PUBLISHING COMPANY
10 - 12 Chester Street
Champaign, Illinois 61820

This book is dedicated to my
encouraging wife

Carolyn McKenzie Still

and my children

Steven McKenzie Still
Shannon Michael Still
Stephanie Michelle Still
Sara Maria Still

This edition is also dedicated to
my parents

Virgil (Mike) and Christina Still

who early on started me
on the garden path.

PREFACE

This text provides information about common and uncommon annuals, biennials, perennials, bulbs, ornamental grasses, herbs, and hardy ferns that are adapted to most climates of the United States and Canada. The fourth edition is larger than the previous edition and I expect that a future edition will be even larger. The learning process of a plantsman is a life-long endeavor and I will continue to discover new plants in my travels.

The idea for this text started developing when I was a student in a herbaceous plants course at the University of Illinois. At that time, I realized that there was no one text that included identification characteristics and the ornamental and cultural features necessary to obtain a complete understanding of the subject. This idea was further reinforced when I became an instructor of herbaceous plants at Kansas State University. I found it impossible to recommend any one book for student use because each had its advantages and disadvantages. This text provides the student, the professional, and the home gardener with illustrations and concise treatment of plant information.

I have had an opportunity to travel extensively in the United States, Canada, Europe, and Great Britain. Information gained in these travels has been incorporated in this expanded fourth edition. There are over 120 new plant descriptions and now a total of 384 color photos. Wildflowers and herbs are two examples of plant groups where coverage has been expanded.

Since the printing of the third edition of the *Manual of Herbaceous Ornamental Plants*, I have received many helpful suggestions of how this text could be enhanced. I am indebted to those individuals who took time to contact me with their suggestions. I have assimilated their comments and incorporated them in the fourth edition.

The art work for the fourth edition was done by Lynda Chandler. Art work for previous editions was by Jeanne E. Cardana, Jackie Neumann, Barbara Williams, Susan Warner, and Lynda Chandler. Proofreading and editing were accomplished by Carolyn Still and Denise Adams. Photographs were taken by the author.

INTRODUCTION

The plants in this text are arranged alphabetically by genus, with one plant type (taxon) discussed per page. Every plant is discussed in a defined manner and one can find a specific plant characteristic in approximately the same location on each page.

Each plant's scientific, common, and family names are the first items under each description. The scientific names are as accurate and current as possible. *Index Hortensis* was consulted for scientific names and common names were collected from many references. The family name was added so the reader can see the common floral or fruit characters that imply a familial relationship among the plants contained in this text. A pronunciation guide was included to aid the reader. I have often heard several pronunciations for the same plant. Some were so different that it was hard to believe the same plant was being discussed by two parties. Although there are no comprehensive rules for the pronunciation of botanical names, the use of the *Pronouncing Dictionary of Plant Names* for this text should provide one standard of use.

The discussion of leaves deals with the overall morphology, size, and color where important. The leaf and flower descriptions can be compared to the line illustrations.

Flowers are discussed in terms of color, form, size, and period of effectiveness (season of flower). This is an important section since the flower is often the major ornamental feature of herbaceous plants. If one wants to have a well-rounded collection of herbaceous plants, one should select plants with various flower colors, sizes, types of flowers, and foliage variety. The plant habits listed are also important for plant placement.

The section on culture discusses the effect of light, moisture, soil, fertility, climate, and other factors that are so important in the successful growth of herbaceous plants.

The utilization of a particular herbaceous plant is often an arbitrary decision. The landscape use chosen by one individual might be completely unacceptable to someone else. The landscape uses listed in this book are possible suggestions for the plant based on size, growth rate, texture, and other factors which effect plant placement.

The propagation section lists the most probable means of seed and vegetative propagation of herbaceous plants.

The information found under diseases and insects is a listing of problems encountered by certain species. When an insect or disease is a particular problem, it is discussed in some detail.

Zone hardiness is commonly applied to survival of plants at minimum temperatures. However, the growth performance of herbaceous plants is also affected by high temperatures, particularly in southern regions. I have compiled performance information from my observations of plant performance in southern zones. It has been traditionally thought that herbaceous plants, especially perennials, are best left to the gardener in northern areas. Fortunately, this is incorrect in many instances. The reader will find that many species are listed as good performers from Zone 4 to Zone 8.

Cultivars are as important in herbaceous plants as they are in woody landscape plants. They are important segments of modern day landscapes. I have tried to list, where feasible, the common and recent introductions of herbaceous plant cultivars.

Some of the plants are discussed under the heading "related species." Plants discussed under this section are useful landscape plants but are often similar enough to the species that unnecessary duplication of material would occur if a separate page were allotted for related species.

The section "additional notes" provides many interesting "extras" about a plant. Some notes may be quite useful, such as listing plants that may have poisonous properties, while other information lists the derivation of a scientific or common name which may provide more meaning to an unfamiliar name.

The last section of each page lists the natural distribution of a particular plant and also lists the life cycle, such as annual, perennial, etc.

In addition to the specific plant information, two other sections provide valuable information. Color prints of 384 different taxa provide the reader with a visual image of growth habits, flowers, and/or fruit.

Lists of plants for specific purposes should provide the reader with a handy reference from which to select plants for special purposes. These lists should prove useful to landscape architecture and landscape design students as a general guide. One can easily add to and delete from these lists as familiarity with herbaceous plants increases.

LEAF MARGINS

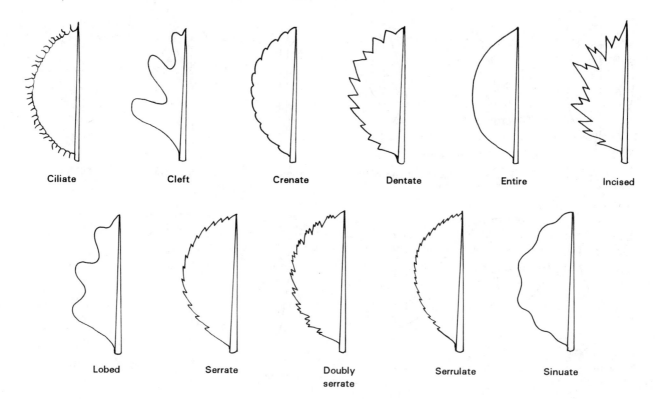

Ciliate   Cleft   Crenate   Dentate   Entire   Incised

Lobed   Serrate   Doubly serrate   Serrulate   Sinuate

LEAF TYPES

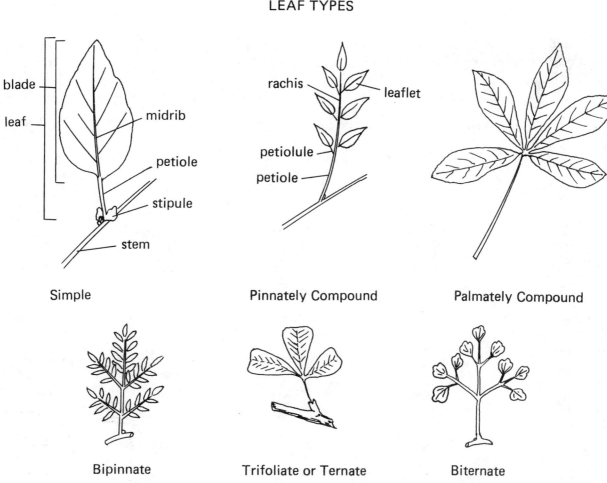

blade   midrib
leaf   petiole
          stipule
          stem

Simple

rachis   leaflet
petiolule
petiole

Pinnately Compound

Palmately Compound

Bipinnate   Trifoliate or Ternate   Biternate

LEAF SHAPES

Elliptic

Filiform

Lanceolate

Linear

Oblanceolate

Oblong

Obovate

Orbicular

Ovate

Reniform or Kidney

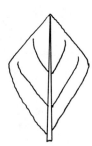
Rhomboid

Spatulate

LEAF APICES

Acuminate

Acute

Cuspidate

Emarginate

Mucronate

Obtuse

LEAF BASES

Auriculate

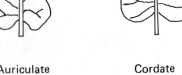
Cordate

Cuneate

Decurrent

Oblique

Obtuse

Peltate

Sagittate

Sheathing

Truncate

INFLORESCENCE TYPES

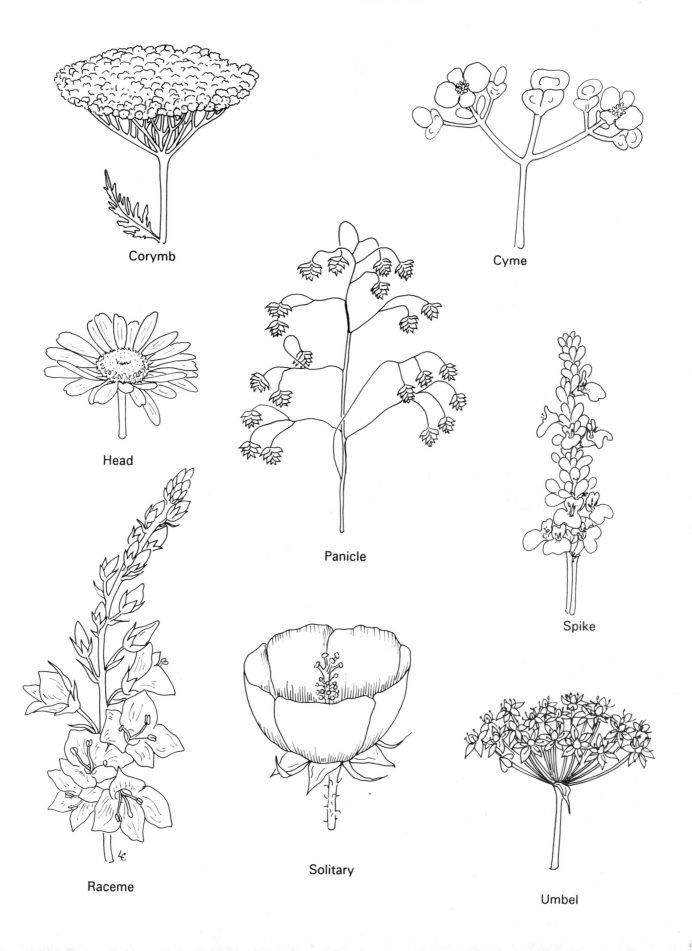

Corymb

Cyme

Head

Panicle

Spike

Raceme

Solitary

Umbel

FLOWER PARTS

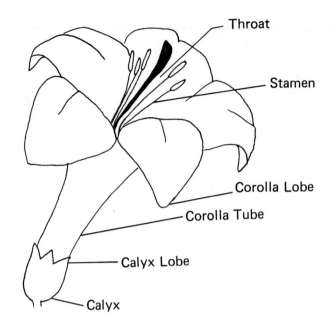

Throat

Stamen

Corolla Lobe

Corolla Tube

Calyx Lobe

Calyx

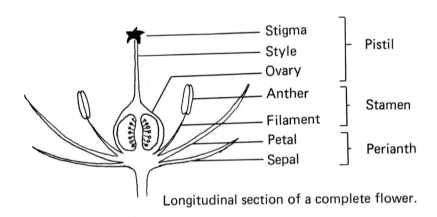

Stigma

Style

Ovary

} Pistil

Anther

Filament

} Stamen

Petal

Sepal

} Perianth

Longitudinal section of a complete flower.

COROLLA TYPES

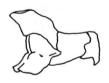

Bilabiate

Campanulate

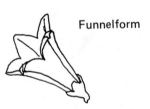

Funnelform

Papilionaceous

Rotate

Salverform

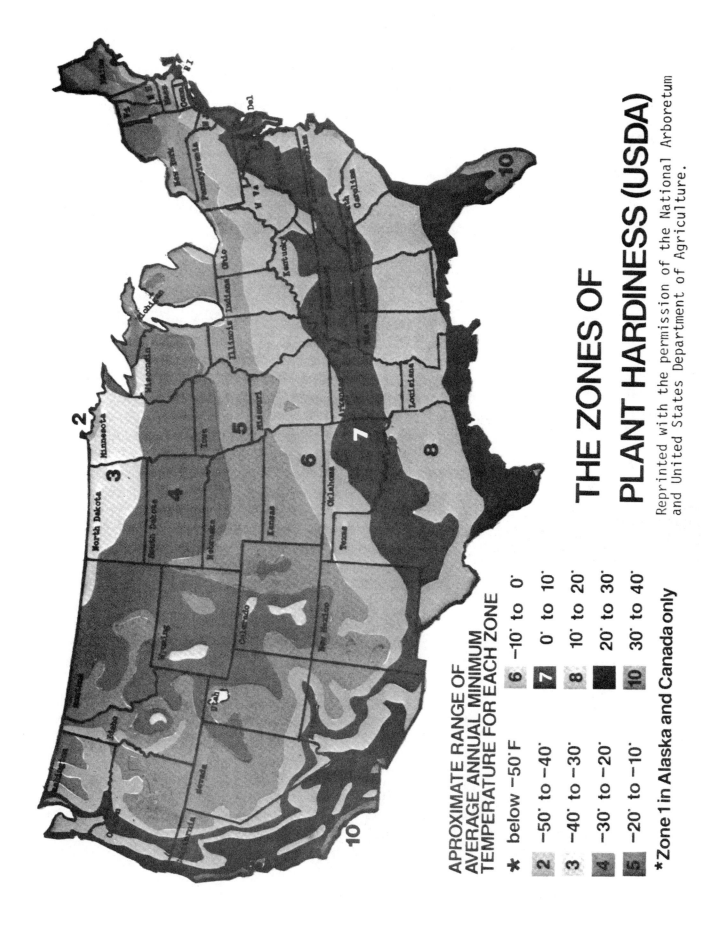

THE ZONES OF
PLANT HARDINESS (USDA)

Reprinted with the permission of the National Arboretum and United States Department of Agriculture.

APROXIMATE RANGE OF AVERAGE ANNUAL MINIMUM TEMPERATURE FOR EACH ZONE

✳ below −50° F		**6**	−10° to 0°
2 −50° to −40°		**7**	0° to 10°
3 −40° to −30°		**8**	10° to 20°
4 −30° to −20°			20° to 30°
5 −20° to −10°		**10**	30° to 40°

*Zone 1 in Alaska and Canada only

SCIENTIFIC NAME/FAMILY: *Abelmoschus moschatus*   Malvaceae
                        (Hibiscus abelmoschus)

                        (a-bel-mos'-chus mos-chā-tus)

COMMON NAME: Musk-mallow, Tropic Jewel Hibiscus

LEAVES: Alternate, 3"–5" long, palmately lobed into 3 to 5 toothed lobes, sparsely pubescent on both surfaces.

FLOWER: Scarlet flower with a white center, 3" to 4" across. The 5-petaled flower resembles a small hibiscus flower. The plant blooms continuously during the summer but the individual flowers last one day.

HABIT: Dense, mounded plant, 18" tall and 18" wide.

SEASON OF BLOOM: Midsummer to frost.

CULTURE: Full sun to partial shade in a fertile, moist, well-drained soil. It performs well in climates with hot summers.

UTILIZATION: Use as a bedding plant or as an edging plant in full sun. I have observed excellent plantings in Georgia where the summers are hot. This is an easily grown annual. Musk mallow is also cultivated in containers where its mounded, flowing habit combines well with taller plants.

PROPAGATION: Seed will germinate in 3 weeks at 75°–80°F. A soil temperature of 80°F will enhance growth and establishment.

DISEASES AND INSECTS: No serious problems.

CULTIVARS:
   'Mischief'—Cherry-red flowers with white centers.
   'Oriental Pink'—Pink flowers with white centers.
   'Oriental Red'—Red flowers with white centers.
   'Pacific' Series—This selection includes scarlet, pink, and mixed colors. 18" tall.

RELATED SPECIES:
   A. manihot (man'-i-hot) (*Hibiscus manihot*)—This species is another tropical perennial that is grown as an annual. It grows 5–6' tall and bears 6" diameter flowers in late summer. Useful as an accent plant or a plant for the back of the border. Plants should be spaced 2' to 3' apart in full sun or partial shade.

Native to Asia.   Annual

See color plate

SCIENTIFIC NAME/FAMILY: *Abutilon hybridum*   Malvaceae

(a-bū'ti-lon hīb'ri-dum)

COMMON NAME: Flowering Maple, Chinese Lantern

LEAVES: Alternate leaves, 3–4", with 3 to 5 lobes. The margins are serrate to crenate-dentate. Leaves may be green but are usually variegated or speckled with white. The leaves resemble variegated red maple leaves.

FLOWER: The showy flowers are solitary on axillary peduncles, usually drooping and are often trumpet-shaped and appear to be made of crepe paper. They are 2" wide and come in various shades and patterns of white, red, yellow and orange.

HABIT: Mounded plant 18"–30" high and 24" wide.

SEASON OF BLOOM: Summer

CULTURE: Full sun or partial shade in moist soil. In areas where day temperatures are often above 90°F, plants should be given afternoon shade. Pinching the stem tips will promote bushy plants. Plants should be spread 18" apart.

UTILIZATION: *Abutilon* is usually treated as a house plant but it can be grown outdoors as an annual. It is useful in the border or in containers. The variegated selections make nice specimen plants.

PROPAGATION: Seeds germinate in 3 weeks at 70°–75°F. Seed early as it takes about 5 months after germination before flowering starts. Cuttings can be taken in the fall before frost or in the spring from plants overwintered in the home or greenhouse.

DISEASES AND INSECTS: No serious problems.

CULTIVARS:
  'Eclipse'—Pink flowers, leaves with yellow variegation.
  'Insigne'—White flowers with red and purple veins.
  'Savitzii'—Foliage variegated green and white.

RELATED SPECIES:
  A. pictum (pik'-tum) (A. striatum)—This shrubby plant to 15 feet is also treated as an annual. The cultivar 'Thompsonii' has 3"–5" long leaves, with 3 or 5 lobes, that are liberally splashed with yellow spots. This 2'–3' tall cultivar has pink flowers and has the same landscape use as *A. hybridum*. The species is widely cultivated in the tropics.

Native to Brazil   Annual

Abutilon pictum

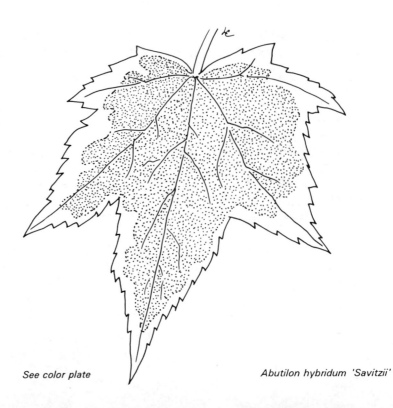

See color plate

Abutilon hybridum 'Savitzii'

SCIENTIFIC NAME/FAMILY: *Acanthus spinosus*   Acanthaceae

(à-kan'thus spī-nō'sus)

COMMON NAME: Spiny Bear's-breeches

LEAVES: Attractive basal leaves are deeply and irregularly pinnatifid; each lobe terminating in a rigid-appearing spine. However, the texture of the foliage is much softer than the appearance would lead one to believe. The shiny dark green leaves are leathery and 18"–24" long and 10"–12" wide.

FLOWER: The flowers are purple, sometimes white, and are borne in spikes atop 2' to 4' flower stalks. Individual flowers are 1" across and subtended by leaf-like, shiny green, often fringed bracts tipped with recurved spines. Intense pain occurs if the unsuspecting gardener unknowingly grabs the flower spike. The corolla is composed of a short tube with an expanded 3-lobed lower lip and no upper lip. Calyx is 4-lobed with 2 lobes smaller than the others.

HABIT: 3' to 4' mounded specimen that is 3' wide.

SEASON OF BLOOM: Midsummer.

CULTURE: *Acanthus* is best grown in partial shade and a well-drained soil. If the summers are cool, it will tolerate more sun and drier soils. Drainage is critical with this species. Plants should be heavily mulched in the fall in northern areas to prevent cold damage. In loose soils, *Acanthus* can spread quickly.

See color plate

UTILIZATION: The bold foliage of *Acanthus* makes it suitable for border use as a background or specimen plant.

PROPAGATION: *Acanthus* can be propagated by division, seed, or root cuttings. Divide every 4 to 5 years in spring. Sufficient moisture must be provided during reestablishment. Fresh seed will germinate in three weeks when kept at 70°F. Root cuttings 2" to 3" long can be taken in the spring. Excessive moving of *Acanthus* leaves fleshy root pieces at each site which grow into new plants.

DISEASES AND INSECTS: Slugs and snails can be problems.

HARDINESS: Zones 5–10.

RELATED SPECIES:

A. mollis (mol'lis), Bear's-breeches. The large glossy leaves are less lobed than those of *A. spinosus*. The flowers are not as abundant as *A. spinosus* but the attractive foliage more than makes up for the scanty flowers. This species is only hardy to Zone 8.

A. mollis var. *latifolius,* (lat-i-fō'li-us). This 3' to 4' variety has larger leaves and is listed as being more cold hardy than the species. It is hardy to Zone 6.

A. mollis var. *spinosissimus* (spī-no-sis'i-mus). This plant has narrower leaf divisions than the above species. The leaf spines are white, stiff, and considerably more vicious than *spinosus.* It is the perfect plant to keep "rug rats" out of your perennial border.

ADDITIONAL NOTES: *Acanthus* is derived from the Greek word *akanthos,* meaning thorn or prickle. It has been called bear's breeches because of the size and appearance of the leaf of some species which is big, broad, and hairy. The *Acanthus* leaf was a favorite decoration in classical structure and was supposed to have served as the pattern for designs on Corinthian architectural columns.

Native to southeastern Europe.   Perennial

SCIENTIFIC NAME/FAMILY: *Achillea filipendulina* (A. eupatorium)   Asteraceae
(Compositae)

(ak-i-lē´à or a-kil´e-a fil-i-pen-dū-lī´nà)

COMMON NAME: Fernleaf Yarrow

LEAVES: Leaves alternate, up to 10″
long, progressively reduced upward,
linear to elliptic, 1–2 pinnatifid into
linear-lanceolate, toothed segments,
leaves are pubescent. They have a
strong spicy odor and fern-like texture.

FLOWER: Heads small, in dense, compound convex corymbs which can be
up to 5″ across. Flower color is yellow.

HABIT: 3′ to 4′; these erect plants may
require staking unless grown in full
sun and dry soil, especially if located
in a windy area. Plants have a spread
of 3 feet.

SEASON OF BLOOM: Late spring to midsummer; removal of faded flowers to
prevent seed formation prolongs the
blooming period.

CULTURE: Full sun, dry soil—no special
needs beyond ordinary well-drained
soil.

UTILIZATION: Border, cut flowers and
dried flowers. If the flowers are cut
before pollen development, the dried
heads will retain their color. I have
kept flower stalks in an urn for a year

See color plate

and the yellow color was nearly as good after a year as when they were first cut.

PROPAGATION: Seeds may be used but sometimes produce inferior plants. Fast
propagation can be achieved with cuttings taken in midsummer. Clumps of mature
plants should be divided every 3 to 4 years. Division is easy.

DISEASES AND INSECTS: There are usually few problems; powdery mildew, rust, and
stem rot are sometimes found.

HARDINESS: Zones 3–8. *Achillea filipendulina* and *millefolium* have performed well in Zone
8, showing good heat tolerance.

CULTIVARS:
'Altgold' (Old Gold)—A hybrid with grey-green leaves and broad, flat, golden yellow
heads, 2 to 3 feet tall. This cultivar is considered a rebloomer.

'Coronation Gold'—A hybrid which is lower growing than *A. filipendulina* and generally requires less staking. Flowers are especially good for drying. A vigorous plant with good heat tolerance. 3' tall.

'Gold Plate'—Tall growing plants 4'–4½', with corymbs to 6" across; mustard-yellow flowers are useful as cut flowers.

'Neugold' (New Gold)—A heavy flowering selection, 2 feet tall, with golden yellow flowers. It is an excellent sturdy, long-lasting, cut flower.

'Parker's Variety'—3½' plant with yellow flowers in 4" diameter heads; plant structure is more open than 'Gold Plate.'

OTHER HYBRID SELECTIONS:

'Anthea'—Alan Bloom, Bressingham Gardens, Diss, England, recently developed this hybrid by crossing A. 'Moonshine' × *A. clypeolata.* It is 18"–20" tall with long serrated silvery leaves. The flower color is slightly paler than 'Moonshine.' The secondary flower heads flower profusely as the terminal flowers decline. This cultivar, which is named after Alan's daughter, has potential as a cut flower.

'Credo'—This is an upcoming cultivar developed by Ernst Pagel in Germany. It is a hybrid of *A. filipendulina* × *A. millefolium.* It has large yellow flowers, a good texture, and best of all, strong stems which eliminate the need for staking.

'Moonshine'—This hybrid of *A. clypeolata* and *A. taygetea* has beautiful silver-gray, feathery foliage and bright yellow flowers. It is 2' tall and may be the best *Achillea* for the garden. It performs well in northern gardens but high humidity and moisture in southern zones often causes melting out. This excellent hybrid was developed by Alan Bloom in the 1950s.

ADDITIONAL NOTES: *Achillea* commemorates Achilles, the Greek hero, who is said to have used *Achillea* for its wound healing properties.

Native to the Caucasus.   Perennial

SCIENTIFIC NAME/FAMILY: *Achillea* × *lewisii* 'King Edward'

(ak-i-lē'à or a-kil'e-a lū-is'ē-i)

COMMON NAME: King Edward Yarrow

LEAVES: Linear, to approximately 1" long, gray-green, and finely dissected.

FLOWER: The daisy-like flowers are 5/16" across and are borne in dense 1½" diameter corymbs atop 6" to 8" stems. Flowers are pale yellow, fading to a creamy-white.

HABIT: 6" to 8" tufted perennial with a 12" spread.

SEASON OF BLOOM: Midsummer.

CULTURE: Full sun, well-drained soil.

UTILIZATION: King Edward yarrow is a very attractive plant for the sunny rock garden or for placement in the border front. The yellow flowers are nicely displayed on a gray-green background.

PROPAGATION: Spring division is the simplest method of propagation.

DISEASES AND INSECTS: Powdery mildew and stem rot are occasional problems.

HARDINESS: Zones 4–8.

ADDITIONAL NOTES: 'King Edward' is a hybrid of *A. clavennae* × *A. tomentosa*.

Hybrid origin.

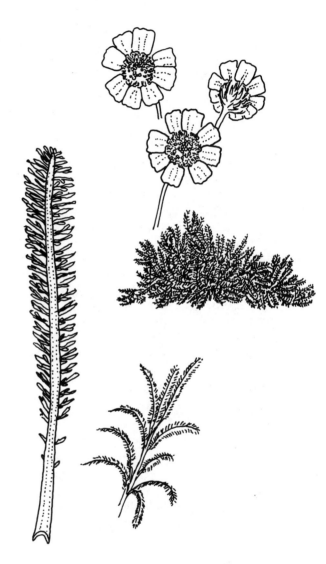

Perennial

SCIENTIFIC NAME/FAMILY: *Achillea millefolium*   Asteraceae
(Compositae)

(ak-i-lē′á or a-kil′e-a mil-e-fōl′i-um)

See color plate

COMMON NAME: Common Yarrow, Milfoil, Sanguinary, Thousand-seal, Nose-bleed.

LEAVES: The strongly aromatic leaves are alternate or in a basal rosette. The simple leaves are finely divided, which creates a soft, fern-like texture. The lower leaves are lanceolate to oblanceolate to 8″ long and have long petioles, upper leaves are lanceolate to linear and are sessile.

FLOWER: Numerous small flowers, ¼″ across, are borne in terminal, flat, dense corymbs from 2″ to 3″ across. The flowers of common yarrow are white; however, the cultivars are superior to the species and will vary in flower color from pink to red.

HABIT: 12″ to 36″ erect growing plant.

SEASON OF BLOOM: Mid to late summer.

CULTURE: This species and its cultivars perform best in full sun and well-drained soils. All are rapid spreaders with a tendency toward lodging. Those in my garden have quickly developed to be a tangled mass. Division will be necessary on a minimum of a 2-year cycle to keep the plant in some reasonable order.

UTILIZATION: *Achillea millefolium* is best restricted to a naturalized site as it is a common weed in areas where the soil is infertile. However, the cultivars are very suitable for massing in the perennial border or for fresh floral arrangements.

PROPAGATION: Division in spring or fall is a very effective method. Although seed can be used for cultivars, there is great variability and several colors will arise when the gardener is expecting one color. It is best to divide plants with excellent color.

DISEASES AND INSECTS: Powdery mildew and stem rot are occasional problems

HARDINESS: Zones 4–8.

CULTIVARS:
    'Cerise Queen'—Rose-pink flowers, 18″–24″ tall.
    'Fire King'—Rose-red flowers, 2″ to 3″ across, borne on 18″ stems with silver-gray foliage.

'New White'—This is a new selection made by Loleta Powell of Powell's Gardens. It is a rich white and is 24″–30″ tall.

'Red Beauty'—Crimson-red flowers, 24″ tall.

'Rosea'—Pink flowers.

'Rubra'—Dark pink flowers.

'White Beauty'—18″–20″ tall plant with clear white flowers.

RELATED SPECIES: The Galaxy hybrids are recent selections developed in Germany by crossing *A. taygetea* × *A. millefolium.* From my observations these cultivars still tend to quickly spread and lodge easily. However, the colors are excellent and add excitement to this species.

'Appleblossom' ('Apfelbute')—Rosy-pink flower heads with an upright and open habit, 3′ tall.

'Fanal' ('Beacon')—Cherry-red flowers with yellow centers, 2′–3′ tall. This cultivar is an excellent red.

'Hoffnung' ('Great Expectations')—Creamy-yellow flowers tinged with peach. 2′ tall.

'Paprika'—Cherry-red, yellow centered flowers which fade to light pink and then to creamy-yellow, 12″–18″ tall.

'Salmon Beauty' ('Lachsshönheit')—Salmon-pink flowers.

'Summer Pastels'—is a 1990 All American winner with a range of pastel colors that include pink, red, white, cream, yellow, salmon, orange, and mauve. They can be used in the border and as fresh or dried flowers.

'Weser River Sandstone' ('Wesersandstein')—Large flowers are light pink, fading to buff.

ADDITIONAL NOTES: *Millefolium* means many-leaved; literally, with a thousand leaves, and refers to the finely dissected foliage which appears to be many small leaves.

Native to Europe and western Asia.   Perennial

SCIENTIFIC NAME/FAMILY: *Achillea ptarmica*   Asteraceae (Compositae)
(ak-i-lē'á or a-kil'e-a tär'mi-kà)

COMMON NAME: Sneezewort, Sneezeweed

LEAVES: Alternate leaves are linear-lanceolate, 1"–3" long, finely toothed, and are borne sessile to the stem.

FLOWER: The small white flowers are borne in ½"–¾" wide heads which are carried in loose corymbs.

HABIT: Sneezeweed presents an untidy appearance of a loose and floppy plant 1½'–2' tall and 2' wide.

SEASON OF BLOOM: Early to late summer.

CULTURE: This species is easily grown in well-drained soil in full sun. Many gardeners consider it too "weedy" for border use because of its invasive habit. The double flowering selections are more popular.

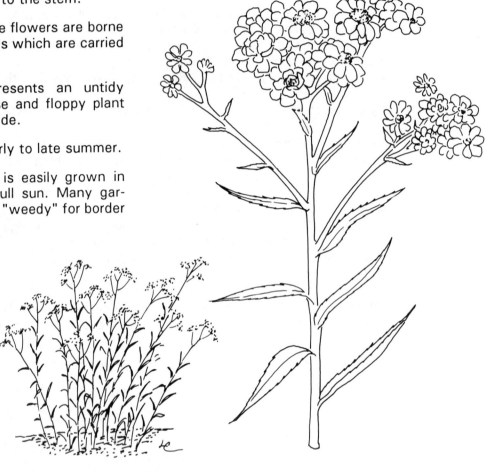

UTILIZATION: Sneezeweed is often relegated to the cutting garden because of its invasive character. The continuous flowering response makes it suitable as a supplier of cut flowers.

PROPAGATION: *Achillea ptarmica* is easily propagated by seed. It has no dormancy requirements. Sneezeweed can also be propagated from fall or spring division or from summer stem tip cuttings.

DISEASES AND INSECTS: There are no serious problems. It is usually difficult to eradicate sneezeweed from the garden.

HARDINESS: Zones 3–9.

CULTIVARS:
'Ballerina'—Double white flowers on plants 12"–18" tall. Also listed as 'Dwarf Ballerina' and *nana* 'Ballerina'.
'Nana Compacta'—Semidouble, white flowers, 18" tall. This selection is listed as a Karl Foerster introduction of 1953. I suspect that it may be very similar to 'Ballerina.'
'Perry's White'—A 1912 introduction with double white flowers, 24" tall with a floppy habit.
'The Pearl'—This selection has been a standard in the industry since 1900. It has double white flowers ½" wide. It is also known as 'Boule de Neige'. 24 inches tall.
'Unschuld'—This cultivar comes true from seed. It is a Benary introduction.

Native to Europe and Western Asia. It has naturalized in North America.   Perennial

SCIENTIFIC NAME/FAMILY: *Achillea tomentosa*

Asteraceae
(Compositae)

(ak-i-lē′á or a-kil′e-a tō-men-tō′sa)

COMMON NAME: Woolly Yarrow

LEAVES: The leaves are linear to lanceolate shaped, pinnately dissected, and very woolly. The segments are very small and present a ferny texture. The foliage is aromatic when crushed.

FLOWER: The yellow flower heads are very small, ⅛″ diameter, and borne in dense 1½″ to 2″ diameter flat-topped corymbs.

HABIT: Mat forming perennial, 6″–12″ tall and 18″ wide.

SEASON OF BLOOM: Early to mid summer.

CULTURE: Plant in full sun and a loose, well-drained soil. Woolly yarrow does poorly in areas with hot and humid weather. In zones warmer than zone 7, new plantings will grow well in early summer but will decline in vigor with the increasing temperatures.

UTILIZATION: It can be utilized in the rock garden, in planting pockets on stone walls, between walking stones, or as a ground cover in sunny areas.

PROPAGATION: Easily produced by division or seed. The spread is fairly quick when the plant is grown in very poor soil.

DISEASES AND INSECTS: No serious problems.

HARDINESS: Zones 3–7.

CULTIVARS:
var. *aurea* ('Maynard's Gold')—gold-yellow flowers are carried on 3″–8″ tall flower stalks.

Native to Europe.

Perennial

SCIENTIFIC NAME/FAMILY: *Aconitum napellus*   Ranunculaceae

(ak-ō-nī'tum nȧ-pel'lus)

COMMON NAME: Garden Monkshood, Helmet Flower

LEAVES: Alternate, 3"–5" wide, palmately veined, divided to the base, each segment again divided to near its base; segments are linear to lance-olate.

FLOWER: Blue or violet, in upright spike-like termi-nal racemes, individual flowers are 1"–2" tall and are shaped like small helmets or hoods with a beak in front.

HABIT: 3' to 4' erect plant that is 12"–18" wide.

SEASON OF BLOOM: Mid to late summer.

CULTURE: *Aconitum* does best in partial shade and soil that is fertile and contains abundant organic matter. If it is placed in full sun, the soil must remain moist to prevent drying which causes stunting.

UTILIZATION: Monkshood is a welcome plant in the perennial border. The dark glossy foliage and dark blue flowers are striking additions to any garden and are good in naturalized areas. The flowers are especially desirable as they appear at a time when there are few blue flow-ers in the landscape. *Aconitum* may also be used for cutting.

PROPAGATION: Clump division can be done in spring or fall; however, the plants are slow to increase and can be left for a number of years before rejuvenation is necessary. *Aconitum* is difficult to propagate from seed.

DISEASES AND INSECTS: Crown rot, verticillium wilt, mosaic, powdery mildew, and cyclamen mite are sometimes problems.

HARDINESS: Zones 4–8.

RELATED SPECIES:
     × *bicolor* (bī'kul-er). This hybrid of *A. napellus* and *A. variegatum* contains a number of the garden hybrids.
        'Bicolor'—Blue and white flowers are borne on wide spreading branches, 3'–4' tall.
        'Blue Sceptre'—This Alan Bloom selection is 24" tall with blue flowers arranged in tighter spikes than the loose habit of 'Bicolor.'

'Bressingham Spire'—Alan Bloom lists this as his finest selection. It is 30″–36″ tall with violet blue flowers in stiff upright panicles. The value of this cultivar lies in the fact that staking is not necessary. It was introduced in 1957.

'Newry Blue'—A 4′–5′ tall plant with navy blue flowers with an upright flowering habit.

'Spark's Variety'—Dark blue flowers, 4′–5′ tall. Staking may be necessary especially if this cultivar is grown in too much shade.

A. carmichaelii (kar-mī-keel′lē-i), Azure Monkshood. 2′–3′ tall, smaller growing than *A. napellus.* It flowers later in the season than the other species. 'Arendsi,' a hybrid selection of *A. carmichaelii* × *A. carmichalii* var. *wilsonii*, is 3′–4′ tall with large hoods of deep blue. It has stiff stems which are sturdy enough to allow the plant to be grown without staking. It is an excellent late flowering monkshood.

A. septentrionale (sep-tin-tri-o-na′-le). This species is the earliest monkshood to flower and has very fibrous roots. The small white flowers are not very significant. The more impressive cultivar 'Ivorine,' with creamy-white flowers and upright habit, was selected from a crop of seedlings in the late 1950s. It is also an Alan Bloom selection.

ADDITIONAL NOTES: *Aconitum* is poisonous. The leaves and roots contain aconitin which is a narcotic alkaloid. One should exercise care in transplanting so that the juice of the leaves or roots does not get into one's mouth. The tuberous roots are quite virulent. They could be confused with Jerusalem artichokes or other root vegetables so it is probably best not to plant *Aconitum* near vegetable gardens or areas where small children might play. The genus *Aconitum* was supposedly named by Theophrastus, who observed large groups of the plants growing near Acona, Greece.

Native to Europe.

Perennial

SCIENTIFIC NAME/FAMILY: *Acorus gramineus* 'Variegatus'   Araceae

(ak'ō-rus gram-in'ē-us var-i-e-gā'tus)

COMMON NAME: Japanese Sweet Flag, Grassy-leaved Sweet Flag

LEAVES: Linear grass-like leaves, ¼" wide and 6"–12" long, with green and white stripes.

FLOWER: The flower is a slender, green spadix up to 3" long. The flowers have little value or decorative appeal.

HABIT: Tufted growth habit, up to 12" tall and 12" wide.

SEASON OF BLOOM: Not important.

CULTURE: *Acorus* requires a moist to wet soil in partial shade to full sun.

UTILIZATION: Useful as a specimen plant in water gardens and bog areas where the soil is constantly moist to wet.

PROPAGATION: Division in the spring.

DISEASES AND INSECTS: No serious problems.

HARDINESS: Zones 6–9.

RELATED SPECIES:
Acorus calamus (kal'a-mus). Sweet Flag. This species has creeping rhizomes and sword-shaped leaves 2' to 3' tall. The rhizomes and leaves have a cinnamon scent when crushed. In earlier days the leaves were strewed on the floor and walks to add a fragrance to perhaps counteract the smells from open garbage. The rhizomes were also used medicinally and had supposed restorative powers. *Acorus calamus* 'Variegatus' has leaves that are boldly variegated green and white, and are 2' to 3' tall. Both plants are usually grown in wet soils including bogs and shallow water. Excellent plants for the water garden. Zones 5–9.

Native to Asia and North America.   Perennial

SCIENTIFIC NAME/FAMILY: *Actaea pachypoda* (A. alba)   Ranunculaceae

(ak-tē'a pak'-ē-pō-da)

COMMON NAME: White Baneberry, Doll's Eyes

LEAVES: Leaves are pinnately to ternately
compound; leaflets are ovate, serrated, or
in some instances cut nearly to the midrib.
The leaves are similar to *Astilbe.*

FLOWER: Very small, white flowers are tightly
clustered in an oblong terminal raceme,
2"–3" long. The flowers are followed by
summer fruit which are ivory white and
borne on bright red, thick pedicels. The
fruit are poisonous if eaten, so caution
should be exercised in gardens where
small children may be present.

HABIT: 18" to 30" tall clump with a 2'–3'
spread.

SEASON OF BLOOM: The flowers are showy
in mid to late spring while the white fruit
debuts in summer.

See color plate

CULTURE: Partial to full shade, in moist, fertile soil. This species grows best in slightly acid
to neutral soil which has a good organic matter content. A woodland garden is usually
the home of this native species.

UTILIZATION: Shaded border or in the woodland wildflower garden. The flowers are not
spectacular, but the white fruit in the late summer make this species a worthwhile
garden investment.

PROPAGATION: Division in late fall or early spring is the easiest method. It can also be
propagated from seed, which takes more patience. *Actaea* will need a period of cold
stratification. If possible, the seed should be harvested when ripe and sown immediately in a cold frame or directly in the soil. Germination will occur the following spring. If
the seeds become dry, either on the plant or after planting, germination is likely to be
delayed. Plants propagated by seed will flower the 3rd year. The easiest seed
propagation method is to sow the seed outside in the fall and let nature provide the cold
stratification.

DISEASES AND INSECTS: There are no serious problems. After establishment, baneberry
is one of the more permanent wildflowers.

HARDINESS: Zones 3–7.

RELATED SPECIES:
   A. rubra (rū'brà), Red Baneberry, Red Cohosh. This species is similar in appearance to
      A. pachypoda except the fruit is red, the leaves tend to be more pubescent, and the
      pedicels are thinner on *A. rubra* than *A. pachypoda.* It is also viewed as an asset for
      the woodland garden.
      'Neglecta'—A white-berried form that is listed in the literature but seldom found in
         commerce in the United States.

A. spicata (spi-kā'-ta), Black Baneberry, Herb Christopher. A European native with white flowers and black fruit. I have seen this species at the Royal Botanic Garden in Edinburgh, Scotland, but I have not seen it in the United States.

ADDITIONAL NOTES: The fruit of *Actaea pachypoda* has a black "eye" opposite the stem end and is responsible for the common name, dolls' eyes.

Native to eastern United States and Canada.   Perennial

SCIENTIFIC NAME/FAMILY: *Adenophora lilifolia*   Campanulaceae

(ad-e-nof'o-ra lil-i-fō'-li-à)

COMMON NAME: Lilyleaf Ladybells

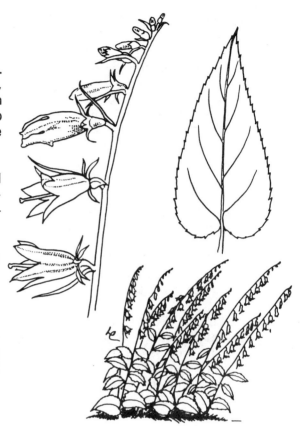

LEAVES: The alternate leaves are of two types. The basal leaves are petioled, cordate-orbicular, 3" long, with a serrated margin. The stem leaves are short-petioled or sessile, ovate to lanceolate shaped, and also serrated. They are 1" wide.

FLOWER: The pale blue flowers are bell shaped and hang downward from terminal racemes. Flowers are ⅝" wide and resemble those of *Campanula.*

HABIT: 18"–24" erect perennial with spire-like inflorescences. It will spread to 2 feet.

SEASON OF BLOOM: Early to midsummer.

CULTURE: Full sun to partial shade in a loose, well-drained soil. Clay soils should be amended with compost or other organic matter. As with all perennials, the money and effort of adding organic matter will far outdistance money and effort spent on fertilizer.

UTILIZATION: Ladybells is useful for adding a blue color to the border in midsummer but remains a relatively unknown perennial.

PROPAGATION: Ladybells does not transplant well, so propagation by division should be kept to a minimum. Cuttings and seed propagation are alternative methods. Stem cuttings can be taken in late spring. The very small seed should be mixed with a fine sand to aid in spreading the seed evenly over the seed flat. The uncovered seed should be germinated at 70°–75°F. Germination will take 2–3 weeks.

DISEASES AND INSECTS: None serious.

HARDINESS: Zones 4–8.

RELATED SPECIES:
   A. confusa (kon-fus'-à) (*A. farreri*), Common Ladybells. This blue-flowered species is taller (3') than *A. lilifolia* but very similar in other features. It is not as heat tolerant as *A. lilifolia.*

ADDITIONAL NOTES: To the novice, and perhaps professionals, ladybells are often confused with bellflowers *(Campanula).* The technical difference between them is that there is a tubular or glandular disk surrounding the base of the style beneath the expanded stamen filaments on *Adenophora. Adenophora* is a derivation of aden, a gland, and phoreo, to bear, and supposedly is in reference to the nectary in the flower.

Native to eastern Asia.

Perennial

SCIENTIFIC NAME/FAMILY: *Adiantum pedatum*   Adiantaceae

(ad-e-ān'tum ped-ā'tum)

COMMON NAME: Northern Maidenhair Fern

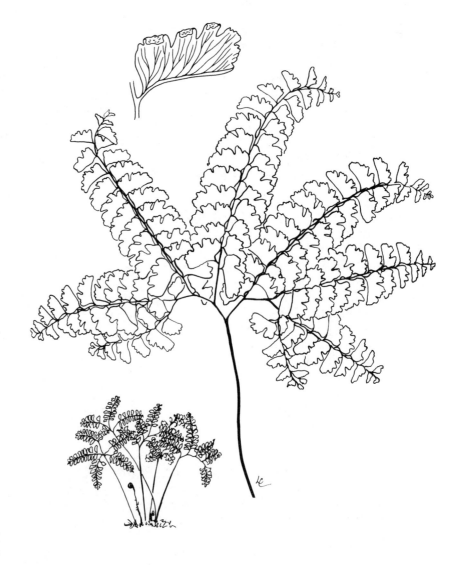

FRONDS: Each frond is branched at the summit of the slender, reddish-brown and polished stalk. The pinnules are oblique at the base and are triangular oblong.

SORI: The sori are borne on the edge of the pinnule.

HABIT: 10"–18" tall, finely textured fern with an 18" spread.

CULTURE: The native haunt of the maidenhair fern is in dim, moist areas in the woods or on shaded hillsides. Consequently, when utilized in residential settings, maidenhair fern should be provided abundant shade and moisture.

UTILIZATION: Excellent fine-textured fern suited for the woodland setting or shaded rock garden. The fine texture is a nice complement to hosta in a shade garden.

PROPAGATION: Maidenhair can be propagated by division in the spring or from spores.

DISEASES AND INSECTS: No serious problems.

HARDINESS: Zones 3 to 8.

ADDITIONAL NOTES: Northern maidenhair is native from Nova Scotia to British Columbia and south to Georgia and Arkansas. The Southern maidenhair fern *(A. capillus-veneris)* is similar but it differs in the way in which the stem branches. If the stem is erect and forks in two, it is Northern maidenhair. When the stem is arched and it does not fork, it is the Southern maidenhair. Southern maidenhair fern grows best in higher pH soils. Zone 7.

Perennial

SCIENTIFIC NAME/FAMILY: *Aegopodium podagraria* 'Variegatum'
(ē-gō-pō'di-um pō-dā-gra'ri-à vãr-i-e-gā'tum)

Apiaceae
(Umbelliferae)

COMMON NAME: Bishop's Goutweed

See color plate

LEAVES: Leaves biternately compound, basal and lower stem leaves with a short, broadly expanding petiole, segments 1½"–3" long, leaves white-margined.

FLOWER: Umbels 1½"–3" wide, 12 to 15 ray flowers, flowers white, not showy.

HABIT: 8" to 10" spreading ground cover.

SEASON OF BLOOM: Late spring to early summer.

CULTURE: Sun or shade with no soil preference. Unvariegated shoots should be removed to prevent reversion of the plant to the green leaf species.

UTILIZATION: Use as a ground cover where it can be restricted, such as between a sidewalk and the house. It is not as invasive as the green leaf species, *Aegopodium podagraria,* but caution should still be used.

PROPAGATION: Plants spread by underground stems. New plants are propagated by dividing old plants in early spring or in early fall when the season's growth has matured.

DISEASES AND INSECTS: In humid, hot weather, *Aegopodium* has severe leaf blight; however, it comes back nicely with the return of drier and cooler weather in the late summer.

HARDINESS: Zone 4 to Zone 8. Plants in Zone 8 perform best in shade.

ADDITIONAL NOTES: Unkempt foliage can be mowed close to the ground and will quickly grow back. Plant can become weedy if not controlled effectively. Never plant in rock gardens where it can spread over choicer plants. *Aegopodium* is derived from the Greek words *aix,* goat, and *podion,* little foot. *Aegopodium* was once thought to cure gout.

Native to Europe.

Perennial

SCIENTIFIC NAME/FAMILY: *Agapanthus hybrids*   Alliaceae
                                                                (Liliaceae)

(ag-à-pan'thus)

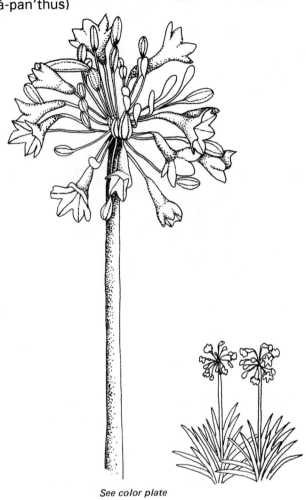

COMMON NAME: Blue African Lily,
   African Lily

LEAVES: Basal leaves, linear-lanceolate, ½" to 2" wide, 12" long,
   dark green. In some instances the
   leaves are evergreen.

FLOWER: The terminal umbel is
   packed with many blue, tubular
   flowers. Hybrid selections will
   vary in the number of flowers per
   umbel from a minimum of 30–40
   up to 100 flowers per umbel.
   Umbel width is 3" to 4" wide.

HABIT: Basal foliage with a leafless
   flower stalk rising 3' to 4'.

SEASON OF BLOOM: Mid to late
   summer.

CULTURE: *Agapanthus* should be
   planted in full sun in sandy, well-
   drained soils. Corms should be
   planted 2" below ground level and
   watered well at establishment and
   during the growing season. The
   plants should not be allowed to
   dry out. However, during the
   winter or dormant period, the corms should be allowed to dry.

See color plate

UTILIZATION: In hardiness zones colder than Zone 8, African lily is utilized as a container
   plant that is placed outside during the summer and brought in during the winter. In
   southern zones, especially California, *Agapanthus* is utilized as a border plant. Very
   useful plant for cut flowers.

PROPAGATION: Division of the rhizomatous roots is the easiest method. Seed can be
   utilized but the time to flower is longer.

DISEASES AND INSECTS: No serious problems.

HARDINESS: Zone 8.

CULTIVARS: Some of the better cultivars are included here:
   'Bressingham Blue'—A deep blue cultivar developed by Alan Bloom in the late 1960s.
      In 1992, Blooms of Bressingham released 'Bressingham Bounty,' which has rich
      blue flower heads that are 8"–10" in diameter.
   'Headbourne hybrids'—This group from England developed from seeds distributed in the
      1950s–1960s by Lewis Palmer from his garden, Headbourne Worthy, near
      Winchester. Many of the cultivars that we know today have come from these
      releases.

'Isis'—Six inch inflorescences of lavender blue flowers. This was the first *Agapanthus* cultivar released by Alan Bloom.

'Loch Hope'—This tall (4'–5'), late flowering selection has deep violet flowers. The intense color is retained until the flowers drop from the plant. Flowers of many cultivars fade to reddish purple.

Hybrid origin.   Perennial

SCIENTIFIC NAME/FAMILY: *Agastache foeniculum*   Lamiaceae
                                                                  (Labiatae)

(Ag-á-stāch'-ē fē-nik'ū-lum)

COMMON NAME: Anise-Hyssop, Blue Giant Hyssop, Fragrant Giant Hyssop, Anise Mint

LEAVES: Opposite leaves, ovate to ovate-lanceolate, serrate margin, 2"–3" long and 1" wide. The leaves have a strong anise fragrance.

FLOWER: Blue flowers, 1/4" long are closely packed into a 4"–5" long terminal spike. The large bracts are violet. Flowers can be dried.

HABIT: *Agastache* has a distinct erect habit, 2–3 times taller than wide, 3' tall. Space 24" apart.

SEASON OF BLOOM: Late summer bloom.

CULTURE: Full sun in moist, well-drained soil.

UTILIZATION: This large species can be used in the perennial border for a bold effect. My first experience with *Agastache* was at the perennial nursery Grafin von Zeppelin in Germany. It was late September and the blue flowers and plant size struck a massive pose in the nursery. The leaves are used in teas, salads, and drinks. It also serves as a bee plant, providing nectar for a light, fragrant honey. Butterflies and hummingbirds are also attracted to this late summer bloomer.

PROPAGATION: The small seeds (300,000/oz.) should be uncovered and germinated at 55°–60° F. Spring or fall division is also possible with this species.

DISEASES AND INSECTS: None serious.

HARDINESS: Zones 5–9.

Native to North America   Perennial

SCIENTIFIC NAME/FAMILY: *Ageratum houstonianum* (A. mexicanum)   Asteraceae
(Compositae)

(aj-ēr-ā'tum, ȧ-jer'ȧ-tum hu-sto'ni-ā-num)

COMMON NAME: Mexican Ageratum, Flossflower

LEAVES: Alternate, ovate to triangular, to 4¾" long, cordate to truncate at base, crenate or rarely dentate, pilose on both sides.

FLOWER: Flower heads to ¼" across, in cymose clusters that are lavender, blue, pink or white depending on the cultivar.

HABIT: 4" to 12"—most often 6" mound-like habit.

SEASON OF BLOOM: May through October. One of the more dependable flowering annuals.

CULTURE: Full sun or partial shade. In areas where summers are hot and dry, light shade may be preferable to full sun.

UTILIZATION: Edging or border. Plant is about as broad as tall. Excellent plant for summer bedding purposes; equally at home in semishade or full sun. I have seen *Ageratum* growing very well in full sun in Zone 8.

PROPAGATION: Seed and stem cuttings. Seeds are small but easy to germinate at 70°F under light. Good uniformity from vegetative propagation.

See color plate

DISEASES AND INSECTS: Basically free from problems; root rot and powdery mildew occasionally appear.

CULTIVARS: Most cultivars are F_1 hybrids which are superior to inbred strains.
    'Adriatic'—Bright violet-blue flowers, early bloomer, uniform growth habit.
    'Bavaria'—Unique cultivar with bicolored blooms of blue ray and white disk flowers, 9"–12" tall and 12" wide.
    'Blue Blazer'—6" midblue flowers, blooms early and continues until frost.
    'Blue Horizon'—Blue flowers are carried on an upright habit.
    'Blue Puffs' ('Blue Danube')—7", midblue flowers, very uniform growth habit, slightly taller than 'Blue Angel.'
    'Blue Ribbon'—Blue flowers, very low, compact habit. The growth habit is similar to sweet alyssum.
    'Blue Tango'—8"–12", early blooming, often when plant is only 3" tall, flowers continuously, powder-blue color.
    'Blue Triomphe'—Midblue flowers—noted for its early flowering and uniform habit.
    'Fine Wine'—Burgundy-red color, compact habit, 6"–8" tall.
    'Hawaii' series—This new series has compact foliage, (6" tall) and intensely colored flowers. Colors include blue, royal, and white.

'North Sea'—8", deep red-purple buds open to violet-blue flowers.
'Royal Delft'—Deep violet-blue flowers, compact habit.
'Spindrift'—Pure white flowers, 6" tall.
'Summer Snow'—6", pure white, first pure white to have size, habit, and earliness similar to 'Blue Blazer.'

ADDITIONAL NOTES: The genus *Ageratum* is derived from *a*, not, and *geras,* old, which indicates that the flowers retain their clear color for a long time.

Native to Mexico, Guatemala and British Honduras.   Annual

SCIENTIFIC NAME/FAMILY: *Ajuga reptans* (A. repens)   Lamiaceae
(Labiatae)

(aj'ū-gȧ; a-jū'gȧ rep'tanz)

COMMON NAME: Bugleweed

LEAVES: Leaves basal, entire or repandate, the basal and stem leaves oblong—elliptic or obovate, narrowed to a margined petiole, rounded at apex, the upper and floral ones elliptic or ovate, sessile, shiny green, square stems.

FLOWER: Flowers usually violet-blue, sometimes red, white or purple, lower whorls of spike distant, the upper ones close. The flowers are quite nice in the spring.

HABIT: 6″ to 9″ dense, mat-like ground cover.

SEASON OF BLOOM: Early to late spring.

CULTURE: Good ground cover in the shade where grass will not grow. Also does well in the sun. Tolerates poor soil.

UTILIZATION: The spreading characteristic of bugleweed makes it a natural as a ground cover. However, placement should be in areas where the advancing growth would be welcome, such as on a bank or in shade areas. It should not be used as an edging near grass areas because it has a tendency to move easily and quickly into these areas.

See color plate

PROPAGATION: *Ajuga* can be propagated by seed, cuttings, division, or tissue culture. Division can be done any time during the year as long as the soil is workable. Seed can be sown in summer or fall.

DISEASES AND INSECTS: Crown rot is the major problem of bugleweed, especially in thick plantings. This can be serious and patches to entire plantings can be destroyed. Plantings should be placed in areas with good air movement, divided every 2–3 years to reduce the crowded conditions, and fungicides used to reduce the infection.

HARDINESS: Zones 4–8.

CULTIVARS:

'Alba'—White flowers and light green foliage.

'Atropurpurea'—Dark bronze-purple leaves. It is also listed as 'Purpurea.'

'Braunherz'—This cultivar has the best deep purple foliage color of any selection available. I first saw it at the Ikast Nursery in Denmark. The foliage gave off a deep purple sheen as the late afternoon sun settled on the leaves. Since then, I have noticed that several nurseries in the United States are building stock and it will soon be more available.

'Bronze Beauty'—Waxy metallic bronze leaves.

'Burgundy Glow'—Tricolored foliage composed of green, white, and dark pink.

'Burgundy Lace'—Blue flowers and shiny leaves with white and pink variegation.

'Catlin's Giant'—8" long leaves make this one of the largest cultivars. It has blue flowers and bronze-green leaves.

'Cristata'—Small, dark green leaves are strongly crinkled. The appearance of this cultivar may remind one of small spinach leaves. The selection is incorrectly listed in the trade as 'Metallica Crispa' ('Crispa').

'Gaiety'—A selection similar to 'Bronze Beauty' but with a darker foliage.

'Jungle Beauty'—This cultivar has an unusual variegation composed of cream, purplish green, and tinges of red and pink. Reversion does occur and the dark purplish leaves and stems should be removed to preserve the true 'Jungle Beauty'. 'Jungle Beauty Improved' is probably a selection from the reversion. It has shiny mahogany-purple leaves forming an 8" mound. It is a vigorous grower that will have flower spikes 12" tall.

'Multicolor' ('Rainbow,' 'Tricolor')—This cultivar has tricolored foliage similar to 'Burgundy Glow' but it is more vigorous.

'Pink Beauty'—Light pink flowers and green foliage.

'Silver Beauty'—Creamy white and green variegated leaves.

RELATED SPECIES:

A. pyramidalis, (pi-ram-i-dā'lis), Upright Bugleweed. The foliage and flowers are similar to *A. reptans* but it does not have the spreading habit. It is a neat clump former and is more suited for edging along grass areas than *A. reptans.*

A. genevensis, (gen-ē-ven'sis), Geneva Bugleweed. This species is 6"–9" tall and tends to be more of a clump former than *A. reptans.* The leaves form a rosette at the base of the plant. It is being used more often because it is faster growing than *A. pyramidalis* but not as rampant as *A. reptans.*

ADDITIONAL NOTES: Foliage is effective year round. *Ajuga* does not take heavy foot traffic. *Ajuga* has stolon-bearing stems, which creates an excellent ground cover; reptans means creeping. Bugleweed mats so heavily that weeds will not grow through the ground cover. There are several different foliage types: light green, purple, and variegated.

Native to Europe.   Perennial

SCIENTIFIC NAME/FAMILY: *Alcea rosea* (Althaea rosea)   Malvaceae

(al-sē'-a̗ rō'zē-a)

COMMON NAME: Hollyhock

LEAVES: Orbicular, shallowly 3-, 5-, or 7-lobed; rugose with an alternate leaf arrangement.

FLOWER: Range in color from white through every shade of yellow, pink, lavender and red to nearly black and are arranged on long wand-like terminal racemes or spikes.
HABIT: 2' to 9' erect plant.

SEASON OF BLOOM: Long blooming period—from midsummer to early fall (June to late August).

CULTURE: Full sun, performs best on well-drained sites.

UTILIZATION: Background in a border or against a fence or wall; sometimes used as a specimen plant.

PROPAGATION: Hollyhock is a half-hardy biennial. Seeds will germinate in 2–3 weeks at 60°F. Plants started during the winter will flower the following summer.

DISEASES AND INSECTS: Anthracnose, rust, leaf spot, spider mites, and Japanese beetle. Rust is very common and will require a fungicide spray program. These problems often promote a ratty foliage appearance but the flowers usually remain attractive.

CULTIVARS:
'Chater's' Series—This popular double flower strain is offered in white, yellow, maroon, purple, salmon, scarlet, and a mix. 6'–8' tall, perennial.
'Indian Spring Mixture'—Single flowers in a mixture of rose, pink, white, and yellow. 6'–8' tall.
'Marjorette'—Double lacy flowers with a mixture of apricot, rose, lavender, pink, lemon and white. 24" tall, All American Selection 1976, annual.
'Nigra'—A novelty selection with chocolate-maroon flowers.
'Pinafore Mixed'—Single and semi-double flowers in colors of pink, carmine, rose, yellow, and white, 3'–3½' tall.
'Powder Puffs Mixed'—Double blooms, 6'–8' tall, red, pink, rose, white, yellow colors.
'Summer Carnival'—Double blooms, 4'–5' tall, wide color range, early bloomer.

ADDITIONAL NOTES: Hollyhock has an indeterminate inflorescence (basal flowers bloom first). In addition to the old fashioned bell-shaped flowers, there are new strains with petals fringed, ruffled or doubled. Hollyhocks may need to be staked in climates with windy weather. *Alcea* originated from the word *altheo*, to cure, since several species possess medicinal properties. It is listed as a perennial to zone 5 in some books.

Native to China.   Biennial

SCIENTIFIC NAME/FAMILY: *Alchemilla mollis* (vulgaris)   Rosaceae

(al-kem-il'à mol'lis)

COMMON NAME: Lady's Mantle.

LEAVES: Basal leaves, orbicular in shape and 2" to 4" wide. Individual leaves are palmately veined and have from 7 to 11 shallow-toothed lobes. The foliage usually has a silk-like pubescence.

FLOWER: Small, yellowish-green or chartreuse flowers are borne in compound cymes. The ⅛" flowers have regular symmetry, are apetalous, and have 4 or 5 sepals.

HABIT: 8" to 10" basal foliage with flower stems up to 18". The spread is 24".

SEASON OF BLOOM: Late spring to early summer.

CULTURE: Lady's mantle grows most easily in a cool and moist summer climate. In this area, full sun is acceptable as is partial shade. In climates which are hot and/or dry, the soils must be moist, fertile, and located in partial shade. The period of flowering will be reduced in hot climates. It will self-sow, which increases the area of the planting. If this becomes a problem, the seed heads should be removed before maturity.

See color plate

UTILIZATION: Lady's mantle is suitable for the front of the border or, if planted in larger groups, used as a ground cover. The fine textured flower inflorescences provide excellent cut flowers, which can be dried for winter floral arrangements. The silken leaves will sparkle when drops of rain or dew collect on the leaves.

PROPAGATION: Easily propagated by seed or division in spring or fall. Fresh seed will germinate quickly. Older seed will require a cold stratification period.

DISEASES AND INSECTS: There are normally no major problems, especially in northern areas. In climates with hot nights, fungal problems may result when rain or irrigation water collects in the depression of the leaves and tight crowns. A fungicide program may be necessary in these areas.

HARDINESS: Zones 4–7.

RELATED SPECIES:

A conjuncta (con-junk'-ta) (alpina). This 6" tall alpine plant is charming. The small leaves are delicately serrated and the backs of the leaves are covered with a shining silk pubescence. This creates a silver edge on the top side of the leaf. The flowers are not as ornamental as *A. mollis.* Zone 5.

A. erythropoda (er-i-thrō-pō'-da). This species has small scalloped blue-green leaves, which are topped with sprays of tiny lime-green flowers.

ADDITIONAL NOTES: *Alchemilla* is probably Latinized from *Alkemelych,* the Arabic name for the plant. The common name, lady's mantle, was derived from the ancient legend that it was used for the adornment of the Virgin Mary.

Native to Europe.   Perennial

SCIENTIFIC NAME/FAMILY: *Allium aflatunense*   Alliaceae (Liliaceae)

(al'i-um a-flat'-u-nen''-se)

COMMON NAME: Persian Onion

LEAVES: Strap-shaped basal leaves are 4″ wide.

FLOWER: Star-shaped lilac flowers are borne in a dense spherical umbel, 4″ wide.

HABIT: Erect plant with 3′ tall scapes.

SEASON OF BLOOM: Late spring.

CULTURE: Full sun and a very well-drained soil. Root rot can occur in heavy clay and poorly drained soils.

UTILIZATION: This ornamental onion can be used in the perennial border and makes an excellent cut flower which will last 2 weeks.

PROPAGATION: Same as *A. karataviense*.

DISEASES AND INSECTS: No serious problems

HARDINESS: Zones 4–7.

CULTIVARS:
'Purple Sensation'—This cultivar has darker purple flowers than the species.

ADDITIONAL NOTES: Introduced by the Van Tubergren bulb company in the early 1900s.

Native to Iran.

Bulb

SCIENTIFIC NAME/FAMILY: *Allium christophii* (A. albopilosum)   Alliaceae
(Liliaceae)

(al'i-um cris-tof'phē-i)

COMMON NAME: Persian Onion,
Star-of-Persia

LEAVES: Leaves 3 to 7 per plant, strap-shaped, to 1" wide. They are sometimes glaucous with a whitish-pubescence on the lower leaf surface.

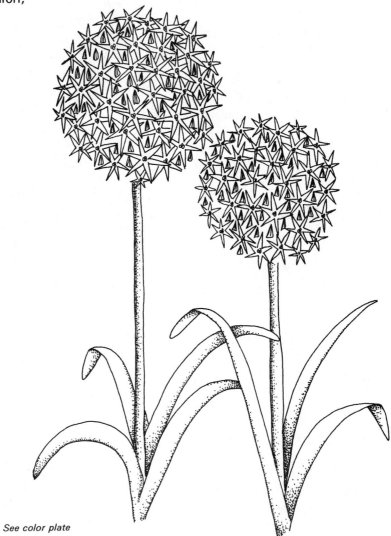

FLOWER: The inflorescence is a many flowered umbel which can be 8" to 10" wide. The outside of the sphere is covered with deep lilac star shaped flowers ½" wide. The dried seed heads are excellent on the plant or in a dried flower arrangement.

HABIT: The flowers are terminal on stout scapes which are 1½' to 2' tall with an 18" spread.

SEASON OF BLOOM: Late spring to early summer.

See color plate

CULTURE: Full sun and a very well-drained soil. The bulbs are planted in the fall. New plantings and established plantings benefit from a winter mulch in areas with severe winters.

UTILIZATION: Useful as a cut or dried flower, in the late spring border, or as a naturalized planting. I have seen it successfully used when planted among bearded iris. The flowers appear in late spring with the remaining iris flowers and the gray-green iris foliage serving as a coverup for the declining *Allium* foliage.

PROPAGATION: Star-of-Persia is not a vigorous grower, but it can be multiplied by digging and separating the bulbs. Seed is another option. It requires a warm-cold-warm stratification for best germination percentages.

DISEASES AND INSECTS: No serious problems.

HARDINESS: Zones 4–8.

Native to Turkestan.   Perennial—hardy bulb

SCIENTIFIC NAME/FAMILY: *Allium giganteum*

(al'i-um jī-gan-tē'um)

COMMON NAME: Giant Onion

LEAVES: Basal leaves, stiff and linear, up to 18″ long, 2″ wide, very smooth leaf surface. If leaves are cut or bruised, they smell like onions.

FLOWER: Lilac-pink flowers are borne in a 5″–6″ wide, globose inflorescence atop a sturdy scape 3′–4′ tall. The flowers color from the top of the inflorescence to the base, changing from green to lilac-pink.

HABIT: 3′ to 4′ erect plant with a 2′ spread.

SEASON OF BLOOM: Late spring to early summer.

CULTURE: Giant onion is very easily grown if placed in full sun and well-drained soil.

UTILIZATION: Due to the height of this species, it is usually utilized in the rear of the border. If the inflorescence is cut in early bloom, it will last 3 weeks. Although the flower scape is sturdy, it may need support in windy, exposed sites. The flower inflorescences are also used in dry arrangements. It is a favorite of floral arrangers.

PROPAGATION: Seed and division of the bulblets. Seed can be sown in early spring and will bloom in 2 to 3 years. The bulblets that form at the base of mature bulbs can be removed in the fall and replanted.

See color plate

DISEASES AND INSECTS: The *Allium* genus is subject to a bulb rot caused by *Sclerotium cepivorum* which prevents the flower stalk from developing. Selection of clean bulbs and removing diseased plants are effective control measures.

HARDINESS: Zones 5–8.

Native to central Asia.

Perennial—hardy bulb

SCIENTIFIC NAME/FAMILY: *Allium karataviense*   Alliaceae (Liliaceae)

(al'i-um ka-rah-ta-vee-en'se)

COMMON NAME: Turkestan Onion

LEAVES: This bulb usually has 2 leaves which are broadly ovate to elliptic, 3" to 4" wide and 6"–10" long. The leaves have a metallic blue-green color and may have a mottled, purple variegation at the base and on the lower leaf surface. The leaves are arranged in a funnel form and are rolled outward at the tip.

FLOWER: Small, silver-lilac flowers are borne in a dense, globose umbel that is 4"–6" wide. The thick flower stalk emerges from the "funnel" created by the two leaves.

HABIT: The bold, erect flower stalk is 10" tall.

SEASON OF BLOOM: Late spring.

CULTURE: Bulbs should be planted 4"–6" deep and 9" apart in a well-drained, sunny location. Clumps can remain undisturbed for years.

See color plate

UTILIZATION: Turkestan onion is valuable in the perennial or mixed border or the rock garden. The foliage is sometimes considerably more ornamental than the dull silver-lilac flowers. The flowers can be cut and used in dry flower arrangements.

PROPAGATION: Plants can be reproduced by offsets, bulblets and seed. Seed will need to be given a warm stratification at 70°F for 3 weeks, placed in the cold at 30°–40°F for 5 weeks and then back into warmer temperatures at 60°F. Plants grown from seed will require 3 years to reach flowering size.

DISEASES AND INSECTS: None serious.

HARDINESS: Zones 4–8.

Native to Turkestan   Bulb

SCIENTIFIC NAME/FAMILY: *Allium moly*

Alliaceae
(Liliaceae)

(al'i-um mō'-le)

COMMON NAME: Lily Leek, Gold-
en Garlic

LEAVES: The leaves are arranged
in 2's. They are basal, lanceolate, narrowed at both ends of
the leaf. The glaucous leaves
are ½" to 1½" wide and 12"
long.

FLOWER: The vivid yellow, star-
shaped flowers are borne in a
loose umbel atop a tall peduncle.

HABIT: 12" tall flowering bulb
which will colonize over time.

SEASON OF BLOOM: Mid to late
spring.

CULTURE: Full sun in a well-
drained soil makes for easy
culture of this bulb.

UTILIZATION: The bright yellow
flowers will brighten up any
spring border. It can also be
used in a naturalized area
where the bulbs will colonize.

See color plate

PROPAGATION: Allowing the plants to colonize will promote self-seeding and production
of offsets. The clumps can be divided after the foliage dies down and the "new" bulbs
can be transplanted in the fall.

DISEASES AND INSECTS: No serious problems.

HARDINESS: Zones 3–9.

Native to southwestern Europe.

Perennial—hardy bulb

SCIENTIFIC NAME/FAMILY: *Allium schoenoprasum*

(al'i-um sken-op'-ras-um)

Alliaceae
(Liliaceae)

COMMON NAME: Chives

LEAVES: The small bulbs of this species produces 1–2 leaves, 6"–10" long. Leaves are dark green, cylindrical and hollow. The hollow leaves distinguish this species from *Allium tuberosum*, which has flat leaves. Leaves have a mild, oniony flavor.

FLOWER: Small, pale purple flowers are carried in dense, globe-shaped umbels atop 18" tall scapes.

HABIT: This species develops into a dense vegetative clump 12" tall with flower stalks to 18".

SEASON OF BLOOM: Late spring to early summer.

CULTURE: Easily grown perennial for sun or partial shade in well-drained soils. Typically, chives will tolerate most situations. The increasing size of the clumps requires division about every 3 years.

See color plate

UTILIZATION: Chives is known best for its culinary use, but it can serve as an edging ornamental. Clipping the leaves for culinary purposes will help keep a neater appearance during the growing season. Clumps of chives supposedly deter Japanese beetles and several leaf diseases. Some recommend it for interplanting among species such as carrots, tomatoes, roses, and grapes. Bees are attracted to the flowers of chives. Space plants 12"–18" apart.

PROPAGATION: Seed or clump division. Seeds should be covered and germinated at 70°F. Clumps can be lifted in spring or fall and divided into smaller clumps of 3–6 plants (bulbs).

DISEASES AND INSECTS: No serious problems.

HARDINESS: Zones 4–8.

CULTIVARS:
'Forescate'—Vigorous grower with showy rose-pink flowers. This cultivar is not common, but a few herb nurseries list it in their catalogs.

Native to northern Europe and northern Britain.   Perennial-hardy bulb

SCIENTIFIC NAME/FAMILY: *Allium senescens* var. *glaucum*

(al'i-um se-nē'-scens glâ'kum)

COMMON NAME: Ornamental Onion

LEAVES: The leaves are linear, flat, ¼" wide, and have a slight twist which gives the entire foliage clump a swirled effect. Foliage color is gray-green and foliage height is 6". If leaves are bruised, the foliage has an onion odor.

FLOWER: The lilac or mauve colored flowers are borne in a globose inflorescence (umbel), 1" wide, atop leafless stalks that grow to 12". The flowering stems are held above the lower swirls of leaves.

HABIT: This species grows into a dense clump which is 12" tall when in flower and 6" wide.

SEASON OF BLOOM: Mid to late summer.

CULTURE: This species is easily grown in ordinary soil in sun or partially shaded sites. Although grown from a bulb, this species is a clump former and is easily lifted and divided as other non-bulbous perennials.

UTILIZATION: The compactness of the clump makes this plant ideal as a border edging. It is utilized in herb and knot gardens for this purpose. A rock garden is another good site for this species as is the top of a low stone wall.

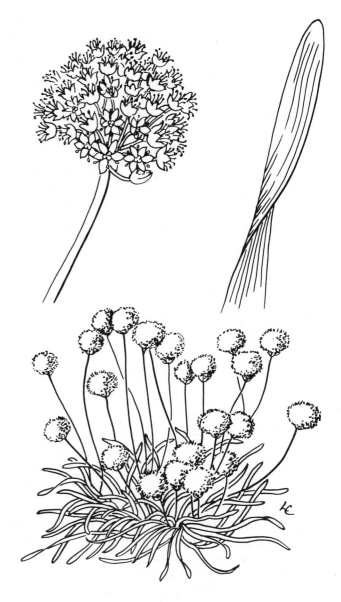

PROPAGATION: Clump can be divided in spring or the fall. Individual bulbs can be separated and used to start new plants.

DISEASES AND INSECTS: None serious.

HARDINESS: Zones 4–8.

RELATED SPECIES: There are several other forms of *A. senescens* in addition to the variety *glaucum.* One selection has bright green leaves, lilac to pink flowers about 2" wide, and it grows 12" tall. This European strain is often listed as ssp. *montanum* and is a sterile form. The second selection is taller growing, has gray-green leaves, and larger, pale mauve flower heads. In the trade, plants or seeds listed as *A. narcissiflorum* are usually this third type of *A. senescens.* The gardener needs to be aware that this species is very variable in relation to the leaves and plant size.

Native to Europe and Siberia.

Perennial—hardy bulb

SCIENTIFIC NAME/FAMILY: *Allium sphaerocephalon*   Alliaceae (Liliaceae)
                        (sphaerocephalum)

(al'i-um sfēr-ō-sef'a-lon)

COMMON NAME: Drumstick Chives, Round-headed Garlic

LEAVES: Upright leaves are semicylindrical, hollow, ⅛" wide and 18" long. There are usually 3–5 leaves per plant.

FLOWER: Two inch diameter flowers are carried at the top of a long, thin scape. The flower buds are green turning to purple. During this change, the flower head has a two-tone effect with a purple top. The flower head is very dense with up to 100 flowers.

HABIT: Tall erect flower stems carry the purple flowers which seem to float in the air. Plants are 2'–3' tall.

SEASON OF BLOOM: Summer

CULTURE: Plant bulbs in a well-drained soil in a full sun location.

UTILIZATION: Drumstick chives is an excellent candidate for a cut flower. In the border where it is in flower for 2–3 weeks, the bulbs should be massed or placed in a grouping for an effective display. Plant bulbs 6" apart.

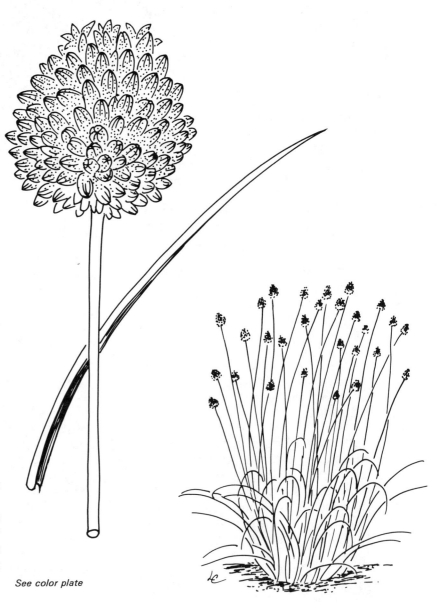

See color plate

PROPAGATION: New plantings can be created by separating the bulblets every 3 years. Seed propagation is the same as *A. karataviense.*

DISEASES AND INSECTS: No serious problems.

HARDINESS: Zones 4–8.

ADDITIONAL NOTES: Introduced in 1594. The flower stems resemble snare-drum sticks. Perhaps that is the reason for the common name.

Native to Central Europe, Southern Europe and Western Asia.   Bulb

SCIENTIFIC NAME/FAMILY: *Allium tuberosum*   Alliaceae (Liliaceae)

(al'i-um tū-be-rō'-sum)

COMMON NAME: Chinese Chive, Garlic Chive, Oriental Garlic

LEAVES: Leaves are ¼" wide, 12" long, with the characteristic onion odor to the crushed foliage. The blue-green leaves of this species are flat compared to the round and hollow leaves of *A. schoenoprasum.*

FLOWER: White flowers are borne in a ½" wide umbel atop an 18" tall scape. The perianth is star-shaped; individual segments are white with faint green to brown lines on the back of the segment.

HABIT: The flower scapes create an upright habit, 18"–24" tall; the leaves create 12" tall clumps.

SEASON OF BLOOM: Mid to late summer.

CULTURE: Chinese chive grows well in sun or partial shade and moist, well-drained soils. Division is required every 3 to 4 years. Flower heads should be removed before seed ripening to prevent unwanted seed dispersal.

UTILIZATION: *Allium tuberosum* is used as an edging ornamental and as a culinary herb. It is often associated with designs for the

See color plate

fragrant garden. This species is known as *gow choy* and has a garlic flavor. The flowers add a nice interest to the late summer season. Dried flower stalks are also used in floral arrangements. Space at 18".

PROPAGATION: Propagation is by seed or division. Seed should be covered and held at 70° F. Germination occurs in 5–7 days.

DISEASES AND INSECTS: No serious problems.

HARDINESS: Zones 4–8.

Native to Southeast Asia   Perennial—hardy bulb

SCIENTIFIC NAME/FAMILY: *Alopecurus pratensis* 'Aureus'

(al-ō-pē-cū′rus prā-ten′sis â′rē-us)

Poaceae
(Gramineae)

COMMON NAME: Golden Foxtail Grass,
   Yellow Foxtail Grass

LEAVES: Leaf blades ¼″ to ⅜″ wide,
   12″–18″ long, flat in cross section,
   narrowing to a fine point. The leaves
   are yellow and green striped.

FLOWER: The early summer flowering
   inflorescence is a very dense, blunt-
   tipped, cylindrical panicle. This 2″–3″
   long inflorescence resembles the
   flower head of timothy *(Phleum pratense).* Flowers are pale green to light
   yellow.

HABIT: Very dense, mounded plant,
   12″–18″ tall.

SEASON OF BLOOM: Spring to early
   summer.

CULTURE: Golden foxtail grass grows
   well in partial shade to full sun in a
   moist, well-drained soil. The flowers
   are not highly ornamental. This colored leaf cultivar should be sheared in
   early summer which will prevent flowering and will intensify the foliage
   color.

UTILIZATION: Grown primarily for the striped yellow foliage, golden foxtail grass is suited
   for the perennial border, rock garden or the edge of a pool.

PROPAGATION: Increase by spring division. Self-seeding can be a problem. Seedlings are
   always the green-leaved species, which can be invasive.

DISEASES AND INSECTS: No serious problems.

HARDINESS: Zones 6–9.

Native to Europe and northern Asia.   Perennial

SCIENTIFIC NAME/FAMILY: *Aloysia triphylla* (A. citriodora)   Verbenaceae

(al-oy-se'-a tri-phil'-la)

COMMON NAME: Lemon Verbena

LEAVES: Leaves are oppo-
site or whorled, in
groups of three, lance-
olate shape, entire or
sometimes a toothed
margin, 2"–4" long
and ½"–1" wide. Fo-
liage has a very distinct
odor of lemon.

FLOWER: Very small white
and pale lavender flow-
ers are borne on axil-
lary spikes or terminal
panicles.

HABIT: Woody shrub
growing to 15' tall in
the tropics. In temper-
ate zones it is treated
as a container plant
with a height of 2' to
4'.

SEASON OF BLOOM: Late
summer and fall.

CULTURE: Full sun in a
fertile, moist soil. In
areas colder than zone 9, lemon verbena must be wintered indoors. Most gardeners will
grow lemon verbena in a container.

UTILIZATION: The strong lemon flavored leaves work well in a blended tea. The leaves can
also be used to enhance drinks, salads, jellies, desserts or other foods or drinks where
lemon flavor is required. Lemon verbena is excellent in potpourri. It is a must plant for
the fragrant garden. The slightest touch of the leaves releases the lemon fragrance.
Lemon verbena was noted in the novel *'Gone With The Wind'*.

PROPAGATION: Summer cuttings is the usual propagation method.

DISEASES AND INSECTS: Spider mites and whiteflies will infest lemon verbena much as
they do other members of the verbena family.

HARDINESS: Zones 9 and 10

ADDITIONAL NOTES: This plant is deciduous and will frequently drop its leaves in the
transition from an outdoor habitat in summer to indoor for the winter.

Native to Chile and Argentina.   Woody perennial used as a container plant

SCIENTIFIC NAME/FAMILY: *Alternanthera ficoidea*   Amaranthaceae

(al-tēr-nan'thēr-à fī-koi'dē-à)

COMMON NAME: Garden Alternanthera, Joseph's-Coat

LEAVES: Leaves opposite, rhombic to narrow-spatulate, ½"–1" long, gradually tapering to a long petiole. Leaves are green in the species but the cultivars have leaves of variegated colors.

FLOWER: The flowers are inconspicuous. The colorful leaves of the cultivars provide the ornamental feature.

HABIT: 6" to 12" rounded plant.

SEASON OF BLOOM: Not significant.

CULTURE: Sun in almost any soil. Easily grown in full sun and a well-drained soil. Best growth will be in soils that are not overly fertile. It can be sheared to maintain a compact habit.

UTILIZATION: Carpet bedding and edging.

PROPAGATION: Cutting or division; homeowners usually buy started plants. Cuttings can be started in sand during February and March at 65°F temperature.

See color plate

DISEASES AND INSECTS: None serious.

HARDINESS: Zone 8.

CULTIVARS:
'Aurea nana'—Green and yellow variegated foliage.
'Bettzickiana'—This cultivar has spoon-shaped leaves marked with red and yellow.
'Haentze's Red Sport'—Pink, yellow, and green variegated foliage.
'Prospect Park'—Purple foliage.

Native to Brazil.   Tender perennial grown as an annual

SCIENTIFIC NAME/FAMILY: *Amaranthus tricolor*   Amaranthaceae

(am-à-ran'thus trī'kul-ẽr)

COMMON NAME: Joseph's Coat Amaranth, Fountain Plant, Tampala

LEAVES: Leaves ovate to oval, 1½"–6" long and mostly 4" wide, abruptly tapering to a long petiole. Foliage is composed of scarlet, gold, and green variegated leaves. Tricolor, of course, indicates three colors, a colorful but coarse effect.

FLOWER: Not significant; color is provided by foliage.

HABIT: 1½' to 5' erect growth habit. Plant 18"–24" apart.

SEASON OF BLOOM: Not important.

CULTURE: Full sun in average to dry soil. Water sparingly after establishment to deter root rot.

UTILIZATION: Background, specimen plant. The bright colors can overwhelm a garden if the plants are not used with discretion; may need staking.

See color plate

PROPAGATION: Seeds germinate in 10–12 days when placed in 75°–80°F. Night temperatures should be at least 65°F for growing on after transplanting.

DISEASES AND INSECTS: Root rot and stem borers can be especially troublesome, particularly on wet sites.

CULTIVARS:
'Early Splendor'—36", pendant scarlet foliage and branches, colors earlier than others.
'Flaming Fountain'— Long willow-like crimson leaves.
'Illumination'—4'–5', upper third of foliage is a bright scarlet with orange and yellow centers.
'Molten Fire'—Dark red foliage with poinsettia-like heads.
'Splendens Perfecta'—36", more uniform than the species, side branches color similar to main shoot.

RELATED SPECIES:
A. caudatus, (kâ-dā'tus), Love-Lies-Bleeding, Tassel Flower. This species has long, drooping inflorescences bearing dark red flowers which are frequently long enough for the tips to touch the ground. The tassel-like flowers last for weeks and are used as cut flowers. 2' to 3' tall.
'Green Thumb.' 18"–24", has erect green spikes. 'Pigmy Touch' is 18"–24" tall and has erect maroon spikes.

ADDITIONAL NOTES: This plant is a "flashy cousin" to the pigweed. *Amaranthus* is derived from *a,* not, and *mairaino,* to wither, which refers to the long-lasting character of the flowers.

Native to India and Philippines.

Annual

SCIENTIFIC NAME/FAMILY: *Amaryllis belladonna*   Amaryllidaceae

(am-à-ril'is bel-à-don'à)

COMMON NAME: Belladon-
na Lily, Naked Lady,
Cape Belladonna

LEAVES: Basal leaves, linear
or strap-like, 18" long,
¾" wide. The leaves
develop in the spring and
often disappear before
the flowers appear in
late summer. In mild
climates the leaves re-
main green throughout
the winter.

FLOWER: Pink lilylike flowers are borne in groups
up to 10 at the tip of a
stout, hollow stem 24–
30" high. Individual
flowers are 3"–3½"
long. Flowers are sweet
scented and contain 6
petals.

HABIT: At flowering, the
plant is an erect scape
with flowers clustered at
the top, 30" tall.

SEASON OF BLOOM: Late
summer.

CULTURE: Full sun or partial
shade in a well-drained
sandy loam soil. Soil
must remain dry during
the dormant period. Sites
in northern California are
ideal because of mois-
ture in spring and fall
and hot, dry summers.

UTILIZATION: In zones 9 and 10, *Amaryllis* can be planted in the perennial border, where it should not be disturbed for several years. In northern climates it can be used in containers although there is little interest after the foliage dies down and until flower spikes appear in summer. Dormant bulbs should be planted in containers large enough to have 4″ between the bulb and the wall of the pot. The neck of the bulb should extend slightly above the soil surface. A very porous soil mix should be used. Water should not be added until flower spikes appear. After foliage develops provide additional water until foliage begins to die. After that the pot should remain dry.

PROPAGATION: Parent bulbs can be lifted in the spring and offsets used for new plantings. Seed will also germinate easily.

DISEASES AND INSECTS: None serious.

HARDINESS: Zones 9–10.

CULTIVARS:
'Cape Town'—Deep rose-red.
'Johannesburg'—Light rose-pink flower with white throat and a yellowish base. This cultivar is a strong bloomer with up to 15 flowers per stalk.
'Kimberley'—Dark carmine-pink flower with a white center.
'White Queen'—White flowers.

Native to South Africa.   Tender bulb

SCIENTIFIC NAME/FAMILY: *Ammobium alatum*   Asteraceae (Compositae)

(a-mō'-bi-um a-lā'-tum)

COMMON NAME: Winged Everlasting

LEAVES: Basal leaves are ovate at the tip and long tapered to the base, 6"–8" long; stem leaves are lanceolate and much shorter. Stems and branches are noticeably winged (see drawing). All vegetative parts are coated with a white tomentose which decreases with age.

FLOWER: The papery textured flower heads are ¾"–1" wide. The disk flowers are yellow and are surrounded by silvery-white bracts which resemble petals.

HABIT: Erect flowering stalks, 3' tall, rise above the basal arching leaves that are 12" high. *Ammobium* should be spaced 12"–15" apart.

SEASON OF BLOOM: Summer

CULTURE: Winged everlasting grows best in full sun and a well-drained, sandy loam soil. *Ammobium* is a derivation from the Greek *ammos*, sand, and *bio*, to live, or thriving in a sandy place.

UTILIZATION: This everlasting can be used as a massing in a bed or border but it is probably more often cultivated for the benefits of the cut and dried flowers. Flowering stems should be cut when the flowers first open and hung upside down in a dry, airy room.

PROPAGATION: Easily produced from seed after 1 week germination. Plants can be started indoors 6–8 weeks before planting. In southern zones, *Ammobium* may be sowed directly in the garden about 6 weeks before frost. The plants will flower the next summer.

DISEASES AND INSECTS: None serious.

CULTIVARS: var. *grandiflorum*. This selection has larger flowers, up to 2" wide.

Native to Australia   Perennial treated as an annual in most climatic areas.

SCIENTIFIC NAME/FAMILY: *Amsonia tabernaemontana*   Apocynaceae

(am-sō'ni-a ta'-ber-nē-mon-ta''na)

COMMON NAME: Willow Amsonia, Blue Stars

LEAVES: The alternate leaves are lanceolate, sessile to the stem, entire, 2" to 6" long, and 1" wide. The foliage turns a clear yellow in the fall and lasts until frost. This is one of the few perennials that have a fall color.

FLOWER: The terminal flower cluster is composed of many star-shaped steel-blue flowers. Individual flowers have flower parts in groups of five.

HABIT: *Amsonia* has an erect growth habit. It is 2 to 3 feet tall and 3' wide.

SEASON OF BLOOM: Late spring to early summer.

CULTURE: Full sun in a moderately fertile soil is ideal. If planted in shade or highly fertile soil, the growth will be open and floppy. The spread is not rapid enough to require frequent division. Cutting the stems back to within 6"–8" of the ground after flowering will increase the density of the plant.

See color plate

UTILIZATION: *Amsonia* should be massed for optimum effect. The cool blue flower color does a good job of toning down adjacent flower colors in the border. It can be used in the front or middle of the border.

PROPAGATION: Seed, spring cuttings, or division in the spring or fall are all suitable propagation methods. Seed germination is enhanced by moist, cold stratification at 34°–40°F for 4–6 weeks. Tip cuttings should be taken in late spring and treated with a rooting hormone. Division is a quick method for increasing the number of plants. However, in a landscape situation, *Amsonia* would not have to be divided for many years.

DISEASES AND INSECTS: No serious problems.

HARDINESS: Zones 3–9.

CULTIVARS:
   var. *salicifolia* (sal-is-i-fō'li-à)—Willowleaf Blue Star—This variety does not stand as erect as the species. The leaves are linear-lanceolate and 5–10 times longer than they are wide. The flowers are blue with white throats.

RELATED SPECIES:

A. ciliata (sil-i-a'ta) (*A. angustifolia*)—Downy Star Flower, Downy Amsonia. The silky, dark green leaves are very thin, which gives rise to a feathery appearance. It is 1' to 3' tall with a 2' to 3' spread. The flowers are pale blue and remain effective for 3 to 4 weeks. it can be grown in the sun or partial shade. Hardiness is Zones 7–10.

A. hubrechtii (hu-brech'-ti-i)—Arkansas Amsonia. This relatively rare species has very fine foliage and the similar clusters of steel-blue flowers. Some of the nurseries specializing in plants for naturalistic landscapes are growing this species.

A. illustris (i-lus'-tris)—This southwest native has shiny broad leaves that have a shape similar to *A. tabernaemontana* and it grows to 3' tall. It is not easily obtained in the nursery trade.

ADDITIONAL NOTES: In the trade, there is an *Amsonia* that is listed as *A. montana* or *A. t.* var. *montana.* What is being offered seems to be smaller than the species. It appears to be a better plant because it does not require a pruning to maintain a tight shape. The nomenclature is confused on this one. The species was named for J. T. Tabernae-montanus, who was a German herbalist.

Native to eastern United States.   Perennial

SCIENTIFIC NAME/FAMILY: *Anaphalis triplinervis*

Asteraceae
(Compositae)

(à-naf'a-lis trip-lin-er'vis)

COMMON NAME: Pearly Everlasting

LEAVES: The leaves are alternate, sessile, and obovate to oblong-ovate.
They are 3"–5" long, 1" wide, with
3–5 main veins. The foliage is gray-
tomentose which creates a silvery
appearance to the plant.

FLOWER: The starry "everlasting" flower
heads are borne in a dense corymb.
Flowers are grayish-white with a
yellow center. Plants are dioecious.

HABIT: A rounded plant 12" to 18" tall
and 12" wide.

SEASON OF BLOOM: Late summer to
early fall.

CULTURE: A well-drained soil in full sun
to partial shade is best for this species. However, when gray foliage
plants are considered, this species is
one of the more tolerant ones when
grown in moist soils. Many gray foliage plants will "melt out" (rot) in
moist soils and/or humid climates.

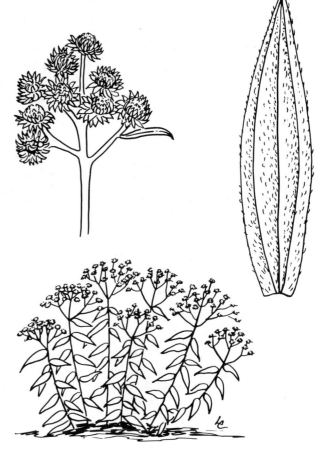

See color plate

UTILIZATION: Good border plant and is
often used as a background perennial for brighter flowers. The pearly everlastings are
good as dried flowers. They should be cut when the yellow centers of the flower head
can be first seen.

PROPAGATION: Division of the clump every 3–4 years is the easiest method.

DISEASES AND INSECTS: This species is very susceptible to larval damage.

HARDINESS: Zones 3–8.

CULTIVARS:
'Summer Snow' ('Sommerschnee')—This Klose Nursery, Germany, introduction (1973)
is a compact cultivar (8"–10") with white flowers and a neat mound of silver-gray
foliage. It is good as an edging perennial for the border.

RELATED SPECIES:
A. margaritacea (mar-gar-it-ā'-se-à). This eastern North American native has gray,
slender leaves and grows to 3' tall. It tends to be more invasive than *A. triplinervis*
but is a better choice if the site experiences periods of drought. Zones 3–8.
Anaphalis cinnamomea, an India native, is nearly identical to *A. margaritacea.* It has
a tighter growth habit than *A. margaritacea* and is only hardy to Zone 5.
A. nubigena (nū-bi-gee'-na). This species is similar to *A. triplinervis* but is only 6"–9"
tall.
Native to Himalayas.

Perennial

SCIENTIFIC NAME/FAMILY: *Anchusa azurea* (A. italica)　　　　　　Boraginaceae

(ang-kū'sȧ a-zū'rē-ȧ or a-zū-rē'ȧ)

COMMON NAME: Italian Alkanet, Italian Bugloss

LEAVES: Alternate, hispid, oblong or lanceolate, up to 6" long; leaves are sessile or clasping at the base, creating a winged petiole.

FLOWER: Bright blue, ¾" diameter, calyx lobes parted almost to base into linear segments; flowers borne in loose racemes.

HABIT: 3' to 5' erect plant with an 18"–24" spread. The habit can become floppy if the soil is too fertile.

SEASON OF BLOOM: Late spring to midsummer.

CULTURE: Best in full sun; will tolerate partial shade. The soils should be moist and well-drained. The growth habit is ungainly and the plant will usually require staking. It does not have much finesse when it falls onto other plants.

UTILIZATION: Border plant, best as single specimens or in groups of three. *Anchusa* may also be naturalized.

See color plate

PROPAGATION: Seed, clump division, and root cuttings. Seeds germinate in 3 to 4 weeks when placed in high humidity conditions at 70°–75°F. *Anchusa* self-sows easily, and volunteer seedlings should be thinned to prevent overcrowding. Division can be done in the spring every 2 years. Commercial production, especially the cultivars, is by root cuttings. Root pieces 2"–3" long can be taken in early spring and laid horizontally in a loose potting soil.

DISEASES AND INSECTS: Crown rot is the only serious problem and will often occur in wet soils.

HARDINESS: Zones 3 to 8. Growth has been good in Zone 8.

CULTIVARS:
　　'Dropmore'—A 1905 introduction with dark blue flowers, 3'–4' tall. This cultivar has an open, floppy habit and often requires staking.
　　'Little John'—This cultivar has dark blue flowers and a compact growth habit with a height of 12"–18".
　　'Loddon Royalist'—purple-blue flowers, 3' tall.

'Opal'—This selection has pale blue flowers and tends toward a floppy growth habit similar to 'Dropmore.'

'Royal Blue' ('Sutton's Royal Blue')—Deep blue flowers, 3' tall. This cultivar was introduced by the Sutton Seed Company.

ADDITIONAL NOTES: *Anchusa* is derived from Greek, and refers to a pigment obtained from the roots which was used as a cosmetic paint for staining the skin.

Native to Mediterranean region; has naturalized in North America.   Perennial

SCIENTIFIC NAME/FAMILY: *Anchusa capensis*   Boraginaceae

(an-kū'så kå-pen'sis)

COMMON NAME: Cape Forget-Me-Not, Summer Forget-Me-Not

LEAVES: Alternate leaves, narrow-lanceolate to linear, 3"–5" long, and ⅓" wide. Leaves and stems are coated with hispid hairs.

FLOWER: Blue flowers with white eyes, ¼" wide, are borne in racemes up to 2" long.

HABIT: Mounded plants with erect stems are 10"–18" tall which varies according to cultivar. Plants should be spaced 12" apart.

SEASON OF BLOOM: Summer.

CULTURE: Full sun or light shade in a fertile, moist, well-drained soil. Bloom is best in cooler climates. If summer heat stall occurs, the plants should be sheared to 6" which will promote flowering upon the return of cooler weather in the fall.

UTILIZATION: Use as an edging or massing in beds or borders.

PROPAGATION: Seed will germinate in 6–14 days at 70°F. Lowering the soil temperature at night enhances germination.

DISEASES AND INSECTS: There are generally few problems. Powdery mildew can be an occasional problem.

CULTIVARS:
'Blue Angel'—Marine blue flowers, 8"–10" tall.
'Blue Bird'—Indigo blue flowers, 18" tall.
'Dawn Mixed'—Mixed colors of blue, pink, and white, 18" tall.

Native to South Africa.   Biennial usually treated as an annual

SCIENTIFIC NAME/FAMILY: *Anemone blanda*   Ranunculaceae

(à-nem'ō-nē bland'à)

COMMON NAME: Greek Anemone, Greek Windflower, Grecian Windflower.

LEAVES: Most leaves emanate from the roots, are long-petioled, twice ternate; segments incised and ovate to obtuse.

FLOWER: Sky-blue for the species; red, white, and pink are available in cultivars. Solitary flowers are 2" across, with 9–14 sepals, which are the showy parts of the flower.

HABIT: 3" to 6" round habit.

SEASON OF BLOOM: Mid spring.

See color plate

CULTURE: Full sun to partial shade in a well-drained soil amended with well-composted organic matter. Although they carry the name windflower, *Anemones* should be sheltered from the wind for best performance. The rhizome-like tubers should be planted in September and October about 2" deep and 4" apart. Better rooting occurs if the tubers are soaked overnight in water before planting. In northern areas, *Anemone* should be handled as one would gladiolus, because Greek anemone is not reliably hardy in areas colder than Zone 5.

UTILIZATION: Sheltered rock garden, in the perennial border, or in semi-shaded naturalized woodland areas. It is also effective as a ground cover with larger bulbs.

PROPAGATION: Seed and division of the tubers. Seed is germinated at 70° to 75° during the spring. Tubers can be dug and divided after the foliage has died. The tubers are washed clean of soil and cut with a knife before the tubers dry. After drying, the tubers are very hard and resemble black, dead sticks. New tubers are relatively inexpensive and unless one wants to perpetuate a special cultivar, purchase of additional tubers may be easier than division. In southern zones the tubers persist from year to year.

DISEASES AND INSECTS: Leaf spot and rhizome rot are sometimes problems but are rarely present.

HARDINESS: Zones 5–8.

CULTIVARS:
    'Blue Star'—Intense blue single flowers, 2"–2½" in diameter.
    'Bridesmaid'—White flowers.
    'Charmer'—Deep pink flowers.
    'Pink Star'—Pink flowers with yellow centers.

'Radar'—Reddish-purple flowers with white centers.

'Rosea'—Clear pink flowers.

'White Splendor'—Double row of pure white sepals, spreads easily. Flowers are long lasting. This cultivar is similar to 'Bridesmaid.'

Native to central Asia.   Perennial—semi-hardy tuber

SCIENTIFIC NAME/FAMILY: *Anemone coronaria*   Ranunculaceae

(à-nem'ō-nē kor-o-nā'ri-a)

COMMON NAME: Poppy Anemone, Lilies of the Field, Windflower

LEAVES: Basal leaves are twice or ternately compound with narrow-cuneate segments; stem leaves cut into many narrow divisions.

FLOWER: Solitary and terminal flower is 1½"–2½" wide, poppy-like, in shades of red, blue, and white. The species has 6–8 sepals but double flowering cultivars exist. In fact, the species is not often used because cultivars with more vibrant colors are more popular.

HABIT: A tuft of bisected basal foliage gives rise to a glabrous scape 8"–12" tall. Poppy anemone is 6"–9" wide.

See color plate

SEASON OF BLOOM: Early spring.

CULTURE: Tubers should be soaked overnight and planted 2″–3″ deep with a 4″–6″ spacing. In warm to moderate climates, tubers may be planted in the fall whereas a spring planting should be done in northern climates. In northern areas the tubers can be planted in a pot in late winter and placed outside for a late spring bloom. Gardeners may treat this anemone as an annual by digging and discarding the tubers following flowering. Even in the best of climates the flowering vigor declines after the tuber has been in the ground for 2 to 3 years.

UTILIZATION: Poppy anemone is an excellent spring blooming plant for the border front or the sunny rock garden. It is also valued as a cut flower.

PROPAGATION: It is best to start with new tubers which are relatively inexpensive.

DISEASES AND INSECTS: No serious problems.

HARDINESS: Zones 6–9.

CULTIVARS:
'DeCaen' hybrids include a number of single selections of various colors. They are: 'Mr. Fokker,' violet-blue; 'Sylphide,' light purple; 'The Bride,' white; and 'Florist Mixture,' mixed colors.
'Hollandia' ('His Excellency')—Scarlet sepals with white bases surrounding a black center. The flowers are large.
'St. Brigid' hybrids—This group contains several semi-double selections of various colors which are: 'Lord Lieutenant,' deep blue; 'Mount Everest,' white; 'The Admiral,' blue; 'The Governor,' scarlet; and a mixture.

Native to the Mediterranean region.   Bulb (tuberous rhizome)

SCIENTIFIC NAME/FAMILY: *Anemone* × *hybrida* (A. japonica)   Ranunculaceae

(à-nem'ō-nē hīb'ri-da)

COMMON NAME: Hybrid Anemone, Japanese Anemone

LEAVES: Leaves are long-petioled and trifoliate. The leaflets usually have 3 lobes and are serrated.

FLOWER: Flowers are 2″–3″ across, white or pink with a silky sheen on the backside of the sepals. The flowers are carried on branching stems that arise gracefully above the dark green foliage.

HABIT: Large mound of foliage topped by many branched flower stems. Height may vary from 2′ to 4′. Plant width is 2 feet.

SEASON OF BLOOM: Late summer and fall.

CULTURE: Morning sun and filtered afternoon light combined with a fertile, moist, humus-rich soil is the best environment. Japanese anemone does poorly in summer drought, exposed and windy sites, and wet winter soils. If the first conditions are fulfilled, the spread of Japanese anemone is reasonably fast. A winter mulch is beneficial in northern climates.

UTILIZATION: Excellent border plant to provide color in the late summer and fall.

PROPAGATION: Division in spring or root cuttings in the winter are propagation methods. Root sections, 3″–4″ long, can be taken when the plant is dormant and placed vertically in a loose propagation medium. The propagation flats can be placed in a cold frame or unheated polyhouse.

See color plate

DISEASES AND INSECTS: No serious problems.

HARDINESS: Zones 4–8.

CULTIVARS:
'Alba'—Single white flowers, 2″–3″ wide, are held on 3′ tall stems.
'Bressingham Glow'—This Alan Bloom introduction has deep rose-magenta semi-double flowers. This cultivar developed from an attempt to produce a red Japanese anemone.
'Hadspen Abundance'—Single pink flowers, 3′ tall.

'Honorine Jobert'—This 1858 introduction is still one of the most popular white anemones. This abundant flowering cultivar is 3'-4' tall.

'Joseph Paxton'—This is the listed name of a 3' to 4' tall plant at Wisley Gardens in England. It is a soft pink with a darker pink center. It may be difficult to obtain.

'Konigin Charlotte' ('Queen Charlotte')—This 3' tall cultivar has semi-double, pink flowers which are 3" in diameter.

'Krimhilde'—A 1909 introduction with salmon pink flowers.

'Luise Uhink'—This selection is more common in Germany than in the United States. It has outstanding white flowers that are 4"–5" wide. It is 4' tall and bears numerous flowers.

'Margarete'—Semi-double dark pink flowers, 24"–36".

'Max Vogel'—This outstanding selection stands 4' tall and has large (4"–5") single pink flowers.

'Pamina'—Pink, semi-double flowers.

'Prinz Heinrich' (Prince Henry)—A 3' cultivar with deep rose, semi-double flowers.

'Whirlwind'—This 1887 release is 4'-5' tall with semi-double white flowers.

RELATED SPECIES:

A. hupehensis (hū-pe-en'sis) var. *japonica* (ja-pon'i-kȧ), Japanese Anemone. This native plant of China was introduced by Robert Fortune in 1844. It has pink, semi-double flowers. The cultivar 'September Charm' has single, silvery pink flowers. The height is 2'-3'. It is also often listed as a cultivar of *Anemone × hybrida*.

A. sylvestris (sil-ves'tris), Snowdrop Anemone. This spring-flowering anemone has white flowers. It is 12"–18" tall and 12" wide. In loose soils it has a tendency to spread quickly. The rate of increase is less in clay soils. It is a suitable plant for the edge of the woods.

A. vitifolia (vit-a-fol'-ē-a), Grapeleaf Anemone. This species is a clump former with white flowers in early fall. The dark green leaves are deeply lobed and resemble grape leaves. Flowering will extend into late fall. White woolly seeds will remain during the winter. 'Robustissima' has mauve pink flowers. It is more tolerant of climate extremes and is hardy to Zone 3.

Hybrid Origin.   Perennial

SCIENTIFIC NAME/FAMILY: *Anethum graveolens*

(a-nē'-thum gra-vē'ō-lenz)

Apiaceae
(Umbelliferae)

COMMON NAME: Dill

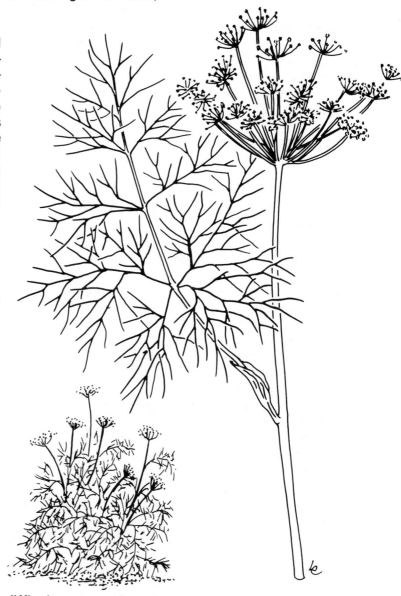

LEAVES: The leaves are divided numerous times, which creates a soft, fine textured feathery appearance. The leaf segments are very thin like the tip of a small needle. Foliage is blue-green. Dill and fennel are similar in appearance. A good distinguishing characteristic between the two is that dill has a hollow stem and fennel has a solid stem.

FLOWER: Numerous tiny yellow flowers compose a flat, compound umbel that is 4" wide. Each small flower has petals rolled inward from all sides of the flower. The elliptical-shaped fruit is flattened and slightly ribbed; 1/16" long.

HABIT: 3' tall erect plant with a feathery texture. Space plants 18"–24" apart.

SEASON OF BLOOM: Mid to late summer.

CULTURE: Full sun and fertile, well-drained soil. Dill will reseed rapidly. Reseeding can be prevented by harvesting the seed head before it is completely mature. Dill may become leggy and will require staking. Pea staking would be a preferred method. Dill is also difficult to transplant due to a taproot.

UTILIZATION: Dill is a staple in the herb garden. Its leaves and seeds are used for cooking. Many people probably associate dill with the making of dill pickles. Personally, I can remember many summers of following my mother down into the basement to check on the progress of the dill pickles in the 10 gallon crock. In the ornamental arena, the lacy foliage and large flower umbels make it an interesting garden plant. It can be used to fill voids or be the mediator between plants with contrasting colors.

PROPAGATION: Dill is propagated from seed. The seed should be covered and held at 70°F. Germination will occur in approximately 7 days.

DISEASES AND INSECTS: None serious.

ADDITIONAL NOTES: The common name is from the ancient Norse word, *dillo*, which means to lull. Medicinal folklore promoted the use of dill to induce sleep.

Native to the Mediterranean region.

Annual

SCIENTIFIC NAME/FAMILY: *Angelica archangelica*   Apiaceae
                        (an-jel'i-ka ark''ān'jel'-i-ca)   (Umbelliferae)

COMMON NAME: Angelica, Archangel, Wild Parsnip

LEAVES: Leaves are biternate; leaflets serrated. Leaflets are 2"–3" long with lower leaves
    sometimes 2'–3' in length. The stem is round, hollow and ridged. The branch resembles
    celery and has a celery fragrance. It has often been called wild celery because of these
    physical features.

FLOWER: Flowers are white or greenish. Many tiny flowers create a round shaped
    compound umbel which can be 6" in diameter.

HABIT: Angelica is a large, coarse-textured herb with a rounded habit. Height varies from
    5 to 8 feet. Plants should be spaced 4–6 feet apart if more than one is used in a
    design.

SEASON OF BLOOM: Early to midsummer.

CULTURE: In northern climates, angelica is grown in full sun. In the southern or far west
    areas, partial shade is more appropriate. Moist and fertile soils enhance the growth of
    angelica. Angelica is considered a biennial or a short-lived perennial. It actually dies
    after flowering and producing seed. The plant will live longer if the flower stalks are
    removed before the seed develops. If this is done, the plant may live for a number of
    years.

UTILIZATION: The stems, seeds, leaves, and roots are all edible and have the taste of
    licorice. Angelica has long been used for culinary purposes. As an ornamental, angelica
    strikes a bold pose in the border due to its size and globe-shaped umbels. A massive
    specimen is prominently displayed in the Queen's Garden at Kew Gardens in London,
    England.

PROPAGATION: Seed is the best means of propagation. Light is needed for germination.
    Seed viability is considered short so seed is often sown as soon as ripening occurs.
    Storing seeds in an airtight container in a refrigerator can extend the period of viability.

DISEASES AND INSECTS: Angelica is usually pest free; however, spider mites, aphids, and
    leaf miners can be occasional problems.

HARDINESS: Zones 4–8.

RELATED SPECIES:
    Angelica gigas—This large, 5'–6' tall, species has large divided leaves. Burgundy
        flowers, carried on 4"–8" wide umbels are produced in great quantities in July and
        August. It is often listed as a biennial; it may be a short-lived perennial. Best growth
        occurs in partial shade. This Korean native was introduced to the United States by
        Barry Yinger.

ADDITIONAL NOTES: Angelica is from Latin for *angelus*, an angel, which alludes to
    valuable healing properties. Other legend has it that this plant blooms each year on May
    8, which is the feast of St. Michael the Archangel.

Native to Europe and Asia.   Biennial

SCIENTIFIC NAME/FAMILY: *Antennaria dioica*   Asteraceae
                                                                              (Compositae)

(an-te-nā'ri-á di-oy'-ka))

COMMON NAME: Rose Pussytoes, Pussytoes

LEAVES: The plant is gray-tomentose throughout. The mat-like basal leaves are oblanceolate to spatulate, to 1" long, while the sparse, alternate stem leaves are narrow lanceolate. The general appearance of this species is like a gray carpet.

FLOWER: The flower heads are composed of only disk flowers and are about ¼" wide. Six to ten heads are densely packed into racemose to corymbose clusters. The flower heads have a white color and have a dry texture that is similar to an everlasting. Plants are dioecious.

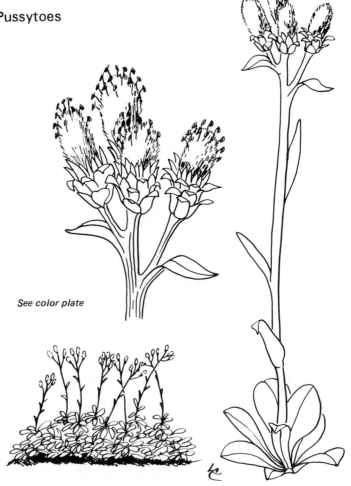

See color plate

HABIT: The creeping mat-like foliage is 2"–3" tall with flower stems growing to 10".

SEASON OF BLOOM: Late spring to early summer.

CULTURE: Pussytoes is easily grown in well-drained, preferably dry soil in full sun. It is so easy to grow that its rapid spread may become a nuisance.

UTILIZATION: The silver-gray foliage and carpet-like growth is useful in rock gardens, planting between paving stones, and planting atop stone walls.

PROPAGATION: Spring or fall division and seed. Seed should be germinated at 65° to 75°F in moist medium. After germination the temperature should be lowered about 10°.

DISEASES AND INSECTS: None serious.

HARDINESS: Zones 3–8.

RELATED SPECIES:
   A. rosea (rō'zē-a), Rose Pussytoes. Light pink flowers on stems 3"–4" tall. The flowers are showier than the above species.

ADDITIONAL NOTES: *Antennaria* is derived from antenna. This refers to the hairs that are attached to the seed, which resemble the antennae of insects.

Native to western United States.   Perennial

SCIENTIFIC NAME/FAMILY: *Anthemis tinctoria*

Asteraceae
(Compositae)

(an'the-mis tink-tō'ri-ȧ)

COMMON NAME: Golden Marguerite, Golden Chamomile, Ox-eye Chamomile.

LEAVES: Alternate, pinnately divided, the segments pinnatifid into ovate or oblong toothed mucronate
lobes; foliage aromatic, leaves white-woolly beneath.

FLOWER: Heads 2″ across, flowers golden-yellow.

HABIT: 2′ to 3′ erect stems and a 2′ width.

SEASON OF BLOOM: Summer, the genus *Anthemis* is
derived from *anthemon,* free flowering, suggesting
profuse blooming.

CULTURE: Full sun and any well-drained soil, tolerates
hot, dry areas. It is short-lived when grown in heavy
clay soils. The plants should be cut back heavily
after flowering to promote basal branches. Division
will need to be done every 2 years.

UTILIZATION: Perennial border or cut flowers that last
for several days. It is a valuable plant for dry and
low fertility soils. It survives with little care.

PROPAGATION: Clump division or stem cuttings taken
in the spring. It can also be grown from seed; seeds
will germinate in 1 to 3 weeks at 68°F.

DISEASES AND INSECTS: Usually none serious.

See color plate

HARDINESS: Zones 3–7.

CULTIVARS:
'E. C. Buxton'—Cream-colored ray flowers with
bright yellow disk flowers are carried on 2′–2½′
stems.
'Grallagh Gold' ('Beauty of Grallagh')—Two foot tall
plants with yellow orange flowers.
'Kelway' ('Kelwayi' or 'Kelway's Variety')—Bright yellow flowers on 2½′–3′ stems.
'Moonlight'—Soft pale yellow flowers, 2′ tall. The flowers fade to near white.

RELATED SPECIES:
A. marschalliana (mar-shal'-ē-ah''-nȧ) (*A. biebersteiniana*), Marshall Camomile. This
12″–18″ tall species has finely cut silvery leaves which have long hairs which have
a silky texture. The 2″–3″ diameter flowers are golden yellow. Flowering is in early
summer but may continue through the summer if the old flowers are removed.

ADDITIONAL NOTES: Many of the above cultivars are probably cultivars of *A. tinctoria* ×
A. sancti-johannis.

Native to eastern Europe

Perennial

SCIENTIFIC NAME/FAMILY: *Antirrhinum majus*   Scrophulariaceae

(an-ti-rī'num mā'jus)

COMMON NAME: Snapdragon, Common Snapdragon, Garden Snapdragon

LEAVES: Opposite or upper leaves alternate, lanceolate to oblong-lanceolate, to 3" in length, glabrous.

FLOWER: Flowers in terminal racemes, purplish-red to white, but cultivars with shades of red, pink, yellow, orange, bronze, and lavender are available.

HABIT: 6" to 48": small 6" to 9"; medium 18" to 24"; tall 3' to 4'. Intermediate most popular—good for bedding or cutting. Tall cultivars need to be staked to prevent lodging.

SEASON OF BLOOM: Early summer to fall (May to October).

CULTURE: Sun to partial shade, well-drained soil. Pinching and removal of old florets are required for good flowering.

UTILIZATION: Cut flowers, border, bedding, edging.

PROPAGATION: Seeds germinate in one or two weeks at 65°–70°F and respond to light. Snapdragons may self-sow with resultant seedlings the following spring. With winter protection it may remain a perennial, but for general garden use, it should be treated as an annual.

DISEASES AND INSECTS: Rust, leaf blights, downy mildew, gray mold, wilt, aphids, and mites. Leaf rust is the most serious problem for the garden snapdragon.

CULTIVARS: Many cultivars are available. A few are described below.
Tall cultivars
'Butterfly' strain—Peloric type flower resembling a penstemon, blend of colors, 30" tall. 'Bright Butterflies' and 'Madame Butterfly Mixed' (A.A.S., 1970) are two available cultivars.
'Rocket' strain—There are at least 10 different types of 'Rocket' snapdragons available. Bred for hot weather tolerance, 30"–36", excellent as cut flowers.

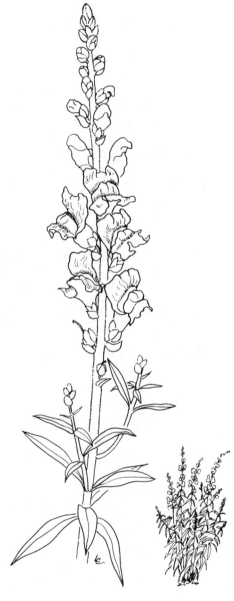

Medium cultivars

'Coronette Mixture'—20"–24", mixed colors.

'Hit Parade Mixture'—18"–24", good for bedding situations.

'Kim Mixture'—12". Wide range of colors. This is a replacement for 'Promenade Mixed.'

'Princess White with Purple Eye'—This 1987 All-American Selection has a white floret and a purple center. It reaches a height of 14" to 16".

'Sonnet' series—22". Wide range of colors. Central spike surrounded by lateral blooms. Plants in this series are self supporting and are excellent as cut flowers.

'Sprite Mixture'—14"–18". Good color range and excellent for cutting and bedding purposes.

Small cultivars

'Floral Carpet' series—Dwarf, 8" very showy plant for edging.

'Floral Showers'—This is an improvement on 'Floral Carpet.' 6"–8" tall spikes. There are 9 colors plus a mix.

'Kolibri Mixture'—6"–9", early flowering, seven colors in the mixture.

'Little Darling'—Peloric flowers, 12", mixed colors, A.A.S. 1971.

'Pixie Mixture'—6"–8", peloric flowers.

'Sweetheart Mixed'—12", double flowers on short spikes.

'Tahiti'—Dwarf selection that is 7"–8" tall. It has good heat tolerance and has dense, full spikes. There are 10 colors and a mix.

ADDITIONAL NOTES: The name *Antirrhinum* relates to the snout or nose shape of the flowers.

Snapdragon is native to the Mediterranean region.   Tender perennial
                                                                      grown as an annual

SCIENTIFIC NAME/FAMILY: *Aquilegia flabellata*   Ranunculaceae

(ak-wi-lē′ji-á flab-el-lā′-tá)

COMMON NAME: Fan Columbine

LEAVES: Leaves are 2 to 3 ternately compound, borne on long petioles; the apex of the leaflet is notched into 2 to 4 lobes. Leaves are glaucous and blue-green.

FLOWER: The waxy, nodding flowers are borne on 1–3 flowering stems. The lilac-blue flowers are 2″ wide and have short incurved spurs.

HABIT: 12″–18″; tall, compact species with a 12″ spread.

SEASON OF BLOOM: Late spring.

CULTURE: Sun or partial shade in a well-drained, moist soil.

UTILIZATION: *A. flabellata* and cultivars are well suited for the rock garden or border front.

PROPAGATION: Seed or careful spring division. The root of this species runs deep, making it harder to transplant. Small plants move more easily than larger ones. Many of the columbines will come true from seed.

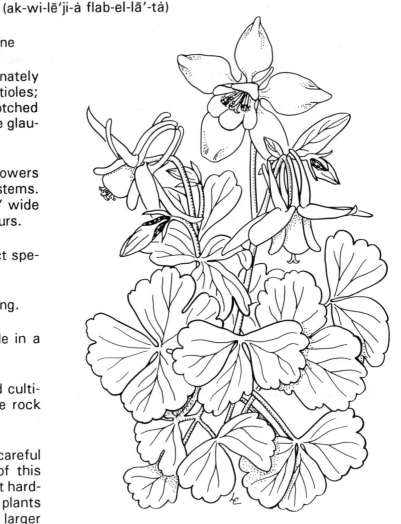

See color plate

DISEASES AND INSECTS: Crown rot, columbine borer, and columbine leaf miner are possible problems. Leaf miner is probably most universal and noticeable. Leaf miner damage usually does not cause lasting harm, but it certainly disfigures the foliage.

HARDINESS: Zones 3–9.

CULTIVARS:
   'Akitensis'—Large blue green leaves create a beautiful backdrop for the blue and white flowers.
   'Mini Star'—This dwarf selection is 6″–8″ tall and has blue sepals and white petals.
   var. *nana*—A compact form that is similar to the species but usually is less than 12″ tall.
   var. *nana alba*—Dwarf cultivar with thick-petalled, creamy-white flowers.

Native to Japan.   Perennial

SCIENTIFIC NAME/FAMILY: *Aquilegia* hybrids   Ranunculaceae

(ak-wi-lē'ji-à)

COMMON NAME: Hybrid Columbine

LEAVES: 2–3 ternately compound; apex of each leaflet deeply incised, petiole long and softly pubescent. Foliage has a gray-green color.

FLOWER: Flowers terminate the branch, hanging or erect; long hollow nectariferous backward-projecting spurs of the 5 petals; 5 sepals, colored like the petals, usually much shorter than the petal-spurs. Colors are red, pink, yellow, blue, white, or purple.

See color plate

HABIT: 1' to 3' erect plant with a 12" spread.

SEASON OF BLOOM: Late spring to early summer.

CULTURE: Full sun to partial shade, with excellent drainage; however, plants will not tolerate an overly dry soil. Light shade will prolong the flowering season. If leaf miner becomes a problem, one should cut the plants down to the ground after flowering. New leaves will develop to create a fresh mound of foliage.

UTILIZATION: Borders and naturalized settings. Because the flowering season ends early, columbines should be planted where their fading leaves will be camouflaged by foliage of other plants. They can also be used as cut flowers.

PROPAGATION: Sow seeds and place in refrigerator for 3 weeks and then germinate them 3 to 4 weeks with 85°F day and 70°F night temperatures. Plants grown from spring-sown seeds do not usually flower the first year. Division can be carefully done in late summer.

DISEASES AND INSECTS: Leaf spots, crown rot, root rot, rust, leaf miner, columbine borer, and aphids can be found on this species. Leaf miner is the most serious problem, especially on the hybrids. A systemic insecticide can be applied in early spring for prevention. Insecticides are not effective after the damage is noticed.

HARDINESS: Zones 3–9.

CULTIVARS:
'Biedermeier Strain'—12" tall, short-spurred flowers that are white, pink, or purple. This cultivar has a stiff growth habit.
'Crimson Star'—30"–36". Crimson and white flowers.
'Dragonfly'—18" tall plants with a mix of colors.
'Maxistar'—24", primrose-yellow flowers.
'McKana Hybrids'—30", a popular strain, mixed colors.

'Mrs. Scott Elliot'—Plants 2½'–3' tall, mixed colors, pastel shades.

'Music' ('Musik')—Plants in this series are 18"–20" tall and are available in 6 different colors. The flowers are large with long spurs. Very good plant for the front or the middle area of the border.

'Nora Barlow'— This 2' to 2½' cultivar has double flowers that are pink and red, tinged with green.

'Song Bird'—This series is known for its vibrant flower colors. Plants are 24"–30" tall.

'Snow Queen'—30"–36", pure white flowers.

'Spring Song'—Large flowers with many petals approaching a double character, multi-colored, 30".

RELATED SPECIES:

A. alpina (al-pī'-nà), Alpine Columbine. This native of Switzerland has a nearly solid blue flower with short, hooked spurs. The leaves are deeply divided into narrow lobes. Plants are 18"–30" tall.

var. *alba*—White flowers.

var. *superba*—Similar to the species but more vigorous and larger than the species. 'Hensol Harebell'—Deep blue flowers, 3' tall. It is a hybrid of *A. alpina* x *A. vulgaris*.

A. canadensis (kan-a-den'sis), Canadian Columbine, Wild Columbine. A 2'–3' tall species with nodding flowers with yellow sepals and red spurs. This North America native is very vigorous and is easily grown. It reseeds readily and will quickly colonize an area. 'Corbett' is a very floriferous, yellow flowered cultivar, 12"–24" tall. It was selected by Richard Simon of Bluemount Nursery, Monkton, Maryland.

A. chrysantha (kris-an'tha), Golden Columbine. This species has yellow flowers with long spurs. It has been used as one of the parents for the long-spurred hybrids.

ADDITIONAL NOTES: *Aquilegia* is a derivation of *aquila,* like an eagle, which may refer to the resemblance of the spurlike petals to an eagle's beak. In southern areas (Zone 8) columbine will survive one year and perform as an "annual."

Hybrid origin.   Perennial

SCIENTIFIC NAME/FAMILY: *Arabis caucasica* (*A. albida*)

(ar'å-bis ka-kas'i-kà)

Brassicaceae
(Cruciferae)

COMMON NAME: Rock Cress

LEAVES: Leaves are tufted and procumbent, basal leaves obovate, tapering toward the base; stem leaves auriculate to sagittate at base. Foliage is covered with very soft stellate pubescence.

FLOWER: White, fragrant flowers borne in racemes; petals ½" long. Individual flowers have 4 petals.

HABIT: 12" spreading plant with an 18" width.

SEASON OF BLOOM: Early spring.

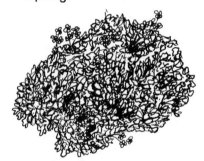

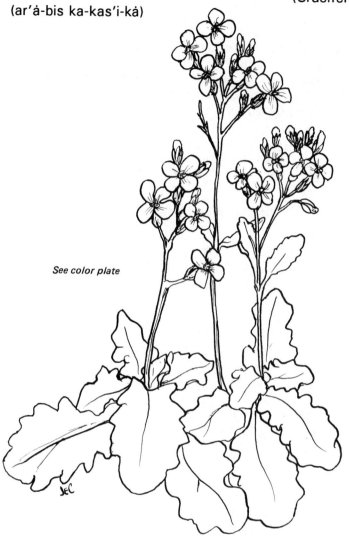

See color plate

CULTURE: Full sun in a very well-drained soil. If the climate is hot and humid, the foliage may "melt out" or show little vigor during the summer. This is what usually occurs in zones higher than Zone 7. The plants should be cut back heavily after flowering to promote a denser growth habit.

UTILIZATION: Rock garden, dry stone wall, in border as an edging plant.

PROPAGATION: Seed, cuttings and division. Seeds of *Arabis* should be germinated under light at 70° (3–4 weeks). Softwood cuttings perform best when taken immediately after bloom.

DISEASES AND INSECTS: Club root, downy mildew, white rust, and lily aphid are sometimes problems but they are usually not a serious concern.

HARDINESS: Zones 4–7.

CULTIVARS:
   'Flore Pleno'—Double white flowers which last longer than the species.
   'Schneehaube' ('Snow Cap')—Single white flowers are abundantly produced on this early flowering cultivar, 8" tall.
   'Spring Charm'—6", rose-tinted flowers.

'Variegata' — Single white flowers are carried above leaves with irregular yellow-white variegation. This characteristic can extend the interest through the season.

RELATED SPECIES:

A. procurrens (prō-kur'-enz). Small dark green leaves form a dense mat above which rises a profusion of sprays of white flowers. A new kid on the block, not as well known as *A. caucasica,* but it is increasing in popularity. It will grow in a variety of conditions, sun or light shade, and in poor, dry soil or relatively fertile soil. Easily propagated by division. Zone 4.

ADDITIONAL NOTES: *Arabis* is the Greek word for *Arabian. Arabis* should be pruned back after flowering to retain a compact plant. Failure to do this will result in plants becoming straggly.

Native to Mediterranean region.   Perennial

SCIENTIFIC NAME/FAMILY: *Arctotis stoechadifolia*   Asteraceae
                                                                                          (Compositae)

(ärk-tō'tis sto-chad-i-fō'li-a)

COMMON NAME: African Daisy, Blue-eyed
African Daisy, Arctotis

LEAVES: Leaves alternate, oblong or obovate, 1"–4" long, lyrate and lobed and
slightly toothed, white-tomentose when
young.

FLOWER: Daisy-like flower heads are 3"
across on peduncles longer than the
leaves; disk flowers violet, ray flowers
creamy-white above, reddish below.

HABIT: Decumbent to trailing stems, 18"–
24" tall and 18" wide.

SEASON OF BLOOM: Summer to fall (June–
September) if faded blooms are removed.

CULTURE: Sun, will withstand drought; can
be planted in dry, sandy soil.

UTILIZATION: Border and possibly cutting.
Arctotis has long stems that make it desirable for flower arrangements, but the
flowers close at night.

PROPAGATION: Seed germinates in two to
three weeks at 60°–70°F.

DISEASES AND INSECTS: Leaf blotch, leaf
spot, root-knot, and root rot. Generally,
none of these are serious.

HARDINESS: Zones 9–10.

CULTIVARS:
var. grandis—Large pearly-white flowers
with steel blue disk flowers, stems 2'
tall. This variety is a larger version of
the species.

ADDITIONAL NOTES: *Arctotis* is derived from *arktos,* a bear, and *otos,* an ear, alluding to
the hairy scales of the pappus.

Native to South Africa.   Annual in most climates

SCIENTIFIC NAME/FAMILY: *Arenaria montana*   Caryophyllaceae

(ar-e-nā'ri-à mon-tā'na)

COMMON NAME: Mountain Sandwort

LEAVES: Opposite leaves, linear–lanceolate, ½"–¾" long, short petioled or
sessile. The stems and foliage are
lightly pubescent.

FLOWER: The profuse white flowers are
¾" to 1" wide and borne in cymes
containing from 2 to 10 flowers.

HABIT: Prostrate growing with 12" long
trailing stems that will grow 6"–8"
tall.

SEASON OF BLOOM: Mid to late spring.

CULTURE: Partial shade or full sun in a
well-drained, moist soil. *Arenaria* has
shallow roots and must be watered
during dry periods of the spring and
summer.

UTILIZATION: Rock gardens, front of the
border.

See color plate

PROPAGATION: Cuttings, division, and
seeds.

DISEASES AND INSECTS: Leaf spot, powdery mildew, and rust have been reported, but
control practices are usually not necessary.

HARDINESS: Zones 4–7.

RELATED SPECIES:
Minuartia verna ssp. *caespitosa* (min-ū-ar'te-a ver'na cās-pē-to'sa) (*A. verna*)—Moss
Sandwort. The moss-like leaves are covered with white flowers in mid spring to
early summer. It is attractive when planted between paving stones or as a ground
cover in a rock garden. The cultivar 'Aurea' has yellow-green foliage. If these
selections are used as fillers in paving stones, it is important that moisture is
provided during dry periods.

Native to northwestern Europe.   Perennial

SCIENTIFIC NAME/FAMILY: *Arisaema triphyllum*   Araceae

(ar-i-sē'ma trī-fīl'um)

COMMON NAME: Jack-in-the-Pulpit, Indian Turnip

LEAVES: Each plant usually has two 3-lobed leaves which are borne on 12" long petioles. The leaf segments are sessile, elliptic shaped, and 9" long. The leaves generally elongate after flowering.

FLOWER: The arrangement of the flower parts of *Arisaema* is unusual and very distinct. The spathe (pulpit or hood) is 4"–7" long with the blade bent forward across the top of the plant. The outside of the spathe is green or purple, and the inside may have a bold pattern of alternating purple and greenish white stripes. The spadix (Jack) is cylindrical with pollen-bearing flowers near the top and a cluster of female flowers near the base. Red berries appear 5–6 months after flowering.

HABIT: 1'–2' tall plant with leaves and flower stalk. There are usually only 2 leaves. Plant is 12" wide.

SEASON OF BLOOM: Early to mid-spring.

CULTURE: Jack-in-the-Pulpit needs a constantly moist to wet site in partial shade. Heavy clay soils should be amended with compost. This species will perform poorly in soils that are not moist.

UTILIZATION: This species belongs in the woodland garden, especially in low, wet areas where other plants may not perform well. It can be interplanted with *Tiarella, Geranium,* and the native *Sedum.* The red berries are eaten by wildlife.

PROPAGATION: Seeds should be gathered when they turn red and the pulp removed immediately. Seeds should then be stratified for 2 months in moist sphagnum moss. If seeds dry out, germination can be delayed for a year. Seeds can be sown indoors or outside. Germination will occur in 2 to 3 weeks. Flowering plants will take three seasons.

DISEASES AND INSECTS: No serious problems.

HARDINESS: Zones 4–9

RELATED SPECIES:
A. *dracontium,* 'Green Dragon'—This species has a single, long-petioled leaf divided into many segments, up to 15. The spathe is light green and terminates in a long, ascending projection that looks like a yellow whip. Orange berries.

Native to eastern United States   Perennial

SCIENTIFIC NAME/FAMILY: *Armeria maritima* (A. vulgaris)   Plumbaginaceae

(är-mē′ri-á má-rit′i-ma)

COMMON NAME: Sea Pink, Sea Thrift, Common Thrift

LEAVES: Linear, to 4″ long, 1-ribbed, and about 1/8″ wide. The evergreen leaves grow in tufts or clumps. The clumps look like mossy cushions.

FLOWER: Flower heads are borne on scapes, flower clusters are pink or white, 1″ across, subtended by scarious bracts; the outer ones shorter than the head.

HABIT: Dense rounded mat 3″–4″ tall with flower scapes up to 12″. The clumps can spread to 12″.

SEASON OF BLOOM: Mid to late spring.

CULTURE: Full sun, adapts very well in dry, infertile soils. Soils moist and high in fertility will cause the dense mats to rot in the center. It is time to lift and divide the plants when they become ragged.

UTILIZATION: Edging, rock garden, cut flowers. This species is very salt tolerant.

PROPAGATION: Seed and clump division. Soak seeds for 6–8 hours and then germinate at 65°–70°F. Clump division should be done if the clump becomes open in the center.

DISEASES AND INSECTS: There are no serious pests.

HARDINESS: Zones 4–8.

See color plate

CULTIVARS:

'Alba'—White flowers, dark green leaves, 5" tall.

'Bloodstone'—Bright red flowers are carried on stems 8"–10" tall. A very excellent plant that is probably a hybrid between *A. maritima* and *A. alliacea.*

'Dusseldorfer Stolz' ('Dusseldorf Pride'). Carmine-red flowers on 6"–8" tall stems. This cultivar was introduced in 1957 but is just now gaining some popularity in the United States.

'Laucheana'—Deep rose pink flowers, large tuft of leaves, 6" tall.

'Ruby Glow'—Ruby colored flowers on 10" stems. This cultivar is similar to 'Dusseldorfer Stolz.'

'Splendens'—Deep red flowers, 8"–10" tall.

'Vindictive'—This cultivar has rosy-red flowers and is a compact 6" tall.

RELATED SPECIES:

A. alliacea (*A. plantaginea*), Plantain Thrift. Plantain thrift is a larger species than *A. maritima.* The leaf is 1"–2" wide with parallel veins and resembles a plantain leaf which gives rise to the common name. The pink flowers are 3/4" wide and the flowering stems are 12"–18" tall. The cultivar 'Bees Ruby' is a hybrid of *A. alliacea* × *A. maritima.* It has shocking pink flowers carried on 18" tall stems.

A. juniperifolia (*A. caespitosa*), Pyrenees Thrift. This rock garden plant from Spain is 2"–4" tall and will grow into a hummock 6" wide. The needlelike leaves are triangular and 3/4" long. The flowers are light pink, 3/8" wide, and carried on 1" tall stems. It should be located in a sunny rock garden in well-drained, gravelly soil. Drainage is most important with this species.

A. pseudarmeria (*A. cephalotes*), Pinkball Thrift. This species has large oblong leaves, 5–7 veined, 3/4" wide, and 6"–8" long. The flower stems are 12" tall and are topped by 1"–2" diameter pink flowers. 'Alba' has white flowers.

ADDITIONAL NOTES: Sea pink is an appropriate common name. On a visit to the Isle of Mull, Scotland, I photographed sea pink in the high tide land of the Firth of Lorn.

Native to Spain, Portugal, and France.   Perennial

SCIENTIFIC NAME/FAMILY: *Arrhenatherum elatius*   Poaceae
                        ssp. *bulbosum 'Variegatum'*   (Gramineae)

(ar-ren-a'ther-um ē-lāt'ē-us bul-bo'-sum var-i-gā'-tum)

COMMON NAME: Variegated Bulbous Oat Grass, Variegated Oat Grass

LEAVES: Leaf blades 1/4" to 1/8" wide, 12"–16" long, lightly pubescent above, smooth beneath. The blue-green leaves have conspicuous white stripes.

FLOWER: The pale green spikelets are borne in a loose and open panicle 4"–8" long. The flowers are not considered ornamental.

HABIT: Low-open spreading grass, 12" tall.

SEASON OF BLOOM: The inflorescence is produced from early to late summer.

CULTURE: Oat grass can be grown in full sun to partial shade in a well-drained soil. It is tolerant of dry soils. The variegated foliage is best in spring and fall. During hot summers, the leaf tips may turn brown. If this occurs, shear the foliage and it will again look good in the fall when the weather moderates.

UTILIZATION: Variegated oat grass is used in the rock garden, perennial border, and as a specimen plant.

PROPAGATION: Increased by division.

DISEASES AND INSECTS: No serious problems.

HARDINESS: Zones 5–8.

Native to Europe.   Perennial

SCIENTIFIC NAME/FAMILY: *Artemisia abrotanum*   Asteraceae (Compositae)

(är-te-miz'i-á or är-te-mē'zhe-a a-brō'-tan-um)

COMMON NAME: Southernwood, Old-Man, Lad's Love

LEAVES: Alternate leaves, divided into very fine, filamentous segments which creates a feathery texture to the foliage. The foliage is green, unlike many of the artemisias, which have silver or grey leaves. The leaves are quite aromatic, with a citrus to camphorlike fragrance.

FLOWER: Yellowish white flowers compose ¼" wide nodding heads in a loose panicle. The flowers are not ornamental.

HABIT: Multiple branched, dense upright subshrub to 4 feet tall and 18" wide.

SEASON OF BLOOM: Mid to late summer.

CULTURE: Southernwood grows well in a dry, well-drained soil in a full sun site. Pruning the plant in early summer will prevent a weedy look later in the season.

See color plate

UTILIZATION: Place this plant in the border or along a garden path where passersby will brush the foliage to release the aromatic fragrance.

PROPAGATION: Semi-hardwood cuttings taken in late summer or early fall work best with this subshrub perennial. Rooting percentage increases with the use of a rooting hormone. If rooting is done in an intermittent mist system, rooted cuttings must be removed quickly to prevent loss from rotting of the cuttings.

DISEASES AND INSECTS: No serious diseases or insects. Wet soils or excessively humid weather will cause the plant to open in the middle.

HARDINESS: Zones 5–9.

Native to southern Europe.   Perennial

SCIENTIFIC NAME/FAMILY: *Artemisia absinthium*

Asteraceae
(Compositae)

(är-te-miz'i-á or är-te-me'zhe-a ab-sin'the-um)

COMMON NAME: Wormwood, Absinthe

LEAVES: Alternate leaves, pinnately divided into 2–3 fingerlike segments, silver-pubescent on the surfaces. Leaves are 2"–5" long. Stems and leaves have a strong acrid odor.

FLOWER: Yellow flowers are borne in drooping heads that are ⅛" wide. The heads are carried in leafy panicles.

HABIT: Erect, bushy perennial 2½' tall and 2' wide.

SEASON OF BLOOM: Late summer.

CULTURE: Full sun and a dry, well-drained soil. As a native plant it is found as a pioneer plant on high pH, sandy-gravelly loam or clay loam soils. It is easily grown.

UTILIZATION: The attractive grey-green foliage provides a nice effect for the herb garden or border. Like other artemisias, wormwood is a good filler for the garden and a separator of clashing plants. Cut branches can be used in wreathes.

PROPAGATION: Wormwood is propagated by division or seed. Seed will germinate in 7–10 days when uncovered at 70°F.

DISEASES AND INSECTS: None serious.

HARDINESS: Zones 4–9.

CULTIVARS: 'Lambrook Silver'—The foliage is more silver colored than the species, 2½' tall. This cultivar was selected by Margery Fish along with 'Lambrook Giant' which is much rarer. 'Lambrook Silver' should be cut back during the summer to promote branching and to prevent a floppy appearance. Zones 4–9.

RELATED SPECIES: A. × 'Powis Castle'—The parents of this hybrid selected by Mr. A. J. Hancock are thought to be *A. arborescens* and *A. absinthium*. The silver foliage is very finely textured, a trait of *A. arborescens,* and derives hardiness from *A. absinthium.* It is 3 feet tall and 4 feet wide. This cultivar lining the walls and terraces of Powis Castle is a sight to behold, well worth the trip to Wales. It is likely that the hardiness is Zone 5; however, this hybrid is just starting to become available in the United States and there has not been a lot of experience gained as yet.

ADDITIONAL NOTES: *Artemisia absinthium* has had a long history of medicinal use. It is most famous for the drink, absinthe. The leaves and flowers were used to create a green-colored drink that was an extremely strong stimulant. Absinthe is illegal in most countries because of the strong and strange effects that it had on those who drank it. Wormwood is not recommended for home remedies due to its "toxic" effect.

Native to Mediterranean region; naturalized through the temperate climate countries.

Perennial

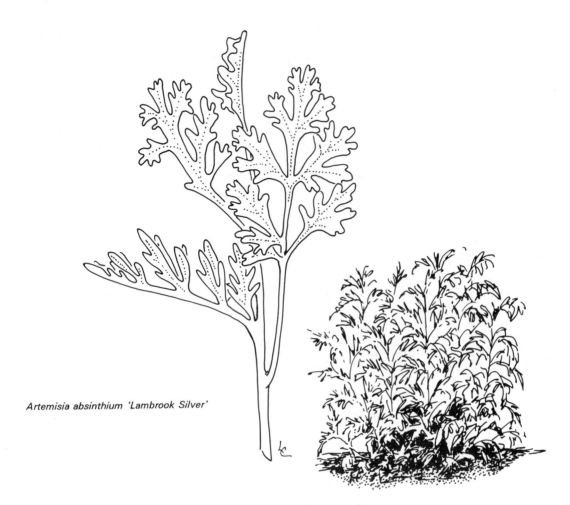

Artemisia absinthium 'Lambrook Silver'

See color plate

Artemisia 'Powis Castle'
See color plate

SCIENTIFIC NAME/FAMILY: *Artemisia dracunculus*

(är-te-miz'i-a or är-te-mē'zhė-a drā-kun'kū-lus)

Asteraceae
(Compositae)

COMMON NAME: Russian Tarragon

LEAVES: Alternate leaves, linear to lanceolate, 1″ to 4″ long, 1/8″ to 1/4″ wide. Leaves have a slight anise odor but not nearly as strong as French tarragon.

FLOWER: Whitish-green flowers in 1/8″ diameter heads are borne in loose spreading panicles. The flowers are not the ornamental feature.

HABIT: Erect growing herb which can grow as high as 5′ tall; however, it will usually be about 3′. Space tarragon 2′ apart in the garden.

SEASON OF BLOOM: Russian tarragon flowers in the summer. The more desirable French tarragon is not grown for flowers and rarely sets seeds.

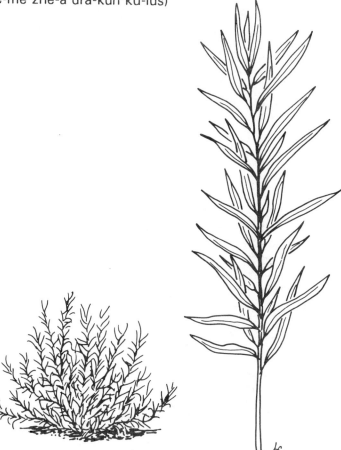

CULTURE: Full sun and a well-drained soil. Wet or acid soils are responsible for poor growth. French tarragon requires more winter protection than Russian tarragon. French tarragon is 2′–3′ tall.

UTILIZATION: The anise flower of French tarragon enhances many foods including vinegars and sauces, meats, and salads. Russian tarragon is a poor substitute and may not be worth the space in the herb garden. The tarragons are generally not used in the ornamental garden.

PROPAGATION: French tarragon can be rooted from cuttings in midsummer. They root in 2 months and must be overwintered in a cold frame or minimum heat greenhouse. It can also be increased by division. Russian tarragon is propagated by seed. The seed germinates easily at 60°–70°F.

DISEASES AND INSECTS: No serious diseases or insects.

HARDINESS: Zones 5–8.

CULTIVARS: 'Sativa'—French Tarragon. This cultivar should be the choice for the producer and gardener. The flavor is superior to the Russian tarragon. French tarragon should be divided and replanted every 3 years to prevent deterioration of the clump.

ADDITIONAL NOTES: Tarragon is a corruption from the French *esdragon*, derived from the Latin *dracunculus*, or little dragon. The dragon connection may have come from the biting taste of the herb or its entangling serpentlike roots. "Dragon" herbs were thought to cure the bites of poisonous animals.

Native to Siberia

Perennial

SCIENTIFIC NAME/FAMILY: *Artemisia lactiflora*   Asteraceae (Compositae)

(är-te-miz'i-a or är-te-mē'zhe-a lak-ti-flō'-ra)

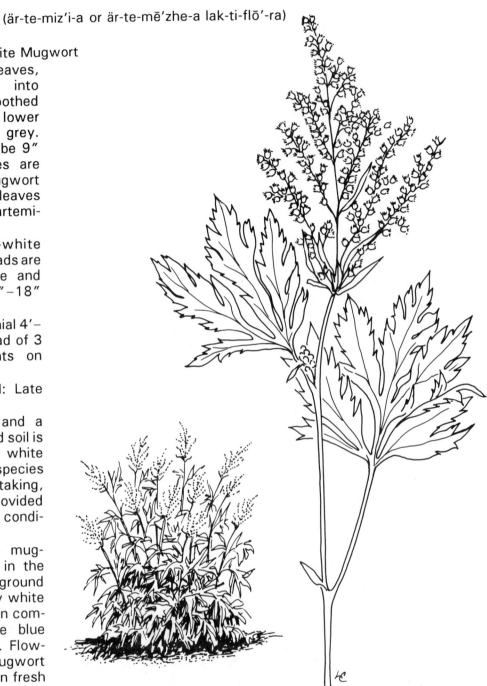

COMMON NAME: White Mugwort

LEAVES: Alternate leaves, pinnately divided into broad-lanceolate toothed or cut segments, lower surface is pale grey. Lower leaves can be 9" long, upper leaves are smaller. White mugwort has the coarsest leaves of the ornamental artemisias.

FLOWER: Creamy-white flowers, flower heads are about 1/16" wide and are borne in 12"–18" long panicles.

HABIT: Upright perennial 4'–6' tall with a spread of 3 feet. Space plants on 2'–3' centers.

SEASON OF BLOOM: Late summer and fall.

CULTURE: Full sun and a moist, well-drained soil is an ideal site for white mugwort. This species will often require staking, especially when provided optimum growing conditions.

UTILIZATION: White mugwort is effective in the border as a background plant. The creamy white flowers are good in combination with the blue asters of autumn. Flowers of white mugwort can also be used in fresh or dried floral arrangements.

See color plate

PROPAGATION: Propagation is usually done by division. In the garden, division is every 3 to 4 years.

DISEASES AND INSECTS: Powdery mildew and leaf rust can be a problem in humid areas.

HARDINESS: Zones 4–8.

ADDITIONAL NOTES: When one talks about artemisias, *Artemisia lactiflora* would probably not be included in the conversation. Nearly all of the ornamental artemisias have fine-textured gray or silver foliage. White mugwort is an oddity because of its green, coarsely toothed leaves and showy flowers. It is the only wormwood that is grown for its flowers.

Native to China.   Perennial

SCIENTIFIC NAME/FAMILY: *Artemisia ludoviciana*

(är-te-miz'i-a or är-te-mē'zhe-a lu-do-vis'e-ā-nȧ)

COMMON NAME: Louisiana Artemisia, White Sage

Asteraceae
(Compositae)

LEAVES: The silver-gray foliage is alternate, lanceolate, to 4" long. The leaves may be toothed to the base or more often only notched at the top. Foliage is aromatic when crushed.

FLOWER: The white flower heads are small and borne in dense panicles. The flower effect is not effective and the foliage is considered the ornamental feature. There are male and female flowers on separate plants.

HABIT: 2'–3' tall erect plant. It develops into a broad spreading clump.

SEASON OF BLOOM: Summer.

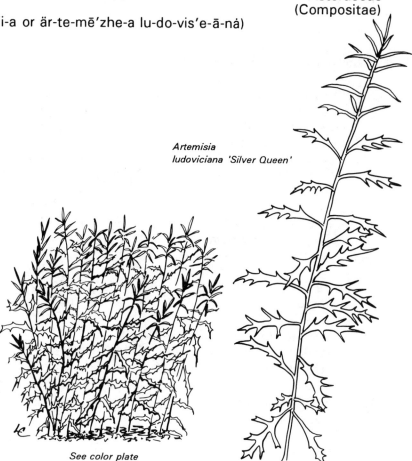

Artemisia ludoviciana 'Silver Queen'

See color plate

CULTURE: Full sun and a well-drained soil are essential. One needs to remember that the roots of gray foliage plants will often rot in wet soil and the foliage may decline in high humidity climates. Division is needed on a regular basis even in clay soils to control the spread of this species. Loose, sandy soils in southern zones, where it can spread quickly, are favorites of white sage.

UTILIZATION: The flowers are not impressive on *Artemisia*, and it is usually considered a foliage plant. Very suitable for massing, filling voids, and complementing the pinks, lavenders, blue and pale yellow flowers found in the border. The foliage can also be dried for decorative use.

PROPAGATION: Division in the spring or summer stem cuttings work well.

DISEASES AND INSECTS: Leaf rust can sometimes be a problem.

HARDINESS: Zones 5–8.

CULTIVARS:
    'Latiloba'—Shorter growing selection (12"–24" high) with gray-green leaves with 3–5 lobes at the tips.
    'Silver King'—A very good cultivar that is more compact than the species and has good bright silver foliage. It is hardy to Zone 3.
    'Silver Queen'—The foliage of this cultivar is deeply cut (see drawing). Excellent plant for cutting flowers. It will quickly spread in loose soils.
    'Valerie Finnis'—Wide, silver-grey leaves, 18"–24" tall.

Native to western United States.

Perennial

SCIENTIFIC NAME/FAMILY: *Artemisia pontica*   Asteraceae (Compositae)

(är-te-miz'i-à or är-te-mē'zhe-a pon'ti-ka)

COMMON NAME: Roman Wormwood

LEAVES: Alternate leaves, divided into many segments, very delicate, ferny texture. Leaves have a grey pubescence on both surfaces.

FLOWER: Open panicles of nodding whitish yellow flower heads. This species is usually grown for its foliage and not for flowers.

HABIT: Dense, low-growing species, 18″ tall and 18″ wide.

SEASON OF BLOOM: Summer.

CULTURE: Full sun and well-drained soil.

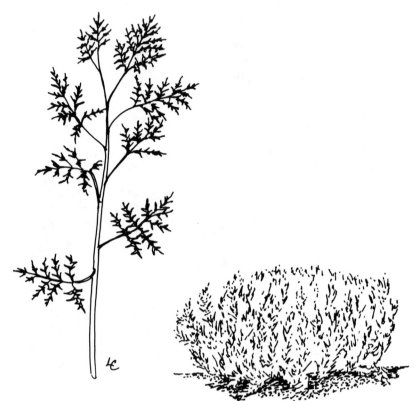

UTILIZATION: Roman wormwood can be invasive, particularly when grown in sandy, loose soils. It is not a selection for the small garden and should be restricted to expansive areas where a quick-covering ground cover is needed.

PROPAGATION: Propagation is by division or stem cuttings.

DISEASES AND INSECTS: None serious.

HARDINESS: Zones 4–9.

Native to southeast and central Europe.   Perennial

SCIENTIFIC NAME/FAMILY: *Artemisia schmidtiana* 'Nana'
                       or 'Silver Mound'

Asteraceae
(Compositae)

(är-te-miz'i-à or är-te-mē'-zhe-a schmit-i-a'na)

COMMON NAME: Wormwood, Angels-Hair, Silvermound Artemisia

LEAVES: Alternate, to 1¾" long, twice palmately divided into linear segments, with silver-white silky hairs, uppermost leaves linear. Foliage has a very soft velvet texture.

FLOWER: The flowers are not spectacular. The chief garden attraction is the foliage.

HABIT: 12"–18" tall and forms a rounded mound about 18" in diameter.

SEASON OF BLOOM: Not important.

CULTURE: 'Silver Mound' should be grown in full sun in well-drained, infertile soil. If grown in fertile, moist soils, the plant height is more than 12" and the clump opens in the middle. The open center can be delayed by trimming the clumps back before they flower. If this selection is grown in a hot and humid climate, the silver, pubescent foliage may rot.

UTILIZATION: Perennial border as a specimen plant or as a contrast to colors of blue, red, and yellow. Greatest value is in borders or rock gardens. 'Silver Mound' also looks good in massed plantings.

PROPAGATION: Stem cuttings. Wormwood rarely spreads, hence propagation by cuttings rather than division is the normal method. Cuttings can be easily rooted during the summer.

See color plate

DISEASES AND INSECTS: Rust is the principal problem.

HARDINESS: Zones 3–7.

ADDITIONAL NOTES: *Artemisia* was named in honor of Artemis, the Greek goddess of chastity.

Native to Japan.

Perennial

SCIENTIFIC NAME/FAMILY: *Artemisia stelleriana*   Asteraceae
(Compositae)

(är-te-miz'i-à or är-te-mē'zhe-a stel-lar''-e-ā'-na)

COMMON NAME: Beach Wormwood, Old Woman, Dusty Miller

LEAVES: Alternate leaves, 2"–3" long, 1" wide. The leaves resemble chrysanthemum leaves that have been cut out of grey felt. This species also resembles the annual Dusty Miller, *Senecio maritima*.

FLOWER: The yellow flower heads are held in narrow, leafy panicles. Individual heads are ¼" wide.

HABIT: Creeping to mounded habit, 12"–24" tall and 2'–3' wide.

See color plate

SEASON OF BLOOM: Early summer.

CULTURE: Full sun and a very well-drained soil. Beach wormwood is sensitive to winter wetness.

UTILIZATION: Attractive when used as a specimen plant in the rock garden or in the dry stone wall. Planted in masses it will function as a ground cover. The silver-grey foliage is a nice complement to blue-flowered plants.

PROPAGATION: Propagated by division or stem cuttings.

DISEASES AND INSECTS: Very susceptible to larval damage in late spring and early summer.

HARDINESS: Zones 3–8.

Native to Asia, naturalized in northern Europe and eastern North America.   Perennial

SCIENTIFIC NAME/FAMILY: *Arum italicum* 'Pictum'   Araceae

(ā'rum i-tal'i-kum pik'tum)

COMMON NAME: Painted Arum

LEAVES: The leaves which rise out of a clump are hastate (spear-shaped) and 12" long. Each leaf is conspicuously marbled with grays and creams with a dark green background. The leaves emerge in the fall. In mild winter climates the leaves will remain over winter. In areas with cold winters, Ohio for example, the leaves die and reappear in the spring as they do on most perennials.

FLOWER: Spathe is whitish-green spotted with purple, spadix is yellow. Spadix does not extend past the middle of the spathe blade. The flowers resemble small Jack-in-the-Pulpit flowers.

HABIT: Clump-forming perennial, 12" to 18" tall and 18" wide.

SEASON OF BLOOM: The greenish white flowers are present for a brief time in the late spring. During midsummer stout stalks carry columns of orange-red berries.

CULTURE: Painted arum is found at its best in partial to full shade in humus enriched soil. During the spring and early summer, the soil should be moist. After the leaves become dormant, the soil can be drier.

See color plate

UTILIZATION: Although the orange-red berries are unusual and striking in midsummer, the variegated foliage is usually considered the ornamental feature. The marbled leaves are treasured by flower arrangers, and the leaves certainly add a class to the garden during the spring in cold climates and fall, winter, and spring in milder climates.

PROPAGATION: The tubers can be divided while the plant is dormant, or arum can be propagated by seed. Seed requires a moist, cold stratification period. Germination is difficult and may require a year for germination to occur.

DISEASES AND INSECTS: No serious problems.

HARDINESS: Zones 5–9.

CULTIVARS:
   A. italicum 'Marmoratum'—Very large leaves which are marbled along the veins with yellow-green. The foliage is not as attractive as 'Pictum.'

Native to southern Europe.   Perennial

SCIENTIFIC NAME/FAMILY: *Aruncus dioicus* (A. sylvester)   Rosaceae

(a-run'kus dī-ō'i-kus)

COMMON NAME: Goat's Beard

LEAVES: The 2'–3' long leaves are alternate and pinnately compound. Leaflets are ovate to ovate-lanceolate, 2" to 4" long, doubly serrate. The dark green foliage looks very much like that of an overgrown *Astilbe.*

FLOWER: The cream colored flowers are very small, ⅛" across. They are borne, however, in dense spikes making large panicles that can be 12" long. *Aruncus* is dioecious, the male plants having showier flowers; however, most nurseries do not separate their *Aruncus* by gender.

HABIT: Large, rounded "herbaceous shrub" growing 4' to 6' tall and 6' wide.

SEASON OF BLOOM: Early summer.

See color plate

CULTURE: The best site is one in partial shade with a moisture-retentive soil. In areas with cool summers, *Aruncus* can be grown in full sun. *Aruncus dioicus* has a large spread. It should be initially placed 4' to 5' between plants to allow for mature spread and to save the labor required to transplant a large *Aruncus*. *Aruncus* will survive in the South, but the best specimens will usually be found above zone 6.

UTILIZATION: Goat's beard looks very nice as a single specimen or placed in the back of the border or the center of an island bed.

PROPAGATION: Division is a suitable method, but it is hard work and the species rarely needs to be divided. Fresh seed should be collected and sown immediately. Hold the seed at 70°–75°F in humid conditions. Old seed should be stratified for 4–6 weeks at 40°F.

DISEASES AND INSECTS: Several leaf spots have been reported. These problems are never serious enough to warrant fungicide control.

HARDINESS: Zones 3–7.

CULTIVARS:
>   var. *astilboides* (a-stil-boi'dez)—This selection is an exact miniature of the species except that it is only 18"–24" tall. Unfortunately, it is not easily found in the trade. It would be an excellent substitute in smaller gardens that are not large enough to handle the size of the species.
>   'Kneiffii'—The leaflets are very finely cut. The margins are strongly serrated and the leaflet is ½" wide. The overall appearance is that of a giant fern. White flowers. 3' tall.

RELATED SPECIES:
>   *A. aethusifolius* (ē-thus-i-fōl'e-us)—This Korean native produces a 6"–8" mound of finely dissected dark green leaves supporting 12" tall spires of cream-colored flowers in early summer. After the flowers fade, the seed-bearing follicles remain during the summer to provide an ornamental effect. It is useful in the border front or the partial shade rock garden. There are no insect or disease problems, but I have noticed damage by voles. Although it was named in 1912, it is a relative newcomer to the perennial industry. It certainly deserves increased use in the perennial border. Some nurseries have it listed as a selection of *Astilbe.*

Native to North America.   Perennial

See color plate

Aruncus aethusifolius

SCIENTIFIC NAME/FAMILY: *Arundo donax*   Poaceae
                                                                   (Gramineae)

(a-run'dō dō'naks)

COMMON NAME: Giant Reed

LEAVES: Leaf blades are 1" to 2" wide and can be as long as 3' to 4'. Leaves are smooth, blue green, alternate on the stem, and arching. The stems are 1¼" in diameter. The leaves resemble those of a corn plant.

FLOWER: The inflorescence is a many-branched panicle, up to 24" long, usually erect, which is at first a reddish brown, turning to white at maturity.

HABIT: Upright, coarsely textured, 12'–16' tall.

SEASON OF BLOOM: Giant reed flowers in late fall. In climates with early frost, it will not bloom.

CULTURE: Full sun and a moist, well-drained soil. The literature reports creeping rhizomes in sandy loam soils. In the clay loam soils of Columbus, Ohio, a clump in the Chadwick Arboretum remained relatively unchanged for 10 years. I have seen the variegated form growing in wet land areas with water over the roots during part of the summer. In late summer, this species has a tendency for one side of the clump to lodge. The stalks may have to be tied together if one wishes to have a neat planting.

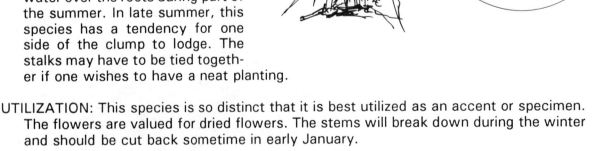

UTILIZATION: This species is so distinct that it is best utilized as an accent or specimen. The flowers are valued for dried flowers. The stems will break down during the winter and should be cut back sometime in early January.

PROPAGATION: Propagated by seed and division. It is a warm season grass. Best results will follow spring division and planting.

DISEASES AND INSECTS: I have seen no problems during 10 years of observation in the Chadwick Arboretum.

HARDINESS: Zone 5. Catalogs and references list Zone 7 for this species. Columbus, Ohio, is in Zone 5/6 and I have seen no hardiness problems with the specimen in the Chadwick Arboretum. Perhaps we have a superior clone that should be asexually produced.

CULTIVARS:

'Variegata' (also known as 'Versicolor') — Variegated Giant Reed. The leaves are striped with green and cream variegation. The variegation is most pronounced on the new growth, especially in the spring. This selection is smaller growing than the species and is hardy to Zones 7–8. I have seen plants growing in Zone 6 but they usually are smaller than those found in Zones 7–8.

ADDITIONAL NOTES: The strong, hollow stems have been used for centuries as a source of reeds for woodwind instruments. *Arundo donax* has freely spread and reseeded in parts of Italy. It is often the main vegetation found in wildlands along railroads and other areas where clean cultivation is not practiced.

Native to southern Europe.   Perennial

SCIENTIFIC NAME/FAMILY: *Asarum europaeum*   Aristolochiaceae

(as'a̱-rum ū-rō-pē'um)

COMMON NAME: Europe-
an Wild Ginger, Shiny-
leaf Ginger.

LEAVES: Evergreen, cor-
date leaf base, 2"–3"
across, glossy green
with fleshy petioles up
to 5" long. The leaves
are kidney-shaped and
leathery.

FLOWER: The flowers are
bell-shaped, greenish-
purple or brown, and
½" long. The single
flowers are borne near
the surface of the soil;
consequently they are
usually not readily no-
ticed. European wild
ginger is noted more
for its lustrous green
foliage.

HABIT: 6" to 10" spread-
ing perennial.

SEASON OF BLOOM: Mid
to late spring.

See color plate

CULTURE: European wild ginger performs best in a shaded soil that is moist and rich in organic matter. The preferred pH is 5.5 to 6.5.

UTILIZATION: Effectively used as a ground cover or edging plant in shaded areas. In mild
winters the foliage will remain evergreen.

PROPAGATION: Wild ginger spreads by rhizomes. Landscape plantings can be easily increased by division in the spring or early fall.

DISEASES AND INSECTS: *Asarum* is relatively pest free.

HARDINESS: Zones 4–7. The species has died out in Zone 8.

RELATED SPECIES:
  A. canadense—Canadian Wild Ginger. Each plant usually has 2 heart-shaped to kidney-
    shaped deciduous leaves that can be up to 7" wide. The leaves and petioles are
    pubescent. It is 6"–12" tall and grows from rhizomes to create a ground cover.
    This species is more heat tolerant than European wild ginger and will survive the
    heat of Zone 8. Early settlers were fond of this plant because it had a flavor similar
    to the Old World Ginger, *Zingiber officinale.* The stems were dried and pulverized
    and used for spice, or sometimes boiled with sugar to make a candied spice.

A. hartwegii (hart-wē′ji-i) — Sierra Wild Ginger. This species is native to California and Oregon. The evergreen leaves are kidney-shaped, about 5″ wide, and are beautifully marked with silver along the veins. It is also called the cyclamen-leaved ginger. Zones 5–7.

A. shuttleworthii (shut-ti-wur′-e-i) (*Hexastylis shuttleworthii*) — Mottled Wild Ginger. This species has mottled evergreen foliage. This species is an excellent selection for southern gardens but is not as cold tolerant as the above species. It is native to the fertile, moist woodlands from Virginia to Georgia and Alabama. Fred Galle, formerly of Callaway Gardens, selected 'Callaway' which has more variegation than the species. It is a very striking plant.

ADDITIONAL NOTES: The common name, wild ginger, probably refers to the pungent odor of the leaves and rhizomes.

Native to Europe.   Perennial

SCIENTIFIC NAME/FAMILY: *Asclepias tuberosa*   Asclepiadaceae

(as-klē'pi-as tū-be-rō'så)

COMMON NAME: Butterfly Weed, Pleurisy Root, Indian Paintbrush, Chigger Flower

LEAVES: Alternate, lanceolate or oblong, 2″–6″ long and ¼″–1″ wide, acute or obtuse, sessile or very short-petioled; foliage is hispid.

FLOWER: Flowers about ¼″ across, in short-peduncled, many-flowered umbels; flowers are orange.

HABIT: 18″ to 36″ tall and 24″ wide.

SEASON OF BLOOM: Late spring to mid-summer.

CULTURE: Butterfly weed is a natural for full sun, dry and infertile soils. I have seen it growing on roadside slopes in Kansas where very little moisture falls. It will not do well in wet soils and it cannot compete with surface rooted trees. However, butterfly weed competes very well with grass, which makes it a good choice for meadow gardens.

See color plate

UTILIZATION: Butterfly weed can be utilized in the border or in meadow areas. It looks nice when planted in groups along the roadside or in other rustic areas. It is also used for cut and dried flower arrangements. The milkweed follicles are attractive in dry flower arrangements. This showy wildflower is attractive to the Aphrodite and Fritillary butterflies. The common milkweed is an important food source for the larvae of the Monarch butterfly.

PROPAGATION: *Asclepias* has a taproot, which makes division harder. However, if one digs deeply when lifting clumps to avoid cutting away the tap root, transplanting is fairly successful. Butterfly weed is easily propagated from seed, terminal cuttings, or from root cuttings. Best germination occurs when fresh seed is used.

DISEASES AND INSECTS: Leaf spots and rusts are sometimes present but control measures are not usually adopted. Generally, butterfly weed is pest free.

HARDINESS: Zones 4–9.

CULTIVARS: Most selections that are sold are orange but there are yellow and scarlet forms in the wild. 'Gay Butterflies' is a selection that was bred for red and yellow; however, most of the flowers are orange.

RELATED SPECIES:

A. incarnata (in-kar-nā'ta) — Swamp Milkweed — This 3' tall plant has clusters of mauve, pink, or white flowers. The leaves are 3"–6" long. It is easily grown in sunny areas in well-drained soil, although it is a wet soil plant in its native habitat. Swamp milkweed is a nice addition to the back of a sunny border or along a sunny pond. This is the plant to place in the garden if hoards of butterflies are desired. Zones 3–9.

ADDITIONAL NOTES: Butterfly weed is slow to emerge in the spring, so careful cultivation is necessary until new growth appears. It is not invasive and requires very little maintenance. *Asclepias* is derived from the name of the Greek god of healing, Asklepios. I have observed excellent plantings of *Asclepias* at Fernbank Science Center, Atlanta, Georgia, and at the University of Georgia Botanic Garden, Athens, Georgia.

Native to eastern North America.   Perennial

SCIENTIFIC NAME/FAMILY: *Asphodeline lutea*   Asphodelaceae (Liliaceae)

(as-fod-e-lī'nē lū'tē-a)

COMMON NAME: Asphodel, King's Spear, Jacob's Rod

LEAVES: Numerous, narrow, linear, gray-green leaves rise from a rhizomatous rootstock. These basal leaves are 8"–10" long and are furrowed. The flower scape has smaller linear leaves which extend up the stem to the inflorescence.

FLOWER: Fragrant, yellow flowers, 1" wide, are subtended by membranous bracts on a 1'–1½' long, tubular raceme. The seed pods develop into a wand of bright green fruit that eventually dries to a crinkled brown fruit, which is attractive.

HABIT: Erect plant, 2'–4' tall and 1' wide.

SEASON OF BLOOM: Late spring to early summer.

See color plate

CULTURE: Full sun and a well-drained soil.

UTILIZATION: Asphodel can be used in the border or the wild garden. The dried flower and fruit scape is used in floral arrangements.

PROPAGATION: Division of the clump should be done in the fall.

DISEASES AND INSECTS: None serious.

HARDINESS: Zones 6–8.

Native to Mediterranean region.   Perennial

SCIENTIFIC NAME/FAMILY: *Asplenium ebenoides*   Polypodiaceae

(as-plē'-ne-um eb-ē-noi'-dez)

COMMON NAME: Dragontail Fern, Scott's Spleenwort

FRONDS: Fronds are pinnatifid and 4"–
12" long. The pinnae are irregular in
shape. The upper ⅓ of the frond tip is
simple (no lobing) giving rise to the
common name of dragontail. The
stipe and lower rachis are dark.

SORI: The sori (groups of sporangia) are
arranged in rows on each side of the
midvein. The sporangia are dark
brown.

HABIT: Narrow, fine erect fronds.

CULTURE: Dragontail fern should be
grown in partial shade (indirect light)
and moist soil that has been enriched
with compost. In native sites, dragontail fern is found growing among
rocks, walls, or ledges. It would perform best in limestone based soils
with a pH near 7.0.

UTILIZATION: This species would enhance a rock ledge in the shaded border or rock garden.

PROPAGATION: Spore propagation is
the principle method. The spores mature in mid to late summer. New
plants are occasionally formed on the
long, narrow apex.

DISEASES AND INSECTS: No problems.

HARDINESS: Zone 5 to 8.

ADDITIONAL NOTES: Dragontail fern is
found natively from Connecticut to
the Mississippi River and south to Alabama.

Perennial

SCIENTIFIC NAME/FAMILY: *Aster amellus*   Asteraceae (Compositae)

(as'tĕr a-mel'lus)

COMMON NAME: Italian Aster

LEAVES: Alternate leaves, basal leaves oblanceolate to obovate, to 5" long and 1" wide, usually entire; stem leaves oblong to lanceolate and sessile. Leaves and stems have a hispid pubescence which creates a rough texture and feel.

FLOWER: Violet-purple daisy-like flowers, 1½"–2½" wide, are borne in a loose, flat-clustered corymb. The center of each flower has a bright yellow eye.

HABIT: Bushy clump of stems with multiple branching at the top, 2'–2½' tall and 1½'–2' wide.

SEASON OF BLOOM: Early fall.

See color plate

CULTURE: Italian aster grows best in a very well-drained, calcareous soil located in full sun. The species has a tendency toward floppiness and will require staking. Fortunately, the cultivars are 12"–24" tall and remain compact unless excess fertility or overcrowding occurs. Poor drainage is also detrimental to optimum growth. Division and transplanting should be done in the spring.

UTILIZATION: Italian aster is a long-blooming plant for the fall border. It is especially effective with the fall-flowering *Sedum* × 'Autumn Joy'.

PROPAGATION: Tip cuttings in spring or division of older plants in the spring are means of propagation. Seed germination can be used for the species.

DISEASES AND INSECTS: Verticillium wilt can be a problem where overcrowding and poor soil conditions are present. Division should be done every 3 years.

HARDINESS: Zones 5–8.

CULTIVARS:
'Brilliant'—Bright pink flowers, 24" tall.
'Dwarf King'—Deep blue-violet flowers, 20" tall.
'King George'—An exceptionally fine old favorite with bright lavender flowers, 24" tall.
'Lady Hindlip'—Pink flowers, similar to 'Pink Zenith'; 2'–3' tall.
'Nocturne'—Deep blue-violet flowers, 24". Some catalogs describe this cultivar as having pink flowers, but the plants that I have observed in my travels have been blue.
'Pink Zenith'—Pink flowers, 24" tall.
'Rudolph Goethe'—Lavender flowers, 24" tall.
'Sonia'—Bold pink flowers are carried on stems 12"–18" tall. This is one of the best pink-flowering types.

ADDITIONAL NOTES: *Aster amellus* is a popular fall plant in Europe, but the interest in the United States has not been kindled. It deserves wider usage, especially in zones 5 and 6. *Aster amellus* is one of the parents of *Aster* × *frikartii.*

Native to Italy.   Perennial

SCIENTIFIC NAME/FAMILY: *Aster × frikartii*

Asteraceae
(Compositae)

(as'ter fri-kart'-ē-i)

COMMON NAME: Frikart's Aster

LEAVES: Alternate leaves, oblong to oblanceolate, to 3" long near the base,
diminishing in size higher on the stem.
Leaves are entire to remotely serrate
near the apex. Both stems and leaves
are lightly pubescent.

FLOWER: Single flowers, lavender with
yellow centers, 2"–3" wide.

HABIT: 2'–3' tall, loose tumbling growth
habit, 3' wide.

SEASON OF BLOOM: Midsummer to fall.
Frikart's aster has a long bloom season. In 1992, *Aster* 'Monch' was in
flower in my garden on November 1
after 3 hard frosts.

CULTURE: Full sun in a well-drained soil
is the optimum placement. In northern
zones, mulch is needed in the winter
(Zone 5). Wet soil in winter can be
detrimental. If one is a tidy gardener,
one may want to stake this tumbling
species but it may look more natural
to allow it to cascade over surrounding plants. This aster should not be
divided in the fall as winter kill can
occur. The stems should remain on
the plant during the winter. Cutting
the foliage back also seems to reduce
winter survival.

See color plate

UTILIZATION: The flower color of this species blends well with other colors and becomes
a very good main character for the summer and autumn border.

PROPAGATION: Division in the spring or stem cuttings are propagation methods. Seed can
be used but the flowers of the seedlings will be many shades of lavender and blue.

DISEASES AND INSECTS: This aster is fairly resistant to mildew although on dry soils it
may appear.

HARDINESS: Zone 5–8. Plants in this Zone 5 will need winter protection.

CULTIVARS: Frikart's aster is an interspecific cross made by Carl Frikart, a Swiss
nurseryman, around 1920. It is a hybrid of *A. thomsonnii* and *A. amellus.* Four
seedlings were selected from this cross with 'Wonder of Stafa' becoming a well known
garden perennial. The other 3 were named after the Bernese Oberland mountains,
'Jungfrau', 'Eiger', and 'Monch'. 'Monch' is the only other selection that is readily

available. Longin Seigler of Switzerland told me that 'Wonder of Stafa' is most popular in Switzerland because the flower is flat and more uniform; whereas, 'Monch' has petals which undulate up and down. He reported that 'Monch' is the easiest to grow.

'Flora Delight'—This cultivar was selected by Alan Bloom from a cross of a dwarf form of *A. thomsonnii* and *A. amellus* 'Sonia.' The flowers have a pale lilac color. It is 24″ tall and is less vigorous than the Frikart hybrids.

'Monch'—This cultivar is more common in the United States than 'Wonder of Stafa'. It is 30″–36″ tall and has a 36″ spread. The lavender blue flowers are supposedly darker than 'Wonder of Stafa' and tends to have sturdier stems.

'Wonder of Stafa'—Lavender-blue flowers, 2½′–3′ tall. Flowers are arranged in a flat plane. The Frikart nursery was located in Stafa, Switzerland, hence the cultivar name of 'Wonder of Stafa'.

Hybrid origin.   Perennial

SCIENTIFIC NAME/FAMILY: *Aster novi-belgii*

Asteraceae
(Compositae)

(as'tĕr nō'-vi-bel'jī)

COMMON NAME: New York Aster, Michaelmas Daisy

LEAVES: Alternate, lanceolate to broadly linear, to 5" long, entire, sessile or auriculate-clasping to the stem. Upper leaf surface has a stiff pubescence while the lower surface has softer hairs.

FLOWER: Heads are 2" across, crowded toward ends of branches in corymbose clusters; ray flowers are usually violet-purple, ¾" long.

HABIT: The species is 3' to 5' tall but shorter cultivars are available.

SEASON OF BLOOM: Late summer to fall.

CULTURE: Michaelmas Daisy performs best in full sun and in well drained soils of average fertility. Most selections will need frequent division. The compact types need division to retain vigor, while the taller cultivars require division to control rapid spread. Pinching can be done to promote compact plants. Tall cultivars will usually need to be staked.

UTILIZATION: Various sites in the perennial border depending upon cultivar height. It is also at home in naturalized areas, particularly meadow-like spots.

See color plate

PROPAGATION: Division and cuttings. Division can be done in early spring or fall by lifting the clumps and replanting the vigorous outside growth and discarding the older center section. This will need to be done every other year to prevent deterioration of the plants. Tip cuttings can be taken in early spring or summer. It is likely that propagation by tip cuttings will reduce the incidence of aster wilt. This fungus is usually present in the root zone area so propagation by tip cuttings my help to clean up the diseased stock plants.

DISEASES AND INSECTS: Powdery mildew and aster wilt are the major problems.

HARDINESS: Zones 4–8.

CULTIVARS: A limited number of cultivars are listed below. There is a wide selection and it is impossible to list all that are available. *Index Hortensis* lists approximately 300 cultivars of *A. novi-belgii.*
  'Ada Ballard'—36", semi-double, lavender-blue flowers, should be staked.
  'Alert'—12"–15", crimson red flowers.
  'Alice Haslam'—12"–15", double dark rose-pink flowers.
  'Audrey'—12", lilac flowers.
  'Bonningdale White'—40", white double flowers with a yellow eye, later September flower.
  'Crimson Brocade'—36", crimson, semi-double flowers.

'Eventide'—36", semi-double violet blue flowers, 2" wide.
'Jenny'—12", red flowers.
'Patricia Ballard'—36", double pink flowers.
'Peter Harrison'—15"–18", pink flowers, profuse bloomer.
'Professor Kippenberg'—12"–15", lavender-blue flowers.
'Red Star'—15", red flowers.
'Snow Flurry'—18", large white flowers.
'Snowball'—10"–12", white flowers with yellow eyes.
'White Lady'—5'–6', white flowers, will need support.
'Winston Churchill'—24", violet-red flowers with yellow center.

RELATED SPECIES:
A. *novae-angliae* (nō'-vē-ang''li-ē), New England Aster. This native species has numerous leaves which are entire, pubescent, and are sessile to the stem, 4"–5" long. The flowers are 1"–2" wide and composed of numerous ray flowers with a yellow center. The species is rarely used as there are superior cultivars available. The bloom period is from late summer to fall. Plants are 4'–6' tall and 4' wide. Zone hardiness is Zones 4–8. Cultivars of this species are tall and usually will require staking.
  'Alma Potschke'—3'–4', bright rose-pink flowers, more compact than other cultivars but support is still required.
  'Barr's Pink'—4', semi-double, rose-pink flowers.
  'Harrington's Pink'—3'–5', salmon-pink flowers, later flowering than other cultivars. Also requires less frequent division.
  'Hella Lacey'—4'–5', violet-blue flowers.
  'Lye End Beauty'—4'–5', excellent ruby-red flowers, requires support.
  'Purple Dome'—A new cultivar named by Mt. Cuba Center in Greenville, Delaware. This selection forms a solid purple mound, 18" tall and 36" wide. The flowers are semi-double, 1½" wide, and cover the plant in early fall. The plant originally came from Mr. Robert Seip of Lennilea Farm in Alburtis, Pennsylvania.
  'September Ruby'—3'–5', ruby red flowers, needs support.

A. *tongolensis* (ton-go-lēn'-sis), East Indies Aster. This compact species has rosettes of dark green leaves over which 2" wide violet-blue flowers are carried. Plants are 1'–2' tall and 1' wide. No support is required for this species. It flowers in summer.
  'Berggarten'—18", 2"–3" violet-blue flowers with orange centers.
  'Napsbury'—15"–18", lavender-blue, orange-eyed daisy.
  'Wartburg Star'—18"–24", lavender-blue flowers with orange centers.

A. *lateriflorus* 'Horizontalis' (lat-er-i-flō'rus), Calico Aster. This 2'–3' tall species is very unique due to its tiny foliage, which becomes a coppery color in late summer. The very small flowers are pale lilac with rosy stamens. The foliage is very attractive even when not in flower. Many gardens in England, especially Great Dixter, use this aster for hedging and massing purposes.

ADDITIONAL NOTES: The compact asters were developed from a crossing of A. *novi-belgii* × A. *dumosus. Aster* is derived from Greek and refers to the star-like shape of the flower.

Native to North America.   Perennial

SCIENTIFIC NAME/FAMILY: *Asteromoea mongolica* (Kalimeris pinnatifida)   Asteraceae
(Compositae)

(as'ter-o-moe-a pin-nāt'i-fid-a)

COMMON NAME: Double Japanese Aster, Orphanage Plant

LEAVES: Alternate, lanceolate, light green leaves about 1/4" long. The entire plant has a fine, airy texture.

FLOWER: Semi-double white flowers with pale yellow stamens are produced in great quantities.

HABIT: An upright, bushy plant, 24" high and 24" wide. It should be spaced 24"–30" apart.

SEASON OF BLOOM: This unusual daisy is in flower from early summer to early fall.

CULTURE: *Asteromoea* does well in well-drained soils in morning sun and afternoon shade sites.

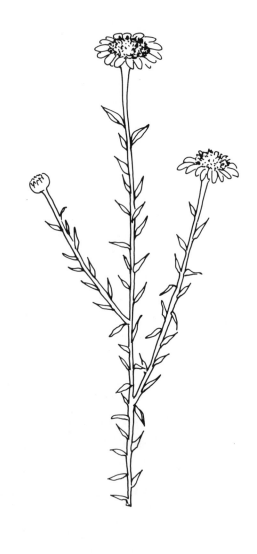

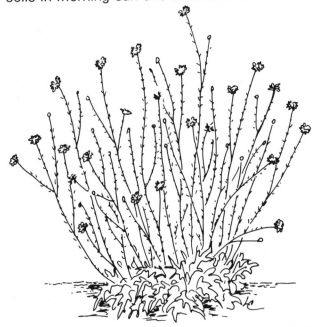

UTILIZATION: Suitable for use in meadow plantings and the herbaceous border. It is valued for its long flowering period.

PROPAGATION: Propagation is by division of the clump in the spring.

DISEASES AND INSECTS: No serious problems.

HARDINESS: Zones 5–8.

ADDITIONAL NOTES: The taxonomic background of this species is confused. Some list the species as *Boltonia indica* or *Kalimeris pinnatifida*. The latter seems to be the more popular of two alternative choices. There is little information or history about this species. Fortunately, that does not prevent it from being a valued white daisy for the summer garden.

Native to Asia.   Perennial

SCIENTIFIC NAME/FAMILY: *Astilbe × arendsii*   Saxifragaceae

(à-stil'bē a-ren'si-i)

COMMON NAME: False Spirea; Astilbe

LEAVES: Leaves are 2–3 ternately compound; leaflets are ovate-oblong, and doubly serrate.

FLOWER: Flower colors are red, pink, white or lavender. Flowers are small in dense, erect or arching panicles about 6″ long.

HABIT: Clump-forming species which is 2′ to 4′ tall and 2′ wide.

SEASON OF BLOOM: Early summer.

CULTURE: Partial shade to full sun. The most important requirement for optimum performance is adequate moisture. Fertile, moist soil will reward the gardener with abundant bloom and lush foliage during the summer. The absence of moisture will result in plants with brown foliage and premature death of leaves. Astilbe should be divided every 3 or 4 years.

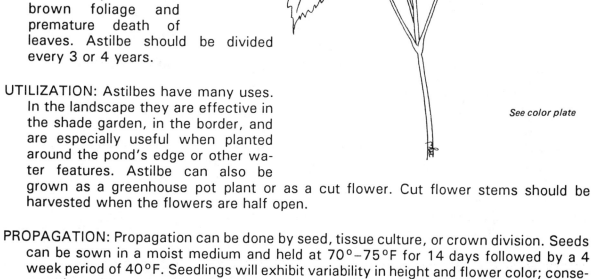

See color plate

UTILIZATION: Astilbes have many uses. In the landscape they are effective in the shade garden, in the border, and are especially useful when planted around the pond's edge or other water features. Astilbe can also be grown as a greenhouse pot plant or as a cut flower. Cut flower stems should be harvested when the flowers are half open.

PROPAGATION: Propagation can be done by seed, tissue culture, or crown division. Seeds can be sown in a moist medium and held at 70°–75°F for 14 days followed by a 4 week period of 40°F. Seedlings will exhibit variability in height and flower color; consequently, cultivar identity will be lost. Tissue culture should probably be restricted to white or pink cultivars. Red cultivars often mutate and the small number of cells used in tissue culture may enhance this characteristic. Tissue cultured propagules should be retained until they flower, so atypical plants can be discarded. Division remains the major method of reproduction. It can be done with equal success in early spring or midsummer (August in Ohio).

DISEASES AND INSECTS: Few diseases affect this plant. Only powdery mildew and wilt have been reported. White fly, black vine weevil and the adult Japanese beetle can be insect problems.

HARDINESS: Zones 4–9.

CULTIVARS: Most of the cultivars available in United States nurseries originated in European nurseries, particularly in Germany, through the breeding efforts of George Arends of Ronsdorf, Germany. He used 4 species in his breeding efforts. They included *A. japonica, A. thunbergii, A. astilboides,* and *A. chinensis.* George Arends introduced more cultivars than any other individual. This important fact is reflected in the naming of this hybrid group as *A.* × *arendsii.* The Arends Nursery is still in operation and managed by the granddaughter of George Arends. In midsummer this nursery is a must stop for anyone with an interest in *Astilbe.* The massed colors of the field-grown stock are remarkable. It is impossible to list all the cultivars available but the following list includes selections that show a variety of heights, colors, and foliage types.

'Amethyst'—Lavender-pink flowers, 24"–30", midseason bloom.

'Brautschleier' ('Bridal Veil')—White flowers, 18"–24" tall, early bloom.

'Cattleya'—Rose flowers, 36" tall, midseason bloom.

'Erica'—Pink flowers, 36", midseason bloom.

'Fanal'—Deep red flowers 24", early bloom. This cultivar was introduced in 1933 and remains a very popular selection. The leaves have a dark bronze color.

'Feuer' ('Fire')—Coral red flowers, 30", midseason bloom.

'Granat'—Carmine-red flowers, 24"–30", midseason bloom.

'Hyazinth' ('Hyacinth')—Lilac flowers, 40", midseason bloom.

'Spinell'—Salmon-red flowers, 30", early bloom.

'Venus'—Rosy-pink flowers, 36", late bloom.

'Weisse Gloria' ('White Gloria')—White flowers, 20", midseason bloom.

Index Hortensis lists other hybrid selections in groupings under the headings of × hybrida, japonica, or simplicifolia. The nomenclature of astilbe is not exact and there are other interpretations that one may find. For this edition, the groupings suggested by *Index Hortensis* will be used.

× Hybrida Group Hybrids:

'America'—Lavender-rose flowers, 28", midseason bloom.

'Bressingham Beauty'—Pink flowers, 42", late bloom. This cultivar was selected as a seedling by Alan Bloom in 1967.

'Etna'—Dark red flowers, 24", early bloom.

'Gloria Purpurea'—Lavender-pink flowers, 24", midseason bloom.

'Irrlicht'—White flowers, 18"–24", early bloom.

'Snowdrift'—Clear white flowers, 24", early bloom. This 1975 introduction by Alan Bloom is one of the whitest astilbes.

Japonica Group Hybrids:

'Bonn'—Rose flowers, 18"–24", midseason bloom.

'Bremen'—Rose-pink flowers, 24", midseason bloom. This cultivar has deep, glossy-green leaves.

'Deutschland'—White flowers, 24", early bloom.

'Emden'—Pink flowers, 24"–36", midseason bloom.

'Europa'—Pale pink flowers, 24", early bloom.

'Montgomery'—Bright red flowers, 20", midseason bloom.

'Red Sentinel'—Red, 24"–30", midseason bloom.

'Rheinland'—Pink flowers, 24", early bloom.

'Washington'—White flowers, 24", midseason bloom.

Simplicifolia Hybrid Group:
'Afrodite'—Rose flowers, 18", late bloom.
'Alba'—White flowers, 20"–24", late bloom.
'Bronce Elegans' ('Bronze Elegance')—Pink flowers, 18" tall, late bloom with shiny bronze-green foliage.
'Dunkellachs'—Dark salmon flowers, 24", late bloom with shiny bronze-green foliage.
'Inshriach Pink'—Pale pink flowers, 12", late bloom with crinkled foliage.
'Sprite'—Pale pink flowers, 12"–18", late bloom with lacy foliage. 'Sprite' is the 1994 Perennial Plant of the Year.
'William Buchanan'—Pale pink flowers, 6"–8", late bloom with curly, shiny dark green foliage.

RELATED SPECIES:
A. × *crispa*—The hybrids of this species are collector's plants for the rock garden. The foliage is very dark green and crinkled. Plant height is 6"–8" tall. 'Lilliput' has salmon-pink flowers and 'Perkeo' has dark pink flowers.
A. × *rosea*—This hybrid resulted from a cross of *A. chinensis* and *A. japonica.* Cultivars include 'Peach Blossom', 3'–4' tall with salmon-pink flowers and 'Queen Alexandra', similar to 'Peach Blossom' but with darker pink flowers.

Native to China, Japan, and Korea.   Perennial

SCIENTIFIC NAME/FAMILY: *Astilbe chinensis* 'Pumila'   Saxifragaceae

(à-stil'bē chi-nen'-sis' pū'mi-la)

COMMON NAME: Dwarf Chinese Astilbe

LEAVES: Leaves are pinnately compound; leaflets are ovate-oblong and doubly-serrate at 2" to 3" long. Foliage is deep green.

FLOWER: The fluffy mauve-pink flowers are borne in stiffly narrow branched panicles which rise above the clump foliage. Flowering is indeterminate.

HABIT: Chinese astilbe is densely stoloniferous with low, compact foliage. Plant height, in flower, is 12" to 15".

SEASON OF BLOOM: Mid to late summer.

CULTURE: Partial shade in a well-drained soil. Best growth will occur in a moist, organic laden soil. However, Chinese astilbe is more tolerant of dry soil than selections of *A. × arendsii*.

UTILIZATION: The stoloniferous growth habit makes this cultivar a candidate as a ground cover or as an edging plant along the front of the border. The late summer bloom is an advantage over other astilbes.

PROPAGATION: Division in spring or fall is an easy method. Seed can be utilized for the species by germinating in moist medium at 65° to 75°F.

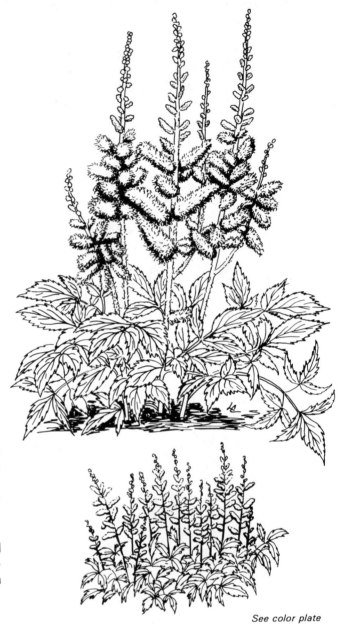

See color plate

HARDINESS: Zones 4–8.

CULTIVARS: Other cultivars of *Astilbe chinensis* include:
   'Finale'—Light pink flowers on spikes 15"–18" tall, midsummer bloom.
   'Intermezzo'—Rose pink flowers, 20"–24", midsummer bloom.
   'Serenade'—Rose-red flowers, 12"–16" tall, midsummer bloom.
   var. *taquetii* (ta-ket'-ē-i) (also listed as a species)—This variety is called the fall astilbe due to its late flower. The cultivar 'Superba' has deep lilac flowers and is 3'–4' tall. 'Purplelanze' is a recent introduction with purple-red flowers.
   'Veronica Klose'—This cultivar is similar to 'Pumila' but the inflorescence is denser and darker pink. It is a 1987 release from the Klose Nursery in Germany.

Native to China.   Perennial

SCIENTIFIC NAME/FAMILY: *Astrantia major*   Apiaceae
                                                            (Umbelliferae)
(as-tran'shi-à mā'jor)

COMMON NAME: Great Masterwort

LEAVES: Lower leaves are palmately cut, usually with 5 lobes, each lobe is toothed or cleft. The stem leaves are simple, not as toothed, and are sessile to the stem.

FLOWER: The umbel of this species differs from the normal umbel found on most members of the carrot family. The creamy-white center of the umbel is surrounded stockade fashion by a ruff of petal-like greenish or pinkish tinged bracts. My wife thinks the bracts look like large ray-like petals curving up to cradle the umbel.

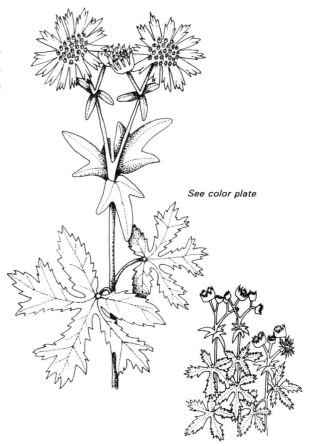

See color plate

HABIT: 2'–3' tall clump with an 18" spread.

SEASON OF BLOOM: Late spring to early summer. In the summer of 1992, plants near the horticulture building at The Ohio State University bloomed sporadically until September 15.

CULTURE: The optimum site would be partial shade with a well-drained soil. If the soil is retentive and maintained in a moist state, masterwort can be grown in full sun.

UTILIZATION: The flowers of this species are unusual and attractive. They are suitable as cut flowers and would add an interesting texture to a summer bouquet. Masterwort is grown commercially as a cut flower in the Netherlands and California. The flowers are also excellent when pressed flat and used in dried flower picture making. It is not a household name in the United States, but it is used in the English borders with good success. Several perennial nurseries in the United States now grow this unusual perennial.

PROPAGATION: Division in spring or fall. Seed propagation requires a cold stratification period.

DISEASES AND INSECTS: Although this species has not been thoroughly evaluated in the United States, there have been no reported problems.

HARDINESS: Zone 4–7.

CULTIVARS:
    'Rosea'—Bright pink bracts.
    'Rubra'—Wine-red flowers, 18".
    'Ruby Glow'—Alan Bloom lists this as a probable natural hybrid of *A. major* × *A. rubra*. It is compact and has a good ruby-red flower color.

'Shaggy'—White flower with an extra long collar of pink bracts. This 24″ tall selection may be from *Astrantia major* ssp. *involucrata* which some people list as a distinct botanical form. It is also called 'Margery Fish.'

'Sunnydale Variegated'—This 1966 introduction has leaves which are elegantly splashed and striped with yellow and cream. The variegation is most intense in the spring and fades in summer.

ADDITIONAL NOTES: *Astrantia* is from Greek for *aster,* a star, and refers to the star-like umbels.

Native to Austria.   Perennial

SCIENTIFIC NAME/FAMILY: *Athyrium filix-femina* (Asplenium filix-femina)   Woodsiaceae
(Polypodiaceae)

(a-ther'ri-um fī'-liks-fem'i-nȧ)

COMMON NAME: Lady Fern

FRONDS: The fronds of lady fern are 2' to 3' tall, 6"– 9" wide, and are twice pinnate. The pinnae are lanceolate and the pinnule are deeply incised. The stalks may be straw-colored, reddish, or brownish and have scattered scales on the lower portion of the stem.

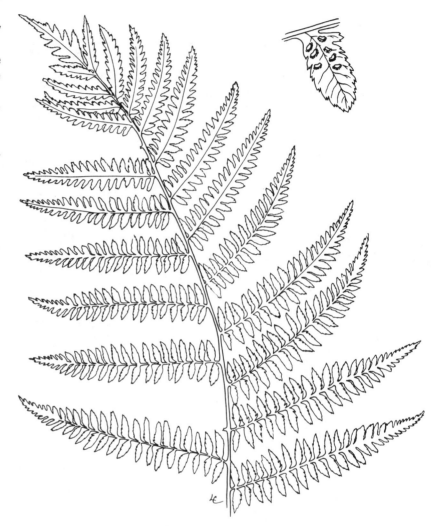

SORI: Sori are curved to horseshoe-shaped and are clustered at the base of the pinnule. Spores ripen in midsummer.

HABIT: Fine-textured, upright growing fern, 2'–3' tall.

CULTURE: Lady fern is relatively easy to grow, especially in comparison to other ferns. It tolerates a wide variety of soil types, even though it performs best in rich soil in a woodland setting. Lady fern will grow well in partial shade.

UTILIZATION: Lady fern is a vigorous growing and useful fern. It combines well with other ferns, is useful as a background plant and looks good when massed along a stream. If lady fern has a disadvantage, it is that the fronds may become tattered and blotched in late summer. However, this condition is probably offset by the gracefulness seen in May and June.

PROPAGATION: Lady fern can be propagated by spores or increased by clump division.

DISEASES AND INSECTS: Woodland ferns are usually pest free.

HARDINESS: Zones 2 to 9.

ADDITIONAL NOTES: This wood and roadside fern is found widely east of the Mississippi River.

Perennial

SCIENTIFIC NAME/FAMILY: *Athyrium nipponicum* 'Pictum'   Woodsiaceae

(a-thēr'i-um nip-pon'-i-kum pik'tum)

COMMON NAME: Japanese Painted Fern

FRONDS: The leaves (fronds) are deciduous, usually drooping, and up to 18" long. The fronds are coarsely divided and are distinguished by a maroon stalk and a maroon flush on the pinnae closest to the stalk. The rest of the pinnae have a gray to glaucous hue. The pinnae are also strongly dissected.

SORI: Flowerless plant.

HABIT: Japanese painted fern is a clump forming fern with fronds 18" long and a plant height of 12" to 18".

SEASON OF BLOOM: None.

CULTURE: Partial to full shade in moist humus-rich soil. It is important that the soil not dry out. Leaf scorch will occur in dry sites.

UTILIZATION: The unique color and texture of the fronds make for attractive combinations when used in border plantings with other species, such as *Hosta* and *Bergenia.* I have seen the Japanese painted fern used nicely to accent small garden sculptures. It can also be utilized in the cool greenhouse for year around enjoyment.

PROPAGATION: Division of the clumps in fall or spring is easy. Spores, which ripen in late summer, can also be used.

DISEASES AND INSECTS: None serious.

HARDINESS: Zones 4–7.

Native to Japan.   Perennial

SCIENTIFIC NAME/FAMILY: *Aubrieta deltoidea*   Brassicaceae
(Cruciferae)

(â-bri-eh'ta del-toid'ē-à)

COMMON NAME: False Rock Cress

LEAVES: Mat-forming foliage, leaves spatulate to rhomboidal, narrowed to a short petiole, with 1 or more teeth on each side; most leaves have a stellate pubescence. Foliage is gray-green.

FLOWER: Rose-lilac to purple, about ¾" wide, calyx cylindrical, about half as long as petals. Individual flowers have 4 petals.

HABIT: 6" prostrate to mounded habit, spreading to 24".

SEASON OF BLOOM: Early to mid spring.

CULTURE: False rock cress performs best in full sun in a well-drained soil of average fertility. It should be trimmed back after flowering to retain a compact form. Failure to perform this operation will result in branches that are long and straggly with a few leaves at the branch tips.

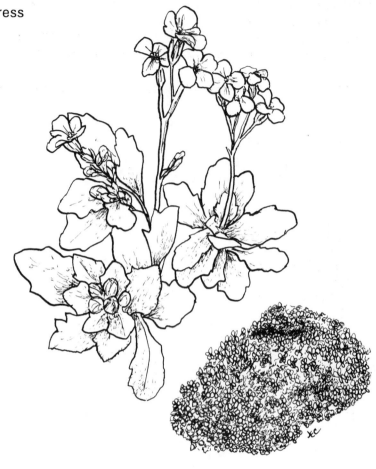

See color plate

UTILIZATION: Rock garden, dry stone walls, edge of perennial border.

PROPAGATION: Seed, division and cuttings. Best germination occurs in 2–3 weeks at 70°F. *Aubrieta* will not flower the first year from seed. Stem cuttings and division can be done in the early spring.

DISEASES AND INSECTS: No serious diseases or insects.

HARDINESS: Zones 4–8. Best growth will occur in northern climates. Plants of the *Brassicaceae* family do poorly in southern areas.

CULTIVARS:
'Aurea'—Golden-green foliage with blue to violet flowers.
'Bengal'—Semi-double flowers in blue, lilac, purple, or red.
'Bob Saunders'—8", large, semi-double reddish-purple flowers.
'Bressingham Pink'—Double pink flowers.

'Campbellii'—Double blue-violet flowers.
'Cascade' series—This 4" selection has individual colors of blue, purple, and red.
'Dr. Mules'—Free flowering plant with blue-violet flowers.
'Henslow Purple'—Bright purple flowers.
'Rosea Splendens'—Bright rose flowers which do not fade.
'Royal Blue'—Dark blue flowers.
'Royal Red'—Flower colors in shades of red and magenta.
'Variegata'—Gold-edged leaves and blue flowers.

ADDITIONAL NOTES: *Aubrieta* was named in honor of Claude Aubriet, a French botanical artist.

Native to Greece and Turkey.   Perennial

SCIENTIFIC NAME/FAMILY: *Aurinia saxatilis* (Alyssum saxatile)   Brassicaceae
(Cruciferae)

(ō-rin'i-à saks-at'i-lis)

COMMON NAME: Basket-of-Gold, Goldentuft
  Madwort, Goldentuft Alyssum

LEAVES: Low branched, basal leaves oblanceolate to obovate-oblong, 2"–5"
  long, entire, sometimes toothed; stem
  leaves smaller and sub-sessile. Leaves are
  gray with stellate pubescence.

FLOWER: Yellow, compact corymbose panicles. Individual flowers have 4 petals.

HABIT: 9" to 12" prostrate habit, 18" wide.

SEASON OF BLOOM: Early to mid spring.

CULTURE: Full sun in a very well-drained
  soil; moist, over-fertilized soil will produce
  a coarse, sprawling habit. The life expec-
  tancy can be increased by cutting the
  plants back by one-third after flowering.

UTILIZATION: *Aurinia* can be found in rock
  gardens and in the front of borders. However, the best displays that I have seen
  have been where it is allowed to trail over
  the edges of rock walls or raised beds.

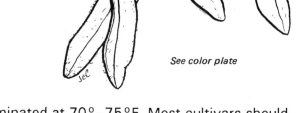

See color plate

PROPAGATION: Seed, division, and cuttings.
  Seeds germinate in 2–3 weeks when germinated at 70°–75°F. Most cultivars should
  be divided in the fall. Stem cuttings can be taken in spring or fall.

DISEASES AND INSECTS: No serious pests.

HARDINESS: Zones 3–7. In southern areas *Aurinia* dies because of summer heat and humidity.

CULTIVARS:
  'Citrinum' ('Silver Queen')—10", lemon-yellow flowers.
  'Compactum'—6"–8", bright-yellow flowers.
  'Dudley Neville'—9", orange buff flowers.
  'Dudley Neville Variegated'—Gray leaves are broadly margined with creamy white.
  'Flore Pleno'—Fully double flowers; less vigor than other cultivars.
  'Sunny Border Apricot'—Apricot colored flowers.
  'Tom Thumb'—Small, 4" tall selection.

ADDITIONAL NOTES: The common name madwort is derived from a mythological belief
  that the plant has powers to calm the troubled mind.

Native to central and southern Europe.   Perennial

SCIENTIFIC NAME/FAMILY: *Baptisia australis*   Fabiaceae
                                                              (Leguminosae)

(bap-tiz'i-á âs-trā'lis)

COMMON NAME: False Indigo, Blue Indigo

LEAVES: Leaves digitate, 3 leaflets, leaflets obo-
    vate, 1½"–3" long, short-pointed, stipules
    to ½" long. Foliage is pea-like and blue-
    green.

FLOWER: Flowers indigo-blue, in long terminal
    erect racemes; individual flowers about 1"
    long. The fruit is a pod 2"–3" long which
    turns black when mature.

HABIT: 3' to 4' erect habit. Taller plants may re-
    quire staking. A mature plant can be 4' wide.

SEASON OF BLOOM: Mid to late spring.

CULTURE: Full sun or partial shade in a well-
    drained soil. It is easily grown in low-fertility
    soils. Plants grown in shady areas will often
    require staking. If grown in sun, staking is
    usually not required.

UTILIZATION: Quite hardy but very slow grow-
    ing, false indigo plants can serve as speci-
    mens or as background plants in borders.
    Baptisia is not invasive; consequently it can
    remain undisturbed for years. The pods are
    quite useful in dried flower arrangements.

PROPAGATION: Seed propagation or division of
    the fleshy roots. Like many legumes, wild
    indigo has a hard seed coat which can cause
    erratic germination. Scarification with acid or
    physical scraping of the seed coat allows

See color plate

moisture and oxygen to enter through the seed coat. Cold stratification at 40°F also
aids uniform germination. The roots can be divided from late fall to early spring.

DISEASES AND INSECTS: No serious problems.

HARDINESS: Zones 3–9. *Baptisia* is an excellent plant in Zone 8.

RELATED SPECIES:
    B. alba (al'ba)—White Wild Indigo. This native of southeastern United States is 2'–3'
        tall and has a 3' spread. White flowers are borne on 12" long racemes. It is later
        flowering than *B. australis.*
    B. leucantha (lū-kan'tha)—Atlantic Wild Indigo. This western species is also called
        prairie wild indigo. It has white flowers and blue-green foliage. Flowering occurs in
        late spring. 3–5 feet tall.
    B. pendula (pen'-du-la). White flower, shiny dark stems, 2–3 feet tall.

B. perfoliata(per-fōl-i-ā'-ta) — Georgia Wild Indigo. The oval-shaped leaves are perfoliate, blue-green, and resemble eucalyptus leaves. The small yellow flowers appear in early summer and are followed by fruit that resemble small, green gooseberries. The flowers and fruit are held in the leaf axils, where they appear as small jewels sitting on a curved plate. It is 2' tall and hardy as far north as Zone 7.

B. tinctoria (tink-to'ri-a) — Yellow Wild Indigo. Flower color is yellow to cream colored. The flowers are probably too small to be an excellent border plant but this native would be welcome in a meadow garden or other informal or naturalized area.

ADDITIONAL NOTES: To encourage profuse flowering, pinch off old blossoms before they form seeds. Easily grown perennial whose foliage remains in good condition all summer. One plantsman describes it as the plant for the person who says, "I can't grow a single thing." *Baptisia* is derived from a Greek word, *bapto*, meaning to dye, because an inferior coloring substance is derived from some species.

Native to eastern North American, Pennsylvania to Georgia, west to Indiana.   Perennial

SCIENTIFIC NAME/FAMILY: *Begonia grandis* (B. evansiana)   Begoniaceae

(bē-gō'ni-à gran'dis)

COMMON NAME: Hardy Begonia, Evans' Begonia

LEAVES: The alternate leaves of this species are thick, succulent and glabrous. They are obliquely cordate at the base, ovate in form, with a serrated margin. The leaves have ruby-red veins and ruby-red lower leaf surfaces.

FLOWER: Flowers are 1" wide, fresh pink, and borne in drooping cymes. Staminate flowers have 4 unequal tepals, while the pistillate flowers have 2 broad tepals.

HABIT: A 2' tall plant with loose sprays of flower clusters over a large clump of broad, green leaves.

SEASON OF BLOOM: Late summer and fall. The pink ovaries remain attractive long after the flowers drop. I have seen good examples of this feature in the middle of October at Swarthmore College, Pennsylvania.

See color plate

CULTURE: In southern zones, hardy begonia should be planted in humus-enriched, moist soil in filtered shade. Further north, in cooler climates, more sun is suitable. The tuberous root must not be allowed to freeze; usually Zone 6 is the northern limit. A winter mulch can extend the hardiness to Zone 5.

UTILIZATION: Useful as a border plant, particularly when combined with woody plants in a shrub border.

PROPAGATION: The easiest propagation method will take very little of the gardener's time. Small bulbils form in the leaf axils, and drop to the soil where they emerge as new plants in the spring. These seedlings are easily transplanted.

DISEASES AND INSECTS: None serious.

HARDINESS: Zone 6–9.

Native to China and Japan.   Perennial

SCIENTIFIC NAME/FAMILY: *Begonia semperflorens-cultorum*   Begoniaceae

(bē-gō′ni-à sem-pēr-flō′renz kul-tō′rum)

COMMON NAME: Fibrous-rooted Begonia, Bedding Begonia, Wax Plant, Wax Begonia

LEAVES: Alternate, glossy, ovate to broad ovate, 2″–4″ long, more or less oblique at base, rounded or obtuse at apex, finely serrulate with ciliate margins, green to bronzy red, or green variegated with white.

FLOWER: Flowers are single or double, borne in small axillary clusters and are white to shades of red or pink.

HABIT: 6″–16″ dense, round habit.

SEASON OF BLOOM: Perpetually in bloom, even well after a light frost (May to October).

CULTURE: Shade. Too few plants grow well in shade and begonia is a good choice for these sites. It will withstand full sun if kept moist.

UTILIZATION: Planters, low edging, carpet bedding, pot plants for indoor landscaping. Begonias are valued for perpetual bloom, low care, profuse bloom, and brilliant flower colors.

PROPAGATION: Seeds, but difficult due to size of seed (2 million/oz). Seeds are scattered on the surface of a moist medium and germinated at a 70°F temperature. From seed to bloom takes about 4½ months. Begonia can also be propagated by leaf cuttings or soft-wood cuttings taken from young shoots in spring or summer.

DISEASES AND INSECTS: *Botrytis* blight, leaf spots, stem rot, powdery mildew, mealybugs, and thrips.

HARDINESS: Zone 10.

CULTIVARS: Most selections of wax begonia are F1 hybrids and are available in many different colors with either green or bronze foliage. The selection is very large and changes annually. It is very easy to quickly peruse the seed catalogs and find 20 different series all of which have many color choices. Selecting your begonia type and color is a great wintertime activity.

RELATED SPECIES: *Begonia* × *tuberhybrida*(tu-ber-hī'-bri-da)—Hybrid Tuberous Begonia. Used as a bedding plant in shaded, protected spots under trees, window boxes, or in hanging baskets. Flowers come in a wide array of colors—white or shades of pink, rose, red, or orange; borne in 3's with 1 male flower between 2 females, or in pairs: male flowers can be 6″ in diameter. *Begonia* × *tuberhybrida* requires a well-drained soil. Plants may be grown from tubers that do not overwinter and must be lifted and replanted in the spring or they may be grown from seed. A popular seeded double type is the 'Non-stop' series which are 8″–10″ tall and have 2½″ wide blooms. Some catalogs list the exposure as full sun. My experience in Ohio indicates that partial shade is required for optimum performance of the 'Non-stop' series. Even in the cooler summer climate of Butchart Gardens, Victoria, British Columbia, tuberous begonias are shaded by trellis work.

Other seed cultivars include:

'Angel' Series—3″–4″ star-shaped flowers are borne in pendant clusters.

'Clips' Mixture—This selection has double, camellia-type flowers, 7″–9″ tall.

'Memory' Series—Very large flowers, 6″–7″, that are similar to 'Non-stop', 10″–12″ tall.

'Musical' Series—Abundant flowering selection with double 2″–2½″ flowers on closely branched, compact plants. It is earlier flowering than 'Non-stop'.

'Pin-Up'—This Fleuroselect winner has single, four-petaled flowers that are white with a deep pink margin.

'Spirit' Series—This group is 6″–8″ tall with more basal-branching than that found with 'Non-stop'.

ADDITIONAL NOTES: Dig begonia before frost and use as a house plant during the winter. *Begonia* was named after Michel Bégon, a patron of botany during the 17th century and the Governor of French Canada. The famous floral carpet created in Brussels, Belgium, each year is made from the flowers of the tuberous begonia. Although I have not seen the "real" thing in Brussels, I was fortunate to see a similar floral carpet created in Columbus, Ohio, to celebrate Ameriflora 92. It is an image that I will always remember.

Native to Brazil.   Annual

SCIENTIFIC NAME/FAMILY: *Belamcanda chinensis* (Pardanthus chinensis)   Iridaceae

(bel-am-kan'dá chi-nen'sis)

COMMON NAME: Blackberry Lily, Leopard Flower

LEAVES: Leaves are equitant, sword-shaped, 1" wide, many-veined, 10" long. The foliage resembles that of German iris.

FLOWER: The flowering stems often reach 4' and carry many flat, star-shaped flowers, 2" across. Flowers are orange, dotted with red. Later, when the capsule splits, the cluster of black seeds resembles a blackberry.

HABIT: 2' to 3' with flower stalks up to 4' tall; erect stems with a width of 2 feet.

SEASON OF BLOOM: Summer.

CULTURE: Blackberry lily will vary in height in relation to soil condition. When grown in full sun in a dry, low fertility soil, the height is nearer to 2'. If the soils are moist and fertile, the flower stalks may extend to 4' which will require staking. This plant is very sensitive to wet soil in the winter. Good drainage is a requirement for optimum growth.

See color plate

UTILIZATION: Perennial border and dried floral arrangements. The shiny black fruit remains effective for many weeks whether on the plant or in a dried arrangement.

PROPAGATION: Blackberry lily can be carefully divided but self-sown seedlings are more easily transplanted. Seeds will germinate in 2–3 weeks at 70°–85°F. *Belamcanda* will bloom the second year from seed.

DISEASES AND INSECTS: Iris borer may attack the fleshy rhizomes. An insecticide program or removal of the dead leaves will reduce the amount of borer infestation.

HARDINESS: Zones 5–10. Blackberry lily performs well over a large climatic range. I have observed excellent plantings at Calloway Gardens, Pine Mountain, Georgia, at the Atlantic Botanic Garden, and in Kansas gardens.

CULTIVARS:
'Freckle Face'—This cultivar is shorter than the species. The flower color is pale orange.

RELATED SPECIES: *B. flabellata.* A 12" tall species with unspotted yellow flowers. In the trade, this species is probably 'Halo Yellow.'

ADDITIONAL NOTES: Needs moderate protection in winter (mulch) to prevent frost heaving. A popular perennial in early times but seldom used today; it deserves a comeback. When not in flower, the plant resembles an iris. The common name, leopard flower was attached to the plant because of the spotted orange flowers.

Native to China and Japan.   Perennial

SCIENTIFIC NAME/FAMILY: *Bellis perennis*   Asteraceae
                                                             (Compositae)
                     (bel'is pĕr-en'is)

COMMON NAME: English Daisy, True Daisy

LEAVES: The 1" to 2" long leaves are spatulate to obovate, glabrous to pubescent, with a crenately-toothed margin. The leaves are arranged in a basal rosette.

FLOWER: Flower heads 1" to 2" across are borne on 3"–6" pubescent scapes. The disk flowers are bisexual and yellow; the numerous ray flowers are white, pink, or red. The flowers may be single or double.

HABIT: 3" to 6" tufted plant with flowers to 8".

SEASON OF BLOOM: Optimum bloom is when the air is still crisp in the morning. Early to late spring is the peak season of bloom with sporadic flowering until fall.

CULTURE: English daisy prefers a cool, moist, fertile soil with abundant organic matter, in full sun to light shade. Although it does well in full sun, the hot summer sun in many parts of the United States is detrimental. The plants must be well watered during the summer and benefit from a light mulch in northern areas. Another method to prevent winter damage is to place the plant in a cold frame.

UTILIZATION: In climates suitable for its growth, English daisy is an excellent plant for the border front, for edging, or for mass effects. It is a good complement to spring bulb plants and is suitable for wild flower beds. In areas where environmental conditions are conducive for growth, English daisy will actually grow in the turf area. In fact the species is a common lawn weed in England.

PROPAGATION: Seeds can be sown in a cold frame in August and then planted out in early spring for flowering during the summer. After flowering, plants can be divided into single crowns. *Bellis* does not come true from seed and to maintain a cultivar, division should be practiced.

DISEASES AND INSECTS: *Bellis* is susceptible to powdery mildew.

HARDINESS: Zones 4–10.

CULTIVARS:
'Dresden China'—Light pink double flowers, 3"–4" tall. Suitable for rock garden use.
'Monstrosa'—3" diameter flowers, 8" tall stems.
'Pomponette'—Button-like double flowers, 6" tall. Usually available in a mix of red, rose, and white.
'Rosea'—Rose-pink ray flowers.

'Smile'—Large flowers are available in bright colors of red, rose, white, or a mix. Compact and uniform plants.

'Super Enorma' Mix—Double flowers in mixed colors of crimson, salmon, rose, and white, 6" tall.

'White Pearl'—White flowers, 3"–4" tall.

ADDITIONAL NOTES: *Bellis* is from the Latin word *bellus* which means pretty.

Native to Europe   Biennial

SCIENTIFIC NAME/FAMILY: *Bergenia cordifolia* (Saxifraga cordifolia)   Saxifragaceae

(bĕr-gen'i-å kōr-di-fōl"i-a)

COMMON NAME: Heartleaf Bergenia, Pig Squeak

LEAVES: Evergreen leaves are produced in clumps; cordate-orbicular, margins undulate-serrate, petioles long and thick, leaves to 12" long. Leaves are glabrous with a fleshy, shiny appearance.

FLOWER: Pink flowers borne on scapes which are just above the foliage. Flowers often are of secondary interest due to the ornamental effect of the foliage.

HABIT: 12"–18" tall clump forming plant that is 12" wide.

SEASON OF BLOOM: Early to late spring.

CULTURE: Full sun or partial shade; adaptable to a wide variety of soils. However, best growth will occur in moisture retentive soils enriched with organic matter. Although the leaves are evergreen, they often become tattered and brown during harsh winters. The flower buds can also be damaged during cold winters.

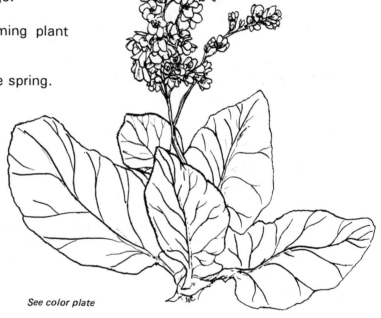

See color plate

UTILIZATION: The foliage of heartleaf bergenia enhances the perennial border, edge of a pool, and the rock garden. *Bergenia* looks best when a number of plants are used to create a mass planting. The shiny, leathery leaves can be used to provide greenery for flower arrangements.

PROPAGATION: Seed or division. *Bergenia* spreads by rhizomes. Spring division of the rhizome is best to allow sufficient root growth before winter. Plants in moist, fertile soil will require division after 4 years, but plants in a drier site can go for several more years without disturbance. The rhizome-like stems can be cut with a knife. The divisions should be transplanted fairly deep into the soil.

DISEASES AND INSECTS: Usually none serious.

HARDINESS: Zones 3–8.

CULTIVARS: There are a number of attractive hybrids that have been selected from crosses of *B cordifolia* and *B. purpurascens.*

'Abendglut' ('Evening Glow')—This 10" tall hybrid has crimson-purple flowers, some being semi-double. The leaves are richly maroon-colored in winter. It was introduced by George Arends Nursery in Germany in 1950.

'Ballawley'—Large leaves, 8"–12" wide, make this cultivar a very useful ground cover in areas with moist soils.

'Bressingham Ruby'—Compact habit, pink flowers, and glossy reddish-purple foliage.

'Bressingham Salmon'—12", salmon flowers.

'Bressingham White'—18", white flowers. 'Bressingham Salmon' and 'Bressingham White' were selected by Alan Bloom after crossing 'Silberlicht' with pink flowering plants.

'Distinction'—An old hybrid with pink flowers similar to *B. cordifolia.*

'Morgenrote' ('Morning Red')—Large bronze-green leaves with dark purplish-red flowers.

'Pugsley's Purple'—Late flowering purple hybrid, 18"–24" tall.

'Silberlicht' ('Silver Light')—This George Arends introduction has white flowers that develop a pink tinge as they age and shiny dark green leaves.

'Sunningdale'—Lilac-carmine flowers are held on 12" tall red stalks. The rounded leaves take on a deep mahogany color in winter.

var. *purpurea*—Darker pink flowers and purple-flushed leaves.

RELATED SPECIES:

B. ciliata (sil-i-a'-ta). This large-leaved species has a dense pubescence on both leaf surfaces. The flowers are pink. The roots are hardy to zone 6 but the leaves are usually deciduous in areas north of Zone 8. 12" tall.

B. crassifolia (kras-si-fō'li-a), Leather Bergenia. The leaves are oval and smaller than those of *B. cordifolia.* The flowers are a light lavender pink. Zones 4–8. 12" tall.

ADDITIONAL NOTES: *Bergenia* is named for Karl August von Bergen, an 18th century botany professor in Frankfort, Germany. Pig squeak comes from the sound made by the finger and thumb rapidly drawn up the leaf blades.

Perennial

Native to Siberia.

SCIENTIFIC NAME/FAMILY: *Bletilla striata*   Orchidaceae

(ble-til'-la strī-ā'tȧ)

COMMON NAME: Chinese Ground Orchid, Hyacinth Bletilla, Hardy Orchid

LEAVES: Three to five leaves arise from pseudo-bulbs. The leaves are pleated, 6"–8" long, broadly linear, and have a papery texture.

FLOWER: The purplish pink flowers are borne on racemes holding 6–10 flowers. The orchidlike flowers are 1"–1½" wide.

HABIT: The leaves are stiffly upright and produce wiry, leafless stems that carry the flowers, 12" tall and 9" wide.

SEASON OF BLOOM: Spring, 2 to 3 weeks.

CULTURE: The pseudobulbs are planted 1"–2" deep in an organic amended soil in partial shade. It is important that the soil does not dry out. A summer drought will cause a reduction in flowering the next spring. In northern areas, the tender pseudobulbs will need to be dug and stored during the winter. A deep mulch of dry leaves will provide winter protection.

UTILIZATION: Useful for the border, rock garden, or in decorative containers. In northern areas, container-grown *Bletilla* can be taken in during the winter and returned outside in the spring.

PROPAGATION: *Bletilla* can be propagated by dividing the pseudobulbs. The tuberlike structures can be removed from the mother plant in the fall. The clump can also be divided by slicing with a knife or shovel.

DISEASES AND INSECTS: There are no serious insects or diseases.

HARDINESS: Zones 5–9.

CULTIVARS:
var. *alba*—White flowers.
'Albostriata'—The leaves are edged with white, flowers are purple. This cultivar is scarce.

Native to China and Japan.   Perennial

SCIENTIFIC NAME/FAMILY: *Boltonia asteroides*   Asteraceae
                                                                 (Compositae)

(bōl-tō′ne-a as-ter-ŏy′-des)

COMMON NAME: White Boltonia, Boltonia

LEAVES: The leaves are alternate, linear
   to lanceolate, up to 5″ long. Most of
   the leaves are sessile and entire. The
   foliage is grayish-green.

FLOWER: The daisy-like flowers of the
   species may be white, lilac to purple.
   They are ¾″ to 1″ wide and are profusely borne in panicles. The flower
   display is impressive.

HABIT: The species is erect, 5′–6′ tall
   and 3′–4′ wide. It often requires staking. The cultivar 'Snowbank' is 3′–4′
   and is self-supporting.

SEASON OF BLOOM: Late summer to
   frost.

CULTURE: Boltonia is easily grown in full
   sun in a well-drained soil with moist,
   organic amended soil. 'Snowbank'
   does not require staking when grown   *See color plate*
   in full sun.

UTILIZATION: 'Snowbank' is a good selection for the fall border. In my garden, 'Snowbank' starts flowering in August and remains in flower to late September or later. It is
   compact enough so staking is not required, but it is open and fine textured enough to
   provide a graceful look to the border. Boltonia is a good complement to other fall-
   flowering perennials like Autumn Joy sedum, Russian sage, and Joe-pye weed. I think
   it is one of the best white flowering perennials for fall bloom.

PROPAGATION: Division in spring or fall and tip cuttings in the spring. The species can
   also be grown from seed.

DISEASES AND INSECTS: There are usually few problems. 'Snowbank' resembles a Michaelmas daisy but appears to be less susceptible to mildew.

HARDINESS: Zones 4–9.

CULTIVARS:
   'Snowbank'—This white flowered cultivar is the preferred choice of the *Boltonia.* Its
      compact habit is an advantage over the species.
   'Pink Beauty'—A compact form, 3′–4′, with pink flowers.

Native to central United States.   Perennial

SCIENTIFIC NAME/FAMILY: *Borago officinalis*   Boraginaceae

(bôr-rā′gō o-fis-i-nā′lis)

COMMON NAME: Borage

LEAVES: Alternate leaves, oval shaped with a round apex. The basal leaves can be 6″–8″ long, long petioled, with bristlelike pubescence, the margins entire but wavy. The upper stem leaves are 3″–6″ long and 1½″–2″ wide. The entire plant has a rough texture with stiff, prickly hairs.

FLOWER: Clear blue flower, ¾″ wide, star-shaped corolla that is wheel shaped and contains 5 petals. The flowers are arranged in an open, drooping raceme. Unopened flower buds are densely pubescent.

HABIT: Round to sprawling habit, 2′–3′ tall and 18″ wide. Space 18″ to 24″ apart.

SEASON OF BLOOM: Midsummer; however, flowering will depend upon when this annual is seeded.

CULTURE: Full sun in well-drained soil is an ideal site for this species. It tends to be a tough, drought-tolerant annual. Borage will self seed and plants can be expected on a permanent basis.

UTILIZATION: In the culinary area, borage is used for flavoring food; it has a cucumber flavor. Borage is used like spinach, and the leaves can be eaten raw, steamed, or sautéed. The stems are also edible. The clear blue flowers are a welcome sight in the summer landscape, but the rough, sprawling habit is not suited for the refined garden. Borage might be better in the herb garden or blended with other plants in the wildflower garden.

DISEASES AND INSECTS: None serious.

Native to Europe.   Annual

SCIENTIFIC NAME/FAMILY: *Brachycome iberidifolia*   Asteraceae
                                                                                    (Compositae)

(brá-kik'ō-mē ī-bē'ri-di-fō'li-a)

COMMON NAME: Swan River Daisy

LEAVES: Alternate, to 3″ long, pinnately dissected into linear segments, rarely entire,
glandular-pubescent to nearly glabrous.

FLOWER: Daisy-like flowers with solid colored
centers. The heads are about 1″ across and
are borne on slender peduncles. Ray flowers
are blue, rose, or white.

HABIT: 9″–14″ round habit and a 12″ spread.

SEASON OF BLOOM: All summer.

CULTURE: Sun with well-drained moist soil.
Doesn't seem to stand hot weather; does
very well in early summer but thins in July
and August.

UTILIZATION: Rock garden, edging, and containers such as window boxes.

PROPAGATION: Seeds should be germinated at
70°F. Germination occurs in 15–20 days.

DISEASES AND INSECTS: Usually none.

CULTIVARS: *See color plate*
    'Blue Splendor'—Flowers are various shades
       of blue, some with yellow centers and others with black centers.
    'White Splendor'—White flowers.

ADDITIONAL NOTES: The name *Brachycome* is derived from the Greek, *brachys,* short,
    and *kome,* hair, referring to the short hairs on the seeds.

Native to Australia.   Annual

SCIENTIFIC NAME/FAMILY: *Brassica oleracea* (Acephala Group)   Brassicaceae
(Cruciferae)

(bras'i-kȧ ol-ēr-ā'sē-a)

COMMON NAME: Flowering Kale, Ornamental Kale

LEAVES: Separate or only in loose rosettes, not making solid heads (*acephala* means head-
less). The leaves are thick and glaucous like cabbage and they are edible. The bluegreen
leaves are showy and open from the center. Centers are usually white or tinged with
pink, red, or purple.

FLOWER: Not important.

HABIT: 10" to 15" tall
with rosette leaves.

SEASON OF BLOOM: Not
important.

CULTURE: Full sun, prefers
moist, well-drained soil.
Low nitrogen rates will
increase foliage color.

UTILIZATION: Bedding
plant, carpet bed, and
specimen plant are
some common uses for
flowering kale. Many of
the theme parks, such
as Walt Disney World,
use flowering kale during the early spring and fall seasons. The vivid color and texture
of the foliage is most attractive.

See color plate

PROPAGATION: Seeds germinate at 70°F and then are grown at 60° for 3–4 weeks. After
a week of hardening off, the plants can be placed outside.

DISEASES AND INSECTS: None serious.

RELATED SPECIES: *Brassica oleracea*, (Capitata Group) Ornamental Cabbage. Flowering
kale and ornamental cabbage are similar and are often sold interchangeably or as a mixture.

CULTIVARS:
Flowering Cabbage:
'Dynasty' Series—plants in this group are 12" tall with semiwavy leaves and tight,
compact heads. The colorful colors include pink, red, white, and a mixture.
'Osaka' Series—Semi-fringed leaves form bright-colored central heads. This group is
very vigorous and colors about a month earlier than other selections. Colors include
pink, red, and white.
'Pigeon'—Compact plants have round, solid heads surrounded by wavy leaves. Red and
white selections.
'Tokyo' Series—These round leaf types are short stemmed and very cold resistant.
They are often used for winter flower beds.

Flowering Kale:
'Chidori'—Fringed leaves with finely ruffled edges. Colors well in warmer climates.
'Nagoya' Series—This group has heavily crinkled leaves and vibrant colors. They are
    early, vigorous, and are suitable for massing in the fall.
'Peacock' Series—Dwarf plants with deeply serrated feathery foliage.
'Sparrow' Series—Dwarf plants, 8″ tall, with finely ruffled leaves and colorful heads
    of red or white.

ADDITIONAL NOTES: *Oleracea* indicates that the plant is edible and *acephala* means head-
    less; consequently, flowering kale does not form heads like other plants in the cabbage
    group. Flowering kale is in the mustard family, which contains plants that grow better
    in cooler temperatures. The colors of the leaves on flowering kale color best in the cool-
    er fall temperatures. Seed is available that will produce leaves with red on green, white
    on green, or a mixture of both. Flowering kale is another member of the *Brassicaceae*
    family which will not survive the hot summers in southern locations.

Native to Eurasia.   Biennial, but usually grown as an annual

SCIENTIFIC NAME/FAMILY: *Briza media*   Poaceae
                                                        (Gramineae)

(bri′zȧ mē′di-ȧ)

COMMON NAME: Quaking Grass,
    Trembling Grass

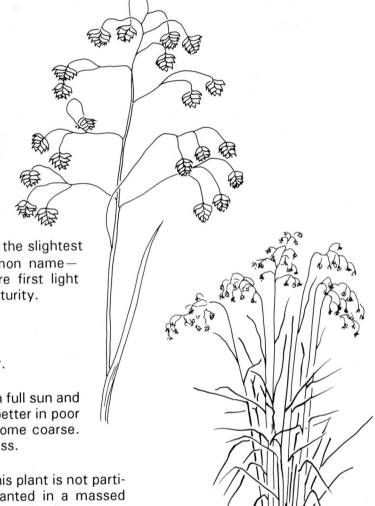

LEAVES: Leaf blades 1/6″ wide
    and 6″ long, flat in cross sec-
    tion, minutely scabrous on the
    margin, blade narrowing to a
    blunt tip. The foliage is medi-
    um green.

FLOWER: Inflorescence is a very
    open panicle, somewhat py-
    ramidal, 6″–8″ long. The
    branches are wide spreading
    and bear loosely attached
    spikelets that shake or quake at the slightest
    breeze; consequently the common name—
    quaking grass. The spikelets are first light
    green and then turn beige at maturity.

HABIT: Upright-open, 24″ tall.

SEASON OF BLOOM: Early summer.

CULTURE: *Briza* should be planted in full sun and
    well-drained soil. It tends to do better in poor
    soils. On fertile soils, it will become coarse.
    Do not over fertilize quaking grass.

UTILIZATION: The overall form of this plant is not parti-
    cularly interesting. It is best planted in a massed
    situation or in naturalized gardens. The flowers are
    excellent for drying and dyeing.

PROPAGATION: Division in spring or fall and seed are
    both suitable methods.

DISEASES AND INSECTS: No serious problems.

HARDINESS: Zones 4–8.

RELATED SPECIES:
    B. maxima (maks′-im-a), Large Quaking Grass. This relative is an annual that grows
        about 18″ tall and bears 1″–2″ long seed heads on drooping stems.
    B. minor (mī′nor), Small Quaking Grass. This annual grass is simply a miniature of *B.
        maxima.*

ADDITIONAL NOTES: *Briza* is from Greek *brizo,* to nod, and refers to the movement of the
    sprays. One book lists 16 common names for *Briza media.*

Native to Europe and Asia.   Perennial

SCIENTIFIC NAME/FAMILY: *Browallia speciosa*   Solanaceae

(brō-wal'i-a spē-si-ō'så)

COMMON NAME: Browallia, Amethyst Flower, Sapphire Flower

LEAVES: Opposite or alternate, narrowly ovate, to 2½" long, obtuse or acute, branches somewhat pendent.

FLOWER: Blue or white star-shaped flower. Flowers solitary, axillary, on very short pedicels. Corolla tube at least 1" long, 2 to 3 times as long as the calyx. Corolla is a dark purple or in some cvs. blue, violet, or white.

HABIT: 8"–16" round habit.

SEASON OF BLOOM: Early to late summer.

CULTURE: Shade to partial shade; flower color is best when plant is shaded from afternoon sun. Over-watering or over-fertilizing will result in a lot of foliage but few flowers.

UTILIZATION: Shade bedding, window boxes, planters, trailing plants for baskets, urns and can be used as an indoor flowering pot plant during the winter.

PROPAGATION: Seed, easy to germinate in 2 to 3 weeks at 70° to 75°F. Seed should be uncovered and exposed to light. Softwood cuttings can be taken in fall or spring.

DISEASES AND INSECTS: None are serious, although *Fusarium* wilt, leafhoppers, and white flies sometimes occur.

CULTIVARS:
'Blue Bells Improved'—Lavender-blue, dwarf branching strain that requires no pinching for good pot plants.
'Blue Troll'—This member of the Troll series has blue flowers on mounded, compact plants, 8"–10" tall.
'Jingle Bells Mixed'—Mixture of the Bells series.
'Marine Bells'—Indigo blue, more compact than 'Blue Bells Improved'; excellent for pots and hanging baskets.
'Silver Bells'— Large snow-white flowers.
'Sky Bells'—Clear powder-blue flowers.
'White Troll'—Pure white flowers, compact growth habit.

ADDITIONAL NOTES: In fall, cut plants back, dig, and move them indoors where they will flower freely all winter. *Browallia* is named in honor of Johan Browall, an 18th century Swedish botanist.

Native to Columbia.   Annual

SCIENTIFIC NAME/FAMILY: *Brunnera macrophylla* (Anchusa myosotidiflora) Boraginaceae

(brun-nē′rȧ mak-rō-fil′ȧ)

COMMON NAME: Siberian Bugloss

LEAVES: Alternate, all leaves strongly cordate or reniform at the base, basal leaves long-petioled, ovate, up to 8″ across; stem leaves smaller with shorter petioles; upper stem leaves nearly sessile. The dark green leaves increase in size from spring to midsummer and provide an excellent foliage effect.

FLOWER: Blue, small (⅛″ – ¼″ across), starlike flowers in branched racemes resemble those of *Anchusa.*

HABIT: 12″ to 18″ round habit which has an 18″ spread.

SEASON OF BLOOM: Early to late spring.

CULTURE: Best growth will occur in partial shade and moist, well-drained soil. In southern zones, dense shade and moist soils are a necessity while plants in northern gardens will grow well with morning sun. Generally little care is needed except when a clump deteriorates in the center, at which time, it should be divided. *Brunnera* freely self-sows but the plants are easily pulled from areas where they are not welcome.

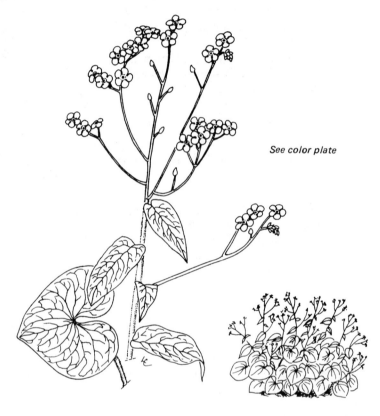

See color plate

UTILIZATION: Excellent for spring display of a true blue flower. Often found in naturalized plantings in semi-shade, the perennial border, or used as a deciduous ground cover in shady, moist areas.

PROPAGATION: Root cuttings, seed and division. Root cuttings made of 1 ½ ″ sections can be planted outside in the spring or in the greenhouse during the winter. Seeds are sown in early fall, while division of the clumps is best done in the spring.

DISEASES AND INSECTS: None serious.

HARDINESS: Zones 3–8. *Brunnera* does well in Zone 8. I have seen nice specimens in the State Botanic Garden of Georgia in Athens.

CULTIVARS:

'Alba'—The flowers of this selection are white rather than the traditional blue.

'Hadspen Cream'—Large, light green leaves with irregular borders of cream color. The leaf margins will become scorched in sunny locations.

'Langtrees'—This selection has dark green leaves with silver spots near the edges of the leaves. It is a very attractive cultivar but relatively unavailable in the United States at this time.

'Variegata'—Large leaves are boldly variegated with creamy-white color. Some leaves are almost entirely white. It is not tolerant to sunny situations or drought, as the leaf margins scorch easily. It must be planted in a moist soil in a shaded site. Green leaf reversions must be removed to retain a variegated plant.

ADDITIONAL NOTES: *Brunnera* is easily cultivated. Although there are 3 species native to Europe, *B. macrophylla* is the only one of garden importance. The genus was named for S. Brunner, a nineteenth century Swiss botanist.

Native to Siberia.   Perennial

SCIENTIFIC NAME/FAMILY: *Buphthalmum salicifolium*   Asteraceae (Compositae)

(būf-thal'mum sal-is-i-fō'-li-um)

COMMON NAME: Willowleaf Oxeye

LEAVES: Alternate leaves, oblong-lanceolate to lanceolate, entire or sparsely toothed margins, 3"–5" long. The basal leaves are petioled while the stem leaves are sessile and clasping. Leaves resemble a willow leaf and often have a whitish pubescence on the lower surface.

FLOWER: Yellow flowers, 1"–2" wide are borne singularly on terminal stems.

HABIT: Erect perennial, 1'–2' tall and 2' wide. The stems are thin and the plant will often topple unless support is provided.

SEASON OF BLOOM: Summer.

CULTURE: Full sun or partial shade in moist soils. This species is tolerant of poor soils. The tidy gardener will opt for staking, but this daisy-like plant also can be allowed to lean on nearby neighbors. Remove spent flowers to prolong the flowering season.

See color plate

UTILIZATION: Useful in the border for its bright yellow midsummer bloom. It is also used as a cut flower.

PROPAGATION: Division can be done in early spring or early autumn after flowering is concluded. Seeds germinate in 3 weeks at 70°–75°F.

DISEASES AND INSECTS: No serious problems.

HARDINESS: Zones 4–7.

CULTIVARS: 'Sunwheel'—Golden yellow flowers, 24"–30" tall.

RELATED SPECIES:

Telekia speciosa (Te-lek'-i-a spē-si-ō'-sum) (*Buphthalmum speciosum*) — Scented Oxeye. The scientific name for this plant is as active as the ball in a tennis match. First it is in one place and then in another. Reference texts and catalogs are also evenly split on the proper name. This oxeye daisy has large, heart-shaped leaves that are pubescent, doubly toothed, and aromatic. It is 4'–5' tall and will spread to 3'. The yellow flowers are 3" in diameter. It can be used at the back of the border. It has a vigorous growth rate and may spread too rapidly for some gardens.

Native to southeastern Europe.   Perennial

SCIENTIFIC NAME/FAMILY: *Caladium × hortulanum*   Araceae

(kả-lā'di-um hôr'ti-lā-num)

COMMON NAME: Fancy-leaved Caladium

LEAVES: Leaf blades sometimes peltate, ovate to lanceolate in outline, basally bifid, cordate, or truncate, flat, undulate, or ruffled, variously variegated with red, rose, salmon, white, or green, petioles as long as or longer than the blade. Leaves are 6" to 18" long.

FLOWER: Not showy.

HABIT: 1' to 2' erect plant.

SEASON OF BLOOM: Not significant.

CULTURE: Full sun to partial shade, prefers fertile, organic soil that is well-drained. *Caladium* needs abundant water during the growing season. *Caladium* will perform poorly in areas of low humidity.

UTILIZATION: Specimen plant, container plant. Excellent for massing in shaded borders.

PROPAGATION: Propagated by removing the tubers from the parent plant at the end of the 4–5 month dormancy period before planting. The tubers are cut into pieces which contain at least two buds (eyes). The tubers are set out when danger of frost is past.

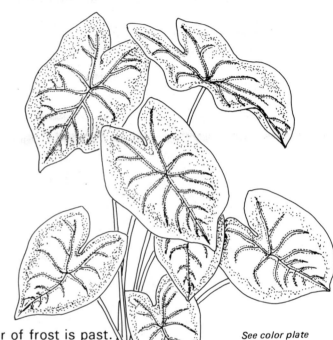

See color plate

DISEASES AND INSECTS: None serious.

HARDINESS: Zone 10.

CULTIVARS: (partial listing)
'Aaron'—White leaves, bordered with bright green.
'Blaze'—Red leaves with scarlet ribs and a light green margin.
'Candidum'—Snow-white leaves with green veins and a green margin.
'Carolyn Wharton'—Pink, with rose veins and a bright green margin.
'Fannie Munson'—Pink leaves with a narrow, green margin.
'Frieda Hemple'—Solid red leaves and a green margin.
'Gypsy Rose'—Green background with deep rose veins surrounded by pink mottles.
'John Reed'—Bright red center and green border.
'June Bride'—White leaves with a faint, lace-like green venation pattern.
'Mrs. F. M. Joyner'—White leaves with scarlet veins that flow outward in shades of pink to white.
'Mrs. W. B. Haldeman'—Watermelon pink leaves with green veins and border.
'Pink Beauty'—Soft pink colors on a deep green background with rose veins.
'Postman Joyner'—Dark red leaves with darker veins and a green margin.
'Red Flash'—Waxy leaves with bright red centers, deep red veins, pink mottling and green edging.
'White Christmas'—White background with green venation that never merges, creating a symmetrical pattern.

ADDITIONAL NOTES: Tubers have to be dug in the fall and stored dry for the winter. The tubers are planted in the spring after danger of frost is past.

Hybrid origin.   Perennial—tender tuber

SCIENTIFIC NAME/FAMILY: *Calamagrostis acutiflora* 'Stricta'   Poaceae
(Gramineae)

(cal'à-ma-gros'-tis a-cūt-i-flō'rà)

COMMON NAME: Feather Reed Grass

LEAVES: The leaves are dull green and hairless. The blades are finely pointed, up to 36″ long, and ½″ wide. The foliage is coarsely textured and rough to the touch.

FLOWER: The green to pinkish flowers are borne in an erect panicle up to 15″ long and ½″ to 1″ wide. The flowers turn a straw color in summer.

HABIT: Slender upright habit, 4'–5' tall and 2' wide.

SEASON OF BLOOM: Early summer. Feather reed grass is one of the first ornamental grasses to flower. The inflorescence is ornamental until late winter. The flowers mature to a Kansas wheat field golden-tan.

CULTURE: *Calamagrostis* is easily grown in full sun and ordinary soil. It is one of the few grasses that will do well in heavy soil. It performs well in moist to wet areas as well as well-drained soils.

UTILIZATION: This species is one of the best medium-sized grasses. It can be used as a specimen, in a massed planting, or along streams, ponds, and other wet areas. Since the maximum height is about 4 feet, feather reed grass is more useful for the smaller garden. The inflorescence is excellent as a dried flower. It is a cool season grass that performs well throughout the hottest days of summer.

PROPAGATION: Division in the spring.

DISEASES AND INSECTS: No serious problems. Ornamental grasses are usually pest and disease free.

HARDINESS: Zones 4–8.

CULTIVARS:
   C. acutiflora 'Karl Foerster'—Karl Foerster's Feather Reed Grass. This cultivar is slightly smaller and blooms 2 weeks earlier than feather reed grass.

RELATED SPECIES:
   C. arundinacea (a-run-di-nā'-se-a) var. *brachytricha* (*Achnatherum brachytricha*), Foxtail Grass or Korean Feather Reed Grass. This selection is 3 feet tall and flowers in late summer. The flowers are rose-purple for 2 or 3 weeks after anthesis and resemble bottle brushes. The foliage and inflorescence only last until early winter versus the later effect of *C. acutiflora* 'Stricta'.
   C. arundinacea, 'Oredam'. The 12″–18″ long leaves have a thin, white variegation. The stems carrying the gold inflorescences are 36″ tall.

Native to Europe.

Perennial

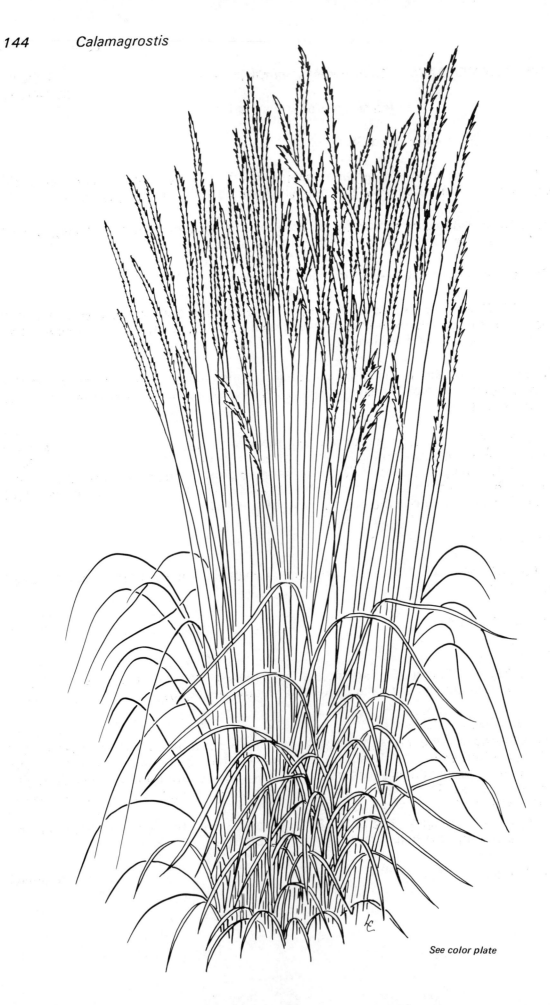

See color plate

SCIENTIFIC NAME/FAMILY: *Calendula officinalis*

Asteraceae
(Compositae)

(kȧ-len′dū-lȧ o-fis-i-nā′lis)

COMMON NAME: Calendula, Pot Marigold

LEAVES: Alternate, thickish, oblong to oblong-obovate, 2″–6″ long, entire or minutely and sparsely denticulate. The leaves often clasp the stem.

FLOWER: Heads solitary, on stout stalks, showy, 1½″ to 4″ across. The head is composed of flat spreading rays, yellowish-white to deep orange, which close at night.

HABIT: 12″–18″ rounded plant.

SEASON OF BLOOM: Early summer to fall (May to September). *Calendula* in Latin means throughout the months and refers to the fact that this plant flowers for many months.

CULTURE: Full sun with well-drained moist soil; does poorly in hot weather.

UTILIZATION: Cutting, bedding, border plant.

PROPAGATION: Seeds germinate in one to two weeks at a constant 70°F and should be covered to exclude light. A second planting may be made for late flowering in the autumn. One may also find that *Calendula* will self-sow.

DISEASES AND INSECTS: Fungal leaf spots, powdery mildew, stem and root rots, aster yellows, cabbage looper, and aphids have been reported. However, these problems usually do not limit the use of this species.

CULTIVARS:
'Bon Bon' series—Earlier blooming, compact selection with yellow, orange or mixed cultivars. Plants are 12″ tall with 3″ wide flowers.
'Coronet'—'Lemon Coronet' and 'Orange Coronet' bloom freely during hot summers.
'Fiesta Gitana' ('Gypsy Festival')—Dwarf, wide color range, double flowers, All Britain Trials Bronze Medal, 1977.
'Geisha Girl'—3″ orange blossoms with incurved petals, 18″–24″.
'Mandarin'—Orange flowers, 2″–3″ wide blossoms, 12″–18″.
'Pacific Beauty'—15″, 4″–5″ flowers, resistant to summer heat; several cultivars of differing colors.
'Touch of Red' Series—Flowers are 3″ wide and the petals have red tips. Plants are 24″ tall and 24″ wide.

ADDITIONAL NOTES: The word *officinalis* means medicinal, and *Calendula* has been used medicinally. The florets were once used for healing wounds and for preventing sickness. They were also used as a country remedy for the treatment of ulcers. The flower heads, after drying, have been used to flavor soups and stews, as well as for coloring butter.

Native to Mediterranean area.

Annual

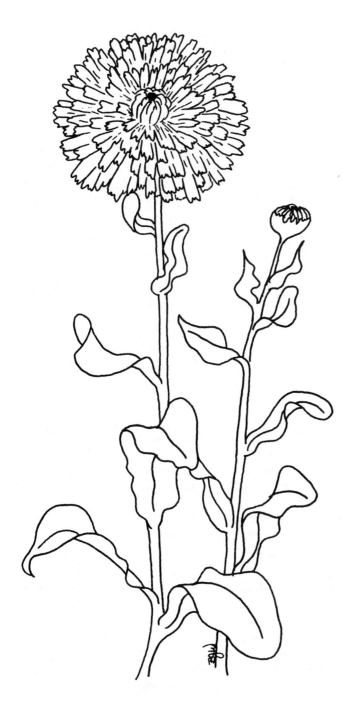

See color plate

SCIENTIFIC NAME/FAMILY: *Callirhoe involucrata*   Malvaceae

(kal-lir'-ō-e in-vol-u-krā'-ta)

COMMON NAME: Poppy Mallow, Winecups, Finger Poppy Mallow

LEAVES: Foliage is hirsute to hispid. The alternate leaves are rounded in outline, very deeply parted, with 5 to 6 lobes arranged in a palmate fashion. Individual leaves are 1½" to 2" wide.

FLOWER: The flowers are solitary and held erect on slender stems. The deep reddish-purple flowers are cup shaped and 2½" wide.

HABIT: A 6"–12" tall plant with procumbent stems which can spread to 3 feet.

SEASON OF BLOOM: Blooms all summer.

CULTURE: Poppy mallow is a sun plant which requires little moisture. Blessed with a long tap root, *Callirhoe* will only need water during periods of prolonged drought.

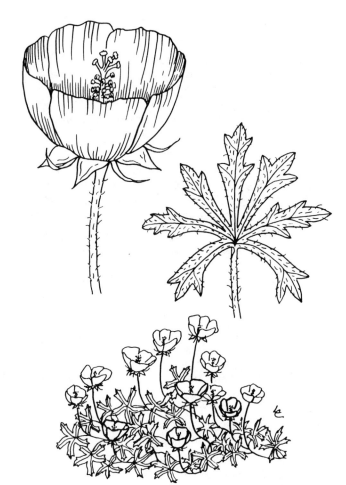

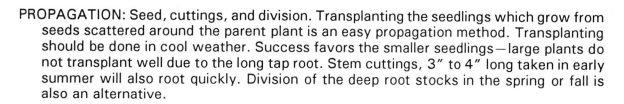

UTILIZATION: Poppy mallow grows quickly during the summer and is useful for the front of the sunny border, in rock gardens, or trailing over a wall.

PROPAGATION: Seed, cuttings, and division. Transplanting the seedlings which grow from seeds scattered around the parent plant is an easy propagation method. Transplanting should be done in cool weather. Success favors the smaller seedlings—large plants do not transplant well due to the long tap root. Stem cuttings, 3" to 4" long taken in early summer will also root quickly. Division of the deep root stocks in the spring or fall is also an alternative.

DISEASES AND INSECTS: None serious.

HARDINESS: Zones 3–9. In zones 8–9 this species will be evergreen.

ADDITIONAL NOTES: *Callirhoe* is a member of the Malvaceae family. It is similar to *Malva* but differs mainly in having petals which are irregularly cut at the apex, unlike the petals of *Malva* which have one notch. *Callirhoe* is derived from the mythical Callirhoe, daughter of Achelous, the river god.

Native to western United States and northern Mexico.   Perennial

SCIENTIFIC NAME/FAMILY: *Callistephus chinensis* (Aster sinensis) Asteraceae
(Compositae)

(ka-lis'te-fus chi-nen'sis)

COMMON NAME: China Aster, Annual Aster

LEAVES: Alternate leaves which are broadly ovate or triangular-ovate to 3½", deeply and irregularly toothed, the blade decurrent into a petiole, the upper leaves becoming spatulate and narrower; stems are hispid.

FLOWER: Flower heads grow as wide as 5" and may have white, creamy-yellow, pink, red, blue, lavender, or purple ray flowers with yellow disk flowers. The colors of China aster are nice because many are tertiary but very vivid and rich. In many cultivars, the head composition may change as the ray flowers may be so numerous that they frequently replace the disk flowers.

See color plate

HABIT: 1'–3' tall-leggy (little foliage). Plants bend from weight of flowers. Consequently, tall plants may need to be staked.

SEASON OF BLOOM: China aster flowers for about 4 weeks. However, there are cultivars for early, midseason, and late summer flowering.

CULTURE: Sun or light shade; prefers neutral to basic soil.

UTILIZATION: Cut flowers, bedding plants. Asters do not rebloom when flowers are cut. Successive plantings will assure continuous bloom.

PROPAGATION: Seeds germinate in 8 to 10 days at 65°–70°F.

DISEASES AND INSECTS: Aphids and red spider mites; mites particularly troublesome in late spring and early summer. Stem rot, which causes plant to rot at surface; dark brown lesions extend up the stem. Aster yellows stops growth and plants turn yellow. The above diseases are not controlled with fungicides. The following procedures can be used to prevent damage:
1. Plant virus or rot resistant varieties.
2. Plant in different areas each year to avoid soil-borne diseases.
3. Spray weekly with insecticide to control leafhoppers, which transmit disease.
4. Discard infected plants away from the garden. Do not place them in the compost pile.

CULTIVARS:

'Color Carpet'—4″ double flowers borne on 8″ tall plants, blooms early August, excellent for border.

'Duchess'—24″ tall, 4″–5″ diameter flowers, wilt-resistant, good for cutting.

'Dwarf Queen'—10″ tall, early July flower, wilt-resistant, mixed colors.

'Dwarf Sparklers' Mix—Spider mum-type flowers, 3″ wide, are carried on 10″ tall stems. Colors include blue, pink, scarlet, and white.

'Milady' Mix—Dwarf, basal branching selection with 4″ diameter flowers. The flowers are mum-like and include the colors of carmine, blue, rose-red, rose, scarlet and white.

'Perfection' Mix—This selection with double flowers is suited for cutting and garden use. Individual flowers have broad incurved petals and are 4″ wide. The stems are 32″ long, making them ideal for cut flower production. Wilt resistant.

'Pinocchio'—6″ dwarf, mixed colors, border and pot plants.

'Pixie Princess'—A mixed color range which includes pink, red, rose, blue, and some whites. It is an early flowering dwarf, 10″ tall.

'Pot'n'Patio'—Compact plants that are 6″ tall are suited for bedding purposes and containers.

'Powderpuffs Mixed'—24″ tall, quilled petals, used as a cut flower.

ADDITIONAL NOTES: *Callistephus* is derived from *kallistos,* most beautiful, and *stephos,* a crown, referring to the appendages of the fruit.

Native to Japan.   Annual

SCIENTIFIC NAME/FAMILY: *Caltha palustris*   Ranunculaceae

(kal'thȧ pa-lus'tris)

COMMON NAME: Marsh Marigold, Kingcup

LEAVES: Stems are hollow on this species. The leaf blades are nearly round and are deeply cordate. Dark green leaves are 3" to 4" wide.

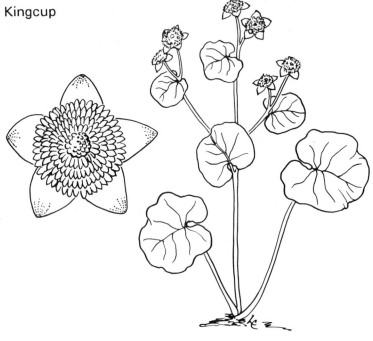

FLOWER: Flowers are bright yellow, 2" wide, contain 5 sepals (no petals) and are borne on long peduncles that raise the flowers above the foliage.

HABIT: Clump forming plant, 12"–18" tall and 18" wide.

SEASON OF BLOOM: Spring.

CULTURE: Marsh marigold will grow in sun or partial shade in moist soil but it is at its best in wet soil.

UTILIZATION: Water gardens, garden ponds, and streams are the best locations, since marsh marigold requires constant moisture. It is most noticeable when grown in masses.

See color plate

PROPAGATION: It is usually done by division.

DISEASES AND INSECTS: None serious.

HARDINESS: Zones 4–9.

CULTIVARS:
  'Alba'—Single white flowers with bold yellow stamens. The flowering is not as profuse as that found on 'Flore Pleno' but 'Alba' is a worthwhile find.
  'Flore Pleno' (flō'-re-plē''no)—The double form (illustrated by the drawing) is very showy and more popular than the species. It blooms longer than the species. It is also listed as 'Multiplex'.

Native to Europe and North America.   Perennial

SCIENTIFIC NAME/FAMILY: *Camassia leichtlinii*   Hyacinthaceae (Liliaceae)

(kȧ-mas'i-ȧ likt'lin-e-ī)

COMMON NAME: Leichtlin Quamash, Camass

LEAVES: The basal leaves are linear to strap shaped, which creates a grasslike appearance. The leaves can be up to 24" long and 1" wide.

FLOWER: Star-shaped flowers are borne in a terminal raceme composed of 20–80 flowers per stem. Each flower has 6 perianth segments with flower colors of blue, purple, white or cream. The flowers twist around the maturing seed capsule as they wither.

HABIT: A 3'–4' tall naked flower stem with a terminal raceme rises above a grass-like clump of foliage 24" tall.

SEASON OF BLOOM: Late spring to early summer.

CULTURE: The ideal site is one that is moist to wet in the spring. Full sun is optimum with some tolerance of partial shade. Planting depth is 4"–6".

UTILIZATION: Use as a border perennial or in the naturalized area. It should be planted in mass for best display. *Camassia* is an excellent cut flower.

PROPAGATION: *Camassia* can be started easily from seed, but flowering will not occur until after 3 or 4 years. Bulb offsets can also be obtained after several years. Commercial production is usually from offsets.

DISEASES AND INSECTS: None serious.

HARDINESS: Zones 5 to 9.

CULTIVARS:
   'Alba' (also listed as ssp. *typica*)—White flowers.
   var. *atroviolacea*—Deep purple flowers.
   'Semi-plena' ('Plena')—White-semidouble, double flowers.

RELATED SPECIES:
   C. quamash (kwä'mash) (esculenta)—Common Quamash. This species has shorter (12") and narrower (½") leaves than *C. leichtlinii*. Total height is 24"–30". Flower colors vary from deep to pale blue to white.

   C. cusickii (kew-sik'-ē-i)—Cusick Quamash. This Oregon native is 3'–4' tall with blue flowers. The leaves can be 2" wide and 18"–24" long. The large bulb can weigh up to 8 ounces. It is the most cold hardy of the *Camassia* species (zone 2).

Native to western United States and British Columbia.   Hardy bulb

SCIENTIFIC NAME/FAMILY: *Campanula carpatica*   Campanulaceae

(kam-pan'ū-là kar-pat'-i-ka)

COMMON NAME: Carpathian Harebell, Carpathian Bellflower, Tussock Bellflower

LEAVES: Stems more or less decumbent or spreading at base, leaves long-petioled, ovate-triangular to broadly lanceolate, 2" long, deeply serrate.

FLOWER: Flowers erect on long, slender, naked, axillary pedicels, corolla, blue-lilac, 1"–2" across, broadly campanulate. Other cultivars are white or purple.

HABIT: The foliage is 4" to 6" tall with a 6" to 12" tall flower pedicel, mounded habit.

SEASON OF BLOOM: Early to midsummer.

CULTURE: Sun or partial shade with a well drained soil of average fertility. Plants will perform poorly in dry or wet soils. Heat and high humidity are also detrimental to optimum growth.

UTILIZATION: Border or rock garden. The small compactness of this plant makes it a natural for edging in perennial borders. It is also at home with alpine plants.

See color plate

PROPAGATION: Seeds will germinate readily from spring sowings (70°), but the many variants of the species are unlikely to reproduce true to type. Older plants can be divided in early spring or August with good success.

DISEASES AND INSECTS: There are no serious disease or insect problems, but slugs and snails can wreak havoc. Protection from slugs is required for optimum growth.

HARDINESS: Zones 3–8.

CULTIVARS:
 var. *alba*—White flowers.
 'Blue Clips'—Large blue flowers on a 6" to 8" tall plant.
 'Bressingham White'—Large flowers and a pure white color.
 'China Doll'—Delicate lavender flowers on stems about 8" tall.
 'Turbinata'—Purplish blue flowers, 6"–9" tall.
 'Wedgewood Blue'—Sky-blue flowers, 6" tall.
 'Wedgewood White'—White flowers, 6" tall.
 'White Clips'—White flowers, 6" to 8" tall.

ADDITIONAL NOTES: *Campanula* has both perennial and biennial species. All are easy to grow and reliable and prodigious in their flowering. *Campanula,* meaning little bell in Latin, takes its name from the customary form of the flowers.

Native to southern Europe.   Perennial

SCIENTIFIC NAME/FAMILY: *Campanula glomerata*   Campanulaceae

(kam-pan′ū-là glom′er-ā-ta)

COMMON NAME: Clustered Bellflower, Danesblood Bellflower

LEAVES: Alternate leaves, the lower leaves are petioled, narrow cordate-ovate, 4″ to 5″ long. The stem leaves are ovate to ovate-oblong, 3″ to 4″ long.

FLOWER: The blue flowers of the species are borne in dense axillary or terminal clusters. Individual flowers are bell-shaped and upward facing.

HABIT: 18″–24″ tall and 12″ wide.

SEASON OF BLOOM: Summer.

CULTURE: Easily grown in sun or partial shade in moist soil. In southern zones partial shade and moist soil are required.

UTILIZATION: Clustered bellflower is a durable perennial, but it is often considered common and is somewhat invasive. Useful in borders and informal areas. For best appearance, plant in groups of at least 3 plants. Bellflower also can be used as a cut flower.

PROPAGATION: Seed, division and stem cuttings can be used. Terminal cuttings, 2″–3″ long should be taken in the summer following flowering. Division is suitable in fall or spring.

DISEASES AND INSECTS: Diseases and insects are usually no problem, but snails and slugs will need attention.

HARDINESS: Zones 3–8.

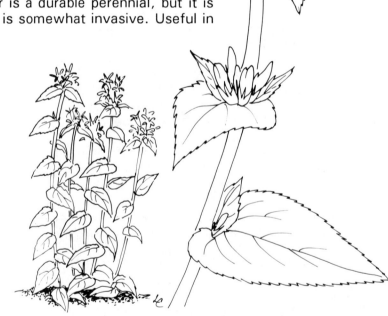

See color plate

CULTIVARS:
'Alba'—White flowers.
var. *acaulis* (à′ca-lis)—Blue-violet flowers, 4″–6″ tall.
'Crown of Snow' ('Schneekrone')—White flowers 18″–24″ tall.
var. *dahurica* (da-hu′ri-ka)—Deep-violet flowers are borne in 3″ diameter clusters, 12″ tall.
'Joan Elliott'—Deep violet flowers, 18″ tall.
'Purple Pixie'—Violet-purple flowers, 18″ tall.
'Superba'—Large violet-blue flowers, 30″ tall. Listed as being more heat tolerant.
'White Barn'—Violet-purple flowers, 12″ tall.

Native to Europe.   Perennial

SCIENTIFIC NAME/FAMILY: *Campanula latifolia*   Campanulaceae

(kam-pan'ū-là lat-i-fō'li-a)

COMMON NAME: Great Bellflower

See color plate

LEAVES: Alternate leaves are oblong-ovate to lanceolate, lower leaves are petioled, 5″–6″ long while the upper leaves are smaller and become sessile higher on the stem. The leaves are rugose, pubescent and have a double-toothed margin. Stems have scattered hairs.

FLOWER: Purplish-blue, bell-shaped flowers are borne in upper leaf axils or in short, terminal racemes. Flowers are 1½″ long with campanulate corollas.

HABIT: This plant forms a sturdy clump of erect, unbranched stems with coarse leaves. It can be 3–5 feet tall with a spread of 2 feet. Plants should be spaced 3 feet apart.

SEASON OF BLOOM: Early summer.

CULTURE: Partial shade in well-drained soil is the optimum placement. It can spread rapidly by running rootstock or seed. The seed pods should be removed to prevent unwanted seedlings.

UTILIZATION: This species is somewhat coarse, needs staking, and is best placed at the rear of informal borders or naturalized areas. There are other bellflowers that make better garden subjects.

PROPAGATION: Propagation is by seed or division during the spring. Highest germination occurs with a stratification of 2–4 weeks at 40°F. Division should be used for the cultivars.

DISEASES AND INSECTS: There are no serious problems.

HARDINESS: Zones 3 to 6.

CULTIVARS:
'Alba'—White flowers with characteristics similar to the species.
'Brantwood'—Large, violet-blue trumpet flowers. One of the better-known selections.
'Gloaming'—An Alan Bloom introduction found as a self-sown seedling. It has an unusual smoky-blue color. This cultivar does not increase rapidly from division and seed production has not produced the original smoky-blue color. 'White Ladies,' another Bloom selection has pure white bells of unusual clarity. It has also proven difficult to propagate and is not easily obtained.
var. *macrantha*—Larger flowers than the species.
var. *macrantha* 'Alba'—White flowers, plant similar to 'Alba.'

Native to Europe.   Perennial

SCIENTIFIC NAME/FAMILY: *Campanula medium* (C. grandiflora)   Campanulaceae

(kam-pan'ū-là mē'di-um)

COMMON NAME: Canterbury Bells

LEAVES: Alternate leaves; rosette leaves are ovate to obovate, to 10" long, margin is crenate-undulate, stem leaves are lanceolate-oblong, 3"–5", and are sessile or clasping. Foliage and stems are covered with a hispid pubescence.

FLOWER: The blue or white flowers are borne 1 or 2 together on stout peduncles in showy, open racemes. The calyx is bristly ciliate with large ovate appendages. Individual flowers are campanulate, 2" long, and inflated at the base.

HABIT: 2' to 3' erect growing biennial, 12" wide.

SEASON OF BLOOM: Late spring to early summer.

CULTURE: Sun or partial shade in moist, well-drained soil of average fertility.

UTILIZATION: Canterbury bells is a biennial that is useful in the border in front of taller growing plants such as delphiniums and hollyhocks. It also produces a long-lasting cut flower.

PROPAGATION: This plant is renewed each year by sowing seed. Seeds can be sown in late spring or summer for bloom the following year. Seed can also be planted indoors under light at temperatures of 70°F and will germinate in 2–3 weeks.

DISEASES AND INSECTS: Crown rot, leaf spot, rust, powdery mildew, foxglove aphids and slugs are occasional problems.

See color plate

CULTIVARS:
'Alba'—White flowers.
'Calycanthema'—Cup and Saucer. The common name refers to the structure of the flower. The calyx is petaloid, 3" wide, flattened, and deeply or shallowly lobed. The calyx resembles a saucer, with the inner corolla shaped like a cup. 'Calycanthema' is available in blue, white, or rose.
'Carillon Dwarf Mix'—12" tall, mixed colors, I first saw this selection in the trial gardens at Wisley Gardens, England. It is a compact plant with many flowers.

Native to southern Europe.   Biennial

SCIENTIFIC NAME/FAMILY: *Campanula persicifolia* (C. amabilis)   Campanulaceae

(kam-pan'ū-lȧ pēr-sik-i-fō'li-ȧ)

COMMON NAME: Peach-leaved Bellflower, Willow Bell-flower, Peach-bells, Paper Bellflower.

LEAVES: Alternate; rosette leaves are oblong-lanceolate, to 8″ long, entire, to crenate margin, glabrous; stem leaves linear to linear-lanceolate, 3″–4″ long, often sessile to the stem.

FLOWER: The deep blue to white flowers are pedicelled and are borne solitary in an elongated terminal or axillary raceme. The 5-lobed corolla is broadly campanulate and 1½″ wide. The calyx lobes are acuminate, entire, and half as long as the corolla.

HABIT: 2′ to 3′ tall and 18″ wide.

SEASON OF BLOOM: Late spring to early summer.

CULTURE: This perennial grows equally well in sun or partial shade in well-drained soils of average fertility. Removal of faded flowers will promote flowering after July.

UTILIZATION: Perennial border, naturalized area, wild flower garden, and cut flowers. This plant displays better when used in a mass planting.

PROPAGATION: Seed, cutting, and division. Division can be done every 3 or 4 years in early spring or fall. Cuttings should be taken in the spring. Seed can be sown in late spring or summer for bloom the following year. Seed can also be planted indoors under light at temperatures of 70°F and will germinate in 2–3 weeks. Not all cultivars will come true to type from seed.

DISEASES AND INSECTS: Slugs can be a problem.

HARDINESS: Zones 3–7.

CULTIVARS:
    'Alba'—White flowers.
    'Coerulea Coronata'—Semi-double purple-blue flowers.
    'Fleur de Neige'—Double white flowers.
    'Grandiflora Alba'—White flowers, 2″ wide.
    'Pride of Exmouth'—Semi-double blue flowers.
    'Telham Beauty'—Porcelain blue flowers, 2″–3″ across, 48″ high.

See color plate

Native to Europe and northeastern Asia.

Perennial

SCIENTIFIC NAME/FAMILY: *Campanula portenschlagiana* (C. muralis)   Campanulaceae

(kam-pan'ū-là por-ten-shlag-i-ā'-nà)

COMMON NAME: Dalmatian Bellflower

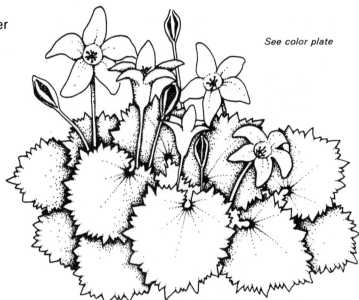

See color plate

LEAVES: Alternate leaves, ovate with a cordate base, sharply toothed, 1" wide.

FLOWER: Flowers are funnel shaped, 5 lobed, lilac-blue, and ½" to ¾" long. Flowers are clustered in a raceme that sits right above the foliage.

HABIT: Creeping, mat-forming perennial, 4" to 8" tall and 12" wide.

SEASON OF BLOOM: Late spring to early summer.

CULTURE: Dalmatian bellflower is easily grown in sun or partial shade in a moist, well-drained soil. If summer temperatures are consistently 90°F or more, bellflowers will require some shade and moisture. Division is needed every 3 to 4 years.

UTILIZATION: Good plant for the border front, rock walls, and rock gardens.

PROPAGATION: Division, cuttings and seed are available methods. Spring division is the simplest method.

DISEASES AND INSECTS: There are no serious diseases or insect problems, but snails and slugs can quickly bring havoc to a planting of *Campanula*.

HARDINESS: Zones 4–8.

CULTIVARS:
var. *alba* (al'ba)—Similar to the species but with white flowers.
'Major'—Lilac-blue flowers that are larger than those of the species.

Native to Yugoslavia.   Perennial

SCIENTIFIC NAME/FAMILY: *Campanula poscharskyana*   Campanulaceae

(kam-pan'ū-là po-shar-skee-ah'na)

COMMON NAME: Serbian Bellflower

LEAVES: Alternate leaves, cordate to ovate shape, margin sharply toothed, leaf surfaces have scattered hairs especially on lower surface. Leaves are 1½"–2½" long, the petiole being two-thirds of the length.

FLOWER: Star shaped, pale blue flowers are borne in loose panicles. Individual flowers are 1/2"–1" wide and face upward.

HABIT: Low spreading creeper, 8"–12" tall and 12" wide.

SEASON OF BLOOM: Late spring and early summer. Flowering will often continue during the summer in cool climates.

CULTURE: Full sun or partial shade in a well-drained soil.

UTILIZATION: Use in the border front, stone walls, and rock gardens in sun or partial shade. It will spread rapidly so it should only be planted in areas where this spread would not be a problem.

PROPAGATION: Propagate by seed or division. Seed should be germinated at 70°–75°F. Divide the plants in spring or fall.

DISEASES AND INSECTS: None serious.

HARDINESS: Zones 3–8.

CULTIVARS:
    'Blauranke' (Blue Gown)—Light blue flowers, 8"–10" tall, good in window boxes and hanging baskets.
    'E. H. Frost'—White flowers, 6"–8" tall.
    'Glandore'—Blue star shaped flowers with a white eye, 8"–10" tall.
    'Lisduggan Variety'—Lavender-rose flowers, 8"–10" tall.
    'Stella'—Deep blue flowers, 8" tall.

RELATED SPECIES:
    C. garganica (gar-gan'-ik-a) *(C. elatines* var. *garganica),* Gargano Bellflower. This species is similar to Serbian bellflower but the leaves are greyish-green. The flowers are lilac and appear in early summer. It is a rapid spreader like Serbian bellflower.
    'Erinus Major', blue flowers, and 'W. H. Paine', deep lavender flowers, are cultivars.

Native to Yugoslavia.   Perennial

SCIENTIFIC NAME/FAMILY: *Canna × generalis*   Cannaceae

(kan'á jen-er-al'is)

COMMON NAME: Canna

LEAVES: Large, to 2' long and 6" wide or wider, simple, entire, with sheathing petioles, foliage may be blue-green, green, or purple.

FLOWER: Flowers 4"–6" across, most are erect or strongly upright, red, yellow, orange, pink, white, variegated, or speckled. Canna is often divided into two groups, the orchid-flowered and the gladiolus-flowered; the latter is generally the more popular.

See color plate

HABIT: 1' to 5' erect plant.

SEASON OF BLOOM: Mid to late summer.

CULTURE: The ideal site is full sun in soils that are rich and fertile. In northern areas the rhizomes should be planted in the spring, after the danger of frost is past, with 4"–6" of soil over the roots. Growth is enhanced with fertilizing once per month with a liquid fertilizer.

UTILIZATION: Primary uses are as container plants, background plants, or in center of formal flower beds.

PROPAGATION: Seed and division. Annual canna is propagated from seeds which have to be scarified. Most cultivars are propagated by division of the rhizomes. Canna freezes off in early fall. Dig after frost and cut off stems about 6"–8" above crown to provide a handle for carrying clump. Store rhizomes over winter in moist peat located in a dark, lightly ventilated room at 45°–50°F. If the rhizomes become too dry, they wither and rot will set in. In spring, cut rhizomes to contain 2–3 "eyes" and start in sand or soil; transplant outside after the frost free date.

DISEASES AND INSECTS: Bud rot, rust, mosaic, aster yellows, Japanese beetle, and the yellow woolly bear caterpillar are noted, but are usually not serious.

HARDINESS: Zone 9.

CULTIVARS:
Rhizome types
Giant Cannas
    'City of Portland'—42", rosy pink flowers and green leaves.
    'Miss Oklahoma'—36", watermelon pink flowers and green leaves.
    'Red King Humbert'—48", orange red flowers, bronze-red foliage.
    'Richard Wallace'—48", golden-yellow flowers, green leaves.
    'Rosamond Cole'—36", scarlet flower with narrow yellow margin.
    'The President'—36", scarlet flowers, glossy green foliage.
'Grand Opera' series—Gladiolus-like flowers in colors of rose, rosy-peach, and canary-yellow.
'Pfitzer's' series—The plants in this group are orchid flowered and were developed by Wilhelm Pfitzer. Colors available are yellow-orange, pink, yellow, and scarlet.
Seed types
'Doc'—18", deep red flowers
'Grumpy'—18", pinkish-red flowers.
'Happy'—18", primrose-yellow flowers.
'Seven Dwarfs Mixed'—A mixture containing red, rose, orange, yellow, and salmon.
'Tropical Rose'—Light pink flowers, 3"–4" wide, velvety green foliage; 24"–30" tall. An All American Selection winner.

ADDITIONAL NOTES: One species of canna is a source of a tropical plant food and source of arrowroot starch (*Canna edulis,* Queensland Arrowroot).

Hybrid origin.   Perennial—tender rhizome. It is often used as an annual.

SCIENTIFIC NAME/FAMILY: *Capsicum annuum* (C. frutescens)   Solanaceae

(kap'si-kum an'ū-um)

COMMON NAME: Bush Red Pepper

LEAVES: Leaves alternate, ovate-elliptic, entire, 1"– 5" long.

FLOWER: The pale white flowers are rotate, 5 toothed, and not particularly showy. *Capsicum* is valued for its colorful black, yellow, red, cream, or purple fruits which are 1"–2" long.

HABIT: 10" to 20" rounded plant at maturity.

SEASON OF BLOOM: The flowering period is not showy. Fruit is borne in midsummer and is retained until frost.

CULTURE: Full sun with a moist soil and good organic matter.

UTILIZATION: Bed, border, carpet beds, and edging.

PROPAGATION: Seed will germinate in 3–4 weeks when held at 70°–75°F.

DISEASES AND INSECTS: None serious.

HARDINESS: Zone 10.

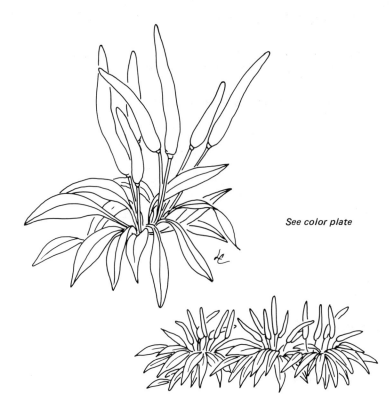

See color plate

CULTIVARS:
'Aurora'—Purple fruit.
'Black Prince'—10", black leaves, black candle-like fruit turn red at maturity.
'Candlelight'—This 1983 AAS winner has a profusion of edible hot peppers that mature to orange and red colors. It is heat and sun resistant and produces fruit until frost.
'Fiesta'—9" globe-shaped plants with 2" long red fruit.
'Fips'—7" conical red and yellow fruit.
'Holiday Cheer'—This AAS winner is usually used as a Christmas pot plant. A compact plant with round fruit that are initially cream turning to a yellow with a purplish blush, and finally red.
'Holiday Flame'—Fruit ripen from a yellow to a bright fiery red.
'Holiday Time'—An AAS winner with flowers and fruit that extend along the stem are carried well above the foliage. Fruit color appears earlier than other cultivars.
'Mosaic'—8"–10", fruit is white with red or purple blotches.

'Red Missile' — Compact plant with 1 ½ " long red fruit at maturity. Suitable for pot plant production.

'Thai Hot' — This selection has small, very hot peppers that can be used to add that special spice for cooking; 8″ tall.

'Variegata' — 10″, foliage is variegated with white, green and light purple.

ADDITIONAL NOTES: *Capsicum* is from the greek word, *kapto,* to bite, and apparently refers to the hot or spicy sensation one tastes when eating a hot pepper.

Native to North and South America.   Annual

SCIENTIFIC NAME/FAMILY: *Carex morrowii* 'Aurea Variegata'   Cyperaceae

(kā'reks mor-rōw'-e-i)

COMMON NAME: Variegated Japanese Sedge

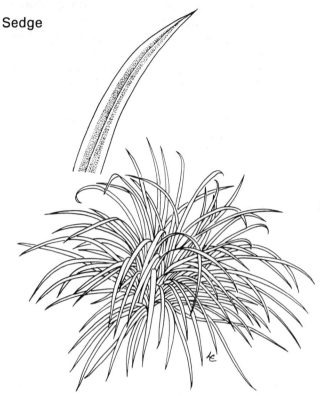

LEAVES: Clustered grass-like leaves arise from the base. Leaves are flat, thick and ¼" to ½" wide. In the cultivar 'Aurea Variegata,' the leaves have golden stripes along the margins. This *Carex* is semi-evergreen.

FLOWER: Not ornamentally important.

HABIT: Densely tufted, mound forming, 12"–18" tall.

SEASON OF BLOOM: Not important.

CULTURE: *Carex* does well in shade, something that is not common to true ornamental grasses. Species such as *Miscanthus* need a sunny site. *Carex* will grow well in moist, well-drained soils.

UTILIZATION: Good selection for massing. Few weeds will venture through a thick covering of *Carex*. It can also be used at the front of shade borders or rock gardens.

PROPAGATION: Division in the spring.

DISEASES AND INSECTS: No serious problems.

HARDINESS: Zones 5–9.

CULTIVARS: Another cultivar of *Carex morrowii* is 'Variegata'. The leaf variegations are white rather than yellow, 12"–18" tall. Zone 6.

RELATED SPECIES:
   Carex conica (kon'-i-kȧ), 'Marginata'. This species has white variegation. It has a finer texture than *C. morrowii* selections. It is an excellent small plant of 6" height.
   C. buchananii (byōō-kan'-an-e-i), Leatherleaf Sedge. This New Zealand plant has a cinnamon brown leaf color. It has a very fine texture with narrow leaves that grow upright from the center of the clump for about 18" and then taper at the ends. This evergreen will grow in sun or light shade in moist soil. The unusual color may be difficult to use in the landscape.
   C. elata 'Bowles Golden' (ē-lā'ta), Bowles Golden Grass. This 24" tall sedge has a clear golden yellow leaf color. The color is very bright and shows well in partial shade areas. Hardy to Zone 6.
   C. muskingumensis (mus-king'-ū-men''-sis), Palm Sedge. The common name is based on the pattern of growth, which has 8" long pointed leaves radiating from the top of rigid upright stems. It is 20" tall and makes a good ground cover, or it can be used in small groupings to create an accent. Hardy to Zone 5. 'Wachtposten' is 36" tall and described as having a better upright growth habit.

C. nigra (nī'grà), Black Sedge. Dark blue-green tufts will create a ground cover that is shade tolerant. It is 6" tall and hardy to Zone 4.

C. ornithopoda ('Variegata') (or-ni-tho'-pō-da), Bird's Foot Sedge. This 4"–6" tall selection should be used in a rock garden in partial to full shade. The creamy white leaves are striped green along the margins. This *Carex* is only hardy to Zone 7.

C. pendula (pen'-du-la), Drooping Sedge. This sedge has dark green leathery leaves which create a mounded habit. Long flower stalks with pendulous blooms emerge from this tuft and sway gracefully over the plant. A plain background is needed so the foliage and flowers are highlighted. It is hardy to Zone 5 and is 2'–3' tall.

ADDITIONAL NOTES: The *Carex* genus includes about 2000 species of rhizomatous grass-like plants. Obviously not all have garden merit but there is a good number that have value. The 1992 catalog of Kurt Bluemel, Inc., Baldwin, Maryland, lists 26 selections of *Carex*.

Native to Japan.   Perennial

SCIENTIFIC NAME/FAMILY: *Catananche caerulea*   Asteraceae
(Compositae)

(kat-ȧ-nan'kē se-rū'lē-a)

COMMON NAME: Cupid's Dart

LEAVES: Leaves are mostly basal, lanceolate to oblanceolate, 8"–12" long, entire or sparsely toothed. Each side of the leaf is tomentose and there are 3 veins that run the length of the leaf.

FLOWER: Flower heads are 2" across, borne on long slender peduncles, blue ray flowers are toothed as if cut off with a pinking shears. The flower is surrounded by strawlike, papery bracts.

HABIT: 18"–24" erect plant with a 12" spread.

SEASON OF BLOOM: Midsummer.

CULTURE: Full sun and a well-drained soil. Wet soil is usually fatal and hardiness is marginal in severe winters.

UTILIZATION: Cut flowers, dried flowers (comparable to strawflower) and as a border plant. Best landscape effects are achieved when cupid's dart is massed.

PROPAGATION: Seed and division. Seeds germinate in 2–3 weeks at 70°F. Spring division is often required every year to maintain good specimens.

DISEASES AND INSECTS: None serious.

HARDINESS: Zones 4–9.

CULTIVARS:
   var. *alba*—Silvery-white flowers, not as attractive as the species.
   'Bicolor'—Flower has white petals and a dark center. Good for dried flower arrangements.
   'Blue Giant'—Pale blue flowers.
   'Major'—Lavender-blue flowers, 30"–36" tall.

ADDITIONAL NOTES: *Catananche* is derived from Greek, *katanangke* which means a strong incentive, as plants were used in love potions in early times.

Native to southern Europe.   Perennial

SCIENTIFIC NAME/FAMILY: *Catharanthus roseus* (Vinca rosea)   Apocynaceae

(ka-thar-an'thus rō'zē-us)

See color plate

COMMON NAME: Madagascar Periwinkle, Rose Periwinkle, Old-maid

LEAVES: Opposite, oblong, 1"–3", rounded and mucronulate at apex, narrowed at base into short petiole. The leaves are glossy dark green.

FLOWER: Typically rose-pink, varying to mauve and white to 1½" across, corolla tube slender, about 1" long.

HABIT: *Catharanthus* cultivars may be prostrate, 3" tall and 18"–24" wide or more upright, 8" to 18".

SEASON OF BLOOM: All summer.

CULTURE: This species performs very well in sun or partial shade in a moist, well-drained soil. It flowers even when subjected to heat stress.

UTILIZATION: Borders, bedding, and ground cover.

PROPAGATION: Seeds germinate at 70°–75°F in dark. Extremely sensitive to overwatering and cold temperatures. Stem cuttings can also be used for propagation.

DISEASES AND INSECTS: Usually none.

CULTIVARS:
'Carpet Series'—Selections in this group are 3" to 4" tall and spread 18" to 24". Color selections are pink, rose, red, white, and mixed.
'Cooler' Series—Round overlapping petals provide a brilliant appearance, 8"–10" tall, good branching habit. 'Grape Cooler,' rosy pink with a darker eye, 'Peppermint Cooler,' white with a rose eye, and 'Blush,' light pink, are available choices.
'Hot Streak' Series—This group is 3"–6" tall and spreads 24" wide. Useful as a ground cover, hanging baskets, and in xeriscape situations. Colors include pink, rose, salmon, white and a mix.
'Little Series'—10", more compact and shapely than other periwinkles, quite uniform, tolerates hot, dry summers.
  'Blanche'—Pure white flowers.
  'Bright Eye'—White flowers with red centers.
  'Delicata'—Pink flowers with rose centers.
  'Mixture'—Blend of 4 colors.
  'Pinkie'—Rosy pink flowers.
'Morning Mist'—Large white flowers with small, rose colored centers, 12"–16" tall.
'Parasol'—This 1991 AAS winner has the largest flowers of any vinca, 1½"–2" wide. The flowers have overlapping petals, which are white with rose eyes. It is a vigorous grower and suitable for commercial landscape use. 12"–18" tall.

'Pink Carousel'—Creeping selection with pink flowers.

'Polka Dot'—Creeping type with white flowers and red eyes.

'Pretty' Series—Cultivars in this group are compact and free flowering and are 12″ tall. 'Pretty in Pink,' pink flowers, and 'Pretty in Rose,' rose purple, are 1991 AAS winners.

ADDITIONAL NOTES: If called upon to suggest bedding plants that come through heat, drought, and even pollution with flying colors, don't forget to mention periwinkle. Periwinkle is hard to beat because it displays glossy deep-green foliage, fine plant form, and a perpetual covering of flowers. It is a super plant for southern sites. The plantings I observed in Georgia were excellent and appeared to thrive in the heat.

Native to Madagascar and India.   Annual

SCIENTIFIC NAME/FAMILY: *Celosia cristata* (C. argenta var. cristata)   Amaranthaceae

(sē-lō'si-à kris-tā'tà)

COMMON NAME: Cockscomb

LEAVES: Alternate, linear to ovate-lanceolate, to 2" long.

FLOWER: Enlarged spikes with fasciated convoluted combs with colors ranging from red, yellow, gold, orange, to pink. Flowers resemble a rooster's comb.

HABIT: 6" to 24", heights and habits vary with cultivars.

SEASON OF BLOOM: Midsummer to fall. Long lasting flowers, up to 8 weeks.

CULTURE: Full sun and tolerates dry, porous soils.

UTILIZATION: Cut flowers, border, edging, bedding and dried flowers.

PROPAGATION: Seeds germinate in 70°–75°F; cover lightly to prevent drying. Plants should be grown at temperatures no lower than 60°F. Cold temperatures may cause permanent stunting of the plants.

DISEASES AND INSECTS: Leaf spots, mites and stem rots are occasional problems.

CULTIVARS: The following cultivars are crested types.
'Empress Improved'—12", crimson-red inflorescences up to 10" across with red leaves.
'Fireglow'—20"–24", globular combs are 6" across and orange-scarlet, (A.A.S. Bronze Medal).
'Jewel Box Mixed'—5"–6", large number of colors, quite dwarf.
'Kardinal Improved'—Large red blooms on 10"–12" tall plants.
'Olympia Mixture'—Mixed colors of yellow, scarlet and deep red on 8" tall plants.
'Toreador'—18"–20", bright red combs to 12" across.

The following cultivars are feather or plume types:
'Apricot Brandy'—This 1981 AAS winner has a bright apricot-orange color, 16".
'Castle' Series—Excellent weather tolerance especially to heat and drought conditions. Colors include scarlet, yellow, mix and pink which was a AAS winner in 1990, 12"–14" tall.
'Century' Series—The large 13" long plumes are carried on 28" tall plants. Selections include cream, fire, red (bronze foliage), rose, yellow and mixture.
'Crusader'—18", vivid-red flowers and bronze foliage, dwarf version of 'Forest Fire.'
'Fairy Fountains'—14", mixture of pink, yellow, scarlet, and gold flowers, plants produce numerous, 4"–6" plumes.
'Fiery Feather'—12", fiery-red spires borne in a pyramid fashion.
'Forest Fire Improved'—24", fiery orange-scarlet plumes with bronzy-red foliage.
'Geisha Series'—This dwarf group, 6"–10", has single colors of orange, scarlet, and yellow along with a mixed selection.
'Golden Feather'—12", golden-yellow form of 'Fiery Feather'.
'Golden Torch'—18", golden yellow plumes, green foliage.
'Golden Triumph'—30", golden-yellow plumes and green foliage.
'Kewpie' Series—Compact plants are 10" tall with 4" long plumes. Basal branching creates flowering side shoots. Selections include orange, red, yellow, and a mixture.
'Kimono Mixture'—Very uniform habit and compact plants that are 6" tall. Flowering is earlier than other cultivars.
'New Look'—Scarlet plumes and basal branching bronze foliage 14"–16" tall.
'Red Fox'—24", carmine-red plumes and green foliage.

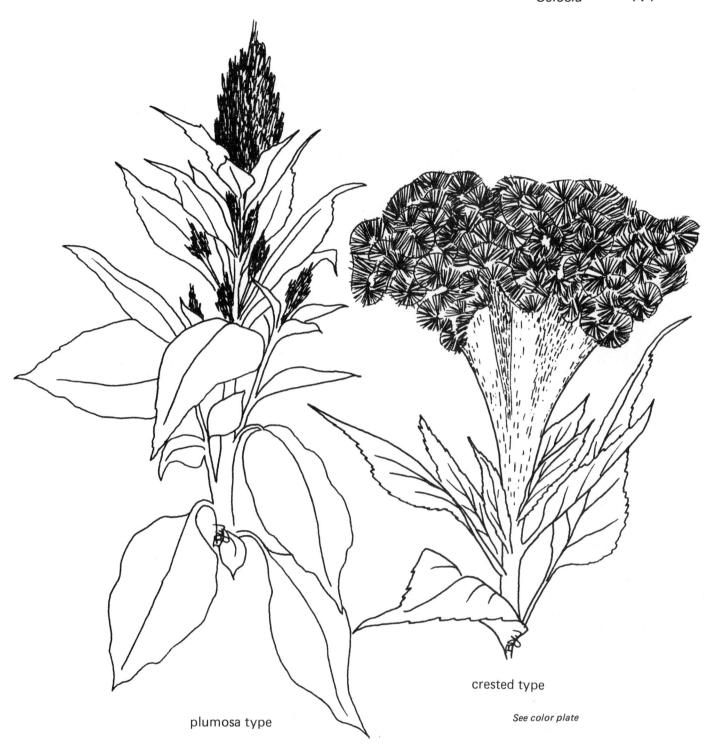

plumosa type

crested type

See color plate

ADDITIONAL NOTES: *Celosia* is from Greek for *burned,* descriptive of the color and character of inflorescences in some varieties. Both cockscomb and plume cockscomb thrive in hot areas.

Native to warm regions of Africa.   Annual

SCIENTIFIC NAME/FAMILY: *Centaurea cyanus*   Asteraceae
                                                              (Compositae)

(sen-tâ-rē'-a or sen-tâ'rē-a sī-an'us)

COMMON NAME: Bachelor's-Button, Cornflower, Bluebottle

LEAVES: Alternate, lower leaves lyrate-pinnatifid or narrowly oblanceolate, entire or with few remote teeth, petioled; upper leaves, linear or lanceolate, entire, sessile, all with grayish pubescence that provides the flowers an excellent setting.

FLOWER: Heads to 1½" across on slender peduncles, flowers classically blue, but are sometimes purple, white, rose, red, or deep wine.

HABIT: 12" to 36" erect plant.

SEASON OF BLOOM: Early summer (May to July), intermittent flowering until frost.

CULTURE: Sun or partial shade, does well in poor soils.

UTILIZATION: Massed in border or beds, either in foreground or background, depending on height. The flower's form and the blue color provide interest and effective color contrast when used in bouquets along with other flowers of white, pastel, or red shades. However, the stem's lack of rigidity limits its use in home floral arrangements.

PROPAGATION: Cover seed with propagation medium and maintain a constant 65°F. Cornflowers have a tendency to reseed and can become persistent in the garden.

DISEASES AND INSECTS: Stem rots, wilt, and rusts.

CULTIVARS:
'Blue Boy'—36", blue flowers, excellent as cut flowers, 2" diameter flower heads.
'Blue Diadem'—24", double blue flowers.
'Imperial' Series (Sweet Sultan)—Old fashioned type with large, fluffy thistle-like flowers in colors of lavender, pink, purple, red, rose, white, and a mix, 18"–24" tall.
'Pinkie'—Pink flowers, tall.
'Polka Dot Mixed'—16", mixed colors.
'Snowman'—White flowers, tall.

ADDITIONAL NOTES: Cornflowers are rather attractive during their main blooming period, but don't expect too much later in the season. An old fashioned annual with some appeal, it should probably be relegated to the cutting garden or mixed border. For massed color in beds, the lower growing strains are preferable; the tall varieties are more vigorous but have a tendency to fall over if not supported. *Cyanus* is from the Greek for *blue,* which is the most common color in this species.

Native to southeastern Europe.   Annual

SCIENTIFIC NAME/FAMILY: *Centaurea hypoleuca* 'John Coutts'   Asteraceae
(Compositae)

(sen-tâ-rē′-a or sen-tâ′rē-a hī-pō-lu′kȧ)

COMMON NAME: John Coutts Knapweed

See color plate

LEAVES: The leaves are of two types, basal or stem. The 12″–18″ long basal leaves are lyrate (lobed in a pinnate manner) and the upper leaves are oblong with a bluntly toothed margin. Both leaf types are dark green on the upper surface and white-tomentose beneath.

FLOWER: The flowers are solitary and borne on stiff stems. Flower heads are 2″ to 3″ wide with white disk flowers and bright pink ray flowers.

HABIT: Mounded plant, 24″ tall and 18″ wide.

SEASON OF BLOOM: Late spring to midsummer. The flowering period is long and one will sometimes get a rebloom in the fall.

CULTURE: 'John Coutts' is easily grown. Place in full sun in moist, well-drained soils. Warm night temperatures will cause the plants to stretch and staking will be required. For this reason, 'John Coutts' performs better in northern areas.

UTILIZATION: The long bloom season makes for an attractive addition to the summer border.

PROPAGATION: Division in spring or fall.

DISEASES AND INSECTS: Stem rot, rust and aster yellows have been reported but are usually not serious problems.

HARDINESS: Zones 4–7.

CULTIVARS:
 'Steenbergii'—This selection is more compact than the species with a longer flowering period. The flowers are carmine purple with white centers.

RELATED SPECIES:
 C. dealbata (de-al-bā'ta)—Persian Cornflower. The lower leaves of *C. dealbata* are 1½' long, long petioled, and pinnately compound. Upper leaves are sessile and pinnately divided. Both leaf types are white-tomentose beneath. The flowers are pink and 2" to 3" across. It is an easy plant to grow but tends to flop over and may need staking. After flowering, I cut back the large stems and flowers, which promotes new growth, making a more refined clump for the summer.

ADDITIONAL NOTES: Many catalogs list 'John Coutts' as a *C. dealbata* cultivar. An explanation is given by Graham Stuart Thomas in his book *Perennial Garden Plants.* He observed several seedlings which were in a planting of *C. dealbata* at Kew Gardens. Thinking they were *C. dealbata* seedlings, he gave the name 'John Coutts' to them in honor of the late curator of the garden, believing that Mr. Coutts had selected them from *C. dealbata.*

Native to Asia.   Perennial

SCIENTIFIC NAME/FAMILY: *Centaurea macrocephala*   Asteraceae
                                                          (Compositae)

(sen-tâ-rē'-a or sen-tâ'rē-a mak-ro-sef'a-la)

COMMON NAME: Globe Centaurea

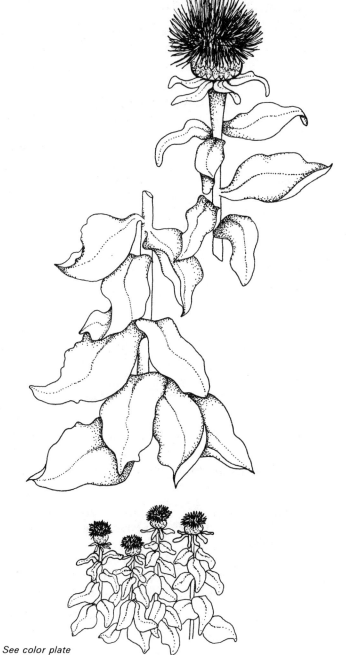

LEAVES: Alternate leaves, ovate-lanceolate to elliptic, scabrous, with an undulating leaf margin. The basal leaves are petioled; stem leaves are slightly decurrent. The stems are pubescent.

FLOWER: The bright yellow flowers are in heads that are 3" to 4" wide. The involucre is composed of 6–8 rows of rusty colored bracts which are scarious and fringed.

HABIT: 3' to 4' erect plant with a 2' spread.

SEASON OF BLOOM: Midsummer for 2 to 3 weeks.

CULTURE: Full sun and a well-drained soil.

UTILIZATION: This giant, thistle-looking plant might be used as a specimen in the border. The flowers are suitable for fresh cut flowers and especially for dried flowers. Since the texture and form are so dominant, one plant may be enough in most gardens.

PROPAGATION: Division in spring or fall and seed.

DISEASES AND INSECTS: No serious problems.

HARDINESS: Zones 3–8.

See color plate

Native to Caucasus.   Perennial

SCIENTIFIC NAME/FAMILY: *Centaurea montana*   Asteraceae
                                                                    (Compositae)

(sen-tâ-rē′-a or sen-tâ′rē-a mon-tā′na)

COMMON NAME: Mountain Bluet, Perennial Bachelor's Button, Mountain Knapweed

LEAVES: Alternate, broadly-lanceolate or obovate-oblanceolate, toothed margin, decurrent to the stem, younger leaves silvery-white. Plant is usually unbranched and many times stoloniferous.

FLOWER: Solitary blue heads are borne on short peduncles, flowers are 2″ wide; involucral bracts have black, fringed margins.

HABIT: 12″ to 24″ erect plant, 12″ wide.

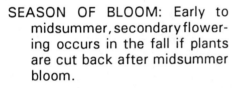

SEASON OF BLOOM: Early to midsummer, secondary flowering occurs in the fall if plants are cut back after midsummer bloom.

CULTURE: Full sun or partial shade, well-drained soil. Most species are fairly drought tolerant.

UTILIZATION: The deep blue flower color is the main attraction. Only a few flowers open at any one time, so the floral impact is never great. To get an optimum effect, this species should be massed in the border. Mountain bluet can be very invasive.

PROPAGATION: Seed or division. Mountain bluet requires frequent division (every 2 years) to maintain desirable plants.

DISEASES AND INSECTS: Stem rot and rust have been reported but they are not serious problems.

HARDINESS: Zones 3 to 8.

CULTIVARS:
  'Alba'—White flowers.
  'Carnea' ('Rosea')—Pink flowers.
  'Violetta'—Dark violet flowers.

ADDITIONAL NOTES: *Centaurea* is derived from the Greek word, *centaur,* meaning famous for healing. Greek mythology claims Chiron the Centaur used the plant to heal a wound in his foot.

Native to Europe.   Perennial

SCIENTIFIC NAME/FAMILY: *Centranthus ruber* (Kentranthus ruber)   Valerianaceae

(sen-tran'thus ru'ber)

COMMON NAME: Jupiter's Beard, Red Valerian

LEAVES: Opposite leaves, lanceolate to ovate shaped, 2" to 3" long. They are glabrous and gray-green, sessile to the stem and are usually entire with some leaves slightly toothed.

FLOWER: The small pink, reddish, or white flowers are fragrant and are borne in large terminal clusters that are 3" wide.

HABIT: Bushy plant, erect, growing 3' tall and 24" wide.

SEASON OF BLOOM: Flowering can occur at different times during the summer. In hot areas, flowering is best in late spring to early summer. Shearing may promote later bloom. In cool regions, *Centranthus* will flower much of the summer.

CULTURE: Full sun in well-drained soils that are neutral or slightly alkaline. It thrives when grown on limestone walls and limestone-based soils.

UTILIZATION: Border plant or sunny, naturalized area. The plant will self-seed, and some gardeners may consider it a nuisance in the border. In England, *Centranthus* looks very nice when allowed to grow and reseed on stone walls. Jupiter's Beard is found throughout England but notable plantings are found at Leeds Castle, Great Dixter, and of course the white limestone cliffs of Dover.

See color plate

PROPAGATION: Basal cuttings and seed are both easy propagation methods. Division can also be done in spring or fall to maintain special colors.

DISEASES AND INSECTS: None serious.

HARDINESS: Zones 5–8.

CULTIVARS:
'Albus'—White flowers, very scarce in commerce.
'Atrococcineus'—Coppery-red flowers.
'Coccineus'—Dark pink flowers.
'Roseus'—Rose flowers.
Most *Centranthus* that you purchase will be seed propagated; consequently, you may have little choice in the "color pedigree" that you receive. If you get a color that you like, increase the plant by basal cuttings or division and pull up seedlings.

Native to Europe.   Perennial

SCIENTIFIC NAME/FAMILY: *Cephalaria gigantea*   Dipsacaceae
(Scabiosa gigantea or Cephalaria tatarica)

(sef-á-lā′ri-á jī-gan-tē′a, jī-gan′-tē-a)

COMMON NAME: Tree Scabiosa, Giant Scabies, Tatarian Cephalaria

LEAVES: Opposite leaves, pinnately compound; leaflets have toothed margins, are pubescent below, and are oblong to oblanceolate. The leaves are carried on wiry stems that are striped or ribbed.

FLOWER: The *Scabiosa*-like flowers are 2″ across, primrose-yellow, and produced at the end of the wiry stems. The flowers are held well above the mass of green foliage. The heads are composed of many 4-parted florets with the marginal florets enlarged and radiating outward.

HABIT: Erect, bushy plant, 5–7 feet tall and 3–4 feet wide. This large species should be spaced 4 feet apart.

SEASON OF BLOOM: Early to mid-summer.

CULTURE: *Cephalaria* grows best in full sun in moist soils. If this species dries out, the margin of the foliage turns black, which quickly leads to a shabby appearance. Even in best conditions, the plant declines in the late summer and should be pruned back after flowering. It may need staking.

UTILIZATION: If room in the border is available, this tall garden plant with the unusual yellow flowers is an excellent addition. The coarseness of the basal foliage can be hidden in the back of the border. After some of the more common species have been used, the gardener should give this species a try.

PROPAGATION: Seed germinates quickly after stratification for 6 weeks at 40°F. Germination temperature is 70–75°F. Division can be used in the home garden and should be done every 2–3 years.

DISEASES AND INSECTS: No serious pests.

HARDINESS: Zones 3–8.

Native to Caucasus.   Perennial

SCIENTIFIC NAME/FAMILY: *Cerastium tomentosum*   Caryophyllaceae

(se-ras′ti-um tō-men-tō′sum)

COMMON NAME: Snow-in-Summer

LEAVES: Opposite leaves, linear-lanceolate, 1″ long and ⅛″ wide, white-woolly tomentose (silver leaves).

FLOWER: White flowers to 1″ across in 3–15 flowered cymes, petals are notched.

HABIT: 3″–6″ tall mat-forming perennial, growing 12″ wide.

SEASON OF BLOOM: Mid to late spring.

CULTURE: *Cerastium tomentosum* performs best in full sun in well-drained soils with low fertility. When planted in moist and fertile soils, *Cerastium* spreads rapidly. The foliage should be cut back after flowering to promote greater plant compactness. In southern zones with heat and humidity, snow-in-summer will "melt out."

UTILIZATION: Snow-in-summer is a good plant for a ground cover in the sunny border, the rock garden, or planting in planting pockets on dry stone walls.

PROPAGATION: Seed, division and cuttings. Seeds germinate easily in 2–4 weeks at 68°F. Division can be done in spring or fall if care is taken to keep a soil ball around the roots when transplanting. Softwood cuttings can be taken in early summer.

See color plate

DISEASES AND INSECTS: No serious problems

HARDINESS: Zones 3–7.

CULTIVARS:
'Columnae'—8″, white flowers, more compact than the species.
'Yo Yo'—free flowering, compact plant, white flowers.
'Silver Carpet' (Silberteppich)—Compact selection similar to 'Columnae'.

ADDITIONAL NOTES: Annual division is often needed to keep this plant in check. One should trim back to encourage new growth. The genus name *Cerastium* is derived from the Greek word *keras,* horn, and refers to the shape of the fruit.

Native to Italy.   Perennial

SCIENTIFIC NAME/FAMILY: *Ceratostigma plumbaginoides*   Plumbaginaceae
(Plumbago larpentiae)

(ser-at-ō-stig'ma plum-ba-ji-noi'd ēz)

COMMON NAME: Plumbago, Leadwort

LEAVES: Leaves alternate, broadly obovate, to 3" long, tapering at base, glabrous except for a strongly ciliate margin. Foliage turns bronzy-red in fall in cooler climates.

FLOWER: Corolla to 1" long, dark blue, about ½" across, sepals and bracts strongly ciliate. The flowers are borne in small dense terminal groups.

HABIT: 8" to 12" tall and spreads 12" to 18".

SEASON OF BLOOM: Summer to late fall.

CULTURE: Partial shade or full sun, well drained soil. Plumbago cannot tolerate soggy conditions or competition from tree roots. Leaves emerge late in the spring.

UTILIZATION: Ground cover for a large rock garden or foreground for shrub border. A nice groundcover planting is displayed at Brookside Gardens, Wheaton, Maryland.

PROPAGATION: Division in the spring or stem and root cuttings are normal propagation methods. Seed germination is also possible. Best results occur when the seed is stratified for 4–6 weeks at 38–40°F.

DISEASES AND INSECTS: No unusual problems exist with this species.

HARDINESS: Zones 5–9.

RELATED SPECIES:
C. *willmottianum* (wil-mot-e-ā'-num)—Chinese Plumbago. This species is similar to *C. plumbaginoides* except for hardiness (Zone 8) and a heavy pubescence on the leaf margin. Chinese plumbago is more drought tolerant than *C. plumbaginoides.*

ADDITIONAL NOTES: Normally grown in zones 6–9, but further north it will survive with a light mulch in the winter. Excellent plantings abound in zone 8. Plumbago should be cut back to ground level in the spring to stimulate new, lush growth. Robert Fortune, the famed nineteenth century plant explorer, discovered plumbago growing in Shanghai, China, in 1846. *Ceratostigma* is derived from the Greek *keras,* horn, and *stigma,* and refers to the shape of the stigma.

Native to China.   Perennial

SCIENTIFIC NAME/FAMILY: *Chasmanthium latifolium* (Uniola latifolia)   Poaceae
(Gramineae)

(kas-man'thi-um lat-i-fōl'-i-um)

COMMON NAME: Northern Sea Oats, Spangle Grass

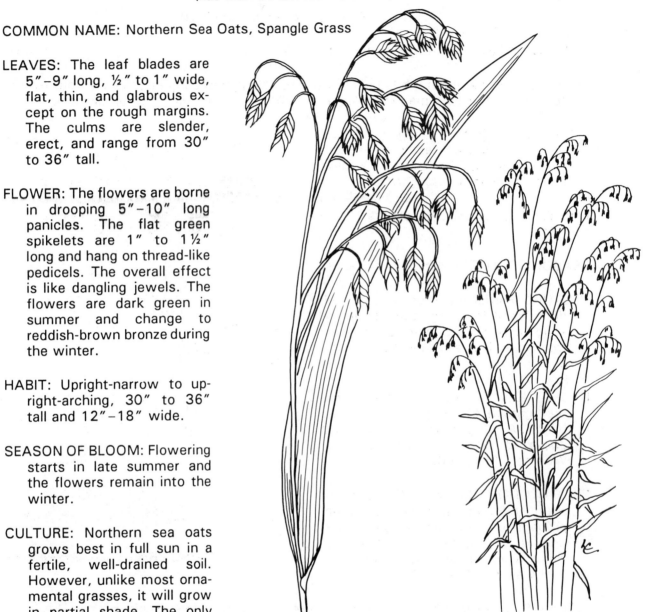

LEAVES: The leaf blades are 5"–9" long, ½" to 1" wide, flat, thin, and glabrous except on the rough margins. The culms are slender, erect, and range from 30" to 36" tall.

FLOWER: The flowers are borne in drooping 5"–10" long panicles. The flat green spikelets are 1" to 1½" long and hang on thread-like pedicels. The overall effect is like dangling jewels. The flowers are dark green in summer and change to reddish-brown bronze during the winter.

HABIT: Upright-narrow to upright-arching, 30" to 36" tall and 12"–18" wide.

SEASON OF BLOOM: Flowering starts in late summer and the flowers remain into the winter.

CULTURE: Northern sea oats grows best in full sun in a fertile, well-drained soil. However, unlike most ornamental grasses, it will grow in partial shade. The only limitation in the shade sites is that the foliage will be darker green in color and the plants will be taller. Plants have a tendency toward self-seeding.

UTILIZATION: Northern sea oats has many uses. It can be an asset to shade gardens, naturalized areas, water gardens, and borders. There is a 3-season interest in Northern sea oats. These occur in the late summer when it is in flower, in the fall when the foliage turns a beautiful bronze, and in the winter as the flowers persist, creating an upright-arching specimen. This can create color in an otherwise depleted garden. Northern sea oats is also valued in dried flower arrangements. The flowers rarely shatter, even if they are harvested when mature. The natural brown flower color is quite attractive.

PROPAGATION: Division and seed. Seed germination may be low because many of the flowers are sterile.

DISEASES AND INSECTS: None serious.

HARDINESS: Zones 4–8.

RELATED SPECIES:
  Uniola paniculata—Sea Oats. Sea oats grows 3' to 6' tall and is found as a native plant on the eastern seacoasts. It has invasive rhizomes, which makes it unpopular for most gardens. It is best utilized for water gardens or on sand dunes situated in full sun.

Native to the United States.   Perennial

SCIENTIFIC NAME/FAMILY: *Chelone lyonii*   Scrophulariaceae

(kē-lō'ne li-ō'ne; li-ō'nē-i)

COMMON NAME: Pink Turtlehead   *See color plate*

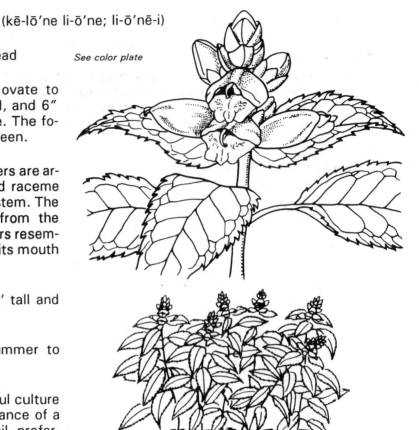

LEAVES: Opposite leaves are ovate to lanceolate, strongly serrated, and 6" long including a 1½" petiole. The foliage is glabrous and dark green.

FLOWER: The hooded pink flowers are arranged in a tightly clustered raceme found at the terminal of the stem. The common name is derived from the fact that the individual flowers resemble the head of a turtle with its mouth open.

HABIT: Dense, upright plant, 3' tall and 2' wide.

SEASON OF BLOOM: Late summer to early fall.

CULTURE: The key to successful culture of turtlehead is the maintenance of a consistently moist to wet soil, preferably humus enriched and in partial shade to full sun. *Chelone* usually will not need staking unless it is too shady. Too much shade will cause the stems to be thin and the plants may not support themselves. Pinching the plant in the spring will also create a bushy plant.

UTILIZATION: Good plant for the area along a stream or pond, border, or in the wild garden.

PROPAGATION: Division, tip cuttings, and seed propagation are suitable propagation methods. Division can be done in the spring or fall. Tip cuttings, 4" long, should be taken in late spring or summer. Seeds require a 6 week stratification period for best germination.

DISEASES AND INSECTS: No serious problems.

HARDINESS: Zones 3–8.

RELATED SPECIES:
 C. glabra (glā'-bra) (*C. obliqua* var. *alba*)—White Turtlehead. This native species of eastern United States is 2'–3' tall and 2' wide. The flowers are white with a tinge of pink. Full sun and consistently moist soil are required for best growth.
 C. obliqua (ob-lee'-kwa)—Rose Turtlehead. This species is very similar to *C. lyonii*—so close that I do not see much difference in form or color. The flowers are darker than those of pink turtlehead and the leaves are distinctly veined. It performs well in moist to wet soils. Hardiness is zones 6–9.

Native to eastern United States.   Perennial

SCIENTIFIC NAME/FAMILY: *Chenopodium botrys* (Ambrosia mexicana)

Chenopodiaceae

(kē-no-pō'di-um bo'-tris)

COMMON NAME: Ambrosia, Sticky Goosefoot

LEAVES: Alternate leaves, 2" long, ovate to oblong with 2–6 deep, rounded lobes. The leaf is distinctively oak-leaf shaped. Leaves and stems have a glandular-hairy, stocky feel and a strong aromatic odor.

FLOWER: Small, yellowish flowers are borne in narrow, nearly leafless panicles, 12" long. The numerous flowers create a fine-textured, feathery plume. Flowers have no petals.

HABIT: This 2' to 3' tall plant is erect in early season but later assumes an arching habit due to the weight of the many flowers.

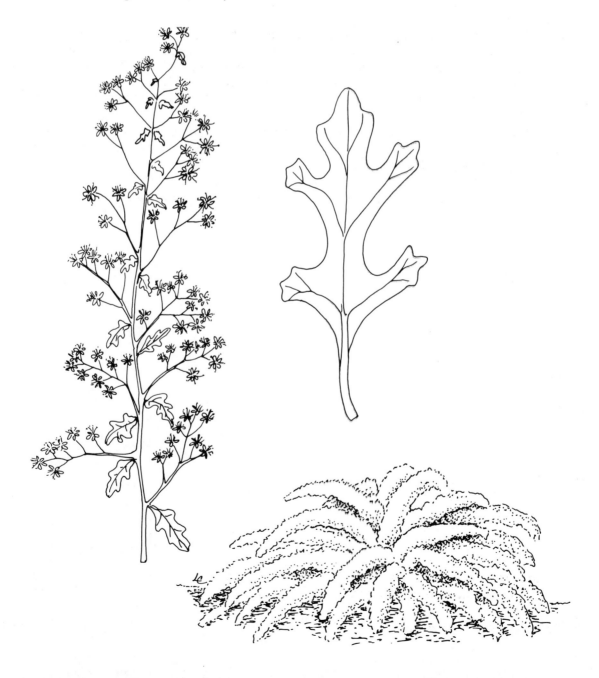

SEASON OF BLOOM: Summer.

CULTURE: Ambrosia is easily grown in full sun and well-drained soils. Self-seeding tends to occur heavily in dry and infertile soils.

UTILIZATION: This member of the goosefoot family is prized for its flower and fragrance. The flowering branches can be formed into wreaths by bending the flowering tops and lacing them into a circle. The highly aromatic flowers and foliage are also used in potpourri.

PROPAGATION: Ambrosia is easily propagated from seed. The seed should be uncovered and will take 3–4 weeks for germination. Seed may be started inside or simply spread on the soil surface after the soil is warm in the spring. Once established, ambrosia will continue to self seed.

DISEASES AND INSECTS: None serious.

RELATED SPECIES:

Chenopodium album, Lamb's quarter. This persistent, self-seeding weed is used for greens by many people and is offered in some herb catalogs. I spent my childhood pulling lamb's quarters from the carrots and other vegetables. Our garden seemed to have enough lamb's quarters to provide greens for all of Macoupin County, Illinois, where I lived. Now it is available in seed catalogs—what a strange world!

ADDITIONAL NOTES: *Chenopodium* is derived from the Greek words, *chen*, a goose, and *pous,* a foot, which is allusion to the supposed resemblance of the leaves to the webbing of a duck's foot.

Native to southern Europe to central Asia. Naturalized in North America.   Annual

SCIENTIFIC NAME/FAMILY: *Chionodoxa luciliae*   Liliaceae
(Hyacinthaceae)

(kī-on-ō-dok'sȧ lu-sil'i-ē)

COMMON NAME: Glory-of-the-Snow

LEAVES: Leaves are basal, ribbon-
like, and dark green.

FLOWER: Vivid blue with a white
center, star-shaped with 6 perianth segments, ¾"–1" in diameter, 6–10 flowers per stem.

HABIT: 3" to 6" erect plant.

SEASON OF BLOOM: Early spring.

CULTURE: Full sun in a well-drained
soil. As with most bulbs, provide
a soil well amended with leaf compost or similar organic matter and
coarse sand. Plant the small bulbs
in the fall at a depth of 2"–3" and
3"–4" apart.

UTILIZATION: Useful as an early
flowering bulb in rock gardens, naturalizing in sunny areas, and in
border foregrounds. Since the

See color plate

flowers are small, a large massing (50–100 bulbs) is required to provide a good display.

PROPAGATION: Propagation is by offsets (bulbs) which form around the older bulbs. *Chionodoxa* can also be propagated from seed, either by self-seeding or seed planted in the spring.

DISEASES AND INSECTS: A serious pest threat to this species is an occasional attack by the stem and bulb nematode. Infected bulbs either do not grow, or, if they develop, fail to flower. Chipmunks and mice are also known to eat the bulbs.

HARDINESS: Zones 4–9.

CULTIVARS:
   var. *alba*—White flowers.
   var. *gigantea*—(may now be considered a species)—Larger flowers (2" wide) and a
      more vigorous grower.
   var. *rosea*—Pink flowers.

ADDITIONAL NOTES: The common name is a literal translation of the genus name from the Greek *chion* (snow) and *doxa* (glory).

Native to Crete, Turkey, and Asia Minor.   Perennial—hardy bulb

SCIENTIFIC NAME/FAMILY: *Chrysogonum virginianum*

Asteraceae
(Compositae)

(kris-sog'ō-num vir-jin-ē-ā'-num)

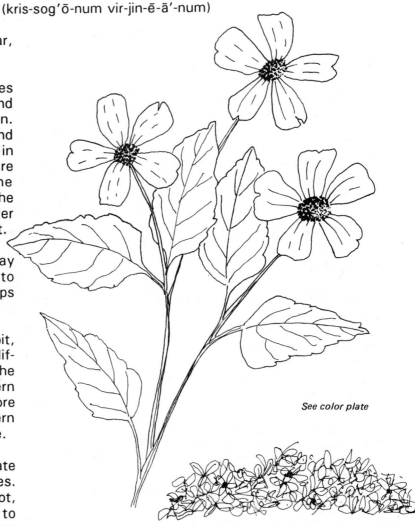

COMMON NAME: Goldenstar, Green and Gold

LEAVES: The opposite leaves are triangular-ovate and have a serrated margin. They are 1"–2" long and have a long petiole. Early in the season basal leaves are predominant, but the stems elongate later. The stems, leaves and flower peduncles are pubescent.

FLOWER: The yellow, five ray starred heads are 1" to 1½" wide. The petal tips are slightly notched.

HABIT: Ground cover habit, 6" to 9" tall. There are different selections in the marketplace. The northern variety is taller and more upright while the southern variety is more prostrate.

See color plate

SEASON OF BLOOM: Climate influences flowering times. If the summers are hot, flowering is mid-spring to early summer. In northern latitudes, flowering will range from spring to early summer. Sporadic flowering will occur during the summer.

CULTURE: Best growth occurs in moist, well-drained soil and partial to full shade.

UTILIZATION: Excellent ground cover for partial shade borders and the woodland edges.

PROPAGATION: This species is easily divided and it will also self sow. Self-sown seedlings can be easily moved to other garden sites.

DISEASES AND INSECTS: No serious problems.

HARDINESS: Zones 5–9. If snow cover is consistent, goldenstar may survive in zone 4. It is worth a try.

CULTIVARS:
'Allen Bush'—8", rapid grower.
'Mark Viette'—6", glaucous leaves
'Piccadilly'—Good prostrate form.
var. *australe*—A good ground cover that spreads faster than the species but the flowers are not as showy.

Native to eastern United States.

Perennial

SCIENTIFIC NAME/FAMILY: *Cimicifuga racemosa*   Ranunculaceae

(sim-i-sif'ū-gȧ, sim-i-si-fug'-ȧ ra-se-mō'sȧ)

COMMON NAME: Black Snake-root, Black Cohosh, Bug-bane

LEAVES: Leaves 2–3 ternate, often again pinnate, leaflets ovate or oblong, cuneate to cordate at the base, incisely toothed, 1″–4″ long.

FLOWER: White, long wand-like racemes up to 3′ long.

HABIT: 4′ to 6′ erect habit when in flower. The width is 2′–4′ at maturity.

SEASON OF BLOOM: Mid-summer.

CULTURE: Full sun to partial shade. For optimum growth in full sun, provide a moist soil with high organic matter. Snakeroot does best in cooler areas. Since it is a native woodland plant, it would also look nice in a naturalized setting.

UTILIZATION: Specimen plant in larger perennial border, shrub border, or massed along the edge of a pond or stream. A dark background, such as a hedge, is useful so that the white flower spires stand out.

See color plate

PROPAGATION: Division in spring or fall is suitable if one wants to increase numbers; otherwise, this plant can be left undisturbed indefinitely. Seed propagation is difficult and fresh seed should always be used if available. Seed needs to be stratified for 6–8 weeks before sowing.

DISEASES AND INSECTS: Leaf spots and rust have been reported but are not serious.

HARDINESS: Zones 3–8. In southern areas I have seen stands of native *Cimicifuga* growing in the mountains of northeastern Georgia, but plants at lower elevations in Georgia tended to suffer from the heat. Perhaps the plants at the lower elevations would have benefited from constant moisture.

CULTIVARS:

var. *cordifolia* (cord-i-fō'-lē-a). 5'–6' tall. This variety has fewer but larger leaflets. The terminal leaflet is heart shaped. It is later flowering than *C. racemosa*.

RELATED SPECIES:

C. ramosa (ra-mō'-sa). This later flowering species (early fall) is 6'–7' tall and has tripinnate foliage and fragrant flowers. This fragrance was highlighted during a visit to Hidcote Manor in England during September. One of the enclosed hedged "rooms" had one side planted with this species. As soon as I walked into the garden, I noticed the fragrance and began to hunt the source. It was outstanding. There are two cultivars available. 'Atropurpurea' is the older selection with bronze-purple leaves and creamy white flowers. 'Brunette' is a recent introduction from the nursery of Greta Peterson in Denmark. It has purplish-black foliage and pinkish white flowers. The foliage is much darker than that found on 'Atropurpurea'.

ADDITIONAL NOTES: *Cimicifuga* is derived from *cimex,* meaning bug, and *fugo,* to flee away, which refers to the insecticidal properties the plants are reputed to contain.

Native to eastern United States.   Perennial

SCIENTIFIC NAME/FAMILY: *Cimicifuga simplex*   Ranunculaceae

(sim-i-sif'u-ġa, sim-i-si-fug'-à sim'-pleks)

COMMON NAME: Kamchatka Bug-
bane

LEAVES: Leaves are ternately compound. Leaflets are ovate or oblong, irregularly toothed, 1½"–3"
long.

FLOWER: The white bottlebrush-like
flowers are arranged in a terminal
raceme. There is usually only one
raceme per stem but there may be
one or two subsidiary racemes
that branch from below. The flower branches are more arching than
those of *Cimicifuga racemosa*.

HABIT: 3' to 4' tall erect plant with
several arching wands with white
flowers arranged in a bottlebrush
fashion. It is 2'–3' wide.

SEASON OF BLOOM: Late summer to
mid-fall. Early frosts may damage
the flowers.

CULTURE: Partial shade is the optimum location. If grown in full sun
the soils need to be moist and fertile. This bugbane will not need attention to staking as *C. racemosa*
may need.

UTILIZATION: Woodland garden or
partially shaded border. Good
plant to extend the flowering
season.

PROPAGATION: Division in spring or fall is acceptable; however, the clumps increase
slowly so division is not a necessity. The species can be seed propagated, although it
appears that the seeds have a complex germination requirement. Some nurseries simply
sow the seeds in ground beds and let nature take its course during summer and winter.
To speed up the process, the seed should be first given a warm stratification
(67°–75°F) for 6–10 weeks and then a cold period (30°–40°F) for 6–8 weeks. The
germination temperature should be kept cool (around 50°F).

DISEASES AND INSECTS: See *C. racemosa*.

HARDINESS: Zones 4–8.

CULTIVARS:

'Braunlaub'—White flowers and very dark green leaves, 4' tall.
'Elstead Variety'—White flowers, later bloom, 4'–5' tall.
'Frau Herms'—Pure white flowers. Introduced by Ernst Pagel, Germany.
'White Pearl' ('Armleuchter')—White-flowering racemes are 2' long, 4'–5' tall. This
selection is most available.

ADDITIONAL NOTES: Sometimes listed as *C. foetida* var. *intermedia*. It is native to Russia.

Perennial

SCIENTIFIC NAME/FAMILY: *Clematis integrifolia*   Ranunculaceae

(klem'à-tis, kle-ma'-tis in-teg-ri-fō'li-a)

COMMON NAME: Solitary Clematis

LEAVES: Opposite leaves, simple and sessile. The leaves have an entire margin, are ovate in shape, 4" long and are widely spaced on thin, sometimes weak stems. The lower leaf surface and margins are covered with a fine pubescence. The leaves are not trifoliate as is often found on other *Clematis* and the foliage is devoid of any climbing properties.

FLOWER: Flowers are solitary, terminal, nodding, and urn-shaped. They are 1 ½ " long and are blue or bluish-purple. There are 4 sepals with tomentum near the margins.

HABIT: Initially the growth habit is upright but it may have a need for support or may simply drape over a low shrub. It is usually about 2' tall but there is variability with heights sometimes reaching 4'.

SEASON OF BLOOM: Early to midsummer.

CULTURE: Clematis requires a warm top and a cool bottom. It can be grown in full sun, but the root zone needs to be cool and moist. One should add as much compost, leaf mold, or peat moss as possible to help retain moisture. Brush staking is usually required to prevent this species and *C. heracleifolia* from sprawling all over the border.

UTILIZATION: Since this clematis is a non-climber, it can be used in the border.

PROPAGATION: Summer stem cuttings, seed, or spring division.

DISEASES AND INSECTS: Blister beetle and tarnished plant bug are sometimes problems.

HARDINESS: Zones 3−8.

CULTIVARS:
 var. *alba*—White flowers.
 'Olgae'—Light blue, fragrant flowers, and twisted sepals. This selection was apparently first grown by Mr. John Treasure of Tenbury Wells, England.

RELATED SPECIES:

C. × *eriostemon* (er-i-ō-stē'mon) 'Hendersonii'—This hybrid has dark blue flowers and an extended bloom season through late summer. It is often listed as a cultivar of *C. integrifolia* but it is now believed to be a hybrid of *C. integrifolia* × *C. viticella.*

C. *heracleifolia* (he-ra'-klē-i-fō''-lē-à)—Tube Clematis. This species is a 2'–3' tall subshrub with compound foliage of 3 leaflets, each leaflet is coarsely toothed. Fragrant, small blue tubular flowers are clustered in the leaf axils or at the tip of the thin stems. The sepals are strongly reflexed. The flowers appear in late summer and are followed by fluffy seed heads. It is a sprawling plant and will require staking. It can also be planted among other plants which will assist in providing support. Best performance occurs in full sun and moist soils.

'Cote d'Azur'—Light blue flowers, similar to the species.

var. *davidiana* (da-vid-i-ā'-na)—Violet-blue flowers, sepals less reflexed, showier than the species. This variety is dioecious while *C. heracleifolia* is monoecious. This selection leans toward a herbaceous quality and *C. heracleifolia* is a subshrub. The variety is easier to divide than the species.

'Wyevale'—Dark blue flowers with attractive crimped sepals; very showy cultivar. It is considered more attractive than the species.

C. *recta* (rek'ta)—Ground Clematis. This rambling clematis has pinnately compound leaves with 5–9 leaflets. The leaflets are 1"–2" long and have entire margins. The plant has fragrant white flowers borne in large clusters which are followed by silvery seed heads. This is a spring blooming shrub clematis. Unless supported, ground clematis, does like the common name suggests: it "crawls" along the ground.

'Flore-plena'—Double white flowers.

'Grandiflora'—Large white flowers.

'Purpurea'—New stems and leaves are purple. This coloration fades to dark green as the foliage expands.

ADDITIONAL NOTES: *Clematis* is from *Klema,* a vine branch, alluding to the vine-like growth habit of most clematis species.

Native to southern Europe.   Perennial

SCIENTIFIC NAME/FAMILY: *Cleome hasslerana* (C. spinosa)   Capparaceae

(klē-ō'mē has-lēr-an'à)

COMMON NAME: Cleome, Spider Flower

LEAVES: Leaves palmately compound, usually with a pair of short spines at the base, 5-7 leaflets which are long-acuminate.

FLOWER: Flowers numerous, rose-purple or white, long-pedicelled, petals about 1" long, stamens 2"-3" long. The spider-like effect of the flower is created by the abnormally long stamens. Cleome has an indeterminate raceme.

HABIT: 3' to 4' tall plant with an 18"-24" spread.

SEASON OF BLOOM: Summer to frost (May to October), flowers continuously.

See color plate

CULTURE: Sun to partial shade. Responds well to abundant moisture.

UTILIZATION: Background, cut flowers; can be used as a temporary shrub.

PROPAGATION: Seed should be chilled for 5 days at 34°F before sowing. Seeds will germinate in 10-14 days when held at 80°F.

DISEASES AND INSECTS: Cleome is trouble-free and easily grown.

CULTIVARS:
'Helen Campbell'—48", white flowers.
'Queen' series—This group consists of plants 4' tall with 5"-6" wide flowers. The color range includes cherry, pink, rose, violet, white, and a mix of the above colors.

ADDITIONAL NOTES: *Cleome* is a super plant for hot areas. Plantings that I have observed in Manhattan, Kansas, and Athens, Georgia, were very vigorous.

Native to southeastern Brazil, Argentina.   Annual

SCIENTIFIC NAME/FAMILY: *Colchicum speciosum*   Colchicaceae
                                                                              (Liliaceae)

(kol'chi-kum spē-si-ō'-sum)

COMMON NAME: Showy Autumn
  Crocus

LEAVES: Leaves 4–6 appearing in
  the spring, broad oblong, 10″–
  15″ long, about 3″–4″ wide,
  obtuse and dark green.

FLOWER: Flowers 4–20, 5″–6″
  across when expanded, appearing in autumn, with a
  slender tube several inches
  long that elevates the purple-
  pink flowers above the ground.
  The tube is 4–5 times longer
  that the individual segments.

HABIT: 12″ erect habit.

SEASON OF BLOOM: Autumn.

CULTURE: Sun or partial shade in
  fertile, moist soil. Heavy fertil-   *See color plate*
  ization is required to promote
  bulb growth.

UTILIZATION: Use in masses near a shrub border or edge of garden. The large flowers will
  appear without the leaves in the fall, whereas the leaves do a solo in the spring. *Colchicum* should be located in a site where the spring leaves can be allowed to die. The
  deteriorating foliage can be unattractive so an allowance should be made for this
  characteristic.

PROPAGATION: *Colchicum* can be left undisturbed for a number of years but if an increase
  is desired, the bulbs can be dug about every 3 years and replanted. It can also be
  propagated from seed, but flowering is 4–5 years removed.

DISEASES AND INSECTS: Leaf smut.

HARDINESS: Zones 5–7.

CULTIVARS:
  var. *album* (al'bum)—Pure white flowers.
  var. *atrorubens* (at-rō-ru'-bens)—Purple-crimson flowers.
  A number of hybrids have been introduced. These have evolved from a varied parentage
  which included *C. speciosum* as one of the parents.
  'Autumn Queen'—Pink with white throat, flowering in late summer.
  'Lilac Bedder'—Violet-purple flowers with darker veins.
  'Lilac Wonder'—Large, vase-shaped flower, amethyst-violet segments with white lines
    near the center.
  'The Giant'—Large flowers, violet with white throat, 10″–12″ tall.

'Violet Queen'—Late summer flower; flowers checkered with purple and white lines in the throat; very distinctive orange anthers.

'Waterlily'—Large double, lilac-pink flowers with up to 20 petals. Flowers may fall over due to the heavy flower. Flowers in the autumn.

RELATED SPECIES:

C. autumnale (a-tum-nā'lē)—Autumn Crocus. This species is one of the earliest to flower, usually in late summer. Pink flowers reach a height of 4"–6" and often there are as many as 6 flowers produced from one corm. Leaves are produced after flowering. They vary in number from 5–8 and may be 10" long. Autumn crocus will often start to flower if left unplanted on a shelf in the potting shed. I have walked into plant centers and found autumn crocus flowering in the display boxes. Zones 5–7.

'Album'—Single white flowers.

'Alboplenum' ('Album plenum')—Double white flowers.

ADDITIONAL NOTES: Bulbs should be planted 3" deep and 6" apart. The dried bulbs and seeds are the source of medicinal colchicum and colchicine, the latter valuable in plant breeding work where it can be used to induce mutations. *Colchicum* derives its name from the Armenian city of Colchis, which is celebrated as the birthplace of Medea and also for its poisonous plants. *Colchicum* has a long history of folklore concerning its poisonous and healing properties.

Native to England, Europe, North Africa.   Perennial—hardy bulb

SCIENTIFIC NAME/FAMILY: *Coleus amboinicus* (Plectranthus amboinicus)   Lamiaceae
(Labiatae)

(kō'lē-us am-boi'-ne-kus)

COMMON NAME: Spanish Thyme, Mexican Oregano, Indian Borage

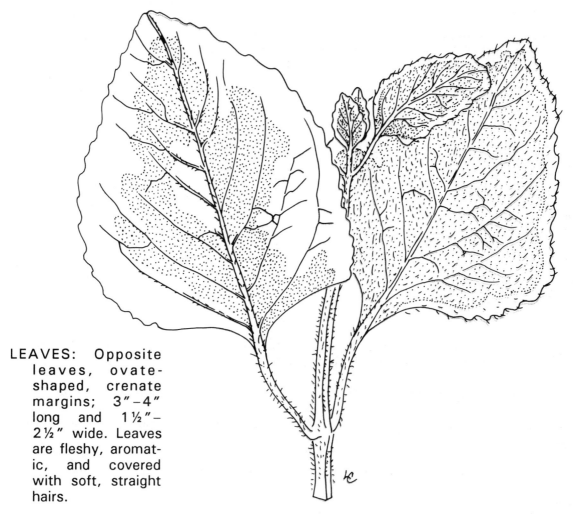

LEAVES: Opposite leaves, ovate-shaped, crenate margins; 3"–4" long and 1½"–2½" wide. Leaves are fleshy, aromatic, and covered with soft, straight hairs.

FLOWER: Pale purple flowers. Plant is grown for foliage effect rather than flowering performance.

HABIT: 12"–18" tall mound.

SEASON OF BLOOM: Not important.

CULTURE: This tender perennial should receive full sun for a few hours each day. Filtered light should be provided during the remainder of the day.

UTILIZATION: Spanish thyme develops into a very admirable foliage plant for hanging baskets; however, it is more popularly used as an exotic herb for the kitchen.

PROPAGATION: Easily propagated by tip cuttings.

DISEASES AND INSECTS: None serious.

ADDITIONAL NOTES: Spanish thyme was introduced into the United States by Cuban refugees in the early 1960s. It is probably native to India or Africa but is commonly found throughout the Caribbean basin, Philippines, Vietnam and Thailand.

Tender perennial

SCIENTIFIC NAME/FAMILY: *Coleus* × *hybridus*   Lamiaceae
(Labiatae)

(kō'lē-us hīb'ri-dus)

COMMON NAME: Coleus

LEAVES: Opposite, membranous, ovate, 3" to 8" long, mostly acuminate, coarsely crenate. Coleus is in the Lamiaceae family indicating the stems are square.

FLOWER: Grown for foliage color, which may be chartreuse, yellow, pink, white, red, maroon or green with multiple leaf patterns. The spike-like flowers with interrupted whorls should be removed for greater profusion of foliage.

HABIT: 9" to 16" tall with a round growth habit, 12" wide.

SEASON OF BLOOM: Not important, however foliage is attractive until frost.

See color plate

CULTURE: Sun to light shade, most types are best in semi-shade. Prefers well-drained, moist soil. Colors are more vivid in partial shade.

UTILIZATION: Edging, borders, planter boxes, hanging baskets, bedding or carpet beds.

PROPAGATION: Seeds germinate at 65°–70°F and should not be covered. Cultivars can be propagated from softwood cuttings which root easily.

DISEASES AND INSECTS: Leaf spots, mealybugs, mites, aphids, and whiteflies.

HARDINESS: Zone 10.

CULTIVARS: The choice in coleus is mind-boggling. There is seemingly a cultivar for every color, leaf shape, and variegation that one can imagine. There are too many cultivars to list individually but the classifications below serve as examples of coleus that can be obtained.
'Carefree' Series—A type of coleus developed by Claude Hope. Carefree coleus is self-branching and remains dwarf and very bushy through the growing season. Leaves are small and closely spaced with deeply and finely lobed margins. Seedlings do not develop normal leaf color until the 3rd set of true leaves.
'Dragon' Series—Vigorous, erect habit, moderately lobed leaves with a clearly defined edge of yellowish-green.
'Fiji' Series—Fringed leaves with the coloration of the 'Rainbow Strain.'
'Jazz' Series—Dwarf habit, 8'–10" tall and 10"–12" spread, similar to 'Wizard.'
'Rainbow Strain'—Medium-sized leaves, striped and mottled with splashes of various colors.

'Saber' Series—Long saber-like leaves give a tropical appearance to these dwarf, basal branching plants.

'Wizard' Series—Large, heart-shaped leaves, basal-branching compact plants, 12″–14″ tall. Suitable for hanging baskets, containers, shady landscape plantings.

ADDITIONAL NOTES: These plants, in much of the literature, are listed under *C. blumei,* but they are of hybrid origin from several species, and it is incorrect to treat them as derivatives of any single species. *Koleos* is the Greek word for sheath, and refers to the arrangement of the stamens.

Native to Java.   Annual; perennial in warm climates

SCIENTIFIC NAME/FAMILY: *Convallaria majalis*   Convallariaceae
(Liliaceae)

(kon-va-lā′ri-à mà-jā′lis)

COMMON NAME: Lily-of-the-Valley

LEAVES: 2 or 3 leaves, 4″–8″ long, 1″–3″ wide, lanceolate-ovate to elliptic.

FLOWER: White, individual flowers bell-shaped, 3/8″ wide, nodding raceme, fragrant.

HABIT: 6″ to 12″ erect plant with a creeping habit.

SEASON OF BLOOM: Midspring.

CULTURE: Full or partial shade, does best in shaded areas. Tolerant of most soil conditions; however, addition of organic matter each year is beneficial. Moist soil is best.

UTILIZATION: Ground cover, cut flowers. *Convallaria* needs room to spread, consequently, it probably should not be placed in the perennial border. Excellent choice as a ground cover beneath shade trees and other shady areas where the aggressive spread is desired.

See color plate

PROPAGATION: Division. Pips (shoots that appear on the rhizome) can be divided and planted in the spring. Division is generally not needed on a regular basis.

DISEASES AND INSECTS: Stem rot, anthracnose, and leaf spots are sometimes seen but are usually not serious.

HARDINESS: Zones 2–7. Shade is a requirement if *Convallaria* is to be grown in southern zones. Even with shade, it will be a struggle in Zone 8.

CULTIVARS:
'Flora Pleno'—Cream-colored double flowers which are larger than the species.
'Fortin's Giant'—Everything on this cultivar is larger than the species. It is 12″–15″ tall with 3/4″ long flowers.
'Rosea'—Pale pink flowers.
'Striata'—(also listed as *C. majalis* 'Albistriata'—Green leaves with thin white stripes and white flowers.

ADDITIONAL NOTES: Occasionally orange-red berries are produced in the fall. These are poisonous and should be removed if young children are present. *Convallaria* is derived from the Latin *Lilium convallium*, meaning lily-of-the-valley.

Native to Europe.   Perennial

SCIENTIFIC NAME/FAMILY: *Coreopsis auriculata*   Asteraceae (Compositae)

(kō-rē-op'sis; kôr-ē-op'sis â-rik-ū-lā'ta)

COMMON NAME: Mouse Ear Coreopsis

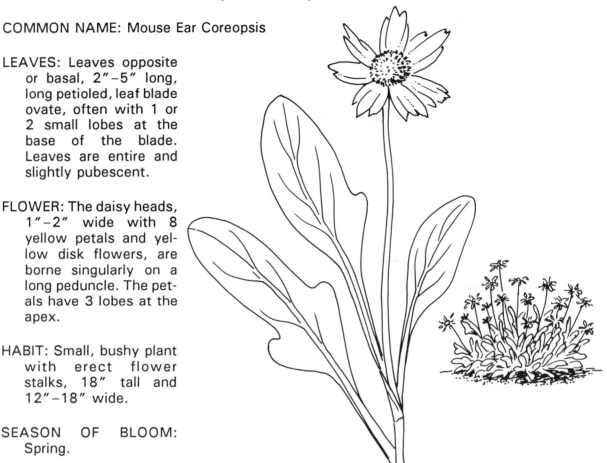

LEAVES: Leaves opposite or basal, 2"–5" long, long petioled, leaf blade ovate, often with 1 or 2 small lobes at the base of the blade. Leaves are entire and slightly pubescent.

FLOWER: The daisy heads, 1"–2" wide with 8 yellow petals and yellow disk flowers, are borne singularly on a long peduncle. The petals have 3 lobes at the apex.

HABIT: Small, bushy plant with erect flower stalks, 18" tall and 12"–18" wide.

SEASON OF BLOOM: Spring.

CULTURE: Best performance will occur in a full sun site with a moist, well-drained soil. Too little moisture during the summer will result in foliage decline. This species should be divided every 2–3 years to maintain vigor.

UTILIZATION: The cultivar 'Nana' is usually the landscape choice in this species. The smaller, compact size makes it an excellent plant for the border front, as an edging plant, or for that special spot in the rock garden.

PROPAGATION: Division or seed. Seed will germinate in 2–3 weeks at 70°F. Division may be done in spring or fall.

DISEASES AND INSECTS: None serious.

HARDINESS: Zones 4–9.

CULTIVARS:
'Nana'—6"–9" tall selection with an abundance of bright yellow flowers in late spring. This selection is stoloniferous, like the species, but is not invasive.

Native to southern United States.   Perennial

SCIENTIFIC NAME/FAMILY: *Coreopsis grandiflora* (C. lanceolata)   Asteraceae
(Compositae)

(kō-rē-op'sis; kôr-ē-op'sis gran-di-flō-'ra)

COMMON NAME: Coreopsis, Tickseed, Lance
Coreopsis

LEAVES: Opposite, leaves usually in a few pairs
or mostly in a tuft near the base, oblong-
spatulate or lanceolate or nearly linear, 2"–
6" long, obtuse, entire or sometimes with 1
or 2 small lateral lobes.

FLOWER: Heads 1½" to 2½" across, on very
long peduncles, about 8 yellow rays, yellow
or chestnut disk flowers.

HABIT: 2' to 3' clump forming plant with erect
flower stems; 12" wide.

SEASON OF BLOOM: Early to late summer.

CULTURE: *Coreopsis* grows very well in full sun
in a well-drained soil. It is tolerant of dry
soils. In fact when grown in moist, fertile
soil, *Coreopsis* has a tendency to tumble. Remove old flowers for continued bloom.

UTILIZATION: Border, cut flowers, good for naturalizing or wild gardens.

See color plate

PROPAGATION: Seed or clump division in the
spring. Seeds which germinate in 2 or 3 weeks at 68°F may produce plants that flower
by summer.

DISEASES AND INSECTS: Leaf spots, rust, powdery mildew, potato aphid, four-lined plant
bug, and spotted cucumber beetle. None are serious problems.

HARDINESS: Zones 4–9.

CULTIVARS: Many of the cultivars are hybrids of *C. grandiflora* and *C. lanceolata.* The
latter is a separate species but there is very little difference between the two species.
The species names are often interchanged in the nursery industry.
'Baby Sun'—Single golden-yellow flowers, 12"–20" tall.
'Badengold'—Bright yellow flowers are borne on long stems from early to late summer.
Individual flowers are up to 4" wide.
'Early Sunrise'—Compact plant, 18"–24" tall, with double yellow flowers. This 1989
All-American Award winner comes true from seed.
'Goldfink'—Compact plant, 10" tall, with 2" wide single yellow flowers.
'Mayfield Giant'—Golden-yellow flowers, 2"–4" diameter, are carried on 2'–3' tall
stems.
'Rotkehlchen'—This 1960 introduction is 12" tall and has yellow flowers with brown
centers.

'Sunburst'—Brilliant, semidouble yellow flowers, comes fairly true from seed, 24″ tall.

'Sunray'—This cultivar was the first perennial to win a Fleuroselect Award in 1980. It is 18″ to 24″ tall and has 4″ wide, golden-yellow double flowers.

ADDITIONAL NOTES: Coreopsis can remain untended in fields or sunny banks where the plants will thrive and multiply indefinitely. Plants tend to sprawl unless supported. Remove faded flowers for continued bloom. *Coreopsis* is from *koris,* a bug, and *opsis,* like; an allusion to the seed, which resembles certain insects.

There are approximately 100 species native to central United States, tropical Africa, and the Hawaiian Islands.
                                                                           Perennial

SCIENTIFIC NAME/FAMILY: *Coreopsis tinctoria*   Asteraceae (Compositae)
(Calliopsis bicolor)

(kō-rē-op'sis; kôr-ē-op'sis tink-tō'-ri-a)

COMMON NAME: Calliopsis, Golden Coreopsis, Tick-seed

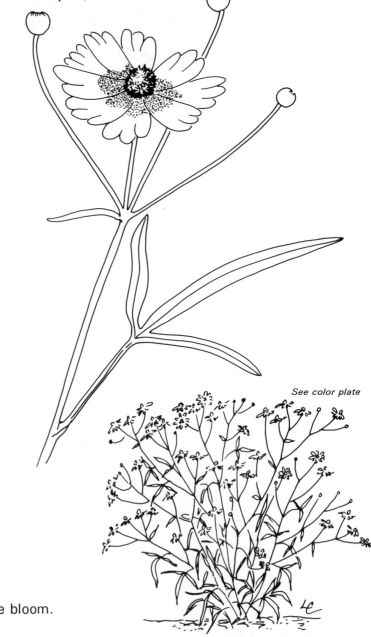

See color plate

LEAVES: Opposite leaves, usually twice divided into linear-lanceolate segments, 2"–4" long. The leaves are very finely cut.

FLOWER: The daisy flowers are borne in loose panicles, on long, slender peduncles. The heads are ¾"–2" across with dark red or purple disc flowers and yellow, orange, or crimson ray flowers. There are usually 8 rays in the single varieties.

HABIT: A multiple-branched species with wiry stems, 2'–3' tall. Space tall selections 12" apart.

SEASON OF BLOOM: Early to midsummer bloom.

CULTURE: Golden coreopsis performs well in full sun, well-drained soils, and hot weather. This species should be dead-headed to keep the plants neat and prolong the bloom.

UTILIZATION: Annual coreopsis is used as a cut flower, in the back of the herbaceous border, or found in wildflower mixes.

PROPAGATION: This annual can be grown from seed started indoors or planted directly into outdoor soil. Seeds will germinate in 5 to 10 days with exposure to light.

DISEASES AND INSECTS: There are no major problems.

Native to eastern United States.   Annual

SCIENTIFIC NAME/FAMILY: *Coreopsis verticillata*

(kō-rē-op′sis; kôr-ē-op′sis vĕr-ti-si-lā′tȧ)

Asteraceae
(Compositae)

COMMON NAME: Threadleaf Coreopsis, Whorled Tickseed, Pot-of-gold

LEAVES: The very fine textured leaves are opposite, sessile, palmately 3-parted, with the division dissected into linear or filiform segments. Leaves are 2″–3″ long. The foliage texture is similar to that of *Cosmos bipinnatus.*

FLOWER: The clear yellow flowers are 1″ to 2″ across and are borne in clusters atop slender peduncles. The disk flowers are yellow; the ray flowers are yellow, sterile and notched.

HABIT: 2′–3′ dense, erect clump, 2′ wide.

SEASON OF BLOOM: Late spring to late summer.

CULTURE: Best growth is in a dry, full sun situation. In fact, it is quite drought resistant and a valued plant in dry sites. Cutting the spent flowers off in the summer will promote an autumn bloom.

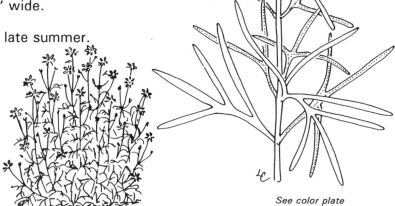

UTILIZATION: This plant makes a showy addition to the dry perennial border, wildflower garden, or naturalized area.

See color plate

PROPAGATION: Division in spring or fall is the simplest method of propagation. Seeds will germinate in 2–3 weeks at 70°. This species will also self-sow.

DISEASES AND INSECTS: None serious.

HARDINESS: Zones 3–9.

CULTIVARS:
    'Golden Showers'—2′ to 3′ tall plant with bright yellow, star-shaped flowers.
    'Moonbeam'—This excellent cultivar has creamy-yellow flowers which are densely produced atop a round hummock of lacy foliage, 18″ to 24″ tall. Good performance in zone 8. Extremely long flower production. A very popular cultivar. It carries the distinction of the 1992 Perennial Plant of the Year as selected by the Perennial Plant Association.
    'Zagreb'—Bright yellow flowers on a plant 12 to 18 inches tall. Flower color is similar to 'Golden Showers.'

RELATED SPECIES:
    C. rosea (rō′-zē′-a). This small, delicate, erect, finely branched plant is 1′–2′ tall and spreads 1′–2′. The flowers are pink with yellow disks, which varies from the normal yellow flower color of the Coreopsis genus. It is a native perennial of eastern United States that has been rediscovered as a "new" perennial. Some catalogs list it as a *verticillata* selection. It spreads quickly and caution should be exercised.

Native from Maryland to Florida, west to Arkansas.   Perennial

SCIENTIFIC NAME/FAMILY: *Cortaderia selloana*

(kôr-tȧ-dē′ri-ȧ sēl-lō-ā′na)

Poaceae
(Gramineae)

COMMON NAME: Pampas Grass

LEAVES: Numerous long, narrow leaves, serrated margins, with tufted hairs at the throat of the sheath.

FLOWER: Silver-white or rose colored inflorescence in a panicle 1½′–3′ long, plumy and fluffy. The best plumes are borne on female plants and one should be sure to obtain a pistillate plant if flowering is desired.

HABIT: 5′ to 12′ erect plant with a 4′–6′ width.

SEASON OF BLOOM: Late summer and fall.

CULTURE: Pampas grass should be planted in full sun and a well-drained soil. During the growing season, it will need abundant water and fertilizer.

UTILIZATION: Best as an isolated free standing specimen or against a background of evergreens; plumes are used for dried arrangements. Pampas grass is a very majestic looking grass.

PROPAGATION: Division and seed. Clumps should be divided in the spring before growth commences. Fall division can be done if the material is potted and overwintered in a minimum heat greenhouse. Seed propagation is possible but seed is not viable for a long period of time. Cultivars will need to be reproduced by clump division.

See color plate

DISEASES AND INSECTS: None serious.

HARDINESS: Zone 8. Some gardeners have reported overwintering success in northern climates by covering the crown with baskets or hay. However, the safest method in northern areas is to plant pampas grass in a container, such as a whiskey barrel, and place it in a greenhouse during the winter.

CULTIVARS:
'Aureo-lineata' ('Gold Band'). The leaves are broad-margined with a rich yellow, 5′–6′ tall.
'Pumila'—Dwarf form with 3′ tall foliage and 6′ tall flower stalks.
'Sunnydale Silver'—The flower heads are a glistening silver and extend well above the foliage. It is a most notable cultivar and a great enhancement for the garden.

ADDITIONAL NOTES: *Cortaderia* means cutting, referring to the leaf margins. Cultivated as a lawn ornamental, also grown commercially for the plumes in California and occasionally as a source of paper in South America.

Native to South America.

Perennial

SCIENTIFIC NAME/FAMILY: *Corydalis lutea*   Fumariaceae
(ko-rid'a-lis lu'tē-a)

COMMON NAME: Yellow Corydalis

LEAVES: Gray-green leaves are 1"–4" wide, long-petioled, and 2 to 3 pinnately compound. The leaflets are obovate and are usually lobed. The foliage has a fern-like appearance.

FLOWER: The yellow flowers are borne in axillary racemes. Flowers are 3/8" to 1/2" long and have a tubular shape with a flared tip. The flowers resemble very small snapdragon flowers and bleeding heart flowers.

HABIT: Lacy mound of foliage, 9"–15" tall and 18" wide.

SEASON OF BLOOM: Late spring to fall. Peak bloom period is during the spring.

CULTURE: Sun or partial shade in well-drained, gravelly soil. *Corydalis* appears to do well when planted around rocks. Best performance will be in partial shade and a slightly alkaline soil. *Corydalis* does not grow as well in North America as it does in Great Britain, where it can be found in any walk or wall crack.

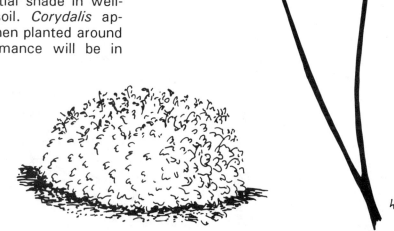

UTILIZATION: This species has been described as a typical cottage garden plant. It self-seeds prolifically and will soon spread into shaded or neglected corners of a garden. It looks especially nice when planted on stone walls or in planting pockets of stone walls. Even though it is often considered a "common" or "weed" plant, the long season bloom is certainly an advantage. Unfortunately, *Corydalis* is not widely available; however, there are several sources in North America.

PROPAGATION: *Corydalis* should be transplanted when small, as it is hard to transplant; fortunately, the plant self seeds and there are usually abundant seedlings. Controlled germination is more difficult because of dormancy requirements. Seeds should be collected when ripe and sown as soon as possible. If purchased seed is used, a warm-cold stratification will probably be needed. The easiest method might be to place seed flats outside in late summer and overwinter the flats outside. This procedure will provide a natural warm and cold stratification.

DISEASES AND INSECTS: There are no pests or diseases.

HARDINESS: Zones 5 to 7.

Native to southeastern Europe. It has naturalized throughout Europe, wherever it is found in garden culture.

Perennial

See color plate

SCIENTIFIC NAME/FAMILY: *Cosmos sulphureus*   Asteraceae
                                                              (Compositae)

(koz'mos sul-fū'rē-us)

COMMON NAME: Yellow Cosmos, Klondike Cosmos, Orange Cosmos

LEAVES: Opposite, pinnately cut into lanceolate or elliptical mucronate lobes, shortly
ciliate.

FLOWER: Heads 2"–3" across, rays 3-toothed at apex, ray flowers are pale gold or
golden-yellow, disk flowers are yellow.

C. sulphureus   C. bipinnatus

See color plate

HABIT: 18″ to 36″ erect plant with fine texture.

SEASON OF BLOOM: Early summer to frost.

CULTURE: Full sun, tolerates dry, porous soils. Heavily fertilized soil promotes foliage instead of flowers.

UTILIZATION: Background plants, cutting flowers.

PROPAGATION: Seeds germinate in one week at 70°F or may be seeded directly into garden.

DISEASES AND INSECTS: Bacterial wilt, canker, aphids, and Japanese beetles are occasional problems.

CULTIVARS:
   C. sulphureus:
   'Diablo'—18″–30″, 2″ semi-double flowers, burnt-orange, A.A.S. 1974.
   'Goldcrest'—24″–36″, golden-orange, double flowers.
   'Ladybird″ Series—Profuse flowering selection with semi-double bloom, 1¼″ wide, and available in orange, scarlet, yellow, and a mixture. Plant height is 12″.
   'Lemon Twist'—Lemon colored flowers, 24″–30″ tall.
   'Sunny Gold'—This dwarf cultivar, 12″–14″, has 1½″–2″ wide, semi-double golden-yellow flowers. Excellent as a bedding annual and for cut flowers.
   'Sunny Red'—This 1987 A.A.S. winner has bright red single flowers with yellow centers. 12″–14″ tall. Good for massed plantings and as a source for cut flowers.
   'Sunset'—24″–30″, semi-double flowers, bright orange-scarlet.

RELATED SPECIES: *C. bipinnatus* (bī-pin-ā′tus) very finely cut foliage, grows to 5′ or 6′. Fast growing annual which lodges easily and should not be used as a bedding plant. Flower colors are red, white, pink, violet, or lavender. Early pinching will make a fuller, stronger plant.

CULTIVARS:
   C. bipinnatus:
   'Early Sensation'—A 3′–4′ tall selection with crimson, rose, pink, or white flowers.
   'Imperial Pink'—A 3′–4′ selection with 4″ diameter, rose-pink flowers.
   'Pinkie'—36″–48″, pink.
   'Purity'—36″–48″, pure white.
   'Radiance'—36″–48″, 4″–6″ flowers, bi-color of deep-rose and rich crimson.
   'Sea Shells'—The petals of this cultivar form fluted "sea shells" which are arranged around a yellow center. Flower colors are creamy-white, pink, and crimson.
   'Sonata' Series—Single, daisy flowers, 40″ tall. 'Sonata White' is a Fleuroselect winner. The mixture contains rose and white colored flowers.
   'Tickle Pink'—Single, white flowers with rose-pink centers, 36″–42″ tall.
   'Yellow Garden'—Single, yellow flowers, 36″ tall. The yellow flower color is unusual for the *Cosmos bipinnatus* species.

ADDITIONAL NOTES: *Cosmos* is from Greek meaning orderly, beautiful, or ornament. Both species perform well in southern gardens. They tend to reseed during the growing season.

Native from Mexico to Brazil.   Annual

SCIENTIFIC NAME/FAMILY: *Crambe cordifolia*   Brassicaceae (Cruciferae)

(kram'bē kor'-di-fol-e-a)

COMMON NAME: Colewort

LEAVES: The basal leaves have long stalks and can be 2' long. The heart-shaped leaves are deeply lobed, coarsely toothed, hispid, and somewhat wrinkled.

FLOWER: The inflorescence on colewort resembles a giant *Gypsophila* inflorescence. The 4-petaled flowers are ⅓" across and are carried on a stout, multiple-branched panicle that may be 5' tall and 3' to 4' wide.

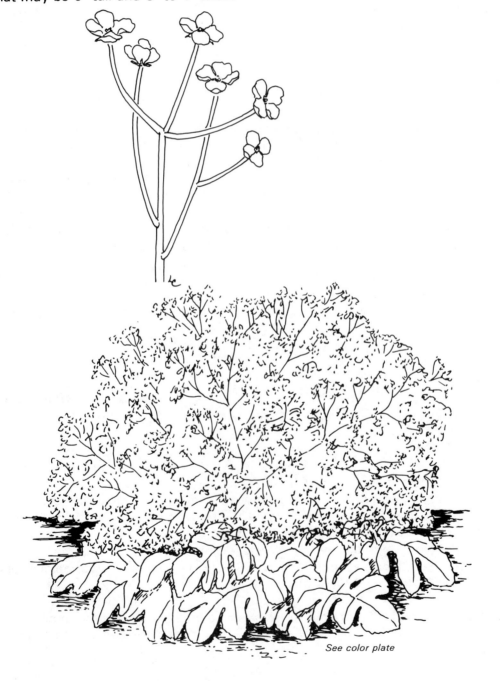

See color plate

HABIT: A large, open inflorescence sits atop a loose, low mound of leaves. This large, round species is 6 feet tall and 4 feet wide.

SEASON OF BLOOM: Late spring to early summer.

CULTURE: *Crambe* should be sited in full sun in a fertile, well-drained, alkaline soil. The large flower panicle may need to be staked.

UTILIZATION: *Crambe cordifolia* is a stately plant that may be used as a specimen plant in the larger garden. A mature plant in full bloom is a sight to behold. It can really light up a garden.

PROPAGATION: *Crambe* is propagated by seed or root cuttings. Sowing seed immediately after ripening works well. Older seed may germinate irregularly and slowly. Germinate at 40°–45°F and keep seed flat moist. Seedlings will flower in 3 years. Pencil-thick root cuttings, 4"–6" long, can be used for asexual propagation.

DISEASES AND INSECTS: None serious.

HARDINESS: Zones 5–9.

RELATED SPECIES:

Crambe maritima (mà-rit'i-ma)—Sea Kale. This 2' tall sand dune species has blue-glaucous, cabbagelike leaves. It has white flowers in early summer. Although usually considered a vegetable, especially in European countries, it can be used as an ornamental in a seashore garden. It is not as desirable as *Crambe cordifolia*. Zones 5–9.

Native to Caucasus, Iran and Afghanistan.   Perennial

SCIENTIFIC NAME/FAMILY: *Crocosmia* × *crocosmiiflora*   Iridaceae

(krō-koz'mi-ȧ krō-koz-me-i-flo'-rȧ)

COMMON NAME: Crocosmia, Montbretia

LEAVES: Sword-shaped leaves in basal clumps. Leaves are 1"–2" wide and 3' long. The leaf blades resemble those of gladiolus.

FLOWER: Orange to orange-red, campanulate to tubular flowers. Flowers are 1½" across in dense, one-sided clusters on 2½'–3' stems which arch near the tip. The buds open from the base to the cluster tip and spent flowers drop cleanly.

HABIT: 1½' to 3' erect plant; one foot wide.

SEASON OF BLOOM: Mid to late summer.

CULTURE: Full sun in moist and well-drained soil. In northern regions above Zone 6 the corms should be dug in the fall and stored in a cool dry place during the winter. Corms should be planted 2"–3" deep and 6"–8" apart.

UTILIZATION: Colorful plant for the border or an excellent plant for cut flowers. *Crocosmia* also is useful for container plantings.

See color plate

PROPAGATION: Montbretia can be propagated by division or by digging the plant and removing the offsets found at the base of the "mother" corm. The normal time for removing the offsets is in the spring before growth starts. Division should be done every 2–3 years to prevent overcrowding which will reduce flowering.

DISEASES AND INSECTS: Spider mites can be a problem.

HARDINESS: Zones 5–9.

CULTIVARS: This interspecific hybrid is a cross between *C. aurea* and *C. pottsii*. Most of the following cultivars have been bred in England.

    'A.E. Amos'—Orange-red flowers, 2' tall.
    'Citronella'—Light lemon-yellow flowers.

'Emily McKenzie'—This cultivar was introduced in 1954 and still is one of the best. It has bright orange flowers with crimson throats. The two colors contrast beautifully.
'His Majesty'—A taller (3') vigorous plant with orange-red flowers.

RELATED SPECIES:

C. masonorum (mas-on-ōr'-um). The flowers on this species point upwards from the stem rather than nodding as seen on other selections. The bright orange-red flowers are earlier in the summer. 'Firebird' is an introduction by Alan Bloom which has "hot" orange-red flowers with open florets.

Alan Bloom has also selected some stunning cultivars by hybridizing *Crocosmia* × *Curtonus* (*Antholyza paniculata*). 'Lucifer' has deep orange-red flowers borne on graceful sprays that extend to 4 feet. It has a long bloom season. 'Spitfire' has orange-red flowers with yellow throats. 'Emberglow' and 'Bressingham Blaze' are similar with darker orange-red color than that found with 'Lucifer'. At present, 'Lucifer' is the most common cultivar in the United States.

Native to South Africa.   Tender corm

SCIENTIFIC NAME/FAMILY: *Crocus vernus*   Iridaceae

(krō'kus vēr'-nus)

COMMON NAME: Dutch Crocus

LEAVES: The leaves are almost grass-like, dark green, curved, and often with a silver-white stripe down the center of each leaf. The leaves are generally shorter than the flowers and appear at the same time or slightly later than the flowers.

FLOWER: Flower color varies from white to purple, often with striped petals. As the flowers appear above ground, they are wrapped in one or two shielding spathes. The flowers can be borne singly, or occasionally in cymes; they have 3 inner and 3 outer segments, creating a globe appearance when the flower is closed. The flowers close at night and remain closed during cloudy days; they are star-like when open in the sunlight.

See color plate

HABIT: 6″ erect growth habit.

SEASON OF BLOOM: Late winter to early spring.

CULTURE: Full sun to partial shade; full shade will tend to keep the flowers closed just as a cloudy day would. The preferred soil is a well-drained sandy loam with well-composted organic matter. Bulbs should be planted in September to November at a depth of 3″, spaced 4″ apart.

UTILIZATION: Crocus are found planted in lawns, rock gardens, and at the base of trees, which creates a spontaneous effect in early spring. One should keep in mind that the crocus planted in the lawn must remain there until the foliage dies, which could be 4 weeks after the start of the lawn mowing season. To a tidy gardener, this could be unnerving.

PROPAGATION: The hybrids produce abundant seeds and naturalize freely. For propagation purposes, these hybrids can be dug every 4 to 5 years and the newly formed corms detached from the mother corm, which usually decays.

DISEASES AND INSECTS: Scab, dry rot, and corm rot are occasional problems. The real problems with crocus are squirrels, chipmunks, rabbits, and mice. There has been many a gardener who has planted crocus in the fall only to find that none emerge in the spring. The "cute" squirrels and chipmunks had a fall snack.

HARDINESS: Zones 3–8.

CULTIVARS:
'Early Perfection'—Violet purple-blue petals with dark edges. A good early-flowering crocus.
'Enchantress'—Light amethyst-purple with a silver sheen and a dark base. Mid-season flowering.
'Flower Record'—Dark purple flowers, often used in containers.
'Jeanne d'Arc'—Pure white flowers.
'Peter Pan'—Pure white flower with orange stigmata.
'Pickwick'—Silver-lilac flowers with darker lilac stripes.
'Remembrance'—Silvery purple flowers, one of the earliest to flower.
'Yellow Mammoth'—Large yellow flowers.
The above hybrids are the product of several years of crossing and are derived from several European species.

RELATED SPECIES:
C. chrysanthus (kris-an'thus)—Golden Crocus. The species has bright orange flowers while the cultivars have varied colors. It is earlier flowering than hybrids of *C. vernus.* By combining the two species, a longer flowering season can be obtained. There are many cultivars and a few are listed below. A more extensive list can be obtained from a specialty bulb catalog.
'Ard Schenk'—Clear white flowers, long-lasting flower.
'Blue Bird'—Lavender blue with cream tinges on the inside of the petals.
'Blue Pearl'—Soft blue with bronze base.
'Blue Peter'—Soft blue with a gold throat.
'E.A. Bowles'—Butter yellow with a bronze veining near the base.
'Goldilocks'—Deep yellow with a purple-brown base.
'Lady Killer'—Purple-violet outside with a white interior.

'Zenith'—Blue flowers, this cultivar is one of the latest flowering.

'Zwanenburg Bronze'—A bronze color on the outside of the petal and a yellow color on the inside make an unusual flower color.

C. speciosus (spe-si-ō'sus)—Showy Crocus. This species is one of the best fall-flowering crocus and is probably the easiest to grow. The flowers emerge while the leaves are very short. Flowers are light blue and have yellow anthers and deep orange stigmas. Plant height is 5"–6". This fall-flowering crocus seeds freely and will increase by offsets.

C. tommasinianus (tom-a-sē-nē-i'nus). This spring flowering species has 4"–6" tall flowers which appear after the leaves have emerged. Pale lavender flowers appear very early in the spring. It seeds freely and is well-suited for large drifts and masses. 'Barr's Purple' has deep purple flowers. Another advantage of this crocus is that it is squirrel resistant, a feature which few other crocus can claim.

ADDITIONAL NOTES: *Saffron,* used to color and flavor food, is manufactured from the dried stigmas of *C. sativus.* About 7000 flowers are required to produce 3 ounces of saffron. In earlier periods, it was used to dye textiles. *Crocus* persists from one year to another in southern zones (Zone 8).

Native to southern Europe.   Perennial—hardy bulb

SCIENTIFIC NAME/FAMILY: *Cuphea hyssopifolia*   Lythraceae

(kū'fē-à his'op-i-fō'-lē-a)

COMMON NAME: False Heather, Elfin Herb

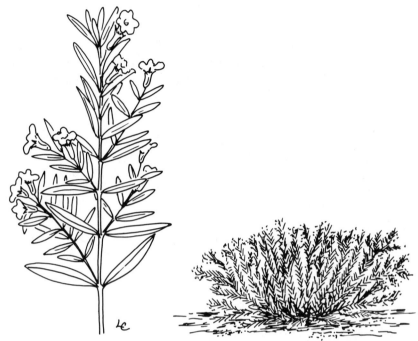

LEAVES: Leaves are opposite or whorled and closely-spaced on the stem. Leaves are ⅜"–¾" long, linear to lanceolate, and sessile.

FLOWER: Delicate, small flowers, ¼" long, are borne in the leaf axils. The 6-petaled flowers are usually lavender but some can be white.

HABIT: 12"–18" tall mound with a similar spread. Space 12" apart.

SEASON OF BLOOM: Summer.

CULTURE: Plant in full sun or partial shade in a well-drained soil. *Cuphea hyssopifolia* is very suitable for long, hot summers.

UTILIZATION: The compact, dense habit of false heather makes it suitable as an edging plant or used in a massed display in a bed. The common name is appropriate, as the flowers and growth habit resemble a small heather.

PROPAGATION: Seed germination will take 7–10 days at 70°F.

DISEASES AND INSECTS: None serious.

Native to Mexico and Guatemala.   Annual

SCIENTIFIC NAME/FAMILY: *Cuphea × purpurea*   Lythraceae
(C. llavea var. miniata)

(kū'fē-á pēr-pū'rē-á)

COMMON NAME: Cigar Plant, Cigar
Flower

LEAVES: Opposite, ovate to lanceolate to 3″ long, acute, short-
petioled, the upper leaves almost
opposite. Leaves and stems are
hirsute.

FLOWER: Borne in terminal racemes,
petals are bright red.

HABIT: 10″–20″; rarely over 12″,
round growth habit.

SEASON OF BLOOM: Midsummer to
fall.

CULTURE: Sun or light shade and
average soil. This species dies at
the first mention of frost.

UTILIZATION: Edging for walks and
borders, window boxes, planters,
or rock gardens.

PROPAGATION: Seeds germinate in
one to two weeks at 70°F.

See color plate

DISEASES AND INSECTS: Whitefly.

CULTIVARS:
'Firefly'—Dwarf, quick-flowering with fiery cerise flowers, 12″ tall.

RELATED SPECIES: *C. ignea,* (ig'nē-á) (*C. platycentra*)—Mexican Cigar Plant. This species
has narrow, glabrous leaves, 1″–2″ long. The 1″ long scarlet flower is tubular with a
black-and-white tip which mimics a newly lit cigarette or cigar; hence the common
name. It has a round growth habit and a height of 12 inches.

ADDITIONAL NOTES: *Cuphea* is derived from *kyphos,* curved, and refers to the shape of
the seed capsule.

Native to Mexico.   Annual

SCIENTIFIC NAME/FAMILY: *Cynoglossum amabile*   Boraginaceae

(sin-ō-glos'um am-a'-bil-ē)

COMMON NAME: Chinese Forget-me-not

LEAVES: Alternate leaves; lower leaves lanceolate to oblong-lanceolate, 2"–8" long, tapering at the base into a winged petiole. Stem leaves are smaller, 2"–3" long, and sessile to the stem. Leaves and stems are covered with short, stiff hairs.

FLOWER: Clear blue flowers, ¼" wide, are carried in spraylike clusters. Each flower has 5 petals. Pink and white forms are also available.

HABIT: 2' tall, upright branching stems creating an irregular to rounded habit. Individual stems are terminated by arching clusters of flowers. Space plants 12" apart.

SEASON OF BLOOM: Summer.

CULTURE: Sow seeds or transplant seedlings into a well-drained soil in full sun or partial shade. Chinese forget-me-not is adaptable and can be successfully grown in wet or dry soils. As a biennial it will often continue to self-seed. In some situations, the seedlings may become too numerous for some gardeners' taste.

UTILIZATION: Chinese forget-me-not is a biennial that is usually used as an annual because it will flower the first year from seed. It can be used in borders and beds. Foliage is coarse, so a mass planting is best. This species can also be used as a cut flower, but the blooms are not long-lasting.

PROPAGATION: Seeds should be covered. Germination occurs in 7–10 days at 70°F. Some gardeners broadcast the seed in the area where they want a mass planting of *Cynoglossum*.

DISEASES AND INSECTS: None serious.

CULTIVARS:
'Firmament'—Sky blue flowers on plants 15" tall.

Native to eastern Asia.   Biennial

SCIENTIFIC NAME/FAMILY: *Cynoglossum nervosum*   Boraginaceae

(sin-ō-glos'-um nĕr-vō'sum)

COMMON NAME: Hairy Hound's Tongue

LEAVES: Alternate leaves; lower leaves 6″– 8″ long, lanceolate, with a short petiole. The upper leaves are oblong, sessile, and 3″–4″ long. Leaves and stems are coated with short, stiff hairs.

FLOWER: Intense blue, forget-me-not-like flowers are produced on the terminal and upper axils of the plant. The ½″ wide flowers start out in a rounded head which uncoils to a 6″–8″ long inflorescence.

HABIT: Bushy, upright plant, 24″–30″ tall and 24″ wide.

CULTURE: *Cynoglossum* should be situated in sun or partial shade in a moist, well-drained soil. It will not tolerate dry situations. Too much fertilizer will create tall and weak plants which may flop.

UTILIZATION: Hairy hound's tongue provides about 4 weeks of bloom in late spring. It is better suited for an informal site rather than a border.

PROPAGATION: Division can be done in fall or spring. Seeds germinate easily in a moist environment at 70°–75°F.

DISEASES AND INSECTS: None serious.

HARDINESS: Zones 4–8.

RELATED SPECIES:
   C. grande (gran'-de)—Pacific Hound's Tongue. A 1′–2′ tall plant with blue flowers. The leaves of this species are mostly basal and long petioled. As a native to the Pacific Northwest, it is sometimes found in gardens in that region. Overall, it is seldom used.

See color plate

Native to Himalayas   Perennial

SCIENTIFIC NAME/FAMILY: *Cypripedium calceolus* var. *pubescens* Orchidaceae

(sip-ri-pē'di-um kal-sē-ō'-lus pū-bes'enz)

COMMON NAME: Yellow Lady's Slipper

LEAVES: Alternate leaves, broadly ovate 3"–8" long. Each leaf is slightly folded and has many veins, which gives the leaf a pleated appearance.

See color plate

FLOWER: There is usually one flower borne at the terminal of a long peduncle. The broad lip is a dull cream to golden yellow and can be from ¾"–2" wide. The lateral petals that extend to the side like wings are greenish yellow to brownish purple and are often twisted.

HABIT: Erect clump, 18"–24" tall and 12" wide.

SEASON OF BLOOM: Mid to late spring.

CULTURE: Lady's slipper can be satisfactorily grown in a neutral to slightly acid soil which has abundant organic matter. As a native plant, it is found in bogs and moist soil sites. It is a difficult plant to establish and is not recommended for the novice gardener. Unfortunately, individuals have attempted to dig this species from the wild. The result is usually a dead plant in the garden and a loss of plant material in the native area.

UTILIZATION: This species would be valued in any woodland setting. Lady's slipper is usually desired by anyone who sees the bright yellow flower pouch.

PROPAGATION: At the present time, there is not a feasible method for commercial propagation of lady's slipper. Lady's slippers purchased from nurseries usually have been collected from the wild. This should be done only when the native site will be destroyed. Digging at other times should not be condoned by the horticulture community.

Lady's slipper can be propagated by careful division in the spring. A soil ball should surround the roots. Even then, establishment will be slow.

DISEASES AND INSECTS: None serious.

HARDINESS: Zones 5–8.

RELATED SPECIES:

Cypripedium acaule (à-cal'ē)—Pink Lady's Slipper. This species has a pink flower borne on a leafless stalk, as there are only 2 basal leaves. It also requires a strongly acid soil (4.5–5.0). It is very difficult to establish in the garden. Zones 5–8.

Native to the southern areas of eastern North America.   Perennial

SCIENTIFIC NAME/FAMILY: *Cystopteris bulbifera*   Woodsiaceae

(sist-op'-ter-is bul-bif'-er-à)

COMMON NAME: Bulblet Bladder Fern

FRONDS: The narrow triangular deciduous fronds are smooth and deeply cut. They are often twice pinnate. The pinnules are deeply lobed or toothed.

SORI: The sori are found in the lobes of the pinnule.

HABIT: 18" to 30" arching frond.

CULTURE: Bulblet bladder fern should be grown in shade in moist soil that has a pH of 7.0 to 7.5. As a native plant it is often found near water; clinging to rocks that are wet from water spray.

UTILIZATION: Excellent plant for rock gardens, especially gardens with running water or pools.

PROPAGATION: Propagation is by clump division in the spring, spore propagation, or from bulbils that are produced on the fronds. The bulbils can be planted and will produce new ferns. The bulblets may also fall off and form new plants in the garden.

DISEASES AND INSECTS: None serious.

HARDINESS: Zones 3 to 8.

RELATED SPECIES:
   C. protrusa (prō-tru'-sa) (*C. fragilis* var. *protrusa*)—Brittle or Fragile Bladder Fern. This fern is similar to the above but it is shorter, 10"–12", and the fronds are wider. It is easily grown in slightly acid to neutral soil in moist shade. Abundant water in the summer will promote new fronds which will cover the older, unattractive fronds.

ADDITIONAL NOTES: This rock and wood fern is found natively from Newfoundland to Georgia.

Perennial

SCIENTIFIC NAME/FAMILY: *Dahlia* hybrids

(däl'ya)

Asteraceae
(Compositae)

COMMON NAME: Garden Dahlia

LEAVES: Opposite or whorled, simple to pinnately dissected or bipinnate, 10" long, including petiole, margins are serrate.

FLOWER: Heads horizontal or sometimes nodding, 2"–3" across but much larger in double forms. Heads in 2's or 3's, but only 2–8 on a stem. Flower color varies with cultivar.

HABIT: 1' to 5', habit varies from round to erect with different cultivars.

SEASON OF BLOOM: Midsummer to frost (July to October).

CULTURE: Sun or partial shade, prefers well-drained, moist soil.

UTILIZATION: Bedding plant (mass for good color) and excellent for cut flowers.

PROPAGATION: Seeds germinate in one to two weeks at a constant 70°F. Cultivars must be propagated vegetatively. Dahlia clumps may be dug in the fall before frost and stored at 30°–50°F and covered with moist vermiculite. The tuberous roots are divided so that each section has at least one shoot.

CULTIVARS: The dwarf seed-grown dahlias are listed below. There is a large class of tuberous-rooted dahlias growing 4'–6' tall and bearing flowers 12" across. There are so many sizes and shapes of dahlias it is almost impossible to characterize. There are tall plants, short plants, marigold-like plants, allium-like plants, and sunflower-like plants. And this is just a modest capsulization. Anytime plant size varies from knee-high to head-high there is bound to be variety.

'Border Jewels'—18"–24", blend of colors, double and semi-double flowers, more dependable during summer than 'Unwins.'

'Early Bird'—15", early flower, excellent color range.

'Figaro Mixture'—This cultivar is one of the newer and better selections. It has a good compact habit, 12" tall, and many bright colors.

'Fresco'—Fully double flowers, wide range of flower colors, and a compact habit. 12" tall.

'Redskin'—15", mixture of colors, bronze leaves, A.A.S. 1975.

'Rigoletto'—15", early flower (1 week before 'Early Bird'), double flowers, mixture of colors.

ADDITIONAL NOTES: Seed-grown dahlias are not very heat tolerant. They also lack uniformity of growth habit and all are usually erratic bloomers. Dahlias grown from tuberous roots are larger than the seed grown annual types and can reach heights of 6'. These larger growing types must be staked. Although *D. pinnata* is commonly used, many of the cultivars available are probably products of the hybridization between *D. coccinea* and *D. pinnata*. *Dahlia* was named for Dr. Anders Dahl, a Swedish botanist who was a pupil of Linnaeus.

Native to Mexico   Annual

SCIENTIFIC NAME/FAMILY: *Darmera peltata*   Saxifragaceae
(Peltiphyllum peltatum)

(dar'-mir-a pel-tā'ta)

COMMON NAME: Umbrella Plant

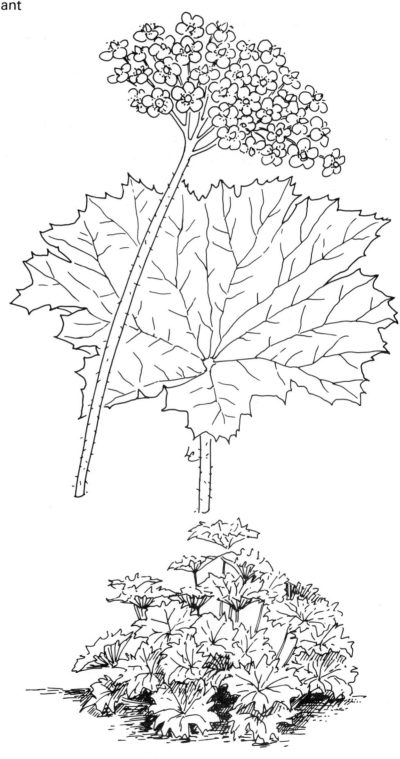

See color plate

LEAVES: Large peltate leaves can be 12" to 18" in diameter. The hairy petioles attach near the center of the leaf blade. Each leaf is conspicuously lobed and toothed and the blade cups in the center. The fall color can be a reddish to coppery color. However, in my garden, they are usually a dreary brown.

FLOWER: Small (1/2") pink to whitish flowers are borne in numerous terminal corymbs that appear before the leaves develop in the spring. The flowers remain effective long after the foliage has developed.

HABIT: The leaf petioles arise directly from a horizontal underground rootstock which creates a rounded mass 3 feet tall and 3–4 feet wide.

SEASON OF BLOOM: The flowers bloom in spring on leafless, hairy stems.

CULTURE: Umbrella plant will perform well in sun or partial shade as long as there is constant moisture. The most successful planting will be found along shaded stream banks, on pond edges, or any area where the roots are cool and moist. The finest plantings that I have seen have been in the bog garden area of Wakehurst Place in England. My trials with *Darmera* in my garden have not been as successful as those at Wakehurst. What an understatement!

UTILIZATION: Umbrella plant is a bold plant that can be used in moist to wet sites. It may be too large for small gardens but certainly has a place in larger sites, especially when combined with other large specimens like *Rheum* and ornamental grasses.

PROPAGATION: *Darmera* is propagated by division in the spring or fall.

DISEASES AND INSECTS: There are no major problems. Leaf scorch can occur, but it is usually a physical problem due to insufficient moisture.

HARDINESS: Zones 5–7. The early spring flowers can be sensitive to frost.

CULTIVARS:
'Nana'—This selection is rare in American gardens but well worth the search. It stands 12"–18" tall, a perfect miniature to the larger species. It would be valuable for use in the small water or bog gardens in residential sites.

ADDITIONAL NOTES: *Darmera* is another American native, Sierra Nevada in California and Oregon, that is commonly found in English gardens but not much in gardens in North America.

Native to California and Oregon.   Perennial

SCIENTIFIC NAME/FAMILY: *Delphinium* × *elatum* (*D. alpinum*)   Ranunculaceae

(del-fin'i-um ē-lā'tum)

COMMON NAME: Delphinium, Larkspur, Candle Larkspur, Bee Larkspur.

LEAVES: Leaves large, palmately 5–7-parted near the base, the upper leaves 3-parted, ultimate segments over ¼" wide.

FLOWER: Flowers in showy racemes or spikes which are often paniculate, usually blue but also red, pink, white, violet, and yellow. Five sepals, the posterior one prolonged into a spur.

HABIT: 4' to 6' erect plant; taller growing types will need staking.

SEASON OF BLOOM: Early to midsummer.

CULTURE: Full sun in a moist well-drained soil. Prefers a slightly alkaline, organic soil with high fertilization. Delphinium should be protected from the wind to prevent lodging.

UTILIZATION: Background, specimen or cutting flowers.

PROPAGATION: Perennial delphinium seeds germinate in three to four weeks at 65°–75°F. Plants started from seed sown in the greenhouse will flower the first year. Seeds may also be sown outdoors in spring or summer to produce plants which flower the following year. Cover the seed for best germination. Delphinium can also be propagated by careful division or by basal cuttings in the spring.

See color plate

DISEASES AND INSECTS: Powdery mildew, fungal blights, *Botrytis* blight, black leaf spot, crown rot, canker, aphids, borers, leaf miner, and mites. The nocturnal slug is also a problem. Delphinium should be planted in uninfested soil, and care should be taken not to contaminate the soil with diseased plants nor to propagate from infected stock.

HARDINESS: Zones 3–7. In southern and western areas, delphinium does well the first year but is only average over time because of the heat.

CULTIVARS:
  'Blackmore and Langdon' Hybrids—The selections of this cutting-grown group from England were very popular in the early 1900s. Flower colors included white, cream, yellow, and blue. However, they were expensive and now have been supplanted by lesser quality mixed-seedlings.
  'Connecticut Yankee'—30", free-flowering, densely branched, with an excellent color range.
  'Dwarf Pacific Hybrid'—Plants in this group are smaller, only 2' tall, and are often treated as annuals. Two selections are 'Blue Fountains' (mixed blues) and 'Blue Heaven,' sky-blue.
  Giant Pacific Hybrid'—This seed-grown hybrid has colors of blue, violet, purple, pink, white, and lavender. Most of the flowers are double.

RELATED SPECIES: *Consolida ambigua,* (con-sol'-i-dȧ am-big-ū'-ȧ) Rocket Larkspur. Hardy annual, 2'–4' tall, blue flowers, useful for massing and for cut flowers.

D. × *belladonna* (bel-a-don'-a)—Belladonna Delphinium. This hybrid is a result of crosses between *D. elatum* and *D. grandiflorum.* These hybrids are smaller and usually only reach 3'–4' tall. They are well-branched with many flower stems of comparable size which differs from *D.* × *elatum* in which there is one major stem with several smaller side branches. Cultivars include:

'Bellamosa'—Dark blue flowers.

'Casa Blanca'—Pure white blossoms.

'Cliveden Beauty'—Sky blue flowers.

'Piccolo'—Azure blue flowers in dense inflorescences.

ADDITIONAL NOTES: Cut back plants after flowering to promote new growth and flowers. Young plants and seeds can be poisonous if eaten. *Delphinium* is derived from the Greek word *delphis,* dolphin, and refers to the flower buds before they expand, which resemble dolphins.

Native to Europe.   Perennial

SCIENTIFIC NAME/FAMILY: *Dendranthema × morifolium*   Asteraceae
                        (Chrysanthemum × morifolium)   (Compositae)

(den-dran'-thē-ma mōr-i-fō'li-um)

COMMON NAME: Hardy Chrysanthemum

LEAVES: Leaves thick, strongly aromatic, lanceolate to ovate, to 3" long, lobed ⅓ to ½" depth of the blade, lobes entire or coarsely toothed, lower surface gray pubescent.

FLOWER: Heads of various sizes and shapes, typically clustered; flower colors are yellow, orange, red, bronze, white, or lavender.

HABIT: Mounded shape, 1' to 3' tall with a spread often equal to the height.

SEASON OF BLOOM: Late summer to frost.

CULTURE: Hardy chrysanthemum should be grown in full sun in a well-drained, moist soil. This species is a heavy feeder and will benefit from fertilizer additions. Hardy chrysanthemum needs to be pinched several times in the late spring and early summer to promote a compact habit. Do not cut back after the first week in August. Flower buds will be cut off with late pinching. In northern areas it is difficult to maintain the hardy chrysanthemum as a permanent species. Gardeners often dig the plants in the fall and overwinter them in a cold frames or cool basement. If plants are left outside it is essential that the soils be well-drained during the winter.

See color plate

UTILIZATION: Border, massing, used for late summer and fall flowering display, and as cutting flowers. The autumn season would be barren without the bright versatile colors of the mum. It has been described as "the last smile of the departing year" because it takes a pretty good frost to discourage a mum! Covering the plants can keep a plant going past that one bad night that often occurs extra early in the fall.

PROPAGATION: Division in the spring is the most common means of reproduction. New plants may also be started from 3" long tip cuttings taken in the spring and summer from vegetative tissue.

DISEASES AND INSECTS: Bacterial blight, leaf spot, stalk borer, leaf miner, aphids, and spider mites are listed problems. Typically, spider mites and aphids will be serious problems and pesticide sprays will be necessary.

HARDINESS: Zones 5–9. Excellent plant for zone 8.

CULTIVARS: The range of cultivars is nearly unending and the choices for the gardener are many. They are available as cushion types, 18" tall; buttons, small double flowers, 18" tall; upright, taller cultivars with large semi-double to double flowers; daisy types, single flowers with yellow centers; and pompons, miniature ball-shaped blooms, 18" tall.

RELATED SPECIES: *D.* × *rubellum* (rū-bell'-um). Members of this species are likely hybrids of *D. zawadskii* but the parentage is unknown. Plants are 2'–3' tall and 3' wide. Leaves are pubescent and deeply lobed. Cultivars flower earlier than the hardy chrysanthemums.

'Clara Curtis'—Rose pink flowers with yellow centers, 2'–3' tall.
'Duchess of Edinburgh'—Dull red flowers, 2' tall.
'Mary Stoker'—Pale yellow flowers with a pink blush, 2'–3' tall.

OTHER SPECIES:
Dendranthema × 'Mei-Kyo'—Double lavender flowers with yellow centers. Flowers do not open until late fall and remain until frost. It is 3' tall and hardy to zones 6–9.

ADDITIONAL NOTES: Mulch during the winter or use a cold frame for winter protection. Mums are heavy feeders, requiring fertilizer and ample water. Chrysanthemums may be transplanted while in bloom which makes them useful for instant landscapes in the fall. *Chrysanthemum* means "golden flower" in Greek. The name is derived from *chryos,* gold, and *anthos,* a flower. The Oriental origin is reflected in the wide usage in frequent images in art forms, in teas, and even as a calming medicinal tea.

Native to the Orient.   Perennial

SCIENTIFIC NAME/FAMILY: *Dennstaedtia punctilobula*   Dennstaedtiaceae
(Dicksonia pilosiuscula)

(den-stet'i-á punk-ti-lōb'-ū-lá)

COMMON NAME: Hay-scented Fern

FRONDS: Fronds are lance-shaped, long-tapering, pale green, 2' to 3' tall and 3" to 5" wide. They are twice to tri-pinnate, which creates a very lacy texture. There are scattered hairs on the rachis and stalk.

SORI: The sporangia (fruit dots) are held on a raised globular receptacle on a recurved toothlet.

HABIT: This fern forms a large clump with graceful, curving fronds.

CULTURE: Hay-scented fern is very adapted for garden use. It tolerates wide variations in sun, moisture and soils. Optimum growth will be in moist, well-drained, slightly acid soils in partial shade.

UTILIZATION: *Dennstaedtia* forms dense mats of light green fronds which smell like freshly mown hay when the fronds are crushed. It can serve as a ground cover fern, especially as a transition fern from the woods to the sunny areas.

PROPAGATION: This fern can be easily propagated by cutting the rhizomatous mats apart in the spring. Spores are usually collected in late summer or fall.

DISEASES AND INSECTS: No pest problems.

HARDINESS: Zones 3 to 8.

ADDITIONAL NOTES: The common name of hay-scented fern comes from the hay smell that occurs when the fronds are crushed.

Native from Canada to Georgia.   Perennial

SCIENTIFIC NAME/FAMILY: *Deschampsia caespitosa*

(de-shamp'si-a ses-pi-tōs'à)

Poaceae
(Gramineae)

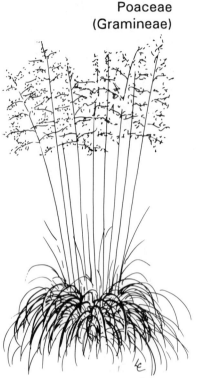

COMMON NAME: Tufted Hair Grass

LEAVES: Leaf blades 1/5″ wide and up to 2′ long. They may
be flat or rolled; the upper surface ribbed lengthwise. The
ribs and margins are scabrous while the lower leaf surface
is smooth. Leaves are dark green.

FLOWER: The inflorescence is a huge, loose panicle, 15″–20″
long and 6″–8″ wide. The spikelets are loosely arranged on
the branches. Flower color can be silvery, light green, or
purple with several colors occurring together in the same
panicle. The inflorescence is very delicate.

HABIT: The leaves create a mound and the stiff stems carry
the flowers well above the mound. Stem height is normally
2′–3′ but some cultivars are taller.

SEASON OF BLOOM: Summer.

CULTURE: *Deschampsia* is a very durable grass. It can be grown in full sun or partial shade
in most soils including moist or dry soils.

UTILIZATION: Tufted hair grass is a versatile grass that can be used in the border, in a rock
garden, or along the water's edge. It has an excellent flower which can be cut to use
dried or left on the plant where it will remain ornamental until late winter. A darker
background such as a hedge will enhance the fine texture of the flowers. The flowering
season is all summer, which makes the grass extra valuable.

PROPAGATION: Division in spring or fall and seed are easy methods. Plants with
attractively colored inflorescences should be propagated by division.

DISEASES AND INSECTS: No problems.

HARDINESS: Zones 4–9.

CULTIVARS:
    'Bronzeschleier' ('Bronze Veil')—Bronze-yellow inflorescence, 3′ tall.
    'Goldgehänge' ('Gold Pendant')—Golden-yellow inflorescence, 3′ tall.
    'Goldschleier' ('Golden Veil')—The flowers and stems turn a bright straw-yellow at
        maturity, 2′–3′ tall.
    'Goldstaub' ('Gold Dust')—Yellow inflorescence, 2′–3′ tall.
    'Schottland' (Scottish tufted hair grass)—4′–5′ tall.
    'Tardiflora'—Late-blooming selection similar in color and habit to the species.
    'Tauträger' ('Dew Bearer')—Slender inflorescence, 3′ tall.

RELATED SPECIES:
    D. vivipara, (vi-rip'-ar-à) Viviparous Hair Grass. This species has an unusual appearance
        due to the loose, open flower panicles that are full of small grass plants (viviparous).
        'Fairy's Joke' is an available cultivar that is 3 feet tall.

Native to Europe.   Perennial

SCIENTIFIC NAME/FAMILY: *Dianthus caryophyllus*   Caryophyllaceae

(dī-an'thus kār-i-ō-fil'us)

COMMON NAME: Annual Carnation, Clove Pink, Divine Flower, Gilliflower

LEAVES: Stems are branched, hard with conspicuous nodes, leaves thick, linear, mostly 3"–6" long, obtuse, stiff at the tips, keeled and gray or powdery gray.

FLOWER: Flowers 1" or more across (to 5" in horticulture cvs.), 2–5 or more to a stem, showy, very fragrant, long-pedicelled, white, pink, red, purple, yellow, or apricot-orange.

HABIT: 1' to 2' erect plant.

SEASON OF BLOOM: Midsummer.

CULTURE: Prefers cool temperatures but requires sun for good blooms; moist, well-drained soil. Soil pH should be neutral to slightly basic.

UTILIZATION: Long-lasting cut flowers, bedding (low compact forms). Center of the plant should be pinched out to promote bushy specimens and abundant flowers.

PROPAGATION: Seed is usually used for bedding plants. Seeds germinate in 2 to 3 weeks at a constant 70°F. However, in the florist trade carnations are readily propagated by softwood cuttings.

DISEASES AND INSECTS: Rust, crown rot, and grasshoppers can be problems.

HARDINESS: Zones 8–10. In most climatic areas, the garden carnation is grown as an annual.

CULTIVARS:
'Chabaud's Giant Improved'—15"–20", large flowers of mixed colors, blooming over a long period.
'Dwarf Fragrance Mixed'—12"–14", compact plants remain upright all season, double flowers are larger and more fragrant than 'Chabaud's Giant Improved'.
'Hellas Stanarthur'—Cream-white flowers with red stripes. This selection has no scent.
'Juliet'—12", large double scarlet flowers, good heat resistance, A.A.S. 1975.
'Knight Series'—Plants in this series are compact, 12" tall, and have very strong stems that need no support. Colors include crimson, orange, scarlet, white, yellow, and mixed.
'Peach Delight'—Light pink flowers, 2'–3' tall.
'Red Riding Hood'—Large 3" wide red flowers on plants 4"–6" tall and 15" wide. Excellent selection for window boxes, baskets, patio tubs, as well as edging and bedding purposes.

'Scarlet Luminette'—This plant is a 1982 A.A.S. and Fleuroselect Bronze Medal winner. The bright scarlet flowers are double and are held on 24″ tall stems.

'Stripes and Picotees'—A mixture with striped and picotee flowers, 2″ wide, with a plant height of 18 inches.

ADDITIONAL NOTES: Annual carnation is similar to greenhouse carnations; the flowers are smaller in size but more fragrant. Annual carnation is not the best bedding flower because it has a tendency to lodge. Taller growing varieties are better for cutting, but need to be disbudded and supported for large blooms. Annual carnation is cultivated in Europe for use in perfume manufacturing. *Dianthus* is derived from *dios,* divine, and *anthos,* a flower; the name is said to have been given by Theophrastus because of the charm and fragrance of the flowers. It is likely that carnation is a corruption of the Latin "carnatio," which means flesh-color. This relates to the flesh-pink color of the original clove pink. However, others think that carnation is from "coronation." The carnation was used in making garlands which were used for crowning nobilities.

Native to southern Europe.   Annual

SCIENTIFIC NAME/FAMILY: *Dianthus chinensis*   Caryophyllaceae

(dī-an'thus chi-nen'sis)

COMMON NAME: China Pinks, Annual Pinks,
Rainbow Pinks

LEAVES: Opposite leaves, basal leaves, usually
gone by flowering, stem leaves 1"–3" long,
exceeding internodes, very narrow to ¼"
wide, margins usually ciliate. Foliage is blue-
gray or frosty looking.

FLOWER: Inflorescence contains a few to 15
flowers, loosely clustered, flowers ½" to 1"
across, slightly fragrant; petals contiguous,
toothed. Colors are red, pink, white, and
bicolored.

HABIT: 6"–12" dense mounded habit.

SEASON OF BLOOM: Early summer to fall.

See color plate

CULTURE: Sun to partial shade, prefers cool summers. Will thrive in soils with high pH (7.0
and above).

UTILIZATION: Edging, bedding.

PROPAGATION: Seed in fall or indoors in spring. *Dianthus* may grow from self-sown seeds
if the winter is not too severe. Seeds germinate in 2 weeks at 70°F.

DISEASES AND INSECTS: Refer to *Dianthus caryophyllus*.

CULTIVARS:
'Carpet' Series—An early flowering series that forms a carpet 6"–8" tall. Five colors
and a mixture provide long season bloom.
'Charms' Series—This group is composed of 6" uniform cultivars that produce clusters
of 1¼" single fringed flowers through the summer.
'China Doll'—10"–12", compact plant with clusters of crimson-red flowers, some with
white markings, A.A.S. 1970.
'Ideal' Series—This group has single flowers with serrated margins. Height is 8"–10"
with a 10" spread. 'Ideal Violet' with a velvety-look is an AAS winner.
'Parfait' Series—A Fleuroselect winner available in scarlet ('Strawberry Parfait') and
crimson ('Raspberry Parfait'). Flowers are fringed with a unique eye pattern.
Selected for early bloom and compact habit.
'Princess' Series—This hybrid of *D. chinensis* and *D. barbatus* has 2" wide, fringed
blossoms. Good for summer edging and bedding. Colors include crimson, scarlet,
salmon, white, and mixed.
'Queen of Hearts'—12"–15", scarlet-red flowers on a bushy, compact plant, A.A.S.
1972.
'Snowfire'—6"–8", fringed white flowers with cherry-red centers, A.A.S. 1978.
'Snowflake'—6"–8", pure white flowers, 2½" across, with serrated edges, spreads
to 12".
'Telstar' Series—Cultivars in this series have received AAS and Fleuroselect awards.
This group was selected for early bloom, compact habit, long bloom season, and
heat tolerance.

RELATED SPECIES:

D. barbatus, (bar-bā'tus)—Sweet William. Sweet William is a biennial but it self-sows so easily that the plant seems to be a constant in the garden. The flowers are dense clusters subtended by narrow green bracts. Most *Dianthus* species have only 1–2 flowers per stem, whereas Sweet William has a flat-topped cluster. This characteristic makes it a favorite among many gardeners. Sweet William is effective in borders, as a bedding plant, in rock gardens, or more recently as a cut flower. A disadvantage to this group is that the flowers are not scented. Division should be used to insure the true colors but seed propagation is usually used for the mixes.

'Indian Carpet' ('Indianerteppich')—Mix of various colors, single flowers, 10" tall.

'Harlequin'—Ball-shaped flower heads of pink and white flowers.

'Spring Messenger' ('Fruhlingsbote')—Very early bloomer, 15" tall.

'Roundabout'—Dwarf, 4"–6" tall, 8"–10" spread, mixed colors.

'Wee Willie'—6" tall, very early bloom, mixed colors.

Native to eastern Asia.   Annual

SCIENTIFIC NAME/FAMILY: *Dianthus plumarius*   Caryophyllaceae

(dī-an'thus plū-mā'ri-us)

COMMON NAME: Cottage Pink, Grass Pink, Garden Pink, Scotch Pink, Pheasant's-eye Pink.

LEAVES: Evergreen foliage forms a mat-like growth. Gray leaves are 1"–4" long, narrow, linear acute and keeled, creating a prominent midrib; margins are finely serrulate.

FLOWER: Rose, pink, white, or bicolored with a darker center. Flowers are fringed, single to semi-double, 1½" across, and fragrant.

HABIT: Dense and rounded habit, 10"–12" tall and 18"–24" wide.

SEASON OF BLOOM: Late spring to early summer.

CULTURE: Full sun and a well-drained alkaline soil is ideal. Cottage pink does not perform well in areas with excessively hot summers. Adding leaf mold or other types of composted material will help overcome dry summer conditions; however, the most rewarding growth will occur along the coasts, particularly to the north.

See color plate

UTILIZATION: Rock garden, edging, and in the perennial border.

PROPAGATION: Seed, cuttings, layering, and division. Seeds are easily germinated in 2 to 3 weeks at 70°, but resultant plants may not be true to type. Cuttings can be taken from vegetative shoots during early summer. Division is best done in the spring and is the propagation method used by most gardeners.

DISEASES AND INSECTS: Leaf spots of various genera cause problems when the weather is humid and the plants are crowded. Plants should be spaced to allow air circulation, and a fungicide should be used when necessary.

HARDINESS: Zones 3–9.

CULTIVARS:

'Aqua'—Fragrant, double white blossoms, 10" tall and 15" wide. This cultivar may be the same as the English pink 'Mrs. Sinkins.'

'Dad's Favorite'—Maroon and white flowers, long blooming, but with little fragrance and a straggly growth habit.

'Essex Witch'—Fragrant flowers in colors of pink, white, and salmon.

'Fadenkienz'—Pink flowers over blue foliage, 10" tall, slight clove fragrance.

'Horatio'—Double pink flower with darker eye, 6"–8" tall, moderate fragrance.

'Lady Granville'—Very fragrant, double white flower with burgundy eye and petal tips.

'Margaret Curtis'—Single white, unfringed flowers with burgundy eyes, 8" tall and 12" wide.

'Rainbow Loveliness' Strain—This selection comes true from seed. Flowers can be white to deep rose to lilac and so deeply fringed that they appear to have no centers. Flowers are very fragrant.

'Rose de Mai'—Very fragrant, long blooming, fringed, semi-double, pale pink flowers, 12" tall.

'Spring Beauty'—Fringed, double flowers, mixed colors, moderately fragrant.

RELATED SPECIES:

D. × *allwoodii* (àl-wood'-ē-i)—Allwood Pinks. This hybrid was developed by Montague Allwood of England, in the 1920s, by crossing *D. plumarius* and *D. caryophyllus*. It has the compact form of the cottage pink and is blessed with the wide range of color from the carnation. The following are some selections of this hybrid. Cultivars can be propagated true to name by cuttings, division, and layering. Zones 5–8.

'Agatha'—Purplish-pink, semi-double flowers, with crimson or scarlet eyes, fragrant. 8″ tall.

'Christopher'—Bright salmon, double flowers, 12″–15″ tall.

'Danielle' (also 'Danielle Marie')—Double coral-orange flowers, long bloom season, 15″ tall and 12″ wide. Listed as a sport of 'Helen.'

'David'—Scarlet flowers, unscented, profuse bloomer, 12″ tall.

'Doris'—A highly recommended cultivar with semi-double salmon-pink flowers with deep pink eyes. Useful as a cut flower and suitable for drying in silica gel for flower crafts. This 10″–12″ selection was introduced by Allwood before 1954.

'Helen'—Double salmon flowers, 8″–12″ tall. It is another popular cultivar introduced by Allwood before 1948.

'Her Majesty'—Large, double white flowers which are fragrant, 10″ tall.

'Ian'—Double red flowers with crimson petal tips, 15″–18″ tall.

'Laced Romeo'—Clove-scented rose-red flowers with cream edged tips, 12″ tall. Introduced by Allwood in 1963.

'Robin'—Bright coral-red flowers, unscented, 12″–18″ tall. It was introduced before 1927 and it is still a popular cultivar.

D. deltoides (del-toi'-dēs)—Maiden Pinks. Maiden pinks forms a wide-spreading mat of loose foliage which creates an excellent ground cover in full sun or partial shade. The flowers last for 8–10 weeks and literally cover the foliage. Additional growth and rebloom occurs if the plants are sheared after flowering. Flower color includes reds, roses, pinks, and whites. Hardy to zones 4–9.

'Albus'—White flowers.

'Brilliancy'—Dark scarlet flowers, 10″ tall. It is a hybrid between *D. deltoides* and *D. chinensis*.

'Brilliant'—Scarlet red flowers.

'Flashing Light' ('Leuchtfunk')—Carmine flowers, dense green foliage, 4″–6″ tall.

'Rosea'—Pink flowers.

'Vampire'—Bright red flowers and dark green foliage, 4″–6″.

D. gratianopolitanus (gra-ti-an-o-pō-li-a'-nus)—Cheddar Pinks. This low-growing species native to Cheddar Gorge in southwest England has glaucous blue-gray, linear foliage and fragrant single flowers. Cheddar pinks is hardy from zones 3 to 9 and is particularly effective in southern zones.

'Bath's Pink'—Pink flowers with fringed petal tips. This selection is one of the finest for southern gardens. Goodness Grows Nursery in Georgia obtained the original plant from Jane Bath, an Atlanta garden designer. The plant had been in her family gardens for many years.

'Karlick'—Fragrant single pink flowers with fringed petals.

'La Bourboule' ('La Bourbille')—Fragrant deeply fringed pink flowers.

'Oakington'—An Alan Bloom introduction with double pink flowers, 4″ tall.

'Petite'—Nice dwarf pink, 3″–4″ tall, with small pink flowers.

'Spotty'—James Fleming of Lincoln, Nebraska, developed this red and white bicolor.

'Tiny Rubies'—Double dark pink flowers, 4″ tall. This is a popular low-growing selection for use in the rock garden and the front of the border.

Native to Europe.   Perennial

SCIENTIFIC NAME/FAMILY: *Dicentra eximia*   Fumariaceae

(dī-sen'trȧ eks-im'-ē-a)

COMMON NAME: Fringed Bleeding-heart, Plume Bleeding-heart, Wild Bleeding-heart, Turkey Corn, Staggerweed

LEAVES: The finely dissected leaves are gray-blue in color. Basal leaves are ternately compound while the highly noticeable stem leaves are dissected. The leaf segments are broadly oblong or ovate.

FLOWER: The heart-shaped, pink to purple flowers are borne in compound racemes. The corolla tapers from a cordate base into a narrow apex, often separating below the middle. The flower scape is nearly as tall as the leaves.

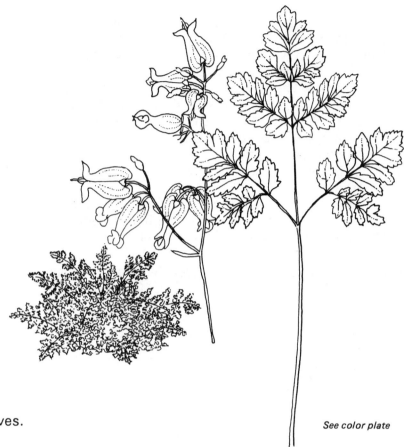

See color plate

HABIT: 12″ to 18″ tall and 18″ wide.

SEASON OF BLOOM: Peak bloom occurs in early summer but with good moisture, flowering continues into the fall. The flowering period is considerably longer than *Dicentra spectabilis.*

CULTURE: A partially shaded site and a well-drained humus soil are ideal. *Dicentra eximia* will not tolerate wet soils in winter or dry soils in summer. Full sun is suitable provided moisture is given during dry periods. The foliage will not die back as that of *Dicentra spectabilis.*

UTILIZATION: This beautiful specimen plant is suitable for the shaded border, the wild flower garden, the rock garden, and as a plant for cut flowers.

PROPAGATION: Division of the fibrous root system can be done in the spring every 3 to 4 years. Root cuttings in summer or fall is also an effective method. Fresh seed may germinate without any preconditioning. Older seed usually requires a warm-cold-warm stratification. It also has a tendency to reseed in the garden.

DISEASES AND INSECTS: Aphids can be an occasional problem.

HARDINESS: Zones 3–9.

CULTIVARS:

'Alba'—Pure white flowers and pale green foliage.

'Boothman's Variety'—Soft-pink flowers with blue-green foliage.

'Stuart Boothman'—Pink flowers with smokey-grey foliage, 16" tall.

There are some very fine cultivars for which the parentage is confusing. The following cultivars may be of *D. eximia, D. formosa,* or hybrids of the two species.

'Adrian Bloom'—Crimson-red flowers, blue-green foliage. It was selected by Alan Bloom as a seedling of 'Bountiful'.

'Baccharal'—The flowers of this hybrid are the darkest red of the cultivars.

'Bountiful'—Deep pink flowers, blue-green foliage. Flowers heavy in spring and autumn with intermittent blossoms during the summer.

'Luxuriant'—Flower buds cherry red, flowers red; blue-green foliage. Flowers intermittently until frost.

'Pearl Drops'—Pearl white flowers on glaucous foliage. This cultivar is the same as 'Langtrees.'

'Silver Smith'—Pure white flowers and blue-green foliage.

'Snowflakes'—White flowers, long bloom period.

'Zestful'—Pink flowers, 12"–15" tall.

Native to the mountain areas of New York and Pennsylvania to Georgia and Tennessee.

Perennial

SCIENTIFIC NAME/FAMILY: *Dicentra spectabilis*   Fumariaceae

(dī-sen'trȧ spek-tab'i-lis)

COMMON NAME: Japanese Bleeding Heart, Lyre Flower, Bleeding Heart

LEAVES: Leaves ternately compound or dissected, segments obovate or cuneate.

FLOWER: Flowers are arranged in simple secund racemes, to 9" long, flowers pendent to 1½" long, basally cordate, outer petals rose-red with tips reflected, inner ones white and exserted. It has been called by many "the living valentine."

HABIT: 2' to 3', branches and flowers create an arching effect. *Dicentra* has a round growth habit.

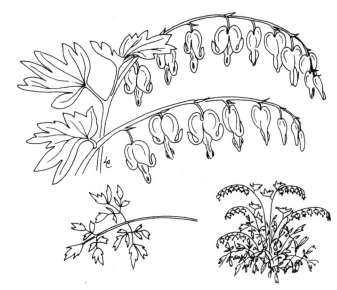

See color plate

SEASON OF BLOOM: Late spring to early summer.

CULTURE: Japanese bleeding heart requires partial shade and adequate moisture during the summer period. If the plants dry out, the foliage will yellow and disappear by early summer. The possible dormancy of this species is a major difference between it and *D. eximia* which does not go dormant during the summer.

UTILIZATION: This is an excellent plant for the shaded border or as a cut flower. Florists also force this bleeding heart in the greenhouse for an early spring flowering pot plant. Since the foliage may die after flowering in the border, a filler plant should be used to cover the bare area.

PROPAGATION: Seeds are sown in late summer for overwintering or they can be stratified for 6 weeks below 41°F before planting. Seeds will germinate in 3 to 4 weeks at 50°– 55°F. Divide clumps in spring or fall. Stem cutting can be rooted if taken in spring after flowering. Root cuttings may also be taken in early spring and set 2" deep in the propagation bench.

DISEASES AND INSECTS: Stem rot, storage rot, wilt.

HARDINESS: Zones 2–9.

CULTIVARS:
'Alba'—White flowers, not as vigorous as the species. 'Pantaloons' is another white that may be a selection of 'Alba'.

ADDITIONAL NOTES: An old-fashioned species which has been a garden favorite for years and will grow strongly for anyone. *Dicentra* is from *dis,* twice, and *kentron,* a spur, which refers to the shape of the corolla. *D. eximia,* in my opinion, is superior to *D. spectabilis* because of the longer flowering season. It has remained in bloom until mid-October at the State of Georgia Botanic Garden, Athens, Georgia.

Native to Asia and North America.   Perennial

SCIENTIFIC NAME/FAMILY: *Dictamnus albus (D. fraxinella)*   Rutaceae

(dik-tam'nus al'bus)

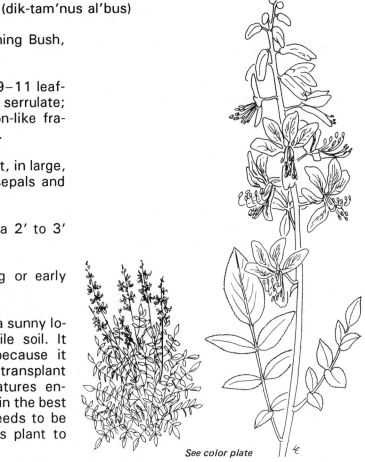

COMMON NAME: Gas Plant, Burning Bush, Dittany, Fraxinella

LEAVES: Alternate, odd pinnate, 9–11 leaf-lets, up to 3″ long, ovate, serrulate; leaves give off a strong lemon-like fragrance when they are crushed.

FLOWER: White, pink or rose-violet, in large, showy, terminal racemes, 5 sepals and petals, 10 stamens.

HABIT: 2′ to 3′ erect plant with a 2′ to 3′ spread.

SEASON OF BLOOM: Late spring or early summer.

CULTURE: Best growth occurs in a sunny location and a moderately fertile soil. It should be left undisturbed because it grows slowly and does not transplant well. Cool nighttime temperatures enhance growth. However, even in the best of conditions, the gardener needs to be patient while he waits for gas plant to reach a mature size.

See color plate

UTILIZATION: Specimen plant in perennial border, glossy green foliage can be used as background, and the seed pods are attractive.

PROPAGATION: Gas plant can be propagated from seed but the process is difficult and time consuming. One method is to cold stratify the seeds for 6–8 weeks before sowing. Some seedlings may emerge but the germination process is long and seeds will continue to germinate for a long period of time. Some nurseries simply harvest the seeds in the fall, sow in seed flats, and place the flats outside during the winter. The natural forces of cold and heat seem to do a good job in promoting germination. Root cuttings taken from dormant plants can also be used for commercial propagation Division is possible but unwise as *Dictamnus* does not transplant well and should not be disturbed after establishment.

DISEASES AND INSECTS: Gas plant is generally pest free.

HARDINESS: Zones 3–9.

CULTIVARS:
var. *purpureus*—Purplish-pink flowers with darker veins on the petals.

ADDITIONAL NOTES: The common name of gas plant is derived from the ability of the plant to exude a volatile gas just beneath the flowers. On a calm summer evening, one is supposedly able to ignite the gas with a match to create a brief blue flame without damage to the flower. The foliage and flowers can cause severe dermatitis on susceptible individuals.

Native to Europe.   Perennial

SCIENTIFIC NAME/FAMILY: *Digitalis grandiflora* (D. ambigua)   Scrophulariaceae

(dij-i-tā'lis, dij-i-ta'lis gran-di-flō'ra)

COMMON NAME: Yellow Foxglove

LEAVES: Leaves are alternate, ovate-lanceolate to 8" long with a serrate margin. The leaves near the base are the largest and they become smaller and sessile as they ascend the stem.

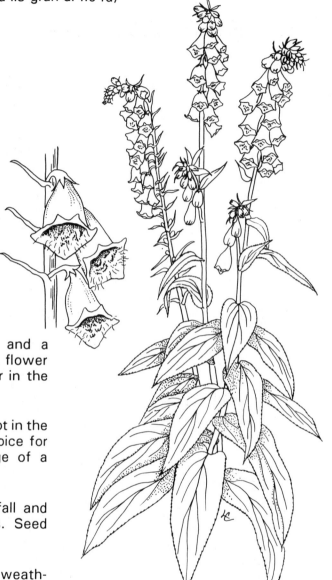

FLOWER: Flowers are large, pendulous and borne in 8"–12" long terminal racemes. The yellow trumpet-shaped corolla is 2"–3" long marked with brown on the interior.

HABIT: 2'–3' tall clump-forming perennial, 18" wide.

SEASON OF BLOOM: Summer.

CULTURE: Easily grown in partial shade and a fertile, well-drained soil. Remove dead flower stalks to promote possible rebloom later in the summer.

UTILIZATION: Yellow foxglove is certainly not in the top 10 of perennials but it is a good choice for the partially shaded border or the edge of a wooded garden.

PROPAGATION: Division in the spring or fall and seed are suitable propagation methods. Seed germinates well at 70°–75°F.

DISEASES AND INSECTS: In hot and humid weather, mildew and leaf spot have been noted as problems.

HARDINESS: Zones 3–8.

CULTIVARS:
'Dropmore Yellow'—There appears to be little difference between this cultivar and the species. It may be more floriferous but other differences are slight. It is not readily available in the United States.

RELATED SPECIES:
D. lutea (lu-te-a)—Small Yellow Foxglove. This species is similar to *D. grandiflora* with some minor differences. The leaves of *D. grandiflora* are sessile while those of *D. lutea* are petioled. The flowers of *D. lutea* are smaller and do not have the brown markings found with *D. grandiflora*. Small yellow foxglove is 2'–3' tall and 12" wide. Propagation is similar to *D. grandiflora*.

Native to Europe.   Perennial

SCIENTIFIC NAME/FAMILY: *Digitalis purpurea*   Scrophulariaceae

(dij-i-tā'lis, dij-i-tal'-is pēr-pū'rē-á)

COMMON NAME: Foxglove, Finger Flower, Fairy Glove, Purple Foxglove.

LEAVES: Alternate, leaves rugose, somewhat downy, the radical ones long-stalked and ovate, the stem leaves short-stalked or sessile, becoming small toward top of stem.

FLOWER: Flowers large, pendulous; borne in a one-sided raceme 1'–2' long, corolla 3" long, purple or sometimes pink, white, rusty or yellow, throat generally spotted, lobes ciliate.

HABIT: 2' to 5' erect plant with basal leaves.

SEASON OF BLOOM: Late spring to early summer.

CULTURE: Partial shade in moist, well-drained locations. Best growth occurs in acid soil with abundant humus and moisture. Foxglove becomes "very tired looking" if grown in dry soils.

UTILIZATION: Border plant, woodlands, natural settings.

PROPAGATION: Seeds sown in late summer will produce plants that flower the following summer. (Seeds germinate best at 70°–80°F and should be exposed to light.) Division of perennial types are best made in the spring.

DISEASES AND INSECTS: Powdery mildew, leaf spot, root and stem rots, aphids, Japanese beetle, mealy bug.

HARDINESS: Zone 4 to zone 9, a good plant for southern gardens.

CULTIVARS:
var. *alba*—White flowers, a good choice for brightening the shade areas of the garden.
'Excelsior Hybrids'—Flowers are borne all around the spike, rather than on one side. Flowers are available in pastel shades of pink, mauve, yellow or white, 3'–5' tall.
'Foxy'—Can be used as an annual, plants started in the greenhouse will flower the first summer, 30"–40" tall.
'Shirley Hybrids'—Many different flower colors, but the flowers are borne on only one side of the spike, 3'–5' tall.

RELATED SPECIES:
D. × *mertonensis* (mer-ton-en'sis)—Strawberry Foxglove. This hybrid was developed by crossing *D. purpurea* × *D. grandiflora*. The coppery-pink flowers are larger than either species, a result of the tetraploid characteristic of the plant. Plants are 3'–4' tall and 2' wide. Division after flowering should be done every two years to maintain plant vigor. Zones 3 to 8.

ADDITIONAL NOTES: Although *Digitalis purpurea* is a biennial, it self sows and remains in the garden much like the hollyhock. *Digitalis* in Latin means finger of a glove, and refers to the shape of the flowers. The common name is connected with English superstitions of fairies. Fox is a corruption of folk, hence little folks gloves, or, more specifically, fairy gloves. The heart stimulant, digitalis, is derived from this plant.

Native to Europe and North Africa.   Biennial

SCIENTIFIC NAME/FAMILY: *Dimorphotheca sinuata*
          (Dimorphoteca sinuata)

Asteraceae
(Compositae)

(dī-môr-fō-thē′kȧ sin-ū-ā′tȧ)

See color plate

COMMON NAME: Cape Marigold, African Daisy

LEAVES: Leaves alternate, oblong to oblanceolate, about 3″ long, coarsely sinuate-dentate, upper leaves oblanceolate.

FLOWER: Heads to 1½″ across, disk flowers yellow, ray flowers orange-yellow, sometimes deep violet at base. Heads are solitary on long peduncles. Other colors are white, salmon, and rose.

HABIT: 12″ to 15″ round habit.

SEASON OF BLOOM: Late spring to fall.

CULTURE: Full sun and well-drained soil. Does well in hot, dry areas.

UTILIZATION: Border plant, bedding, useful as cut flowers but they do close at night.

PROPAGATION: Seed should be germinated at 70°F, and should be covered.

DISEASES AND INSECTS: Blight, downy mildew, rust, aster yellows, and leafhoppers can occur but none are serious problems.

CULTIVARS:
    'Aurantiaca Mixture'—12″ tall, 3½″ single flowers in bright yellow, buff, and orange shades.
    'Glistening White'—8″ tall, 3½″ pure white flowers surround a shiny black center.
    'Orange Improved'—12″ tall, flowers early with 3″ deep orange flowers.
    'Salmon Beauty'—12″ tall, deep salmon-pink flowers.

ADDITIONAL NOTES: Cape Marigold is a minor bedding plant and is grown as a tropical perennial in South Africa. *Dimorphotheca* is derived from the Greek words *dis,* twice; *morphe,* shape; and *theba,* fruit, which refers to the 2 types of fruit found in the flower head. A closely related species (*Osteospermum*) is grown as a perennial in many gardens in England. There are many hybrid cultivars of white, pink, blue, and yellow that brighten the mixed borders during the summer. I have seen little *Osteospermum* used in the United States.

Native to South Africa

Annual

SCIENTIFIC NAME/FAMILY: *Disporum lanuginosum*   Convallariaceae
(Liliaceae)

(dī-spō'rum là-nū-ji-nō'sum)

COMMON NAME: Fairy Bells,
Yellow Mandarin

LEAVES: The alternate leaves are ovate to oblong-ovate, 2" to 4" long. The simple, dark leaves are sessile or clasping to the stem. Leaves have an attractive leathery texture, are slightly downy on the lower leaf surface and have parallel veins.

FLOWER: The 1" long flowers are lemon-yellow, bell-shaped, and are either solitary or borne in a small, umbel cluster.

HABIT: 2' to 3' tall, erect plant with spears of bamboo-like stems topped by the nodding flower clusters.

SEASON OF BLOOM: Spring.

CULTURE: Partial shade to shade conditions, moist, well-drained soil and a soil pH of 5.0–6.0 are conditions for optimum growth.

UTILIZATION: Woodland garden or the partially shaded border. This species is one of our less available native plants.

PROPAGATION: Taking divisions from the ever-increasing clumps in the spring is an easy propagation method.

DISEASES AND INSECTS: No serious problems.

HARDINESS: Zones 3–8.

RELATED SPECIES:
   D. maculatum (mak-ū-lā'-tum)—Nodding Mandarin. This species is similar but the flowers are speckled white and are showier than *D. lanuginosum.* The required growing conditions are the same.

ADDITIONAL NOTES: *Disporum* is derived from *dis,* meaning two, and *spora,* meaning seeds, and is in reference to the paired ovules.

Native to eastern North America.   Perennial

SCIENTIFIC NAME/FAMILY: *Disporum sessile* 'Variegatum'   Convallariaceae
(Liliaceae)

(dī-spō'rum ses'il var-i-e-gā'-tum)

COMMON NAME: Variegated Japanese Fairy Bells

LEAVES: The bamboo-like stems are slightly zig-zag and are erect. The ovate to lance-shaped leaves are up to 4″ long and are carried sessile to the stem. Most of the leaves are edged in white with the variegation sometimes running down the veins.

FLOWER: Greenish-white flowers, 1″ long, borne solitary or in 2's or 3's.

HABIT: Erect stems create a mounded habit 12″ to 24″ tall.

SEASON OF BLOOM: Spring.

CULTURE: See *D. lanuginosum*.

UTILIZATION: The variegated leaves are a better asset than the green-white flowers. Good plant for the partially shaded border or woodland garden.

PROPAGATION: Division in the spring.

DISEASES AND INSECTS: None serious.

HARDINESS: Zones 4–8.

Native to Japan.   Perennial

See color plate

SCIENTIFIC NAME/FAMILY: *Dodecatheon meadia*   Primulaceae

(dō-dē-kath'ē-on mē'dē-a)

COMMON NAME: Common Shooting-star

LEAVES: Leaves ovate to spatulate, obtuse tips, 6″ to 9″ long, narrowed into a winged petiole. Leaf margins are usually entire.

FLOWER: The flowers are arranged in an 8 to 20 flowered umbel that terminates a stout scape 9″ to 18″ tall. The nodding flowers have 5 reflexed petals. The stamens are attached at the throat of the corolla and the anthers converge into a cone. Flower colors can be white, pink, lavender, or purple.

HABIT: Shooting-star has a basal foliage clump which resembles a clump of spinach. Three or four flower peduncles rise from the clump 9″–18″.

SEASON OF BLOOM: Late spring.

CULTURE: Shooting-star is native to a woodland site and best growth will occur if the site chosen closely mimics the native habitat. The best site is in partial to full shade in a well-drained, but constantly moist, humus-enriched soil. The foliage dies back during the summer season. Water must not stand on the crown during winter.

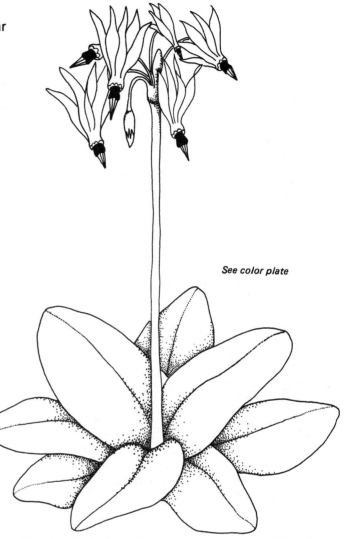

See color plate

UTILIZATION: Excellent plant for the shaded woodland garden and rock garden. Since the foliage goes dormant in the summer, a cover of foam flower *(Tiarella)* would be effective.

PROPAGATION: Fall division of the dormant plant is an easy method. Seed germination can be erratic due to a requirement for low temperature stratification.

DISEASES AND INSECTS: There are no insect or disease problems.

HARDINESS: Zones 4–8.

CULTIVARS:
    forma *alba*—White flower, 12″.

Native to eastern United States.   Perennial

SCIENTIFIC NAME/FAMILY: *Doronicum orientale* (*D. caucasicum*)   Asteraceae
(Compositae)

(dō-ron'i-kum ôr-i-en-tā'le)

COMMON NAME: Leopardsbane

See color plate

LEAVES: Alternate, basal leaves long-petioled, deeply cordate. The stem leaves are of two types: lower leaves are petiolate and subcordate, while the upper stem leaves are ovate, cordate-clasping with those near the flower linear-lanceolate. All leaves are coarsely dentate.

FLOWER: Yellow, solitary head, 2″ across on a peduncle 12″–15″ long.

HABIT: 18″–24″ tall and 12″–18″ wide.

SEASON OF BLOOM: Early to mid-spring.

CULTURE: Leopardsbane can be placed in the sun in cool climates but requires partial shade in hot climates. It is shallow rooted so the soil should be cool and moist. A mulch will help in this regard. It is important to keep the soil moist during periods of drought.

UTILIZATION: Useful in the perennial border and as a cut flower. It is very effective when combined with *Myosotis* for the spring border. Leopardsbane should not be massed because the leaves deteriorate during the summer and a void is left. Best planted near perennials with spreading foliage so the space will be filled in during the summer.

PROPAGATION: Seed and division. Best germination occurs when seeds are lighted and provided a 70°F temperature. Plants are easily divided in the spring or after flowering.

DISEASES AND INSECTS: There are few diseases or insects that affect leopardsbane. Powdery mildew, crescent-marked lily aphid, and sawfly have been reported, but they are not common.

HARDINESS: Zones 4–7. *Doronicum* is not heat tolerant and performs poorly in southern zones.

CULTIVARS:

'Finesse'—Yellow-orange flowers with slender ray flowers, 15″–18″ tall. It is a 1976 introduction by Benary which comes true from seed.

'Magnificum'—Large yellow flowers, 24″–30″ tall, early bloom. This cultivar also comes true from seed.

× 'Miss Mason' ('Mme. Mason')—This hybrid of *D. orientale* × *D. austriacum* has more persistent foliage than the species. It has an early bloom and a longer flowering period. Cutting back may encourage a second bloom.

'Spring Beauty' ('Fruhlingspracht')—This 15″–18″ cultivar has golden-yellow flowers. It was introduced by H. Hagemann of Germany in 1962. A very nice cultivar that should be in the garden.

ADDITIONAL NOTES: The common name leopardsbane arose because arrows were once dipped in the juice of one species for hunting leopards.

Native to southeastern Europe.

Perennial

SCIENTIFIC NAME/FAMILY: *Dryopteris cristata* (Aspidium cristatum)   Aspleniaceae
(Polypodiaceae)

(drī-op'tēr-is kris-tā'tà)

COMMON NAME: Crested Shield Fern, Common Shield Fern

FRONDS: The fronds are 18" to 30" long, 3" to 6" wide and twice pinnate. The pinnae of fertile fronds turn toward the apex of the frond, making each frond appear as a staircase.

SORI: The sori (fruit-dots) are large, round, rusty-brown, and borne halfway between the midrib and the margin.

HABIT: Erect fern, 18" to 30" tall. The fertile fronds are more erect than the sterile fronds.

CULTURE: Grow this species in a lightly shaded area with a moist soil.

UTILIZATION: Good species for a wet, shady area.

PROPAGATION: This species is propagated by clump division or spores.

DISEASES AND INSECTS: None serious.

HARDINESS: Zones 3 to 7. In zones 6 and 7 the fronds are evergreen.

ADDITIONAL NOTES: Native to wet areas from Newfoundland to Kentucky.

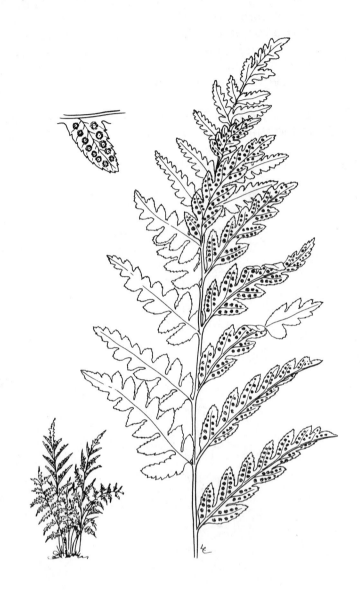

Perennial

SCIENTIFIC NAME/FAMILY: *Dryopteris erythrosora*   Aspleniaceae
                                                                (Polypodiaceae)

(drī-op′tēr-is er-i-thrō′sor-à)

COMMON NAME: Autumn
   Fern, Japanese Red
   Shield Fern

FRONDS: Fronds can be 30″
   long, 8″−12″ wide and
   twice pinnate. The ex-
   panding leaf buds (cro-
   siers) are first a copper-
   pink color, later unfolding
   to shades of bronze-
   green, and at maturity a
   dark shiny green. In fact,
   the common name, Au-
   tumn fern, is due to the
   autumn-like color of the
   new fronds. The stalk
   and rachis are covered
   with dark brown or black
   scales.

SORI: The sori are circular
   and arranged along the
   midrib of the pinnules.

HABIT: Erect fern with out-
   ward-curving fronds, 3
   feet tall.

CULTURE: This fern requires
   a loose, well-drained soil
   that is moist and enriched with humus. Open shade is an ideal light exposure. This fern
   is best in garden soils that never dry out.

UTILIZATION: Autumn fern is a good choice for a specimen plant in the woodland garden
   or the Japanese formal garden. The colors of the developing fronds is a striking feature.

PROPAGATION: Spores and division.

DISEASES AND INSECTS: No problems.

HARDINESS: Zones 5−8.

Naive to Japan and China.   Perennial

SCIENTIFIC NAME/FAMILY: *Dryopteris marginalis*   Aspleniaceae
(Polypodiaceae)

(drī-op'tēr-is mar-ji-nā'lis)

COMMON NAME: Marginal Shield-fern

FRONDS: Evergreen fronds are lanceolate to ovate-oblong, bipinnate, 15" to 20" long and 5"–8" wide. The fronds have a leathery texture. There are brown scales on the petiole and rachis.

SORI: The species name, marginalis, refers to the location of the sori on the edge of the pinnae.

HABIT: The fronds are clustered in a vase-like arrangement in a symmetrical fashion. Fronds are 18" to 24" tall.

CULTURE: The best location for this species is a cool, shady site which is protected from sun and drying winds. The soil should be moist and enriched with humus.

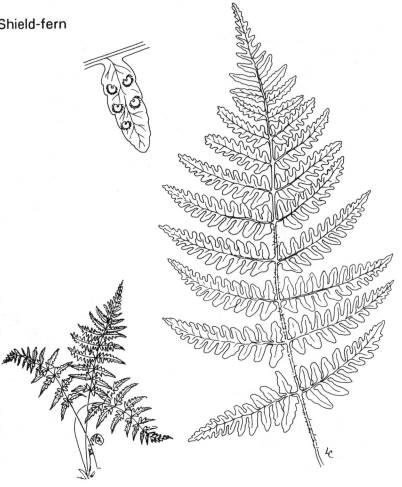

UTILIZATION: The evergreen foliage allows marginal shield-fern to be used as a year-round feature in the shaded rock garden or woodland garden. The deep green color of the fronds compliments the colors of most wildflowers, especially the whites and reds.

PROPAGATION: Spores may be collected in late summer. Small crowns found near the main rosette can be carefully separated and transplanted.

DISEASES AND INSECTS: No problems.

HARDINESS: Zones 3 to 8.

ADDITIONAL NOTES: Marginal shield fern is found from Nova Scotia to Minnesota and south to Alabama and Oklahoma.

Perennial

SCIENTIFIC NAME/FAMILY: *Dryopteris carthusiana* (*Aspidium spinulosum*) Aspleniaceae
(Polypodiaceae)

(drī-op'tēr-is kar-thōō'-si-a-na)

COMMON NAME: Toothed Wood Fern

FRONDS: Fronds are oblong-
ovate, two to three pin-
nate, 2' to 3' long and 4"
to 6" wide. The pinnules
on the lower side are
longer than those on the
upper side. The stalk has
brown chaff.

SORI: The brown sori are
round and are equally
distributed on each side
of the midvein.

HABIT: Erect fern with out-
ward-curving fronds.

CULTURE: Best growth oc-
curs in partial shade, in
moist and acid soils.

UTILIZATION: Toothed wood
fern makes an attractive
accent plant or massed in
a woodland setting.

PROPAGATION: Clump divi-
sion and spores are the
propagation methods.

DISEASES AND INSECTS:
No problems.

HARDINESS: Zone 3 to 8.

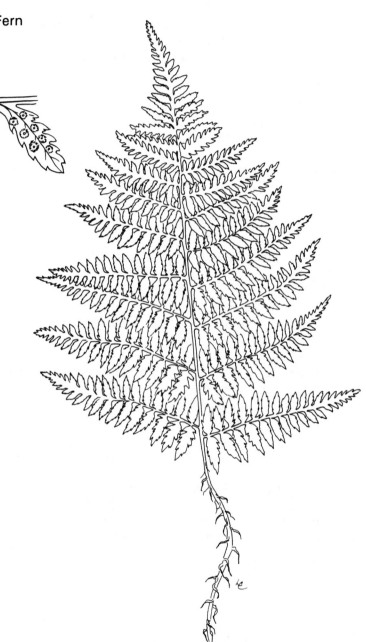

ADDITIONAL NOTES: Toothed wood fern is native from Labrador and Newfoundland to
Idaho, and south to North Carolina.

Perennial

SCIENTIFIC NAME/FAMILY: *Dyssodia tenuiloba*   Asteraceae
(Compositae)

(dis-od'ē-à ten-ū-i-lōb'à)

COMMON NAME: Dahlberg Daisy, Golden-Fleece

LEAVES: Lower leaves opposite, upper ones alternate ¾" long, pinnately parted into 7–11 linear-filiform, bristle-tipped segments, margins glandular.

FLOWER: Heads to ½" across, disk flowers yellow, ray flowers golden-yellow-orange. Flowers are small and dainty.

HABIT: Spreading habit, 6"–8" tall and 15"–18" wide.

SEASON OF BLOOM: All summer.

CULTURE: Full sun, well-drained soil; takes heat well.

UTILIZATION: Dahlberg daisy is an excellent plant for edging, bedding, or hanging baskets.

PROPAGATION: Flowering from seed propagation in 4 months. May be started indoors to take advantage of the long blooming season. Germinating temperature is 65°–70°F.

See color plate

DISEASES AND INSECTS: May get aster yellows, but generally not a common problem.

ADDITIONAL NOTES: Dahlberg daisy is refined, neat, and always in flower. Useful for low edgings, variety in the border, and for bright garden accents. It is a minor bedding plant that performs consistently well but remains unknown and seldom used. I enjoy seeing lesser-known plants tastefully used as it really adds variety to the landscape.

Native to south central Texas and Mexico.   Annual

SCIENTIFIC NAME/FAMILY: *Echinacea purpurea*
(Rudbeckia purpurea)

Asteraceae
(Compositae)

(ek-i-nā′sē-ȧ pĕr-pū′rē-ȧ)

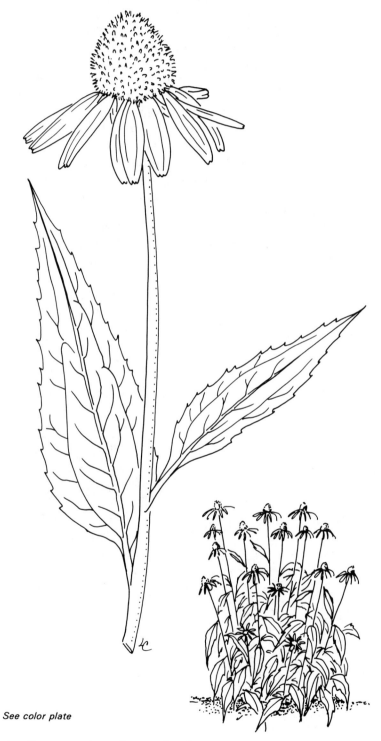

See color plate

COMMON NAME: Purple Coneflower, Hedge Coneflower, Black Sampson, Purple Echinacea, Purple Rudbeckia.

LEAVES: Alternate, lower leaves ovate to broadly lanceolate, coarsely toothed, long-petioled, upper stem leaves narrower, nearly entire, sessile. Leaves are 4″–8″ long and dark green.

FLOWER: Heads solitary on stout terminal peduncles, rays purple, sometimes white, spreading or drooping; disk flowers, brown cone. The flowers always remind me of purple badminton birds (shuttlecocks).

HABIT: 2′ to 4′ erect plant, 2′ wide.

SEASON OF BLOOM: Summer.

CULTURE: Full sun, drought resistant; best in a well-drained soil. Light shade will enhance the richer colors in hot weather.

UTILIZATION: Border, cutflower, and naturalized area. Soft-textured plants should be planted nearby to offset the rigid texture of the purple coneflower.

PROPAGATION: Clump division in the spring every 4 years. Root cuttings have also been successful, particularly in commercial situations. Seeds do not come true to type and take 2 or more years to flower.

DISEASES AND INSECTS: Leaf spots and Japanese beetle.

HARDINESS: Zones 3 to 8. The *Echinacea* that I observed at various gardens in zone 8 were excellent.

CULTIVARS:

'Abendsonne'—This German cultivar was used by Alan Bloom to produce a number of seedlings from which he chose 'Robert Bloom'. Other seedlings were grown on to create 'Bressingham Hybrids' which have light rose to red flowers.

'Alba'—Cream-white flowers, seed grown selection.

'Bright Star'—Bright rose-red, 2"–3", daisy-like flowers with maroon centers, plants 2'–3' tall, does not produce well from root cuttings.

'Crimson Star'—Crimson-red flowers, 24"–30" tall. It is a new release from Springbrook Gardens, Mentor, Ohio.

'Robert Bloom'—Vigorous, free-branching plant, carmine-purple flowers with orange centers, plants are 2'–3' tall.

'Magnus'—Rosy-purple flowers with broad, non-drooping petals.

'The King'—Coral-crimson flowers with maroon or brown centers, This cultivar was popular in earlier years but it has now been superseded by better cultivars like 'Robert Bloom'.

'White Lustre'—Coarse leaves and dull white rays, leaves tend to reflex, prolific bloomer even in dry areas. Good performance in zone 8.

'White Swan'—White flowers, 2'–3' tall, excellent as a cutflower.

ADDITIONAL NOTES: The stiff and coarse habit of *Echinacea* fits well in a naturalized area. *Echinacea,* is derived from a Greek term for hedgehog, which apparently refers to the scales of the receptacles, which are prickly.

Native to eastern United States.   Perennial

SCIENTIFIC NAME/FAMILY: *Echinops ritro*

Asteraceae
(Compositae)

(ek'i-nops rī'tro)

COMMON NAME: Small Globe Thistle

LEAVES: Alternate, pinnatifid into lanceolate, acuminate, spinose-toothed segments, the upper surface rough and setose and deep green; the lower surface white tomentose, basal leaves much larger and petioled. Leaves are thistle-like with spiny tips.

FLOWER: Heads 1½"–2" across, dark blue, on tomentose peduncles, outer bristle-like bracts about half as long as the acuminate inner bracts. The flower heads provide a nice color long before the actual flowers open, which prolongs the flowering season.

HABIT: 3' to 4' erect plant with a 2'–3' width.

SEASON OF BLOOM: Summer for 6–8 weeks.

CULTURE: Full sun and well-drained soil. Although globe thistle will tolerate partial shade, best results are obtained in full sun. Flower color is more intense in areas with cool nights.

UTILIZATION: Cut and dried flowers, border, or specimen plant. Flowers will retain blue color if they are cut just as the flower starts to open. The flowers are attractive to bees.

PROPAGATION: Clump division or root cuttings in spring. Plants will flower the same season. Seeds may be sown in the spring but inferior types often result. Seeds will germinate in 1 to 4 weeks at 68°–75°F.

DISEASES AND INSECTS: Easily grown with no serious pests.

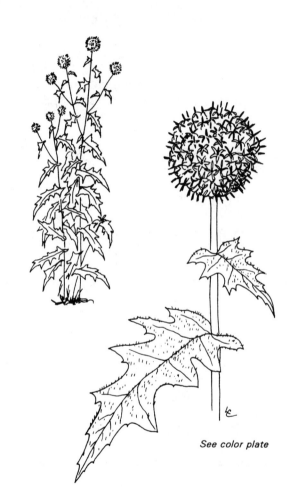

See color plate

HARDINESS: Zones 3–8. *Echinops* is a perennial that tolerates hot climates; consequently, it performs well in southern areas.

CULTIVARS:
  'Taplow Blue'—Excellent cultivar, steel-blue flower heads with a silvery overcast, up to 3" in diameter. Plants are 4'–5' tall.
  'Taplow Purple'—Violet-blue flowers which are not as ornamental as those of 'Taplow Blue'.
  'Veitch's Blue'—Steel blue flowers which are darker than 'Taplow Blue'. There are numerous flower heads on stems 3'–3½' tall.

ADDITIONAL NOTES: Group smaller plants around the base of globe thistle to conceal the lower foliage, which usually deteriorates. *Echinops* in Greek means "like a hedgehog" and refers to the spiny involucral bracts.

Native to southeastern Europe.

Perennial

SCIENTIFIC NAME/FAMILY: *Elymus arenarius* (glaucus)   Poaceae
                                                            (Gramineae)

(el'-i-mus ar-ē-nā'ri-us)

COMMON NAME: Blue Lyme Grass, Blue Wild Rye

LEAVES: The leaf blades are 18" to 24" long, ¾"
   wide, flat or inrolled, rigid and sharply pointed.
   Leaves are rough on the upper surface and
   smooth beneath. Margins are minutely hairy.
   The foliage has a light blue-gray color.

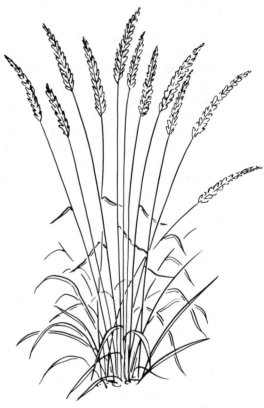

FLOWER: The flowers are produced in a stiff,
   compact spike that is 6"–12" long and ½" to
   1" wide. Flowers are blue-gray, becoming buff
   to brown with age. When mature, they resemble the fruit spikes of wheat.

HABIT: Large tuft overtopped by stiff wheat-like
   spikes, 2' to 3' tall.

SEASON OF BLOOM: Midsummer.

CULTURE: Full sun in most soil types, moist, wet,
   or dry. It can be invasive if grown in light soils.
   Bottomless containers can be placed in the soil
   around the roots to help prevent spread.

UTILIZATION: It is grown mainly for the foliage   *See color plate*
   color, the flowers are not outstanding. If
   contained, it can be grown in a border. How-
ever, a more likely utilization would be a naturalized area or in bank stabilization
situations. In these sites, the spreading roots are an advantage. It is too invasive for the
small garden.

PROPAGATION: Division in the spring or fall.

DISEASES AND INSECTS: No problem.

HARDINESS: Zones 4–9.

ADDITIONAL NOTES: Lyme grass is a dune grass of North America. In disturbed beach
   areas of the Outer Banks in North Carolina, lyme grass has been replanted to stabilize
   the sand dunes.

Native to Europe.   Perennial

SCIENTIFIC NAME/FAMILY: *Epimedium × rubrum*   Berberidaceae
(E. alpinum var. rubrum)

(ep-i-mē'di-um ru'brum)

COMMON NAME: Red Barrenwort

LEAVES: Leaves basal and cauline, usually biternate, leaflets
ovate, acuminate, serrate margin, base cordate.

FLOWER: Crimson flower, flushed
with red or yellow, inflorescence compound with 10–20
flowers; flowers 1″ across,
spurs slightly upturned.

HABIT: 8″–12″ tall and 12″
wide, mounded growth habit.

SEASON OF BLOOM: Midspring.

CULTURE: Optimum growth occurs in partial to full shade in
moist soils containing copious
amounts of organic matter.
Dry conditions should be
avoided. The old foliage should
be clipped back in early spring
to allow full appreciation of
the flowers.

See color plate

UTILIZATION: Rock garden, perennial border and as a ground cover for shade. The last use
is probably the one of prime interest. *Epimedium* will grow quite well under trees, a
situation in which few other perennials will perform well. The semi-evergreen foliage
is red in the spring. Clumps increase slowly so initially spacing should not be more than
12″ apart. Although slow to establish, *Epimedium* is an excellent ground cover at
maturity.

PROPAGATION: Division can be done in spring or fall.

DISEASES AND INSECTS: This plant is generally pest free.

HARDINESS: Zones 4–8.

RELATED SPECIES:
   E. grandiflorum (gran-di-flō'rum)—Longspur Epimedium. 12″ tall, pink flowers; one of
      the largest species. 'Rose Queen' has large, spurred flowers which are dark pink.
      The new foliage is reddish and matures to a dark green. 'White Queen' has silvery-
      white flowers. 'Lilofee' is a new cultivar from Pagels in Germany which is 12″ tall
      and has purple flowers. Zones 5–8.
   E. × perralchicum (per-ral-kē'kum) 'Frohnleiten'.—This hybrid selected in Germany is
      8″–12″ tall. The yellow flowers are held well above the foliage on very narrow
      stems. Zones 5–8.

E. pinnatum (pin-nā'tum)—Persian Epimedium. Yellow flowers, 8"–12" tall. This species forms a dense mat of almost evergreen, all basal foliage. The entire plant is hairy. The var. *colchicum* is grown for its larger flowers.

E. × *versicolor* (ver'-si-col-or)—Bicolor Barrenwort. This cross between *E. grandiflorum* and *E. pinnatum* var. *colchicum* is 10"–12" tall with yellow flowers. The cultivar 'Sulphureum' is one of the best epimediums available and tends to tolerate dry, shady situations better than others. 'Versicolor', 8"–10" tall has mauve-pink flowers with a pale yellow center. Zones 5–8.

E. × *warleyense* (war-lē-yen'-se). This hybrid is 8"–10" tall and forms a loose mat of foliage. It is more suited for the wild garden than the role of a tidy ground cover. The flower has a brownish-coppery color which is a different color than found in other epimediums.

E. × *youngianum* (yung-ē-ā'-num)—Young's Barrenwort. Cultivars of this hybrid tend to be the shortest barrenworts with heights of 6"–8". 'Niveum' has white flowers and 'Roseum' has rose to lilac colored flowers. Both are fine selections for small gardens. This white flowering species is smaller than other *Epimedium,* about 8" tall.

Hybrid origin.   Perennial

SCIENTIFIC NAME/FAMILY: *Equisetum hyemale*   Equisetaceae

(ek-wi-sē'tum hī-e-mā'-lē)

COMMON NAME: Scouring Rush, Horsetail

LEAVES: The leaves of the horsetail family are scale-like and are marginally united into a sheath around each node. The obvious feature of scouring rush is the evergreen stem which is hollow, conspicuously jointed and furrowed by many ridges. The stems look like bamboo canes without leaves.

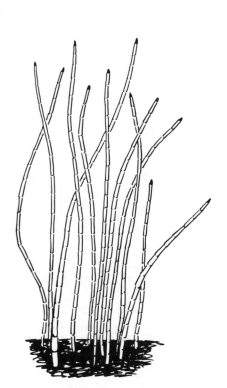

FLOWER: The flowering structure of *Equisetum* is the sporophyll borne at the stem terminal. The flower is not ornamentally important.

HABIT: The stems grow in a very erect habit, 3' to 5' tall.

SEASON OF BLOOM: Not important.

CULTURE: Scouring rush can be grown in sun or partial shade in moist to wet soil.

UTILIZATION: Horsetail is useful for moist to wet areas either in water gardens or at the edge of pools and streams. It can be used as a striking accent plant. However, caution is needed as horsetail is aggressively stoloniferous. It can be planted in a sunken pot which will contain the stoloniferous growth.

PROPAGATION: It is easily propagated by division.

DISEASES AND INSECTS: None serious.

HARDINESS: Zones 4–9.

ADDITIONAL NOTES: *Equisetum* is from *equus,* horse, and *seta,* bristle. The barren stems supposedly made one think of a horse's tail.

Native to Europe, Asia, and North America.   Perennial

SCIENTIFIC NAME/FAMILY: *Eranthis hyemalis*   Ranunculaceae

(ē-ran'this hī-e-mā'lis)

COMMON NAME: Winter Aconite

LEAVES: Leaves mostly basal from the tuber, leaves orbicular, long-petioled, palmately dissected nearly to the base, these segments again lobed, cauline leaf beneath the single flower forms an involucre.

FLOWER: Yellow, sessile, about 1" wide, equalled or exceeded by the calyx-like involucre. Flowers resemble those of buttercup.

HABIT: 3" to 6" erect plant.

SEASON OF BLOOM: Late winter to early spring.

See color plate

CULTURE: Partial shade to full sun. Plants in full sun should be planted in moist soil. *Eranthis* is easily grown if the soil is well-drained, cool, and moderately moist. Consequently, growth is often best in cool, shaded areas. Tubers should be planted in early fall so that they will become well rooted before winter. Plant tubers 3" deep and 6" apart and mulch well.

UTILIZATION: *Eranthis* is best displayed in masses, excellent in naturalized areas or the sunny slope for very early spring bloom. There is a sloping bank at the Tyler Arboretum near Philadelphia that looks like a yellow carpet in the early spring.

PROPAGATION: Seed and division. Seed is sown in June and July and may take 8–9 months to germinate. It will be 4 years before one can expect blooms. Tubers will not need disturbance for several years, after which time they can be lifted and cut into several pieces. Under favorable conditions *Eranthis* will also self-sow, which helps increase the display.

DISEASES AND INSECTS: None serious.

HARDINESS: Zones 3–7.

ADDITIONAL NOTES: *Eranthis* is derived from the Greek *er,* spring, and *anthos,* flower, meaning the flower of spring. Winter aconite flowers very early, often when snow is still on the ground.

Native to Europe and Siberia.   Perennial—hardy bulb

SCIENTIFIC NAME/FAMILY: *Erianthus ravennae*   Poaceae
(Gramineae)

(er-i-an'thus rav-en-nā'e)

COMMON NAME: Plume Grass, Ravenna Grass

LEAVES: Leaf blades are 24"
to 30" long, 1" wide, V-
shaped in cross section,
narrowing abruptly to an
attenuated point. The
leaves are coarsely pubescent on both surfaces. A
clear white stripe runs
down the middle of the
leaf.

FLOWER: The plume is silver,
changing to gray as it
matures. The inflorescence
can be 24" long and up to
9" wide. The lower portion
of the panicle is very hairy.

HABIT: Upright habit, 10'–14'
tall. A mature clump of
Ravenna grass can have
30–40 stalks rising to 14'.
It is certainly a dominant
accent plant.

SEASON OF BLOOM: Late
summer.

CULTURE: Full sun and a very
well-drained soil. Heavy
clay soils that remain wet
will reduce vigor and possible survival.

UTILIZATION: This species has a good architectural form as well as having flowers suitable
for drying. It can be used as a specimen, for an accent, or screening. It is considered
by many as a northern substitute for pampas grass *(Cortaderia selloana).* The plumes
are narrower than those of pampas grass. The flower stalks should be removed in early
winter before they fall over. The foliage may be left until early spring.

PROPAGATION: Division in the spring.

DISEASES AND INSECTS: No serious problems.

HARDINESS: Zones 5–9.

Native to southern Europe.   Perennial

SCIENTIFIC NAME/FAMILY: *Erigeron* hybrids

Asteraceae
(Compositae)

(ē-rig′ēr-on or ē-rij′-er-on)

COMMON NAME: Fleabane

LEAVES: Alternate, leaves glabrous except for ciliate margins, lower leaves oblanceolate to spatulate, narrowed to winged petioles, uppermost leaves mostly lanceolate, sessile.

FLOWER: Heads 1″–1½″ across, borne at the tips of the corymbosely clustered branchlets, rays are very numerous and are violet-blue; disk flowers are yellow.

HABIT: 1½′ to 2′ erect plant with a 2′ spread.

SEASON OF BLOOM: Midsummer with sporadic flowers into the fall.

CULTURE: Full sun, well-drained soil and only moderately fertile. Good drainage is a requirement.

UTILIZATION: Cut flowers, rock gardens. In perennial borders the plants should be in groups of at least three. Fleabanes are good plants to try in light sandy soils.

See color plate

PROPAGATION: *Erigeron* can be propagated by clump division, cuttings, and seed. Seed germinates in 2 weeks when held at 70°–75°F. Division should be done in the fall every 2–3 years. Shoot tip cuttings should be taken before flower buds form.

DISEASES AND INSECTS: Downy mildew, powdery mildew, leaf spots, rusts, and aphids.

HARDINESS: Zones 2–8.

CULTIVARS: The following cultivars are hybrids resulting from 4 different parents: *E. speciosus*, *E. speciosus.* var. *macranthus*, *E. glaucus* and *E. aurantiacus*.
'Adria'—Very large, violet-blue flowers, 24″ tall.
'Azure Fairy'—Semi-double lavender-blue flowers, 30″ tall.
'Dominator'—Dark purple flowers, 24″ tall.

'Dunkelste Aller' ('Darkest of All')—Violet-blue flowers, slightly lighter than 'Dominator', 24″ tall. This is a widely used cultivar.

'Elstead Pink'—Light pink flowers, 12″–18″ tall.

'Foerster's Liebling'—Bright pink semi-double flowers, excellent as a cut flower, 18″–24″ tall. (Also listed as 'Foerster's Darling'.)

'Prosperity'—Lavender blue flowers, 18″ tall.

'Rosa Triumph'—Rosy pink, semi-double flowers, 24″ tall.

'Rotes Meer' ('Red Sea')—Red flowers, 24″ tall.

'Sommerabend' ('Summer Night')—Single, lavender flowers, 24″ tall.

'Sommerneuschnee' ('New Summer Snow')—White flowers with a pink blush, prolific bloomer, 24″ tall.

'Strahlenmeer' ('Shining Sea')—Light violet flowers, 24″–30″ tall.

'Wuppertal'—Lilac flowers, 24″ tall.

ADDITIONAL NOTES: Flowers are similar to the fall asters. Fleabanes are much more popular in Europe than in the United States. Frequent removal of old blossoms will prolong the blooming season. The genus *Erigeron* goes way back to Theophrastus, and in Greek means "old man in spring." This is in reference to the downy young leaves of several species.

Native to Oregon and British Columbia.   Perennial

SCIENTIFIC NAME/FAMILY: *Erodium reichardii* (E. chamaedryoides)   Geraniaceae

(ē-rō'di-um rikh ard'-ē-ī)

COMMON NAME: Heronsbill, Storksbill

LEAVES: Leaves are round to ovate, deeply crenate; 1" – 2" in length with a very long petiole. Leaves have a sparse, hispid pubescence.

FLOWER: Solitary white flowers with rosy veins are borne very close to the foliage. The flowers are 1/3" wide.

HABIT: Dense cluster of foliage creates a hummock that is 2"–3" tall and 6"–9" wide.

SEASON OF BLOOM: Late spring to early summer.

CULTURE: The members of the *Erodium* genus are often found in well-drained, gravelly loam soils in full sun. Too much moisture is fatal to this alpine plant.

UTILIZATION: Heronsbill is a natural for the rock garden, trough garden, or the dry stone wall. In well-drained soils, it can also be used as an edging plant along the walk or front of the border.

PROPAGATION: This species can be increased by seed or root cuttings. Take 1"–2" root pieces in March.

DISEASES AND INSECTS: None serious.

HARDINESS: The listed hardiness of this species varies from Zone 5 to Zone 7. The difference is due to the small size of heronsbill which allows it to be insulated by snow in colder regions. In areas absent of snow the hardiness is reduced considerably.

CULTIVARS:
'Album'—White flowers. Zone 7.
'Roseum'—Pink flowers, darker venation. This cultivar is probably most available. Zone 7.
'Roseum Plenum'—Double pink flowers, 10 petals instead of the normal 5 petals. Zone 7.

RELATED SPECIES:

E. chrysanthum (kris-anth'-um)—Silvery foliage highlights this 5″ tall clump. Flowers are yellow, and male and female flowers are found on separate plants. Late spring bloomer. Often grown for foliage alone. Rare but available from a few nurseries. Zone 6.

E. petraeum ssp. *crispum* (pe-trī'um kri'spum) (*E. chelanthifolium*)—Light grey foliage, white flowers with pink veins, 8″ tall. Zone 6.

E. petraeum ssp. *glandulosum* (gland-ū-lō'sum) (*E. macradenum*)—Lacy green foliage with deep pink flowers with dark venation, 8″ tall. Zone 6.

E. 'David Crocker'—Siskiyou Rare Plant Nursery, Medford, Oregon, lists this selected seedling. It has very silvery foliage, white flowers with a raspberry-pink blotch in the center. They feel that it is similar to *E. petraeum* ssp. *crispum.*

ADDITIONAL NOTES: There are 60 species of *Erodium* with only a few in cultivation. Many of the cultivated selections are only of interest to plant collectors. Selections of *Erodium reichardii* are most common.

Native to Corsica and Balearic Islands.   Perennial

SCIENTIFIC NAME/FAMILY: *Eryngium amethystinum*   Apiaceae
(Umbelliferae)

(e-rin'ji-um a-me-this'ti-num)

COMMON NAME: Amethyst Sea
Holly, Sea Holly, Eryngo

LEAVES: Rigid, obovate or oblong-
ovate, bipinnatifid, spinulose-
toothed, lower leaves with long
petioles; upper leaves, clasping,
pinnately parted, spinose-toothed.
Leaves are deeply cut and spiny.

FLOWER: Heads ovoid-globose, ½"
or more long, blue; bracts are long
and lanceolate.

HABIT: 1½' to 2', erect plant that
seldom requires staking.

SEASON OF BLOOM: Midsummer.

See color plate

CULTURE: Full sun in sandy, dry areas, particularly during the winter. This plant is the
solution for those dry, sunny, infertile, sandy loam soils.

UTILIZATION: Single specimen or in three's; massing is not effective. Sea holly has a bold
texture. It can also be used for dried floral arrangements.

PROPAGATION: Division, but plant develops long tap root so transplanting is difficult.
Seeds may be germinated in 1–2 weeks at 65°–75°F.

DISEASES AND INSECTS: Sea-holly is relatively pest free.

HARDINESS: Zones 3–8.

RELATED SPECIES: *E. planum* (pla'num). 3' tall with blue flowers, heart-shaped leaves.
Best planted in naturalistic areas. Many nurseries incorrectly label *E. planum* as
E. amethystinum. E. planum is taller and has less interesting flowers and lacks the
colorful stems of *E. amethystinum.* Zones 5–9.

ADDITIONAL NOTES: The sea-holly probably deserves more frequent cultivation because
of its tolerance to dry sandy areas. The unique flower provides an interesting subject
for dried floral arrangements. Flowers picked when fully open will retain their color
when dried. *Eryngium* is Greek for thistle.

There are over 200 species of *Eryngium* which are found mainly in Mediterranean regions.
Perennial

SCIENTIFIC NAME/FAMILY: *Eryngium bourgatii*   Apiaceae
(Umbelliferae)

(e-rin'ji-um boor-ga'-tē-i)

COMMON NAME: Mediterranean Sea Holly, Mediterranean Eryngo

See color plate

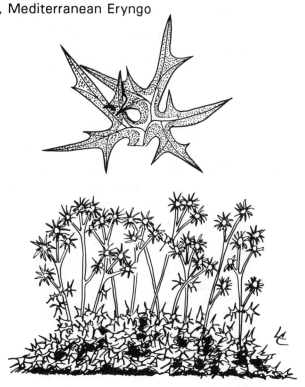

LEAVES: The alternate leaves are of two types. The basal leaves are nearly orbicular, 2" wide, palmately parted in 3 to 5 lobes nearly to the leaf base. Leaf segments are 3 lobed and spinose toothed. Stem leaves are sessile and deeply dissected. All leaves are white veined.

FLOWER: Blue flower heads are 3/4" long and are surrounded by 9 to 15 involucral bracts which are unequal in length. Bracts can be entire with a pointed tip or have sparse spines on the margin. The bracts create a very unusual and attractive collar around the teasel-like flower head.

HABIT: 18"–24" tall and 18"–24" wide.

SEASON OF BLOOM: Summer.

CULTURE: Same as *E. amethystinum.*

UTILIZATION: The white-veined foliage is the classy ornamental feature; the flowers are of secondary importance. Use in the border for summer foliage effect.

PROPAGATION: Division is possible but the long tap root will make transplant success difficult. Propagation by root cuttings is possible and is the commercial method for the species not coming true from seed. Seeds should be moistened and kept warm for 2 to 4 weeks at 68°–72°F. After this period, place in cold for 4–6 weeks at 36° to 40°F. After the cold period, raise the temperature to 65° to 75°F.

DISEASES AND INSECTS: None serious. (No insect would want to tackle the rigid, spiny leaves!)

HARDINESS: Zones 5–8.

CULTIVARS:
    'Oxford Blue'—Deep silver-blue flower heads.

RELATED SPECIES:
    E. alpinum (al-pi'num)—Bluetop Sea Holly, Alpine Sea Holly. This species has the finest
        flowers of the *Eryngium* genus. The attractive flowers are composed of large blue
        cones surrounded by frilled blue involucral bracts. The bracts are feather-like
        compared to the stiff bracts on other sea holly. The cut flowers of the species and
        its cultivars are excellent and will last at least two weeks in water. Optimum growth
        occurs in full sun and well-drained soil. This species is 18"–24" tall and 24" wide.
        Zones 4–8.
    'Amethyst'—Metallic blue flowers, 30"–36" tall.
    'Blue Star'—This cultivar may be the best sea holly for cut flowers. It has a deep
        blue inflorescence to which nothing else compares. I was first introduced to this
        cultivar in 1992 when I visited the nursery of Gunter Fuss in Konigslutter,
        Germany. It is my hope that 'Blue Star' will make its way to the United States
        where it could be used as a cut flower or in the border.
    'Opal'—Similar to 'Amethyst', only shorter at 2 feet.
    'Superbum'—Dark blue flowers, 24"–36" tall.

    E. giganteum (ji-gan-te'um; ji-gan'-te-um)—Stout Sea Holly. The silver bracts of this
        species are like spiny holly leaves rather than the narrow, spine-tipped bracts of
        other species. It is a biennial but often performs as a perennial because it self-seeds.
        The plant may change location from year to year due to the self-seeding habit. It is
        4'–6' tall and 4' wide. Zones 4–8.

Native to Europe.   Perennial

SCIENTIFIC NAME/FAMILY: *Erysimum asperum* (Cheiranthus allionii)   Brassicaceae (Cruciferae)

(e-ris'i-mum as-per'-um)

COMMON NAME: Siberian Wallflower, Alpine Wallflower, Blister Cress

LEAVES: Alternate, lanceolate, to 3" long, acute, tapering at both ends, often bunched beneath the flowers. Leaves and stems have an appressed pubescence and have a grayish cast similar to *Matthiola incana* 'Annua'.

FLOWER: Yellow or orange flowers borne in terminal racemes. *Erysimum* is a member of the Brassicaceae family; consequently, each flower has 4 petals.

HABIT: 15" to 18", erect growing plant.

SEASON OF BLOOM: Midspring.

CULTURE: Full sun or light shade, well-drained soil. Plants should be cut back after flowering.

UTILIZATION: The early spring fragrance and bright color of this plant make it a desired plant for the border or as a rock garden addition.

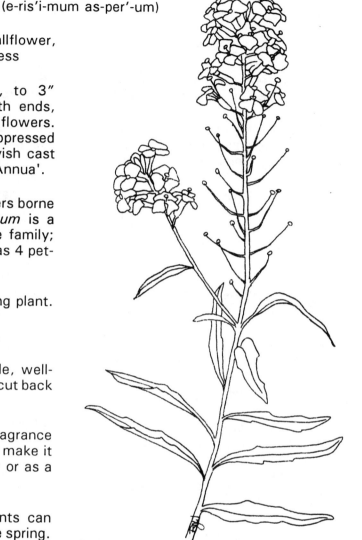

PROPAGATION: Established plants can be multiplied by division in the spring. For biennial use, seed can be sown outside in late summer or started inside at a temperature of 55°–65°F for 1 week.

DISEASES AND INSECTS: Bacterial wilt, club root, gray mold, and white rust.

HARDINESS: Zones 3–7.

RELATED SPECIES:
E. linifolium (li-nif-o'le-um)—Alpine Erysimum. This species has purple flowers which places it as the odd man out since most wallflowers have yellow to orange colors. The stems are 12" long and carry narrow gray green leaves that are evergreen in milder climates. The flowers are a nice beginning for the spring season. 'Variegatum' has variegated foliage and lilac flowers. *Erysimum linifolium* can be propagated by seed, by division in the fall, or tip cuttings taken after flowering. Zones 5–8.

ADDITIONAL NOTES: *Erysimum asperum* is very similar to *Cheiranthus cheiri* which is the English wall flower. The two genera differ slightly in ovary and fruit characters. Some plant catalogs list *Cheiranthus cheiri* as the genus for Siberian wallflower. *Erysimum* in Greek means blister-forming. Some species of this genus are said to produce blisters.

Native to Rocky Mountains.   Perennial, but often treated as a biennial

SCIENTIFIC NAME/FAMILY: *Erythronium americanum*   Liliaceae

(er-i-thrō'ni-um a-mer-i-kā'num)

COMMON NAME: American Trout Lily, Dog-tooth Violet, Adder's Tongue, Fawn Lily

LEAVES: Each corm produces 2 leaves which are 4"–8" tall, oblong or spatulate with an acute tip. They are conspicuously mottled with maroon-purple spots.

FLOWER: A 1" to 2" wide, nodding, yellow lily-shaped flower is borne atop a single stalk. The sepals are yellow on the inside and purple on the back. The petals are also yellow but have a purple streak on the mid-rib.

HABIT: The erect leaves and flower stalks create a small clump 6"–9" tall. Self sowing may eventually form drifts of this native species.

SEASON OF BLOOM: Mid to late spring.

CULTURE: Trout lily is a native species that should be grown in the moist to damp shade garden at a preferred pH of 5 to 6. Soil preparation will include adding copious amounts of humus or other types of organic matter.

UTILIZATION: *Erythronium* is a natural for the wild garden. It is planted for its interesting mottled leaves and early development in the garden. It is best to interplant trout lily with other plants such as hardy ferns so there is interest in the garden during the later spring and summer.

PROPAGATION: Propagation by seed is enhanced by using fresh seed and alternating warm-cold-warm temperatures. Start the seed in moist, warm temperatures, 70°–75°F for 4–6 weeks. Transfer to cool storage at 30°–35°F for 4–6 weeks and then place in warm temperatures. This cycle is similar to the natural fall, winter, spring cycle found in nature. It will take 4 years to develop a flowering plant from seed. Offsets can be obtained from mature plants which will take 2 years to reach flowering size.

DISEASES AND INSECTS: No serious problems.

HARDINESS: Zones 3–8.

RELATED SPECIES:

E. albidum (al'-bi-dum), White Trout Lily. The nodding flowers are a gleaming white with a blush of yellow at the base. It is 6"–12" tall. The leaves of this selection are narrower than *E. americanum.* The corms produce stolons so drifts can be established.

E. dens-canis (dens-ka'-nis), Dog Tooth Violet. This native of central Europe has been cultivated since 1596 and is commonly grown in Europe. It is a shorter growing species, 4" to 6" tall, purple. Cultivars include:

'Charmer'—White flowers mottled with purple.

'Frans Hals'—The outside petals are purple with a greenish-bronze basal spot.

'Lilac Wonder'—Purple petals with a chocolate-brown basal spot.

'Pink Perfection'—Clear bright pink flowers.

'Purple King'—Mauve flowers are edged with white and the centers have dark brown spots.

'White Splendor'—Large white flowers.

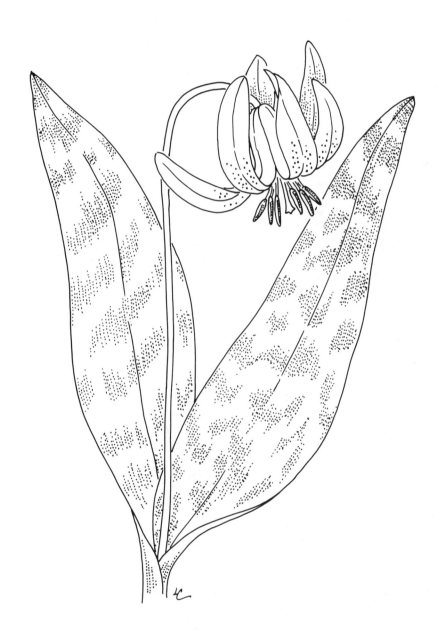

ADDITIONAL NOTES: Some people have suggested the common name fawn lily because the two leaves suggest the ears of a fawn. Others proposed trout lily because the leaf spots were mindful of trout markings.

Native to eastern North America.   Perennial

SCIENTIFIC NAME/FAMILY: *Eschscholzia californica*   Papaveraceae

(e-shōl'si-à kal-i-fôr'ni-kà)

COMMON NAME: California Poppy

See color plate

LEAVES: Leaves alternate, ternately dissected into linear or oblong segments, long-petioled, glabrous, mostly basal. Foliage is blue-gray-green.

FLOWER: Flowers deep orange to pale yellow, petals ¾"–2½" long, rim of receptacle expanded. Other colors available are bronze, scarlet, rose or white.

HABIT: 12" to 15" round habit with an equal spread.

SEASON OF BLOOM: Summer.

CULTURE: Full sun, well-drained sandy soil. Will tolerate some shade and will grow in quite dry and otherwise adverse sites.

UTILIZATION: Bed, border, naturalized areas.

PROPAGATION: Plants will bloom 45 to 60 days from seed. The plants will often self-sow, particularly in mild climates where it performs as a perennial. Although seeds can be germinated in 2 weeks at 70°F, they are hard to transplant. I have also seen plants that have self-sown at Dawes Arboretum, Newark, Ohio.

DISEASES AND INSECTS: Usually none, although bacterial blight, leaf mold and powdery mildew are sometimes reported.

CULTIVARS:
'Ballerina Mixed'—3" fluted blossoms, bright mixed colors.
'Dalli'—This 1991 Fleuroselect Gold Medal winner has bicolored flowers with scarlet petals and yellow centers. It is more compact than other California poppies.
'Mission Bells'—12", double and semi-double, crinkled margins, various color combinations as well as solid colors.
'Monarch Mixed'—This mixture has single and semi-double flowers with colors of red, orange, pink, and yellow.
'Thai Silk Mixed'—Flower petals have a silky, fluted form and wavy edges. Colors include red, pink, orange and gold.

ADDITIONAL NOTES: The plant is easy to grow with attractive foliage and very brightly colored flowers. The colorless juice is reported to be mildly narcotic and to have been used by Indians in California as a toothache remedy. *Eschscholzia* is named after Dr. Eschscholtz, a naturalist and physician, who was part of a Russian botanical expedition to the United States in 1815–1818.

Native to California and Oregon.

Perennial in mild climates; performs as an annual in northern areas.

SCIENTIFIC NAME/FAMILY: *Eupatorium coelestinum*   Asteraceae
(Compositae)

(ū-pȧ-tō′ri-um sē-les′ti-num)

COMMON NAME: Mist-flower, Hardy Ageratum,
Blue Boneset

LEAVES: Opposite, triangular-ovate, 1½"–3"
long, obtuse or acute, truncate or abruptly
contracted at the base, coarsely toothed.

FLOWER: Heads in compact clusters, 35–70
flowers, each flower about ½" across, in
dense corymbs. Flowers are bluish purple and
look very much like the flowers of Mexican
ageratum.

HABIT: 24" tall erect habit with a spread of
18"–24".

SEASON OF BLOOM: Midsummer to frost.

CULTURE: Best performance occurs when planted in full sun and soils with moisture. Cutting
back several times during the summer will
promote lateral breaks creating a fuller habit.

UTILIZATION: Cutting flowers and late season
bloom are the chief merits of this rangy
looking plant. Frequent division is needed to
prevent the plant from spreading. Staking
may also be required.

PROPAGATION: Clump division in the spring is
the usual and easiest method. Seeds require
moist, cold stratification for 4–6 weeks. Tip
cuttings in the spring can also be used.

DISEASES AND INSECTS: Powdery mildew, aphids and leaf miner.

HARDINESS: Zones 5–10.

CULTIVARS:
'Alba'—White flowers.

ADDITIONAL NOTES: Plant spreads very easily, so it is best to keep it away from choice
perennials. Blooms in late summer and early autumn when it is difficult to find showy
perennials. Excellent color combination with yellow or white chrysanthemums. Plants
appear late in the spring, so early cultivation should be done with care so the shallow
roots are not damaged. *Eupatorium* is named for Mithridates Eupator, ancient king of
Pontus, who was said to have employed one of the eupatoriums for medicinal use.

Native to eastern United States.   Perennial

SCIENTIFIC NAME/FAMILY: *Eupatorium purpureum*

Asteraceae
(Compositae)

(ū-pȧ-tō'ri-um pur-pur'-e-um)

COMMON NAME: Joe-Pye Weed

LEAVES: The leaves of this American native are whorled, with usually 3 to 5 leaves at each node. The 8"–12" long leaves are strongly serrated and have lanceolate shapes. The stems are canelike and often are purple at the nodes. The related species *Eupatorium maculatum* has purple spotted and mottled stems. Crushed foliage has a vanilla scent.

FLOWER: Many small individual purple flowers combine together to create large terminal corymb-like panicles that can be up to 18" in diameter.

HABIT: This giant of the garden reaches dimensions of 5–7 feet tall and 3–4 feet wide. If grown in the shade, the height can be greater than 7 feet.

SEASON OF BLOOM: Late summer and fall.

CULTURE: Joe-pye weed responds best to full sun and abundant moisture. Plants in dry sites will show scorch and an overall lack of vigor. Although tall, it will respond to heavy pruning in June, which will reduce the ultimate size. I have seen this done effectively at Saul Nurseries near Atlanta, Georgia. After early pruning, they had plants that were flowering at 4 feet.

UTILIZATION: This is a very effective plant for naturalizing in the landscape, especially near water. It is also a good companion plant to ornamental grasses and perennials such as *Rudbeckia nitida* found in wide borders. Joe-Pye weed is a magnificent structural plant from the distance.

PROPAGATION: Plants can be divided in the spring on a 3 year rotation. Seed germination improves with cold treatment.

DISEASES AND INSECTS: This species is not tolerant of high summer temperature. There are usually no serious pest problems.

HARDINESS: Zones 4–9.

RELATED SPECIES:
 maculatum (mak-ū-lā'-tum) 'Atropurpureum'. Plants in the nursery industry sold as Joe-pye weed are probably this species. It is about the same height as Joe-pye weed but the stems are purple spotted and mottled. The flower heads contain nearly twice as many flowers as *Eupatorium purpureum.*
 maculatum 'Gateway'. This cultivar is smaller, 5–6 feet, with large mauve-pink flowers at the top of reddish stems.

ADDITIONAL NOTES: Until recently, Joe-pye weed was not considered to be of garden merit, especially since it was commonly seen on the moist roadsides in eastern United States. *Eupatorium purpureum* is another example of an American native that has made good in Great Britain but does not have a loyal following in North America.

Native to eastern North America.

Perennial

See color plate

SCIENTIFIC NAME/FAMILY: *Euphorbia characias* ssp. *wulfenii*   Euphorbiaceae

(ū-fôr'bi-á kar-a-sī'-as wul-fe'-nē-i)

COMMON NAME: Mediterranean Euphorbia

LEAVES: The evergreen leaves are arranged in close spirals on the thick, pithy stems. The blue green, glaucous, leaves are alternately arranged, oblong lanceolate, 4" long, and taper to a short petiole.

FLOWER: The clustered flowers make round to cylindrical dense masses of chartreuse to lime green colors. They appear to be huge lime green bottle brushes terminating each stem. This color remains with little fading until the seeds ripen.

HABIT: Upright stems create a dome-shaped plant that can be 4 feet tall and 3 feet wide. Spacing should be at 3 feet.

SEASON OF BLOOM: Late winter to early spring.

CULTURE: This *Euphorbia* can be grown in full sun and a well-drained soil. It is fairly drought resistant. When the flowers are faded, late spring, the flower stem should be cut out at the base, which makes way for the new shoots which are emerging.

UTILIZATION: This shrubby evergreen perennial can be used in the border for year round effect in those regions that have a climate similar to the Mediterranean.

PROPAGATION: Terminal cuttings taken after flowering can be used.

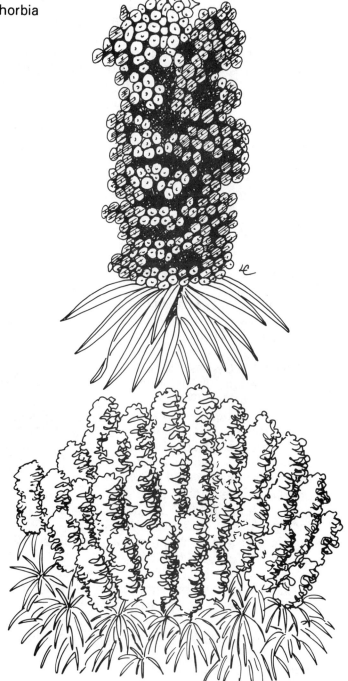

See color plate

DISEASES AND INSECTS: There are no serious problems.

HARDINESS: Zones 8–9.

CULTIVARS:
  'Lambrook Gold'—The bracts of this selection by Margery Fish are almost golden. An excellent cultivar but relatively unavailable.

Native to western Mediterranean.   Shrubby evergreen perennial

SCIENTIFIC NAME/FAMILY: *Euphorbia cyparissias*   Euphorbiaceae

(ū-fôr′bi-á sī-pár-iss′ē-ás)

COMMON NAME: Cypress Spurge

LEAVES: Numerous leaves, linear, to 1 ½″ long, entire, floral leaves whorled and ovate-cordate, very soft foliage, milky sap exudes from broken stems or foliage.

FLOWER: Yellowish flowers in many-rayed umbels; as the flowers mature, the color becomes purplish to reddish.

HABIT: 10″ to 12″ spreading habit.

SEASON OF BLOOM: Mid to late spring.

CULTURE: Full sun, does well on dry banks where little else will grow. *Euphorbia* becomes invasive when grown in moist, fertile soil.

UTILIZATION: Cypress spurge can spread rapidly by underground stems. This invasiveness tendency limits the use of this species. It can be considered of value when it is planted in soils where other perennials would grow poorly. I have seen it effectively used on dry, south facing slopes. It cannot be considered a suitable plant for the border unless annual division is done. The foliage dies to the ground in the winter.

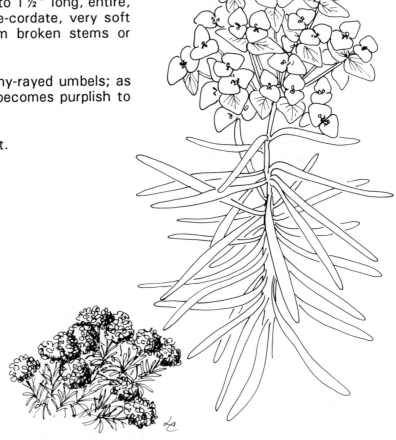

See color plate

PROPAGATION: Cypress spurge can be left undisturbed indefinitely if it does not become invasive. It may be carefully divided in spring or fall.

DISEASES AND INSECTS: Blight is sometimes a problem of the flowers and foliage.

HARDINESS: Zones 4–8.

RELATED SPECIES:
   E. corollata (kō-rōl-lā′-ta), Flowering Spurge. 1′–3′ tall, with numerous white bracts in summer. It resembles baby's-breath and provides the same fine-textured effect. Leaves turn red in the fall. Zones 4–9.
   E. marginata (mar-jin-ā′-ta), Snow-on-the-Mountain. 1 ½′ tall, green leaves marked with white. At one time a popular annual in many gardens, but it is often now considered a weedy annual. The latex is sometimes corrosive to the skin and may cause burns.

ADDITIONAL NOTES: Needle-like leaves create an effect of a large bottlebrush. *Euphorbia* honors Euphorbus, the physician to a Mauritanian emperor.

Native to Europe.   Perennial

SCIENTIFIC NAME/FAMILY: *Euphorbia griffithii*   Euphorbiaceae

(ū-fôr'bi-á grif'ith-e-i)

COMMON NAME: Griffith's Spurge

LEAVES: The alternate leaves are sessile, lanceolate, with a pinkish to reddish midrib, 3" to 4" long. Fall color can be yellow to red.

FLOWER: The flowers are borne in terminal cymes with orange-red tinged bracts. As found with many *Euphorbia*, the bracts create the noticeable "flower color."

HABIT: Erect plant with a mounded outline, 2'–3' high. It should be spaced at 2 feet.

SEASON OF BLOOM: Early summer.

CULTURE: This *Euphorbia* performs best in partial shade in southern zones and will tolerate full sun in northern sites. It is important to grow this perennial in moist, well-drained soils. It does creep by rhizomes but the spread is not excessive.

UTILIZATION: Griffith's spurge is a bold plant, useful for warm color schemes. It can be used in the middle or back of the border or island bed. Even after the colorful bracts fade, the gardener is left with a mounded herbaceous shrub that graces the garden through the remainder of the summer.

See color plate

PROPAGATION: This species can be propagated from seed at 70°F. The cultivars should be propagated by terminal cuttings in midsummer.

DISEASES AND INSECTS: No serious problems.

HARDINESS: Zones 5–8.

CULTIVARS:
'Dixter'—The foliage has a reddish blush on the back of the leaves and veins. The bracts are a brilliant orange-red. It came to commerce from the garden of Christopher Lloyd at Great Dixter, Northiam, England. Mr. Lloyd may have obtained it from Miss Hilda Davenport-Jones of England. It is not as common as the following cultivar.
'Fireglow'—This selection has fiery-orange bracts, red midveins, and orange-brown stems. It was introduced by Alan Bloom in 1954. In his book, *Hardy Perennials,* he discussed that *E. griffithii* started to be sold in the early 1950s but it was a leggy grower with weak stems. To build up stock, he raised some from seed. In this group of plants, he found one with sturdier stems and deep orange bracts. He gave it the name of 'Fireglow'.

Native to the Himalayas.   Perennial

SCIENTIFIC NAME/FAMILY: *Euphorbia myrsinites*   Euphorbiaceae

(ū-fôr'bi-à mir-sin-ī'tēz)

COMMON NAME: Myrtle Euphorbia

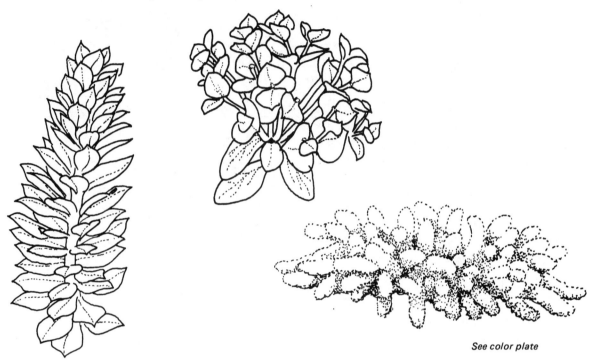

See color plate

LEAVES: The fleshy, glaucous blue-green leaves are borne in close spirals which resemble a whorled leaf arrangement. Individual leaves are obovate to obovate-oblong, ½" long, abruptly short-mucronate, and sessile. The leaves remain on the plant during the winter and retain their blue-green attractiveness when protected from winter sun and wind.

FLOWER: Unisexual flowers are contained in several cyathia in 7–12 rayed umbels. The greenish flowers, which are inconspicuous, are subtended by attractive pale yellow bracts.

HABIT: 6"–8" prostrate plant with 12"–18" long trailing stems.

SEASON OF BLOOM: Spring.

CULTURE: Full sun and a well-drained soil, preferably on the dry side. Plant hardiness is increased when grown in well-drained sites.

UTILIZATION: Although one can find *Euphorbia myrsinites* used in the perennial border, it is especially suitable for rock outcroppings such as rock gardens, rock walls, and stone retaining walls. The foliage is especially effective when the stems can trail over the wall.

PROPAGATION: Division and seed are normal propagation methods. Division in the spring should be done carefully so there is a minimum damage to the thick, fleshy roots. Seed can be sown in the fall or early spring. Smaller seedlings are easier to dig and transplant than larger established plants.

DISEASES AND INSECTS: None serious.

HARDINESS: Zones 5–9.

Native to Mediterranean region.   Perennial

SCIENTIFIC NAME/FAMILY: *Euphorbia polychroma* (*E. epithymoides*)   Euphorbiaceae

(ū-fôr'bi-à pol-e-kro'ma)

See color plate

COMMON NAME: Cushion Euphorbia, Cushion Spurge

LEAVES: Alternate leaves, oblong to 2", entire, short petioled or sessile, and oblong-ovate. The foliage remains green during the summer and turns a dark red in autumn. A milky sap exudes from broken stems or foliage.

FLOWER: The flowers of *Euphorbia* are borne in a cyathium. The cyathia are produced in umbel-like cymes which are borne terminally on the stem. The greenish unisexual flowers have no petals or sepals and are inconspicuous. The showy portion of the inflorescence is created by the 1" wide, brightly colored chartreuse-yellow, involucral bracts.

HABIT: 12"–18" symmetrical mound-like plant that is 18" wide.

SEASON OF BLOOM: Spring.

CULTURE: Full sun and well-drained soil. This plant does best when the soil is kept somewhat dry. A moist, fertile soil may promote invasiveness. Cushion spurge is long lived and dislikes frequent transplanting. In southern zones cushion spurge performs better in a partially shaded location.

UTILIZATION: The neat semi-spherical mound shape of this plant makes it useful as a specimen plant or as a plant for the herbaceous border.

PROPAGATION: Division and seed are the normal propagation methods. Division in the spring should be done carefully so there is minimum damage to the thick, fleshy roots. Seeds can be sown outdoors or started indoors at a temperature of 65°–70°F. Germination takes 15–20 days. Tip cuttings can also be taken after flowering.

DISEASES AND INSECTS: None serious.

HARDINESS: Zones 4–8.

ADDITIONAL NOTES: The milky sap produced by *Euphorbia* can produce a skin irritation similar to poison ivy on some individuals. As a precautionary measure, gloves should be worn when handling *Euphorbia.*

Native to eastern Europe.   Perennial

Abelmoschus moschatus   p. 2

Achillea × 'Apple Blossom'   p. 11

Abutilon hybridum 'Savitzii'   p. 4

Actaea rubra   p. 17

Acanthus spinosus   p. 5

Aegopodium podagraria 'Variegatum'   p. 21

Achillea filipendulina 'Gold Plate'   p. 8

Agapanthus hybrids   p. 22

Ageratum houstonianum p. 25

Allium giganteum p. 35

Ajuga reptans 'Catlins Giant' p. 28

Allium karataviense p. 36

Alchemilla mollis p. 31

Allium moly p. 37

Allium christophii p. 34

Allium schoenoprasum p. 38

Allium sphaerocephalon p. 40	*Amsonia tabernaemontana* p. 49
Allium tuberosum p. 41	*Anaphalis triplinervis* p. 51
Alternanthera ficoidea 'Bettzickiana' p. 44	*Anchusa azurea* 'Loddon Royalist' p. 52
Amaranthus tricolor p. 45	*Anemone blanda* p. 55

Anemone coronaria   p. 57

Aquilegia flabellata var. nana   p. 68

Anemone × hybrida 'Max Vogel'   p. 60

Aquilegia × 'McKana Hybrids'   p. 69

Antennaria rosea   p. 64

Aquilegia × 'Nora Barlow'   p. 70

Anthemis tinctoria 'E. C. Buxton'   p. 65

Arabis caucasica   p. 71

Arenaria montana   p. 74

Artemisia × 'Powis Castle'   p. 81

Armeria maritima   p. 77

Artemisia lactiflora   p. 84

Artemisia abrotanum   p. 80

Artemisia ludoviciana   p. 85

Artemisia absinthium 'Lambrook Silver'   p. 81

Artemisia schmidtiana 'Nana'   p. 87

Artemisia stelleriana   p. 88

Asarum europaeum   p. 94

Arum italicum 'Pictum'   p. 89

Asclepias tuberosa   p. 96

Aruncus dioicus   p. 90

Asphodeline lutea   p. 98

Aruncus aethusifolius   p. 91

Aster amellus 'Pink Zenith'   p. 101

Aster × frikartii 'Monch'   p. 103

Astrantia major   p. 111

Aster novae-angilae 'Lye End Beauty'   p. 105

Aubrieta deltoidea   p. 115

Astilbe × 'Erica'   p. 108

Aurinia saxatilis   p. 117

Astilbe chinensis 'Serenade'   p. 110

Baptisia australis   p. 118

Begonia grandis   p. 120

Bergenia cordifolia   p. 127

Begonia semperflorens-cultorum   p. 121

Boltonia asteroides   p. 130

Begonia × tuberhybrida   p. 122

Brachycome iberidifolia   p. 133

Belamcanda chinenis   p. 123

Brassica oleracea 'Dynasty Pink'   p. 134

Brunnera macrophylla 'Langtrees' p. 139

Calendula officinalis p. 145

Buphthalmum salicifolium p. 140

Callistephus chinensis p. 148

Caladium × hortulanum p. 142

Caltha palustris p. 150

Calamagrostis acutiflora 'Stricta' p. 143

Campanula carpatica p. 153

Campanula glomerata 'Joan Elliott'   p. 154

Campanula portenschlagiana   p. 159

Campanula latifolia 'Brantwood'   p. 156

Canna × generalis   p. 161

Campanula medium   p. 157

Capsicum annuum   p. 163

Campanula persicifolia 'Alba'   p. 158

Catharanthus roseus 'Grape Cooler'   p. 168

Celosia cristata 'Apricot Beauty'   p. 170

Cerastium tomentosum   p. 180

Centaurea hypoleuca 'John Coutts'   p. 173

Chelone obliqua   p. 184

Centaurea macrocephala   p. 175

Chionodoxa luciliae   p. 187

Centranthus ruber   p. 177

Chrysogonum virginianum   p. 188

732

Cimicifuga racemosa   p. 189

Coleus × hybrids   p. 198

Cimicifuga ramosa 'Brunette'   p. 190

Convallaria majus 'Striata'   p. 200

Cleome hasslerana 'Helen Campbell'   p. 194

Coreopsis grandiflora   p. 202

Colchicum speciosum   p. 195

Coreopsis grandiflora 'Baby Sun'   p. 202

Coreopsis tinctoria   p. 204

Cosmos sulphureus 'Diablo'   p. 209

Coreopsis verticillata 'Moonbeam'   p. 205

Cosmos bipinnatus 'Sonata Mixed'   p. 208

Cortaderia selloana 'Sunnydale Silver' p. 206

Crambe cordifolia   p. 210

Corydalis lutea   p. 207

Crocosmia × *crocosmiiflora*   p. 212

Crocus vernus   p. 214

Darmera peltata   p. 227

Cuphea ignea   p. 218

Delphinium × elatum   p. 229

Cynoglossum nervosum   p. 221

Dendranthema × morifolium   p. 231

Cypripedium calceolus var. pubescens   p. 222

Dianthus chinensis   p. 237

Dianthus plumarius 'Margaret Curtis' p. 239

Dicentra spectabilis 'Alba' p. 243

Dianthus deltoides 'Brilliancy' p. 240

Dictamnus albus p. 244

Dianthus gratianopolitanus 'Tiny Rubies' p. 240

Digitalis grandiflora p. 245

Dicentra × 'Luxuriant' p. 241

Digitalis purpurea p. 246

Dimorphotheca sinuata　　　　　p. 248

Dyssodia tenuiloba　　　　　p. 258

Disporum sessile 'Variegatum'　　　　　p. 250

Echinacea purpurea　　　　　p. 259

Dodecatheon meadia　　　　　p. 251

Echinops ritro　　　　　p. 261

Doronicum orientale　　　　　p. 252

Elymus arenarius　　　　　p. 262

Epimedium × youngianum 'Roseum'   p. 264

Eryngium amethystinum   p. 272

Eranthis hyemalis   p. 266

Eryngium alpinum 'Blue Star'   p. 274

Erianthus ravennae   p. 267

Eschscholzia californica   p. 278

Erigeron × 'Rosa Triumph'   p. 268

Eupatorium purpureum   p. 282

Euphorbia characias ssp. wulfenii   p. 283

Euphorbia polychroma   p. 288

Euphorbia cyparissias   p. 284

Euphorbia wallichii   p. 289

Euphorbia griffithii   p. 285

Festuca cinerea 'Elijah Blue'   p. 291

Euphorbia myrsinites   p. 287

Filipendula ulmaria 'Aurea'   p. 293

Filipendula vulgaris   p. 294

Galanthus nivalis   p. 304

Foeniculum vulgare 'Purpurascens'   p. 296

Galega orientalis   p. 305

Fritillaria imperialis   p. 297

Galium odoratum   p. 307

Gaillardia × *grandiflora*   p. 302

Galtonia candicans   p. 308

Gaura lindeimeri   p. 310

Geranium macrorrhizum 'Bevan's Variety'   p. 316

Gazania rigens 'Mini-star Tangerine'   p. 311

Geranium psilostemon   p. 317

Geranium endressii 'Wargrave Pink'   p. 314

Geranium sanguineum   p. 318

Geranium × 'Johnson's Blue'   p. 315

Geranium cinereum 'Lawrence Flatman'   p. 319

Gerbera jamesonii   p. 320

Gypsophila paniculata   p. 327

Geum × 'Mrs. Bradshaw'   p. 322

Hakonechloa macra 'Aureola'   p. 328

Gillenia trifoliata   p. 323

Helenium autumnale   p. 329

Gomphrena globosa   p. 325

Helianthemum nummularium 'Fire Dragon'   p. 331

Helianthus annuus 'Teddy Bear'   p. 332

Heliopsis helianthoides var. scabra 'Gold Greenheart' p. 337

Helianthus × multiflorus 'Meteor'   p. 333

Helleborus argutifolius var. corsicus   p. 339

Helichrysum bracteatum   p. 334

Helleborus orientalis   p. 340

Helictotrichon sempervirens   p. 335

Hemerocallis species   p. 342

Hesperis matronalis   p. 346

Hibiscus moscheutos   p. 354

Heuchera micrantha 'Palace Purple'   p. 349

Hosta × 'Francee'   p. 358

Heuchera sanguinea   p. 351

Hosta × 'Gold Tiara'   p. 358

Hibiscus coccineus   p. 352

Hosta sieboldiana 'Frances Williams'   p. 358

Hosta sieboldiana 'Elegans'   p. 358

Hypoestes phyllostachya 'Confetti White'   p. 365

Houttuynia cordata 'Chameleon'   p. 360

Hyssopus officinalis   p. 366

Hyacinthus orientalis   p. 361

Iberis sempervirens   p. 368

Hypericum calycinum   p. 363

Impatiens New Guinea hybrid   p. 373

Impatiens wallerana 'Super Elfin Lipstick' p. 371

Iris ensata p. 379

Imperata cylindrica 'Red Baron' p. 373

Iris hybrids p. 380

Ipomoea purpurea p. 375

Iris pumila p. 381

Iris cristata 'Shenandoah Sky' p. 376

Iris pallida 'Variegata' p. 382

Iris pseudacorus 'Variegata'   p. 383

Kochia scoparia   p. 388

Iris sibirica   p. 385

Lamiastrum galeobdolan 'Herman's Pride'   p. 390

Isatis tinctoria   p. 386

Lamiastrum galeobdolan 'Variegatum'   p. 390

Kniphofia × 'Little Maid'   p. 387

Lamium maculatum 'Beacon Silver'   p. 392

Lavandula angustifolia   p. 395

Liatris spicata   p. 402

Leontopodium alpinum   p. 398

Ligularia dentata 'Desdemona'   p. 404

Leucanthemum × *superbum*   p. 399

Ligularia × *hessei*   p. 405

Leucanthemum pacificum   p. 400

Ligularia 'The Rocket'   p. 406

Limonium latifolium p. 408

Liriope muscari 'Lilac Beauty' p. 414

Linum perenne p. 411

Lobelia cardinalis p. 415

Linum flavum 'Compactum' p. 412

Lobelia splendens p. 416

Liriope muscari 'Variegata' p. 414

Lobelia erinus p. 417

Lobularia maritima p. 419	*Lychnis × arkwrightii* p. 425
Lunaria annua 'Variegata' p. 421	*Lychnis viscaria* 'Splendens Plena' p. 425
Lupinus × 'Noble Maiden' p. 422	*Lychnis coronaria* 'Abbotswood' p. 426
Lychnis chalcedonica p. 425	*Lysimachia clethroides* p. 428

Lysimachia nummularia 'Aurea'　　　　p. 429

Matthiola incana 'Annua'　　　　p. 437

Lysimachia punctata　　　　p. 430

Mimulus guttatus　　　　p. 443

Lythrum salicaria　　　　p. 431

Miscanthus sinensis 'Kleine Fontaine'　　　　p. 446

Macleaya cordata　　　　p. 433

Miscanthus sinensis 'Variegatus'　　　　p. 446

Miscanthus sinensis 'Zebrinus'　　　　p. 446

Muscari armeniacum　　　　p. 454

Miscanthus sinensis 'Kaskade'　　　　p. 446

Nepeta × faassenii 'Six Hills Giant'　　　　p. 458

Molinia caerulea 'Variegata'　　　　p. 449

Nicotiana alata 'Nicki Formula Mix'　　　　p. 459

Monarda didyma 'Croftway Pink'　　　　p. 452

Nierembergia hippomanica var. violacea　　　　p. 460

Nipponthemum nipponicum   p. 462

Oenothera speciosa   p. 465

Ocimum basilicum 'Dark Opal'   p. 463

Omphalodes cappadocica   p. 466

Oenothera missourensis 'Greencourt Lemon' p. 464

Opuntia humifusa   p. 470

Oenothera tetragona   p. 464

Origanum vulgare 'Aureum'   p. 471

Ornithogalum umbellatum   p. 475

Paeonia suffruticosa   p. 481

Osmuda cinnamomea   p. 477

Panicum virgatum   p. 483

Pachysandra procumbens   p. 478

Papaver nudicaule   p. 485

Paeonia × 'Bowl of Beauty'   p. 479

Papaver orientale   p. 486

Pelargonium × *hortorum* 'Sprinter Salmon'   p. 495

Penstemon barbatus 'Elfin Pink'   p. 501

Pennisetum alopecuroides   p. 497

Perovskia atriplicifolia   p. 503

Pennisetum orientale   p. 498

Persicaria virginiana var. filiformis 'Painter's Palette' p. 505

Pennisetum setaceum 'Rubrum'   p. 499

Petasites japonicus   p. 507

Petroselinum crispum   p. 510

Phlox paniculata 'Mt. Fujiyama'   p. 519

Phalaris arundinaceae var. picta   p. 512

Phlox subulata   p. 520

Phlomis russeliana   p. 514

Phygelius aequalis 'Yellow Trumpet'   p. 522

Phlox divaricata 'Fuller's White'   p. 515

Physalis alkekengi   p. 524

Physostegia virginiana   p. 525

Polygonatum biflorum   p. 533

Platycodon grandiflorus   p. 526

Polygonatum odoratum 'Variegatum'   p. 534

Polemonium caeruleum   p. 530

Polygonum affine 'Superba'   p. 535

Polemonium reptans var. alba   p. 532

Polygonum bistorta 'Superbum'   p. 536

Polygonum amplexicaule   p. 537

Potentilla tridentata   p. 548

Polygonum capitatum 'Magic Carpet'   p. 538

Primula × polyantha   p. 550

Portulaca grandiflora   p. 544

Primula japonica   p. 551

Potentilla × 'William Rollison'   p. 547

Prunella grandiflora 'Pink Loveliness'   p. 552

Pulmonaria angustifolia p. 553

Puschkinia scilloides p. 559

Pulmonaria longifolia 'Roy Davidson' p. 555

Ranunculus acris 'Flore Pleno' p. 560

Pulmonaria saccharata 'Mrs. Moon' p. 557

Rehmannia elata p. 562

Pulmonaria saccharata 'Sissinghurst White' p. 557

Rheum palmatum 'Bowles Variety' p. 563

Ricinus communis 'Red Spire'   p. 565

Rudbeckia hirta var. pulcherrima 'Goldilocks'   p. 573

Rodgersia pinnata   p. 566

Rudbeckia fulgida   p. 574

Rodgersia podophylla   p. 567

Rudbeckia nitida   p. 575

Rodgersia tabularis   p. 568

Ruta graveolens   p. 577

Sagina subulata   p. 579

Salvia officinalis 'Icterina'   p. 585

Salpiglossis sinuata 'Splash'   p. 580

Salvia officinalis 'Purpurascens'   p. 585

Salvia coccinea   p. 581

Salvia splendens   p. 587

Salvia farinacea   p. 583

Salvia × superba 'Viola Klose'   p. 590

Salvia viridis   p. 591

Sanvitalia procumbens   p. 597

Sanguisorba canadensis   p. 592

Saponaria ocymoides   p. 598

Santolina chamaecyparissus   p. 595

Scabiosa caucasica 'Butterfly Blue'   p. 605

Santolina virens   p. 596

Sedum kamtschaticum var. ellacombianum   p. 610

762

Sedum × 'Autumn Joy' p. 611

Sidalcea malviflora 'Loveliness' p. 620

Sedum maximum 'Atropurpureum' p. 612

Silene dioica p. 622

Sempervivum tectorum p. 614

Sisyrinchium striatum p. 624

Senecio cineraria p. 615

Smilacina racemosa p. 625

Solidago hybrids p. 626

Stachys macrantha p. 634

Spartina pectinata 'Aureo-marginata' p. 629

Stipa gigantea p. 636

Spigelia marilandica p. 630

Stokesia laevis p. 637

Stachys byzantina 'Silver Carpet' p. 633

Stylophorum diphyllum p. 639

Symphytum grandiflorum   p. 641

Tagetes patula 'Queen Sophia'   p. 645

Symphytum × rubrum   p. 642

Tanacetum coccineum   p. 647

Symphytum × uplandicum 'Variegatum'   p. 642

Tanacetum vulgare var. crispum   p. 651

Tagetes erecta 'Inca Gold'   p. 643

Tellima grandiflora   p. 653

Teucrium chamaedrys   p. 654

Thalictrum speciosissimum   p. 660

Teucrium fruticans   p. 656

Thermopsis caroliniana   p. 662

Thalictrum aquilegifolium   p. 657

Thunbergia alata   p. 664

Thalictrum rochebrunianum   p. 660

Thymus praecox ssp. arcticus 'Lanuginosus'   p. 665

Thymus serpyllum p. 666

Tiarella wherryi p. 670

Thymus × 'Doone Valley' p. 668

Tigridia pavonia p. 671

Thymus × *citriodorus* 'Aureus' p. 668

Tradescantia × *andersoniana* 'Osprey' p. 675

Tiarella cordifolia p. 669

Tricyrtis formosana p. 677

Trillium grandiflorum   p. 678

Uvularia grandiflora   p. 687

Trollius × cultorum   p. 681

Veratrum viride   p. 689

Tropaeolum majus   p. 682

Verbascum chaixii 'Album'   p. 691

Tulipa greigii 'Red Riding Hood'   p. 686

Verbena × hybrida   p. 693

Verbena rigida   p. 695

Veronica spicata ssp. incana   p. 704

Verbena tenuisecta   p. 697

Veronicastrum virginicum   p. 706

Veronica austriaca ssp. teucrium 'Royal Blue'   p. 700

Viola tricolor   p. 708

Veronica spicata 'Icicle'   p. 702

Zinnia angustifolia 'Classic'   p. 720

HERBACEOUS PLANTS FOR SPECIAL PURPOSES

PLANTS WITH FRAGRANT FOLIAGE OR FLOWERS

Achillea sp. (foliage)
Allium sp. (foliage)
Aloysia triphylla (foliage)
Anthemis tinctoria (foliage)
Arabis caucasica (flower)
Artemisia sp. (foliage) (A. abrotanum, A. absinthium, A. dracunculus 'Sativa', particularly)
Chenopodium botrys (foliage)
Convallaria majalis (flower)
Dendranthema × morifolium (foliage)
Dianthus caryophyllus (flower)
Dianthus plumarius (flower)
Dictamnus albus (flower)
Erysimum asperum (flower)
Foeniculum vulgare (foliage)
Fritillaria imperialis (flower)
Galium odoratum (foliage)
Geranium macrorrhizum (foliage)
Hemerocallis hybrids (flower)
Hosta sp. (flower)
Houttuynia cordata 'Chameleon' (foliage)
Hyacinthus orientalis (flower)
Hyssopus officinalis (foliage)
Iris hybrids (flower)
Lathyrus latifolius (flower)
Lavandula angustifolia (flower & foliage)
Leucojum vernum (flower)

Lobularia maritima (flower)
Lycoris squamigera (flower)
Matthiola incana 'Annua' (flower)
Melissa officinalis (foliage)
Mentha sp. (foliage)
Mirabilis jalapa (flower)
Monarda didyma (foliage)
Muscari armeniacum (flower)
Nepeta × faassenii (foliage—cat attractant)
Nicotiana alata (flower)
Ocimum basilicum (foliage)
Oenothera sp. (flower)
Origanum sp. (foliage)
Paeonia sp. (flower)
Papaver nudicaule (flower)
Pelargonium graveolens (foliage)
Pelargonium × hortorum (foliage)
Primula vulgaris (flower)
Rosmarinus officinalis (foliage)
Ruta graveolens (foliage)
Salvia officinalis (foliage)
Santolina chamaecyparissus (foliage)
Tagetes erecta (foliage)
Tagetes patula (foliage)
Thymus sp. (foliage)
Viola cornuta (flower)
Viola odorata (flower)

PLANTS FOR CUT FLOWERS

Abelmoschus moschatus
Achillea sp.
Aconitum napellus
Agapanthus hybrids
Alchemilla mollis
Allium sp.
Ammobium alatum
Anthemis tinctoria
Antirrhinum majus
Aquilegia hybrida
Armeria maritima
Astrantia major
Boltonia asteroides
Buphthalmum salicifolium
Calendula officinalis
Callistephus chinensis
Campanula medium
Catananche caerulea

Celosia cristata
Centaurea cyanus
Centaurea macrocephala
Cleome hasslerana
Convallaria majalis
Coreopsis sp.
Cosmos sulphureus
Crocosmia × crocosmiiflora
Dahlia hybrids
Delphinium × elatum
Dendranthema × morifolium
Dianthus caryophyllus
Dicentra sp.
Doronicum orientale
Echinacea purpurea
Echinops ritro
Erigeron hybrid
Eryngium sp.

PLANTS FOR CUT FLOWERS (con't.)

Eupatorium coelestinum
Foeniculum vulgare
Gaillardia sp.
Gerbera jamesonii
Geum hybrids
Gladiolus × *hortulanus*
Gomphrena globosa
Gypsophila sp.
Helenium autumnale
Helichrysum bracteatum
Heliopsis helianthoides
Heliotropium arborescens
Heuchera sp.
Iris sp.
Kniphofia hybrids
Lavandula angustifolia
Leucanthemum × *superbum*
Liatris sp.
Lilium sp.
Limonium sp.
Lobelia cardinalis
Lupinus 'Russell Hybrid'
Lysimachia clethroides
Lythrum salicaria
Macleaya cordata
Matthiola incana 'Annua'
Molucella laevis
Monarda didyma

Narcissus cvs.
Nicotiana alata
Nigella damascena
Paeonia lactiflora
Papaver nudicaule
Papaver orientale
Penstemon sp.
Phlox paniculata
Physostegia virginiana
Platycodon grandiflorus
Rudbeckia sp.
Salpiglossis sinuata
Salvia sp.
Scabiosa sp.
Sedum spectabile
Stokesia laevis
Tagetes sp.
Tanacetum coccineum
Tanacetum parthenium
Thalictrum sp.
Thermopsis caroliniana
Tithonia rotundifolia
Trollius sp.
Tropaeolum majus
Tulipa cvs.
Veronica spicata
Viola sp.
Xanthisma texanum
Zinnia elegans

PLANTS FOR ATTRACTING BUTTERFLIES AND BEES

Achillea sp.
Ageratum houstonianum
Alcea rosea (nectar & larval food)
Anaphalis sp. (nectar & larval food)
Anethum graveolens (larval food)
Antennaria sp. (nectar & larval food)
Armeria sp.
Aruncus dioicus
Asclepias tuberosa
Aster sp. (nectar & larval food)
Aubrieta deltoidea
Aurinia saxatilis
Baptisia australis
Borago officinalis
Calendula officinalis
Centaurea cyanus
Centranthus ruber

Cimicifuga sp.
Cleome hasslerana
Coreopsis sp.
Cosmos sp.
Dendranthema × *morifolium*
Dianthus barbatus
Dictamnus albus
Echinacea purpurea
Echinops sp.
Erigeron sp.
Eupatorium coelestinum
Foeniculum vulgare (larval food)
Gaillardia sp.
Geranium sp.
Gomphrena globosa
Helenium autumnale
Helianthus sp. (nectar & larval food)

PLANTS FOR ATTRACTING BUTTERFLIES AND BEES (con't.)

Heliotropium arborescens
Hemerocallis sp.
Hesperis matronalis
Hibiscus moscheutos
Iberis sempervirens
Lathyrus latifolius
Lavandula angustifolia
Liatris sp.
Lobelia cardinalis
Lobelia erinus
Lobularia maritima
Leucanthemum × *superbum*
Lupinus sp. (larval food)
Lythrum salicaria
Marrubium vulgare
Matthiola incana 'Annua'
Mentha sp.
Monarda didyma
Nepeta × *faassenii*
Opuntia humifusa

Petroselinum crispum (larval food)
Phlox paniculata
Polygonum sp. (nectar plants and larval food)
Ratibida columnifera
Rudbeckia sp.
Ruta graveolens (larval food)
Salvia sp.
Scabiosa sp.
Sedum spectabile
Sedum 'Autumn Joy'
Solidago sp.
Symphytum sp.
Tagetes patula
Thymus sp.
Tropaeolum majus (larva food)
Verbena sp.
Vernonia sp.
Viola sp. (larval food)
Zinnia sp.

PLANTS FOR FULL SHADE

Actaea sp.
Adiantum pedatum
Ajuga reptans
Arisaema triphylla
Arum italicum 'Pictum'
Asarum sp.
Asplenium ebenoides
Athyrium filix-femina
Athyrium nipponicum 'Pictum'
Begonia semperflorens-cultorum
Browallia speciosa
Brunnera macrophylla
Caladium × *hortulanum*
Convallaria majalis
Cystopteris bulbifera
Darmera peltata
Dennstaedtia punctilobula
Dicentra sp.
Disporum sp.
Dodecatheon meadia
Dryopteris sp.
Epimedium sp.
Erythronium americanum
Fuchsia × *hybrida*

Galium odoratum
Hosta sp.
Impatiens wallerana
Lamiastrum galeobdolan var. *variegatum*
Lamium sp.
Liriope spicata
Luzula nivea
Matteuccia struthiopteris
Mertensia virginica
Omphalodes cappadocica
Osmunda regalis
Pachysandra procumbens
Pachysandra terminalis
Phyllitis scolopendrium
Polygonatum sp.
Polystichum sp.
Pulmonaria sp.
Smilacina racemosa
Stylophorum diphyllum
Tiarella cordifolia
Torenia fournieri
Uvularia sp.
Vancouveria hexandra
Viola odorata

PLANTS FOR CONSTANTLY MOIST TO WET SOILS

Acorus gramineus 'Variegatus'
Adiantum pedatum
Aruncus dioicus
Asplenium ebenoides
Astilbe × *arendsii*
Athyrium nipponicum
Caltha palustris
Campanula glomerata
Chelone lyonii
Cimicifuga sp.
Cystopteris bulbifera
Darmera peltata
Dodecatheon meadia
Dryopteris sp.
Equisetum hyemale
Filipendula ulmaria
Hibiscus coccineus
Hibiscus moscheutos
Houttuynia cordata
Iris ensata
Iris pseudacorus

Ligularia sp.
Lobelia cardinalis
Lobelia siphilitica
Lysimachia sp.
Lythrum salicaria
Matteuccia struthiopteris
Myosotis sylvatica
Petasites japonicus
Phalaris arundinacea var. *picta*
Phlox divaricata
Phyllitis scolopendrium
Physostegia virginiana
Polygonum sp.
Polystichum sp.
Primula sp.
Ranunculus repens
Rodgersia sp.
Smilacina racemosa
Spartina pectinata
Tradescantia × *andersoniana*
Trollius europaeus

PLANTS SUITABLE FOR SUNNY, DRY CONDITIONS

Achillea sp.
Amaranthus tricolor
Antennaria dioica
Anthemis tinctoria
Arabis caucasica
Arctotis stoechadifolia
Arrhenatherum elatius 'Variegatum'
Artemisia sp.
Asclepias tuberosa
Aubrieta deltoidea
Aurinia saxatilis
Briza media
Callirhoe involucrata
Catharanthus roseus
Celosia sp.
Centaurea montana
Cerastium tomentosum
Chasmanthium latifolium
Coreopsis sp.
Cosmos sp.
Dimorphotheca sinuata
Dyssodia tenuiloba
Echinacea purpurea
Echinops ritro
Elymus arenarius

Erianthus ravennae
Eryngium sp.
Eschscholzia californica
Euphorbia sp.
Festuca cinerea
Filipendula vulgaris
Gaillardia sp.
Gaura lindheimeri
Gazania rigens
Gomphrena globosa
Goniolimon tataricum
Helianthemum nummularium
Helianthus sp.
Helictotrichon sempervirens
Hemerocallis hybrids
Hordeum jubatum
Iberis sempervirens
Kochia scoparia f. *trichophylla*
Leontopodium alpinum
Liatris sp.
Limonium sp.
Lonas annua
Malva alcea
Mirabilis jalapa
Miscanthus sp.

PLANTS SUITABLE FOR SUNNY, DRY CONDITIONS (con't.)

Ocimum basilicum
Oenothera sp.
Opuntia humifusa
Panicum virgatum
Pennisetum sp.
Perovskia atriplicifolia
Phalaris arundinacea var. *picta*
Phlomis russeliana
Phlox subulata
Physostegia virginiana
Polygonum cuspidatum var. *compactum*
Portulaca grandiflora
Potentilla sp.
Rudbeckia sp.

Santolina sp.
Sanvitalia procumbens
Saponaria ocymoides
Sedum sp.
Sempervivum tectorum
Senecio cineraria
Sorghastrum avenaceum
Stachys byzantina
Tanacetum vulgare
Thymus sp.
Tithonia rotundifolia
Verbascum chaixii
Xanthisma texanum
Yucca sp.
Zinnia elegans

PLANTS WITH SHOWY FRUIT OR DRIED FLOWER OR FRUIT POTENTIAL

Achillea sp. (flower)
Actaea sp. (fruit)
Alchemilla mollis (flower)
Allium sp. (flower)
Ammobium alatum (flower)
Anaphalis triplinervis (flower)
Arum italicum 'Pictum' (fruit)
Arundo donax (flower)
Asclepias tuberosa (fruit)
Baptisia australis (fruit)
Belamcanda chinensis (fruit)
Capsicum annuum (fruit)
Catananche caerulea (flower)
Celosia sp. (flower)
Chasmanthium latifolium (fruit)
Chenopodium botrys (flower)
Cortaderia selloana (flower)
Deschampsia caespitosa (flower)
Echinops ritro (flower)
Erianthus ravennae (flower)
Eryngium sp. (flower)
Eupatorium sp. (flower)
Gomphrena globosa (flower)
Gypsophila sp. (flower)
Helichrysum bracteatum (flower)
Hyssopus officinalis (flower)

Lavandula angustifolia (flower)
Limonium sp. (flower)
Lonas annua (flower)
Lunaria annua (fruit)
Macleaya cordata (flower)
Marrubium vulgare (flower)
Mentha sp. (flower)
Miscanthus sp. (flower)
Molucella laevis (flower)
Nigella damascena (fruit)
Origanum sp. (flower)
Paeonia sp. (flower)
Panicum virgatum (flower)
Papaver orientale (fruit)
Physalis alkekengi (fruit)
Salvia farinacea (flower)
Salvia viridis (flower)
Satureja montana (flower)
Sedum sp. (flower)
Solidago sp. (flower)
Sorghastrum avenaceum (flower)
Spartina pectinata (flower)
Stipa pinnata (flower)
Tanacetum parthenium (flower)
Tanacetum vulgare (flower)
Thymus sp. (flower)
Zinnia elegans (flower)

PLANTS FOR ATTRACTING HUMMINGBIRDS

Ajuga reptans
Alcea rosea
Antirrhinum majus
Aquilegia sp.
Asclepias tuberosa
Campanula sp.
Cleome hasslerana
Delphinium elatum & hybrids
Dianthus sp.
Dicentra sp.
Digitalis sp.
Fuchsia × *hybrida*
Gladiolus × *hortulanus*
Heuchera sanguinea
Hemerocallis sp.

Hibiscus moscheutos
Impatiens wallerana
Ipomoea purpurea
Kniphofia hybrids
Lilium sp.
Lobelia cardinalis
Lupinus hybrids
Mirabilis jalapa
Monarda didyma
Nicotiana alata
Penstemon sp.
Petunia × *hybrida*
Phlox drummondi
Salvia sp.
Tropaeolum majus

PLANTS USED AS GROUND COVERS

Achillea tomentosa
Aegopodium podagraria 'Variegatum'
Ajuga reptans
Antennaria dioica
Arabis caucasica
Arenaria montana
Armeria maritima
Artemisia stelleriana
Asarum sp.
Astilbe chinensis 'Pumila'
Aubrieta deltoidea
Catharanthus roseus
Cerastium tomentosum
Ceratostigma plumbaginoides
Chrysogonum virginianum
Convallaria majalis
Corydalis lutea
Dianthus gratianopolitanus
Duchesnea indica
Epimedium sp.
Euphorbia cyparissias
Festuca cinerea
Galium odoratum
Geranium sp.
Helianthemum nummularium
Helleborus sp.

Hosta sp.
Houttuynia cordata 'Chameleon'
Hypericum calycinum
Lamiastrum galeobdolan var. *variegatum*
Lamium maculatum
Liriope spicata
Lysimachia nummularia
Pachysandra terminalis
Phalaris arundinacea var. *picta*
Phlox stolonifera
Phlox subulata
Polygonum sp.
Portulaca grandiflora
Potentilla tridentata
Potentilla verna
Pulmonaria sp.
Sagina subulata
Sanvitalia procumbens
Sedum sp.
Stachys byzantina
Symphytum grandiflorum
Thymus sp.
Tiarella cordifolia
Vancouveria hexandra
Veronica spicata ssp. *incana*
Waldsteinia fragarioides

PLANTS WITH EVERGREEN FOLIAGE

Ajuga reptans
Armeria maritima
Asarum europaeum
Bergenia cordifolia
Carex morrowii 'Aurea Variegata'
Dryopteris marginalis
Equisetum hyemale
Euphorbia myrsinites
Festuca cinerea
Helleborus sp.

Iberis sempervirens
Liriope spicata
Liriope muscari
Opuntia humifusa
Pachysandra terminalis
Phlox subulata
Polystichum acrostichoides
Sedum (some species)
Sempervivum sp.
Teucrium chamaedrys
Yucca sp.

PLANTS FOR FOLIAGE EFFECTS

Acanthus spinosus
Acorus gramineus 'Variegatus'
Actaea pachypoda
Adiantum pedatum
Aegopodium podagraria 'Variegatum'
Ajuga reptans
Alchemilla mollis
Allium senescens
Alopecurus pratensis 'Aureus'
Alternanthera ficoidea
Amaranthus tricolor
Arenaria montana
Armeria maritima
Arrhenatherum elatius 'Variegatum'
Artemisia sp.
Arum italicum 'Pictum'
Arundo donax 'Variegata'
Asarum sp.
Asplenium ebenoides
Astilbe sp.
Athyrium sp.
Begonia semperflorens-cultorum
Bergenia cordifolia
Brassica oleracea
Brunnera macrophylla
Caladium × *hortulanum*
Calamagrostis acutiflora 'Stricta'
Carex morrowi 'Aurea Variegata'
Cerastium tomentosum
Coleus × *hybridus*
Cystopteris bulbifera
Darmera peltata
Dennstaedtia punctilobula
Dianthus gratianopolitanus
Dryopteris sp.

Elymus arenarius
Eryngium bourgatii
Euphorbia cyparissias
Euphorbia marginata
Euphorbia myrsinites
Festuca cinerea
Galium odoratum
Hakonechloa macra 'Aureola'
Helictotrichon sempervirens
Helleborus sp.
Heuchera sp.
Holcus mollis 'Variegatus'
Hosta sp.
Hypericum calycinum
Hypoestes phyllostachya
Imperata cylindrica var. *rubra*
Iberis sempervirens
Iris pallida 'Variegata'
Iris pseudacorus 'Variegata'
Kochia scoparia f. *trichophylla*
Koeleria glauca
Lamiastrum galeobdolan var. *variegatum*
Lamium sp.
Lavandula angustifolia
Lychnis coronaria
Lysimachia nummularia 'Aurea'
Matteuccia struthiopteris
Miscanthus sp.
Molinia caerulea 'Variegata'
Ocimum basilicum 'Dark Opal'
Ophiopogon planiscapus 'Arabicus'
Opuntia humifusa
Origanum vulgare 'Aureum'
Osmunda regalis
Pachysandra terminalis

PLANTS FOR FOLIAGE EFFECTS (con't.)

Pennisetum sp.
Perovskia atriplicifolia
Phalaris arundinacea var. *picta*
Phyllitis scolopendrium
Polygonatum odoratum 'Variegatum'
Polygonum capitatum 'Magic Carpet'
Polygonum cuspidatum var. *compactum*
Polystichum sp.
Potentilla verna
Pulmonaria saccharata
Rodgersia sp.
Ruta graveolens

Sagina subulata
Salvia officinalis (variegated cultivars)
Santolina sp.
Sedum sp.
Sempervivum sp.
Senecio cineraria
Setcreasea pallida
Stachys byzantina
Teucrium chamaedrys
Thymus sp.
Veratrum viride
Veronica spicata ssp. *incana*
Yucca sp.

GLOSSARY

achene: small, dry, indehiscent, one-seeded fruit with a tight, thin outer wall.

acuminate: apex whose sides are gradually concave and tapering to a point.

acute: apex whose sides are straight and taper to a point.

alkaline: having a pH of more than 7.

alternate: term usually applied to the arrangement of leaves or branches on a stem; parts are situated one at a node on different sides of a stem.

anther: pollen-bearing structure of the stamen, borne at the top of the filament, or sessile.

apetalous: without petals.

apex: tip or terminal end.

apiculate: terminated by a short, sharp, flexible point.

appressed: closely or flatly pressed to a structure, as leaves appressed to a stem.

areole: the spine-bearing sunken or raised spot on the stem of cacti.

ascending: curving indirectly or obliquely upward.

attenuate: gradually tapering to a long tip

auricle: an ear-shaped lobe, generally used to describe the base of leaves or petals.

auriculate: bearing an auricle or auricles.

awn: a bristlelike appendage.

axil: the upper angle that a petiole or peduncle makes with the stem that bears it.

axillary: in the axil.

background plant: a plant similar to a hedge or screen plant but often is flowerless and provides a backdrop or frame for smaller or showier plants.

basal: pertaining to the extremity of an organ by which it is attached to its support; said of leaves when at base of plant only.

bed: a garden spot with definite dimensions that stands as a distinct landscape entity; may be composed of one or many plant species.

bifid: two-cleft, as in the apices of some petals or leaves.

bipinnate: twice pinnate.

bisexual: stamen(s) and pistil(s) present and functional in the same flower.

biternate: twice ternate; a structure basically ternate, but whose primary divisions are again each ternate (*ex.,* leaves of some columbines).

blade: expanded part of a leaf or petal.

border: a garden spot similar to a bed, but generally including more than one plant type and often is flanked by larger plants or walls. Plants described only as border plants often have a rangy or irregular growth habit that makes them undesirable as specimens or difficult to mass.

bract: a much-reduced leaf, often scalelike and usually associated with a flower or inflorescence.

bristly: covered with stiff, strong hairs or bristles.

bulb: usually an underground modified leaf bud which consists of a short, thick stem and fleshy scales, and serves as a storage organ.

bulbil: small bulb that arises in the leaf axil.

calyx: the outer set of perianth segments or floral envelope of a flower, usually green in color and smaller than the inner set.

campanulate: bell shaped.

capsule: dry, dehiscent fruit composed of two or more united carpels.

carpet bedding (carpet bed): plants that, due to their evenness of growth, symmetry, and/or lateral spreading qualities, produce a flat-topped or carpet appearance; usually requires close planting.

cauline: pertaining to the stem, as stem leaves.

chaff: a thin, dry membranous scale or bract.

chaffy: similar to chaff in texture.

ciliate: marginally fringed with hairs.

clasp: describing a leaf base that partly surrounds the stem.

claw: the constricted petiolelike base of petals and sepals of some flowers (*ex.,* petals of flowers of the mustard family, or *Cleome*).

cleft: divided to or nearly to the middle into lobes.

cleistogamous: production of seeds by self-pollination in the unopened flower.

colchicine: a mutagenic chemical extracted from *Colchicum* that, when applied to a plant, often doubles the chromosome number.

compound: a leaf of two or more leaflets. *Ternately compound* when the leaflets are in 3's; *palmately compound* when three or more leaflets arise from a common point; *pinnately compound* when arranged along a common rachis or, if only three are present, at least the terminal leaflet is petioled; *odd pinnate* if a terminal leaflet is present and the total number of leaflets for the leaf is an odd number; *even pinnate* if no terminal leaflet is present and the total is an even number.

container plant (pot, planter, or box plant): plant with one (or both) of two qualities: (1) drought tolerance and willingness to stand root constriction; (2) upright growth combined with lateral spread.

contiguous: touching or in contact; no fusion.

convex: curved like the outer surface of a sphere.

convolute: rolled up or twisted together lengthwise.

cordate: heart shaped, ovate with a sinus and rounded lobes, generally referring to leaf bases.

corm: a solid, swollen part of a stem, usually found underground.

corolla: the inner circle or second whorl of floral envelopes; when the parts are separate and distinct, they are *petals,* and the corolla is *polypetalous;* when united in whole or in part, the distal parts are *teeth, lobes, divisions,* or *segments,* and the corolla is *gamopetalous.*

corymb: a nearly flat-topped, indeterminate inflorescence with the outer flowers opening first.

crenate: rounded teeth on leaf margin.

crown: the base of a plant, where stem and root meet.

culm: the stem of plants in the *Gramineae* family, which includes grasses and bamboos.

cultivar: a plant within a species that is distinguishable from the species by one or more characteristics (morphological, physiological, chemical, etc.) and that, when reproduced sexually or asexually, retains the characteristics. Cultivar is a contraction of *cultivated variety.*

cuneate: wedge shaped with straight sides; attached at the narrow end.

cuspidate: an apex abruptly and concavely constricted into an elongated, sharp-pointed tip.

cutting: a section of a plant (stem, root, or leaf) capable of initiating roots and used for propagation.

cutting flower: a broad term describing any plant that produces flowers, floral parts, stems, or leaves that keep their ornamental qualities after being cut from the plant and/or are useful in floral arrangements.

cutting garden: an individual bed or border or collection of them that is planted specifically for the production of cutting or drying flowers.

cyathium: an inflorescence characteristic of *Euphorbia.* The unisexual flowers are condensed and congested with a cuplike involucre from which they emerge at anthesis (*pl.*—cyathia).

cyme: a more or less flat-topped, determinate inflorescence whose outer flowers open last.

cymose: of or arranged in cymes.

deciduous: not persistent, falling off at the end of a functional period, as petals of many flowers.

decumbent: reclining or lying on the ground with the tip ascending.

decurrent: extending down the stem.

dentate: teeth on the leaf margin whose apices are perpendicular to the margin and do not point forward.

denticulate: slightly or minutely dentate.

diffuse: loosely or widely spreading; open form.

digitate: palmate, compound leaf with the leaflets arising from one point, shaped like a hand.

dimorphic: occurring in two different forms, as the leaves of ferns in which the fertile fronds have a different form than the sterile fronds.

dioecious: with unisexual flowers; the staminate and pistillate flowers are on separate plants.

disk flower: the tubular flower in the center of the normal composite inflorescence.

dissected: divided into narrow segments.

division: plant propagation by dividing parts (crown, suckers, tubers) and planting segments capable of producing roots and shoots.

downy: covered with fine, soft hairs, pubescent.

dry stone wall: a wall made of loose stones (uncemented or unbonded). If the wall is utilized as a retaining wall, plants may be placed on top or on the face of the wall. These plants are usually trailing or vinelike plants and are often considered rock garden plants.

drying flower: any plant that produces flowers, floral parts, stems, or leaves that are known to be preservable by air, chemical drying, or pressing.

edging plant: a plant similar to a hedge plant; edging plants generally have a mounded appearance, lending softness to the bed or border margins.

elliptic: oblong, narrowed to rounded ends and wider near the middle.

entire: a margin with no teeth or crenations.

equitant: leaves that overlap in 2 ranks, like a fan (*ex.,* leaves of *Iris*).

even pinnate: pinnately compound leaf with no terminal leaflet.

evergreen: a plant whose foliage remains green and functional for more than one growing season.

exserted: protruding, sticking out, as stamens exserted from a corolla.

fall: one of the parts of the outer whorl of the perianth in genera such as *Iris,* usually broader than those in the inner whorl; often drooping or reflexed.

fasciated: abnormally flattened, and appears to have several units fused together.

fibrous root system: a root system composed of many branched rootlets, many lateral rootlets, and usually lacking a main or taproot development.

filament: usually refers to the stalk that bears the anther in a stamen.

filiform: threadlike, long and slender.

filler: nondescript plants (at least when massed or for most of the year) used in a garden area to back up, surround, or "fill" around a specimen plant; filler plants should be green for most of the season.

floret: the individual small flower, especially when part of a dense inflorescence.

floriferous: flower bearing.

formal garden: a landscape laid out mainly in straight lines, which may incorporate intricate bed designs, hedges, and/or specimen plants of extreme or contrived shapes.

formal landscape plant: a plant that is rigid, dense, or compact in form or can be pruned to be so.

frond: a fern leaf.

funnelform: the corolla tube gradually widens (*ex.,* corollas of morning glory).

gamopetalous: petals united, at least at the base, to form a corolla of one piece; the corolla coming off from the inflorescence as a single unit.

genus: a closely related and definable group of plants comprising one or more species. Common characteristics of a genus are the similarities of flowers and fruits (*pl.* — genera).

glabrous: without any hairs, no pubescence.

gland: generally a secreting organ, but often refers to projections that appear glandlike.

glaucous: covered with a waxy bloom or whitish material that rubs off readily.

globose: a round or spherical shape.

glossy: shining, reflecting more light than if lustrous.

graft: a grafted plant; the junction of two pieces of living tissue, the upper portion *(scion)* and lower portion or root *(stock).*

groundcover plant: any plant that spreads laterally to "cover the ground" surrounding the plant. Though low vining or trailing plants usually make good ground covers, larger arching plants will also serve effectively. The best ground covers are usually those that reproduce themselves asexually on surrounding ground and form a dense mat that serves as a mulch against soil evaporation and weed growth.

group: a semitechnical term used to describe an assemblage of similar cultivars within a species or interspecific hybrid.

hairy: pubescent with long hairs.

hastate: arrowhead shape with the basal lobes turned outward.

head: a short, dense inflorescence of variable form, as in the *Asteraceae* (daisy) family, *Eryngium,* or many clovers.

hedge: plants that have a naturally dense growth habit and will grow together to form a tight, continuous line when planted in a row. These plants may also function as screen plants and usually will stand shearing, though they do not require it.

hirsute: pubescent with coarse or stiff hairs.

hispid: short, stiff hairs.

incised: cut, often severely or irregularly.

indeterminate: type of inflorescence in which the terminal flowers open last, thus the growth or elongation of the main axis is not arrested by the opening of the first flowers.

indoor pot plant: a plant that will tolerate pot culture and indoor conditions of lower light and humidity.

inflorescence: arrangement of flowers on a plant; flowering part of a plant; or the flowering habit of a plant.

informal garden: a landscape casually designed with few straight lines. An informal garden may be incorporated in a wild area or may be planned to appear wild.

informal landscape plant: a plant that is loose, often straggly, in growth habit, that may propagate itself asexually, and that usually appears similar in form and texture to temperate American native plants.

internode: part of the axis between the nodes.

involucre: one or more whorls or close spirals of small leaves or bracts standing close beneath a flower or an inflorescence.

involute: rolled inward or toward the upper surface.

joint: stem section of *Opuntia.*

keeled: ridged, like the bottom of a boat.

laciniate: cut into narrow, pointed lobes.

lanceolate: much longer than wide, tapering to the apex, like a lance.

landscape: any definable or singularly distinct space, whether artificially arranged and designed or natural, that includes all objects and structures in that area.

landscaping: the process of arranging soil, water, plants, and structures to develop a space with a particular tone or appearance.

lateral: borne at or on the side, as flowers, buds, branches.

layering: a propagation practice. Roots are formed on stems which come in contact with the soil.

leaflet: a foliar unit of the compound leaf.

ligule: (1) a strap-shaped organ (2) (in grasses) a minute projection from the top of the leaf sheaths (3) the strap-shaped corolla in the ray flowers of composites.

limb: the expanded, and usually terminal, part of a petal, or of a gamopetalous corolla as distinguished from the often constricted tube.

linear: long and narrow, as in blades of grass.

lobe: usually a division of a leaf, calyx, or petals cut to about the middle (i.e., midway between the margin and midrib).

lyrate: cleft into a nearly pinnate appearance with the terminal lobe being the largest.

massing: using large groups of plants or large plants to provide mass or visual bulk in a garden planting. Massing is also used to achieve landscape balance and/or proportion and may serve as filler or specimen as well.

membranous: parchmentlike texture.

midrib: the midvein or primary rib of a leaf or leaflet.

monoecious: with unisexual flowers; the staminate and pistillate flowers are on the same plant.

mucro: short, sharp, abrupt tip.

mucronate: abruptly terminated by a mucro.

mucronulate: minutely mucronate.

naturalistic garden (wild garden): a garden developed through plantings that either add to an existing native site or completely create an area that appears native. The creation of such a garden may be as simple as the addition of non-native flowering water plants to a swampy area or the further massing of existing plants to make a showier garden. The wild garden may have foreign species; it can be shady or sunny, a deep woods, or a meadow. Plants used are usually loose in habit, often spreading, and, if not native, then similar in growth and appearance to the species that are native.

naturalizing effect: this is achieved in beds or gardens by use of plants with loose or broad growth habit or those which multiply by roots or stems. Naturalizing plants are usually the same as those used to add unity and continuity to a garden.

nectary: nectar-secreting gland which may appear as a pit, scale, or protuberance.

node: site on the stem where one or more leaves are attached.

oblanceolate: inversely lanceolate.

oblique: lopsided, slanting, with unequal sides, as the leaves of *Begonia.*

oblong: longer than broad; rectangular; sides nearly parallel.

obovate: inversely ovate, broadest above the middle.

obtuse: rounded.

odd-pinnate: pinnately compound leaf with a terminal leaflet.

opposite: two structures at a node arranged on opposite sides of the stem, as leaves at a node.

orbicular: circular.

oval: widest at the middle and rounded on each end.

ovate: egg shaped in outline, broadest below the middle.

palmate: radiating from a common base in a fanlike pattern, as leaflets of palmately compound leaf.

panicle: indeterminate, branching inflorescence; the individual branches are either raceme- or corymb-like.

paniculate: bearing panicles.

parted: incised or cleft not quite to the base.

pedicel: the stalk of a flower or fruit when in a cluster or when solitary.

peduncle: stalk of a flower cluster, or of a solitary flower when the inflorescence consists of only one flower.

peltate: the petiole is attached inside the leaf margin; such a leaf is often shield shaped or circular.

pendent: drooping.

perianth: a collective term that includes both the corolla and calyx as a unit; used when it is difficult to distinguish one series from another.

petal: one unit of the corolla of a polypetalous flower, usually colored and more or less showy.

petaloid: petal-like; a structure other than a petal, which resembles a petal.

petiolate: bearing a petiole.

petiole: stalk of a leaf.

pilose: shaggy with soft hairs.

pinna: primary division or leaflet of a pinnate leaf.

pinnate: compounded with the leaflets or segments along each side of a common axis or rachis.

pinnatifid: pinnately cleft or parted.

pinnule: a secondary pinna or leaflet which is the ultimate and finest division of a pinnately decompound leaf.

pistil: female portion of the flower, composed of an ovary, style, and stigma.

pistillate: female, having no functional stamens in the flower.

pleated: folded lengthwise.

plumose: featherlike, plumy.

plumy: featherlike.

pod: a general term which refers to a dry, dehiscent fruit.

pot plant: see container plant.

procumbent: lying prone without rooting.

prostrate: refers to lying flat on the ground.

pubescent: covered with short, soft hairs.

punctate: with translucent or covered dots, depressions, or pits.

raceme: simple, indeterminate inflorescence with pedicelled flowers.

racemose: (1) racemelike, having flowers in racemelike inflorescences that may or may not be true racemes; (2) borne in a raceme or a racemelike inflorescence, as racemose flowers.

rachis: axis of a compound leaf or an inflorescence.

radiate: spreading from or arranged around a common center; radiate flowers are characteristic of composite flowers.

radical: leaves that arise from the root or crown, generally referred to as basal or rosette leaves.

ray flower: a flower with a straplike corolla above a short tube. Ray flowers are present on the margin of the flower head in many species, particularly the *Asteraceae*.

receptacle: a torus; the distal end of a flower-bearing axis, usually more or less enlarged, flattened, or cuplike, on which some or all of the flower parts are borne.

reflected: to fold back upon itself.

reflexed: bent abruptly backward or downward.

reniform: kidney-shaped.

repandate: weakly sinuate margin; one slightly uneven.

revolute: rolled toward the back, as a leaf margin tightly or loosely rolled on the lower side.

rhizome: an underground stem that bears nodes, buds, or scalelike leaves.

rhombic: having four nearly equal sides but unequal angles; diamond shaped.

rib: conspicuous vein of a leaf.

rock garden: a term that has numerous applications in different gardening circles. In this book, a rock garden is a sunny, sandy, or dry garden spot having either natural or placed rock outcropping (see also **dry stone wall**).

rosette: a crown of leaves radiating from a stem and at or close to the surface of the ground.

rotate: wheel shaped or saucer shaped; a gamopetalous corolla with a flat, circular limb at right angles to a short or obsolete tube.

rugose: wrinkled.

sagittate: shaped like an arrowhead, with the basal lobes pointed down or inward.

salverform: pertaining to a corolla that has a slender tube and an abruptly expanded flat limb extending at right angles to the tube.

scabrous: rough or gritty to the touch; rough-pubescent.

scallop: semicircular curves along an edge, as a scalloped leaf margin.

scape: a leafless peduncle arising from the basal rosette of a few or no basal leaves; sometimes a few scalelike leaves or bracts may be borne on it; a scape may be one or many flowered.

scarious: thin, dry, and membranous, often more or less translucent.

scorpioid cyme: a coiled, determinate inflorescence. The flowers or branches develop alternately to the left or right.

screen: for herbaceous plants, screen plants are those that grow tall, grow broad, and stay full to the ground so that views are blocked.

secund: flowers are borne on a one-sided inflorescence (*ex., Dicentra*).

segment: parts of a leaf or flower that are deeply divided but are not compound.

sepal: one of the parts of the calyx; usually a green foliaceous element subtending the corolla.

septum: a partition or cross wall.

serrate: sawtoothed; teeth pointed forward.

serrulate: minutely serrate.

sessile: without a stalk.

setose: covered with bristles.

sheath: any elongated, tubular structure enveloping an organ or part, as the basal part of a grass leaf, which surrounds the stem.

silicle: the short fruit of the crucifers.

silique: elongated fruit of some crucifers, usually 3 times as long as wide.

simple: usually refers to a leaf that is not compound or an inflorescence that is not branched.

sinuate: strong, wavy margin.

sinus: an indentation or recess in a margin between two lobes or division of a leaf or other expanded organ.

solitary: borne singly or alone.

sorus: the clusters of sporangia in ferns, usually on the lower leaf surface (*pl.*—sori).

spadix: thick or fleshy flower spike, usually surrounded or subtended by a spathe; found in members of *Araceae.*

spathe: a leaf or bract subtending or surrounding a flower inflorescence.

spatulate: spoon shaped.

species: the basic unit of plant classification. The species name consists of two words, the first *(generic name)* representing the genus, the second *(specific epithet)* identifying the particular member of the genus. The two names together provide the species name. Species is both singular and plural.

specimen: an individual plant, group of plants, or bed that is sufficiently colorful, massive, or distinctive in shape or texture to have stronger visual interest than surrounding plants and so provide focalization.

spike: (1) a usually unbranched, elongated, simple, indeterminate inflorescence, whose flowers are sessile; the flowers may be bunched or remote; (2) a seemingly simple inflorescence, whose flowers may actually be composite heads, as in *Liatris.*

spikelet: one part of a compound inflorescence often related to the clusters in a grass inflorescence. It is composed of flowers and their subtending bracts.

spine: strong, stiff, sharp-pointed outgrowth on a leaf, stem, or other plant organ.

spinose: beset with spines.

spinulose: bearing small spines.

sporangium: a spore case; a sac or body bearing spores (*pl.*—sporangia).

sporophyll: leaflike organ that bears spores.

spreading plant: a plant that multiplies the plant body through asexual reproduction. The term is also applied to low groundcover plants that may not multiply, but the stems of which spread laterally over the surface of the ground.

spur: a tubular or saclike projection from a flower and usually from a sepal or petal, as in columbine.

stalk: a supporting unit of a leaf, flower, or fruit.

stamen: the pollen-bearing organ of a seed plant, usually composed of anther and filament.

stellate: starlike, hairs having radiating branches; also hairs once or twice forked are considered stellate.

stipe: the petiole of a fern leaf.

stipule: an appendage at the base of the petiole, often one at each side, varying in form from foliarlike to glandlike.

stolon: a stem that runs horizontally across the ground and roots at the nodes or the apex.

stoloniferous: bearing slender stems that grow on or just below the surface and root at the tips.

strigose: with sharp, stiff, straight, and appressed hairs.

style: elongated part of a pistil between the stigma and the ovary.

subtend: situated between and close to, such as a bract just below a flower, especially when the bract is prominent or persistent.

subulate: awl shaped, linear and tapering from the base to a sharp apex.

succulent: fleshy, usually thick and juicy.

temporary shrub: a herbaceous plant that grows rapidly and densely to acquire the mass and rigidity of woody plants.

tendril: modified leaf or stem, often filiform, that twines about an object for support.

tepal: a segment of a perianth which is not clearly differentiated into a recognized corolla and calyx.

terete: cylindrical, or at least circular in cross section.

terminal: distal or at the tip.

ternate: in threes; also divided into three parts, as a ternate leaf.

tetraploid: containing four rather than the usual two sets of chromosomes.

throat: the opening into the lower end of a gamopetalous corolla; the point where the limb joins the tube.

trifoliate: having three leaflets.

tomentose: densely woolly; the hairs soft and matted.

toothed: refers to a margin that is broken up into small, regular segments.

truncate: applied to bases or apices; cut off at right angles to the primary axis.

tuber: a short, thick organ, usually an underground stem.

tuft: clump of hairs growing close together.

turgid: swollen or filled to firmness.

umbel: indeterminate inflorescence, usually but not necessarily flat topped, with the pedicels and peduncles arising from a common point. An umbel resembles the stays of an umbrella.

undulate: wavy, as on a leaf margin.

variety: a subdivision of a species that exhibits inheritable characteristics that are perpetuated through both sexual and asexual propagation.

vein: vascular rib of a leaf or flower.

venation: the arrangement of the veins.

villous: having long, soft, shaggy hairs that are not matted.

viscid: sticky.

water edge plant: plants that either require or desire large amounts of water or have the coarse texture or large leaves usually associated with water plants.

whorl: three or more leaves, flowers, or other organs emanating around the stem from one node.

wild garden: see **naturalistic garden**.

wing: a thin, membranous appendage.

woolly: having long, soft, matted hairs.

SCIENTIFIC NAME INDEX

COMMON NAME INDEX

SCIENTIFIC NAME/FAMILY: *Euphorbia wallichii*   Euphorbiaceae
(Euphorbia longifolia)

(ū-fôr′bi-à wol ich′-ē-ī)

COMMON NAME: Wallich Spurge

See color plate

LEAVES: The alternate, oblong-lanceolate leaves are 3″–4″ long and 1/2″ wide. There is a conspicuous white midrib on each leaf.

FLOWER: Three large bracts, 4″–6″ diameter, encircle the true flowers. The eye-catching bracts are greenish-yellow. Additional leafy bracts subtend the showy bracts.

HABIT: Dense, mounded species, 24″ high and 12″–18″ wide. This species should be spaced at 18″.

SEASON OF BLOOM: Early summer.

CULTURE: Best growth occurs in partial shade, although it will tolerate full sun. Moist conditions are also essential for optimum performance.

UTILIZATION: Useful plant for the border. Even without flowers, the foliage remains in good condition until the fall.

PROPAGATION: Asexual propagation is by 2″–3″ terminal cuttings after flowering. Plants can also be produced from seed. A cold treatment at 40°F for 4–6 weeks can be beneficial. Germinate at 70°F.

DISEASES AND INSECTS: There are no major problems.

HARDINESS: Zones 6–9.

Native to the Himalayas.

Perennial

SCIENTIFIC NAME/FAMILY: *Festuca cinerea* (*F. glauca*)

(fes-tū′kȧ sin-e-rē′-a)

COMMON NAME: Blue Fescue

LEAVES: Low tufted grass with many stems and fine leaves. The evergreen leaves have an attractive blue color.

FLOWER: Flower stems carry terminal panicles of slender, nodding, spikelets. Many gardeners do not consider the flowers to be highly ornamental and remove them as soon as they begin to fade. The blue foliage is an ornamental aspect. Other gardeners enjoy the starburst effect of the fine foliage and fine flower stems.

HABIT: Blue fescue is a dense, hemispherical clump grass, 6″–10″ tall with an 8″ spread.

SEASON OF BLOOM: Summer.

CULTURE: Blue fescue should be planted in full sun and well-drained soil. It will tolerate dry, infertile soils. Heavy, wet soils are deleterious to blue fescue.

UTILIZATION: Use as an edging plant or planted in mass on a bank or anywhere a ground cover is needed. Blue fescue is a clump-forming grass and should be planted close if a solid cover is desired. The foliage color is deeper blue when the plant is grown in full sun and dry soil. Blue fescue is salt tolerant and would be useful for seashore plantings.

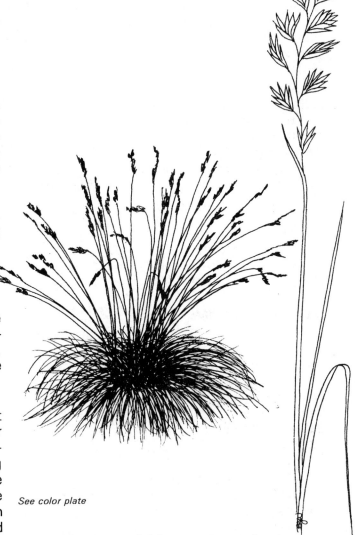

See color plate

PROPAGATION: The species can be propagated from seed. However, the cultivars should all be propagated asexually by division in the spring or fall.

DISEASES AND INSECTS: It is seldom bothered by insects or diseases.

HARDINESS: Zones 5–8. Blue fescue also performs well in southern gardens.

CULTIVARS: A number of cultivars are available and are noted for their various foliage colors and sizes. Most are products from German nurseries such as Klose, Hagemann, zur Linden, and Arends. Fortunately, these cultivars are becoming more available in the United States. The following are a few of the selections.
'Azurit'—Deep blue foliage, 12″–16″ tall, Klose Nursery introduction, 1982.
'Blaufink' ('Blue Finch')—Silver-blue foliage, 4″–8″, Klose Nursery, 1974.

'Blaufuchs' ('Blue Fox")—Excellent steel blue foliage, 6"–10", Klose, 1974.

'Blauglut' ('Blue Glow')—Dark blue foliage, 8"–12", Klose, 1972.

'Elijah Blue'—An excellent cultivar with powdery blue foliage. Lois Woodhull, The Plantage, Long Island, New York, selected this fine cultivar that is 6"–10" tall.

'Meerblau' ('Blue Sea')—Blue-green foliage, 6"–10", Klose, 1972.

'Palatinat'—Silver platinum blue foliage, 6"–12".

'Seeigel' ('Sea Urchin')—Foliage has a sea green color, 6" tall. Introduced by Peter zur Linden, Linne, Germany.

'Solling'—Bluish, grey-green foliage, 6"–10", introduced by Hagemann. This cultivar does not set flowers which eliminates the need for deadheading.

RELATED SPECIES:

F. scoparia (skō-pa′ri-a)—Bear Skin Fescue. This fescue has very fine, dark green, prickly leaves that develop into a hummock 4"–6" tall and 12" wide. In early summer, delicate flowers are borne about 8" high. These turn to a contrasting straw color at maturity. This fescue is most suited for a rock garden or rock wall. 'Pic Carlit' is only 2"–3" tall. It is also good for a sunny rock garden or perhaps in a scree.

Native to Europe.   Perennial

SCIENTIFIC NAME/FAMILY: *Filipendula ulmaria*   Rosaceae

(fil-i-pen′dū-là ul′-mar′-i-à)

COMMON NAME: Queen-of-the-Meadow

LEAVES: Leaves are alternate, 4″–8″ long, and pinnately compound with 7 to 9 leaflets. Lateral leaflets are ovate and doubly serrate while the terminal leaflet is palmately divided into 3 or sometimes 5 lobes. Leaflets have impressed venation which creates a crinkled texture. The foliage is white-tomentose beneath.

FLOWER: Flowers are white, 1/4″ wide, and borne in dense paniculate cymes. 'Flore Pleno' has double flowers.

HABIT: Thin erect flower stems rise above the large mound of pinnately compound foliage, 4 feet tall and 3 feet wide.

SEASON OF BLOOM: Early to midsummer.

CULTURE: Queen-of-the-meadow should be planted in moist, humus rich soil in partial shade. It will even tolerate soggy soil. Best performance will occur in cooler climates but satisfactory growth will result in hot climates if adequate shade and moisture is provided.

See color plate

UTILIZATION: Foliage and flowers are useful in the border. The height allows it to be utilized in the rear of the border.

PROPAGATION: Propagate by division or seed. Division will require the use of a knife to divide the tough root system. In the garden, this species self-sows freely so one will usually have more than enough seedlings. However, purchased seed may require a warm-cold stratification to get consistent germination.

DISEASES AND INSECTS: Mildew is sometimes a problem. This species is especially prone to infection if the soil is dry or the plant is under stress.

HARDINESS: Zones 3–9.

CULTIVARS:
'Aurea'—White flowers and yellow foliage, 3–4 feet. The yellow foliage is at its brightest in spring and fades to a greenish-yellow in summer. Flowers should be removed before they seed to prevent seedlings, which are green, not yellow, and very vigorous.
'Flore Pleno'—Double white flowers make this cultivar more attractive than the species, 3–4 feet. 'Flore Pleno' seems to be particularly susceptible to mildew.
'Variegata'—Foliage has a mixture of green and yellow blotches.

RELATED SPECIES:
F. palmata (pal-mā′ta)—Siberian Meadowsweet. Leaves of this species are palmately lobed into 7–9 lobes and are white tomentose beneath. Pink flowers are borne in 6″ wide flattened heads during early summer. Plant height is 3′–4′ with a width of 3′. Although the flowers last only several weeks, the foliage creates a bold texture which is an asset for the garden. However, the soils must remain moist during the growing season or the attractive leaves will brown on the edges and drop prematurely. 'Elegans' has pink flowers on stems more compact than the species. 'Nana' ('Digitata Nana') has pink flowers and is 8″–12″ tall.
F. rubra (rū′brá)—Queen-of-the-Prairie. This native North American species is the tallest of the cultivated *Filipendula*. It grows 6 to 8 feet tall and bears large, fluffy plumes of pink to peach flowers. A dominant accent plant that may be too large for the small garden. This species performs poorly in areas with hot and dry summers. 'Venusta' is a deeper pink flowering cultivar. Zones 3–9.

Native to Europe.   Perennial

SCIENTIFIC NAME/FAMILY: *Filipendula vulgaris* (F. hexapetala)   Rosaceae

(fil-i-pen'dū-lá vul-gā'ris)

COMMON NAME: Dropwort Meadowsweet

LEAVES: Most of the leaves are basal with a few smaller leaves on the flower stems. Leaves are pinnately compound, 6"–12" long and 1" to 2" wide. The leaflets are sessile to the rachis.

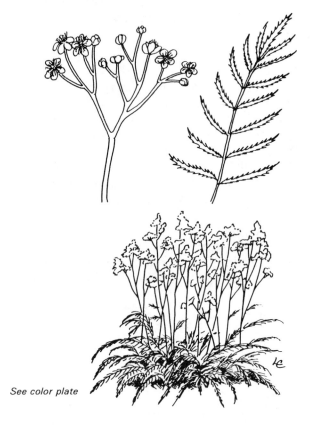

FLOWER: The flowers are white and are often tinged red on the outside, particularly when in bud. The numerous 5 to 6 petaled small flowers are arranged in a terminal panicle.

HABIT: The carrot-like foliage creates a small mound above which the slender flower stalks rise to 2–3 feet and are topped by the fleecy panicles of white flowers. Plant width is 2 feet.

SEASON OF BLOOM: Late spring to early summer.

See color plate

CULTURE: This species is easily grown in sun or partial shade in a fertile, loam soil. It is tolerant of dry and infertile sites. Dropwort self-seeds in abundance, but the seedlings pull easily, which makes maintenance less of a chore.

UTILIZATION: The fine textured foliage and wispy flowers are good in the border.

PROPAGATION: Dropwort can be propagated by division. Clumps of this species can be separated by gently pulling the roots apart. Other species require the use of a knife. Seed should be germinated at 65°–75°F in a constantly moist germination medium.

DISEASES AND INSECTS: Powdery mildew is sometimes a problem. A suitable fungicide will give sufficient control.

HARDINESS: Zones 3–8.

CULTIVARS: 'Flore Pleno'—This double flower selection has white flowers which resemble very small white roses. It is shorter than the species (15") and is used as an edging plant. One disadvantage to this selection is that the flower stems will tumble when weighted down by rain. Support may be needed.

ADDITIONAL NOTES: *Filipendula* is derived from *filum*, meaning a thread, and *pendulus*, meaning hanging, and refers to the tubers which hang from the root system.

Native to Europe.   Perennial

SCIENTIFIC NAME/FAMILY: *Foeniculum vulgare*

Apiaceae
(Umbelliferae)

(fē-nik'ū-lum vul-gā'-rē)

COMMON NAME: Fennel

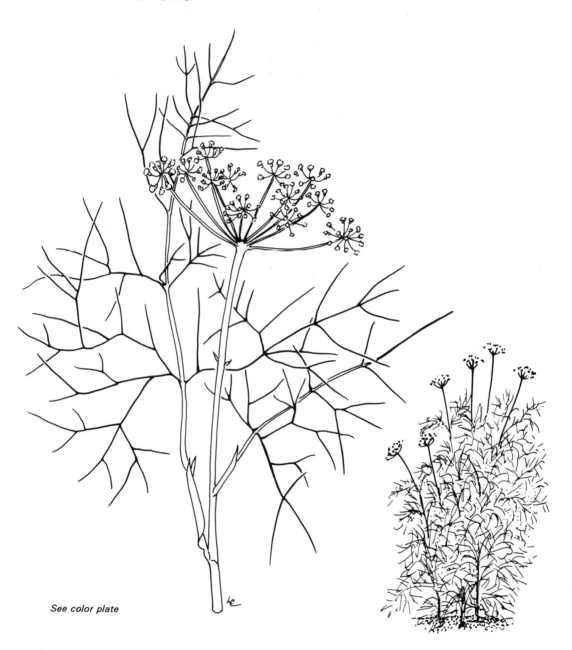

See color plate

LEAVES: Leaves are repeatedly pinnately compound. The ultimate leaf segments are threadlike, almost like hair. The thin segments create a very feathery texture. The broad petioles wrap around the stems at the joints. *Foeniculum* resembles dill but its foliage is light green rather than the blue-green foliage of dill. Stems of fennel are solid and those of dill are hollow.

FLOWER: Numerous greenish yellow flowers are found in large, flat umbels.

HABIT: 4' tall erect plant with feathery texture. Space plants 18"–24" apart.

SEASON OF BLOOM: Summer flowering. The yellow flowers are a nice contrast to the green foliage.

CULTURE: Full sun in most soils except heavy, wet clay loams. Fennel may need supplemental fertilizer to maintain plant vigor. Unless the plant is being grown for seed, the spent flowering stems should be removed to prevent unwanted seedlings.

UTILIZATION: Fennel is used for massing, filling voids, and as a facer plant for leggy perennials. Fennel is also grown for the leaves, stems, and seeds which are used in a wide variety of cooking recipes. The taste of fennel is similar to anise or licorice.

PROPAGATION: Seeds are easily germinated in 2 weeks at 70°F.

DISEASES AND INSECTS: None serious.

HARDINESS: Zones 4–9.

CULTIVARS:
'Purpurascens'—Copper Fennel. The young foliage is a deep dark bronze which contrasts nicely with lighter-colored foliage. It can be used as an accent in the border or the herb garden.
var. *azoricum* (à-zōr′-i-kum), Florence Fennel—This variety is an annual that is grown for its succulent bulbous root stalk, which is eaten raw or cooked.

ADDITIONAL NOTES: *Foeniculum* is derived from *foenum*, which is the Latin for hay, which refers to the hay-like fragrance of fennel.

Native to Mediterranean region.   Perennial

SCIENTIFIC NAME/FAMILY: *Fritillaria imperialis*   Liliaceae

(frit-i-lā′ri-à im-pēr-i-ā′lis)

COMMON NAME: Crown Imperial, Imperial Fritillary

LEAVES: Alternate, lanceolate to 6″ long, wavy margin, about 1″ wide, glabrous.

FLOWER: Various shades of yellow, orange, or red. The pendulous flowers, 2″ long, are clustered at the terminal of a stout, naked stem. The large inflorescence, composed of many individual flowers, is topped by a sheaf of small leaves that forms a tuft of green above the flowers. The flowers have a slight skunk-like odor. A drop of nectar forms near the tip of each petal, appearing to defy the laws of gravity.

See color plate

HABIT: 3′ to 4′ erect habit, 12″ wide.

SEASON OF BLOOM: Spring.

CULTURE: Shade to partial shade in a moist soil. *Fritillaria* performs best when planted in a deep, rich soil. Prepare the site by removing the top soil and mixing in well-decayed organic matter. The bulbs should be planted 6″ deep and spaced at 8″–12″. A thick organic mulch should be applied in the fall.

UTILIZATION: Useful for planting among shrubs, in the herbaceous border, and in naturalized shaded gardens.

PROPAGATION: Crown imperial can be left undisturbed for 6 years or more. It can easily be increased by removing the offsets which form around the mother bulb.

DISEASES AND INSECTS: Leaf spot, rust, and mosaic are minor problems with this species. Be sure to plant the bulbs on their sides to keep water from settling in the centers of the bulbs and causing rotting of the bulbs.

HARDINESS: Zones 5–8.

CULTIVARS:
'Aurora'—Vivid orange-red flowers, strong grower, 48″.
'Flava' ('Lutea')—Lemon yellow flowers.
'Flava Maxima'—Stronger grower than 'Flava' with larger flower heads.
'Rubra'—Orange brown flowers.

RELATED SPECIES:
F. persica (per′-si-cà). This vigorous grower from Persia has dark plum-purple flowers and green flower-stems. It should be planted in a sheltered location. Zone 6.

ADDITIONAL NOTES: *Fritillaria* is a derivation of *fritillus,* a chessboard, and refers to the checkered colors of the flower, *F. meleagris.*

Native to Iran.   Perennial—hardy bulb

SCIENTIFIC NAME/FAMILY: *Fritillaria meleagris*   Liliaceae

(frit-i-lā'ri-à mel-ē-ā'gris)

COMMON NAME: Checkered Lily, Snake's-head,
    Guinea-Hen Flower

LEAVES: Alternate leaves, linear to oblanceolate,
    3"–6" long.

FLOWER: The drooping flowers are usually soli-
    tary, some 2 or 3, and are mottled and veined
    with bronze, gray, purple, and white colors.
    The 2" bell-shaped flowers are composed of 6
    segments.

HABIT: 9" to 15" erect growing plant.

SEASON OF BLOOM: Spring.

CULTURE: Best performance occurs in full sun to
    light shade exposures and moist, well-drained
    soil. Moisture needs to be abundant throughout
    the year.

UTILIZATION: Checkered lily should be massed in
    the border or naturalized area to increase its
    effectiveness.

PROPAGATION: Checkered lily can be propagated
    by division of the bulbs after the foliage dies
    following flowering.

DISEASES AND INSECTS: None serious.

HARDINESS: Zones 3–8.

CULTIVARS:
    'Alba'—White flowers.
    'Charon'—Deep purple flowers.
    'Poseidon'—Purplish-pink flowers.

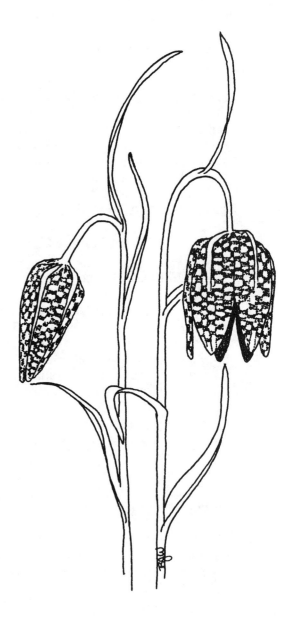

Native to Norway and England through middle Europe to the Caucasus.

Perennial—hardy bulb

SCIENTIFIC NAME/FAMILY: *Fuchsia × hybrida*   Onagraceae

(fū'shȧ, fūk'si-ȧ hī'brid-ȧ)

COMMON NAME: Fuchsia, Lady's-Eardrops

LEAVES: Opposite, ovate-cordate, 2"–5" in length, acute apex, toothed margin.

FLOWER: Pink to dull red, calyx tube cylindrical, 2"–3" long, 4 sepals ½" long, petals bright red, ½" long, stamens and style exserted. Flowers are very showy, generally pendulous and borne axillary or in terminal racemes or panicles.

HABIT: 1 ½' to 3' rounded habit with trailing branches.

SEASON OF BLOOM: Summer.

CULTURE: Since fuchsia is often grown as a container ornamental, the following discussion will be directed toward that use. A suitable potting medium is one with 75% loam soil, 15% coarse builder's sand, and 10% leaf mold. Fuchsia should be kept damp, but not wet. A hanging basket during the summer needs water every day, and during dry, windy periods, it may require watering twice per day. Fuchsia should be grown in indirect light, not full sun. To promote heavy bloom, the plants should be pinched back, which will create a bushy form. It is a good idea to mist the leaves in the morning and afternoon in very hot weather.

UTILIZATION: Hanging baskets, containers, and trained to tree form on standards. Hanging baskets of fuchsia are most effectively placed at eye level for full appreciation of the blooms.

PROPAGATION: The most effective method of propagation is by cuttings taken in spring or late summer.

DISEASES AND INSECTS: *Botrytis* blight, rust, aphids, Japanese beetle, mealybugs, mites, scale, thrips and whitefly. These problems are not common.

HARDINESS: Zone 10.

CULTIVARS:
'Crusader'—Double violet corolla with white sepals and rosy red tube.
'Display'—Pink blossoms and quite floriferous.
'Flying Cloud'—Double, white flowers with a trace of pink in the stamens.
'Mrs. Victor Reiter'—White tube and sepals, deep rose corolla.
'Orange Drops'—Orange flowers.
'Pink Chiffon'—Double, cream-pink flowers, ruffled corolla.
'Swingtime'—Double, white corolla and red sepals.
'Voodoo'—Nearly a double-double type flower, purple corolla, deep crimson sepals.

ADDITIONAL NOTES: Fuchsia can be maintained as a pot plant for about 3 years by storing during the winter. Before a hard frost, place the container in a storage area at about 40°F and water once a month or enough to keep the old wood from drying. In February bring the plant out to the light and prune back hard to the old wood. This will induce branching and will not harm flowering, since fuchsia flowers on new growth. Cultivars of *F.* × *hybrida* are probably derived from *F. fulgens* and *F. magellanica*. *Fuchsia* is named for Leonhard Fuchs, a 16th century German physician and herbalist.

Hybrid origin.   Perennial treated as an annual

SCIENTIFIC NAME/FAMILY: *Gaillardia* × *grandiflora*   Asteraceae
(Compositae)

(gā-lär'di-à gran-di-flō'ra)

COMMON NAME: Blanket Flower

LEAVES: Alternate or basal, leaves sometimes pinnately lobed. 8"–10" long including the petiole; upper leaves entire, sessile. Most leaves are hirsute and are gray-green in color.

FLOWER: 3"–4" head, yellow ray flowers and yellow or purple disk flowers.

HABIT: 2' to 3' plant with erect or sprawling stems that spread 2 feet.

SEASON OF BLOOM: Summer.

CULTURE: Full sun and a light, well-drained soil. *Gaillardia* will not survive in heavy clay soils, particularly during the winter.

UTILIZATION: Perennial border and cut flowers. *Gaillardia* will flower continuously, even without dead heading.

PROPAGATION: Seed, division, root cuttings. Seed will germinate in 3 weeks when exposed to light and 70°–75°F temperatures. Divide plants in the spring. New growth that appears away from the old crown can be dug and transplanted.

DISEASES AND INSECTS: Leaf spot, powdery mildew, aster yellows, leafhoppers, and four-lined plant bug are sometimes noted but none of these are serious.

HARDINESS: Zones 3–10. It has proven to be a good selection for dry soils and areas where summer temperatures are 90°F plus.

CULTIVARS:

'Baby Cole'—Dwarf, less than 8", red flowers with yellow margins.

'Bremen'—Dark-scarlet flowers with yellow tips, 24" tall.

'Burgunder' ('Burgundy')—Large, wine red flowers, 24"–30" tall.

'Dazzler'—24"–36", golden-yellow flowers with maroon centers.

'Fackelschein' ('Torchlight')—Red flowers with yellow margins, heads 5"–6" wide, 36" tall.

'Kobold' ('Goblin')—Red flowers with yellow margins, 9"–12" tall. This is an excellent cultivar.

'Monarch Strain'—30", flowers in various combinations of red and yellow.

'Sun God'—Bright yellow rays with brown disc flowers, 24"–30" tall.

'Yellow Queen'—24"–30", golden yellow flowers.

'Monarch Strain' can be grown from seed. The other cultivars should be propagated asexually to retain trueness to type.

ADDITIONAL NOTES: *Gaillardia* × *grandiflora* is a cross between *G. aristata* and *G. pulchella*.

Native to western United States.   Perennial

SCIENTIFIC NAME/FAMILY: *Gaillardia pulchella* (*G. drummondi*)

(gā-lär'di-ȧ pul-kel'-ȧ)

Asteraceae
(Compositae)

COMMON NAME: Gaillardia, Blanket Flower, Indian Blanket

LEAVES: Lower leaves oblanceolate to spatulate, 5"–6" long, toothed or pinnately lobed, sessile or short-petioled, upper leaves oblong or oblanceolate, usually entire, sessile, pubescent.

FLOWER: Heads 2" across, long-peduncled, involucre bracts green, with a short papery base; disk flowers yellow or with red tips, ray flowers red, tipped with yellow, or entirely yellow or red.

HABIT: 1½' to 2' round habit.

SEASON OF BLOOM: Summer and fall.

CULTURE: Full sun, will tolerate most garden soils and will withstand hot winds and drought better than most flowering plants.

UTILIZATION: Cut flowers, bedding plants, window boxes and planters due to ability to tolerate dry soils.

PROPAGATION: Best seed germination occurs under light in two to three weeks at 70°F.

DISEASES AND INSECTS: No serious problems.

CULTIVARS:
'Butterscotch Bronze'—12", yellow with red centers, slightly larger flowers than 'Raspberry Red'.
'Lollipops'—18", colors range from lemon yellow to deep orange or scarlet.
'Raspberry Red'—10", deep scarlet flowers.
'Red Plume'—Double, bright red flowers cover a dense mound 12"–14" tall. This AAS winner has excellent heat and drought tolerance.

ADDITIONAL NOTES: *Gaillardia* performs well in the garden, yet seems to have little appeal to gardeners. *Gaillardia* is named for Gaillard, a French patron of botany. It really reminds one of the rich colors of the Indian blankets woven by American natives. The colors and color arrangements are bold and simple mixes of primary colors—red and yellow.

Native to American West—descendents of wild plants of the area.   Annual

SCIENTIFIC NAME/FAMILY: *Galanthus nivalis*   Amaryllidaceae

(gà-lan'thus ni-vā'lis)

COMMON NAME: Common Snowdrop

LEAVES: There are generally only
2 or 3 leaves, which are linear
and glaucous, ¼" wide and
6" long.

FLOWER: Pure white except for a
green crescent around the
notch of the inner segments.
The solitary drooping flower is
about 1" across and is
borne on a slender
pedicel.

HABIT: 6" erect plant.

SEASON OF BLOOM: Early
spring.

CULTURE: Partial shade to
full shade, performs
best in cool, moist,
well-drained soil en-
riched with organic

See color plate

matter. Top dressing with well-rotted manure each fall is beneficial. In September, plant
the bulbs 4" deep and 4" apart.

UTILIZATION: Snowdrops look best when naturalized in the grass; but they are also
effective when planted among deciduous shrubs, at the edge of woodlands, or in
clumps in the shaded herbaceous border. Wherever the location, they should have the
look of spontaneity. They should not be planted in straight rows. Generally a mass
planting of smaller bulbs like *Galanthus* looks best.

PROPAGATION: The most common method is to dig and divide 4- to 5-year old clumps
immediately after flowering in midspring. Seeds can also be used but require a 4-year
wait for flowers.

DISEASES AND INSECTS: Gray mold is sometimes found in the bulbs. Before planting,
remove any scales that contain the small black sclerotia.

HARDINESS: Zones 3–7.

CULTIVARS: 'Flore Pleno'—Double flowers.

RELATED SPECIES: *G. elwesii* (el-wes'-ē-ī), Giant Snowdrop. 9"–12", flowers are larger
than *G. nivalis* and appear in early spring. Zones 4–7.

ADDITIONAL NOTES: *Galanthus* is derived from *gala,* milk, and *anthos,* a flower, which
refers to the pure white flower color.

Native to Europe.   Perennial—hardy bulb

SCIENTIFIC NAME/FAMILY: *Galega officinalis*

(gā-lē'ga o-fis-i-nā'-lis)

Fabaceae
(Leguminosae)

COMMON NAME: Common Goat's Rue

LEAVES: Alternate, pinnately compound leaves with 11–17 leaflets. Leaflets are oblong, entire, and usually have a mucronate tip.

FLOWER: The purplish-blue pea-like flowers are 1/2" long and are assembled on a 4"–6" long terminal raceme. Fruit is a 1" to 1½" long pod.

HABIT: 2' to 3' erect perennial.

SEASON OF BLOOM: Early to late summer.

CULTURE: Full sun and moist, well-drained soil is the optimum placement but *Galega* will also tolerate light shade.

UTILIZATION: Goat's rue could be a good addition to the summer border because it is easily grown and has a long bloom period. However, it is relatively unknown and will probably stay that way unless it is promoted.

See color plate

PROPAGATION: Division in spring or fall and seed are suitable methods. Seeds should be propagated at 65°–75°F in a moist medium.

DISEASES AND INSECTS: Aphids, cutworms, and powdery mildew.

HARDINESS: Zones 3–7.

RELATED SPECIES:
  G. × *hartlandii* (hart-lan'-dē-ī). This species, a hybrid of *G. officinalis* × *G. patula,* is 2'–4' tall with bicolored flowers of blue-violet and white. Cultivars available are selections of this hybrid. These cultivars are usually found in European gardens.
  'Alba'—White flowers
  'Her Majesty'—Lilac flowers, 4 feet tall.
  'Lady Wilson'—Large racemes of mauve flowers, 4 feet tall.

G. orientalis (or-i-en-tā'lis)—Caucasus Goat's Rue. This species is similar to *G. offici-nalis* but has pubescent stems and can be invasive. The violet-blue flowers are borne on erect racemes, 4 feet.

ADDITIONAL NOTES: *Galega* is derived from the Greek, *gala,* for milk, and *ago,* to lead. *Galega* has been used in the past as feed for goats and other dairy animals.

Native to Europe.   Perennial

SCIENTIFIC NAME/FAMILY: *Galium odoratum* (Asperula odorata)   Rubiaceae

(gā'li-um ō-do-rā'tum)

COMMON NAME: Woodruff, Sweet Woodruff, Woodroof

LEAVES: Leaves are arranged in whorls of 6–8 and are sessile to the stem, lanceolate; 1½" long, ¼"–½" wide; leaves are bristle-tipped and finely toothed or rough on the margin. The leaves and stems, when crushed, emit a very pleasant odor of new-mown hay.

FLOWER: White, fragrant flowers, 1/8"–1/4" long, borne in loose branching cymes.

HABIT: 6" to 8" ground cover with erect stems.

SEASON OF BLOOM: Late spring.   *See color plate*

CULTURE: For full season growth, the plant should be placed in a partial to full shade site with moist, well-drained soil. If grown in a dry, sunny area, the foliage may die down completely before summer's end. *Galium* will quickly spread and cover large areas if consistent moisture is provided.

UTILIZATION: Woodruff is an old-fashioned perennial that is useful for the rock garden, naturalized area, as a ground cover, or as an edging plant in the shaded border. The fragrant dried foliage is excellent for sachets or potpourris. I have also used the fresh foliage for flavoring springtime punch drinks.

PROPAGATION: Division in the spring or fall.

DISEASES AND INSECTS: None serious.

HARDINESS: Zones 4–8.

ADDITIONAL NOTES: *Galium* is derived from the Greek word, *galion* which was the name of the plant described by Dioscorides as one used for curdling milk.

Native to Europe, North Africa, and Asia.   Perennial

SCIENTIFIC NAME/FAMILY: *Galtonia candicans*   Hyacinthaceae
(Liliaceae)

(gâl-tō'ni-à kan'di-kanz)

COMMON NAME: Summer Hyacinth

LEAVES: The basal leaves are 2–3 feet long, 2" wide and have a conspicuous midvein.

FLOWER: Clear white bell-shaped flowers are borne in a loose raceme of 20–30 flowers atop a stout, leafless scape. The individual flowers are 1½" long and hang from 1"–2" long pedicels.

HABIT: The basal clump of leaves gives rise to leafless scapes that are 2'–4' tall. The overall effect is vertical.

SEASON OF BLOOM: This bulb is a summer bloomer with a bloom period of approximately 4 weeks.

CULTURE: Summer hyacinth should be grown in full sun with fertile, moist, well-drained soil during the growing season. After flowering, the plants should be dry during the dormant season. Staking may be necessary if this plant is grown in the shade or infertile soil. In these situations, the flower scapes are not sufficiently sturdy to hold up the heavy flowers. The foliage should be cut back after flowering, as the plants will have an unkempt appearance when the leaves die back. The large bulbs (some to 5" diameter) should be planted in the spring with the tops just below the surface. In gardens colder than Zone 6, the bulbs need to be dug in the fall and stored for planting the following spring.

See color plate

UTILIZATION: Good plant for the summer border, where the tall spikes of flowers create a noticeable effect for many weeks. It is also effective in containers such as half whiskey barrels.

PROPAGATION: *Galtonia* can be produced from seed or offsets. The offsets are not abundantly produced but can be lifted in the spring. These will flower in 2 years. Seed is usually the best way to increase stock. Seed is sown in late summer and held at nighttime temperatures of at least 55°F. About 12–15 months after germination, the bulbs can be transplanted to containers. It takes about 3 years to produce a flowering bulb from seed.

DISEASES AND INSECTS: There are no special problems, however, bulb rot can occur if drainage is poor.

HARDINESS: Zones 6–9.

ADDITIONAL NOTES: The *Galtonia* genus is named in honor of Francis Galton, a British botanist who traveled extensively in South Africa, the native site of *Galtonia.*

Native to South Africa.   Tender bulb in northern areas

SCIENTIFIC NAME/FAMILY: *Gaura lindheimeri*   Onagraceae

(gaw'ra lind-hi'-mer-i)

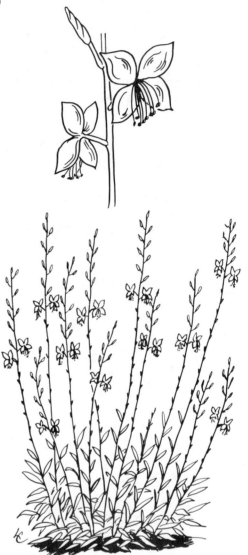

COMMON NAME: White Gaura

LEAVES: Alternate leaves are lanceolate, sessile, and 1½" to 3" long.

FLOWER: Flowers are white fading to pink as they age. The flowering spike continues to elongate during the bloom period with only a few flowers in bloom at the same time. The old flowers drop neatly and there is a new crop throughout the long bloom season. Individual flowers have four reflexed petals and usually 8 stamens.

HABIT: *Gaura* is somewhat vase-shaped with wand-like flowering stalks growing to 5 feet tall.

SEASON OF BLOOM: Early summer to frost. In cool summer climates, the bloom will be delayed until late summer.

CULTURE: Full sun in a well-drained soil. Unless a sandy loam soil is available, the planting bed for *Gaura* should be raised to provide adequate drainage. *Gaura* has a long tap root so watering is usually only needed in the driest parts of the summer.

UTILIZATION: The long season of bloom and adaptability to hot summers makes this species a useful selection for the southern garden border. One of the better plantings I have seen was at the Ziegler Nursery, near Zurich, Switzerland.

See color plate

PROPAGATION: *Gaura* is easily grown from seeds germinated at 65°–75°F in moist medium or by transplanting self-sown seedlings which reach flowering size after 1 year. The seedlings can be moved keeping in mind that the spade must go deep to prevent injury to the root system. Clumps will seldom need division.

DISEASES AND INSECTS: No serious problems.

HARDINESS: Zones 5–9.

ADDITIONAL NOTES: *Gaura* is derived from *gauros* meaning superb.

Native to Louisiana, Texas, and Mexico.   Perennial

SCIENTIFIC NAME/FAMILY: *Gazania rigens* (*G. splendens*)   Asteraceae
(Compositae)

(gā-zā'ni-à rī'jenz)

COMMON NAME: Gazania,
Treasure Flower

LEAVES: Leaves mostly in basal rosettes, rarely on the stem, densely white-tomentose below, green and glabrous above, simple, linear-lanceolate, 4"–5" long, tapering to a long winged petiole, or some with 1–2 large lateral lobes.

FLOWER: Heads large and showy, 2"–3" across, on glabrous peduncles longer than leaves, rays orange, yellow, pink or red with a dark ring about the base of the ray flowers. *Gazania* ray flowers grow together at the base while those on *Arctotis* are separate.

See color plate

HABIT: 6" to 12" tall plant with basal leaves and long stalked flowers.

SEASON OF BLOOM: Early summer to frost.

CULTURE: Full sun, tolerates light and sandy soils even in dry and windy conditions.

UTILIZATION: Border, flower bed, edging.

PROPAGATION: Gazania is a perennial grown as an annual. Seed can be sown indoors and will flower the first summer. As a perennial in warm climates it can be propagated by cuttings or division of clumps. Best seed germination occurs at 60°F and under dark conditions.

DISEASES AND INSECTS: Usually none.

CULTIVARS:
'Chansonette'—8"–10" compact selection, mixed colors, 2" diameter blooms.
'Daybreak Series'—This cultivar is available in colors of bronze, yellow, orange, and a mixture. It flowers 2 to 3 weeks earlier than 'Chansonette' or 'Mini-star'.
'Mini-star Series'—Large 2½" diameter flowers, 8" tall stems. 'Mini-star Tangerine', an All American and Fleuroselect winner, has an orange-gold flower color. 'Mini-star Yellow', a Fleuroselect winner, has pure yellow flowers.
'Morning Star Mix'—8" tall plants, 2½" diameter blooms of mixed color.
'Starburst Mixture'—Large flowers and bright flower colors.
'Sunshine Giants'—8", extra large flowers up to 4" across, wide range of colors, tetraploid.

ADDITIONAL NOTES: Gazania can be moved from the garden in the fall and potted as a house plant. Flower stalks rise 6″–12″ directly from the ground and bear single daisy-like blossoms which close at night and on cloudy days; hence they have little value as cut flowers. *Gazania* is named for Theodore of Gaza (1398–1478), who translated the botanical works of Theophrastus from Greek into Latin. This is an excellent plant, particularly for dry and hot sites, and I recommend it for northern and southern gardens.

Native to South Africa.   Perennial treated as an annual

SCIENTIFIC NAME/FAMILY: *Gentiana septemfida*   Gentianaceae

(jen-shi-ā´na sep-tem-fi´da)

COMMON NAME: Crested Gentian

LEAVES: The opposite leaves are ovate, sessile to nearly clasping, and ½″ to 1″ long.

FLOWER: The dark blue corolla is trumpet-shaped, 1″ long, and has a white throat. The corolla is lobed and has pleats or appendages between the lobes. The flower is solitary and borne on the terminal of a short, upright stem.

HABIT: Low spreading plant, 4″ to 6″ tall and 12″ wide.

SEASON OF BLOOM: Mid to late summer.

CULTURE: Crested gentian can be grown in sun or partial shade. The optimum soil is one that is moist, gravelly, and well-drained. The soil pH can be acid or slightly alkaline.

UTILIZATION: Crested gentian is an easily grown old-reliable that has value as rock plant in the sun.

PROPAGATION: Gentian is most easily propagated by seed. Seeds need a precooling before sowing. The young plants should be kept in pots until transplanting. The young roots must not be damaged.

DISEASES AND INSECTS: None serious.

HARDINESS: Zones 3–8 .

RELATED SPECIES:
Gentiana asclepiadea (as-klep-e-ad´-e-a), Willow Gentian. This species is 18″ to 24″ tall, has 2″ to 3″ long leaves, and large tubular deep blue flowers, 1½″ long. It is not as tolerant of soil and exposure as *G. septemfida*. Willow gentian should be planted in a neutral to slightly acid, humus-rich soil that is constantly moist and cool.

ADDITIONAL NOTES: *Gentiana* was named for King Gentius, 500 BC, who was reported to have discovered medicinal virtues of the root of yellow gentian, *G. lutea.*

Native to Asia Minor.   Perennial

SCIENTIFIC NAME/FAMILY: *Geranium endressii*   Geraniaceae

(je-ra′ni-um en-dres′-sē-ī)

COMMON NAME: Pyrenean Crane's-bill

LEAVES: Basal, 2″–3″ wide; deeply 5-lobed, lobes sharply cut, pubescent. The petioles are 4″ to 10″ long. In cool moist climates, such as the Pacific Northwest, the foliage is evergreen; otherwise the foliage is deciduous in cold winter climates.

FLOWER: Pink flowers, ½″ to 1″ wide, borne in terminal 2 flowered clusters.

HABIT: Mounded and creeping ground cover; 12″ to 18″ tall and 18″ wide.

SEASON OF BLOOM: In climates with cool summers, it will flower most of the summer; in hot areas, flowering is usually restricted to late spring and early summer.

See color plate

CULTURE: Climate dictates the culture of this species, in areas of cool summers, it can be grown in sun and tolerates dry shade conditions. However, in hot summer climates, partial shade and moist soil are required.

UTILIZATION: Useful as a ground cover or massed in the front of the border or in an island bed.

PROPAGATION: Division in spring or fall, summer cuttings, or seed are all suitable methods for increasing this species.

DISEASES AND INSECTS: Leaf spot diseases are occasional problems.

HARDINESS: Zones 4–8.

CULTIVARS: 'Wargrave Pink'—A popular cultivar with salmon-pink flowers. It is more vigorous than the species.

RELATED SPECIES: *G.* × *oxonianum* (ox-on-ē-ā′-num). This species is a cross between *G. endressii* and *G. versicolor.* It is a vigorous, free flowering plant with broad mounds of attractive foliage.
    'A.T. Johnson'—Silvery-pink flowers.
    'Claridge Druce'—Grayish-green foliage and purple-pink flowers with purple tracery on the petals.
    'Rose Clair'—Light pink flowers; this cultivar is intermediate in color between 'A.T. Johnson' and 'Wargrave Pink'.

Native to Pyrenees.   Perennial

SCIENTIFIC NAME/FAMILY: *Geranium himalayense* (G. grandiflorum)   Geraniaceae

(je-rā′ni-um him-a-lā′enz)

COMMON NAME: Lilac Crane's-bill

LEAVES: Leaves deeply 5–7 parted, to 3″–6″ wide, lobes broadly rhombic-obovate, incisely-toothed to pinnately parted.

FLOWER: Two flowers borne on axillary peduncles to 8″ long; flowers 1½″–2″ wide, petals are lilac blue with purple veins.

HABIT: 2″ to 18″, each plant forms a clump 12″–15″ wide.

SEASON OF BLOOM: Early summer.

CULTURE: Lilac cranesbill can be grown in full sun in regions with cool summers. In climates with hotter summers, this geranium should be placed in partial shade. Soils should be moist and well-drained.

UTILIZATION: Positions in the perennial garden or in a rock garden. A sprawling habit makes this plant suited for placement along the garden path.

See color plate

PROPAGATION: Division every four years in the spring. Species may be also started by seeds, which germinate in 1 to 4 weeks at 70°F.

DISEASES AND INSECTS: Leaf spots and four-lined plant bug.

HARDINESS: Zones 4–8.

CULTIVARS:
'Gravetye' (var. *alpinum*)—Flowers are 2″ wide and deep blue. Plants are 12″ tall with deeply lobed foliage and wrinkled flowers.
'Plenum' ('Birch Double')—Double, pale purple-violet flowers which are smaller than the species. This cultivar is not as vigorous.

RELATED SPECIES: G. × 'Johnson's Blue'—This cultivar is one of the best even though the habit is somewhat sprawling. The flowers have a clear blue color. There is minimal seed set so flowering occurs over a longer time period. It is a hybrid of *G. pratense* and *G. himalayense.*

ADDITIONAL NOTES: *Geranium* is derived from the Greek word for crane which refers to the similarity of the beaked fruit to the bill of a crane.

Native to Turkestan, India, and Tibet.   Perennial

SCIENTIFIC NAME/FAMILY: *Geranium macrorrhizum*   Geraniaceae

(je-rā'ni-um mak-ror-rhiz'-um)

COMMON NAME: Bigroot Geranium

LEAVES: The basal leaves are palmately lobed with 5 to 7 lobes which are cut nearly to the leaf base. Each lobe in turn has 3 to 5 notches at the tip. The foliage is pubescent and aromatic.

FLOWER: Pink flowers are arranged in a terminal cluster. The stems are 2 times as long as the sepals and petals. Each flower is about 1" wide. Dark red calyces are inflated like small balloons.

HABIT: Wide spreading mound, 12"–18" tall and 15" wide.

SEASON OF BLOOM: Late spring to early summer.

See color plate

CULTURE: In hot summer regions, *Geranium macrorrhizum* should be grown in partial shade. If the summers are cool, it can be grown in full sun. It is adaptable to most soil types including those of higher pH. Best growth will occur on well-drained soils with good humus content.

UTILIZATION: Excellent plant to be used as a deciduous ground cover or a plant for the border front. Very few weeds are capable of penetrating the dense cover of a mature plant. It is one of the easiest geraniums to grow.

PROPAGATION: Division of the roots is the easiest propagation method. The stems are arranged in rosettes and these can be removed and treated as cuttings. Seed can also be used. In fact, it spreads easily by self-seeding.

DISEASES AND INSECTS: No serious problems.

HARDINESS: Zones 3–8.

CULTIVARS:
'Album'—The white flower is highlighted by a pinkish-red calyx and long protruding stamens and anther. 10"–12".
'Bevan's Variety'—Deep magenta flowers, 12".
'Ingwersen's Variety'—Pale-pink flowers with glossy leaves, 12" tall.
'Spessart'—Soft pink flowers, 12" tall.
'Variegatum'—Magenta-pink flowers, leaves variegated with cream, yellow, and a bit of red around the leaf edges.

RELATED SPECIES:

G. cantabrigiense (can-ta-brig-i-en'-se) (*G. dalmaticum* × *G. macrorrhizum*). 'Biokova' is a natural hybrid of these species. The flowers are white and have a pink blush in the center. Sterile flowers produce a longer-flowering season. It is suitable as a ground cover or for rock gardens.

G. pratense (pra-ten'se), Meadow Cranesbill. This species of northern Europe is one of the taller and more vigorous of the cranesbill. It is 2'–3' tall and will usually require staking. The flowers are dark blue and 1½" wide. The flowering period is short lived due to a tendency toward heavy seed production. Best growth occurs in full sun in soils with abundant moisture.

'Mrs. Kendall Clark'—Large finely-veined light blue flowers, 24" tall.

'Plenum Album'—Double white flowers.

'Plenum Caeruleum'—Double pale blue flowers.

'Plenum Violaceum'—Double purple flowers.

'Kashmir Purple' and 'Kashmir White' were once listed as cultivars of *G. pratense* but are now found under *G. clarkei.* Regardless of their nomenclature location, they are fine hardy geraniums. Both plants have upward-facing flowers which cover the plant in late spring and early summer.

G. psilostemon (si-los'tē-mon), Armenian Geranium. This radiant species is still more common on the European continent than it is in North America. Plants are 3' to 4' tall with shocking red flowers with jet black centers. It is a color that grows on you or knocks you on your heels. The fluorescent color is highlighted if the plants are placed in front of a dark background.

'Bressingham Flair'—Flowers of this Blooms Nursery introduction have more pink in the petals and are not as vivid as the species, 30" tall.

Native to southern Europe.   Perennial

SCIENTIFIC NAME/FAMILY: *Geranium sanguineum*   Geraniaceae

(je-ra′ni-um san-gwin′ē-um)

COMMON NAME: Bloodred Geranium

LEAVES: Leaves are circular in outline with 5–7 narrow lobes and 1½″–2″ wide. The leaf surfaces have scattered hispid hairs and the stems and flower peduncles have spreading white hairs. The foliage turns red to maroon after the first hard frost.

FLOWER: The magenta flowers are carried on 1-flowered axillary peduncles. The flowers have 5 petals and are 1″ to 1½″ wide.

HABIT: 6″ to 12″ tall clump-forming perennial which will spread 24″.

SEASON OF BLOOM: Late spring to early summer.

CULTURE: The preferred site is partial shade. However, *G. sanguineum* is one of the geraniums that can tolerate full sun even in long, hot summers. Moist, humus-rich soils will promote spread.

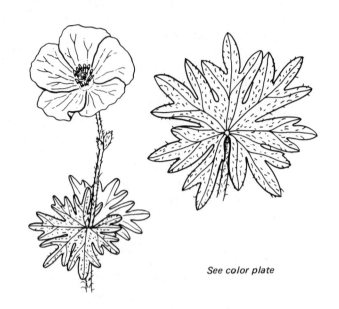

See color plate

UTILIZATION: Excellent selection for the border front, rock garden, or ground cover in partial shade to full sun.

PROPAGATION: Tip cuttings, division, or by seed. Geraniums rarely need division. However, division can be obtained by digging to the side and removing a side piece of roots. If this is done carefully, the clump will not have to be lifted. The species can be propagated by seed germinated at 65°–75°F in a moist medium.

DISEASES AND INSECTS: Leaf spot and rusts may sometimes appear but geraniums are generally considered pest free.

HARDINESS: Zones 3–8.

CULTIVARS:
'Album'—Pure white flowers, 10″–12″ tall.
'Aviemore'—Clear pink flowers, 12″ tall.
'Elspeth'—Pink flowers, dark green leaves turning a nice red color in the fall.
'Jubilee Pink'—Soft pink flowers, 12″ tall.
'Shepherds Warning'—Reddish pink flowers, 4″–6″ tall.
var. *striatum*—Light pink flowers with reddish veins. It is 6″–8″ tall and may be the best cultivar. It is also sold as 'Lancastriense' or 'Prostratum'.

RELATED SPECIES:

G. cinereum (sin-er'-ē-um). Members of this species are small in stature and often are used at the border front or in rock gardens. They are viewed as alpine geraniums. The leaves have 5–7 lobes and are dissected almost to the leaf base. This spring-blooming plant has a purplish pink flower with dark veins on the petals. Optimum growth occurs in zones 5–7 when planted in a well-drained soil. There are some attractive cultivars with *G. cinereum* as one of the parents.

'Ballerina'—This alpine beauty is 4"–6" tall and produces lilac-pink flowers with dark eyes and crimson veining on the petals. Most of the flowers are sterile, which produces a long bloom period. Alan Bloom selected this cultivar from seedings of *G. cinereum* × *G. cinereum* var. *subcaulescens.*

'Lawrence Flatman'—Alan Bloom also selected this cultivar, which is very similar to 'Ballerina'. He described it as being more vigorous with a deeper flower color. Both cultivars are excellent plants and will provide grace and charm to any rock garden. Alan named this cultivar to honor Lawrence Flatman, a long-time employee of the company.

Native to Europe and Asia.   Perennial

SCIENTIFIC NAME/FAMILY: *Gerbera jamesonii*   Asteraceae
                                                                        (Compositae)

(jĕr′-bē rȧ; gĕr′-bē rȧ jam-sōn′-ē-ī)

COMMON NAME: Transvaal Daisy, Gerbera, Barberton Daisy, Veldt Daisy

LEAVES: Leaves are basal, mature leaves very woolly beneath, petioles 6″–8″ long, the blade 5″–10″ long, pinnately lobed or parted.

FLOWER: Heads to 4″ across, with showy orange-flame colored strap-shaped rays. Many color forms are known in the cultivated strains ranging from shades of yellow, salmon, pink or red with petals arranged in single or several rows.

HABIT: 12″ to 18″ tall plant with prostrate leaves and erect flower stems.

SEASON OF BLOOM: Early summer to fall.

CULTURE: Full sun to partial shade, well-drained soil. In zone 8 *Gerbera* may overwinter if covered with a nonmatting mulch such as evergreen boughs, pine needles, or salt hay. Compost or bark mulches should not be used.

UTILIZATION: Cut flowers, bedding plants.

PROPAGATION: Can be grown from seed and germinates in one or two weeks at 70°F. It is important to use fresh seed. In southern zones where it will overwinter, division can be done carefully in the spring.

DISEASES AND INSECTS: No serious problems.

HARDINESS: Zone 8.

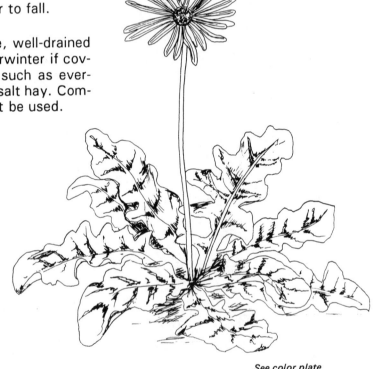

See color plate

CULTIVARS:
'Chorus Line'—8″–12″ tall with 4″ to 5″ wide blossoms, full color range.
'Happipot Mix'—Good for pots, planters, and window boxes. Colors include red, rose, pink, salmon, orange, yellow, and cream. This selection is often utilized for greenhouse pot production of *Gerbera*.
 ·di Gras Mixed'—F₁ hybrid with many brilliant colors. Good early-flowering
   ·tion.
       Strain'—Double flowers.
         x Mixed'—Double flowers, 4″ across, thick stems, variety of colors.

       Perennial plant that is grown as an annual. May be dug in the fall
     ·inter house plant. *Gerbera* is named for Traugott Gerber, a German

Africa and Asia.   Perennial treated as an annual

SCIENTIFIC NAME/FAMILY: *Geum* hybrids   Rosaceae
                (generally hybrids of *G. coccineum* × *G. quellyon*)

(jē'um)

COMMON NAME: Geum, Avens

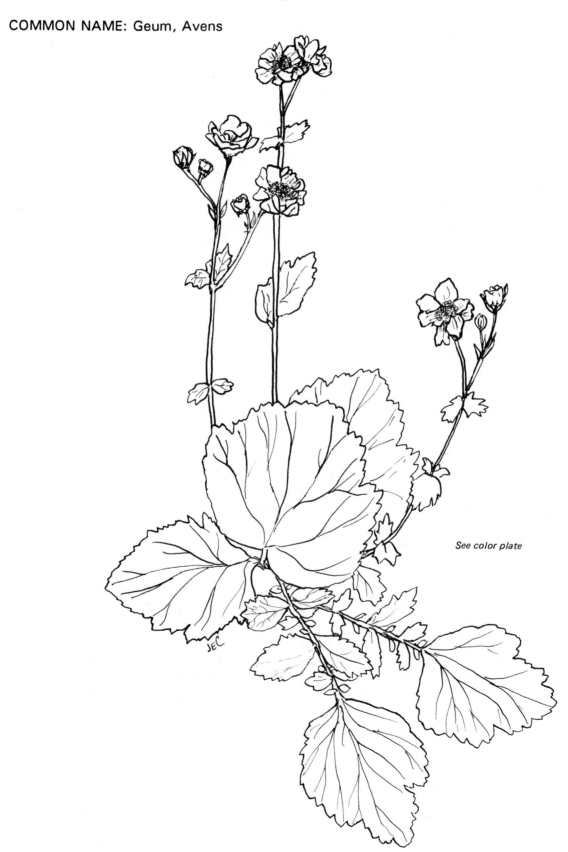

See color plate

LEAVES: Pinnate with large terminal lobe, to 6" long, leaflets unequally toothed and pubescent; many leaves are basal.

FLOWER: Scarlet, orange or yellow, erect and single, to 1" wide; some cultivars are double.

HABIT: 18"–24" tall plant with prostrate leaves and erect flower stems. It has an 18" spread.

SEASON OF BLOOM: Late spring to early summer.

CULTURE: Geum requires extra care in site selection. They perform best in cool climates with full sun and well-drained soil rich in organic matter to retain moisture during the summer. Geum is not reliably winter-hardy in all areas of the country. Wet winter conditions are usually fatal. Annual division seems to prolong the longevity.

UTILIZATION: Massing in the perennial border or as cut flowers. The smaller cultivars can be used in the rock garden. With proper location, the gardener will be rewarded with a very showy display. The orange and yellow flowers complement the blue flowers of forget-me-nots and *Brunnera*.

PROPAGATION: Seed and division. Germination occurs in 3–4 weeks at 70°–85°F. Division done in late summer will provide flowering-size plants for the following year.

DISEASES AND INSECTS: Hardiness and site requirements are usually the only problems, although spider mite populations can build to troublesome levels on occasion.

HARDINESS: Zones 5–7. *Geum* will grow in southern gardens but it is not an outstanding plant. It is best planted in cooler areas.

CULTIVARS:
  'Fire Opal'—Red flowers with bronze shading, 2"–3" wide.
  'Lady Stratheden'—24", golden-yellow, semi-double flowers, comes true from seed.
  'Mrs. Bradshaw'—24", orange-red double flowers, comes true from seed.
  'Princess Juliana'—Bronzy-orange, semi-double flowers.
  'Red Wings'—Scarlet, semi-double flowers, 24" tall.
  'Starkers Magnificent'—Apricot-orange, double flowers, 15" tall.

RELATED SPECIES:
  G. × *borisii* (bor'-is-ē-ī). This hybrid has orange, single flowers on stems that are 9"–12" high with a spread of 12". It has a wider geographic range and performs well in zones 3 to 7.
  G. reptans (rep'tanz), Creeping Avens. Solitary pale yellow flowers are borne on trailing branches which send up stems 6"–8" tall. This native of the European Alps should be located in full sun in soils that are alkaline and very well-drained. Without these conditions, creeping avens does not last long in the garden. Zones 4–7.

Hybrid origin.   Perennial

SCIENTIFIC NAME/FAMILY: *Gillenia trifoliata*   Rosaceae
(Poteranthus trifoliatus)
(gil-lē′-ne-a trī-fō li-ā′-ta)

COMMON NAME: Bowman's Root, Indian-Physics

LEAVES: *Gillenia* has alternate, sessile leaves which are trifoliate or 3-parted. Leaflets are sharply serrated and the veins are impressed.

FLOWER: Flowers have 5 petals which are very narrow and assume a star-shape. They are white or blushed with pink and are borne in large, loose panicles. The red calyces, which are also ornamental, persist after the petals drop.

HABIT: 2′ to 3′ tall, erect, branching plant, 3′ wide.

See color plate

SEASON OF BLOOM: Late spring to midsummer.

CULTURE: Performs well in partial shade or sun in a moist, well-drained soil. It is tolerant of drier soils.

UTILIZATION: Well suited for the border. It probably should be massed because of its airy texture. Good plant for placement in the mixed border of woody shrubs and perennials.

PROPAGATION: Spring or fall division or by seed. Seed propagation may be difficult and may require a warm-cold stratification period. Sowing outside in the fall may provide the warm-cold period with germination occurring in the spring. Placing tip cuttings under mist also works well.

DISEASES AND INSECTS: None serious.

HARDINESS: Zones 4–8.

ADDITIONAL NOTES: *Gillenia* is named after Arnold Gille, a German physician who wrote horticulture articles in the seventeenth century.

Native to the eastern United States.   Perennial

SCIENTIFIC NAME/FAMILY: *Gladiolus* × *hortulanus*   Iridaceae

(glad-i-ō'lus hôr-tu-lān'us)

COMMON NAME: Gladiolus, Gladiola

LEAVES: Basal and cauline, sword-shaped, 1"–2" wide, many veins. The leaves are erect.

FLOWER: Flowers showy, in one-sided spikes, each flower from 2"–4" across, in many shades and markings, the upper perianth sometimes hooded. There are hundreds of named cultivars.

HABIT: 1' to 5' erect plant.

SEASON OF BLOOM: Summer. Successive plantings should be made to insure flowers for continuous cutting.

CULTURE: Full sun in moist, well-drained soil with good air circulation. They should be located away from trees and shrubs. Although gladiolus will grow in nearly any soil, one should avoid very sandy or heavy clay soils. Fertilization and watering should be increased when flowers start to develop.

UTILIZATION: Cutting flowers.

PROPAGATION: Division of the corms. Dig the corms before a hard fall freeze, cut the tops to ½" above the corm and spread thinly to dry. After drying, remove the old mother corm and old roots from the new corms. Store over winter at 35°–40°F. Corms should be dusted with an insecticide or naphthalene (moth flakes) before storage.

DISEASES AND INSECTS: Fusarium rot, mosaic, *Botrytis* leaf and flower spot, rust, dry rot, aphids, thrips, and corn borer. Although the potential problems are many, gladiolus is relatively easy to grow.

HARDINESS: Zone 9.

CULTIVARS:
Large-flowered hybrids—2'–4½', vigorous, robust growth habit and a wide array of colors. Individual blooms may be 4"–8" in diameter.
Butterfly and miniature hybrids—1½'–4', many flowers per stem, each bloom is 1½"–3½" in diameter, often with ruffled petals. These hybrids are more expensive because the corms are small and do not multiply as rapidly as other types.
Primulinus hybrids—1½'–3', less vigorous but have a more graceful habit than the large-flowered hybrids. A wide variety of color is available.

ADDITIONAL NOTES: *Gladiolus* is a derivation of *gladius,* meaning sword, and is in reference to the sword-shaped leaves.

Hybrid origin.   Perennial—tender corm.

SCIENTIFIC NAME/FAMILY: *Gomphrena globosa*   Amaranthaceae

(gom-frē'nȧ glō-bō'sȧ)

COMMON NAME: Gomphrena, Globe Amaranth

LEAVES: Opposite, leaves oblong to elliptic, to 4" long, entire with ciliate margins.

FLOWER: Flower has a clover-like appearance due to the globular, dense, long-peduncled heads which are purple, white, pink, or yellow and closely subtended by 2 broad, leafy bracts.

HABIT: 9" to 24", rounded growth habit.

SEASON OF BLOOM: Summer.

CULTURE: Sun, well-drained soil; will tolerate hot weather, wind, and rain without looking poor.

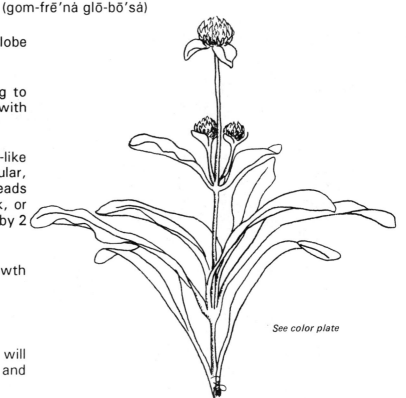

See color plate

UTILIZATION: The taller cultivars are good for cut and dried flowers. The smaller selections are suitable for bedding purposes and as edging plants. The small globe shapes are unique in the garden and a good texture change, especially massed.

PROPAGATION: Seed should be soaked in water for 3 to 4 days before seeding. Cover seed with ¼" of soil to prevent light exposure. Germinate 70° to 75°F with bottom heat.

DISEASES AND INSECTS: Damping off in seeding stage; otherwise fairly pest free.

CULTIVARS:
'Buddy' Series—9" tall plants used for bedding, edging, or cut flowers. Available in reddish purple or white.
'Lavender Lady'—Lavender flowers, 1½" diameter, 24" tall.
'Strawberry Fields'—Bright red flowers, popular plant for dried floral arrangements, 24" tall.
'Tall Mixture'—24" tall, flower colors include purple, silver, white, pink, and orange.
'Woodcreek' Series—Tall selection with large flowers, good for cut flowers, 24"–30" tall. This series is available in 7 colors and a mixture.

ADDITIONAL NOTES: *Gomphrena* is long on dependability and short on popularity. This old fashioned garden flower is easy to grow, tough, and drought resistant but is little used. For drying, pick just as the flowers open fully, hang upside down to dry. The flower heads will hold their color indefinitely. *Gomphrena* is derived from Latin, *gromphaena*, a type of Amaranth. *Gomphrena* is an excellent plant for late season color, particularly in southern areas where the seasons are longer.

Native to tropics.   Annual

SCIENTIFIC NAME/FAMILY: *Gypsophila elegans*   Caryophyllaceae

(jip-sof'i-là el'e-ganz)

COMMON NAME: Annual Baby's-Breath, Chalk Plant.

LEAVES: Leaves linear-lanceolate, 1"–2" long, 1–3 veined, glabrous.

FLOWER: Borne in panicled cymes, bracts, scarious, petals ¼" to 1" long, with purple veins. Flower colors of cultivars include rose and purple. Plants have a misty, airy appearance when in flower.

HABIT: 12" to 24" round habit with a fine texture.

SEASON OF BLOOM: Flowers for only 6 weeks starting in early summer. For a continuous bloom during the summer, successive plantings about every 2–3 weeks should be made.

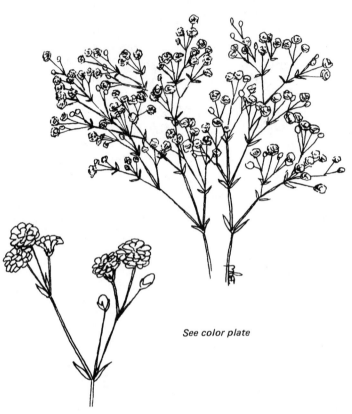

See color plate

CULTURE: Well-drained sunny location, low nutrient soil with a high pH (7–7.5). Perennial baby's breath will not overwinter in a moist soggy soil.

UTILIZATION: Cutting garden, dried flowers, rock gardens. Tall plants will often need staking. Pea staking is a good choice for baby's breath.

PROPAGATION: Both annual and perennial types can be started with seed. Both types will germinate at 70°–80°F after 10 days. Perennial plants are also divided in spring or fall, although fleshy roots make division difficult. Terminal cuttings can be taken after flowering. Tissue culture labs are now producing large amounts of clonal material.

DISEASES AND INSECTS: *Botrytis* blight, aster yellows, and leafhoppers.

CULTIVARS:
'Covent Garden'—24"–36", large and full-petaled white flowers.
'White Giant'—Larger flowers than 'Covent Garden'.

RELATED SPECIES:
G. paniculata (pan-ik-ū-lā'-ta)—Perennial Baby's-Breath. *Gypsophila* is a perennial that has a use in every garden. It can be used as a filler to cover areas vacated by oriental poppies, common bleeding hearts, and spring bulbs, as well as its classical use as a cut flower. Hardy to zones 3–9.
'Bristol Fairy'—24", white double flowers, excellent for borders or cutting, repeat bloomer.
'Compacta Plena'—Semi-double flowers, white, 15"–18" tall.
'Double Snowflake'—36", double white flowers.

'Flamingo'—24", double, pink flowers.

'Perfecta'—30", white, double flowers. Larger flowers than 'Bristol Fairy'.

'Pink Fairy'—18", double pink flowers which bloom until frost.

'Pink Star'—Pink flowers, 18" tall.

'Rosenschleier' ('Rosy Veil')—Semi-prostrate selection with pale pink semi-double flowers, 15" tall.

G. repens (rē'penz)—Creeping Baby's-Breath. This perennial is low growing, 6", with white flowers from late spring until frost. It is an excellent plant for front of borders, rock gardens, or dry stone walls. It is especially attractive when it trails over stone walls. Plant in full sun and very well-drained soil. 'Rosea' and 'Dorothy Teacher' are pink-flowered selections. Creeping baby's breath is native to Europe. On an afternoon trip to the top of Mt. Stanserhorn near Lucerne, Switzerland, I was able to view this baby's breath in its natural habitat.

ADDITIONAL NOTES: *Gypsophila* comes from the Greek *gypsos,* or gypsum, and *philos,* or friendship and alludes to the plants' preference for gypsum rock.

Native to Europe and northern Asia.   Annual

SCIENTIFIC NAME/FAMILY: *Hakonechloa macra* 'Aureola'

(ha-kon'-ē-klō''à mak'ra â-rē-ōl'à)

Poaceae
(Gramineae)

COMMON NAME: Golden Variegated Hakonechloa

LEAVES: Leaf blades, 3/8" wide, 8" to 12" long, bright yellow with slender green lines creating a striped pattern.

FLOWER: The yellowish green flowers are borne in an open panicle up to 6" long and 2" wide. The flowers are not particularly showy; consequently, this selection is usually utilized for the foliage effect.

HABIT: Dense, mounded clump, 12"– 18" tall. This mound looks like the hairdo of Moe of the Three Stooges.

SEASON OF BLOOM: Late summer.

CULTURE: Full sun or partial shade in a well-drained soil. Leaf coloration will be best in partial shade.

UTILIZATION: This selection, when planted as a specimen or massed in a group, provides color and interest in the front of the border. It also brightens the darker areas of the garden.

PROPAGATION: This variegated form must be increased by division. The species can be propagated from seed.

See color plate

DISEASES AND INSECTS: No problem.

HARDINESS: Zones 6–9. *Hakonechloa* grows in Columbus, Ohio, zone 5, but plant quality varies from one year to the next. I would guess that plant survival is related to soil conditions as much as cold temperatures. Plant in well-drained soils for best results.

CULTIVARS:
The species, *Hakonechloa macra,* has bright green foliage. Two other cultivars include 'Albo-aurea'—foliage variegated with white and yellow and green and 'Albo-variegata'—foliage variegated with white and green. These 2 cultivars are not as vigorous as 'Aureola' and are rarely found in the trade.

Native to Japan.   Perennial

SCIENTIFIC NAME/FAMILY: *Helenium autumnale*   Asteraceae
(Compositae)

(he-lē'ni-um â-tum-nā'lē)

COMMON NAME: Sneezeweed, Helen's
Flower, Yellow Star, False Sunflower,
Swamp Sunflower

LEAVES: Alternate, leaves decurrent,
creating a winged effect, leaves
linear-lanceolate to elliptic or ovate-
lanceolate, to 6" long, usually serrate,
nearly glabrous.

FLOWER: Heads to 2" wide, receptacle
nearly globose to hemispherical, colors are yellow, reddish brown or
orange. Flowers are daisy-like.

HABIT: 2½' to 6' erect plant, three feet
wide.

SEASON OF BLOOM: Late summer to
frost.

CULTURE: Sneezeweed is adaptable to
many different climates. Optimum
growth occurs in full sun and a moist,
well-drained soil. Dry soils should be
avoided. Most of the cultivars are tall
and will require staking before the
summer flowering season. Foliage should be cut back at least 1/3 after flowering.

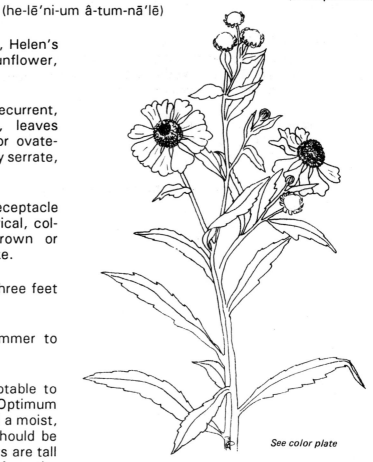

See color plate

UTILIZATION: *Helenium* is a tall plant that is best used at the back of the border or in the
center of island beds. Cultivar selection is varied and includes many different bright
colors which are useful for the late summer and early fall borders. Shorter cultivars will
reduce the need for staking. Sneezeweed is also used as a cut flower.

PROPAGATION: Clump division should be every third year to prevent over-crowding. Seeds
can be used, but cultivars will not come true to type. Germination occurs in 1 to 2
weeks at 70°F.

DISEASES AND INSECTS: Powdery mildew is the major problem and is accelerated by dry
conditions.

HARDINESS: *Helenium* does well in zones 3–8. In areas of high night temperatures, the
flowers of sneezeweed become smaller and the need for staking increases.

CULTIVARS:
'Brilliant'—Bronze flowers, prolific bloomer.
'Bruno'—2½'–4', sturdy habit, mahogany-red flowers, excellent in zone 8.
'Butterpat'—Clear yellow flowers, excellent for cutting, 3'–4'.
'Crimson Beauty'—2'–3' tall, mahogany flowers.
'Kugelsonne'—Yellow flowers, 4'–5' tall.
'Moerheim Beauty'—4' tall, bronze-red flowers.
'Pumilum Magnificum'—Light yellow flowers, 5' tall.

'Riverton Beauty'—Lemon yellow flowers with purplish black disk flowers, sturdy 4' stems, excellent in zone 8.

'Wyndley'—Coppery brown flowers, 2'-3' tall.

RELATED SPECIES:

H. hoopesii (hoop'-sē-ī). This species flowers earlier (early to midsummer) than *H. autumnale.* The yellow flowers are held on stems 2'-4' tall. It is not as tolerant of hot summers as *Helenium autumnale.*

ADDITIONAL NOTES: Tall heavy stems need to be staked. Pinch plant back about 6 weeks before blooming to encourage branching and reduce height. *Helenium* is named after Helen of Troy.

Native to eastern and south central United States.   Perennial

SCIENTIFIC NAME/FAMILY: *Helianthemum nummularium*   Cistaceae

(hē-le-anth'-em-um num-mū-lar'-ē-um)

COMMON NAME: Sunrose, Rock Rose

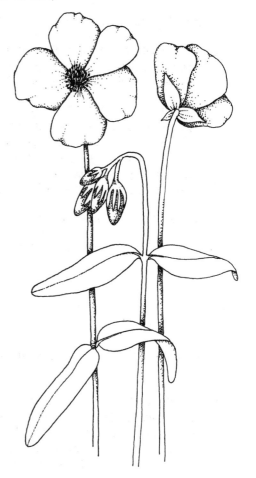

LEAVES: Gray-green leaves are usually opposite, ovate to lanceolate in shape. They are 1"–2" long and are gray-tomentose on the lower leaf surfaces. Margins are flat or slightly revolute.

FLOWER: The flower colors are numerous and include yellow, orange, red, pink, and bicolors. The symmetrical flower contains 5 petals, 5 sepals, and numerous stamens. Flowers are about 1" wide and have a crepe paper–like texture.

HABIT: Low-growing mound with procumbent branches, 6"–12" tall and 12"–18" wide.

SEASON OF BLOOM: Late spring to early summer.

CULTURE: It is very important that this species be planted in a well-drained, sandy loam soil, which is dry and alkaline. Sun rose does not perform well in fertile soils. Prune the plants in early spring to create a dense mat of growth. The plants should be again pruned after flowering. A mulch is needed for winter protection.

UTILIZATION: Use as a ground cover, in the perennial border, rock garden, or rock wall. It grows well on dry, sunny slopes where other plants would do poorly under heat and drought conditions.

PROPAGATION: Spring division or summer tip cuttings.

DISEASES AND INSECTS: None serious.

HARDINESS: Zones 5–7.

See color plate

CULTIVARS: There are endless named cultivars. A few of the selection are:
'Amy Baring'—Apricot yellow flowers, 4" high.
'Ben Heckle'—Orange flowers with a red eye, performs well in the heat.
'Ben Nevis'—Tawny orange-gold flowers, 10"– 12" tall, green foliage. *Index Hortensis* lists 17 cultivars that begin with "Ben."
'Cerise Queen'—Double, rose-red flowers.
'Firedragon'—Flame-orange flowers, gray foliage.
'Jubilee'—Double yellow flowers.
'Raspberry Ripple'—Red and white bicolor, 6", upright habit.
'Rose Queen'—Rose-pink flowers, performs well in the heat.
'St. Mary's'—Large white flowers, green foliage.
'Wisley Pink'—Soft pink on gray foliage.
'Wisley Primrose'—Soft yellow flowers, gray foliage.

Native to Europe.   Perennial

SCIENTIFIC NAME/FAMILY: *Helianthus annuus*   Asteraceae
                                                               (Compositae)

(hē-li-an'thus an'ū-us)

COMMON NAME: Common Sunflower

LEAVES: Mostly alternate, ovate, to 1' long, trun-
    cate to cordate at base, dentate; scabrous-bristly
    above, hispid beneath, petioles to 1' long.

FLOWER: Heads 3"–6" across in wild specimens,
    sometimes 14" in cultivation; disk flowers red or
    purple, ray flowers orange-yellow. In addition to
    the garden types, there is the giant common sun-
    flower, which grows as tall as 10', with a single
    yellow blossom 8"–14" across.

HABIT: 2' to 10' erect plant with a coarse texture.

SEASON OF BLOOM: Summer.

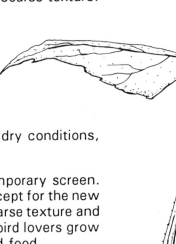

See color plate

CULTURE: Sun, tolerates heat and dry conditions,
    almost any soil type.

UTILIZATION: Background as a temporary screen.
    Difficult to use in a landscape except for the new
    cultivars, because of a rough, coarse texture and
    rangy, leggy appearance. Many bird lovers grow
    sunflower to shell for winter bird food.

PROPAGATION: Seeds germinate in two to three
    weeks at 68°–86°F.

DISEASES AND INSECTS: Leaf spot, powdery
    mildew, rust, stem rot, aphids, seed midges, and
    cutworms often contribute to the ragged appearance of this plant.

CULTIVARS:
    'Italian White'—4', pure white cream colored flowers up to 4" across.
    'Lemon Queen'—Lemon yellow flowers with dark centers, 4"–5" diameter, 5 feet tall.
    'Orange Sun'—Apricot-orange, double flowers on stems 3½ feet tall.
    'Russian Giant'—Choose this cultivar if you want to have the tallest sunflower on the
        block. It is 8'–10' tall.
    'Sunspot'—2' tall plants have full size 10" diameter heads. It is a great plant for the
        family garden.
    'Teddy Bear'—24", single and double flowers, yellow.
    'Valentine'—Bright lemon-yellow blossoms. 6" diameter, 5' tall. Cut flowers will last
        2–3 weeks in water with floral preservative.

ADDITIONAL NOTES: Grown in many countries for its seed oil, as well as for the edible
    seeds. The name *Helianthus* is derived from *helios*, the sun, and *anthos*, a flower. The
    annual, crop-like nature of this plant is evident as it grows brown and dry in the fall,
    suggesting a plant ready for harvest.

North American origin.   Annual

SCIENTIFIC NAME/FAMILY: *Helianthus × multiflorus*

Asteraceae
(Compositae)

(hē-li-an'thus mul-ti-flō'rus)

COMMON NAME: Perennial Sunflower

LEAVES: The leaf arrangement varies with position. The lower leaves are often opposite while the upper ones are alternate. Leaves ovate to ovate lanceolate, 3" to 8" long, serrate. The leaves are coarse textured above and pubescent beneath.

FLOWER: Bright yellow heads, 3"–5" wide are borne solitary at the terminal. Some cultivars are so "double" that very few or no disk flowers remain.

HABIT: Large erect mass, 3' to 5' tall, 3' wide.

SEASON OF BLOOM: Midsummer to fall.

CULTURE: Sunflower is easily grown in full sun in a well-drained soil. It will need space so allow 2' to 3' between it and other plants.

UTILIZATION: Large specimen for the border or island bed. One plant will usually suffice in an average size garden.

PROPAGATION: Division in fall or spring. Division may be needed every 3 to 4 years. In my own experience, it was 3 years after my Kansas "sonflower" arrived that "daughter-flower" appeared!!

DISEASES AND INSECTS: No serious problems.

HARDINESS: Zones 4–8.

CULTIVARS:
'Capenoch Star'—Lemon yellow, 3½'.
'Flore Pleno'—Double yellow flowers resemble dahlias, 3'–5'.
'Loddon Gold'—Deep yellow, double pompom flowers, 5'.
'Meteor'—Semidouble, gold-yellow flowers, 5' tall.
'Morning Sun'—Single yellow flowers with yellow-brown centers, 5' tall.
'Soleil d'or'—Gold pompom flowers, 3"–4" wide, on multibranched stems 4'–5' tall.
'Triomphe de Gand'—Clear yellow, semidouble flowers, 3' to 4'.

RELATED SPECIES:
H. angustifolius (an-gus-ti-fo'lē-us)—Swamp Sunflower. Leaves are narrowly lanceolate, up to 8" long, and scabrous above and pubescent beneath. It is native to low wetland areas and requires full sun, good fertility, and abundant moisture. This sunflower flowers later in the fall and is covered with 2"–3" wide yellow flowers. Hardy to zones 6–9. *Helianthus salicifolius,* willowleaf sunflower, is similar but the leaves are narrower and smoother than *H. angustifolius*. The flower color and habit are similar. It is hardy to zone 3, making it a possible choice for the northern garden.

ADDITIONAL NOTES: *H. × multiflorus* is a hybrid cross between *H. annuus × H. decapetalus.*

Hybrid origin.   Perennial

SCIENTIFIC NAME/FAMILY: *Helichrysum bracteatum*

(hēl-i-krī'sum brak-tē-ā'tum)

Asteraceae
(Compositae)

COMMON NAME: Strawflower

LEAVES: Leaves alternate, oblong-lanceolate, 3" to 5" long, tapering to a short petiole, glabrous or nearly so.

FLOWER: Heads to 2½" across; involucral bracts rigid, glossy, the outer ones short, the inner ones petal-like; elongated; yellow, orange, red, salmon, rose, white, or purple. The papery feeling "petals" are actually bracts.

HABIT: 1½' to 3'. Habit varies from round to erect depending upon cultivar utilized.

SEASON OF BLOOM: Mid through late summer.

CULTURE: Sun and a well-drained, moist soil.

UTILIZATION: Fresh cut flowers or dried flowers. Strawflowers are the most brilliant of all flowers suitable for drying.

PROPAGATION: Seeds germinate best when exposed to light and 70°–80°F. Germination occurs in 7 days.

DISEASES AND INSECTS: Stem rot occurs in wet soils.

See color plate

CULTIVARS:
   'Bikini' Series—This series includes a mixture as well as colors of crimson, gold, pink, and white. 'Hot Bikini' has bright fiery red flowers. It was a 1977 Fleuroselect Bronze medal winner. Plants are 12" tall.
   'Frosted Sulphur'—Pastel sulphur yellow with a silvery white blush, 30" tall.
   'Monstrosum'—30", large flower heads with a greater number of bracts, 6 solid colors plus a mixture available. 'Tall Tetraploid' strain and 'Swiss Giants' mixture are similar selections.
   'Silvery Rose'—Pink-tinged rose-colored flowers with a silvery white blush, 30" tall.

ADDITIONAL NOTES: To dry, cut the flowers just before the center petals open, strip off the foliage and hang the flowers upside down in a dry, shady place. Flowers will retain their color. *Helichrysum* is derived from *helios*, sun, and *chrysos*, gold, and refers to the bright colors of the petal-like bracts.

Native to Australia.
Annual

SCIENTIFIC NAME/FAMILY: *Helictotrichon sempervirens*   Poaceae
(Avena sempervirens)   (Gramineae)

(hē-lik-tō-tri′kon sem-per-vī′renz)

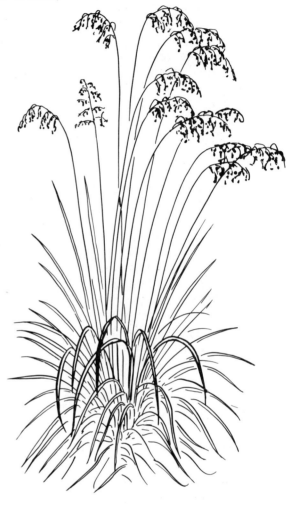

COMMON NAME: Blue Oat Grass, Ornamental Oats

LEAVES: Leaf blades up to 18″ long, ½″ wide, tapering to a fine point, slightly hairy, light glaucous blue. Foliage is semi-evergreen.

FLOWER: Inflorescence is a drooping, one-sided panicle, up to 6″ long, arching at the tip of the stems. The spikelets are sparsely borne, initially a pale blue, maturing to a light brown. The flower resembles those of some of the cereal grains.

HABIT: Round hummock of blue leaves topped by arching flower heads, 2′ to 3′ tall with a similar spread.

SEASON OF BLOOM: This species flowers in early summer, but it is primarily grown for its blue foliage.

CULTURE: Full sun in a well-drained soil. *Helictotrichon* is very durable and can perform well for many years in low-fertility soils.

UTILIZATION: Ornamental oats is a very attractive foliage plant and should be sited so the form can be fully displayed. It is suitable for the rock garden or as a border specimen.

See color plate

PROPAGATION: Increase by division in spring or fall.

DISEASES AND INSECTS: Rust can be a problem in areas of excessive humidity or moist conditions.

HARDINESS: Zones 5–8.

CULTIVARS: 'Saphirsprudel' ('Sapphire Fountain')—This 1982 introduction from the Klose Nursery in Kassel, Germany, is more resistant to leaf rust.

Native to Europe.   Perennial

SCIENTIFIC NAME/FAMILY: *Heliopsis helianthoides* var. *scabra*

Asteraceae
(Compositae)

(hē-li-op'sis hē-li-an'thoi-dēz skā'bra)

COMMON NAME: Sunflower Heliopsis, Hardy Zinnia, Orange Sunflower, False Sunflower

LEAVES: Opposite or whorled leaves, lanceolate-ovate to oblong-ovate, to 4½" long, serrate, petioles are 1½" long.

FLOWER: Heads solitary, showy, yellow ray flowers are large, and the disk flowers brownish-yellow; other cultivars have orange flowers. Stems and leaves have sandpapery textures.

HABIT: 3' to 4' erect and loosely branched.

SEASON OF BLOOM: Midsummer to fall.

CULTURE: Full sun or partial shade and moderately fertile soil that does not dry out during the summer.

UTILIZATION: Utilized in the perennial border, also for cutting.

PROPAGATION: Division in fall or spring. Also by seeds, which germinate in 1 to 2 weeks at 68°F. Cultivars are propagated by division or cuttings, the species by seed.

See color plate

DISEASES AND INSECTS: None serious, although aphids may occur on plants grown on infertile soil.

HARDINESS: Zones 3–9. A good plant for southern gardens.

CULTIVARS:

'Goldgefieder' ('Golden Plume') — 3½' tall, double yellow flowers, prolific bloomer, June to September flowers.

'Goldgrunherz' ('Gold Greenheart') — 3' tall, double yellow flowers with emerald green centers, good for cutting or drying.

'Incomparabilis' — 3' tall, semi-double, rich yellow flowers with dark centers and overlapping petals.

'Karat' — Large single yellow flowers on 4' stems; may need protection from wind.

'Mars' — Yellow-orange flowers, 4'–5' tall.

'Patula' — Semidouble yellow flowers on 4' tall stems.

'Sommesonne' ('Summer Sun') — Double golden yellow flowers, 3' stems, excellent for cutting. This cultivar will come fairly true from seed.

Native to North America.   Perennial

SCIENTIFIC NAME/FAMILY: *Heliotropium arborescens*   Boraginaceae

(hē-li-ō-trōp'-i-um ar-bō-res'enz)

COMMON NAME: Heliotrope

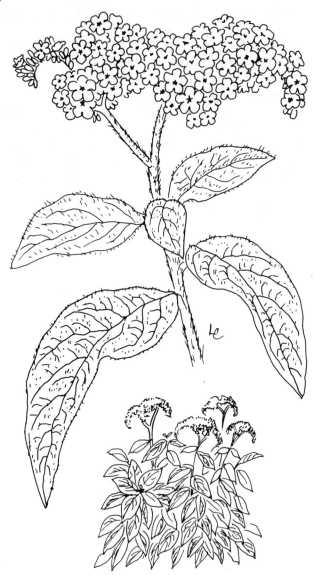

LEAVES: The leaves are simple and alternately arranged on the stem. Leaves are 1" to 3" long, elliptic or oblong-lanceolate, with impressed venation. All parts of the plant are pubescent.

FLOWER: The 5-petaled flowers are small, ¼" long, and are borne in a scorpioid cyme. Flower colors are violet, purple, or white. They have a strong fragrance similar to vanilla. In southern Europe, this species is cultivated for perfume.

HABIT: Rounded habit, 12" to 18" tall, spreading 12"–15" wide.

SEASON OF BLOOM: Summer.

CULTURE: Heliotrope should be planted in full sun in a fertile and well-drained soil. It will require abundant water during drought periods.

UTILIZATION: This species can be used as an accent plant in mixed beds, borders, and containers. It is also a good addition to the cutting garden. In the Victorian period, *Heliotrope* was a favorite container plant.

PROPAGATION: Seed will germinate in 3 weeks at 75°–80°F. Cuttings can also be used.

DISEASES AND INSECTS: No serious problems.

CULTIVARS:
   'Lemoine's Giant'—Blue, violet, and lavender flowers are borne in large inflorescences that are 6" to 10" wide. This cultivar is 24" to 30" tall.
   'Marine'—Navy blue flowers in clusters to 10" wide. Plant height is 15" to 18".

ADDITIONAL NOTES: *Heliotrope* is one of the plants that made its way across the United States in covered wagons.

Native to Peru.   Tender perennial utilized as an annual

SCIENTIFIC NAME/FAMILY: *Helleborus argutifolius* var. *corsicus*   Ranunculaceae

(hel-le'-bōr-us ar-gu-ti-fo'lē-us)

COMMON NAME: Corsican Hellebore

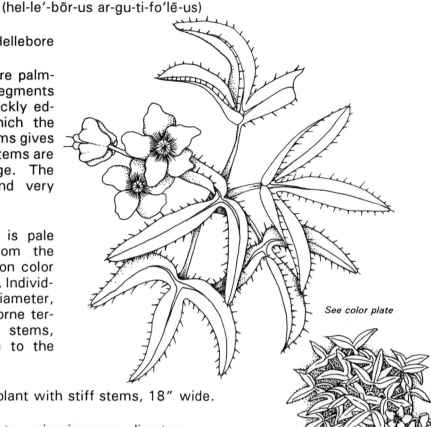

See color plate

LEAVES: The basal leaves are palmately divided into 3 leaf segments which have very stiff prickly edges. The manner in which the leaves are held on the stems gives the appearance that the stems are carrying claw-like foliage. The foliage is gray-green and very attractive.

FLOWER: The flower color is pale green, which differs from the white or pinkish to maroon color of other hellebore species. Individual flowers are 2½" diameter, with 5 sepals, and are borne terminally on long flower stems, which tend to lean due to the weight of the flowers.

HABIT: An 18"–24" bushy plant with stiff stems, 18" wide.

SEASON OF BLOOM: Winter to spring in warm climates.

CULTURE: Partial shade to full sun in a well-drained soil. This hellebore is fairly drought tolerant and is the best hellebore for southern California. If this species is well established, it will tolerate more sun than other hellebores. Winter protection will generally be needed even in southern zones.

UTILIZATION: The bold-textured foliage is sure to add class to any partially shaded border.

PROPAGATION: Division can be done successfully if it is carefully done. Seeds may take 2 years to germinate because of the stratification requirements. This natural process can be speeded up by a warm stratification (70°F) for 8–10 weeks followed by cool stratification of 30°–40°F for 8–10 weeks. Collecting and sowing seeds immediately may also beat the dormancy requirement.

DISEASES AND INSECTS: None serious.

HARDINESS: Zones 6–8.

RELATED SPECIES: *H. foetidus* (fet'-id-us) — Stinking Hellebore. The evergreen leaves are deeply lobed and divided into 3–9 narrow segments. Plant height is 18"–24" with a spread of 18". The cup-shaped, nodding flowers are light green and malodorous. The specific epithet, *foetidus,* means fetid or stinking. This species is hardy to zones 6–8 but it is not especially tolerant of summer heat.

ADDITIONAL NOTES: Corsican hellebore produces a leafy stem one year which flowers the second year. The leaves die and make way for succeeding shoots to develop.

Native to Corsica.   Perennial

SCIENTIFIC NAME/FAMILY: *Helleborus orientalis*   Ranunculaceae

(hel-le'bōr-us or-i-en-tā'-lis)

COMMON NAME: Lenten Rose

LEAVES: Dark evergreen, leathery leaves, are divided into 7–9 segments, sharply serrated on the margins. The leaves are often attractive throughout the year. However, in northern climates scorching can occur on the edges in the winter.

FLOWER: The nodding flowers are 3"–4" wide and composed of 5 showy sepals. Flower colors vary from purple to pink to cream-colored, and the sepals may be spotted on the inside.

HABIT: 15"–18" tall and 15" wide.

SEASON OF BLOOM: Early spring.

CULTURE: Lenten rose does best in partial to full shade and humus-enriched soil. It is not tolerant of high temperatures and is at its best in moist, well-drained soils. The evergreen leaves can become scorched unless they are covered by snow during the winter. If this occurs, cut out the old leaves and new ones will quickly fill in.

UTILIZATION: Useful for that special place in the border or near a walk or the patio where the flowers can be displayed during the early flowering period. The early season flowers and evergreen foliage are sufficient reason to utilize this plant.

PROPAGATION: Seed and division. Although seed propagation may be used, it is a very slow process. Division is more successful in the spring and is accomplished by carefully separating the crown to create sections with new leaf buds and several roots. New plants can be obtained from the seedlings that are produced in the fertile soil near the plants.

DISEASES AND INSECTS: Black spot and crown rot.

HARDINESS: Zones 4–9.

RELATED SPECIES:
   H. niger (ni'jer)—Christmas Rose. The leaves of this species are less serrated than *H. orientalis* and are duller green. Flowers are white with pink shading. There is great variation in flower color, size, and how early the flowers appear. Christmas rose flowers earlier than the Lenten rose. Zones 3–8. 'Potter's Wheel' has large white flowers with green eyes. It must be vegetatively propagated.

ADDITIONAL NOTES: *Helleborus* is derived from the Greek words *helein,* to injure, and *bora,* food, and refers to the bitter tasting leaves and roots which are poisonous when eaten.

Native to Europe.   Perennial

See color plate

SCIENTIFIC NAME/FAMILY: *Hemerocallis* species   Liliaceae

(hem-er-ō-kal′is)

COMMON NAME: Daylily

LEAVES: Long linear leaves, 1′–2′, ½″–1″ wide.

FLOWER: 5–9 flowers, often fragrant; 3″–4″ long, tube ½″–1″, pedicels 1″–2″ long with small, lanceolate bracts, lobes about ¾″ or less broad. Flowers are borne on a leafless stem called a scape. Flowers can be obtained in almost any color of the rainbow. They generally last one day.

HABIT: Plants in flower range in height from 12″ to 3′ or 4′, depending upon the cultivar. Daylily forms large clumps with erect flower stems.

SEASON OF BLOOM: Early summer to frost. By selecting particular cultivars, the bloom can be extended from May until October.

CULTURE: Full sun or partial shade for pastel colors, which fade in the sun. Daylily does best in soils well supplied with organic matter and well-drained. High soil fertility leads to rank growth and poor flowering. The heavy root system competes well with tree roots.

UTILIZATION: Daylilies are appropriate for borders; dwarf types are suitable for rock gardens.

PROPAGATION: Divide clumps in fall or spring every 4 to 6 years by separating into rooted segments, each with about 3 shoots. This process is somewhat difficult as the fibrous root system is dense and hard to separate. Seeds require 6 weeks of stratification and then 3–7 weeks for germination at 60°–70°F.

DISEASES AND INSECTS: None serious; the average daylily is so hard to kill that it may one day become the symbol of abandoned or overgrown gardens.

HARDINESS: Zones 3–9.

CULTIVARS: There are literally thousands of cultivars for the daylily fancier to choose. Hybridizers, led by the late Dr. A. B. Stout, New York Botanical Garden, have introduced countless numbers of selections with new shadings, petal formation, and sizes.

ADDITIONAL NOTES: Daylily is easy to culture and the plants multiply freely. They are permanent and are generally not palatable to insects. *Hemerocallis* is Greek meaning "beautiful for a day" which refers to the flowers' being short-lived. Daylily has a wide distribution, and fine specimens are found in northern and southern gardens.

Individuals desiring additional information about *Hemerocallis* would benefit from membership in the American Hemerocallis Society, 3803 Greystone Drive, Austin, TX, 78731.

Native to central Europe to China and Japan; however, most selections are now hybrids.
Perennial

See color plate

SCIENTIFIC NAME/FAMILY: *Heracleum mantegazzianum*   Apiaceae
                                                                    (Umbelliferae)

(her-à-klē'um man-te-gaz-ē-ā'-num)

COMMON NAME: Giant Hogweed

LEAVES: The huge basal leaves are ternately compound and up to 3' long. Leaflets are large, triangular-lanceolate shaped and deeply cut.

FLOWER: Thousands of tiny white flowers compose a giant umbel inflorescence that can be 4' wide. There are not many plants with flowers larger than those of the giant hogweed. The flower stems are hollow.

HABIT: Upright flower stems stand 8'–10' tall over a large mound of coarse-textured basal leaves. The clump can be 4'–6' wide.

SEASON OF BLOOM: Summer.

CULTURE: Grow in full sun or partial shade in a moist, fertile soil. The huge seed heads must be removed to prevent self-sowing and unwanted spread of the plant.

UTILIZATION: The size of this species limits its use to accent or specimen status in large gardens such as parks. It looks nice near large ponds or streams where it is at home in the moist soils. Giant hogweed is not for the small garden.

PROPAGATION: Propagate by seed. A warm stratification followed by cold stratification enhances germination. Sowing seed as soon as it is ripe is also an appropriate method.

DISEASES AND INSECTS: There are no major problems.

HARDINESS: Zones 3–9.

ADDITIONAL NOTES: The sap of this species can be very irritating to some individuals. To those with sensitive skin, severe blistering can occur. The severity tends to be worse if the temperature is hot and there is a bright sun. One should wear long sleeves and gloves when handling the plant.

Native to Caucasus.   Biennial

SCIENTIFIC NAME/FAMILY: *Hesperis matronalis*   Brassicaceae
                                                                (Cruciferae)

(hes'per-is mat-tro-na'lis)

COMMON NAME: Dame's Rocket, Sweet Rocket, Dame's Violet

LEAVES: The alternate leaves are 2"–4" long, lanceolate shaped, with fine teeth along the margin. They are sessile or borne on short petioles.

FLOWER: White or purple 4-petaled flowers are borne in loose, terminal racemes. A sweet fragrance is evident, especially in the evening.

HABIT: Dame's rocket is a multiple-branched, shrubby type plant that is 3–4 feet tall with a 2 foot spread.

SEASON OF BLOOM: Late spring to early summer.

CULTURE: This self-seeding biennial performs best in partial shade. Consistent moisture is required for a long bloom season. High pH soils seem to be preferred. Deadheading may promote a second flush of flowers. The mother plants die after flowering but the seeds are easily germinated in the garden and plants persist for years. Annuals or later emerging perennials should be used to fill in the gaps created by the dying plants.

See color plate

UTILIZATION: The haphazard self-seeding provides white or purple islands in the cottage garden or naturalized area. The white flower types will stand out in the shade garden more so than the purple selections.

PROPAGATION: The species can be propagated from seed at 70°F in 7–10 days. The double forms must be propagated by terminal cuttings or division.

DISEASES AND INSECTS: There are no serious problems.

HARDINESS: Zones 3–8.

CULTIVARS:
   var. *alba plena*—White double flowers with a nice fragrance.

Native to southern Europe and Asia.   Biennial

SCIENTIFIC NAME/FAMILY: *Heuchera americana*   Saxifragaceae

(hū′kĕr-á a-mer-i-kā′na)

COMMON NAME: American Alumroot

LEAVES: Leaves are mostly basal, rounded, with cordate bases. The leaf blades are 3″ wide, have toothed and lobed margins with scattered stiff pubescence on the upper and lower leaf surfaces. The young foliage is flushed and veined coppery-brown, the mature foliage a deep green.

FLOWER: The flowers are greenish or red-tinged and ¼″ long. Many urn-shaped flowers are arranged in panicles on stems 12″–18″ long.

HABIT: The basal leaves create a mounded clump. The flower stems are thin and very erect, rising to 18″.

SEASON OF BLOOM: Late spring to early summer.

CULTURE: Full sun or partial shade, well-drained moist soil with good organic matter content. In southern zones, coralbells do best in partial shade. If grown in cool summer regions, coralbells will bloom longer if the old flowers are removed. *Heuchera* is shallow rooted and the clumps soon get bare and take on a woody character. Applications of loam or organic mulch to the crowns postpone the need for division for about 3 years. After 3 years, the clumps should be dug, the woody crown discarded, and the divisions planted deeply, to the level of the leaves.

See color plate

UTILIZATION: Unlike other *Heuchera* species and cultivars, *Heuchera americana* is more often used for its foliage effect than for the flowers. It is an excellent choice as a foliage plant in the woodland garden. American alumroot is one of the best *Heuchera* for southern gardens.

PROPAGATION: Clump division in spring or fall, seed, or by leaf cuttings. The entire leaf plus a short piece of the stem should be taken.

DISEASES AND INSECTS: No serious problems.

HARDINESS: Zones 4–9.

CULTIVARS:

'Dale's Strain'—Silver-blue marbled foliage, 12"–15" tall, makes an excellent ground cover and is fairly tolerant of dry soils. It is seed propagated.

'Garnet'—This cultivar is a clump-forming ground cover suited for dry and sunny or shady sites. Its main asset is the deep garnet winter foliage and the bright garnet foliage in the spring. It will create a solid carpet of vegetation in one year when planted on 12"–15" spacing. 'Garnet' was introduced by the Mt. Cuba Center for the Study of Piedmont Flora, Greenville, Delaware.

'Pewter Veil'—The foliage of this 1993 introduction has metallic silver leaves with an underlay of purplish color.

RELATED SPECIES:

H. micrantha (mi-kran'-tha)—Small-flowered Alumroot. This species is a native of western North America. The leaves are 2"–4" long and are grey-green and heart shaped with round lobes. Plants grow 12"–24" tall and 12" wide. Since this species is native to the Pacific Northwest it does not perform well in other areas where the temperatures fluctuate widely. However, there are several good cultivars of this species available in commerce.

'Palace Purple'—This cultivar has ivy-shaped foliage with greenish purple to dark purple color. Plants are 15"–18" tall with a similar spread. 'Palace Purple' is often seed propagated so variability occurs in foliage color. Poorly colored plants should be rogued out of the nursery or garden. The origin of 'Palace Purple' is questioned as is the species to which it should be assigned. The most common story is that it was discovered at Kew Gardens in the late 1970s and awarded an Award of Merit from the Royal Horticultural Society. At that point Allen Bush, Holbrook Farm and Nursery, Fletcher, North Carolina obtained seed and 'Palace Purple' has "grown" from that point. In 1991 the Perennial Plant Association selected it as the Perennial Plant of the Year. It is found listed as *H. micrantha, H. micrantha* var. *diversifolia, H. micrantha* var. *versicolor, H. villosa* and *H. americana.* I am most comfortable with *Heuchera micrantha* 'Palace Purple.' Regardless of which species lays claim to 'Palace Purple,' it is still a desirable plant to incorporate into the shade border.

'Bressingham Bronze'—The large crinkled leaves are bronze-purple on the upper surface and a bright purple below. As with other *H. micrantha,* the off-white flowers extend above the foliage but are often more of a nuisance than an attraction. 'Bressingham Bronze' is vegetatively propagated. Adrian Bloom selected this cultivar from a collection of seedlings in his garden near Diss, England.

'Montrose Ruby'—Leaves are dark purple with silver mottling. Nancy Goodwin, Montrose Nursery, obtained seedlings by using 'Palace Purple' and *H. americana* 'Dale's Strain' as parents. Some plants display a mottled dark purple foliage with a nice shine while others, due to seedling variability, show mottling but more green with maturity.

'Pewter Moon'—This cultivar has a dark maroon reverse to the leaves, which are marbled on top with a pewter overlay. The lower leaf surfaces are purple. Creamy-pink flowers appear in late spring. Plants are 10"–12" tall. I was introduced to this cultivar at Richalps Nursery in the Land of Nod, Headley Down, England in the summer of 1992. Rod Richards, owner of Richalps, had crossed 'Palace Purple' with *H. cylindrica* 'Greenfinch' to produce 'Pewter Moon.'

'Ruffles'—This cultivar has strongly ruffled leaves which are not found in other *H. micrantha* selections.

× *Heucherella tiarelloides*—This selection is an intergeneric hybrid between *Heuchera brizoides* × *Tiarella cordifolia.* × *Heucherella* is a slow-growing ground cover with salmon-pink flowers. The culture is similar to *Heuchera.* × *Heucherella* 'Bridget Bloom'—a hybrid cross of *Heuchera brizoides* × *Tiarella wherryi* made by Alan Bloom has dainty pink flower spikes rising above nice basal foliage.

Native to eastern United States.   Perennial

SCIENTIFIC NAME/FAMILY: *Heuchera sanguinea*   Saxifragaceae

(hū'kĕr-ȧ san-gwin'ē-ȧ)

COMMON NAME: Coral Bells, Alum Root, Crimson Bells

LEAVES: Mostly basal, reniform to ovate-orbicular, ¾" to 2" across, base cordate, lobed and dentate, glandular-pubescent, borne on hairy petioles 1½"–5" long.

FLOWER: Flowers ¼"–½" long, bell shaped, in cymose panicles on stems 10"–20" long. Flower colors are red, pink, or white.

HABIT: Plants of *H. sanguinea* are usually 12"–20" tall and 12" wide while cultivars of *H. × brizoides* tend to be larger at 24"–30".

SEASON OF BLOOM: Late spring to early summer; flowering can be prolonged by removing faded flower stalks and watering during dry periods.

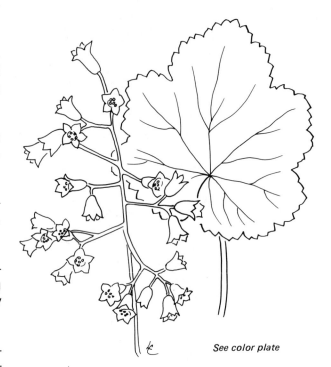

See color plate

CULTURE: Full sun or partial shade, in well-drained soil with good organic matter content. Drainage is most important and growth will be poor in heavy clay soils, especially ones with an acid pH. Coral bells performs best when placed in partial shade in southern gardens. Flowering can be prolonged by removing faded inflorescences.

UTILIZATION: Coral bells can be used at the front of the border, as a source for cut flowers, and to attract hummingbirds and bees to the garden.

PROPAGATION: Division, seed, stem and leaf cuttings. Divide when center of plant becomes woody, perhaps every 3 years. Leaf cuttings are made in late fall, entire leaf plus short segment of petiole can be rooted in sand. Seeds germinate easily in spring, which provides flowering plants the following year. Seeds germinate in 3 weeks when exposed to light and 70°F.

DISEASES AND INSECTS: Stem rot, strawberry root weevil, and mealy bug.

HARDINESS: Zones 3–8.

CULTIVARS: Extensive breeding work has resulted in a number of good hybrids, which are often listed as selections of *H. × brizoides*. Blooms Nursery, Diss, England, has been responsible for many of the hybrids.
   'Bressingham Blaze'—Fiery-red flowers with marbled leaves.
   'Bressingham Hybrids'—Hybrid of mixed colors in shades of white, pink, and coral-red. This cultivar is usually seed propagated.

'Chatterbox'—Rose-pink flowers, June to September flowering period.

'Cherry Splash'—Cherry red flowers over leaves with white and gold splashes. A 1993 introduction by Terra-Nova Nursery, Portland, Oregon.

'Firebird'—Deep scarlet flowers, 15"–18" tall.

'Frosty'—Very heavy silvered foliage and bright red flowers.

'Green Ivory'—White flowers, 24"–30" tall.

'June Bride'—White flowers on 15" stems.

'Matin Bells'—Coral-red flowers, June to September flowering period.

'Pluie de Feu' (Rain of Fire)—Cherry-red flowers, 18".

'Pretty Polly'—Pale pink flowers, 10"–12" tall.

'Red Spangles'—Deep red flowers and dark green foliage. This selection may be the darkest red of all available cultivars.

'Scarlet Sentinel'—Red flowers, 30" tall.

'Scintillation'—Red flowers, 24"–30" tall.

'Silver Veil'—Foliage of this new cultivar has a silver overlay. The silver color is more solid than that found on 'Snow Storm'.

'Snowflakes'—White flowers.

'Snow Storm'—The foliage of this cultivar is variegated with dense white speckling and the flowers are cerise colored. It is a striking plant but may not be dependable in hot summer climates. It has proved to be a popular cultivar in England and Europe.

'White Cloud'—White to cream colored flowers, 18".

For Canadian gardens, H. H. Marshall, Research Station, Morden, Manitoba, recommends the following cultivars:

'Brandon Glow'—Darker flowers than 'Brandon Pink' and shorter in stature.

'Brandon Pink'—Deep pink flowers in late spring to early summer.

'Northern Fire'—Currant-red at the tips to delft-rose at the base of the sepals.

Dan Heims, Terra-Nova Nursery, Portland, Oregon, is selecting several hybrids which are being produced by tissue culture. In the future look for selections with cup-shaped leaves, green picotee leaf edges, metallic sheens, and chocolate stipples. Things are definitely changing with coral bells.

ADDITIONAL NOTES: Plants are shallow rooted and subject to frost heaving. To help alleviate heaving, crowns should be set 1" below soil level and mulched. *Heuchera* honors a German botanist of the 18th Century, J. H. von Heucher.

Seventy species are native to the Rocky Mountains.   Perennial

SCIENTIFIC NAME/FAMILY: *Hibiscus coccineus*   Malvaceae

(hī-bis'kus kok-sin'ē-us)

COMMON NAME: Scarlet Rose Mallow

LEAVES: This rose mallow has 5"–6" wide leaves which are palmately lobed into 3, 5, or 7 jagged finger-like lobes. The lobes are very slender, almost skeleton-like, and are remotely toothed.

FLOWER: The deep red funnel-shaped flowers are 5"–6" wide. The flowers are borne on long peduncles that arise out of the leaf axils. There are 10 or more involucral bracts which are very narrow, 1¼" long, and curved upward. The bracts are much shorter than the calyx lobes.

HABIT: Narrow, upright plant, 6'–8' tall and 3 feet wide.

SEASON OF BLOOM: Mid to late summer.

See color plate

CULTURE: *Hibiscus coccineus* is found as a native plant in wet land areas such as swamps and marshes. Consequently best performance will occur in similar areas, but it is tolerant of drier soil. It can be planted in full sun or light shade.

UTILIZATION: This species is very dominant because of its size. It can be placed in the border, or it can add a touch of grace around the edge of a pond or along a stream.

PROPAGATION: Species can be propagated by seed, cultivars by division.

DISEASES AND INSECTS: Japanese beetle and stalk borer have been occasional problems.

HARDINESS: Zone 5–9.

RELATED SPECIES: Robert Darby of Iowa City, Iowa, has developed several superior hybrids by using a genetic makeup derived from the crossing of *H. moscheutos, H. militaris, H. palustris,* and *H. coccineus.* These selections have multiple branching up and down the stem compared to the species, which has multiple stems with very little branching. These cultivars are also hardy to zone 4 and have performed well in Iowa City. They are propagated by tissue culture by some nurseries.

'Ann Arundel' —Large pink flowers, up to 9" wide, 4'–5' tall. Mr. Darby patented this selection in 1984.

'Lady Baltimore'—Pink flowers with a satiny red center, 4' tall. This patented selection was released in 1978.

'Lord Baltimore'—Vibrant red flowers with ruffled overlapping petals, 10" diameter flowers, 4'–5' tall. Mr. Darby had flowering plants in 1955 with sales starting in 1961.

Other breeding efforts by Dr. Harold F. Winters of Silver Springs, Maryland, have produced the following cultivars.

'Blue River II'—Clear white flowers, 12" diameter, 4'–5' tall. It was developed from a cross of *H. militaris* and *H. moscheutos.*

'Sweet Caroline'—This new cultivar has pink flowers that are 9" wide on stems 4'–5' tall.

Native to eastern United States coastal area.   Perennial

SCIENTIFIC NAME/FAMILY: *Hibiscus moscheutos*   Malvaceae

(hī-bis′kus mos-kö′tos)

COMMON NAME: Rose Mallow, Hibiscus, Mallow Rose, Wild Cotton, Swamp Rose

LEAVES: Leaves alternate to 8″ long, lanceolate to broad ovate, unlobed or shallowly 3- or 5-lobed, green above, white-pubescent beneath.

FLOWER: Flowers single, borne in axils, petals 3″–5″ long, which create a flower 6″–12″ wide. Flower colors are red, white, pink, and bicolors.

HABIT: 3′ to 8′, most about 5′. *Hibiscus* grows as a large multi-stemmed shrub.

SEASON OF BLOOM: Midsummer to frost.

CULTURE: Full sun or partial shade, in soils with high organic matter. *Hibiscus* will tolerate moist conditions, in fact, naturalizing on a large scale is possible in troublesome wet areas.

UTILIZATION: Best use is as single specimens in the border planting. Durable stems allow use of the plant in windy areas. Other uses might be as temporary summer screens and hedges or massed along the edge of a pond or lake.

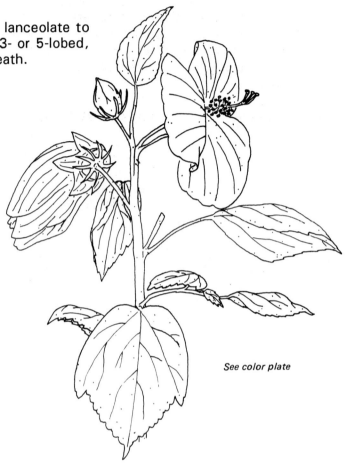

See color plate

PROPAGATION: Seeds may be sown in spring or fall with good results. Division in spring or fall is the usual method of propagating cultivars. Plants flower the second year after division. Plants can be allowed to remain indefinitely as roots do not spread underground.

DISEASES AND INSECTS: Leaf spots, canker, rust, blight, aphids, white fly, scale, and Japanese beetle. Japanese beetle and white fly are major concerns.

HARDINESS: Zones 4–9.

CULTIVARS:
    'Disco Belle'—Small plants, 18″–24″ tall, available in red or white colors.
    'Poinsettia'—Red flowers, 5′ tall.
    'Radiation'—Pink flowers, 5′ tall.
    'Southern Belle'—Red, pink, or white flowers, 4′–6′ tall. Seed propagated.

ADDITIONAL NOTES: Although rose mallow is tall, it seldom needs staking. Rose mallow appears to perform well in climatic zones 4 and warmer.

Native to wetland areas on the eastern seaboard from Massachusetts to Florida and can be found as far west as Michigan and Alabama.   Perennial

SCIENTIFIC NAME/FAMILY: *Holcus mollis* 'Variegatus' ('Albo-variegatus')   Poaceae
(Gramineae)
(hol'kus mol'lis vãr-i-e-gã'tus)

COMMON NAME: Variegated Velvet Grass

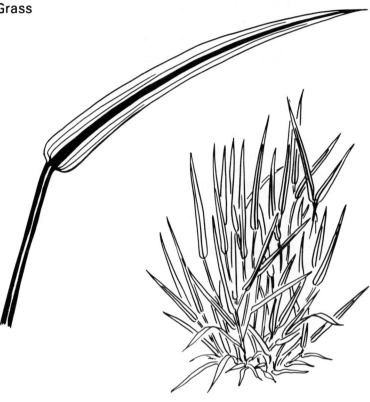

LEAVES: The velvety leaf blades are
½" wide, 6"–8" long, flat in
cross section, softly hairy, with
broad margins of pure white with
a narrow strip of green in the
middle.

FLOWER: The greenish-white spikelets are borne in a narrow, oblong
panicle. The flowers are not ornamental and will possibly detract
from the foliage.

HABIT: Low, open, spreading clump,
4"–10" tall.

SEASON OF BLOOM: The flowers are
produced in late spring to midsummer but are not considered ornamental.

CULTURE: Full sun to partial shade in
a well-drained soil. Velvet grass
performs poorly in areas with hot summers. This species has a creeping rhizome root
system which may need confining if grown in fertile, sandy loam soils.

UTILIZATION: Foreground of borders or as ground cover. The leaf color and texture are
good contrasts.

PROPAGATION: Increase by division in the spring or fall.

DISEASES AND INSECTS: No serious problems.

HARDINESS: Zone 4–7.

CULTIVARS:
H. lanatus (la-na'-tus) 'Variegatus.' Both species, *H. lanatus* and *H. mollis*, have
variegated forms. Both are small, dainty grasses. However, *H. lanatus* tends to be
a more tufted grass, whereas *H. mollis* is a creeping form. Catalogs list both types;
however, I am not sure that there is a difference in the plants offered. They may be
the same species under different names.

Native to Europe.   Perennial

SCIENTIFIC NAME/FAMILY: *Hordeum jubatum*   Poaceae
                                                            (Gramineae)

(hôr'dē-um joo-bā'tum)

COMMON NAME: Squirreltail
    Grass, Foxtail Barley

LEAVES: Leaves are scabrous,
    1/8" wide, and 5" to 8"
    long.

FLOWER: The flowers are 3"
    to 4" long, very silky, with
    very long awns. The com-
    mon name refers to the
    bushy appearance of the
    flower head which resem-
    bles a squirrel's tail.

HABIT: Tufted grass which is upright and
    open. The texture is very fine. Height
    is 18" to 24".

SEASON OF BLOOM: Late spring to early
    summer.

CULTURE: Squirreltail grass grows well in
    full sun in moist or dry soils. It has
    the potential to become weedy be-
    cause it self-sows.

UTILIZATION: *Hordeum jubatum* is very
    showy in flower because the plant
    becomes a mass of silky, nodding
    blossoms. Peak ornamental effect is
    during the early summer. After flow-
    ering, it has no interest in late sum-
    mer, fall or winter. The flowers readily
    fall apart at maturity and easily self-
    sow. It is suitable for fresh flowers
    but the dried flowers shatter with
    age.

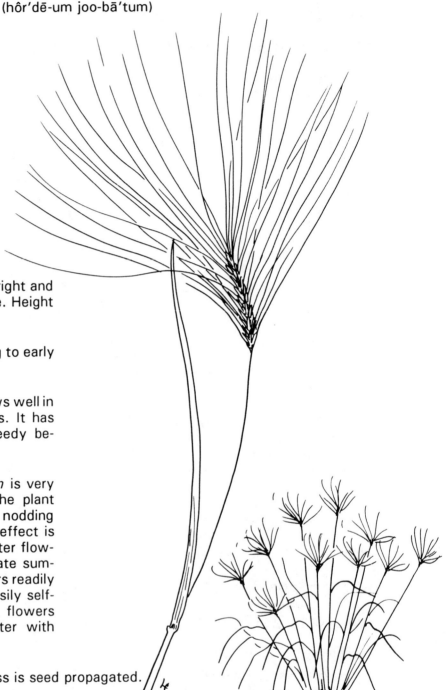

PROPAGATION: Squirreltail grass is seed propagated.

DISEASES AND INSECTS: None serious.

HARDINESS: Zones 5–8. This species is a short-lived perennial that is usually treated as
    an annual.

Native to North and South America.   Perennial

SCIENTIFIC NAME/FAMILY: *Hosta plantaginea* (*H. subcordata*)   Liliaceae

(hos'tá plan-tā-jin'e-á; plan-ta-jin-ē'-á)

COMMON NAME: Fragrant Plantain-
Lily, August Lily, Fragrant Hosta

LEAVES: Basal leaves, long-petioled,
blades ovate to cordate-ovate, to
10" long, 4"–6" wide with 7–9
veins on each side of the midrib,
yellow-green and glossy.

See color plate

FLOWER: White, fragrant, trumpet-
shaped flowers, 4" long and
borne on 1½'–2½' scapes.

HABIT: 1½' to 2½' with flower
scapes to 2½'. This plant assumes a mound habit.

SEASON OF BLOOM: Late summer.

CULTURE: Full to partial shade,
good organic matter content for
water retention. Partial shade is
far better than full sun, which,
except in cooler, moist areas,
causes the leaves to yellow and scorch on the edges.

UTILIZATION: Shade of tall trees provides a good microclimate. Border, rock gardens, pools
and massed plantings in the shade. Good for naturalized areas. Excellent specimen
plant.

PROPAGATION: Clump division in spring, however, *Hosta* has no need for regular division
but should be initially spaced at 3' to 4' intervals. Seeds that are sown in the spring will
not produce flowering plants for 3 years.

DISEASES AND INSECTS: Leaf spots, crown rot, chewing insects, and slugs which can
disfigure the foliage.

HARDINESS: Zones 3–8. If provided shade, *Hosta* performs very well in zone 8.

CULTIVARS:
  'Aphrodite'—Unusual hosta with double white fragrant flowers over large, glossy green
    heart-shaped leaves, 24" tall. An introduction from China in 1940 that is now
    available in Europe and North America.
  Hosta plantaginea has also been used as one of the parents to produce several hybrids
    that have good garden merit.
  'Honeybells'—Light green foliage and fragrant lavender flowers, 24" tall.
  'Royal Standard'—Rich green, deeply veined foliage and fragrant white flowers, 2'–3'
    tall. It is a probable hybrid between *H. plantaginea* and *H. sieboldii*.
  'Sweet Susan'—This hybrid of *H. plantaginea* × *H. sieboldii* has glossy green leaves
    and fragrant, lilac flowers. It was the first hybrid introduced with violet, scented
    flowers. It is not widely used since more garden-worthy hostas have been
    produced.

RELATED SPECIES:

H. sieboldiana (sē-bōl-dē-ā'-na) — Siebold Hosta. The gray-green foliage is covered with a waxy blue bloom. Long petioled leaves with 12–14 pairs of deeply impressed veins may be up to 12" wide and develop a clump 4' wide. Cultivars of this species are excellent accent or specimen plants. The lilac flowers barely extend above the foliage and are not especially attractive.

'Elegans' — An excellent specimen hosta with steel blue leaves and light lavender flowers. It is 3' tall and 3'–4' wide. 'Elegans' is still a popular hosta even though it has been in commerce since 1905 when it was released by the George Arends Nursery of Ronsdorf, Germany.

'Frances Williams' (also called 'Yellow Edge') — Large, round, heavily textured blue leaves with gold borders and nearly white flowers, 3' tall and 3'–4' wide. This cultivar is at the top of the American Hosta Society's popularity poll. Frances Williams was brought to the "hosta world" by Mrs. Frances R. Williams, who discovered the plant in a row of grey-green hostas at the Bristol Nurseries, Bristol, Connecticut in 1936. The name 'Frances Williams' did not exist until 1963.

'Golden Sunburst' — Large, round, golden leaves with pure white flowers, 24" tall. This name was selected by the American Hosta Society's Nomenclature Committee to describe the gold-leaved sports of *H. sieboldiana* 'Frances Williams'.

'Northern Halo' — This sport of *H. sieboldiana* 'Elegans' has glaucous, blue-green leaves with irregular, creamy white margins. Flowers are similar to 'Elegans'. This selection was a result of tissue culture.

Other hybrids of hosta are produced yearly and entire books and book chapters are required to adequately describe the fantastic selections that are available. The following hostas are some of my favorites and have performed well in Ohio.

'Francee' — Dark green, slightly rugose leaf, with a regular, narrow, pure white margin. Pale lavender flowers appear in late summer, 24" tall.

'Ginko Craig' — Light green leaves with thin bands of white at the leaf margins. Blue-violet, bell-shaped flowers are carried well above the foliage. The leaves are 6"–8" tall with flower stalks extending to 12". 'Ginko Craig' can be used as an edging plant or for the front of a border.

'Golden Tiara' — Small, heart-shaped leaves are medium-green with 1/4" wide margins of chartreuse-yellow. Lavender-purple flowers appear in midsummer. A compact habit at 12"–14" makes this cultivar a good one for edging and the border front. Tissue culture production has resulted in the 'Tiara' series.

'Gold Standard' — The leaves unfurl to a chartreuse-green with an irregular green margin. If adequate sun is provided, the blade will turn bright gold providing a vivid contrast to the deep green margin. Useful in the border and excellent for providing foliage for the flower arranger.

'Krossa Regal' — Greyish-blue leaves sit atop tall stems that form a beautiful vase-shaped clump 3'–4' tall. The flower stalks extend another 2' and bear lavender flowers. In my garden it stands as the "beacon" of the border. It is a most impressive specimen. 'Regal Splendor' is a Walters Gardens introduction with a creamy yellow to white border on the leaf.

ADDITIONAL NOTES: Weeds will not grow under massed plantings of *Hosta*. *Hosta* is a plant that has a beauty in foliage and flowers and in certain situations has an aristocratic stature. It is a dependable perennial that requires little care. The taxonomy of the *Hosta* genus is confused and many incorrect names are present in the trade. *Hosta* was named for Nicolaus Thomas Host, a 19th-century Austrian physician. The common name plantain-lily is in reference to the resemblance of the leaves to those of the lawn weed, plantain. Additional information about *Hosta* can be obtained from the American Hosta Society, 5300 Whiting Ave., Edina, MN 55435

Native to China and Japan.   Perennial

SCIENTIFIC NAME/FAMILY: *Hosta undulata* (*H. lancifolia* var. *undulata*)   Liliaceae

(hos'tá un-dū-lāt'-á)

COMMON NAME: Wavy-leaved Plantain-Lily

LEAVES: Basal leaves, blades elliptic
to ovate, to about 6" long, with
about 10 veins on each side of
midrib, striped lengthwise with
cream or white, sharply pointed,
strongly undulate, abruptly narrowed into a winged petiole.

FLOWER: Many flowers, about 2"
long, pale lavender gradually widening and funnelform, borne on a
scape about 1' tall.

HABIT: 12" to 18" mounded growth
habit with a width of 18".

SEASON OF BLOOM: Midsummer.

CULTURE: Light to moderate shade
and moist soil. Withstands conditions in full sun better than other
species of *Hosta.*

UTILIZATION: Border, rock garden,
near pools, as an edging plant or
ground cover. Foliage is good from
spring until frost.

PROPAGATION: Clump division in
spring. Plants can be left undisturbed indefinitely. Plants grown
from seed will flower in 3 years.

DISEASES AND INSECTS: See *Hosta
plantaginea.*

HARDINESS: Zones 3–8.

CULTIVARS:
'Albo-marginata'—Irregular white
margin with a center of medium green on the leaf blade. The variegation is a reverse
of the species. Plants are 12" tall and 18" wide. In England, this cultivar is known
as 'Thomas Hogg'.
'Erronema'—This is a green leaf sport that is larger and more vigorous than the species.
Leaves are 7"–9" long and 5" wide. Flower stems are 3½' tall. It is a "Plain Jane"
but a very durable hosta that performs well in large plantings in dense shade.
'Univittata'—The green leaf margins are wider on this cultivar which creates a more defined narrow strip of white in the center of the blade. This is a vigorous grower that
can be 2'–3' tall.

Native to China and Japan.   Perennial

SCIENTIFIC NAME/FAMILY: *Houttuynia cordata* 'Chameleon'   Saururaceae

(hŏt-tē'nē-a kor-dā'ta)

COMMON NAME: Houttuynia

LEAVES: The leaves of this species with the creeping rhizomes are alternate. They are ovate, 2" to 3" long, cordate, and attractively variegated yellow, green, bronze, and red. The variegation is very striking in full sun but does fade to greens and maroons in shaded sites.

FLOWER: The inflorescence is a ½" to 1" long spike, which contains a cluster of small, petal-less florets surrounded by four petal-like bracts.

HABIT: 6" to 9" tall mound with potential for spreading by rhizomes.

SEASON OF BLOOM: Early summer.

CULTURE: Houttuynia can be grown in moist to wet soil in sun or partial shade. This species has the potential to be very invasive because of its creeping rootstock. I have seen instances where it has almost covered Crimson Pygmy barberry.

See color plate

UTILIZATION: Ground cover or border planting with care taken that it is not placed where it will overrun choicer perennials.

PROPAGATION: It can be increased by division in fall or spring and by cuttings in the summer.

DISEASES AND INSECTS: None serious.

HARDINESS: Zones 5–8.

CULTIVARS:
   H. cordata. This species has dark metallic green leaves and is 18" tall. It is also very invasive and does not have the advantage of the Joseph's coat foliage as does the cultivar 'Chameleon'. 'Plena' has double white flowers and purple-tinged green leaves.

ADDITIONAL NOTES: The bruised foliage has a most pungent citrus-type odor. It is very difficult to characterize the odor. Some have described it as fragrant, while others have described it as cheap perfume laced with diesel fuel. Take your pick.

Native to Japan.   Perennial

SCIENTIFIC NAME/FAMILY: *Hyacinthus orientalis*   Hyacinthaceae
(Liliaceae)

(hī-ȧ-sin'thus ôr-i-en-tā'lis)

COMMON NAME: Hyacinth, Dutch Hyacinth, Common Hyacinth, Garden Hyacinth

LEAVES: 3–4 basal leaves, strap-shaped, many parallel veins, margins are upturned, which creates a shape like the keel of a boat; leaves can be 1" wide and up to 12" long.

FLOWER: Various colors depending upon cultivar chosen. Individual flowers are about 1" long, the 6 perianth segments are wide spreading and reflexed, and they are extremely fragrant with a sweet odor. There are 15 to 30 or more flowers per inflorescence, which is a cylindrical raceme that terminates a rigid scape.

HABIT: 6"–10", erect growth habit.

SEASON OF BLOOM: Spring.

CULTURE: Full sun in normal, fertile, garden soil is suitable, but best growth will be in a soil amended with a composted leaf matter and sand. Before planting, the soil should be dug deeply (15") to allow good root growth essential in hyacinth growing. Plant in mid-autumn to allow good root development before the onset of freezing temperatures. Plant the bulbs 6" deep and about 9" apart. After the blooms fade, remove them to prevent exhaustion of the bulb through fruit development. Bulbs can be left in place for several years, but the flowers will likely be smaller each year. When they become too small for a good display, dig and discard them.

UTILIZATION: Hyacinth is generally perceived as too rigid and formal for naturalizing. Best results occur when hyacinths are massed in the perennial bed and border. Also used for forcing in the home.

PROPAGATION: Unlike many of the other "bulb" plants, hyacinth increases very slowly. Although bulblets are produced, they take several years to reach flowering size. The chief requirement for increasing bulblet size is a rich, deeply cultivated, sandy soil with a high water content. In most areas of the world, these characteristics are in direct contradiction. In Holland, however, the water level is high enough that water is always available to the bulb roots even though the soil is sandy. Propagation is also increased by cutting a mature bulb crosswise to a depth of ½" before planting. Small bulblets will form at the cut. The homeowner should purchase new bulbs every 2 to 3 years.

DISEASES AND INSECTS: No serious problems.

HARDINESS: Zones 3–7.

ADDITIONAL NOTES: The many grades of hyacinth sold are based on bulb size. Top size, for example, is 7½" or more in circumference. The larger the bulb, the larger the flower. For borders, it might be better to use a slightly smaller bulb so the resultant flower is not so heavy that staking is required. A top-heavy flower can easily lodge during spring winds and rains. There are many colors from which to choose: blue, red, pink, rose, white, yellow-orange, and mixtures. A fall bulb catalog should be consulted for the various cultivars available. *Hyacinthus* is named after Hyakinthos, the Spartan youth of Greek mythology who was accidently killed by Apollo, the legend stating that hyacinths sprang up where his blood was shed.

Native to Syria, North Africa, and from Greece to Asia Minor.   Perennial—hardy bulb

See color plate

SCIENTIFIC NAME/FAMILY: *Hypericum calycinum*   Clusiaceae
(Guttiferae or Hypericaceae)

(hī-per'i-kum kal-i-sī'num)

COMMON NAME: Aaron's Beard, St. Johnswort, St. Andrew's-Cross

LEAVES: Opposite leaves are borne on 4-angled stems. The 2"–4" long leaves are ovate-oblong to oblong in shape with a small point at the tip. The evergreen leaves are glabrous, have an entire margin, and are glaucous on the lower surface.

FLOWER: The large, bright yellow flowers, 2"–3" wide, are solitary or in groups of 2–3. The flowers have 5 petals and 5 sepals with numerous, erect stamens that produce a powder puff appearance at the center of the flower. This species has 5 styles at the time of pollination, but in early anthesis the styles appear as one.

HABIT: Stoloniferous, ground cover growing 15"–18" high and spreading 24" wide.

SEASON OF BLOOM: Summer.

See color plate

CULTURE: Aaron's beard is a drought-tolerant species suitable for full sun or partial shade. Flowering is decreased in shady areas. In northern climates the leaves often turn brown with exposure to desiccating winds. If this occurs, the plants should be cut back in early spring. This species will quickly cover a large area, so maintenance division may be required every 2–3 years.

UTILIZATION: A most useful ground cover for barren areas that need a quick ground cover with an attractive summer long flower. It has the ability to cover the soil surface in dry, shady areas.

PROPAGATION: Propagation is by seed, division, or cuttings. Cuttings are taken from vegetative shoots in late spring. Division can be done in spring or fall.

DISEASES AND INSECTS: None serious.

HARDINESS: Zones 5–9.

Native to southeastern Europe.   Perennial

SCIENTIFIC NAME/FAMILY: *Hypoestes phyllostachya*   Acanthaceae

(hī-pest'ēz fil-ō-stak'ē-à)

COMMON NAME: Polka-dot Plant, Pink Polka-dot Plant, Freckle-face

LEAVES: The opposite leaves are ovate, thin, dark green and marked with lavender-pink spots. The leaf blades are 1½" to 2½" long and the narrow petiole is 1½" to 2" long.

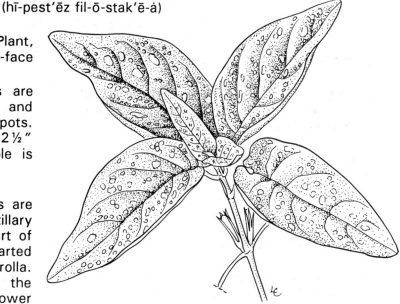

FLOWER: The lavender flowers are borne in terminal and axillary cymes in the uppermost part of the plant. The calyx is 5-parted and is shorter than the corolla. The corolla is two-lipped, the upper one is 3-lobed and the lower is entire.

HABIT: Loosely branched plant, 1' to 2' tall and 12" wide.

SEASON OF BLOOM: Summer. In comparison to the brightly spotted foliage, the flowers are insignificant.

See color plate

CULTURE: This annual performs very well in full sun in a moist and well-drained soil. It will grow fairly well in partial shade, but the habit is more open. Pinching the plants grown in sun or partial shade will promote a bushier plant.

UTILIZATION: As a garden plant, *Hypoestes* is very useful for a mass display. The speckled leaves provide an unusual effect to the garden. Polka-dot plant is probably better known as an indoor foliage plant. Plants grown as garden subjects can be dug in the fall, pinched back, and taken into the home.

PROPAGATION: Polka-dot plant is easily grown from seed or tip cuttings, which can be taken from the over-wintered plants.

DISEASES AND INSECTS: Polka-dot plant has no serious problems.

CULTIVARS:
   'Confetti' Series—Bold spotted foliage, available in colors of burgundy, red, rose, white, and a mixture.
   'Pink Splash'—The pink spots are larger on this selection.

ADDITIONAL NOTES: In the trade, this species is incorrectly listed as *H. sanguinolenta*.

Native to Madagascar.   Annual

SCIENTIFIC NAME/FAMILY: *Hyssopus officinalis*   Lamiaceae
                                                                    (Labiatae)

(hi-sō'pus o-fis-i-nā'lis)

COMMON NAME: Hyssop

LEAVES: Leaves opposite, linear to lanceolate, entire margin, 3/4" to 1¼" long and 1/8" to 1/4" wide. Foliage has a strong camphorlike odor. The stems are square, which is characteristic of the mint family.

FLOWER: Blue-violet flowers, corolla 1/2" long, tubular, calyx is 1/4" long. Flowers are arranged in whorls on dense spikes.

HABIT: Round, compact habit, 24" tall and 18" wide. Space plants 18" apart.

SEASON OF BLOOM: Late spring to mid summer.

CULTURE: Full sun to partial shade in a very well-drained soil. Hyssop performs well in dry areas. Old flower heads should be removed. Other than this practice, hyssop requires little maintenance.

UTILIZATION: Hyssop has been known as a cleaning herb due to its strong camphorlike odor. In early times it was scattered around the floors of sickrooms and placed into kitchens to improve the smell. The leaves and flowers were used to add flavor to salads, soups, meats, and stuffings. Flowers and leaves were dried for teas. In herb gardens hyssop can be clipped into a hedge for edging in the knot garden. Hyssop can also be used in the informal border. It is an excellent plant for attracting butterflies, hummingbirds, and bees. I know no one who currently cooks with hyssop.

PROPAGATION: Seed, cuttings, or division. Seed will germinate in 21 days when held at 70°F. Transplants will be ready 10 weeks from seed. Division can be done in spring or fall. Stem cuttings are successful from spring to summer.

DISEASES AND INSECTS: None serious.

HARDINESS: Zones 4-9.

CULTIVARS:
  'Albus'—White flowers.
  ssp. *aristatus*—Compact plant, narrow leaves, blue-purple flowers.

ADDITIONAL NOTES: Some catalogs list *Hyssopus officinalis* with flowers of blue, white, or pink. Seed of blue hyssop will occasionally produce a white or pink-flowered plant. These plants, if propagated by division, will keep their pink or white flowers. However, in most cases, the flower color of *Hyssopus officinalis* is blue.

Native to Europe and Asia; naturalized in North America.   Perennial

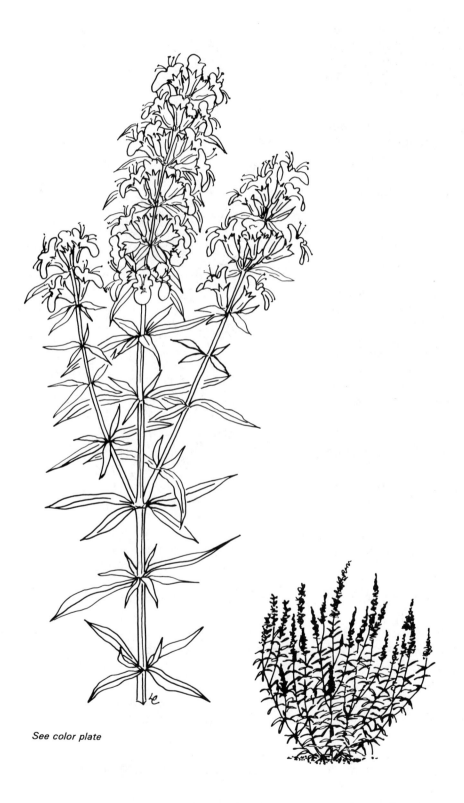

See color plate

SCIENTIFIC NAME/FAMILY: *Iberis sempervirens*   Brassicaceae
             (ī-bē'ris sem-pẽr-vī'renz)   (Cruciferae)

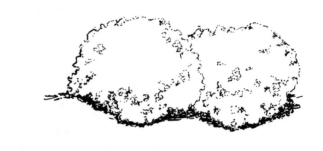

COMMON NAME: Evergreen Candytuft, Edging Candytuft

LEAVES: Alternate leaves are evergreen and glabrous, linear to narrow oblong, to 1" long, blunt apex and entire margin. Stems are semi-woody.

FLOWER: White, 1" wide racemose inflorescences that cover the entire plant.

HABIT: 6" to 12" tall with a spread of 24".

SEASON OF BLOOM: Spring.

CULTURE: Full sun and a well-drained soil are particularly important in winter. Flowering will be better in full sun than partial shade. In cold climates with little snow, the evergreen foliage benefits from a light covering of evergreen branches to reduce sunscorch and desiccation.

UTILIZATION: Rock gardens and edging. The glossy, evergreen foliage is a pleasing accent even after the flowers have faded.

See color plate

PROPAGATION: Seed, cuttings and division. Germinate seeds at 60°–65°F for 3 weeks. Cuttings taken in midsummer root easily. Clump division can be done in spring or fall.

DISEASES AND INSECTS: Club root, which attacks many members of the mustard family, may infect candytuft.

HARDINESS: Zones 3–9. I have seen excellent plantings of *Iberis* from zone 3 to zone 9.

CULTIVARS:
'Alexander's White'—Very dense growing and floriferous plant, 8"–10" tall.
'Autumn Beauty'—Pure white flowers, flowers in the spring and again in the fall, 8"–10".
'Little Gem' ('Weisser Zwerg')—Clear white flowers, 5"–8" tall.
'Nana' (known as 'Pygmaea' in trade)—Prostrate growth habit, 4" tall with white flowers.
'Purity'—Very white flowers, quite floriferous, 8" tall.
'Snowflake' ('Schneeflocke')—10", large leaves and large white flowers.
'Snowmantle'—8" compact mound, smaller than 'Snowflake'.

RELATED SPECIES:

I. gibraltarica (jib-ral-tar'-ik-a) — Gibraltar Candytuft. This tender perennial is a compact clump former with 1" long evergreen leaves that are toothed near the tip. It has lilac-pink flowers with white centers arranged in flat clusters which do not elongate. Plants are 9"–12" tall and spread to 12". In northern areas it functions as a self-sown annual or it can be started from seed each year.

I. umbellata (um-bel-lā'-ta) – Annual Candytuft, Globe Candytuft. This annual candytuft has an erect habit, grows 8"–16" tall, and has pink, red, lilac, or violet flowers, which are not fragrant.

ADDITIONAL NOTES: After flowering, the stems should be cut back at least 2" to promote vigorous growth and prevent the semi-woody clumps from opening in the center. *Iberis* is derived from Iberia, because many of its species are native to Spain.

Native to southern Europe.   Perennial

SCIENTIFIC NAME/FAMILY: *Impatiens balsamina*   Balsaminaceae

(im-pā'shi-enz bal-sam'-in-à)

COMMON NAME: Touch-Me-Not, Garden Balsam, Rose Balsam

LEAVES: Alternate, to 6" long, lanceolate, acuminate, deeply serrated.

FLOWER: Axillary, short-pedicelled, covered by leafy shoots, 1"–2" across, white to yellow, pink, purple, or dark red, often spotted. Flowers resemble small rose or camellia flowers.

HABIT: 8" to 36" depending upon cultivar. Habit is usually erect.

SEASON OF BLOOM: Early summer to fall.

CULTURE: Sun or shade, moist, light sandy loam. Balsams do best in rich, light soil containing leaf mold or other types of compost.

UTILIZATION: Small cultivars can be used for bedding and edging purposes, the species is suitable for borders.

PROPAGATION: Seed requires about 8 days for germination when exposed to a constant 70°F soil temperature. Balsam is susceptible to damping off and will not tolerate wet or cold weather.

DISEASES AND INSECTS: Damping off.

CULTIVARS:
'Carambole' Series—10"–14" tall, double flowers carried at the top of the plant. Available in scarlet, rose, violet, white, and mixed colors.
'Tom Thumb Dwarf'—More compact and uniform than bush-flowered balsam, double flowers held above the foliage.

ADDITIONAL NOTES: Seed pods, when ripe, burst upon touch; hence, the common name—Touch-Me-Not. Also the name is derived from *impatiens,* impatient, and refers to the elasticity of the valves of the seed pods, which discharge the seeds when ripe.

Native to India and China.   Annual

SCIENTIFIC NAME/FAMILY: *Impatiens wallerana*   Balsaminaceae

(im-pā'shi-enz wâl-er-ā'nȧ)

COMMON NAME: Sultana, Patient Lucy, Busy Lizzie.

LEAVES: Alternate (the upper leaves sometimes opposite), ovate to elliptic, mostly 1½"–4" long, acute to cuspidate, crenate-denticulate, mostly cuneate and decurrent on petiole, green or reddish on both surfaces; foliage is glossy.

FLOWER: Flowers solitary or in axillary or terminal racemes, 1"–2" across, lower sepal to 2" long, with a slightly curved spur. Flowers may be single, double, and come in all colors, including bicolored types.

HABIT: 6" to 18", compact, mound habit.

SEASON OF BLOOM: Early summer to frost.

CULTURE: *Impatiens* is typically considered an annual for shade areas. However, it can also be successfully grown in partial shade and full sun areas. The essential requirement for growing *Impatiens* in full sun is a moist, organic amended soil. Dwarfness in *Impatiens* is influenced by water and fertilizer. For example, a cultivar listed as 12" tall may grow to 15" to 18" in a garden with higher watering and fertilizing regimes.

UTILIZATION: Around trees in shaded area, in planters on patio, hanging baskets.

PROPAGATION: Seeds germinate in two to three weeks at a uniform 70°F. Maximum germination occurs when seeds are exposed to light but not direct sunlight.

DISEASES AND INSECTS: Damping off during germination and slugs.

CULTIVARS: For a complete listing of the various cultivars available, one should consult a seed catalog. There are many color types under each of the hybrids listed in this partial listing.

'Accent' Series—This cultivar has a wide color range, 18 colors and a mix, as well as a basal branching habit, and large flowers. Selected for early bloom.

'Blitz' Series—Large 2½" wide blossoms highlight this durable cultivar. It is recommended for pots and hanging baskets. Seven colors and a mix.

'Dazzler'—8"–10" tall, free-flowering selection performing best in shady areas, 12 colors.

'Fantasia'—10"–12" compact with basal branching. This cultivar has a baker's dozen of colors.

'Futura'—10"–12", compact, vigorous, taller than 'Super Elfin', 10 colors plus a mixture.

'Mini' Series—6"–8", more compact than 'Super Elfin'. The compact, non-stretching habit creates a nice carpet-like effect.

'Novette' Series—6"–8", 9 colors, earlier bloom than 'Super Elfin'.

'Soda Pops' Series—Early bloomer with large flowers on compact plants with basal branching, 16 colors and a mixture.

'Splash' Series—8"–10" tall, early flowers, bright colored flowers in 7 colors.

'Sun and Shade' Series—Strong grower suited for pots, baskets, window boxes, and bedding purposes. Available in 17 different colors.

'Super Elfin'—8"–10", 15 colors, basal branching and free-flowering. This cultivar is probably the single largest-selling impatiens.

'Twinkles'—8"–10", early flowering, free-flowering, bicolors.

RELATED SPECIES: New Guinea Impatiens—This group of plants was developed from species collected in New Guinea. These exotic-appearing plants have variegated leaves and extra-large flowers. Propagation is done by cuttings as well as seed.

Native to eastern Africa.   Annual

See color plate

SCIENTIFIC NAME/FAMILY: *Imperata cylindrica var. rubra* 'Red Baron'   Poaceae
(Gramineae)

(im-pĕr-ā'ta si-lin'dri-ka ru'brȧ)

COMMON NAME: Japanese Blood Grass, Red Baron Blood
  Grass

LEAVES: Leaf blades 1/4" wide and 12" to 18" long. The
  key identification feature for this grass is the bright red
  coloration of the leaves, which appears in early summer
  and lasts until late autumn. There is
  nothing else like it in the ornamental
  grass world.

FLOWER: 'Red Baron' does not produce
  flowers.

HABIT: Upright stems, 12"–18" tall.
  Clumps slowly spread by rhizomes to
  form small colonies.

SEASON OF BLOOM: Not important.

CULTURE: Best growth occurs in full sun
  and moist, well-drained soils. It tolerates partial shade but the color intensity is lessened. Poor growth is a
  certainty in heavy, poorly-drained soil
  or hot, dry areas.

UTILIZATION: Used in groups or masses
  in the border. The summer-long brilliant red color is very attractive. The
  foliage color is enhanced when the
  plants are located so morning or afternoon light backlights the foliage.

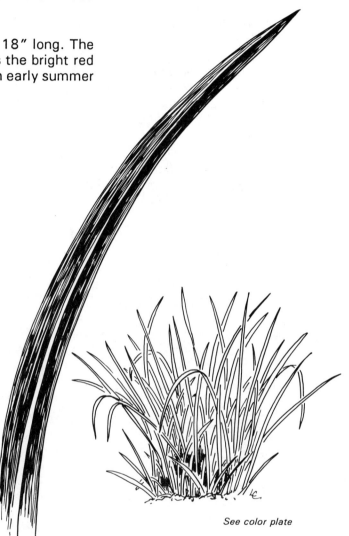

See color plate

PROPAGATION: Propagate by spring
  division. Some 'Red Baron' has been
  produced in tissue culture. However, this practice is questionable due to possible
  mutations resulting in the green-foliage types which are very aggressive. The species,
  Imperata cylindrica, a green-leaved African native, is very aggressive and is listed as a
  noxious weed in the United States. If any part of 'Red Baron' blood grass reverts to
  green, it should be removed immediately.

DISEASES AND INSECTS: No serious problems.

HARDINESS: Zones 5–9.

Native to Japan.   Perennial

SCIENTIFIC NAME/FAMILY: *Inula ensifolia*   Asteraceae
                                                            (Compositae)

(in'ū-lá en-sif-ŏl'e-a)

COMMON NAME: Swordleaf Inula

LEAVES: The alternate leaves are very narrow and linear-lanceolate, to 4" long. The margin is serrulate with ciliate hairs; the rest of the leaf is glabrous. Leaf bases are attenuate (tapering) or sessile to the stem.

FLOWER: Yellow flower heads are 1" to 2" wide, borne solitary or in small clusters.

HABIT: 12"–24" tall, round clump with a width of 18".

SEASON OF BLOOM: Early summer for about 6 weeks.

CULTURE: Full sun or partial shade in well-drained soil. It is fairly heat tolerant and performs well in southern zones.

UTILIZATION: Front of the border.

PROPAGATION: Propagate by clump division in spring or fall or by seed.

DISEASES AND INSECTS: Mildew is an occasional problem.

HARDINESS: Zones 3–8.

CULTIVARS:
'Compacta'—Globose, compact form, 12" tall.
'Goldammer'—Golden yellow flowers, 8"–10" tall.

RELATED SPECIES:
I. royleana (roy-le-a'-na)—Blackbud Inula. Basal leaves are ovate or oblong with a winged petiole. The upper leaves are cordate or auriculate at the base. The flowers are wider (3"–4") than those of *I. ensifolia.* The orange-yellow petals are very narrow and often droop. 18"–24" tall. This species has stout, unbranched stems.
I. magnifica (mag-nif'i-ka). This species is suited for the middle to rear of the border. It is 5'–6' tall and carries yellow flowers up to 6" wide. The stems are purple-speckled. Zones 3–8.

ADDITIONAL NOTES: A different taxa that is very similar to *I. ensifolia* is *Bupthalmum salicifolium* (būf-thal'mum sālis-i-fō'li-um). It is taller growing (24") and a little earlier in flower.

Native to Europe.   Perennial

SCIENTIFIC NAME/FAMILY: *Ipomoea purpurea*   Convolvulaceae
(Convolvulus purpureus)

(i-pō-mē′á pẽr-pū′rē-á)

COMMON NAME: Morning-glory

LEAVES: Alternate, broadly cordate-ovate, entire, to 5″ long; leaves and stems are pubescent.

FLOWER: Trumpet-shaped flowers can be single or double, 2″–3″ long. The corolla may be purple, blue, pink, or white with a lighter-colored tube.

HABIT: 8′ to 10′ twining vine.

SEASON OF BLOOM: Summer. Individual flowers are open in the morning and often close in the afternoon. On cloudy days the flowers remain open during the day.

See color plate

CULTURE: Morning-glory does best in full sun in well-drained soil. High fertility and moisture will produce abundant foliage but few flowers.

UTILIZATION: The fast growing vine can reach 10 feet in 2 months′ time. It is useful for covering a screen or trellis. However, quite a few plants are needed, as a plant tends to grow in a long strand rather than branching laterally.

PROPAGATION: Seed should be scarified by nicking the seed coat with a file or soaking in warm water for 24 hours before sowing. The seed can be planted outside or started indoors. Germination will occur in 7 days at 70°–85°F.

DISEASES AND INSECTS: None serious.

ADDITIONAL NOTES: *Ipomoea* is derived from the Greek words *ips*, bindweed, and *homoios,* similar, and refers to the similarity of *Ipomoea* to bindweed *(Convolvulus).* In fact, don't even breathe the name morning-glory to agronomists lest they bring out the weed killer. It is called morning-glory because the flowers open mostly in the morning.

Native to the Tropics, naturalized in North America.   Annual

SCIENTIFIC NAME/FAMILY: *Iris cristata*   Iridaceae

(ī'ris kris-tā'tȧ)

COMMON NAME: Crested Iris, Crested Dwarf Iris

LEAVES: The narrow pointed leaves are arranged in clusters arising from a network of rhizomes. Individual leaves are 4" to 10" long and ¾" wide.

FLOWER: Crested iris has the typical iris flower composed of 3 sepals, 3 petals, and 3 petaloid styles. The sepals, which are 1½" to 2¼" long, are blue to violet and marked with a central white or yellow band having 2 crested ridges. The shorter petals are bluish to violet. The flowering stems are shorter than the leaves, and the showy flowers are often nestled within the clumped foliage.

HABIT: 6" ground cover spreading by rhizomes.

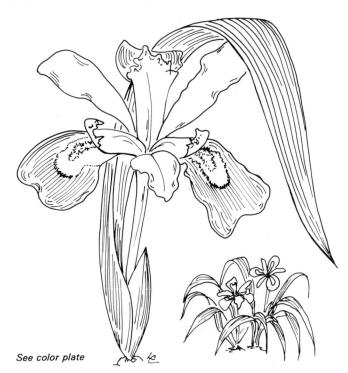

See color plate

SEASON OF BLOOM: Early to midspring.

CULTURE: The ideal site for this species is a partial shade exposure with a few hours of direct light each day. The soil should be well-drained and is best when amended with sand or leaf mold. Highly fertile soils tend to promote excess vegetative growth, and the clumps have a tendency to "open up." Plants are more likely to succeed on a slope as opposed to a flat or poorly drained site. Crested iris can be grown in full sun if the soils are constantly moist.

UTILIZATION: Crested iris is useful in the front of the herbaceous border, in the rock garden, in the woodland garden, and naturalized sites. It is effective as a seasonal ground cover and edging plant.

PROPAGATION: *Iris cristata* is easily propagated by division in the early fall. If crested iris is provided space to spread, division will not be needed. Seeds should be sown as soon as they are collected in the fall. Seeds that dry will germinate sporadically over a 2-year period.

DISEASES AND INSECTS: Slugs can be a problem.

HARDINESS: Zones 3–9.

CULTIVARS:
   'Alba'—White flowers.
   'Shenandoah Sky'—Pale blue, 6" tall.
   'Summer Storm'—Deep blue, 6" tall.

RELATED SPECIES:

I. tectorum (tek-tō′rum), Japanese Roof Iris. This 12″ tall iris has 6″ wide blue flowers in late spring. Best growth occurs in a sandy-loam soil that is slightly acid and of low fertility. It flowers best in hot summers and full sun or partial shade. 'Alba' is a white flowered cultivar. The common name comes from the fact that this species has been grown on thatched roofs in the Orient. *Tectorum* is derived from *tectum,* Latin for roof. Zones 4–9. The leaves are evergreen if the temperature does not drop below 20°F.

Native to southeastern and south central United States.   Perennial

SCIENTIFIC NAME/FAMILY: *Iris ensata (kaempferi)*   Iridaceae

(ī′ris en-sā′tà)

COMMON NAME: Japanese Iris

LEAVES: Stems are often branched, leaves are sword-shaped, 2′ or more long, with a prominent raised midrib.

FLOWER: Flowers are often at least 6″ across, in colors from white to blue, purple, reddish-purple, and lavender-pink. The flowers are often veined, marbled, or speckled with a contrasting color. The perianth is divided into 6 segments. The outer 3 segments (falls) are very large and nearly horizontal while the 3 inner segments (standards) are short and also resemble the falls. This creates a wide, flat flower and this group is sometimes called the "flat-top iris." The falls are beardless.

See color plate

HABIT: 18″ to 24″ foliage and flowering stem to 3′, erect habit with an 18″ spread.

SEASON OF BLOOM: Early to midsummer.

CULTURE: Full sun or partial shade is satisfactory. The soil requirements are quite exacting. Inferior growth will result unless the soil is acid, amended with organic matter, and able to retain abundant moisture during the growing season. Soils with high pH are fatal to this plant.

UTILIZATION: Since moist soil is preferable, plantings are an excellent choice around fountains, pools, streams, particularly where a reflection in the water is possible. They are also suitable for borders if the soil conditions are satisfactory. Japanese iris is outstanding en masse or as a specimen.

PROPAGATION: Division in spring or fall. Japanese iris can be left undisturbed for many years.

DISEASES AND INSECTS: Japanese iris does not have the problems associated with the tall bearded iris. However, it is susceptible to iris thrips.

HARDINESS: Zones 4–9.

CULTIVARS: Although not as extensive as the tall bearded iris, there is a good number of cultivars from which to choose. A partial list includes:

'Activity'—Pale blue flowers with purple veins.
'Cry of Rejoice'—Deep purple flowers with a yellow heart.
'Darling'—Soft lilac flowers.
'Emotion'—Double white flower with a soft blue edge and yellow heart.
'Kagari Bi'—Rose-pink flowers with silver veins.
'Pink Lady'—Large, clear pink flowers.
'Ruby King'—Royal purple flowers with white veining.
'Waka Murasaki'—Double, large purple flowers, later flowering.

RELATED SPECIES:

I. laevigata (lev-e-ga'-ta)—Rabbitear Iris. This related species has 2"–3" wide flattened lavender blue flowers. It requires constantly moist soils and only grows well in bogs, along stream banks, or with its roots submerged in water. 'Alba' has white flowers and 'Variegata' has attractive leaves with cream variegation on the margins. If the environmental conditions of this species can be met, it is a marvelous specimen.

Native to Japan and eastern Siberia.   Perennial

SCIENTIFIC NAME/FAMILY: *Iris* hybrids   Iridaceae

(ī′ris)

COMMON NAME: Bearded Iris

LEAVES: Sword-shaped, to 1½′ long and 1½″ wide, glaucous.

FLOWER: One or more flowers per stem, perianth divided into 6 segments, the outer 3 segments (falls) drooping and broad with a beard down the center, the inner 3 segments (standards) usually erect and arching. Flower colors are numerous and vary with the cultivar.

HABIT: 2′ to 4′ erect plant for the tall bearded iris.

SEASON OF BLOOM: Late spring to early summer.

CULTURE: Full sun and a well-drained soil are essential. Good drainage will aid in preventing bacterial soft rot, and a sunny site promotes maximum flowering. Bearded iris performs best in a nearly neutral soil.

UTILIZATION: A very useful and distinctive flower for the perennial border. Utilized for early spring color in the border after the spring-flowering bulbs have finished.

PROPAGATION: Division of the rhizomes after flowering (until August) is the normal method. The rhizomes are separated into segments with one set of leaves in a fan and several feeding roots. These are set 1″ deep, the leaves are cut back to 6″, and the foliage should face outward away from the center of a group planting.

See color plate

DISEASES AND INSECTS: Bearded iris is quite susceptible to the iris borer. This larva tunnels in the rhizomes, causing mechanical damage and opening the rhizomes to bacterial soft rot. Control of the borers is a preventive program. In the spring when new growth is about 3″ begin an insecticide spray program and repeat at weekly intervals for 2 weeks. Infected rhizomes should be dug and discarded. Fall cleanup should include removing the old foliage which may harbor eggs of the borer.

HARDINESS: Zones 3–10.

RELATED SPECIES: The bearded iris has been highly hybridized and it is a good bet that the first iris grown by a gardener is likely to be a bearded iris and more specifically a tall bearded iris. There are hundreds of cultivars from which to choose and new cultivars are introduced yearly.

   The logical classification for bearded iris is dwarf (less than 15″), intermediate (15″–28″), and tall (over 28″). These classifications have been further divided by The American Iris Society. Dwarf bearded iris is divided into miniature (4″–10″ and standard (10″–15″) while the intermediate is divided into intermediate, table, and border iris.

Miniature dwarf bearded iris. This iris is the earliest to flower with several 2"–3" diameter flowers. It is often used in rock gardens or in niches of rock walls. Excellent drainage is required.

'Already'—Deep wine-red flowers, 8" tall.

'Blue Frost'—Light blue flowers, 6" tall.

'Brite'—White flowers, 8" tall.

'Sky Baby'—Ruffled blue flowers, 8" tall.

Standard dwarf bearded iris. This group is larger than the miniatures with 3"–4" wide flowers and the bloom period is 7–10 days later. They are suited for use at the front of the border as well as in the rock garden.

'Bingo'—Velvet purple flowers, 12" tall.

'Early Sunshine'—Yellow flowers, 15" tall.

'Red Dandy'—Wine-red flowers, 10" tall.

'Sunlite Trail'—Yellow flowers, 14" tall.

Intermediate bearded iris. Plants in this group have a flowering time between the dwarf and the tall bearded types.

Tall bearded iris. The greatest number of cultivars resides in this group. One can spend long hours during the winter perusing the catalogs that highlight this important plant for the perennial garden. There are just too many cultivars available to provide a meaningful list in this book. The reader would benefit from consulting catalogs and The American Iris Society for cultivar information.

ADDITIONAL NOTES: The tall bearded iris previously was referred to as *Iris germanica*, German Iris. However, because of the extensive hybridization that has occurred, the cultivars are no longer typical of German iris. Several hundred cultivars are currently offered by nurseries. In fact, there are nurseries that deal exclusively with iris. Tall bearded iris can be obtained in nearly every color of the rainbow, in fact, iris is Greek for rainbow.

Hybrid origin.   Perennial

SCIENTIFIC NAME/FAMILY: *Iris pallida*   Iridaceae

(ī'ris pal'lid-a)

COMMON NAME: Sweet Iris, Orris Root

LEAVES: This old fashioned bearded iris
    has leaves up to 24" long. They are
    gray-green and sword-blade shaped,
    like the bearded iris.

FLOWER: Two to three flowers per
    spathe. Flowers are fragrant, bluish
    purple and 3" long. They have 3
    erect standards and 3 falls similar to
    the bearded iris.

HABIT: Rigid, erect growth habit 3' tall
    and 2' wide.

SEASON OF BLOOM: Late spring or
    early summer.

CULTURE: Orris root is very easily
    grown and very durable. There are
    many patches of this species doing
    very well with no care in forgotten
    gardens where a home or farmhouse
    once stood. Full sun and well-drained
    soil are sufficient. Division is not
    required on a regular basis.

See color plate

UTILIZATION: This species is not used as much as the flashier hybrids, although it may be
    a better garden plant than many selections. The variegated leafed cultivars are used,
    and they add an accent to a border planting.

PROPAGATION: Clump division in summer.

DISEASES AND INSECTS: *Iris pallida* is susceptible to the iris borer but it seems that it is
    able to survive without application of insecticides.

HARDINESS: Zones 4–8.

CULTIVARS:
    'Argentea Variegata'—Cream and white streaking on the edges of blue-green leaves.
        Flowers are clear blue. Some catalogs may list this as 'Zebra'.
    'Variegata' (formerly 'Aurea-variegata')—Plants have foliage with golden-yellow-stripes
        and pale blue flowers.

ADDITIONAL NOTES: *Iris pallida* is one of the species from which orris is extracted. The
    powdered dry rhizome is used in the production of some perfumes.

Native to Europe.   Perennial

SCIENTIFIC NAME/FAMILY: *Iris pseudacorus* (lutea)   Iridaceae

(ī'ris sued-ak-or'-us)

COMMON NAME: Yellow Flag, Yellow Iris

LEAVES: Sword-shaped leaves, 1" wide, 3' to 5' long, and usually glaucous.

FLOWER: Flowers light yellow, the falls are 1½" or less wide; the standards are narrow, ¼" to ¾" long, erect. There is a brown blotch on the falls.

HABIT: Upright clump, up to 5' tall and 24" wide.

SEASON OF BLOOM: Late spring to early summer.

CULTURE: Yellow flag can be grown in full sun if the soil is moist to wet. In drier situations and hotter summers, yellow flag should be placed in partial shade. The seed pods should be removed to prevent self-seeding, especially if yellow flag is grown in a moist site.

UTILIZATION: Excellent plant for the edge of streams and ponds, especially in the variegated form. It can also be used in borders that have a moisture retentive soil. This species could quickly colonize in a suitable site.

PROPAGATION: Division or seed propagation. Seeds need to be covered and germinated at a warm temperature (72°F) and high humidity.

See color plate

DISEASES AND INSECTS: No serious problems.

HARDINESS: Zones 3–9.

CULTIVARS:
   var. *bastardii*—Creamy yellow flowers, 4 feet tall.
   'Golden Queen'—Larger yellow flowers without the brown blotches on the falls.
   'Variegata'—In spring the newly emerged leaves are striped with pale yellow markings. As the leaves mature they turn green by midsummer. The foliage is very striking in the spring.

ADDITIONAL NOTES: Yellow flag is native to Europe but has naturalized so well in many parts of the United States that it seems it is native to the North American country.

Native to Europe.   Perennial

SCIENTIFIC NAME/FAMILY: *Iris reticulata*   Iridaceae

(ī'ris re-tik-ū-lā'tȧ)

COMMON NAME: Netted Iris

LEAVES: Linear, 8"–10" long at flowering, later to 18", 4-angled, usually 2–4 per plant.

FLOWER: Violet-purple, perianth tube 3"–6" long, falls ovate, ½" wide, yellow crests, standards erect, 2½" long and ¼" wide; violet scented.

HABIT: 3" to 9" erect plant.

SEASON OF BLOOM: Early spring.

CULTURE: Full sun and a fertile, well-drained soil which is slightly alkaline is ideal. Plant bulbs 2"–4" deep and space at 2" in the fall.

UTILIZATION: Excellent plant for rock gardens and sunny borders or along streams. When massed, the fragrant blossoms resemble clumps of violets. The bulbs must be planted in large numbers to create a good display.

PROPAGATION: The bulbs of netted iris are very small and can be undisturbed for several years. For multiplication, they can be lifted, divided, and replanted in the fall.

DISEASES AND INSECTS: Ink spot and *Fusarium* basal rot.

HARDINESS: Zones 5–9.

CULTIVARS:
'Cantab'—Pale blue flower with a yellow blotch and white rimmed.
'Clairette'—Sky blue and dark purple bicolor.
'Edward'—Bright blue flowers.
'Gordon'—The standards are blue and falls are violet.
'Hercules'—Dark red violet flowers.
'Ida'—Blue flowers with yellow ridges.
'Jeannine'—Purple-violet falls with orange edges. This selection has a good fragrance.
'Joyce'—Sky blue flowers, with orange central ridge on the falls.
'Natascha'—Ivory-white falls with a golden yellow blotch.
'Pauline'—Purple-violet flowers with a white blotch.
'Spring Time'—Blue standards and dark blue falls with white lines.

ADDITIONAL NOTES: The specific epithet, *reticulata*, is probably derived from the net-like pattern on the scales of the bulb.

Native to Caucasus.   Perennial—hardy bulb

SCIENTIFIC NAME/FAMILY: *Iris sibirica*   Iridaceae

(ī′ris sī-bir′i-ka)

COMMON NAME: Siberian Iris

LEAVES: Leaves linear, ½″ wide, sheaths split
into slender fibers.

FLOWER: Perianth divided into 6 segments; the
outer 3 (falls) are reflexed, round-oblong, ¾″
wide, the inner 3 (standards) are broad-
lanceolate, erect, and shorter than the falls
(the falls are beardless). Flowers are white,
blue, purple, and violet.

HABIT: 2′–4′ erect plant. Most plants are in the
3′ range. Clumps are 18″–24″ wide.

SEASON OF BLOOM: Late spring.

CULTURE: Full sun or partial shade. Although
they will tolerate a poor, dry soil, best
growth is obtained in fertile, moist, slightly
acid soils.

UTILIZATION: Use in the perennial border. Siberian iris is a bridge plant in the bloom se-
quence between German iris and the Japanese iris. The foliage is refined and the large
clumps have an upright vase-shaped growth
habit. After flowering, the flower stalks bear
2″–3″ seed pods, which turn brown and remain on the plant during the winter. An
orangish fall color also develops on the foliage.

PROPAGATION: Spring division is best but is
needed infrequently.

DISEASES AND INSECTS: There are no serious
problems. This species is not as susceptible
to the iris borer or soft rot as the tall bearded iris.

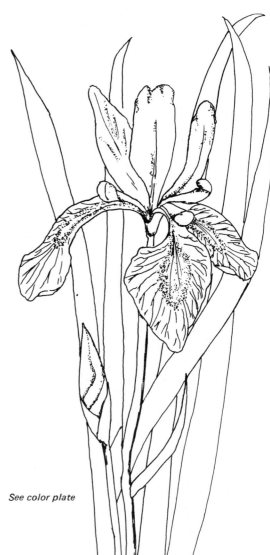

See color plate

HARDINESS: Zones 3–9. Siberian iris may be the best iris for southern gardens.

CULTIVARS: The selection in Siberian iris is very large. I counted 213 cultivars in one
catalog.
  'Caesar's Brother'—Blue to nearly black flowers, 36″.
  'Dreaming Spires'—Lavender and royal blue flowers, 30″.
  'Ego'—Rich blue, wide falls, 30″.
  'Flight of Butterflies'—Blue petals with a faint blue to white coloring between the veins
    on the falls, 30″.
  'Little White'—White flowers, 12″–18″ tall.
  'Placid Waters'—Blue flower, wide falls, 30″.
  'Sea Shadows'—Blue and turquoise flowers, 36″.
  'Snow Queen'—Pure white flowers, 24″–30″.
  'Sparkling Rose'—Rose colored flowers, 30″.
  'Tealwood'—Dark violet flowers, 36″.
  'White Swirl'—White with a bit of yellow, 36″.

Native to central Europe.   Perennial

SCIENTIFIC NAME/FAMILY: *Isatis tinctoria*   Brassicaceae (Cruciferae)

(i'-sā-tis tink-tor'-e-a)

COMMON NAME: Woad, Dyer's Woad

LEAVES: Alternate leaves, oblong to lanceolate, 4" long. The stem leaves are clasping or auricled. Foliage is bluish green.

FLOWER: Yellow flowers, ¼" wide, are
borne in terminal panicles. Each flower
has 4 petals and 4 sepals. Fruit is a
black, flat, pendulous, 1-seeded silicle.
First year growth is vegetative, flowering
occurs during second year.

HABIT: Erect plant with a loose habit, 4' tall.
Space plants 18" apart.

SEASON OF BLOOM:
Mid to late spring.

CULTURE: Performs
well in well-
drained soils with
full sun exposure.
Some lodging will
occur. Pea staking
would be best
with this species.

See color plate

UTILIZATION: The
fluffy clouds of
yellow flowers are
nice in a herba-
ceous border of
spike and round
flowers. It is best used at the back of the border. The flowers are long lasting and are
excellent in fresh bouquets. Some arrangers use the black seed heads in dried
arrangements. Woad is also used as a natural blue dye for yarns and fabrics. A pink dye
can also be obtained when young leaves are combined with an alum mordant.

PROPAGATION: Seed germination requires about 10 days. Once established, woad will
self-sow freely.

DISEASES AND INSECTS: Woad, as a member of the mustard family, can be susceptible
to club root and cabbage maggot. Plant this species away from related crops.

ADDITIONAL NOTES: Woad has been grown as a dye for over 2000 years. It was the
principle blue dye in Europe until indigo was imported from the Far East. Warriors in the
British Isles used a blue paste from fermented woad leaves to check bleeding and as
a war paint.

Native to central Europe, Mediterranean region, and central Asia.   Biennial

SCIENTIFIC NAME/FAMILY: *Kniphofia hybrids* (Tritoma)   Liliaceae

(nip-hō'fi-ȧ)

COMMON NAME: Torch Lily, Red-Hot Poker, Tritoma, Poker Plant

LEAVES: Linear-sword shaped, to 3' long, 1" wide, gray-green, strongly keeled, margins often rough.

FLOWER: Individual drooping flowers are tubular in shape. Arranged in dense racemes at the top of the flowering stems. The flowers are massed on the top 6"–10" of the scape. Flower colors are red and yellow on the species, with a greater variety available on the cultivars.

HABIT: 2' to 4' erect plant with a width of 3 feet.

SEASON OF BLOOM: Summer.

CULTURE: Full sun, well-drained soils are required for successful growth. Heavy, soggy soils are nearly always fatal for this species. Wet soils in winter will cause the rhizomatous roots to rot.

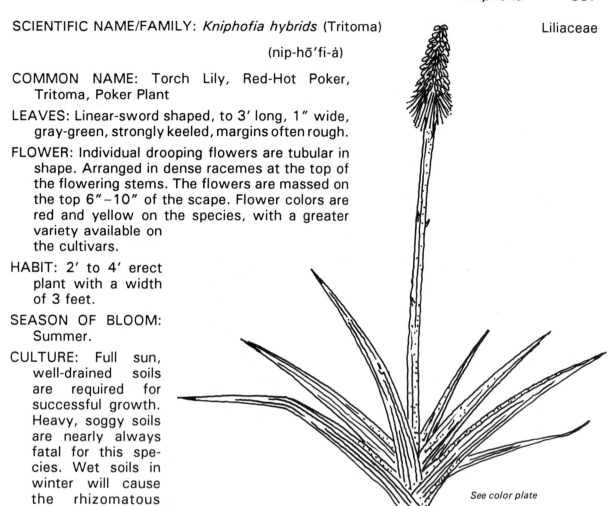

See color plate

UTILIZATION: Single specimens or plantings in borders of not more than 3 together. Cut flowers are also a possible use.

PROPAGATION: Seeds may be sown in the spring; however, flowering plants will not be obtained for 2 to 3 years. Division in the spring is generally recommended. *Kniphofia* may build up to a clump size of 2½'–3' wide, but will not need division for many years.

DISEASES AND INSECTS: None serious.

HARDINESS: Zones 5–9. *Kniphofia* performs well in southern zones.

CULTIVARS:
'Alcazar'—Clear red flowers, 40" tall.
'Bressingham Comet'—Flower spikes have red top flowers and yellow flowers below.
'Earliest of All'—Coral flowers, earlier bloom than other cultivars, and very hardy, 2½'.
'Innocence'—Narrow flower spikes turn from coppery-orange to pale yellow and then to cream, 30" tall.
'Little Maid'—Creamy-white spikes, 2' tall. Introduced by Beth Chatto of England.
'Primrose Beauty'—30", primrose yellow flowers.
'Royal Standard'—3', top flowers red; lower, yellow to cream color.
'Springtime'—Top flowers red; lower ones are white.

ADDITIONAL NOTES: The name of the genus pays tribute to J. J. Kniphof, an eighteenth century professor in Germany. Many of the cultivars are listed as selections of *K. uvaria*. This species was first introduced in 1705 and is about 4' tall. The flowers are scarlet on the upper half of the inflorescence and yellow on the lower half.

Native to Africa.   Perennial

SCIENTIFIC NAME/FAMILY: *Kochia scoparia f. trichophylla*   Chenopodiaceae
(K. childsii)

(kō'ki-à skō-pā'ri-à trik-ō-fil'à)

COMMON NAME: Summer Cypress, Burning Bush, Firebush, Belvedere

LEAVES: Alternate, linear-acute, usually ciliate, the larger leaves to 2" or more long, narrowed to a short petiole, many smaller ones very narrow with a short petiole. The light green foliage, which turns red in cool autumn weather, is the ornamental feature of the plant. The fall color is very bright, hence the common names, burning bush and firebush.

FLOWER: Inconspicuous.

HABIT: 2' to 3' erect growth habit with a fine-textured branching habit.

SEASON OF BLOOM: Not significant.

CULTURE: Full sun, will tolerate hot weather but prefers a moist, well-drained soil.

UTILIZATION: Hedge, screen, background for a border. Resembles an evergreen hedge, columnar or pyramidal to globular habit. I have seen plantings at Fernbank Science Center, Atlanta, Georgia, and Manhattan, Kansas, used very effectively as hedges.

See color plate

PROPAGATION: Seeds germinate at 70°F after soaking seed in water for a day. Start 6 weeks before outside planting desired.

DISEASES AND INSECTS: None serious.

CULTIVARS:
'Acapulco Silver'—This All American Selection Bronze Medal winner has lime-green foliage which is sprinkled freely with silver variegation. 36" tall.

ADDITIONAL NOTES: Handsome, medium height temporary hedge. Nicely shaped plants fill out tightly to form very uniform, upright, rounded mounds of fine-textured foliage. Rated as one of the toughest annuals, even in highly polluted areas. In a warm climate, it could become a nuisance because it self-sows and is very vigorous. To prevent this, the plant should be cut down before the seed matures in the fall. *Kochia* is named for Wilhelm Daniel Josef Kock, a 19th century botany professor.

Native to Europe, Asia—naturalized in North America.   Annual

SCIENTIFIC NAME/FAMILY: *Koeleria glauca*   Poaceae
                                                        (Gramineae)

(kol-er'-i-á glâ'kà)

COMMON NAME: Large Blue June Grass

LEAVES: The narrow leaf blades are involute or flat,
    glaucous above and slightly pubescent beneath.
    The leaves are blue-gray and evergreen to semi-
    evergreen.

FLOWER: The flowers are silvery-white and borne in
    2" to 4" long panicles held on stems rising
    8"–12" above the foliage.

HABIT: This grass forms a hedgehog-like clump of
    foliage 12" tall and 12" wide. Flowers extend
    8"–12" above the leaves.

SEASON OF BLOOM: Early summer.

CULTURE: *Koeleria* should be grown in full sun and
    in a well-drained soil. It does not tolerate heavy,
    wet soils and shade areas.

UTILIZATION: The size of this species and the
    foliage color make it useful for rock gardens or
    the foreground of perennial borders. Although
    the flowers are short stemmed, they are suited
    for fresh and dried arrangements.

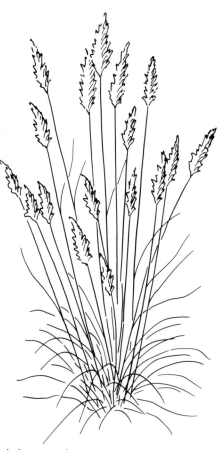
Koeleria macrantha

PROPAGATION: *Koeleria* can be propagated from
    seed. Cover the seeds lightly, keep the germina-
    tion medium moist at a temperature of 70°F. Division can also be done in spring or fall.

DISEASES AND INSECTS: None serious.

HARDINESS: Zones 6–9.

RELATED SPECIES:
    K. argentea (ar-jen'tē-a)—Silver Hairgrass. The foliage of this species is 1/8"–1/4"
        wide, 10" long, grayish green on the top and silvery beneath. Full sun and well-
        drained soil are absolute requirements. Silver hairgrass is a useful plant for massing,
        grouping, or as a ground cover.
    K. brevis (bre'-vis)—Blue Hairgrass. This species is similar to large blue hairgrass except
        for its smaller size. Its 4"–6" tall clump makes it useful as an accent in the rock or
        trough garden. As is found with other *Koeleria*, a well-drained soil in a full sun site
        is a requirement.
    K. macrantha (ma-kran'tha)—June grass. June grass forms more of a vertical clump
        than other *Koeleria* species (see drawing). It has foliage 12"–18" tall with flower
        stalks extending 12"–18" above the foliage. This species can be used in naturalized
        areas and in drifts and masses.

Native to central Europe and Siberia.   Perennial

SCIENTIFIC NAME/FAMILY: *Lamiastrum galeobdolan* 'Variegatum'   Lamiaceae
(Labiatae)

(lam-ĭ-ā'-strum gal-ē-ob'-dō-lan văr-i-e-gā'tum)

COMMON NAME: Variegated Yellow Archangel

See color plate

LEAVES: Opposite, cordate-ovate leaves, 1"–2" long with crenate-dentate margins; basal leaves are long-petioled. The leaves have silver variegation throughout except on the midribs and the margins.

FLOWER: Yellow, hooded and double lipped, borne in axillary or terminal whorls of 5 to 15 flowers, corolla tube 2–3 times longer than calyx, ½" to ¾".

HABIT: 12"–18" spreading plant. It will easily spread 18"–24" in a short period of time.

SEASON OF BLOOM: Late spring to early summer.

CULTURE: Well-drained soil in full or partial shade is the optimum site for this species. However, it is fairly adaptable and can make reasonable growth in dry shade areas. If plants become leggy, the stems can be cut back to about 6″ and regrowth will quickly occur.

UTILIZATION: Variegated yellow archangel should be used in woodland or shade areas as a ground cover. It is very useful for covering areas in the dry shade where little else will grow. Its aggressive nature precludes its use in perennial borders where it may crowd out other perennials.

PROPAGATION: Division of the plants in the spring or terminal cuttings in spring are practical propagation methods.

DISEASES AND INSECTS: Slugs and snails will need to be controlled.

HARDINESS: Zones 4–9.

CULTIVARS:
'Herman's Pride'. Green leaves with silver mottling. The leaves of this cultivar are more lanceolate and regularly marked than the leaves of the species. This cultivar is more of a clump former and is not as aggressive as 'Variegatum.'

ADDITIONAL NOTES: The species is also known under the names of *Lamium galeobdolan* and *Galeobdolan luteum.*

Native to Europe.   Perennial

SCIENTIFIC NAME/FAMILY: *Lamium maculatum*   Lamiaceae
                                                              (Labiatae)

(lā'mi-um mak-ū-lā'tum)

COMMON NAME: Spotted Deadnettle

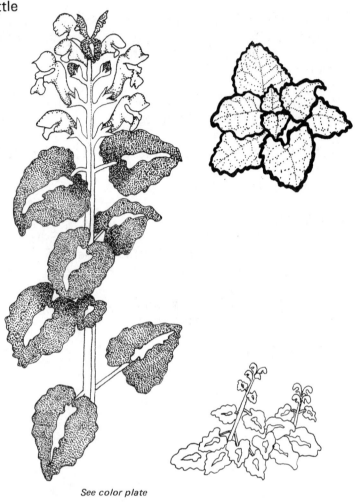

LEAVES: Square stems, opposite leaves, both have a bristly pubescence. Leaves ovate, with a cordate base and crenate-dentate margin, with gray-green to cream-green blotches near the midrib of the leaves.

FLOWER: Mauve-pink hooded flowers, ½" to 1" long, borne in the whorls.

HABIT: Wide-spreading, clump, 8"–12" tall.

SEASON OF BLOOM: Late spring to midsummer.

CULTURE: This selection should be placed in partial to full shade in moist, well-drained soil. It performs exceedingly well in deep shade. If soils become too dry, as would be found in a dry shade area, *Lamium maculatum* will become straggly and open spaces will occur.

See color plate

UTILIZATION: Ground cover for the shade garden or as an edging plant for the border. It may be too vigorous for some garden situations.

PROPAGATION: Division in spring or fall. Cuttings can be taken at any time during the growing season.

DISEASES AND INSECTS: No serious insect or disease problems. Exposure to full sun may scorch the leaves.

HARDINESS: Zones 3–8.

CULTIVARS:
  'Album'—White flowers with leaves similar to the species.
  'Aureum'—Yellow leaf form, pink flowers. Shade and moist soil is required for this yellow leaf selection. It is not as aggressive as the species.
  'Beacon Silver' ('Silbergroschen')—This German introduction from the Klose Nursery has silver leaves with narrow green borders and pink flowers. It is a popular cultivar with foliage that stands out in the shade garden.

'Chequers'—Leaves of this selection are green with a wide silver stripe in the center. The green margins are broader than those of 'Beacon Silver'. The flowers are pink. Plant height is 9"–12" when in flower.

'Shell Pink'—Flowers are pale pink on plants 8" tall.

'White Nancy'—This newer cultivar has silver leaves, like 'Beacon Silver', and white flowers. In fact, it is often listed as a white-flowering version of 'Beacon Silver'. The white flowers appear to be fresher and more vibrant than the pink of 'Beacon Silver'.

Native to Europe and North America.   Perennial

SCIENTIFIC NAME/FAMILY: *Lathyrus latifolius*   Fabaceae
                                                              (Leguminosae)

(lath'i-rus lat-i-fō'li-us)

COMMON NAME: Perennial Sweet Pea,
    Everlasting Pea

LEAVES: Even pinnate leaves, leaflets
    ovate-lanceolate, to 4" long, acute
    and mucronate, prominently 3–5
    veined, leaflike stipules, tendrils stout
    and branched.

FLOWER: Flowers large, several to many
    on peduncles exceeding the leaves,
    1" across in colors of pink, red, pur-
    ple, white, yellow, or blue.

HABIT: 4' to 8' vine.

SEASON OF BLOOM: Summer.

CULTURE: Full sun, well-drained soil.

UTILIZATION: The climbing sweet pea
    can be placed on a trellis, fence, or
    other structures.

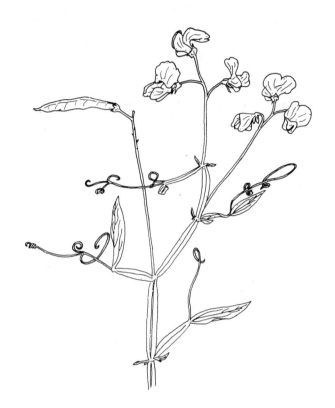

PROPAGATION: Seeds in late spring will germinate in 2 to 3 weeks at 55°–65°F. Before
    planting seeds should be soaked in water or if only a few seeds, the seed coats should
    be scarified by using a nail file. Clump division is also a possibility.

DISEASES AND INSECTS: No serious problems.

HARDINESS: Zones 4–8.

CULTIVARS:
    'Pink Pearl' ('Rosa Perle')—Pink flowers.
    'Red Pearl'—Red flowers.
    'White Pearl' (Weisse Perle)—White flowers.

RELATED SPECIES: *Lathyrus odoratus* (ō-do-rā'tus), Annual Sweet Pea. Annual sweet pea
    is best germinated by soaking the seed for several days, covering the seed with ½" of
    soil and germinating at 55°F. Annual sweet pea can develop into a nicely mounded
    ground cover. The flowers are borne above the foliage and they come in a wide color
    range.

ADDITIONAL NOTES: Both the annual and perennial sweet peas were favorites in the past
    but now find little favor among the gardening public. I still remember, as a small child,
    my mother collecting flowering branches of sweet pea for exhibiting at the county fair.
    Lathyrus is the Greek name for pea.

Native to Europe.   Perennial

SCIENTIFIC NAME/FAMILY: *Lavandula angustifolia*

Lamiaceae
(Labiatae)

(lá-van'dù-là an-gus-ti-fō'li-a)

COMMON NAME: True Lavender, English Lavender, Lavender

LEAVES: Opposite or whorled, leaves oblong-linear or lanceolate, to 2" long, entire; younger leaves often clustered in axils, white tomentose, square stems.

FLOWER: Flowers lavender or purple, ¼" – ½" long, in 6–10 flowered whorls forming interrupted spikes. Flowers are aromatic and have been used to make sachets and potpourris. Often called the "queen of herbs."

HABIT: 12"–24" depending on cultivar. True lavender has a compact, rounded growth habit.

SEASON OF BLOOM: Summer.

CULTURE: Full sun, well-drained soil. Plants grown in heavy soils will have soft growth, which can create a hardiness problem.

UTILIZATION: Rock gardens, cut flowers (planted in masses or small hedges), and used for sachets and potpourris.

PROPAGATION: Stem cuttings in summer, seeds, or clump division in the fall work well. Seeds germinate in 2 or 3 weeks at 70°F after 5 weeks of stratification. Cuttings should be taken from side shoots (non-flowering).

DISEASES AND INSECTS: Leaf spot, root rot, four-line plant bug, caterpillars, and Northern root-knot nematode have been reported, but none are serious pests.

HARDINESS: Zones 5–9.

CULTIVARS:

'Gray Lady'—Grey foliage and lavender-blue flowers, fast, compact grower, 18" tall.

'Hidcote'—Deep violet-blue flowers, silver-grey foliage, 18"–24" tall. 'Hidcote' was grown by Major Lawrence Johnston at Hidcote Manor in Gloucestershire, England, before 1950.

'Jean Davis'—15"–18" tall, pinkish white flowers, blue-green foliage.

'Munstead'—Early flowering, compact grower with lavender-blue flowers similar to 'Hidcote'. 'Munstead' was grown by Gertrude Jekyll at Munstead Wood, Surrey, England, and introduced into the trade in 1916. Also listed by the synonym 'Munstead Dwarf'.

'Twickel Purple'—Dark violet flowers with grey foliage, 18".

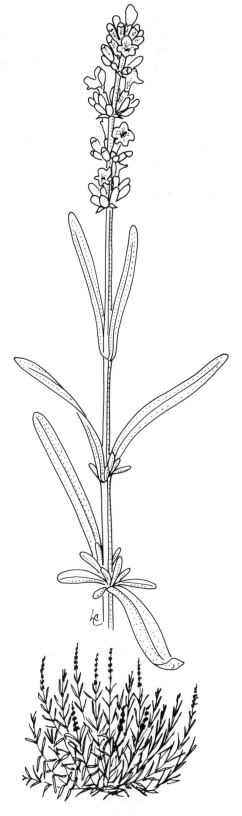

See color plate

RELATED SPECIES:

L. × *intermedia*—Lavandin. This is a natural interspecific hybrid of *L. angustifolia* × *L. latifoliia.* The differences are slight between lavender and lavandin. The latter has longer flower bracts and flowers later in the season. 'Grosso', a common cultivar, has violet flowers.

L. stoechas—French Lavender. This half-hardy perennial has purple flowers with purple bracts that extend vertically from the flowers. The variety *pedunculata* has magenta pink flowers with purple bracts. Both are excellent as pot plants. Hardiness is zones 6-9.

ADDITIONAL NOTES: Each year—cut lavender back to just above last year's point of growth. The plants can grow undisturbed for an indefinite period of time. *Lavandula* is Latin for *to wash,* referring to the use of lavender in the bath. Oil of lavender, used in perfume, is distilled from the flowers of true lavender.

Native to Mediterranean region.　　　　　　　　　　　　　　　　　　　Perennial

SCIENTIFIC NAME/FAMILY: *Lavatera thuringiaca*   Malvaceae

(la-vat'-er-a thū-ring-ī-a'-ka)

COMMON NAME: Tree Mallow

LEAVES: The alternate leaves have maple-like shapes, 3 to 5 lobes, have toothed margins, and are 3" long and 2"–3" wide.

FLOWER: The rose-pink mallow flowers (similar to single hollyhocks) have 5 petals and are 2–3 inches wide. The flowers can be borne solitarily in the axils or form a loose, terminal raceme.

HABIT: Bushy, erect shrub which is 4–5 feet tall and wide. Space this species 3 feet apart.

SEASON OF BLOOM: Summer.

CULTURE: Mallow thrives in average soil in full sun conditions. It is an easily grown perennial.

UTILIZATION: An erect, long blooming species suitable for the rear of the border.

PROPAGATION: Propagation is by seed.

DISEASES AND INSECTS: As with other mallows, Japanese beetle can be a serious problem.

HARDINESS: Zones 5–8.

Native to central and southeastern Europe.   Perennial

SCIENTIFIC NAME/FAMILY: *Leontopodium alpinum*   Asteraceae
                                                        (Compositae)

(lē-on-to-pō′di-um al-pī′-num)

COMMON NAME: Edelweiss

LEAVES: The silver-gray tomentose leaves are
    alternate, linear to oblanceolate, 2″ to 3″ long.
    The newer leaves are more pubescent than ma-
    ture leaves; consequently, the upper portions of
    the plant, which include the flower bracts, are a
    striking silver-gray color.

FLOWER: The silver heads, ¼″ across, are clustered
    closely together and are surrounded by a tuft of
    white-woolly floral bracts which are much longer
    than the flower head cluster. This creates a
    silver star 1″ to 2″ across. The true flowers are
    yellow, but their importance is minimal when
    compared to the silver-gray floral bracts.

HABIT: Edelweiss is a 6″–10″ tall tufted perennial.

SEASON OF BLOOM: Late spring to early summer.

CULTURE: *Leontopodium* is often considered to be
    a plant grown only in the mountains. However,
    it can be utilized as a garden plant if proper
    cultural needs are met. It performs best in an
    alkaline soil which is well-drained, preferably a
    sandy loam, and a full sun site. Most edelweiss,
    lost in heavy, moist soils, succumb to crown rot.

UTILIZATION: Rock gardens or as an edging in the
    border front if the soils are well-drained. Too
    often the soil in the border is not as well-drained
    as the soil mix in a well-prepared rock garden or
    trough.

See color plate

PROPAGATION: Seed propagation or careful division. The seeds are very small and may
    need to be mixed with a carrier such as a fine sand to get even distribution. Rather than
    cover the seeds, just firm them into the germination medium. Edelweiss slowly spreads
    by stolons, and division is needed only for propagation.

DISEASES AND INSECTS: No serious problems.

HARDINESS: Zones 2–7.

ADDITIONAL NOTES: *Leontopodium* is a derivation of *leon,* a lion, and *pous,* a foot. The
    flowers and floral bracts supposedly resemble a lion's paw.

Native to the Alps Mountains.   Perennial

SCIENTIFIC NAME/FAMILY: *Leucanthemum* × *superbum*   Asteraceae
(Chrysanthemum x superbum)   (Compositae)
(lū-kan'thē-mum sū-pĕr'bum)

COMMON NAME: Shasta Daisy

LEAVES: Leaves alternate, coarsely toothed, lower leaves oblanceolate, to 1' long including petiole; upper leaves, lanceolate, sessile, coarsely and bluntly toothed.

FLOWER: Heads terminating the long stems, 2"–3" across, with broad and obtuse white rays, disk flowers yellow.

HABIT: 1'–3' tall and 2' wide; smaller cultivars have a round habit.

SEASON OF BLOOM: Early summer to frost.

See color plate

CULTURE: Shasta daisy grows best in fertile, moist and well-drained soils. The soil needs to be especially well-drained during the winter. In hot summer climates, this species should be in partial shade; in cooler regions, full sun is good. Divide every 2–3 years to retain vigor and compactness. Taller growing selections should be pinched to keep them compact. Deadhead for better appearance and to promote rebloom.

UTILIZATION: Cutting garden or in borders where they are effective as singles or in groups of three.

PROPAGATION: Seeds, sown in the spring, produce a variety of first class plants. Maintain seeds at 70°–75°F for 10–14 days. Clumps should be divided every other spring. One can also dig the stolon-like shoots and plant in the fall.

DISEASES AND INSECTS: Leaf spots, stem rots, four-lined plant bug, and leaf miner are occasional pest problems.

HARDINESS: Zones 5–9. Shasta daisy varies in hardiness. It is seldom long-lived in areas north of zone 5, and in my experience it is not always hardy in zone 5.

CULTIVARS:
'Aglaya'—Frilled double flowers, 3" wide, 2' tall.
'Alaska'—Large single white flowers with yellow centers, 3" wide, 2'–3' tall plants. Hardy to zone 4.
'Cobham Gold'—Double cream-colored flowers with deep yellow centers, 15"–18" tall.
'Diener's Double'—Double flowers, 24"–30" tall.
'Esther Read'—Double flowers, 18"–24" tall.
'Everest'—Large flowers, 3"–4" wide on stems 3'–4' tall.
'Little Miss Muffet'—Semi-double, creamy white flowers, 8"–12" tall.
'Little Princess'—Single flowers, compact plants, 12" tall.
'Majestic'—Large, single white flower (4"–5" wide) with a small yellow center, 3' tall.
'Marconi'—Semi-double white flowers, up to 5" wide, on 3' tall stems.
'Polaris'—Huge flowers, some 7" wide, are carried on 3' tall stems.

'Silver Princess'—Creamy white flowers with yellow centers, 8"–12" tall. It is similar to 'Little Miss Muffet'.

'Snowcap'—This cultivar selected by Alan Bloom is compact, 12"–15" tall, and flowers profusely. It appeared as a self-sown seedling in Mr. Bloom's nursery.

'T. Killin'—Single flowers with double rows of petals and crested yellow centers. It has thick sturdy stems which makes it desirable as a cut flower. 24"–30" tall.

'Wirral Pride'—Flowers have an obvious center crest, 2'–3' tall.

RELATED SPECIES:

L. pacificum (pà-sif'-i-kum). Silver and Gold Chrysanthemum. This species has an attractive foliage with silver on the edges and lower leaf surfaces. This creates a frosty appearance to the mounded plant. In mid to late fall, many small yellow button flowers cover the foliage. Plant in well-drained soil for best growth. It is useful in the border, as a specimen, or ground cover for dry, sandy areas. Unfortunately for northern gardeners, it is not reliably hardy above zone 6.

ADDITIONAL NOTES: Double flowering cultivars perform best in partial shade. Shasta daisy needs good air circulation and should not be crowded. Luther Burbank is often credited with the shasta daisy as we know it today. Since his experiments were done near the white peaks of Mt. Shasta in California, the common name is understandable.

Hybrid origin.   Perennial

SCIENTIFIC NAME/FAMILY: *Leucojum vernum*   Amaryllidaceae

(lū-kō'jum vēr'num)

COMMON NAME: Spring Snowflake

LEAVES: Leaves are linear and straplike, 6″ to 9″ long, ½″ wide, obtuse.

FLOWER: Pure white with a green crescent on all 6 segments. The 6 segments of the perianth are nearly equal length, which is different from *Galanthus*, where the external segments are longer than the internal segments. The single flowers droop and are bell-shaped and have a sweet fragrance.

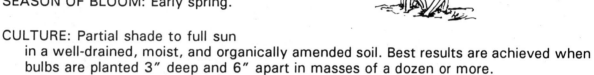

HABIT: 6″ to 12″, round habit.

SEASON OF BLOOM: Early spring.

CULTURE: Partial shade to full sun in a well-drained, moist, and organically amended soil. Best results are achieved when bulbs are planted 3″ deep and 6″ apart in masses of a dozen or more.

UTILIZATION: Ideal for naturalizing in grass, plantings around shrubs or trees, and in the rock garden.

PROPAGATION: Under most conditions, it is necessary to remove the bulbs from the soil only for the purpose of multiplication. This is normally done, after the foliage has turned brown, by digging and separating the bulbs. Plants produced by seed propagation will take 4–5 years to flower.

DISEASES AND INSECTS: None serious.

HARDINESS: Zones 3–9.

RELATED SPECIES:
L. aestivum (es'-tiv-um) — Summer Snowflake. 12″–18″, white flowers in April to June, borne 3 or 4 per scape.
L. aestivum 'Gravetye Giant'. Larger flowers than the species, 2–8 per scape.
L. autumnale (a-tum-nā'lē) — Autumn Snowflake. 9″–12″, white flowers, shaded with pink at the base, appear in the fall. This species has thread-like leaves which develop after flowering. It is harder to establish than other members of *Leucojum*. Plants require excellent drainage. Successful gardeners will use this species in the rock garden or containers near the patio. Zones 5–9.

ADDITIONAL NOTES: *Leucojum* is of Greek origin; *leukos,* meaning white, is in reference to the color of the flowers.

Native to central Europe.   Perennial—hardy bulb

SCIENTIFIC NAME/FAMILY: *Liatris scariosa*   Asteraceae
                                                                    (Compositae)

(lī-ā'tris skār-i-ō'sȧ)

COMMON NAME: Tall Gayfeather, Blazing Star, Button Snakeroot

LEAVES: Alternate, lower leaves broad-lanceolate, to 5" long and
    1" wide, with petioles to 4" long, upper leaves much smaller
    and punctate.

FLOWER: Heads to 1" across, 25–50 flowered, in a racemose or
    occasionally paniculate inflorescence, flowers are rose,
    lavender, or white.

HABIT: 1½' to 3' tall plant with stout, erect stems. Plant width is
    24".

SEASON OF BLOOM: Midsummer to late fall.

CULTURE: Sun or light shade in well-drained soils. One should
    avoid soggy soil situations during the winter.

UTILIZATION: Cutting, superb for drying, and beautiful in the
    border. *Liatris* looks best when planted sparingly rather than in
    large masses, which creates a regimented feeling.

PROPAGATION: Seeds will germinate in 3 to 4 weeks at 65°–
    75°F. From seed to flower takes 2 years. The woody corms or
    rhizomes can also be divided in the spring and should be
    divided approximately every 4 years. Cultivars should be
    asexually propagated.

DISEASES AND INSECTS: In southern areas, the Southern root-
    knot nematode may be a problem.

HARDINESS: Zones 3–9. *Liatris* is tolerant of hot summers, which
    makes it suitable for southern areas.

CULTIVARS:
    'September Glory'—Deep purple flowers that open simulta-
        neously in mid to late summer. Plants are 3' to 4' and may
        need staking due to a tendency to lodge.
    'White Spires'—A sport of 'September Glory' with pure white
        flowers. Like 'September Glory', it may need staking.

See color plate

RELATED SPECIES:
    L. pycnostachya (pik-nos-tak'-e-a) Kansas Gayfeather—Tall-growing species with purple
        or pinkish-lavender flowers. Stems of the species have a large number of leaves.
        Very susceptible to damage during wet winters. This species is 3'–5' tall, making
        it too tall for most gardens.
    L. spicata (spi-ka'-ta)—Spike Gayfeather. This species or its cultivars are most
        commonly used by gardeners. Plants are 2'–3' tall and 2' wide. Although shorter
        than other species, spike gayfeather will usually require staking after the first year.
        It is an excellent species to grow for cut flowers as well as providing a vertical
        accent in the perennial border.
    'Floristan Violett'—Violet flowers, 36" tall.
    'Floristan White' ('Floristan Weiss')—Creamy-white flowers, 3' tall. Good selection
        for southern gardens.

'Kobold'—Compact cultivar, 18"–30", with dark purple flowers. It produces many flowers spikes which can be used as cut flowers. 'Kobold' is one of the best cultivars for the border.

ADDITIONAL NOTES: *Liatris* starts flowering at the top and moves downward. This is different than most spike flowers, which start at the bottom.

Native to North America.   Perennial

SCIENTIFIC NAME/FAMILY: *Ligularia dentata*   Asteraceae
                        (Senecio clivorum)   (Compositae)

(lig-ū-lā′ri-á den-tā′tá)

COMMON NAME: Bigleaf Goldenray, Ragwort

LEAVES: The leathery, textured leaves are basal (alternate on the stem) long-petioled, and are 2′ to 3′ long. Leaf blades are orbicular or reniform shaped, have deeply cordate bases, dentate margins, and are 8″ to 12″ wide.

FLOWER: The yellowish-orange daisy flowers are borne in corymbose heads that are 3″ to 6″ wide. The heads are on stems that rise 3′ to 4′.

HABIT: Mounded habit, 3′ to 4′ tall and 4′ wide.

SEASON OF BLOOM: Midsummer to early fall.

CULTURE: It should be planted in moist to wet soils, bogs and streamsides are good locations, and in filtered shade or the north side of buildings in climates where the summer temperatures go above 80°–85°F. A moist soil can be created by lining the planting hole with perforated plastic film or newspapers and backfilling with an organic amended soil mix. This procedure will aid in moisture retention in gardens that are not blessed with a bog or stream.

UTILIZATION: The bold foliage and flowers of *Ligularia dentata* make for imposing specimen plants which make nice additions to areas alongside water.

See color plate

PROPAGATION: The species is easily propagated by seed, while the cultivars should be produced by division.

DISEASES AND INSECTS: No serious problems.

HARDINESS: Zones 4–8.

CULTIVARS:
'Desdemona'—The striking feature of this cultivar is the lower leaf surface and stem, which are purple. It is 3′ to 4′ tall. It is listed as being more heat tolerant than other cultivars. 'Othello' is very similar to 'Desdemona', but it is not as compact and the flowers are smaller. I cannot see much difference between these two cultivars.
'Orange Queen'—Gold-orange flowers, green leaves, 4′–5′ tall.
'Sommergold'—Bright yellow flowers, green leaves, compact form, 30″–36″ tall.

RELATED SPECIES:

  L. × 'Gregynog Gold'. This hybrid of *L. dentata* × *L. veitchiana* is a good specimen plant with handsome, heart-shaped leaves and orange flowers arranged in a tall, conical spire. It can reach 6' tall.

  L. × *hessei* (hess'-ē-i). This hybrid has leathery, kidney-shaped leaves with small dentate teeth on the margins. Orange-yellow flowers are carried in a short panicle. Plants are 4'–5' tall and 2'–3' wide.

Native to China.   Perennial

SCIENTIFIC NAME/FAMILY: *Ligularia* 'The Rocket'
(Senecio)
(lig-ū lā'ri-à)

Asteraceae
(Compositae)

COMMON NAME: Rocket Ligularia

LEAVES: The leaves are both basal and alternate on the stems. Leaves are hastate-cordate to triangular, 8"–12" long, dentately toothed. The stems and the veins at the base of the leaf blade are purple-black

FLOWER: Small, bright yellow flowers are carried in long, wandlike racemes 4' to 6' high. The racemes tower above the foliage like rockets on a launch pad.

HABIT: Large clump of foliage topped by erect flower stems. Flower stems grow 5' to 6' tall.

SEASON OF BLOOM: Early to midsummer.

CULTURE: The optimum culture of *Ligularia* places the gardener between a rock and a hard place. 'The Rocket' should be placed in full sun to prevent the long racemes from leaning toward the light, which will occur in lower light settings. However, when planted in full sun, the leaves wilt in midday even when the moisture is optimum. The wilted leaves recover at night. As a compromise, a filtered shade situation in moist soil is probably the best solution. The soil should be well amended with organic matter.

UTILIZATION: This species makes an imposing specimen, can be used in groupings, and is especially effective alongside water. Plants grown in dry soil will be a disappointment to the gardener.

PROPAGATION: 'The Rocket' should be propagated by division to insure trueness.

DISEASES AND INSECTS: No serious problems.

HARDINESS: Zones 5–8.

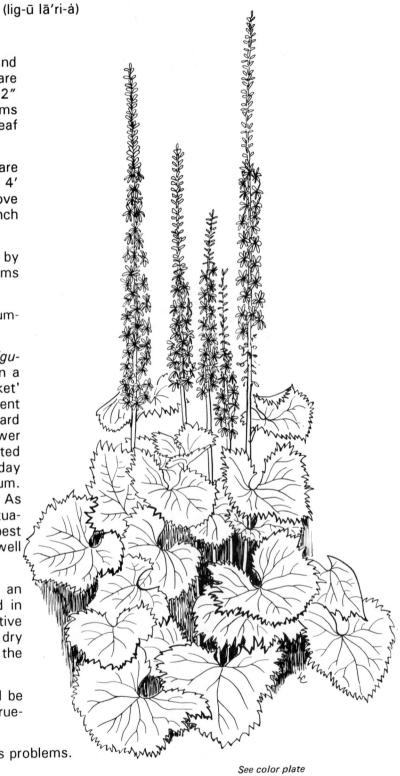

See color plate

ADDITIONAL NOTES: 'The Rocket' can be found assigned to different species. Many references list it under *L. stenocephala* while some classify it as a cultivar of *L. przewalskii.* Both species are closely related and will easily cross-pollinate. This indicates that 'The Rocket' could actually be a hybrid.

Perennial

SCIENTIFIC NAME/FAMILY: *Lilium* sp.   Liliaceae

(lil'i-um)

COMMON NAME: Garden Lily

LEAVES: Many leaves, crowded, narrowly lance-
    olate, 4"–6" long, ½"–¾" wide, 5–7 veins.

FLOWER: Flowers few to many, nodding, open
    and spreading, with colors of white, orange,
    scarlet, rose, pink, or yellow.

HABIT: 2' to 6' erect plant.

SEASON OF BLOOM: Early to midsummer.

CULTURE: Full sun or partial shade. Provide
    fertile soil and mulch to keep the root zone
    cool. Drainage is very important for this
    species. Bulbs should be planted in the fall.

UTILIZATION: Border or cut flowers. Lilies are
    excellent as single specimens or in solid
    masses. Best planted to come up through or
    behind shorter plants which also support the
    stems.

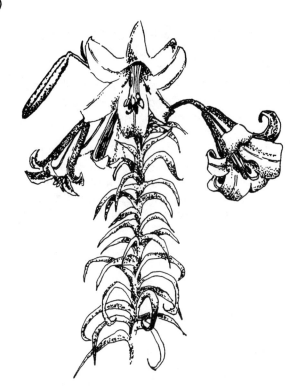

PROPAGATION: Propagation of *Lilium* may be done in several ways and all are satisfactory.
    Seed: Sow in early spring in shallow rows. Small bulblets are dug in the fall and
        replanted in the spring. Seed grown plants will take several years to flower.
    Division: Clumps can be divided in the fall and split into individual bulbs. Virus disease
        may be transmitted through asexual division.
    Bulbils: L. tigrinum and other species produce shiny black bulbils in the leaf axils. These
        may be harvested in August and sown immediately. After leaves appear in the
        spring, these plants may be reset. Plants will flower in several years.
    Scales: Scales may be removed from the mother bulb and planted in the greenhouse
        or outside in shade. The plants are replanted in the spring and then reset in the fall
        to a permanent location.

DISEASES AND INSECTS: Insects are generally not a problem; however, aphids can
    transmit lily mosaic which distorts the blossoms and mottles the foliage. Basal bulb rot
    is also a problem in poorly drained soils.

HARDINESS: Zones 5–9.

CULTIVARS: Although there are a wide number of reliable and popular species, the hybrid
    lilies are more often found in popular perennial catalogs. The selections available are too
    numerous to list in this text as selection will often be based on the preference of each
    gardener.

ADDITIONAL NOTES: *Lilium* is the old Latin name similar to the Greek *leirion,* a lily.
    Membership in the North American Lily Society, Inc., is a must for individuals with a
    strong interest in hardy lilies. Information can be obtained by writing to the Society at
    Box 476, Waukee, IA 50263.

Hybrid origin.   Perennial—hardy bulb

SCIENTIFIC NAME/FAMILY: *Limonium latifolium* (Statice latifolia)   Plumbaginaceae

(lī-mō'ni-um lat-i-fō'li-um)

COMMON NAME: Sea-Lavender, Statice, Wideleaf Sea-Lavender

LEAVES: Basal leaves, oblong-elliptic, to 10" long, narrowed to a petiole about as long as the blade, leathery.

FLOWER: Scape tall and very much branched, inflorescence strongly spreading until almost spherical, corolla blue-violet. Flowering scape creates a very airy texture 24"–30" tall and 24" wide.

HABIT: 24"–30", basal leaves and erect flower stems. The multiple-branching creates a round habit.

SEASON OF BLOOM: Mid to late summer.

CULTURE: Full sun, well-drained soil (light sandy loam). A heavy soil may create weak stems that will require staking.

UTILIZATION: Borders, cut flowers, and dried bouquets. To dry flowers, cut before they are fully open and hang upside down in a shady, airy place.

PROPAGATION: Seeds will germinate in 3 to 4 weeks at 65°–75°F. Division can be done in very early spring. Clumps may remain indefinitely and are best left undisturbed to improve each year. To obtain additional plants, a portion of the clump can be carefully removed which will cause minimum disturbance.

See color plate

DISEASES AND INSECTS: Crown and root rots can be problems. Wide spacing increases air circulation which reduces the incidence of diseases.

HARDINESS: Zone 3–9. The *Limonium* species perform well in southern zones.

CULTIVARS:
   'Violetta'—Deep violet-blue flowers. This flower is used for the ornamental flower bed as well as for the production of cut flowers.

RELATED SPECIES:

Goniolimon tataricum (gon-ē-o-lī'-mon tà-tar'-i-kum)—German Statice. This species is more compact (squat) than *Limonium.* It grows 12"–18" tall and has rose-pink flowers. The bracts are silvery-white. In my experience, it requires less staking than *Limonium. Goniolimon* is listed in most catalogs as *Limonium dumosum* or *Limonium tataricum.* It is a popular florists' flower.

ADDITIONAL NOTES: Very salt resistant and would be good for sea-side planting. *Limonium* is derived from the Greek *leimon,* a meadow, and alludes to salt meadows, as it is native to those areas.

Native to Russia.   Perennial

SCIENTIFIC NAME/FAMILY: *Limonium sinuatum* (*Statice sinuata*)   Plumbaginaceae

(lī-mō'ni-um sin-ū-ā'tum)

COMMON NAME: Notchleaf Statice

LEAVES: Leaves basal, lyrate-pinnatifid, mostly 4"–8" long, lobes and sinuses rounded, terminal lobe bearing a bristle, branches 3–5 winged, the wings below the forks divided into 3 linear-lanceolate appendages.

FLOWER: Spikelets 3–5 flowered in short one-sided spikes, corolla yellowish-white, calyx blue, lavender, rose or white. Flowers are paper-textured. Bright colored calyx remains after the corolla drops.

HABIT: 1½' to 2' erect plant.

SEASON OF BLOOM: Summer to fall.

CULTURE: Sun, requires dry porous soils. Wet soils are an invitation for root rot.

UTILIZATION: Dried and cut flowers; they can be cut before fully expanding and hung in a cool area to dry. Plants can also be massed in the beds or borders.

PROPAGATION: Seed should be covered lightly with soil and germinated at 70°F. Statice has a long taproot and does not transplant easily. Germination occurs in 2–3 weeks. Statice is available in cleaned (decorticated) or uncleaned seed. Cleaned seed can be sown more easily and precisely.

DISEASES AND INSECTS: Root rot can infect plants grown in poorly drained soils.

CULTIVARS:
   'American Beauty'—Deep rose.
   'Apricot'—Pastel shade.
   'Blue Bonnet'—Sky blue.
   'Gold Coast'—Canary yellow.
   'Iceberg'—Pure white.
   'Kampf's Blue'—Deep blue.
   'Modra'—Dark blue, more branched than other statice.
   'Petite Bouquet' Series—Dwarf habit, 12" tall, available in blue, salmon, white, yellow, and a mixed color. Good selection for borders and bedding purposes.

ADDITIONAL NOTES: *Limonium* is salt tolerant and grown under ocean-side conditions.

Native to Mediterranean region.   Annual

SCIENTIFIC NAME/FAMILY: *Linum perenne* (L. sibiricum)   Linaceae

(lī′num pĕr-en′e)

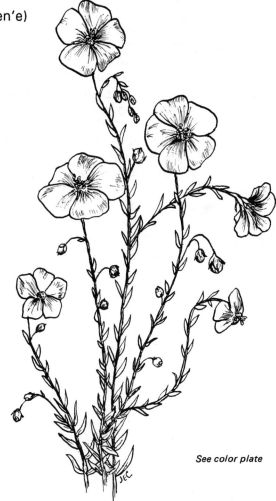

COMMON NAME: Perennial Flax

LEAVES: Alternate, linear to lanceolate, 1″ long; lower section of the stem usually leafless or partially so; upper leaves 1-ribbed.

FLOWER: Sky blue, 1″ wide, usually in a many-branched panicle. Individual flowers last only one day, but they are produced in such profusion that the plant is always in bloom.

HABIT: 24″ upright growing plant with arching stems. Plants are 12″–18″ wide.

SEASON OF BLOOM: Late spring and summer.

CULTURE: Flax doesn't require specialized site conditions. A site in full sun with a light, well-drained soil is suitable. Soggy soil in the winter will reduce the winter hardiness and result in plant decline.

UTILIZATION: Rock garden and the perennial border. Flax is very suitable for an area that needs a light, airy texture. It is a very suitable species for wild gardens. Flax cannot be used as a cut flower because the petals often drop after one day.

See color plate

PROPAGATION: *Linum* is best propagated by seed or cuttings. Division can be done but it is difficult; the root system is coarse and sparse. Seeds can be germinated in 7 to 14 days at 65° to 70°F. Cuttings can be taken in the summer. Flax is usually short-lived, normally 3 to 5 years. However, the plants will often self-sow in the garden.

DISEASES AND INSECTS: Grasshoppers and cutworms are occasional pests.

HARDINESS: Zones 5–8. Excellent plant in zone 8.

CULTIVARS:
'Album'—Off-white flowers that fade when grown in full sun, 18″ tall.
var. *alpinum*—Alpine Flax—Clear blue flowers are carried on stems 8″–12″ tall. It is a nice choice for the rock garden.
'Diamant' (also listed as 'Nanum Diamant')—White flowers, 16″ tall.
'Saphir' (also listed as 'Sapphire' or 'Nanum Sapphire')—Compact form, 12″ × 12″, with clear blue flowers. One of the best for the rock garden.

RELATED SPECIES:
L. capitatum (cap-i-tā′-tum). This species from the mountains of Bulgaria has yellow flowers and is 12″ tall.

L. flavum (fla'vum)—Golden Flax. This species has leathery leaves and 1" wide yellow waxy flowers. It has a height of 15"–18", making it suitable for the rock garden or border front. 'Compactum' is smaller at 6"–9". 'Gemmell's Hybrid' is a small plant that I saw at Harlow Car Gardens near Harrogate, England. It was 10"–12" tall and was covered with bright yellow flowers. I have not seen this cultivar offered in any European or United States nursery. One reference indicates that it may be a hybrid of *L. campanulatum* × *L. elegans.*

L. narbonense (nar-bon-en'-se)—Narbonne Flax. This flax species has clear blue flowers with white eyes. Narbonne flax is more robust and has larger flowers than perennial flax. Plants are 18"–24" tall and 18" wide. 'Heavenly Blue' is more compact than the species (12"–18") and has dark blue flowers. Zones 5–9.

L. suffruticosum ssp. *salsoloides* (suf-fru-ti-ko'-sum) (sal-sol-oi'-dez) var. *nanum.* This selection is long on name and short on height. It is a low growing rockery plant that is 2"–4" tall and 12" wide. The flowers are white and veined with lilac. It should be used in the rock or trough garden.

ADDITIONAL NOTES: *Linum* is a derivation of *linon,* the classical word for flax and the root of linen, flax being a recognized fiber for clothing since ancient times.

Native to Europe.   Perennial

SCIENTIFIC NAME/FAMILY: *Liriope spicata* (L. graminifolia)   Liliaceae

(lir'-i-ōp or li-rī'ō-pē spī-kā'tȧ)

COMMON NAME: Creeping Lily-turf

LEAVES: Evergreen grasslike leaves, 18" long and ¼" wide, serrulate margin. In northern areas, the foliage is a dark green until January and then turns to a pale green-brown color due to winter damage.

FLOWER: The small flowers, ¼" wide, are pale violet to white and are arranged in terminal racemes atop erect, light violet-brown scapes 8"–10" tall. Blue-black berry like fruit are often present in the fall.

HABIT: This stoloniferous evergreen perennial is 8"–12" tall with flower scapes to 10". It forms a heavy, almost impenetrable mass.

SEASON OF BLOOM: Summer.

CULTURE: Creeping lily-turf can be grown in sun or shade. Although optimum growth will occur in light shade and a moist, fertile soil, creeping lily-turf is suitable for dry, sunny areas. Old foliage should be removed in the spring to promote new growth. This can easily be done by mowing the foliage with a rotary mower.

See color plate

UTILIZATION: The most common use of lily-turf is as a ground cover. It spreads by rhizomes and can quickly crowd out everything, including grass and weeds. *Liriope spicata* is useful for preventing soil erosion or for planting in areas where tree roots are so thick that little else will grow.

PROPAGATION: Division in the spring is a common propagation practice.

DISEASES AND INSECTS: None serious.

HARDINESS: Zones 4–10.

RELATED SPECIES:

Liriope muscari (mus-ka'-ri) — Blue Lily-turf. This species of *Liriope* is the plant of choice in southern gardens. The leaves are 1" wide and 12"–18" long, which creates a larger plant than *L. spicata*. The lilac-purple flowers in late summer are more noticeable than those of creeping lily-turf. Plants can be grown successfully in heavy shade although the spread will be slower. Blue lily-turf is widely used in zones 6–10 as a ground cover.

'Christmas Tree' — Lilac flowers that are wider at the base and tapering toward the tip as seen in the shape of a Christmas tree.

'Gold Banded'—Leaves are variegated with a gold band down the middle; lavender flowers.

'John Burch'—Variegated foliage and crested lavender flowers. The tip of the flower resembles the cockscomb found on *Celosia.*

'Lilac Beauty'—This cultivar is a good flowering selection with stiff, lilac flowers held above the foliage.

'Majestic'—Violet-blue flowers which are larger than the species.

'Monroe's White' ('Munroe's White')—Good white-flowered cultivar that grows slower than other cultivars.

'Silvery Midget'—Variegated foliage, violet flowers, 8" tall.

'Silvery Sunproof'—The variegated leaves are nearly white when grown in full sun but fade to green or yellowish-green in shade areas. 10"–12" tall.

'Variegata'—This cultivar is probably the most common variegated form. The leaf margins are lined with cream and the flowers are lilac colored.

ADDITIONAL NOTES: *Liriope* is named in honor of the Greek woodland nymph, Liriope, the mother of Narcissus.

Native to China and Japan.   Perennial

SCIENTIFIC NAME/FAMILY: *Lobelia cardinalis*   Lobeliaceae

(lō-bē'li-á kär-di-nā'lis)

COMMON NAME: Cardinal Flower, Indian Pink, Scarlet Lobelia, Red Lobelia, Red-birds

LEAVES: Alternate, sessile or short-petiolate, oblong-lanceolate, acute or acuminate apex, serrulate or irregularly serrate; leaves to 4" long.

FLOWER: Scarlet, sometimes pink or white; flowers in bracted racemes, corolla tube to 1½", 3 lower lobes are very narrow and reflexed, anthers are exserted.

HABIT: 3' or 4' erect plant with a spread of 2'.

SEASON OF BLOOM: Early to late summer.

CULTURE: Partial shade and moist soil are the best growing conditions. Full sun is suitable in regions with cool summers. The soil should be amended with compost and a mulch applied to retain soil moisture. Native *Lobelia* is found along streams or damp meadows.

UTILIZATION: Useful for the perennial border or the naturalized garden located in the shade.

PROPAGATION: Seed and clump division. Seeds can be easily germinated at 70°F, or self-sowing generally occurs. Since cardinal flower self-seeds, a familiarity with the appearance of the young foliage is needed so the plants are not mistakenly removed as weeds. Basal rosettes that surround the flowering stalk can be divided in the fall.

See color plate

DISEASES AND INSECTS: No serious problems.

HARDINESS: Zones 3–9.

CULTIVARS:
   'Alba'—White flowers, 2'-3' tall. It should be grown from cuttings for true white colors.
   'Heather Pink'—Soft pink flowers highlight this cultivar that is similar to the species in all other areas.

RELATED SPECIES:

L. siphilitica (sif-il-it'-ik-a)—Great Blue Lobelia. This lobelia is another native of eastern United States that requires partial shade and constant moisture for optimum growth. The blue flowers appear later than those of cardinal flower. It is 2'–3' tall and 18" wide. Suitable for use in the border or in naturalized plantings.
'Alba'—White flowers, 2'–3' tall.

L. splendens (splen'denz) (also listed as *fulgens*)—Mexican Lobelia. This species is similar to cardinal flower. It has more pubescence on the leaves, slightly larger flowers, and the stems have a reddish hue. Although the flowers are showier, Mexican lobelia is not very cold hardy (zone 7).
'Bees' Flame'—Hot red flowers and purplish-red foliage. Plant height is 5 feet.
'Queen Victoria'—Bright red flowers and reddish leaves. This is a popular cardinal flower particularly in England. 5 feet tall.

L. × speciosa (spe-si-o'-sa)—This hybrid group has very large red flowers and bronze foliage. Wray Bowden of Ottawa, Canada, developed this tetraploid group by crossing *L. siphilitica*, *L. cardinalis*, and selections of *L. splendens*. Plants are more vigorous and all plant parts are larger and thicker than the parent plants. These cultivars are hardy to zone 3.
'Oakes Ames'—Scarlet flowers and bronze stems and leaves.
'Robert Landon'—Cherry red flowers, good hardiness and performance in Canada.
'Wisley'—Red flowers which are lighter than those of 'Oakes Ames'.

ADDITIONAL NOTES: There are over 200 species of *Lobelia,* though few are worthy of garden cultivation. *Lobelia* is named for Mathias de l'Obel (Lobel) a Flemish botanist and physician of the 16th century.

Native to eastern half of the United States and Canada.   Perennial

SCIENTIFIC NAME/FAMILY: *Lobelia erinus*   Lobeliaceae

(lō-bē'li-á er-rī'nus)

COMMON NAME: Lobelia, Edging Lobelia

LEAVES: Alternate, lower leaves elliptic to obovate, upper leaves linear, ½"–1" long, all serrate.

FLOWER: Flowers in loose racemes, corolla ½"–¾" long, blue or violet, throat yellowish or whitish, anthers slightly exserted, usually blue, but white and purple-red colors are available.

HABIT: 4" to 8", usually about 6", habit is round or spreading to 18".

SEASON OF BLOOM: Spring to frost.

CULTURE: *Lobelia erinus* should be grown in partial shade in hot areas. It can be grown in full sun if the soils are moist and the summers cool. The key to good growth is adequate moisture.

See color plate

UTILIZATION: Edging, ground cover, rock gardens.
Trailing pendula types are suitable for hanging baskets, and window boxes.

PROPAGATION: Seeds germinate in 2 or 3 weeks at 70°–80°F, but seedling growth is slow. Start indoors 10 to 12 weeks before transplanting outdoors after frost. Mature plants, if potted in the fall and kept over winter, can be used to provide new growth for cuttings.

DISEASES AND INSECTS: No serious problems.

CULTIVARS:
Bedding types:
'Blue Gown'—5", deep-blue, free flowering.
'Blue Moon'—('Cobalt Blue')—True-blue flowers, 5"–6".
'Blue Skies'—5", globe-shaped plant, sky-blue flowers.
'Cambridge Blue'—4"–6", light blue flowers.
'Crystal Palace'—5", dark blue flowers with bronze-green foliage.
'Heavenly'—8", flowers twice as large as 'Crystal Palace', sky blue, vigorous and free flowering. 'Heavenly' germinates best at 50°F.
'Palace' Series—Early flowering, two weeks earlier than 'Blue Moon'. Available in blue, blue with white eye, and white.
'Paper Moon'—Pure white flowers cover a compact and ball-shaped plant.
'Rosamond'—Deep carmine-red blossoms with white eyes.
'Wedgewood Blue'—Dark blue blossoms, free flowering, and compact habit.
'White Lady'—4"–6" white flowers.

Pendula types:
'Blue Cascade'—Light blue flowers.
'Red Cascade'—Purple-red flowers with a white eye.
'Fountain' Series—Trailing habit with a height of 6"–8". Available in crimson, blue, lilac, rose, white, and a mix.
'Sapphire'—Navy-blue with white eye.

ADDITIONAL NOTES: *Lobelia* is better in cool areas of the country. It often goes out of bloom in periods of extreme heat; yet usually comes back with moderating temperature. After the first blooming period, shear back lightly and fertilize to maintain good flowering through the summer.

Native to Cape of Good Hope.   Annual

SCIENTIFIC NAME/FAMILY: *Lobularia maritima* (*Alyssum maritimum*)   Brassicaceae
(Cruciferae)

(lob-ū-lā'ri-à mà-rit'i-ma)

COMMON NAME: Sweet Alyssum

LEAVES: Alternate, lanceolate or linear, entire, tapering to the base, fine-textured plant. Leaves are ¾–1" long and ⅛" wide.

FLOWER: Flowers are white, pink, or lavender. They are very profuse and are held on very thin pedicels. Flowers vary in size and are fragrant.

HABIT: 4"–8" tall and 10"–15" spread.

SEASON OF BLOOM: Late spring until frost.

CULTURE: Sweet alyssum is easily grown in full sun or partial shade in a wide variety of soils. Soils must be well-drained.

UTILIZATION: Edging, rock garden, and massing. Used in bulb beds as a carpet plant to hide the dying leaves of bulb plants such as daffodils.

PROPAGATION: Seeds require 8 days to germinate when exposed to light and 70° temperature. Water management is important because sweet alyssum is susceptible to damping off.

DISEASES AND INSECTS: Damping off in seedling stage.

See color plate

CULTIVARS:
'Easter Bonnet'—Compact and uniform growth habit; pink, violet, and a mix are available.
'New Carpet of Snow'—3"–4", dwarf, spreading habit, white flowers.
'Oriental Night'—4", dark violet-purple, compact habit.
'Rosie O'Day—4", low spreading to 10" wide, lavender-rose flowers.
'Royal Carpet'—4", violet-purple, free flowering, 10" wide.
'Snow Crystals'—White flowers are larger than standard cultivars, good heat tolerance, 4"–6" tall.
'Snowdrift'—4", white, not as vigorous as 'Carpet of Snow'.
'Wonderland' Series—4", compact and free flowering, cerise-rose, white, or purple flowers.

ADDITIONAL NOTES: Sweet alyssum ranks high as a standard bedding plant. With reasonable care, it is easily grown; however, a midsummer slump is not uncommon in extreme heat. Flowering resumes with cooler weather. Purple forms do best in cooler temperatures. This heat decline is particularly prevalent in southern gardens.

Native to Mediterranean area.   Annual

SCIENTIFIC NAME/FAMILY: *Lonas annua* (*L. inodora*)   Asteraceae
(Compositae)

(lōn'as an'ū-à)

COMMON NAME: Yellow Ageratum, Golden
Ageratum

LEAVES: Alternate, pinnately divided into
entire linear segments. The plant texture
is very open.

FLOWER: Yellow, disk flowers only, borne in
dense corymbs, 1"–2" across.

HABIT: 12" tall with a round growth habit.

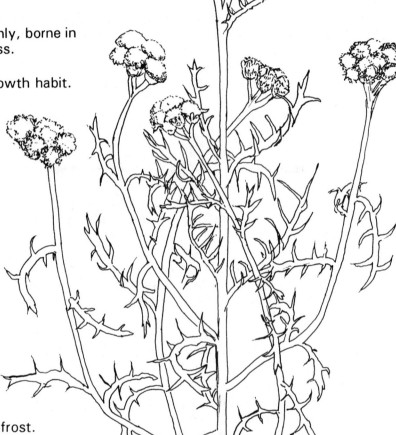

SEASON OF BLOOM: Spring to frost.

CULTURE: Full sun and well-drained soil; a
light, sandy, infertile soil is preferred.

UTILIZATION: A minor bedding plant with
little horticultural value. Often sold as a
novelty plant to complement *Ageratum*
although there is no relationship except
for the common name. The flowers dry
well.

PROPAGATION: Seed can be started in the greenhouse or sown where the plants are to
grow. Greenhouse-sown seeds can be germinated in one week in the dark at
70°F.

DISEASES AND INSECTS: None serious.

Native to Italy and northwestern Africa.   Annual

SCIENTIFIC NAME/FAMILY: *Lunaria annua* (*L. biennis*)   Brassicaceae
(Cruciferae)

(lū-nā′-ri-ȧ an′ū-ȧ)

COMMON NAME: Money Plant, Honesty,
Bolbonac, Silver Dollar, Penny Flower,
Dollar Plant, Moneywort, Moonwort

LEAVES: Alternate, simple, broad-ovate,
cordate leaf base, coarsely toothed,
upper leaves sessile or subsessile.

FLOWER: Flowers are pink or
purple, borne in terminal
racemes. The flowers are
not very showy; money
plant is valued more for its
fruit, which is a flat and
nearly orbicular silicle with
a satiny, paper-white septum.

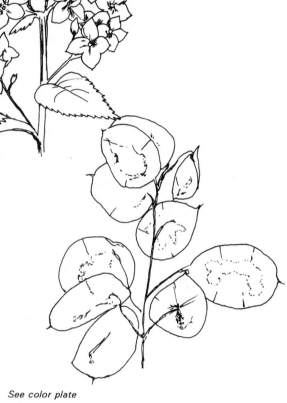

HABIT: 2′ to 3′ erect plant that is taller than it is
broad.

SEASON OF BLOOM: The flowers are present in
late spring, while the showy fruit does not
develop until midsummer.

CULTURE: Sun or partial shade in a well-drained
soil.

UTILIZATION: Most often used for dried floral
arrangements. It is one of the old-fashioned
everlastings. The plant somewhat resembles
a weed and should be reserved for the cutting garden instead of a prize site in the
annual or perennial borders. The dried circular
fruits resemble silver dollars.

See color plate

PROPAGATION: Easily propagated from seeds. Germinate at 65°–75°F for 2–3 weeks.
Money plant is a biennial and will flower the second year. After establishment, *Lunaria*
self-seeds, so there is always a group of fresh plants.

DISEASES AND INSECTS: Leaf spot, stem canker, and club root, none of which are serious
enough for control measures.

CULTIVARS:
var. *alba*—White flowers.
'Variegata'—Leaf margins are marked with white. The flowers are pink.

RELATED SPECIES:
Lunaria rediviva (re-di-vēv′-a). This species is a perennial that has been known since the
16th century. However, it is seldom grown even though the ornamental qualities
are good. The flowers are pale lilac-white and are sweetly scented. The papery seed
cases found in the autumn are elliptic and not round like the seed cases of *L. annua.*
This money plant is 2′ tall. Hardiness has not been established in the United States.

ADDITIONAL NOTES: *Lunaria* is derived from *Luna,* the moon, which is in reference to the
shape of the fruit.

Native to southern Europe.   Biennial

SCIENTIFIC NAME/FAMILY: *Lupinus* 'Russell Hybrid'   Fabaceae
                        (lū-pī'nus)   (Leguminosae)

COMMON NAME: Russell Hybrid Lupine

LEAVES: Leaves long-stalked, petioles 6"–
    12", palmately compound, 9–16 leaflets,
    lanceolate to oblanceolate, 2"–6" long,
    acute, glabrous above and sparsely pu-
    bescent below.

FLOWER: Flowers showy, in terminal ra-
    cemes, 1'–2' long, flowers papiliona-
    ceous (butterfly-like) and about ½" long.

HABIT: 3' to 4' erect plant.

SEASON OF BLOOM: Early summer.

CULTURE: Sun or partial shade in cool, moist
    areas. Best in acid soils. These plants
    cannot be recommended for universal
    cultivation because of their sensitivity to
    hot summers. Better performance is
    achieved if the seed or plant roots are
    treated with a legume inoculant.

UTILIZATION: Cut flowers or border. The
    lupine may need staking.

PROPAGATION: Seeds should be germinated
    at alternating 80°F day and 70°F night
    temperatures after soaking for 24 hours
    in water. Covered seeds will germinate in
    30 days and will bloom the 2nd year.
    Russell Hybrid lupine can also be propa-
    gated by cuttings taken in early spring with a small piece of root or crown attached.

See color plate

DISEASES AND INSECTS: Powdery mildew, rusts, lupine aphid, and four-lined plant bug.
    None of these pests are serious.

HARDINESS: Zones 4–6.

CULTIVARS: George Russell of York, England, a railroad crossing guard and home
    gardener, developed the Russell Hybrid by improving on the common blue and white
    lupine. He began a breeding project at age 60 and by the time he was 75, his seedlings
    were renowned. Russell kept no records, consequently, the exact parentage of this
    group is unknown. Russell Hybrid is by far the showiest and most popular of the many
    types of lupines. It is 3'–4' high with pea-like flowers of every color imaginable.
    'My Castle'—Brick red flowers, 2'–3' tall.
    'Noble Maiden'—Ivory-white flowers, 2'–3' tall.
    'The Governor'—Marine blue and white flowers, 2'–3' tall.

ADDITIONAL NOTES: Lupine is a derivation of *lupus,* a wolf. The origin of the name
    apparently is associated with the deep-rooted character of the plant, which was
    incorrectly believed to reduce the fertility of the soil. In fact, several of the species are
    used for restoring fertility to depleted soils. In areas where the climate is ideal for
    lupines, this species will be an asset to the perennial garden. Lupine is not widely
    grown in the midwest or the south. Lupines are easily grown in the northwest and will
    perform in the northeast or mountain areas of the southeast. A winter mulch is needed
    in cold regions.

This genus has about 3000 species, which are largely from North America.   Perennial

SCIENTIFIC NAME/FAMILY: *Luzula nivea*   Juncaceae

(lu-zu'-là niv'ē-a)

COMMON NAME: Snowy Wood Rush

LEAVES: Grasslike leaves are 3/8" wide and 18" long. The leaves are flat, conspicuously ribbed, and have dense hairs on the margins. *Luzula* has evergreen leaves.

FLOWER: White flowers are borne in an umbel-like inflorescence terminating the flowering stems. There are 3–8 flowers per inflorescence.

HABIT: Tufted perennial sedge 18" to 24" tall. Space 12" apart.

SEASON OF BLOOM: Summer.

CULTURE: Snowy wood rush should be grown in a partial shade to full shade location in a moist, humus enriched soil. Best performance will be in a slightly acid soil.

UTILIZATION: *Luzula* is suitable for groups or massing in the border. It is a useful grasslike plant for the partially shaded border where many ornamental grasses would not grow well.

Luzula nivea

PROPAGATION: *Luzula* can be divided in spring or fall. It can also be propagated from seed.

DISEASES AND INSECTS: None serious.

HARDINESS: Zones 4–9.

RELATED SPECIES:

Luzula sylvatica (sil-vat'-i-ca) (*L. maxima*) (maks'-i-ma), Greater Wood Rush—The evergreen leaves of this species are glabrous, which can be used to distinguish *L. sylvatica* from *L. nivea* in the vegetative state. The spring flowers of *L. sylvatica* are chestnut brown and borne in a loose, terminal cyme inflorescence. Flower stems can reach 2½' but the size is usually closer to 18". Culture and use are similar to those of *L. nivea.* Greater wood rush is native to Europe and Asia.

Native to Central Europe.   Perennial

Luzula sylvatica

SCIENTIFIC NAME/FAMILY: *Lychnis chalcedonica*   Caryophyllaceae
(lik'nis chal-sē-don'i-kȧ)

COMMON NAME: Maltese Cross, Jerusalem Cross, Scarlet Lightning, London Pride

LEAVES: Opposite, leaves ovate to lanceolate, acute, stem leaves clasping, 2"–4" long with rounded or cordate bases; stems and leaves are sparsely hispid.

FLOWER: Scarlet; dense terminal head is composed of 10–50 flowers. Petals are 2-lobed. Flower heads 3" to 4" in diameter.

HABIT: 2' to 3' erect plant with an 18" spread.

SEASON OF BLOOM: Summer.

CULTURE: Maltese cross performs well in sun or partial shade. Soils should be moist, well-drained, with good fertility. Without these requirements, Maltese cross will be short-lived. Even with the best of conditions, *Lychnis* usually has a 3–4 year life span.

UTILIZATION: Small massings will add a bold color to the perennial border in the summer.

PROPAGATION: Seed or division. Clumps can be divided every third year in the spring or fall. Seed propagation is easy with best germination at 68°F.

DISEASES AND INSECTS: Leaf spots, root rot, rusts, smut, and white fly.

HARDINESS: Zones 3–9. *Lychnis* is a good plant for southern gardens.

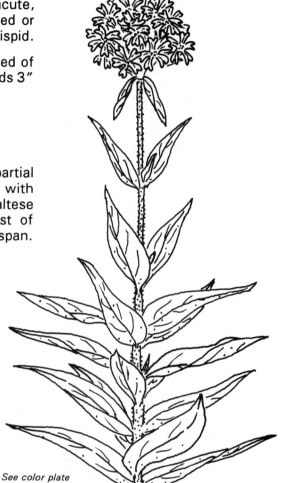

See color plate

CULTIVARS:
'Alba'—White flowers.

RELATED SPECIES:
L. × arkwrightii (ark-rīt'-ē-ī). This hybrid of *L. chalcedonica* and *L. × haageana* is 18"–24" tall and has orange-red flowers and bronze-purple leaves. Flowering is in early summer. Hardiness is questionable and winter mulches will probably be required north of Zone 6. 'Vesuvius' has orange-scarlet flowers.
L. flos-jovis (flos-jo'-vis)—Flower-of-Jove. This 18" tall species has reddish-purple flowers and white-woolly foliage. It blooms in spring.
L. × haageana (hâg-ē-a'-na)—Haage Campion. 12"–15" tall, orange-scarlet flowers to 2" wide, summer bloom. Requires constant moisture during hot summers. This *Lychnis* is a favorite of slugs and control measures will be required. Zones 3–9.
L. viscaria (vis-kar'-ē-a)—German Catchfly. This species forms a clump 12"–15" tall and 8"–10" wide. The flower stems are viscid, and it is this characteristic that gives rise to the common name—Catchfly. The flowers are reddish purple and appear in late spring to early summer. Zones 3–8.
'Alba'—White flowers.
'Splendens Plena'—Magenta-pink, double flowers. This cultivar is the best selection in the species.

ADDITIONAL NOTES: *Lychnis* is from a Greek word meaning lamp and refers to the fiery red flowers.

Native to Russia.   Perennial

SCIENTIFIC NAME/FAMILY: *Lychnis coronaria*   Caryophyllaceae

(lik'nis kor-o-nā'ri-à)

COMMON NAME: Rose Campion, Mullein Pink

LEAVES: Opposite leaves, oval or oblong to ovate, up to 5" long. The lower leaves have a petiole, the upper leaves are sessile. The stems and leaves are grayish-white and densely pubescent.

FLOWER: Single magenta-pink flowers are 1" wide and are borne on very long peduncles. The flowers are profusely produced.

HABIT: Erect, many branched perennial, 2' to 3' tall and 18" wide.

See color plate

SEASON OF BLOOM: Late spring through early summer.

CULTURE: Rose campion grows best in full sun and well-drained soil. It does not perform as a true perennial with plants dying after several seasons. Although it is not long-lived, it easily self-sows and never seems to disappear.

UTILIZATION: The flowers are nearly fluorescent. Fortunately, the vivid flowers are softened by the gray foliage. Rose campion can add an intense spot of color to the border and is often used as an accent. The foliage alone makes this species a worthwhile garden addition.

PROPAGATION: Seed propagation is more reliable than division, which is difficult. Seeds placed in 70°F conditions will germinate in 3 weeks.

DISEASES AND INSECTS: No serious problems.

HARDINESS: Zones 4–8.

CULTIVARS:
'Abbotswood Rose'—Brilliant magenta flowers on a compact plant, 24" tall.
'Alba'—White flowers.
'Atrosanguinea'—Carmine-red flowers.
'Oculata'—White flowers with a light pink eye.

Native to southern Europe.   Perennial

SCIENTIFIC NAME/FAMILY: *Lycoris squamigera*   Amaryllidaceae

(lī-kō'ris sqä-mi'jer-ä)

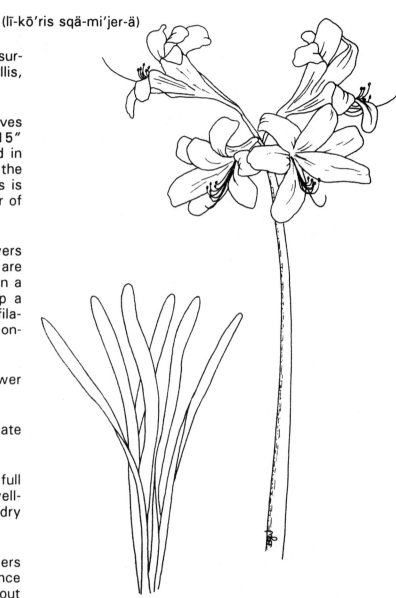

COMMON NAME: Magic Lily, Resur-
rection Lily, Hardy Amaryllis,
Autumn Amaryllis, Naked Lily

LEAVES: The 1″ wide basal leaves
are linear to strap-shaped and 15″
long. The leaves are produced in
the spring and die back to the
ground by early summer. This is
similar to the foliage character of
Colchicum autumnale.

FLOWER: The fragrant lily-like flowers
are rose-lilac or pink and are
3″–4″ long. They are borne in a
4- to 12-flowered umbel atop a
leafless scape. The white filaments and yellow anthers are conspicuous.

HABIT: 18″–24″ erect leafless flower
scapes.

SEASON OF BLOOM: Mid to late
summer.

CULTURE: *Lycoris* grows well in full
sun or partial shade in a well-
drained soil. The soil should be dry
during the dormant period.

UTILIZATION: The bright pink flowers
are very showy. However, since
the flowers are borne without
leaves, it is better to place the plants at the back of the border or interplanted with
perennials that have good late-summer foliage. The wild flower garden and perennial
border are possible choices. The declining foliage during the late spring can be a
detriment.

PROPAGATION: Propagation is usually by bulb offsets. Bulbs can be dug after the foliage
dies in midsummer and the offsets transplanted immediately.

DISEASES AND INSECTS: None serious.

HARDINESS: Zones 5–9.

ADDITIONAL NOTES: *Lycoris* is named in honor of a Roman beauty, the mistress of Mark
Antony, who was famed for intrigues. One may assume that the disappearance of the
leaves and then reappearance of the flowers in the fall is the intriguing aspect of this
plant.

Native to Japan.   Perennial—hardy bulb

SCIENTIFIC NAME/FAMILY: *Lysimachia clethroides*   Primulaceae

(ly-si-mok'-ē-a or lī-si-mā'ki-ȧ kleth'roi-dēz)

COMMON NAME: Gooseneck
   Loosestrife,   Japanese
   Loosestrife

LEAVES: Alternate, ovate-lanceolate, tapering base and apex, 3"–6" long,
   revolute margin; stems and leaves pubescent.

FLOWER: White, in slender curving racemes that create the "gooseneck"
   appearance characteristic of this
   plant. Flowers are 3" to 6" long.

HABIT: 2'–3' erect plant with a 2'–3'
   spread.

SEASON OF BLOOM: Summer.

CULTURE: Optimum growth occurs in full
   sun in moist, well-drained soil. This
   species can be quite invasive especially in a loose soil such as a sandy
   loam. Gardeners should be prepared
   to lift sections of the plant each year
   to retard the spread.

UTILIZATION: Best in the informal perennial border or naturalized in moist
   woodlands or other areas of partial
   shade. Loosestrife should be planted
   3' from the nearest small plant to
   lessen the chance of invasion.

See color plate

PROPAGATION: If loosestrife is planted far enough away from choicer perennials, division
   will not be required for a number of years. Seed can be used to start plants.

DISEASES AND INSECTS: No serious problems.

HARDINESS: Zones 3–8.

ADDITIONAL NOTES: The leaves of loosestrife often turn a bronzy-yellow in the fall.
   Lysimachia may have been a direct translation of the Greek loosestrife, which refers to
   peacemaking. Literature reports that Pliny stated that branches of loosestrife, when laid
   on the shoulders of quarreling, yoked oxen promoted "instantaneous and perfect
   reconciliation."

Native to China and Japan.   Perennial

SCIENTIFIC NAME/FAMILY: *Lysimachia nummularia*   Primulaceae

(ly-si-mok'-ē-a or lī-si-mā'ki-ȧ num-ū-le'ri-ȧ)

COMMON NAME: Moneywort, Creeping Jenny, Creeping Charlie, Wandering Sally, Wandering Jenny

LEAVES: Opposite, orbicular, nearly 1" long, leaf base obtuse, rounding or slightly cordate, short petioles of about ½". The specific epithet *nummularia* is derived from the Latin word *nummus,* coin, and refers to the small, almost circular, leaves.

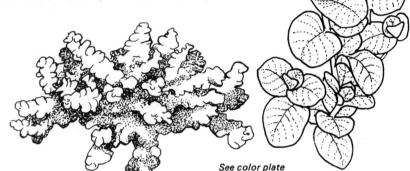

FLOWER: Large quantities of yellow cup-shaped flowers about ½"– ¾" across, solitary and axillary. The co-rolla is rotate or cam-panulate, 5-lobed and sparsely dark-dotted; calyx is 5- or 6-lobed.

See color plate

HABIT: Moneywort is a low creeping plant which roots at the nodes of the long trailing stems. Plants are 2"–4" tall and can spread to 24".

SEASON OF BLOOM: Late spring is the peak period of bloom, with sporadic flowering until midsummer if the soil is kept moist.

CULTURE: Moneywort is easily cultivated and appears to adapt to most situations. It will grow in sun or shade and prefers a moist soil; it will not thrive in a dry soil. The cultivar 'Aurea' should be grown in full sun to enhance the yellow foliage.

UTILIZATION: A useful plant to cover banks, stone walls, etc. Its use as a border plant is limited because of its invasive nature. The creeping stems could become a nuisance in the lawn or soon spread into other perennials. A 6" clump that I transplanted covered a 3' square area after 1 year. The cultivar 'Aurea' could brighten a dull area, especially if its invasive habit would not be a problem. Other uses would be in hanging baskets or for naturalization along the edges of streams, lakes, or pools.

PROPAGATION: Moneywort is easily propagated by division or cuttings. In fact, moneywort grows so well that one could easily supply divisions to his neighbors.

DISEASES AND INSECTS: None serious.

HARDINESS: Zone 3–8.

CULTIVARS:
'Aurea'—Yellow foliage.

ADDITIONAL NOTES: On occasion I have noticed that the foliage of 'Aurea' has reverted to green.

Native to northern Europe, but naturalized in eastern United States.   Perennial

SCIENTIFIC NAME/FAMILY: *Lysimachia punctata*   Primulaceae

(ly-si-mok'-ē-a or lī-si-mā'ki-a̍ punk-tā'ta)

COMMON NAME: Yellow Loosestrife

LEAVES: The leaves are whorled in groups of four, occasionally in three's. They are 1" to 3" long, ovate-lanceolate, with an entire margin. The stems and leaves are pubescent.

FLOWER: The bright yellow flowers are 3/4" wide and are clustered in the leaf axils. The corolla lobes are glandular-ciliate.

HABIT: Erect plant, 18"–30" tall and 12" wide.

SEASON OF BLOOM: Late spring to early summer.

CULTURE: This species is easily grown in sun or partial shade in moist soil. In moist, fertile soil, the spread will be very rapid and it will soon be invasive. If the soils are drier, a partially shaded site should be selected.

See color plate

UTILIZATION: Yellow loosestrife should be used where it can spread with abandon and not overrun choicer perennials. It is a good choice for broad sweeps in the wilder parts of a garden.

PROPAGATION: Division in spring or fall and seed are easy methods. The seeds may need a stratification period.

DISEASES AND INSECTS: Whitefly is an occasional insect pest.

HARDINESS: Zones 4–8; better performance occurs in the northern zones compared to zones 7–8.

Native to Europe.   Perennial

SCIENTIFIC NAME/FAMILY: *Lythrum salicaria*   Lythraceae

(lith'rum sal-i-kā'ri-á)

COMMON NAME: Purple Loosestrife, Spiked Loosestrife, Black Blood, Red Sally

LEAVES: Leaves opposite or whorled, lanceolate, 2"–
4" long, rounded or cordate and clasping at the
base.

FLOWER: Reddish purple, individual flowers about 1"
diameter on dense spikes 1' long.

HABIT: 3' to 5' erect plant, 2'–3' wide.

SEASON OF BLOOM: Mid to late summer.

CULTURE: Full sun in any soil, damp or dry. *Lythrum*
is an excellent plant for the perplexing wet areas.

UTILIZATION: Effective in border, or in sunny semi-
wild conditions; useful in naturalized areas such as
along streams or in low, wet areas. For the garden
area, *L. salicaria* is not as suitable as the cultivars
below. *Lythrum salicaria* will freely self-sow and
take over wet land areas. In this process most
other vegetation is choked out. In some areas of
the United States, *Lythrum salicaria* has nearly
ruined waterfowl areas. Fortunately, the named
cultivars do not appear to have this seeding tendency.

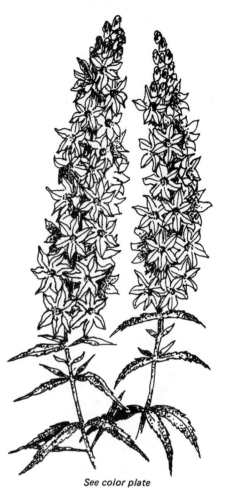

See color plate

PROPAGATION: Seedlings exhibit variation; consequently, division in spring or fall is the
custom. The roots are tough and woody and division will be slightly difficult. Cultivars
may also be propagated from stem cuttings.

DISEASES AND INSECTS: Japanese beetle has been noted as a serious pest.

HARDINESS: Zones 3–9.

CULTIVARS:
'Firecandle'—Bright rose-red flowers, 3' tall.
'Roseum Superbum'—Rose-purple flowers, vigorous grower, 3' tall.
'The Beacon'—Dark red flowers, 36"–42" tall.

RELATED SPECIES:
L. virgatum (vir-ga'-tum). This species is very similar to *L. salicaria* and to the casual
observer it would be difficult to identify the differences between the two species.
Lythrum virgatum has narrower leaves which are acute at the base and do not clasp
the stem. Cultivars of this species and related hybrids are less likely to produce seed
and become invasive. Many of the hybrids involving *L. virgatum* are products of the
breeding program from the Agriculture Research Station, Manitoba, Canada. The
late Dr. Skinner was responsible for these selections.

'Dropmore Purple'—Deep purple flowers, 3' tall. This cultivar is a hybrid of *L. salicaria* and *L. virgatum*.

'Happy'—This selection may be the best for the small garden. It is only 15"–18" tall, which is less than half the height of other cultivars. The flowers are dark pink.

'Morden Gleam'—Flower color is deep rose-pink. Plant height is 3½'. This cultivar is a hybrid of *L. virgatum* 'Morden Pink' × *L. alatum*.

'Morden Pink'—This pure pink flowering cultivar was introduced in 1937 as a bud sport of *L. virgatum*. The pink flowers are profusely produced from mid to late summer.

'Morden Rose'—Rosy-red flowers and dark foliage, 3' tall. This is another cross of *L. virgatum* 'Morden Pink' × *L. alatum*. It is more tolerant of hot, dry weather.

'Robert'—Bright pink flowers on a compact plant, 2'–3' tall.

ADDITIONAL NOTES: *Lythrum* is derived from *lythron*, blood, which is an allusion to the color of the flowers.

Native to Europe but has naturalized easily in North America.   Perennial

SCIENTIFIC NAME/FAMILY: *Macleaya cordata* (Bocconia cordata)   Papaveraceae

(mak-lā'á kor-dāt'-á)

COMMON NAME: Plume Poppy, Tree Celandine

LEAVES: Alternate, leaves petioled, cordate at base, about 7 lobes which are sinuate or dentate. Leaves are light green on the upper surface with gray-white pubescence on lower surface. Leaves 6"–8" long.

FLOWER: Cream-colored flowers in elongated terminal panicles to 1' long.

HABIT: 6' to 10' upright growth which has a 6' width.

SEASON OF BLOOM: Mid to late summer.

CULTURE: Full sun in moist, well-drained soils. High fertility soils and shade locations accelerate the invasive tendency of *Macleaya*. Despite its size, *Macleaya* does not require staking.

UTILIZATION: Specimen plant, flowers for cutting or drying. The large size of this plant makes the rear of the border an appropriate site, or it can be effectively used as a specimen plant.

PROPAGATION: Division in spring should be done every 3 to 4 years to reduce the size of each clump. Seed sown in the spring is a suitable method for increasing plant numbers. It also abundantly self-sows.

See color plate

DISEASES AND INSECTS: Anthracnose is a problem during warm, wet weather.

HARDINESS: Zones 3–8. I have seen good plantings of plume poppy as far south as Calloway Gardens, Pine Mountain, Georgia.

RELATED SPECIES:
  M. microcarpa (mī-kro-kar'-pa). This 7' species is similar in appearance to *M. cordata*. *M. microcarpa* has pinkish colored flowers, rather than white, and is considered more invasive than *cordata*. The major difference between these two *Macleaya* is that the flowers of *cordata* have 24 to 30 stamens whereas the flowers of *microcarpa* have 8 to 12 stamens.

ADDITIONAL NOTES: Large scalloped leaves are tropical in appearance and resemble fig leaves. *Macleaya* is not recommended for the small garden or as a low maintenance perennial because of its invasive habit. The genus *Macleaya* honors Alexander Macleay, a former secretary of the Linnean Society of London.

Native to China and Japan.   Perennial

SCIENTIFIC NAME/FAMILY: *Malva alcea*   Malvaceae

(mal'vȧ al'sē-ȧ or al-sē'-ȧ)

COMMON NAME: Hollyhock Mallow

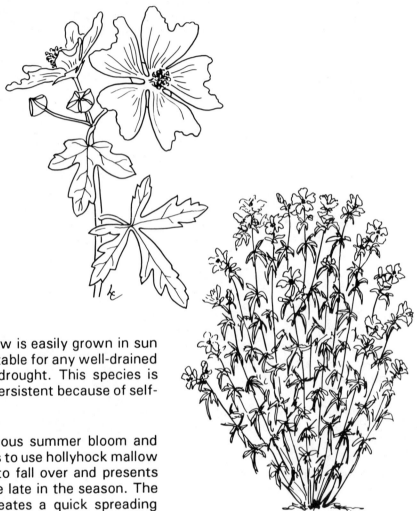

LEAVES: The alternate leaves are 3-to-5 palmately lobed with stellate pubescence. They are 2" to 3" wide.

FLOWER: The 1½" wide pink flowers are borne in long-blooming spikes. Each one of the five petals has a conspicuous notch at the tip.

HABIT: 3'–4' tall, loosely branched perennial. It is 18" wide.

SEASON OF BLOOM: Early to late summer.

CULTURE: Hollyhock mallow is easily grown in sun or partial shade. It is suitable for any well-drained soil and is tolerant of drought. This species is short-lived but usually persistent because of self-sown plants.

UTILIZATION: The continuous summer bloom and pink flowers are reasons to use hollyhock mallow in the border. It tends to fall over and presents an unkempt appearance late in the season. The self-seeding feature creates a quick spreading perennial which may be a problem in the small garden.

PROPAGATION: Division in fall or spring and seed are the normal propagation methods.

DISEASES AND INSECTS: Japanese beetles are a problem in areas where this pest is found. Spider mites and foliar diseases can also occur.

HARDINESS: Zones 4–8.

CULTIVARS:
  'Fastigiata'—A selection with ascending branches and a neater outline. Most of the plants found in the gardens are probably 'Fastigiata'.

Native to Italy.   Perennial

SCIENTIFIC NAME/FAMILY: *Marrubium vulgare*   Lamiaceae (Labiatae)

(ma-rū'bi-um vul-gā're)

COMMON NAME: Horehound

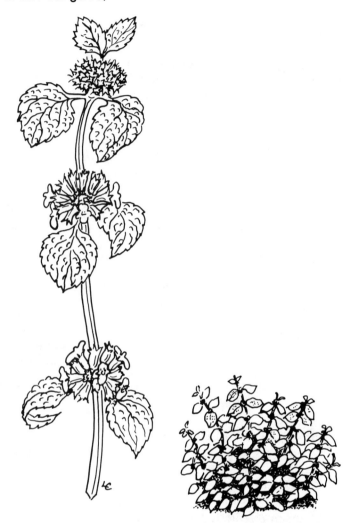

LEAVES: Leaves opposite, round to ovate, crenate margin, ½"–1½" long; lower leaves petioled, upper leaves sessile. Leaves and stems are densely pubescent, which gives a white, woolly appearance to stems and leaves. The upper leaf surface has a wrinkled appearance.

FLOWER: Small, white flowers are borne in dense whorls. The tubular calyx is divided at the margin into 10 hooklike segments. Flowers are not especially ornamental.

HABIT: Erect perennial, 18". Space 12"–18" apart in the garden.

SEASON OF BLOOM: Flowering is during the summer.

CULTURE: Horehound is a very easy plant to grow; in fact, it can sometimes become invasive. Grow in full sun in a well-drained soil. Horehound performs very well in sandy, dry soils. Flowers should be removed to prevent self-seeding.

UTILIZATION: Most people probably know horehound as an old-fashioned candy flavoring. It is still used as an ingredient for some over-the-counter and prescription drugs, particularly in cough syrups. An old time cough remedy is made by mixing honey and horehound tea. As an ornamental, horehound is usually placed in the herb garden. Some gardeners use it as a bee plant.

PROPAGATION: *Marrubium* is propagated by seed, cuttings or division. Seed should be germinated at 65° to 70°F. Cuttings can be taken during the summer, and division can be done in spring or fall.

DISEASES AND INSECTS: None serious.

HARDINESS: Zones 4–9.

RELATED SPECIES:

Ballota nigra, (bal-lot'-a nī'-gra) Black Horehound. Strong-smelling weed that even cattle will not eat. *Marrubium* should not be confused with this foul-smelling species.

ADDITIONAL NOTES: Some say that *Marrubium* is derived from *Maria urbs*, an ancient Italian city. Other references say the name is a derivation from the Hebrew *marrob* (for bitter juice) and that *Marrubium* was one of the bitter herbs which the Jews were ordered to take for Passover.

Native to southern Europe, Asia, and North Africa.   Perennial

SCIENTIFIC NAME/FAMILY: *Matteuccia struthiopteris*   Aspleniaceae

(mat-tō'si-ȧ strut-hi-op'ter-is)

COMMON NAME: Ostrich Fern

FRONDS: The fern leaves (fronds) occur in 2 forms (dimorphic). The outer sterile fronds are very lacy, the inner fertile fronds bear spores. The pinnules (leaflets) are often revolute, petioles are 4-sided and the rachises are grooved on the upper surface.

SORI: The ostrich fern is a flowerless plant. Plants are reproduced by spores produced in special sacs (sporangia) often clustered into compact groups (sori) on the lower surface of fertile fronds.

HABIT: In its native swampy area, ostrich fern will grow to 7', but in cultivated sites growth is usually to 4'.

SEASON OF BLOOM: Not applicable.

CULTURE: Ostrich fern should be planted in the shade in a slightly acid, high humus soil with good moisture. Moisture is very important because leaves will quickly scorch if the soil becomes dry.

UTILIZATION: A planting of ferns is a garden treasure any time of the year. The tender fiddleheads that pop up in the spring are very interesting while the lush green summer colors are very refreshing. Ostrich ferns can also be used as companion plants to spring bulbs or wildflowers. After the spring flowers have faded, the ferns will hide the dying foliage.

PROPAGATION: Division in the spring is a suitable method.

DISEASES AND INSECTS: None serious.

HARDINESS: Zones 4–7.

ADDITIONAL NOTES: The common name of ostrich fern refers to the sterile fronds which are shaped like the tail feathers of a bird.

Native to eastern United States.   Perennial

SCIENTIFIC NAME/FAMILY: *Matthiola incana* 'Annua'   Brassicaceae
                                                                                                          (Cruciferae)

(ma-thī'ō-lá in-kā'na)

COMMON NAME: Common Stock, Ten-Weeks Stock, Gilly-
flower

LEAVES: Alternate, gray-pubescent with branched hairs,
leaves oblong to oblanceolate, 2"–6" long, including
the narrow petiole-like base, very obtuse, entire.

FLOWER: Flowers are about 1" long and are borne in
terminal racemes on heavy pedicels. Flowers are often
double. Colors are white, blue, yellow, pink, purple, and
the flowers are nicely fragrant.

HABIT: 12" to 30" erect plant.

SEASON OF BLOOM: Early to midsummer.

CULTURE: Full sun or light shade,
cool location with moisture. Hot
weather slows the flowering of
stock.

UTILIZATION: Cutting and bedding.
Spicy fragrance is an asset.

PROPAGATION: Seed germinates in
two weeks at 70°F. Seeds are
sown in late winter indoors for
spring bloom and outdoors in
spring for summer bloom.

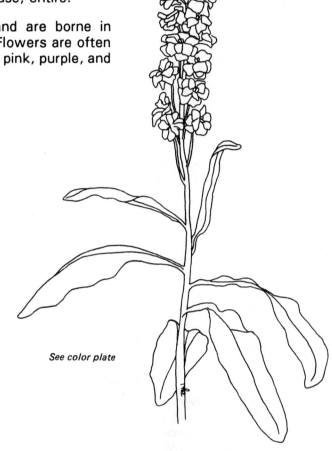

See color plate

DISEASES AND INSECTS: Root rot,
bacterial blight, and flea beetles.
Do not overwater or crowd stock.

CULTIVARS:
'Dwarf Ten-Week'—12", compact, branched plant with large double flowers, mixed
colors.
'Early Giant Imperial'—30", double flowers, mixed colors.
'Midget' Series—Compact, 10" tall, early flowering. Good plant for bedding purposes.
Flower colors include lavender, red, rose, violet, white, and a mix.
'Miracle' Series—Upright, tall stock with a height of 3' and a width of 18". Colors
include crimson, blue, gold, lavender, pink, white, and a mix.
'Trysomic Dwarf 7-Week'—12"–15", wide color range, blooms over long period, even
in hot weather.

RELATED SPECIES:
M. longipetala ssp. *bicornis,* (lon-ji-pet'-a-la bik-or'nis) Night Scented Stock. The flowers
of this species are highly fragrant. It is often planted close to decks, patios, and
other outdoor living areas. The flowers are single and much smaller than the flowers
of the common stock.

ADDITIONAL NOTES: Since *Matthiola* is in the Brassicaceae family, early planting will
produce good flowering before heat stress develops. *Matthiola* is named for Pierandrea
Mattioli, a 16th century Italian physician and botanist.

Native to Mediterranean region.   Annual

SCIENTIFIC NAME/FAMILY: *Melissa officinalis*   Lamiaceae (Labiatae)

(mē-lis'à o-fis-i-nā'lis)

COMMON NAME: Lemon Balm, Balm, Bee Balm

LEAVES: Opposite leaves, ovate shaped, crenate or serrate margin, 1"–2" long and 1" wide. The leaves and stems are covered with long, silky hairs.

FLOWER: Pale yellow or whitish flowers are borne in clusters in the leaf axils. The corolla is tube shaped, two lipped, and ½" long. The flowers are not particularly ornamental.

HABIT: Lemon balm has a tumbled, upright appearance and often appears weedy. 3' tall and 3' wide.

SEASON OF BLOOM: Summer.

CULTURE: Full sun or partial shade in a well-drained soil. Wet soils in winter may cause older plants to die, but seedlings generally develop to assume their place in the garden.

UTILIZATION: Lemon balm can be used for a tea or the chopped leaves are nice additions to salads, stews, and soups. It serves as a bee plant, particularly useful in attracting bees to new hives. In the ornamental area, the species is probably too weedy and is often limited to the herb garden. However, the gold and variegated leaf cultivars are more useful for the perennial border.

PROPAGATION: Lemon balm is propagated by seed, spring division, or summer cuttings. Seed should be uncovered and germinated at 70°F. Cultivars should be asexually propagated.

DISEASES AND INSECTS: Powdery mildew is an occasional problem.

HARDINESS: Zones 4–9.

CULTIVARS:
'Aurea'—Golden Lemon Balm. Yellow variegated foliage in the spring. The variegation fades in the summer. 3' tall.

ADDITIONAL NOTES: *Melissa* is Greek for bee, referring to its quality as a bee plant. Pliny noted that bees chose lemon balm over other plants.

Native to southern Europe and North Africa.   Perennial

SCIENTIFIC NAME/FAMILY: *Mentha suaveolens*   Lamiaceae (Labiatae)

(men'thȧ swa-vē-ō'lenz)

COMMON NAME: Apple Mint

LEAVES: Opposite leaves are sessile or short petioled. The leaves have an oblong to ovate shape with an obtuse apex. The 1"–2" long leaves are serrate and pubescent, particularly on the lower surface. Stems are 4-angled. Pineapple mint (see drawing) has white to cream colored blotches on the leaves. Apple mint has light green foliage. Both apple and pineapple mint have a faint fruity fragrance to the crushed foliage.

FLOWER: The whitish or pink flowers are borne in dense whorls on a terminal spike.

HABIT: 18"–24" tall, erect plant. Space mint 18" apart.

SEASON OF BLOOM: Summer.

CULTURE: Full sun or partial shade in moist soils. Leaf variegation is better on less fertile soils. Gardeners will find that mint is often harder to get rid of than it is to start. Some mints can be very aggressive and can quickly overrun other plants. In semi-wild areas, mint can be allowed to spread. Cutting on a frequent basis will promote additional branching and lusher appearing plants. In smaller gardens, mints should be placed in containers sunk into the soil.

UTILIZATION: Variegated pineapple mint is a nice variegation effect for the partial shade garden. Apple and pineapple mint have fruity flavors and are used to flavor and garnish drinks. Pineapple mint is particularly good as a garnish because the thick leaves do not wilt quickly.

PROPAGATION: Propagation is usually by cuttings or division. Cross breeding occurs easily with the mints; consequently, seed propagation will not produce the exact species or cultivar.

DISEASES AND INSECTS: Verticillium wilt, mint rust, mint anthracnose, spider mites, aphids, mint flea beetles. Mint is a tough plant and the above pest problems are usually not major problems.

HARDINESS: Zones 5–9.

CULTIVARS:
'Variegata'—Pineapple Mint. Leaf margins are irregularly banded with white or cream colors. 18"–24" tall. This selection is not as invasive as many of the mints.

Native to southern Europe.   Perennial

Mentha suaveolens 'Variegata'

'Apple mint'

SCIENTIFIC NAME/FAMILY: *Mertensia virginica*   Boraginaceae

(mĕr-ten′si-á vĕr-jin-i′ca)

COMMON NAME: Virginia Bluebells, Cowslip, Roanoke Bells, Bluebells

LEAVES: Alternate, basal leaves elliptic to 8″ long and 2″–5″ wide, long stalked; stem leaves are smaller and nearly sessile. All leaves are glabrous and have an entire margin.

FLOWER: Flowers are borne in nodding clusters; corolla is trumpet-shaped, about 1″ long, with a purple tube and blue limb.

HABIT: 12″ to 24″ erect plant which usually grows in clumps.

SEASON OF BLOOM: Early spring.

CULTURE: *Mertensia* grows best in shaded areas where the soil is cool and amply supplied with organic matter and water.

UTILIZATION: Suited for small areas in the shaded rock garden or perennial border. Bluebells should not be massed in the border because the foliage dies down by early summer, leaving a void. They should be planted among perennials with spreading summer foliage, such as hosta, so the voids will not be obvious. Annuals can also be used to cover the open areas created by the dormant plants.

PROPAGATION: Division should be done in the spring.

DISEASES AND INSECTS: There are a few fungal diseases but none are serious enough to warrant control methods.

HARDINESS: Zones 3–9.

ADDITIONAL NOTES: Virginia bluebells are a symbol of spring and add a quality to any perennial planting. *Mertensia* is named for Franz Carl Mertens, a 19th century botanist.

Native to North America.   Perennial

SCIENTIFIC NAME/FAMILY: *Mimulus guttatus*   Scrophulariaceae

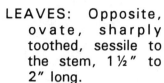

(mim'ū-lus gu-tā'tus)

COMMON NAME: Common Monkey Flower

LEAVES: Opposite, ovate, sharply toothed, sessile to the stem, 1½" to 2" long.

FLOWER: The tubular trumpet-shaped 2-lipped flowers are yellow with red or brown dots on the lip and throat. Flowers are 2½" long. The common name, monkey flower, refers to the spots, which sometimes resemble a face.

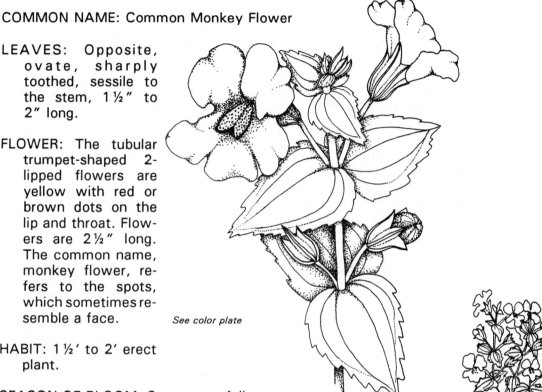

See color plate

HABIT: 1½' to 2' erect plant.

SEASON OF BLOOM: Summer to fall.

CULTURE: Monkey flower does best in full sun in a fertile, humus soil. In northern areas, it is treated as an annual. *Mimulus* will not tolerate summer heat.

UTILIZATION: In warm zones as the southern tier of states, monkey flower is used in the perennial border. In other climates, it is used as a colorful annual. It is a useful plant along moist stream banks or in hanging baskets.

PROPAGATION: Seed propagation is the usual method.

DISEASES AND INSECTS: No serious problems.

HARDINESS: Zones 9–10.

CULTIVARS:
'Mystic Mix'—Flowers of orange, rose, yellow, scarlet, wine, and ivory are profusely borne on compact plants, 10"–12" tall.

RELATED SPECIES:
Mimulus × *hybridus* (hi'-brid-us). This hybrid of *M. guttatus* × *M. luteus* has several cultivars which are utilized as annuals in the garden or in hanging baskets.
'Calypso Mixture'—Compact branching plant with wide range of colors and patterns.
'Malibu' Series—This series includes yellow and orange flower selections which are 10"–12" tall and free-flowering.
'Velvet' Series—Early blooming, 12" tall.
    'Royal Velvet'—Deep maroon with bright yellow throat.
    'Yellow Velvet'—Bright yellow flowers with deep red spots in the throat.

Native to North America.   Annual

SCIENTIFIC NAME/FAMILY: *Mirabilis jalapa*   Nyctaginaceae

(mi-rab'i-lis'; mī-rab'i-lis jal'op-à)

COMMON NAME: Four-O'Clock, Marvel
of Peru, Beauty-of-the-Night

LEAVES: Opposite, leaves deep green,
ovate, 2"–6" long, acuminate, truncate, or cordate at base, with petioles
almost half as long as blades.

FLOWER: Flowers about 1" across, involucre containing only one flower;
calyx trumpet-shaped, the tube 1"–
2" long. Flowers open in late afternoon and are white, red, yellow, pink,
or striped. Flowers are fragrant.

HABIT: 18" to 30"—bushy shrublike
mass.

SEASON OF BLOOM: Summer to frost.

CULTURE: *Mirabilis* is an easily grown
tender perennial that tolerates most
any soil site. It can be grown in sun or
partial shade and is tolerant to heat
stress and pollution.

UTILIZATION: Border or use as temporary plantings until shrubs are planted.

PROPAGATION: Seed or from tuberous roots, which can be dug and stored during the
winter to prevent freezing. Seed will germinate in 7–10 days at 70°F.

DISEASES AND INSECTS: Leaf spot, root rot, rust, and Japanese beetle. These problems
are not often found, however.

HARDINESS: Zones 9–10.

CULTIVARS:
'Jingles'—Smaller and more branched than the species. Striped colors of yellow, red,
rose, white, pink, and salmon.

ADDITIONAL NOTES: Good in urban areas—tolerates smoke, dust, and most any other
pollution. The name *Mirabilis* means wonderful in Latin, and refers to the colors of the
flowers. The flowers of this species open in late afternoon, hence the common name,
Four O'Clock.

Native to tropics.   Tender perennial, often used as an annual.

SCIENTIFIC NAME/FAMILY: *Miscanthus sinensis*   Poaceae
(Gramineae)

(mis-kan'thus sī-nen'sis)

COMMON NAME: Chinese Silver Grass, Eulalia, Japanese Silver Grass

LEAVES: Leaf blades are mostly basal arising from a large clump. Leaves are flat, 3' to 4' long, 3/8" wide, tapered to a slender tip, and sharply serrate.

FLOWER: The flowers are pale pink to reddish and are borne in a loose, terminal panicle that is 8"–10" long. The flowers are long lasting when dried.

HABIT: Upright clump growing 8 feet tall with a 3'–4' spread.

SEASON OF BLOOM: The actual bloom period of the species is fall but the flower effect of the plume lasts nearly all winter. In northern zones, flowering starts in early October.

CULTURE: Full sun is the main requirement and most soils are suitable. In general, *Miscanthus* performs poorly in shaded areas. *Miscanthus* is a warm season grass that transplants best in the spring.

UTILIZATION: The various selections of *Miscanthus* can be utilized as specimens, screens, and in park settings, massings, small show gardens, and as fresh or dried art flowers. Most cultivars are enjoyable through most of the winter season.

PROPAGATION: Division in the spring. All cultivars of this species should be produced by division.

DISEASES AND INSECTS: The ornamental grasses are usually low maintenance in relation to insect and disease problems.

HARDINESS: Zones 5–9 for the species. Other *Miscanthus* species and cultivars will vary slightly.

CULTIVARS:
  'Adagio'—Silver gray foliage and pink to white blooms. It is 4' tall with a 2' spread. Hardy to zones 7–9.
  'Arabesque'—This 4'–5' compact cultivar blooms in August. Zones 5–9.
  'Autumn Light'—Excellent hardy selection with a good yellow fall color, 6'–7' tall. Zones 4–9.
  'Cabaret'—Leaves of this selection have milky white, linear-striped centers. The flowers are white with a pink tint. Yellow fall color. This is an excellent variegated form.
  'Condensatus'—Early bloom, coarse texture, and more vigorous than *Miscanthus sinensis*, 7'–8' tall.
  'Cosmopolitan'—Broad green leaves with white margins, a reverse form of 'Cabaret', 6'–8' tall. Zones 7–10.
  'Goliath'—This is a vigorous selection with foliage to 7' and flowers another 2'–3' above the foliage. A very dramatic grass that is suitable for screening purposes.
  'Gracillimus'—Maiden Grass has an upright habit, 5'–7' tall with narrower leaves than the species. Coppery-colored flowers appear in late fall. It has a very fine texture and is very suitable as a specimen or in groupings. This is one of the older cultivars but one that is still widely used.
  'Graziella'—Showy silvery-white flowers on slender foliage, 5'–6' tall. The flowers set high above the foliage.

'Grosse Fontaine'—A large cultivar with a fountain-like growth habit, early silver plumes, 6'–7' tall.

'Kaskade'—A cascade of silver and pinkish plumes rise from the foliage. It is one of the best summer-flowering *Miscanthus*, 5'–7' tall.

'Kleine Fontaine'—A cultivar noted for its large plumes, early flowering, and compact growth, 3'–4' tall.

'Malepartus'—Pinkish plumes turn silver in early summer. Blooms are held high over the foliage which turns bronze in the fall.

'Morning Light'—This grass has a narrow strip of white on the leaf margin. The thin, fine-textured leaves appear silver at a distance. The arching foliage grows 4'–5' tall with flower stems to 6 feet. The reddish-bronze flowers appear in late fall. This is an excellent *Miscanthus* for the garden.

'Nippon'—Compact cultivar with a reddish bronze fall color, 4'.

'Puenktchen'—Foliage is marked with gold bands similar to 'Zebrinus' but the overall plant texture is finer, 5'–7' tall.

'Purpurascens'—An excellent, compact cultivar with outstanding orange-red fall color. Later in the fall, the foliage turns to a reddish brown that remains well into the winter. 3'–4' tall.

'Sarabande'—Fine silvery foliage with silver flowers. It may become a replacement for 'Gracillimus'.

'Silberfeder' ('Silver Feather')—Silvery white flowers develop in August and are carried high above the foliage. It is an excellent cultivar that remains attractive well into the winter. Plant height is 6'–8'.

'Silberspinne'—Graceful plant with narrow leaves and silvery flowers, 4'–5'. It is similar to 'Gracillimus'.

'Strictus'—Porcupine grass has bright yellow horizontal variegation. The narrow, upright form is accented by stiff, vertical leaves. Zebra grass has a floppy growth, whereas porcupine grass is tight and upright. 'Strictus' is hardy to zone 4.

'Variegatus'—The leaves are 1/2" to 3/4" wide with white stripes. The growth form is loose and mounded. It is tolerant to shade but will flop in too much shade. This is one of the oldest cultivars and still widely used in gardens.

'Yaku Jima'—This dwarf cultivar is from the Yaku Jima island in Japan. The total plant height is 3'–4' with the foliage a compact 18". A good selection for the small garden. Newer cultivars like 'Nippon' have a better separation of foliage and flowers.

'Zebrinus'—6'–7', loose growing, with horizontal yellow bands on the leaves. It is useful as a specimen plant, a screen, accent plant, or to add interest in a water garden. Plants will flop with age and may require staking.

RELATED SPECIES:

M. floridulis (flō-rid'-ū-lis) (*M. sinensis* 'Giganteus')—Giant Chinese Silver Grass. This species is certainly the giant of the *Miscanthus*. It grows 12' to 15' high. Excellent as a screen or background plant for smaller grasses. The flower plume develops in mid-September and provides a super winter effect. The stems are very strong and are resistant to the winter ravages of ice, wet snow, and wind. Stems will persist until spring or later unless cut down.

M. sacchariflorus var. *robustus* (sak-kar-i-flō'-rus rō-bust'-us)—Giant Silver Banner Grass. 5'—8' tall, useful for edges of ponds and streams. It is slightly invasive but grows well in normal soil conditions or those with temporary flooding.

M. transmorrisonensis, (trans-mōr-ris-sōn-en'-sis) Evergreen Miscanthus, Formosa Maiden Grass. This evergreen species is hardy to zone 7. Narrow green leaves form dense clumps 2'–3' tall and wide. Silky, reddish brown flower plumes arch out from the plant giving the clump a feathery, airy texture. It is an attractive accent plant for the middle to back of the border. The fine-textured flowers catch the breeze and add movement to the garden.

Native to eastern Asia.   Perennial

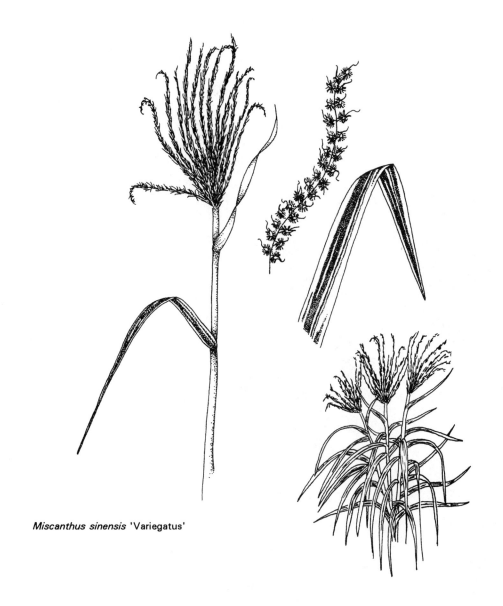

Miscanthus sinensis 'Variegatus'

See color plate

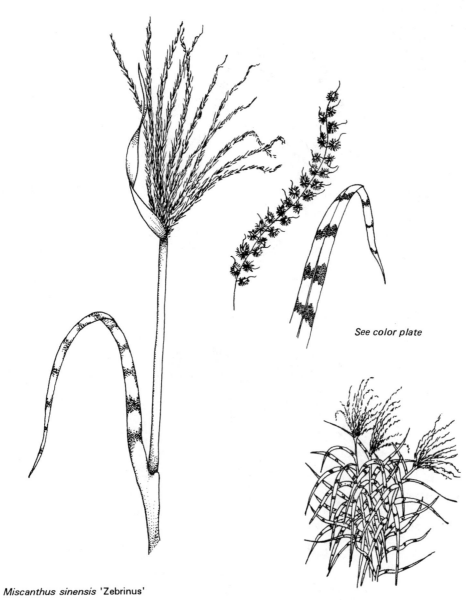

See color plate

Miscanthus sinensis 'Zebrinus'

SCIENTIFIC NAME/FAMILY: *Molinia caerulea* 'Variegata'

Poaceae
(Gramineae)

(mō-lē'-ni-a se-ru'-le-à)

COMMON NAME: Variegated Purple Moor Grass

LEAVES: Leaf blades ½" wide, to 18" long, tapering to a narrow point. The leaves and leaf margins are sparsely pubescent. 'Variegata' is the selection most often grown in this species. The leaves of 'Variegata' are longitudinally striped with white. The degree of variegation tends to be variable with some selections having a finer variegation than others.

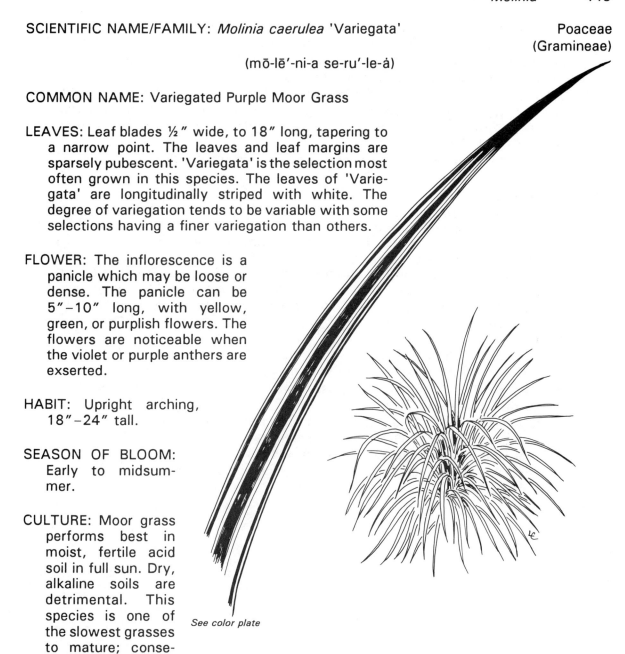

FLOWER: The inflorescence is a panicle which may be loose or dense. The panicle can be 5"–10" long, with yellow, green, or purplish flowers. The flowers are noticeable when the violet or purple anthers are exserted.

HABIT: Upright arching, 18"–24" tall.

SEASON OF BLOOM: Early to midsummer.

CULTURE: Moor grass performs best in moist, fertile acid soil in full sun. Dry, alkaline soils are detrimental. This species is one of the slowest grasses to mature; conse-

See color plate

quently, large plants should be planted if a quick display is desired. In the fall, the flowers and foliage break off at the base of the stems. This species is one of the few grasses that will shed the previous year's foliage.

UTILIZATION: Moor grass can be utilized as a specimen plant, massing in the foreground of the perennial border, as a ground cover, in the rock garden, or along a pond.

PROPAGATION: Division in the spring is the best method. Seed can be used but it will take a long time for the plants to flower.

DISEASES AND INSECTS: No problems.

HARDINESS: Zones 4–9.

CULTIVARS: Other cultivars besides 'Variegata' include the following selections:

'Dauerstrahl'—Compact growth with arching flowers creates a round habit, 2' tall. Introduced in 1982 by the Klose Nursery, Germany.

'Heidebraut' (Heather Bride)—Compact foliage with erect flowering stems, 2'–3' tall.

'Moorflamme'—Compact habit with an attractive orange-red fall color, 1'–2' tall.

'Moorhexe'—The Hagemann Nursery, Langenhagen, Germany, introduced this cultivar in 1963. The flowers are purplish and are carried on very fine textured stems, 24"–30" tall.

'Strahlenquelle'—Flower stems are more arching than the species, 2'–3' tall.

RELATED SPECIES:

M. caerulea. ssp. *arundinacea* (a-run-din-āc'ē-a) Tall Moor Grass. This grass is similar to *M. caerulea* except it is taller. The foliage grows 2'–3' tall and the flowering stems rise 3'–4' above the foliage. The stems are long and thin and are set in motion at the slightest breeze. One might call it the dancing grass. In the fall, the foliage and flowers turn yellow and then mature to a dull gold. The stems are nearly transparent and look best if placed in the landscape with a darker background. Like *M. caerulea,* tall moor grass is a slow grower and large-sized clumps should be planted. Small divisions may take 3 to 4 years to produce a mature plant. Zones 5–9.

'Bergfreund'—A bright yellow fall color highlights this cultivar, 5'–6' tall.

'Karl Foerster'—An older selection with flower stems 6'–7' tall.

'Skyracer'—This 7'–8' tall moor grass has a robust growth rate. It was introduced by Kurt Bluemel of Baldwin, Maryland.

'Staefa'—This selection is shorter with flower stalks 4'–5' tall.

'Transparent'—The 5'–6' tall flowering stems appear transparent. This cultivar will require a dark background for effective display.

'Windspiel'—Tall-growing selection with golden-colored flowers, 6'–7' tall.

Native to Europe.   Perennial

SCIENTIFIC NAME/FAMILY: *Molucella laevis*   Lamiaceae
                                                             (Labiatae)

(mo-lū-sel'á lē'vis)

COMMON NAME: Bells of Ireland, Irish Bells, Shellflower, Molucca Palm

LEAVES: Opposite, leaves long-petioled, rounded-subcordate ¾" to 1¼" long, with coarse rounded teeth.

FLOWER: Calyx inflated, to ¾" long, 5-angled, with 5 small thorns, light green; corolla white.

HABIT: 2' to 3' erect plant, 18" wide.

SEASON OF BLOOM: Summer; however, the green bells are the calyx of the flower; and the tiny, fragrant, white flowers tucked in the center of the bells are inconspicuous.

CULTURE: Full sun with well-drained, moist soil.

UTILIZATION: Border, cut and dried flowers. *Molucella* may need staking in an exposed area.

PROPAGATION: Seed should be pre-chilled at 50°F for 5 days, followed by exposure to light and alternating day and night temperature of 85° and 50°, respectively. Seed should not be covered. *Molucella* may be transplanted if the taproot is placed straight down. Generally the seed is sown in place due to transplanting difficulty.

DISEASES AND INSECTS: Crown rot has been reported in commercial fields.

ADDITIONAL NOTES: Bells-of-Ireland is grown for its shell-like calyx, which is persistent, and used either fresh (green) or dried (tan) in floral arrangements.

Native to Western Asia, Mediterranean region.
                                                             Annual

SCIENTIFIC NAME/FAMILY: *Monarda didyma* (M. coccinea)   Lamiaceae
(Labiatae)

(mō-när′dȧ did′i-ma)

COMMON NAME: Beebalm, Oswego Tea, Monarda, Bergamot, Horsemint, Red Balm

LEAVES: Opposite, ovate to ovate-lanceolate, 3″–6″ long, serrate-dentate; leaves are villous-hirsute to glabrous. The foliage has an aroma when crushed, and the stem is decidedly 4-angled.

FLOWER: Scarlet-red, the 2″–3″ tubular flowers are borne in single or double whorls creating dense heads.

HABIT: 2′–4′ tall and 3′ wide.

SEASON OF BLOOM: Summer.

CULTURE: Full sun and good soil moisture retention are ideal. Plants placed in a shaded area will have a tendency to spread faster. *Monarda* is not drought tolerant. Dead heading will prolong the period of bloom.

UTILIZATION: Beebalm should be located where its spreading tendencies will not be harmful; naturalizing is good. If placed in the perennial border for a bold effect, division will be required every 3 years to prevent rampant spread. Beebalm attracts bees and hummingbirds.

PROPAGATION: *Monarda* can be started from seeds, softwood cuttings or by dividing the clumps in the spring. Seed will germinate in 2–3 weeks at 60°–70°F.

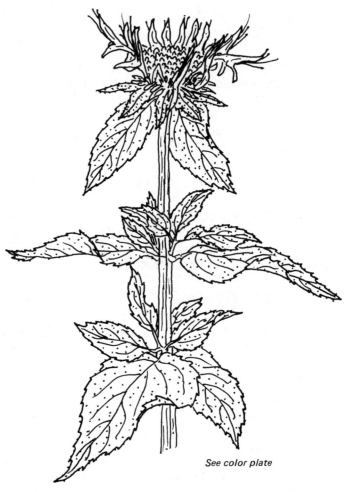

See color plate

DISEASES AND INSECTS: Powdery mildew and rust can be problems when the clumps become too large and air circulation is reduced. Dry soils promote the incidence of powdery mildew.

HARDINESS: Zones 4–9.

CULTIVARS:

'Adam'—Clear red flowers, profuse bloom, 2′–3′ tall.

'Blaustrumpf' ('Blue Stocking')—Unlike the name suggests, the flowers are violet-blue.

'Cambridge Scarlet'—Bright scarlet flowers, vigorous grower, 3′ tall.

'Croftway Pink'—Soft pink flowers, 3′–4′ tall.

'Donnerwolke'—Violet flowers, 3′ tall.

'Fishes'—White flowers with a pink blush.

'Kardinal'—Pinkish red flowers.

'Mahogany'—Deep wine-red flowers, 3′ tall.

'Morgenrote'—Salmon-red flowers, early bloomer.

'Prairie Night' ('Prarienacht')—Purplish violet flowers, 3′ tall.

'Schneewittchen' ('Snow White')—Creamy white flowers, 3′ tall.

'Violet Queen'—Deep purple flowers.

RELATED SPECIES: *M. fistulosa* (fis-tu-lo'-sa) — Wild Bergamot. This native species has pale lavender flowers which are not as showy as *M. didyma.* It is not widely used as a garden plant but it is more tolerant to dry conditions and is less susceptible to powdery mildew. Wild bergamot is best suited for the naturalized garden.

ADDITIONAL NOTES: Beebalm is also called oswego tea because John Bartram discovered early settlers near Oswego, N.Y., steeping the leaves to make tea. Bergamont flavoring is presently used in Earl Grey blended tea. The common name of beebalm resulted from the attraction of bees by the fragrance. Beebalm is an excellent native plant found throughout eastern North America; consequently, it should do well in cultivated gardens from the north to the south. The genus was named for Nicolas Monardes, a 16th century Spanish physician and botanist.

Native to eastern North America.   Perennial

SCIENTIFIC NAME/FAMILY: *Muscari armeniacum*   Liliaceae

(mus-kā'rī är-mēn-i-ā'cum)

COMMON NAME: Armenian Grape
Hyacinth

LEAVES: 6–8 basal leaves, up to
12" long, exceeding the scape,
¼" wide.

FLOWER: Blue, individual flowers
are urn-shaped and are borne in
a dense raceme on a 6"–9"
flower scape. The flowers are
slightly fragrant.

HABIT: 6" to 9" flower stalk,
leaves may be several inches
taller, erect habit.

SEASON OF BLOOM: Early spring.

CULTURE: Full sun or partial shade.
Although *Muscari* will grow in
most sites, they grow best in
cool, moist sites. Plant bulbs 3"
deep and 4" apart in the fall.

UTILIZATION: Grape hyacinth
seems to look best in open
areas, among shrubs, edges of
the rock garden, grassy slopes,
or as naturalized drifts.

See color plate

PROPAGATION: *Muscari* is easily
increased by removing the offsets which form about the old
bulbs. This can be done every 4 to 5 years. Although seed propagation is an alternative,
blooms will not develop until after 4 years.

DISEASES AND INSECTS: This species is generally free of diseases or insects.

HARDINESS: Zones 4–8.

CULTIVARS:
'Blue Spike'—Double flowers, medium blue.
'Cantab'—6" sky blue flowers.
'Christmas Pearl'—Bluish violet, 8" tall.
'Heavenly Blue'—More intense blue than species.
'Saphir'—Deep blue flowers with a white rim. The flowers are sterile, which makes
them long lasting.
'Spring Creation'—Double blue flowers, 8" tall.

RELATED SPECIES:
M. botryoides, (bot-re-oi'-dēz) Common Grape Hyacinth. Smaller and less robust than
M. armeniacum. Pale blue flowers borne on flower stems longer than the leaves.
Zones 2–8.
var. *album*—Pure white flowers.

Native to Asia Minor.   Perennial—hardy bulb

SCIENTIFIC NAME/FAMILY: *Myosotis sylvatica* (M. oblongata)   Boraginaceae

(mī-ō-sō'tis sil-vat'i-kȧ)

COMMON NAME: Garden Forget-me-not, Woodland Forget-me-not

LEAVES: Alternate, simple and entire, oblong-linear to oblong lanceolate, mostly sessile, ½"–1½" long.

FLOWER: Tiny light blue flowers with yellow centers, ⅓" wide, borne in loose terminal racemes. Corolla is rotate to salverform and 5-lobed; calyx is 5-lobed.

HABIT: 6"–8" tall and 6" wide.

SEASON OF BLOOM: Spring is the peak bloom period; sporadic flowering will occur until midsummer.

CULTURE: This plant prefers a moist soil in light shade; however, it is adaptable to all sites. Plants should be mulched to provide winter protection.

UTILIZATION: *Myosotis sylvatica* can be used effectively with bulbs during the spring. Forget-me-not is also used in the perennial border, rock garden, or in the naturalized or wildflower garden. I feel they are especially effective as a carpet of blue in the woodland region.

PROPAGATION: *Myosotis* can be propagated by seeds, cuttings, and division. Cuttings root best in summer, with division being better in late summer. Seeds germinate in 8–14 days when placed in the dark at 55°–70°. Plants may also be started from spring sowing outside, or the plants readily seed each year.

DISEASES AND INSECTS: Powdery mildew and red spider.

HARDINESS: Zones 3–8.

CULTIVARS:
var. *alba*—White flowers.
'Blue Ball'—Round plants with indigo blue flowers.
'Victoria Blue'—Gentian blue flowers, early flowering.
'Victoria Rose'—Pink flowers, early flowering.

ADDITIONAL NOTES: *Myosotis* is from the Greek words *mus,* mouse, and *ous,* ear, and refers to the mouse-like shape of the leaves.

Native to Europe and Asia, with some naturalized in North America.   Perennial

SCIENTIFIC NAME/FAMILY: *Narcissus* (species and hybrids)   Amaryllidaceae

(när-sis'us)

COMMON NAME: Daffodil, Narcissus, Jonquil

LEAVES: For trumpet daffodil, the leaves are basal, straplike, ¾" wide and up to 15" long, and are glaucous green. There are hundreds of cultivars of the genus *Narcissus*. Leaf and flower character may differ with the cultivar selected.

FLOWER: The flowers of *Narcissus* are distinctive in form. There may be 1 or several flowers on a scape, subtended by a spathe, the perianth is white or yellow, often salverform, with a long and tubular or short and ringlike corona (trumpet) separate from the filaments. The corona may be the same color or different from that of the perianth. Corona colors are white, yellow, orange, orange-red, pink shades, and for novelty, a green.

HABIT: 6" to 24" depending upon selection, erect growth habit.

SEASON OF BLOOM: Early to mid spring.

CULTURE: Full sun or partial shade in well-drained soil. Lighter soils will need no amendments, but coarse sand and organic material should be added to heavy clay soils. Plant bulbs in the fall at a depth of 5"–6" and space 6"–12" apart. In lighter soils, a planting depth of 8" can be used.

UTILIZATION: Daffodil is probably one of the best bulbs for naturalizing. Daffodils are easily grown, the bulbs multiply rapidly, and they do not need to be disturbed for several years. Massing in the perennial border is also effective.

PROPAGATION: Easiest propagation is by division of the dormant bulbs that are produced at the sides of the parent bulb; do this after the foliage has died.

DISEASES AND INSECTS: Bulb rots are generally the most frequent problems with narcissus culture. To control these problems, plant high quality bulbs in well-drained sites.

HARDINESS: Zones 4–8. *Narcissus* and *Crocus* may be the two best bulbs for southern areas.

ADDITIONAL NOTES: There is some confusion over the correct name for this genus. Narcissus, daffodil, and jonquil are three names that are tossed around freely, and many people think all three are synonymous. This is partially true. *Narcissus* is the generic name and also is used as a common name. Daffodil is a common name that was carried to other countries by English-speaking people. Jonquil, however, should refer to a specific type of narcissus, and should not be used as a general term. The true jonquil, *N. jonquilla*, has a reedlike leaf and sweet-smelling flowers. There are 11 major divisions of *Narcissus* which are based on flower proportions, such as trumpet length. These were adopted in 1950 by the Royal Horticulture Society. This standard is generally used by exhibitors and judges at flower shows.

According to Greek mythology, *Narcissus* is a classical Greek name which honors a beautiful youth who became so entranced with his own reflection that the gods turned him into a flower.

Native to Europe and the Mediterranean region.   Perennial—hardy bulb

SCIENTIFIC NAME/FAMILY: *Nepeta × faassenii*   Lamiaceae
(Labiatae)

(nep′e-tȧ; ne-pē′ta fâs-sen′ē-ī)

COMMON NAME: Catmint

LEAVES: Opposite leaves are lanceolate to oblong-ovate and the leaf margin is coarsely crenate to dentate. The foliage is pubescent, silvery gray, and aromatic with a mint fragrance. Stems are square.

FLOWER: The lavender to blue trumpet-shaped flowers are borne in an interrupted raceme. The floret is 2-lipped; the upper lip is 2-lobed, the lower is 3-lobed. Plants flower in late spring and early summer and often bloom a second time if the plant is cut back one-half after the first flowering period.

HABIT: This species has a spreading to erect habit. Selections vary from 18″ to 36″ tall.

CULTURE: Catmint grows well in ordinary well-drained soil and full sun.

UTILIZATION: Useful for creating a ribbon of blue in the border front or as a filler.

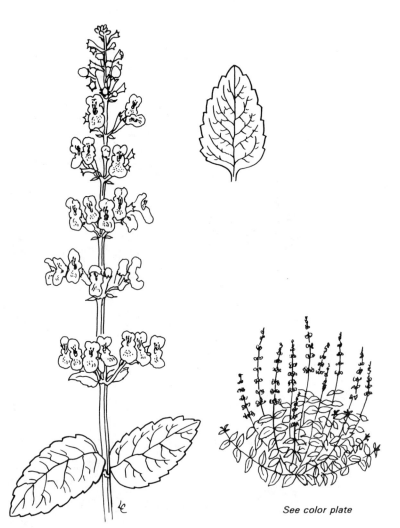

See color plate

PROPAGATION: *N. × faassenii* is sterile and must be propagated by division. *Nepeta mussinii*, a similar species, is propagated by seed.

DISEASES AND INSECTS: None serious.

HARDINESS: Zones 3–8.

CULTIVARS:
  'Six Hills Giant'—This hybrid is twice as large as *N. × faassenii*. It is used for the same landscape purposes and is propagated by division.

RELATED SPECIES:
  Nepeta mussinii (mu-sē′nē-ī). This seed-propagated relative to *N. × faassenii* is often substituted for *N. × faassenii*. It is not as free flowering as *N. × faassenii,* and it may produce self-sown seedlings. *Nepeta × faassenii* is a hybrid of *N. mussinii × N. nepetella.*
  'Blue Wonder'—Dark blue flowers, 12″–15″ tall.
  'Snowflake'—Creamy white flowers.

Hybrid origin.   Perennial

SCIENTIFIC NAME/FAMILY: *Nicotiana alata*   Solanaceae

(ni-kō-shi-ā'na a-lā'ta)

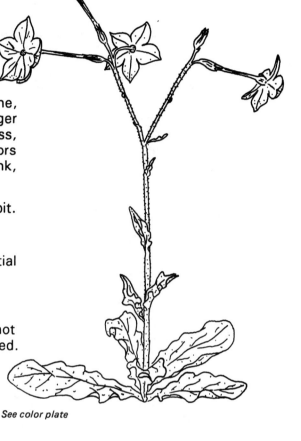

COMMON NAME: Flowering Tobacco, Jasmine Tobacco, Ornamental Tobacco

LEAVES: Alternate, viscid-pubescent, strongly scented, often basal leaves, ovate to elliptic 4"–8" long, decurrent.

FLOWER: Inflorescence a short, few-flowered raceme, corolla tube 2"–4" long, expanding into a larger throat 5/16" in diameter, limb about 1" across, irregular, deeply cut into broadly ovate lobes. Colors are white, lavender, crimson, maroon, green, pink, lime, and yellow.

HABIT: 12"–24", clumps attain a round growth habit.

SEASON OF BLOOM: Early summer to fall.

CULTURE: Optimum growth occurs in full sun or partial shade in well-drained, moist soil.

UTILIZATION: Border, bedding, cut flowers.

PROPAGATION: For best germination, seed should not be covered; a constant 70°F should be maintained.

DISEASES AND INSECTS: Flowering tobacco is subject to many of the same fungus and virus diseases that affect smoking tobacco. However, they are rarely serious enough to warrant control measures. Colorado potato beetle and tobacco flea beetle are insect pests.

See color plate

CULTIVARS:

'Domino' Series—Plants of this F_1 hybrid are more compact and earlier flowering than the Nicki series. The foliage has a rugose texture. Colors in this series include crimson, lime green, pink with white eye, purple, red, white, and mix.

'Lime Green'—18", lime green flowers.

'Merlin' Series—Compact plant, earlier flowering than the 'Domino' series. Colors in this series include crimson, lime, purple, white and a mix.

'Metro' Series—Dwarf plants with vibrant colors, 12"–14" tall. Colors include lilac, lime, red, rose, white, and a mix.

'Nicki' Series—This series includes plants with pink, rose, red, lime, white, and mixed colors. 'Nicki-Red' is an All American Selection award winner.

'Sensation Mixed'—30", mixed colors.

'Starship' Series—Compact plants, 10"–12", available in colors of lemon-lime, red, rose-pink, white, and a mixture. These plants are excellent for mass planting.

'Tinkerbell Mixture'—10"–12", mixed colors include red-rose, pink, white, and lime-yellow.

ADDITIONAL NOTES: Juice of the leaves is poisonous. Flowering tobacco gives a continuous display of nicely scented flowers and makes a fine showing in sunny beds. Medium height plants may, however, become a bit open and rangy toward summer's end. *Nicotiana* was named after Jean Nicot (1530–1600), a French consul. *N. tabacum* is the species used for tobacco.

Native to Brazil.   Annual

SCIENTIFIC NAME/FAMILY: *Nierembergia hippomanica* var. *violacea*   Solanaceae
(N. caerulea)

(nē-rem-bĕr'gi-à hip-ō-man'i-kà vī-ō-lā'sē-à)

COMMON NAME: Nierembergia, Cup Flower

LEAVES: Alternate, simple, entire, linear-lan-ceolate, to 1" long, diffusely branched.

FLOWER: Corolla violet with yellow-throats, corolla tube to 5/8" long, limb 1½" across, salverform to cup shaped.

HABIT: 6" to 9", round growth habit.

SEASON OF BLOOM: All summer—peak bloom is in late summer.

CULTURE: Sun or light shade. If planted in areas that have hot and dry summers, light shade is preferred.

UTILIZATION: Edging, window boxes, and rock gardens.

PROPAGATION: Tender perennial grown as an annual. Seeds germinate in 2 weeks at 80°F.

DISEASES AND INSECTS: Usually none.

See color plate

CULTIVARS:
'Mont Blanc'—This new cultivar produces 1" wide white flowers throughout the season. It is 6" tall and 12"–15" wide. The quality of this cultivar is indicated by its receiving the 1993 All American Selection and Fleuroselect Gold Medals.
'Purple Robe'—6", violet blue flowers that do not fade in summer sun; flowers freely during summer.
'Regal Robe'—6", deep purple flowers, which retain color even under strong sunlight, free flowering.

ADDITIONAL NOTES: Without reservation, *Nierembergia* could be recommended as a fine bedding and edging plant for sunny conditions. The compact, fine-textured mounds are literally covered with nonfading lavender-blue, star-shaped blooms all summer. However, most homeowners are unfamiliar with this plant and demand is small. *Nierembergia* is named for Juan Nieremberg, a 16th century Spanish Jesuit.

Native to Argentina.   Annual

SCIENTIFIC NAME/FAMILY: *Nigella damascena*   Ranunculaceae

(nī-jel'a dam-à-sē'na)

COMMON NAME: Love-in-a-Mist, Devil-in-the-Bush

LEAVES: This species is one of the finest textured plants available. The leaves are pinnately to palmately parted and the segments are filiform.

FLOWER: The solitary flowers are at the end of the stems. The blue flower is 1½" across and is surrounded at the base by a finely cut involucre. The common name, Love-in-a-mist comes from the thought that the blue flowers are nestled in a misty moss of fernlike foliage.

HABIT: Erect, many-branched annual, 18"–24" tall and 18" wide.

SEASON OF BLOOM: Summer.

CULTURE: *Nigella* is easy to grow in full sun and ordinary soil.

UTILIZATION: *Nigella* can be massed in the border or used for cut and dried floral arrangements. Cut flowers are long lasting and the color and texture works well in arrangements. An added attraction for arrangers is the dried seed capsule which is 1" in diameter. It is shaped like an egg and is covered with bristles and branched spines. Hence the second common name, Devil-in-the-bush.

PROPAGATION: Seeds started indoors during February will produce flowering and fruiting plants the same year.

DISEASES AND INSECTS: None serious.

CULTIVARS:
'Miss Jekyll' Series—Double flowers with arching green centers. Available in colors of dark blue, rose, sky blue, white, and a mix. Plants are 24" tall.

Native to southern Europe.   Annual

SCIENTIFIC NAME/FAMILY: *Nipponanthemum nipponicum*   Asteraceae
(Chrysanthemum nipponicum)   (Compositae)

(nip-pon'-an'thē-mum nip-pon'-i-kum)

COMMON NAME: Nippon Daisy,
Nippon Chrysanthemum

LEAVES: The leaves are crowded
on the upper part of the stem.
They are thick, somewhat succulent, and rather stiff in comparison to other chrysanthemums. Oblong and spatulate in
shape, they have a bluntly
serrate to dentate leaf tip. The
dark green leaves are alternate
and are 1½" to 3½" long.
Nippon daisy is a shrubby
perennial and the lower foliage
often falls from the stem.

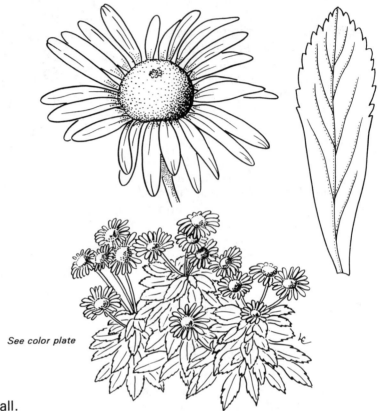

FLOWER: The flower heads are
single with white ray flowers
and yellow disk flowers, 1½"
to 3½" diameter.

See color plate

HABIT: Rounded, shrubby perennial, 3 feet tall.

SEASON OF BLOOM: Mid to late fall.

CULTURE: Nippon daisy is easily grown in full sun and ordinary, well-drained soil. In southern areas, it should be pinched several times until mid-July. This prevents early set of
buds and helps develop a compact plant. In northern zones, pinching may not be a good
idea since it will delay bloom. Consequently, an early frost may leave an unsightly and
unfulfilled legacy.

UTILIZATION: The late season bloom is an added attraction to prolong the color in the fall
border. It is an especially good selection in climates where a long, sunny fall can be expected.

PROPAGATION: Nippon daisy is difficult to divide because of its shrubby character. Spring
tip cuttings are the easiest propagation method.

DISEASES AND INSECTS: None serious.

HARDINESS: Zones 5–9.

Native to Japan.   Perennial

SCIENTIFIC NAME/FAMILY: *Ocimum basilicum*   Lamiaceae (Labiatae)

(ō'-sē''-mum bȧ-sil'ē-kum)

COMMON NAME: Sweet Basil, Common Basil

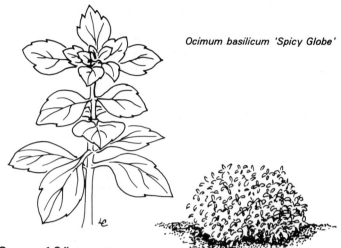

Ocimum basilicum 'Spicy Globe'

LEAVES: Opposite, leaves petioled, ovate, 2"–4" long, entire or toothed, foliage has a pleasing fragrance; square stem.

FLOWER: Inflorescence racemose, corolla about 5/16" long, white or purplish. The flowers should be removed to promote vegetative growth.

HABIT: 1' to 2', round growth habit. Space 12" apart.

SEASON OF BLOOM: Midsummer, not significant; grown for the foliage effect.

CULTURE: Full sun, moist, well-drained soil. Basil is very sensitive to cold temperatures and should not be transplanted outside until the temperatures have warmed. Mulching helps conserve soil moisture. To maintain a compact plant, basil should be pruned every 2 to 3 weeks. The leaves from these prunings can be used in culinary pursuits.

UTILIZATION: Basil has been made famous by its use in tomato sauce and pesto. The leaves can be used fresh, dried, or frozen. Best flavor is found in fresh leaves. Basil is an excellent herb for many meat and vegetable dishes. Basil is used in the herb garden and as an ornamental in borders, beds, pots, and window boxes. The green, dark, or ruffled foliage types add color, texture, and a nice scent to the ornamental garden. Several selections have received the prestigious All American Award for bedding plants.

PROPAGATION: Seeds can be germinated with 70°F bottom heat and grown at a 65°F minimum temperature. Seed should be uncovered. Germination takes 4 days.

DISEASES AND INSECTS: Slugs and snails can be serious.

CULTIVARS:
'Citriodorum'—Lemon Basil. Lemon-scented leaves, white flowers, 12" tall.
'Crispum'—Lettuce Leaf Basil. Very large, crinkled textured leaves, white flowers; good selection for salads.
'Dark Opal'—This 1962 All American Selection winner has been a standard in the industry with its purple-bronze leaves and compact growth habit.
'Green Bouquet'—This cultivar is very compact with lime green foliage, excellent ornamental.
'Purple Ruffles'—This 1987 All American Selection Winner has glossy purple leaves that are deeply serrated and ruffled. The mature height is 18" to 24".
'Spicy Globe'—Dwarf, compact selection; excellent plant for pot culture. Leaves are 1" long.

ADDITIONAL NOTES: Dig plant in fall for indoor use in a windowsill planter. *Ocimum* is from the Greek word *okimom* for an aromatic herb.

Native to India, Africa, and Asia.   Annual

SCIENTIFIC NAME/FAMILY: *Oenothera missouriensis*   Onagraceae

(ē-nō-thē'rȧ mis-su-rē-en'sis)

COMMON NAME: Ozark Sundrop

LEAVES: The alternate leaves have long, tapering petioles and lanceolate-shaped blades. The margins are entire, and the leaf blades are 2" to 4" long. The stems have stiff, appressed hairs.

FLOWER: Flowers canary yellow, 3"–4" wide, petals shallowly toothed, with a mild fragrance. The fruit is 2" to 3" long, leathery or woody, and it is broadly 4-winged.

HABIT: Sprawling plants which may be 9" to 12" tall and 12" wide.

SEASON OF BLOOM: Summer.

CULTURE: Ozark sundrop should be grown in full sun and a well-drained soil. It is quite tolerant of poor soils and drought conditions. Drainage is extremely important. Plants grown in poorly drained soils usually die from root rot.

See color plate

UTILIZATION: The trailing habit of this species makes it a natural for the raised bed or rock garden in full sun. It is also used along a walk to soften the edgelines of a pathway.

PROPAGATION: Seeds may be sown in spring or fall and will germinate in 1 to 3 weeks at 75°F. Named cultivars can be produced from division in early fall or spring.

DISEASES AND INSECTS: Root rot will occur in wet soils.

HARDINESS: Zones 3–7. This species is successfully grown at the Agriculture Research Station, Morden, Manitoba.

CULTIVARS:
'Greencourt Lemon'—This selection has wavy, lance-shaped, grey-green leaves. The flowers are pale yellow and the plants flower intermittently until fall. 'Greencourt Lemon' is an excellent plant for the rock garden or border front.

RELATED SPECIES:
O. tetragona (tet-ra-go'-na)—Common Sundrops. A hardy species with soil requirements similar to *O. missouriensis.* Lemon yellow flowers are borne on 2' plants in early summer. It is listed in many catalogs as *O. fruticosa* var. *youngii* or *O. youngii.* The cultivars are considered better garden plants than the species.
'Fireworks'—Deep yellow flowers, 2"–3" wide are carried on 18" stems.
'Highlight'—2" wide yellow flowers are borne on 18" plants.
'Yellow River'—Canary yellow flowers up to 2½" in diameter. Plants are 18" tall.
Some references list *O. tetragona* as a subspecies of *O. fruticosa.* This is certainly possible as the plants seem to be mixed in the trade and listed as *O. tetragona* or *O. fruticosa.*

ADDITIONAL NOTES: Plant is late to appear in the spring, so its location should be marked. *Oenothera* is Greek for wine tasting. Folklore claims the roots of some species were used as relishes with after-dinner wines.

Native to United States.   Perennial

SCIENTIFIC NAME/FAMILY: *Oenothera speciosa*   Onagraceae

(ē-nō-thē′rȧ spē-si-ō′sȧ)

COMMON NAME: White Evening Primrose, Showy Primrose, Showy Evening Primrose

LEAVES: Alternate leaves, linear to lance-olate, to 3″ long. The leaves are remotely dentate or pinnately lobed and have a soft pubescence.

FLOWER: The 1″–2″ diurnal flowers are borne in the axils of the upper leaves. There are 4 white to pinkish petals. The flower color usually starts white and matures to pink. The flower buds appear to nod.

HABIT: *Oenothera speciosa* is a 6″–24″ tall sprawling to erect plant. Space 18″ apart.

SEASON OF BLOOM: Summer.

CULTURE: This primrose should be plant-ed in infertile, well-drained soil in full sun. In these conditions, compact plants are the result. If placed in a fertile, moist soil, rampant growth will occur which will quickly cover more desirable plants, especially when planted in a border.

UTILIZATION: This native plant is useful for meadow plantings, gravelly road-side banks, or other areas where the soil is of poor quality. Although the flowers are produced in great quantity over a long period, this species is too invasive for the refined border. It will survive high humidity and performs well in southern states.

PROPAGATION: Propagation is by seed or division.

DISEASES AND INSECTS: No serious problems with this species.

HARDINESS: Zones 3–8.

See color plate

RELATED SPECIES:

    O. berlandieri (ber-lan-dē-er′-ē)—Mexican Evening Primrose. This species, also listed as *Oenothera speciosa* var. *childsii* (child-sē-ī), forms compact, prostrate plants, 6″ to 12″ tall. The 1″–2″ diameter flowers are rose-colored. The cultivar sold as 'Rosea' may be the same. Hardiness of Mexican evening primrose is Zones 5–10.

Native from Missouri to Mexico and southeastern United States.   Perennial

SCIENTIFIC NAME/FAMILY: *Omphalodes cappadocica*   Boraginaceae

(om-fa-lō′dēz kap-pa-dos′ik-à)

COMMON NAME: Navelwort, Navelseed, Cappadocian Navelwort

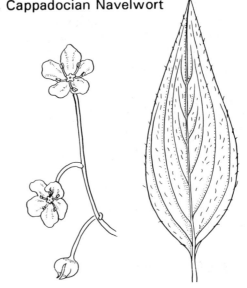

LEAVES: This forget-me-not look-alike has two leaf types. The basal leaves are ovate to lanceolate, 4″ long, densely pubescent. The apex is acute and the leaves are long-petioled. The stem leaves are smaller and nearly sessile. Leaf arrangement is alternate.

FLOWER: The bright blue flowers, 1/3″ wide, are borne on long pedicels in elongated racemes. Flower parts are arranged in fives. Veinlike markings radiate from the center of the flower, giving the corolla a starlike appearance.

HABIT: Navelwort is a low-growing tufted perennial 8″–10″ tall and 12″ wide.

See color plate

SEASON OF BLOOM: Mid to late spring.

CULTURE: Best performance will occur in filtered or full shade in moist, humus soils. However, navelwort will tolerate dry shade, which makes it an attractive choice for gardens with dry shade conditions.

UTILIZATION: Use in shade gardens, especially dry shade or in the front of the north- or east-facing border.

PROPAGATION: Division in the fall or spring is the easiest propagation method for home gardeners. Seeds are another source of propagules.

DISEASES AND INSECTS: Slugs can be a problem.

HARDINESS: Zones 6–9.

RELATED SPECIES:
O. verna (ver′na), Creeping Navelwort, Blue-eyed Mary. This closely related species has broad, heart-shaped leaves and slightly larger, bright blue flowers. It spreads rapidly and is a fine plant for the woodland garden as well as a ground cover under shrubs. It is also easily increased by division in fall and spring. *O. verna* 'Alba' has pure white flowers.

ADDITIONAL NOTES: The genus name is derived from *omphalos,* the navel, and *eidos,* resemblance, and refers to the shape of the seeds.

Native to Europe and Asia.   Perennial

SCIENTIFIC NAME/FAMILY: *Onopordum acanthium*   Asteraceae
(Compositae)

(on-op-or'dum ak-anth'e-um)

COMMON NAME: Scotch Thistle, Cotton Thistle, Silver Thistle

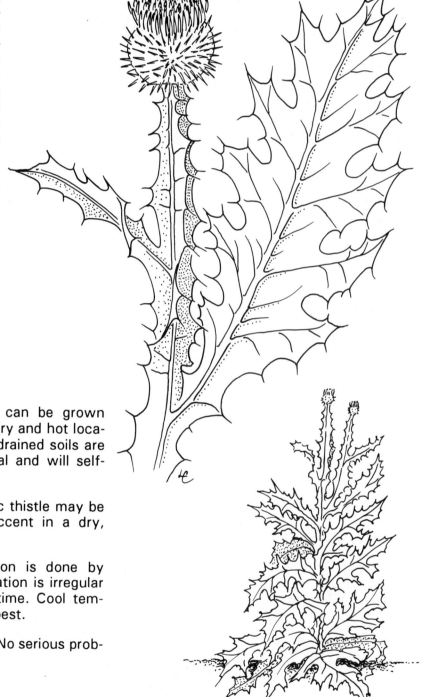

LEAVES: Leaves and stems are white tomentose throughout the plant. Leaves are alternate, oblong, pinnately lobed and spiny toothed. Lower leaves are up to 24" long and 12" wide. Leaf bases are decurrent to the stem.

FLOWER: The thistle-like flower heads are 1 ½" – 2" wide and are borne singly on the branches. Flower color is pale purple, sometimes white.

HABIT: Stiff, erect specimen, 6'–8' tall and 3' wide.

SEASON OF BLOOM: Late spring to early summer.

CULTURE: Scotch thistle can be grown successfully in a very dry and hot location. Full sun and well-drained soils are required. It is a biennial and will self-sow.

UTILIZATION: This gigantic thistle may be used as a dramatic accent in a dry, sunny border.

PROPAGATION: Propagation is done by seeds although germination is irregular over a long period of time. Cool temperatures at 40°F are best.

DISEASES AND INSECTS: No serious problems.

HARDINESS: Zones 5–8.

ADDITIONAL NOTES: *Onopordum* is an old Greek name that is possibly from the Greek *onos*, an ass, and *perdo,* to consume, which must refer to asses eating thistles. Frankly, I cannot imagine any human or animal eating a Scotch thistle.

Native to Europe, central Asia, and naturalized in areas of North and South America.

Biennial

SCIENTIFIC NAME/FAMILY: *Ophiopogon japonicus* Convallariaceae (Liliaceae)

(ō-fi-ō-pō'gon ja-pon'i-kus)

COMMON NAME: Dwarf Mondo Grass, Dwarf Lilyturf

LEAVES: This tufted perennial has numerous grasslike leaves, 8"–15" long, and 1/8" wide. Leaves are curved, creating a mound habit. Leaves of this species are often confused with *Liriope.* The leaves of mondo grass are narrower than those of *Liriope.*

FLOWER: Light blue flowers, 3/16" long, are borne on short, terminal racemes which are nearly hidden by the foliage. A metallic blue fruit, about the size of a pea, is produced during the summer. The fruit is also hidden in the foliage.

HABIT: Turflike clumps develop into a 12" tall ground cover.

SEASON OF BLOOM: Summer.

CULTURE: Mondo grass is tolerant to full sun, but best performance will be in partially shaded sites with moist, well-drained soils.

UTILIZATION: *Ophiopogon* is an excellent edging plant and ground cover for mild climate areas. *Liriope spicata* is a better choice for areas north of zone 6.

PROPAGATION: Mondo grass is easily propagated by division. Seeds can also be used but they must be soaked for at least 24 hours to remove the pulp surrounding the seed. Seeds will germinate in 5–6 weeks.

DISEASES AND INSECTS: Slugs and snails can disfigure the foliage.

HARDINESS: Zones 7–9.

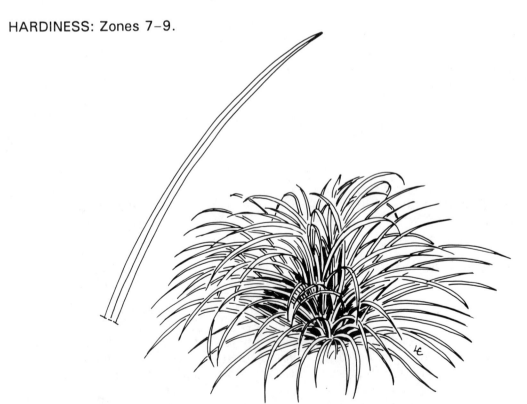

CULTIVARS:
    'Nana'—Compact selection, 3″ tall. It always appears to be neatly clipped due to its size.
    var. *variegatus*—Leaves have white margins.

RELATED SPECIES:
    O. planiscapus (plan-is-cap′-us) 'Arabicus' (known as 'Nigrescens' and 'Ebony Knight' in the trade)—Black Mondo Grass. The leaves of this recent introduction are nearly black and the plants are 6″ tall. The flower spikes carry pinkish flowers which rise slightly above the foliage. This selection increases slowly and will not develop as a ground cover as quickly as dwarf mondo grass. The black foliage contrasts beautifully with lighter-colored foliage found in ferns and hostas. It is listed as zone 6 in catalogs, but I suspect best performance will be in climates of zone 7 and warmer. A snow cover is beneficial in northern zones.

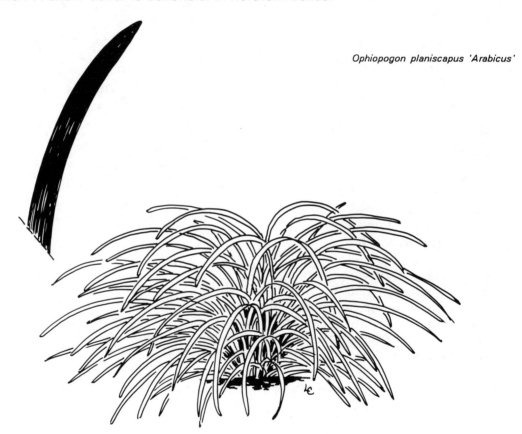

Ophiopogon planiscapus 'Arabicus'

Native to Japan and Korea.   Perennial

SCIENTIFIC NAME/FAMILY: *Opuntia humifusa* (O. compressa)   Cactaceae

(ō-pun'shi-å hū-mi-fū'så)

COMMON NAME: Prickly Pear Cactus

LEAVES: Thick, fleshy sections (joints) are orbicular to obovate, 2"–6" long; the areoles are sparse, usually spineless except those on the edge which contain 1 or 2 slender spines ¾" long.

FLOWER: The yellow frilled flowers are borne toward the upper part of the joints; 2"–3" across.

HABIT: 8"–12" clump forming plant.

SEASON OF BLOOM: Early summer. A dark red 1" oblong fruit will sometimes follow flowering. The fruit is inedible.

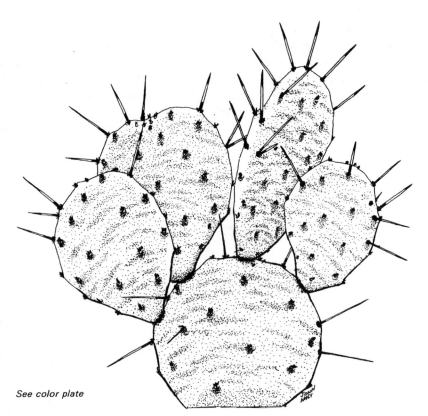

See color plate

CULTURE: *Opuntia* performs well in full sun and very well-drained soils. Moist or wet soils are particularly troublesome for proper growth. The segments become somewhat limp and shriveled during the winter but regain their turgor during the growing season. On the smooth surface of the cactus there are small, red-brown hairs which detach easily and lodge under the skin. Care should be taken in cultivating around the plants.

UTILIZATION: Prickly pear serves as a good specimen plant for the dry rock garden, sunny border, or for a stone wall.

PROPAGATION: New plants can be propagated by placing the fleshy, oval pads in slightly moist sand. Division and seed can also be utilized.

DISEASES AND INSECTS: None serious.

HARDINESS: Zones 5–10.

ADDITIONAL NOTES: *Opuntia* is derived from the Greek name for a different plant which grew around the ancient town of Opus in Greece. Some species of Opuntia have edible fruit. *Opuntia tuna* can be found in markets and varies from pear-shape to round and has a yellowish-rose color when ripe. It is sweet and juicy; and it may be peeled, sliced, chilled, and served with lemon juice or with cream and sugar.

Native to North America.   Perennial

SCIENTIFIC NAME/FAMILY: *Origanum marjorana*   Lamiaceae
(Marjorana hortensis)   (Labiatae)

(ō-rig'å-num mar-jor-ā'-na)

COMMON NAME: Sweet Marjoram, Annual Marjoram, Knotted Marjoram

LEAVES: Opposite leaves, ovate to obovate, grey-green, pubescent, 1/4"–1/2" long. The leaves have a mild oregano fragrance. The fragrance is milder than *Origanum vulgare.*

FLOWER: Small, purplish or whitish flowers form clustered raceme or panicle inflorescences, 1/2"–3/4" long.

HABIT: As an annual, sweet marjoram has a dense, mounded habit 12" tall with a 12"–15" spread. It should be spaced 18" apart. In mild climates where sweet marjoram maintains a perennial status, the height can be 24".

SEASON OF BLOOM: Mid to late summer.

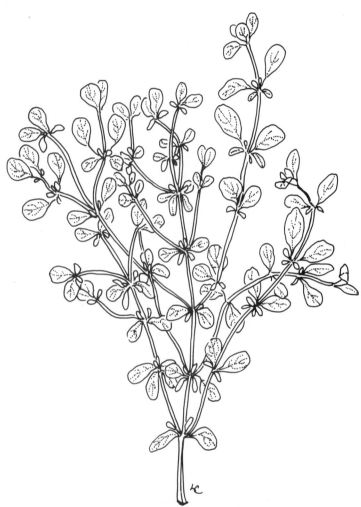

CULTURE: Sweet marjoram performs best in a well-drained, alkaline soil in full sun. Unlike many herbs, sweet marjoram has a stronger flavor when grown in a nutrient rich soil. The flavor is strongest if cutting is done right before the flower buds open.

UTILIZATION: The leaves and flowers of sweet marjoram are used fresh or dried in recipes. It can be used in nearly all meat recipes and is found as a flavoring in vinegars, soups, herb butters, and stuffings. It is usually found commercially as whole or ground leaves. Sweet marjoram is usually used in the herb garden and does not have major ornamental applications. However, variegated forms of *Origanum vulgare* are used to add accents to the garden.

PROPAGATION: Seed should be uncovered and germinated at 65°–70°F. Sweet marjoram seed is very small at 165,000 seeds per ounce.

DISEASES AND INSECTS: None serious.

HARDINESS: Zone 9. Sweet marjoram is usually grown as an annual.

ADDITIONAL NOTES: The ancients revered sweet marjoram as a gentle, calming herb. Newly married couples in Greece were crowned with garlands of sweet marjoram at their weddings. Ancient legend reported that anointing yourself before sleep would allow you to dream about your future spouse. Present day citizens probably associate sweet marjoram more with turkey dressing than marital bliss. However, I guess marital bliss can be disrupted if the turkey dressing is bad.

Native to North Africa and southwest Asia.

Tender perennial usually treated as an annual

SCIENTIFIC NAME/FAMILY: *Origanum vulgare*   Lamiaceae (Labiatae)

(ō-rig'à-num vul-gā're)

COMMON NAME: Oregano, Wild Marjoram

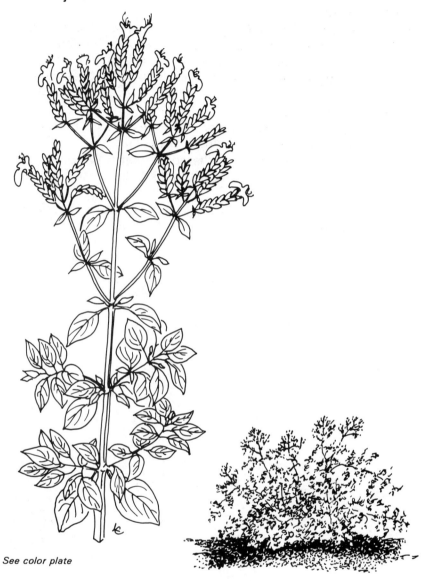

LEAVES: Opposite leaves, ovate shaped, long petioled, sparsely pubescent, ½" to 1" long. The margins are sometimes toothed but are usually entire. Stems are square.

FLOWER: White or pinkish-purple flowers are borne in 1"–1½" terminal or axillary spikelets. Individual flowers are ¼" long, 2-lipped, with 4 protruding stamens.

HABIT: Round to slightly sprawling habit, 24" tall and 18"–24" wide. Space 18" apart.

SEASON OF BLOOM: Mid to late summer.

CULTURE: Plant oregano in full sun and a well-drained soil. Plants should be cut back before flowering to promote new growth. Gold leaf varieties will need partial shade to prevent leaf scorch.

See color plate

UTILIZATION: Oregano is best known for its use in tomato sauce that finds its way onto Italian cuisine and pizza. There are few children and teenagers who cannot tell you what the spice is on their favorite pizza. Oregano is found in the cuisines of Greece, Brazil, Mexico, Italy, and Spain. Oregano has a stronger flavor than its cousin, marjoram. The variegated or yellow-leaved forms of *Origanum vulgare* are used in herb gardens and borders. The cultivar 'Aureum' is particularly useful because of its bright golden-yellow foliage in the spring. It is a nice complement to the red flowering coralbells (*Heuchera sanguinea*).

PROPAGATION: Propagation is by seed, spring division, or cuttings. *Origanum vulgare* seed is very small (350,000 seeds/oz.) and should not be covered. Germination success is best at 70°F. Although seed propagation is successful, it is best to produce oregano from cuttings. *Origanum vulgare* produced from seed often does not have much flavor and it is better to select flavorful plants from asexual means or to select other species if using seed (see below).

DISEASES AND INSECTS: Root rot, fungal diseases, aphids, spider mites, and leaf miners have been noticed.

HARDINESS: Zones 4–8.

CULTIVARS:
'Aureum'—Golden Oregano. Golden yellow leaves create a striking mound 8"–12" tall. The leaves have a mild savory flavor. The leaves will scorch in full sun. The purple or white flowers should be cut off so as to not detract from the gold foliage.
'Variegatum'—Gold Variegated Marjoram. Green leaves are marbled with gold.

RELATED SPECIES:
Oregano describes a flavor and not a genus. There are many selections of oregano that are found in other genera or species.
O. ssp. *hirtum* (hĕr'tum) (heracleoticum), Winter marjoram. This selection has tender, sweet, spicy leaves. Many herbalists consider it superior in flavor to *Origanum vulgare.* 18" tall.
O. onites (on-ē'-tez)—Cretan oregano. Strong oregano flavor. Tender perennial that is usually grown as an annual in a pot.

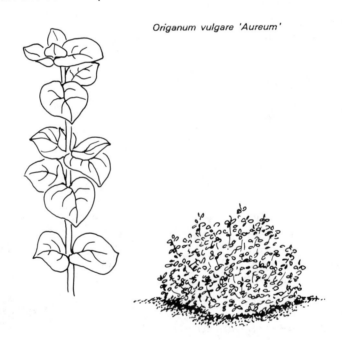

Origanum vulgare 'Aureum'

Native to Mediterranean region and central Asia.
Origanum vulgare is naturalized in the eastern United States.   Perennial

SCIENTIFIC NAME/FAMILY: *Ornithogalum umbellatum*   Hyacinthaceae
                                                              (Liliaceae)

(ôr-ni-thog'a-lum um-bel-lā'-tum)

COMMON NAME: Star-of-Bethlehem

LEAVES: The bulbs pro-
    duce a tuft of narrow
    (1/8″ wide), smooth
    leaves, each 9″ to 12″
    long. The foliage has a
    grass-like appearance.

FLOWER: There are 10 to
    20 flowers carried on a
    corymb-like flower
    structure. The star-
    shaped, pure white
    flowers are 1″ to 2″
    wide and are striped
    green on the outside of
    the segment. The green
    is hardly noticeable
    when the flowers are
    fully opened. The flow-
    ers open late in the
    day, usually just before
    noon, and close before
    night.

HABIT: The tufted foliage
    creates a mound that is
    6″–9″ tall and 6″
    wide. The bulbs quickly
    multiply and it isn't
    long before this species
    will colonize an area.

SEASON OF BLOOM: Late
    spring.

CULTURE: This species is
    easily grown in full sun
    or partial shade in most
    soil situations. After
    the bulbs become es-
    tablished, they are
    drought tolerant.

See color plate

UTILIZATION: Star-of-Bethlehem is suitable for the very informal to wild garden, but it is
    probably too invasive for most situations. The bulbs increase very rapidly, and self-
    sown seedlings are also common.

PROPAGATION: The easiest propagation method is to dig the bulbs after flowering, remove
    the daughter bulbs, and replant in the desired area.

DISEASES AND INSECTS: There are no serious problems. As with many bulbs, rot can occur in poorly drained soils.

HARDINESS: Zones 4 to 9.

RELATED SPECIES: The following species are not as invasive as the Star-of-Bethlehem and are more suited to gardens and as cutting flowers.

arabicum (a-rab'i-kum), Arabian Star Flower. The individual flowers are pure white with a jet black ovary. They are quite large, often over 2" in diameter. The flower spikes can rise 2 feet above the ground. This species is tender in zones colder than 8 and needs to be lifted in the fall. It is useful as a cut flower as well as in the border.

nutans (nū'tanz), Drooping Star-of-Bethlehem. The white flowers have a green midrib on the outside of the petals. Flower spikes of 3–12 flowers are carried on 12"–18" stems. It is in flower in late spring and early summer. This species is tolerant to partial shade and is often used at the edge of wooded areas or in partially shaded borders. Hardy in Zones 5–9.

thyrsoides (ther-soi'-dēz), Chincherinchee. This species is known more as a cut flower than a plant for the perennial border. However, that shouldn't stop the gardener from using it in the garden as well as buying it in the florist shop. The ¾" diameter flowers are white and borne in clusters of 12–30 flowers. As a cut flower, it will last for weeks on end, either in water or intact on the plant. The common name is quite strange and is listed as an onomatopoetic expression. Supposedly, it is the expression of the sound made when the peduncles are rubbed against one another. It is hardy in Zones 7 to 9. In northern areas, this species can be enjoyed as an annual because the bulbs are relatively inexpensive.

Native to the Mediterranean region.   Bulb

SCIENTIFIC NAME/FAMILY: *Osmunda regalis*

(os-mun′dȧ rē-gā′lis)

Osmundaceae
(Polypodiaceae)

COMMON NAME: Royal Fern

FRONDS: Fronds of the royal fern are 4′ to
6′ tall. The sterile fronds are twice-
pinnate with oblong pinnules. The fronds
look like large locust leaves. When the
fronds unfurl, they have a wine red color
which becomes green as the fronds mature.

SORI: The sporangia on the fertile fronds are
found in bright brown clusters at the apex
of the fronds.

HABIT: Average size clumps are 3′ tall but I
have seen fronds as tall as 5 feet.
Clumps are 3′ wide.

CULTURE: Royal fern should be grown in
shaded areas in moist to
wet soils with an acid pH.

UTILIZATION: Graceful and
grand large fern suited for
the border, as an accent,
or along the water's edge.

PROPAGATION: Spores should
be collected and sown as
soon as they are mature, in
the spring. Royal fern

See color plate

develops a massive clump which is hard to divide. It's better to use a spade than a
knife to complete this task.

DISEASES AND INSECTS: None serious.

HARDINESS: Zones 3 to 10.

RELATED SPECIES:
   O. cinnamomea (sin-na-mo′me-a) — Cinnamon Fern. This relative has two different types
      of fronds. The fertile fronds look like cinnamon sticks rising above the foliage in the
      spring. The sterile fronds are yellowish-green and are pinnately compound. Plants
      are 36″ tall. Cinnamon fern also requires a moist, acid soil in a partially shaded site.
      If the soil is wet, it can be grown in full sun. This fern is an excellent choice for
      planting at the edge of the water.
   O. claytoniana (klā-to-nē-ā′-na) — Interrupted Fern. This fern has fertile pinnae on the
      lower half of the sterile fronds. This feature creates an interruption to the sterile
      frond and is responsible for the common name. Plants are 2′–3′ tall.

ADDITIONAL NOTES: Royal fern is found in swampy areas from Canada to Florida.

Perennial

SCIENTIFIC NAME/FAMILY: *Pachysandra terminalis*   Buxaceae

(pak-i-san'dra tẽr-mi-nā'lis; tẽr-mi-nâl'is)

COMMON NAME: Japanese Pachysandra

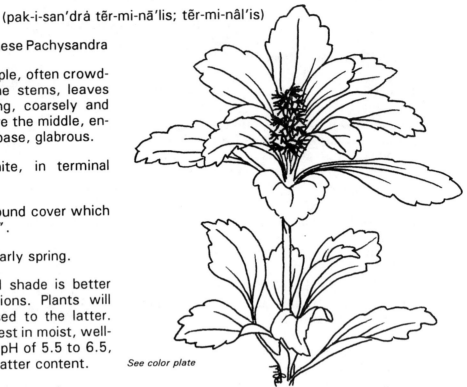

LEAVES: Alternate, simple, often crowded at the end of the stems, leaves obovate, 2"–4" long, coarsely and bluntly toothed above the middle, entire and cuneate at base, glabrous.

FLOWER: Flowers white, in terminal spikes, 1"–2" long.

HABIT: 6" to 8" tall ground cover which will spread 12"–18".

SEASON OF BLOOM: Early spring.

CULTURE: Light to full shade is better than full sun locations. Plants will yellow when exposed to the latter. *Pachysandra* does best in moist, well-drained soils with a pH of 5.5 to 6.5, and good organic matter content.

See color plate

UTILIZATION: Ground cover, slopes or level ground. Does very well in dense shade; is suitable for growing beneath trees.

PROPAGATION: Division or rooted stem cuttings in spring or early summer. Cuttings root readily with 1000 ppm IBA.

DISEASES AND INSECTS: *Volutella pachysandrae,* leaf blight, can be serious enough to ruin a planting. Root rot, *Euonymus* scale, and leaf blight can also cause significant damage.

HARDINESS: Zones 5–9.

CULTIVARS:
'Green Carpet'—Foliage grows low to the ground, forming a low, neat ground cover. Foliage color is a deeper green than the species.
'Variegata' ('Silver Edge')—Leaves are prominently mottled with white, is not as vigorous as the species.

RELATED SPECIES: *P. procumbens* (prō-kum'-benz)—Allegheny Spurge, Allegheny Pachysandra. The dull green leaves are coarsely toothed at the apex of the leaf blade and are entire at the tapered base. Plants are usually deciduous in northern zones and semi-evergreen to evergreen in southern zones. The term evergreen is loosely used as the leaves become very tired looking and tattered during the winter and are best removed in the early spring. Flowers are white with a pinkish tinge and tend to be hidden by the foliage. Plants are 9"–12" tall and 12" wide. Allegheny spurge is not as vigorous as Japanese spurge and does not form the massive ground cover display. However, Allegheny spurge is more attractive as an individual clump. Hardy in zones 5–9.

ADDITIONAL NOTES: *Pachysandra* is derived from the Greek *pachys,* thick, and *andros,* man, and refers to the thick stamens.

Native to Japan.   Perennial

SCIENTIFIC NAME/FAMILY: *Paeonia* hybrids   Paeoniaceae

(pē-ō'ni-ā)

COMMON NAME: Peony, Chinese Peony, Hybrid Peony

LEAVES: Alternate, biternate, leaflets elliptical to lanceolate, entire or sometimes lobed. Leaves 6" to 8".

FLOWER: Various colors, depending upon cultivars selected. Flowers are 3"–6" across, very fragrant, outer sepals leaflike, 8 or more petals, which are large and broad. Flower types include single, double, and anemone. The peony fragrance can be very sweet and overwhelmingly strong.

See color plate

HABIT: 3' tall plant with equal spread creating a round growth habit.

SEASON OF BLOOM: Late spring to early summer. Selection of early, midseason, and late blooming cultivars will provide a succession of bloom for about 6 weeks.

CULTURE: Full sun or light shade, the latter to prevent fading of some of the pastel-colored flowers. Requires a well-drained site and a deep, fertile soil. Too much shade inhibits flowering as does competition from tree roots or a late spring freeze.

UTILIZATION: Specimen plant in the perennial border and for cut flowers. The flowers are very showy. In addition, the foliage is an asset, from the reddish tint of the young shoots in spring to deep green during the summer. In the Midwest, it is tradition to count on peonies for the cemetery for Memorial Day. In fact, the Sunset Cemetery on Sunset Avenue in Manhattan, Kansas, has one of the most extensive plantings and beautiful arrays of peonies I have ever seen.

PROPAGATION: It often takes 5 to 7 years to produce a flowering plant from seed; consequently, division is the normal propagation method. In late summer, the large clumps can be cut into sections containing 3 to 5 eyes (buds). These divisions should be set about 1" below the soil surface. Deeper planting delays or inhibits flowering. Normal establishment time is 3 years before full blooming is experienced.

DISEASES AND INSECTS: *Botrytis* blight and *Phytophthora* blight are the most common and serious problems of peony. Both require good sanitation procedures to help prevent spread of infection. The shoots of the plant should be removed each fall and destroyed. They should not be placed on a compost pile. A fungicide program can also be used to control *Botrytis* blight.

HARDINESS: Zones 3–8. In zone 8, some selections of peony will be marginal because of a lack of chilling hours. However, there are still a number of selections that can be used. The gardener should plant early season flowering cultivars that have single or Japanese flower forms. These selections do not retain as much moisture as the double types which reduces the incidence of diseases.

RELATED SPECIES:
   P. tenuifolia (ten-ū-i-fō'li-a)—Fernleaf Peony. This species has a finely divided foliage which warrants the common name—fernleaf. The single flowers are deep red. The cultivar 'Flore Plena' has double flowers. Culture is the same as that of the *P. hybrids.* Zones 3–8.

ADDITIONAL NOTES: Gardeners interested in this group would benefit from membership in the American Peony Society, 250 Interlachen Road, Hopkins, MN, 55343. *Paeonia* is of Greek derivation from the name of the physician Paeon. Pluto changed Paeon into a flower in gratitude for Paeon's successful cure after Hercules defeated Pluto.

Native to China, Mongolia, and Siberia.   Perennial

SCIENTIFIC NAME/FAMILY: *Paeonia suffruticosa* (P. arborea)   Paeoniaceae

(pē-ō′ni-ā su-frö-ti-kō′så)

COMMON NAME: Tree Peony

LEAVES: Alternate, leaves are biternate, leaflets stalked, ovate to broad-oval with 3 to 5 lobes, whitish beneath. Leaves are 10″ to 12″ long.

FLOWER: Red, rose pink, white and into the yellow ranges, usually solitary, 6″–8″ across, 8 or more petals.

See color plate

HABIT: 3' to 5' erect and coarsely branched shrub that will have a 3'–4' width.

SEASON OF BLOOM: Mid to late spring.

CULTURE: Full sun or light shade. Tree peony requires a well-drained and deep, fertile soil. Too much shade will inhibit flowering as will competition from tree roots. A windbreak is desirable for large specimens.

UTILIZATION: This exotic and spectacular flowering plant should be utilized as a focal point in the perennial border. It is useful as an intermediate plant between the herbaceous and shrub borders. One plant may produce 75–100 blossoms during the 2-month flowering period.

PROPAGATION: Seed and grafting. Propagation from seed is complicated by epicotyl dormancy. Seeds are planted in moist medium, rooted and then transplanted and placed at 40°–50°F or outside during the winter for 90 days. This overcomes the shoot dormancy, and the plant develops normally in the spring. Plants from seed are generally not true to type, and a wait of several years is required before flowers develop. Cultivars are grafted in late summer using *P. lactiflora* as a rootstock. Grafts are callused in a sand-peat medium and potted in the fall. Young plants should be planted 6"–10" deep to encourage the grafted plant to initiate roots.

DISEASES AND INSECTS: Stem wilt, San Jose scale, and leaf blight. Stem wilt is caused by cankers that girdle the stem. There is no control except digging infected plants to prevent spread of the disease.

HARDINESS: Zones 4–7.

CULTIVARS:

The tree peony has had a long and glorious history since it was discovered in southern China some 1600 years ago. For centuries it was the principal flower in the Chinese Imperial Palace Gardens. Chinese plant breeders developed more than 300 variations of tree peony with a wide variation in colors. Today there are several good American varieties, developed by the late A. P. Saunders of Hamilton College. Also, the Japanese have hybridized many fine selections. Due to the large number, I have listed only a few cultivars.

'Alhambra'—Bright golden flowers with crinkled petals. Vigorous grower with semi-double flowers.

'Chinese Dragon'—Semi-double, crimson flowers. Petals are slightly crinkled. Foliage is finely dissected.

'Hesperus'—Flowers are single, rose-pink with yellow undertones. Petals are crinkled.

'Iphigenia'—Velvet, deep red flowers, semi-double.

'Joseph Rock'—Pure white petals are accented with purple inner flares. Flowers are semi-double.

'Leda'—Mauve-pink flowers are streaked with plum color. The flares have a deeper color which highlights the intensity of the blossom.

'Marchiness'—Single flowers are creamy-mauve to very light yellow with a rose blush.

'Roman Gold'—Single bright yellow flowers are carried on a compact plant.

'Summer Night'—Rose-pink with a bronze blush.

'Yachiyo Tsubaki'—Single coral-pink flowers.

Native to China.   Perennial

SCIENTIFIC NAME/FAMILY: *Panicum virgatum*   Poaceae
                                                              (Gramineae)

(pan'i-kum ver-gā'-tum)

COMMON NAME: Switch Grass

LEAVES: Leaves are 2' to 3' long, ⅝" wide, and are flat and glabrous. The culms are up to 5' tall. The foliage is green in summer, changing to yellows and red in the fall, and finally to beige during the winter months.

FLOWER: The flowers are borne in a large, finely textured and dainty panicle which can be 2 feet long. The spikelets are up to ¼" long. Flowers are dark red to purple and turn beige as they mature.

HABIT: The flower stems create an upright habit above the mounded foliage.

SEASON OF BLOOM: Mid to late summer.

CULTURE: Switch grass grows best in full sun and a moist soil. It is tolerant of dry soils and will grow in partial shade. However, in partial shade, the plant is more open and tends to fall over. In dry soils, the plant will spread slowly. Switch grass performs well in seacoast areas and tolerates windy sites and salt spray.

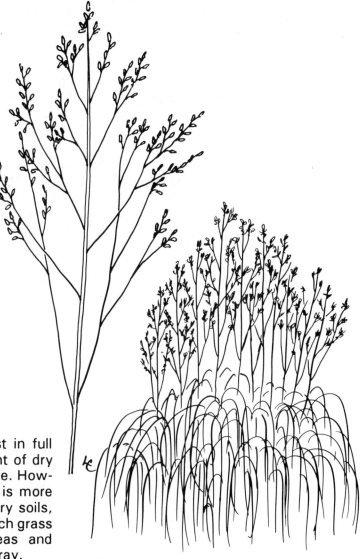

See color plate

UTILIZATION: Best use would be as a massing or screening plant. The flowers are good in fresh or dried arrangements or, if left on the plant, they will last until early winter. The foliage will remain attractive until late winter. Some gardeners use switch grass as a wildlife grass for winter cover.

PROPAGATION: *Panicum* is a warm season grass that can be propagated by seed or division of the clumps in the spring. All cultivars should be propagated by division as they do not come true from seed.

DISEASES AND INSECTS: None serious.

HARDINESS: Zones 5–9.

CULTIVARS:

'Haense Hermes'—Red foliage color develops in midsummer and lasts until frost. The foliage and whitish gray seed heads create a very attractive contrast. This cultivar is also more compact at 3'–3½' tall.

'Heavy Metal'—This cultivar has stiff, metallic-blue leaves which create a tight upright habit. Plant height is 3'–4' tall. The foliage turns bright yellow in the fall.

'Rehbraun'—Red foliage color, 3' tall. The foliage of this cultivar is more of a reddish-brown rather than bright red. It is not as attractive as the other red-leaved types.

'Rotstrahlbusch'—Very red foliage color which is considered to be the reddest of all selections.

'Squaw'—3'–4' tall red foliage switch grass.

'Strictum'—This is an older cultivar with blue-green leaves and an upright growth habit. It is an early bloomer. Plant height is 5'–6' tall.

'Warrior'—Tall cultivar with reddish-brown fall color, 4'–5' tall.

RELATED SPECIES: *P. clandestinum* (clan-des'-tī-num)—Deer Tongue Grass. The foliage of this species is unlike switch grass; in fact, it more resembles bamboo than it does *Panicum.* Leaves are 3/4' to 1' wide and 6"–8" long. Deer tongue grass is 3'–4' tall and is most effective in mass plantings in partial shade where the soils are moist. The growth is floppy so naturalized sites are most appropriate for this species. Hardy to zones 5–9.

Native to the United States.   Perennial

SCIENTIFIC NAME/FAMILY: *Papaver nudicaule* (P. macounii)   Papaveraceae

(på-pā'vẽr nū-di-kâ'le)

COMMON NAME: Iceland Poppy, Arctic Poppy

LEAVES: Leaves mostly basal, petioled, pinnately lobed or cleft, 6". The foliage is often hirsute.

FLOWER: The fragrant flowers are 2"–4" across, saucer shaped, and are orange, yellow, salmon pink, red, or white. The individual flowers are borne on long leafless peduncles. The petals have a crepe paper–like texture.

HABIT: This plant has low clump-like foliage with flowering scapes up to 18". Plants are narrow with a 12" spread.

SEASON OF BLOOM: Spring to early summer. Iceland poppy has a longer blooming season than oriental poppy.

CULTURE: Full sun or partial shade. Iceland poppy requires a well-drained soil. In areas where the summers are extremely hot and humid, the flowering period will be restricted to the spring period.

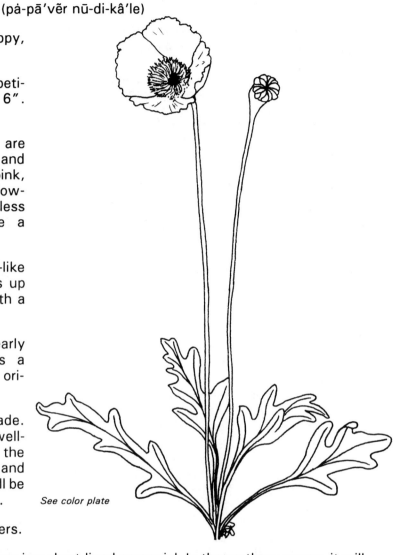

See color plate

UTILIZATION: Border or cut flowers.

HARDINESS: Zones 2–7. This poppy is a short-lived perennial. In the northern zones, it will remain in the garden for 2–3 years, while in the south it seldom will last more than a year due to the summer heat.

CULTIVARS:
'Champagne Bubbles'—This F_1 hybrid is vigorous and has a wide range of bicolors and solids including bronze, orange, scarlet, and yellow. 12" to 18" tall.
'Oregon Rainbows'—This selection has a wide color range and some flowers have 2 to 3 colors. Many blossoms are semidouble. The flowers are large and the stems are sturdy, which makes this cultivar useful as a cut flower. 15" to 20" tall.
'Popsicle'—Flowers are 3"–4" wide and are available in many colors including rose, pink, yellow, red, orange, and apricot.
'Sparkling Bubbles'—16" tall plants with a wide range of colors.
'Summer Breeze'—This cultivar was selected for its long season of bloom. Available in a wide selection of colors.
'Wonderland Series'—12"–14" compact plants with large flowers and thick, short stems. There is an orange selection and a mixture containing red, orange, rose, pink, yellow, cream, and white flowers. The shorter, thicker stems make this cultivar a good choice for windy sites.

Native to North America.   Perennial

SCIENTIFIC NAME/FAMILY: *Papaver orientale* (P. bracteatum)   **Papaveraceae**

(pȧ-pā'vẽr ôr-i-en-tā'le)

COMMON NAME: Oriental Poppy

LEAVES: Hispid, leaves to 12" long and regularly pinnatifid, the segments oblong-lanceolate and sharply lobed or toothed. Broken stem or leaves exude a white milky sap.

FLOWER: Flowers showy, 4"–6" across, petals 4 or 6, borne on long peduncles with coarse appressed white hairs, flower colors are orange-red, white, deep red or pink, often with a mound of black pollen-bearing stamens in the center of the flower.

HABIT: 2' to 4' erect plant with an oval habit.

SEASON OF BLOOM: Late spring to early summer.

CULTURE: Oriental poppy can be grown in full sun or partial shade in well-drained soil. Wet soil conditions in winter lead to rapid decline. A mulch is useful during the first winter after planting or transplanting. The foliage of oriental poppy dies after flowering; consequently, other plants must be planted around the poppy to conceal the dying foliage or vacant space. *Gypsophila paniculata* is a good example of a plant to use for this purpose.

See color plate

UTILIZATION: This species is useful as a border plant or cut flower. Oriental poppies are very dominant visually so they need companion plants that are more subdued to create a good balance. Poppies that are grouped together usually compete with each other for the viewer's attention.

PROPAGATION: 4"–6" root cuttings of dormant plants taken in mid to late summer, or division in the fall. Poppies, however, do best if left undisturbed. The very fine seeds of poppy should be covered lightly and will germinate in 1 to 2 weeks at 55°F. Plants will bloom the 2nd year. Cultivars should be produced by asexual methods.

DISEASES AND INSECTS: No serious problems.

HARDINESS: Zones 3–7.

CULTIVARS: Oriental poppy remains a popular plant although there are few nurseries still propagating the cultivars by root cuttings. Much of the production is by seed propagation in which the quality and trueness of type cannot be guaranteed. Springbrook Gardens in Mentor, Ohio, is a major producer of poppies by root cuttings and has 34 cultivars listed in their catalog. The Countess von Zeppelin Nursery in Laufen, Germany, is known for introduction of oriental poppy cultivars. The following cultivars are a very small listing of potential garden poppies.
'Allegro'—Bright scarlet flowers, compact habit at 16" tall.
'Big Jim'—Crinkled petals of deep red. This is one of the better red color selections.

'Carousel'—White flowers with orange margins.
'China Boy'—Orange flowers with white bases.
'Glowing Embers'—Crimson-red flowers.
'Mrs. Perry'—Salmon pink flowers.
'Warlord'—Very deep red color on large blooms.
'Watermelon'—Watermelon pink flowers.

RELATED SPECIES: *P. somniferum* (som-nif'-er-um)—Opium Poppy. This species is usually thought of as the source for the opium drug, edible seeds and an edible oil. It is also used as a short-lived ornamental in southern zones where it reseeds each year. In northern zones, opium poppy is treated as an annual. The plant is 2'–3' tall with little side branching. It has gray-green foliage and large flowers that can be 5" wide. Flower colors are usually red, pink, purple or white.

ADDITIONAL NOTES: *Papaver* is the Latin name for poppy. The common name was derived from *popig,* which was an Anglo-Saxon term for sleep. This refers to the use of seeds from certain species to make a drink to induce sleepiness.

Native to the Mediterranean region.   Perennial

SCIENTIFIC NAME/FAMILY: *Patrinia triloba*   Valerianaceae
                        (Patrinia palmata)

(pat-rin'-ē-a trī-lō'-ba)

COMMON NAME: Elvis-eyes,
Patrinia

LEAVES: The opposite leaves
are palmately lobed into 3
to 5 segments which are
irregularly and coarsely
toothed. They are 3" long
and borne on 2"–3" long
petioles.

FLOWER: Small, light yellow
flowers (1/4") are borne in
3"–4" wide clusters atop
wiry, brownish stems.

HABIT: Erect flower stems
protrude from a basal
clump of leaves. Height is
12"–18". Plant 12" apart.

SEASON OF BLOOM: Early
summer.

CULTURE: This species grows
well in partial shade to full
sun sites in cool, moist
soils.

UTILIZATION: It is very suitable for the lightly shaded
native woodland setting.

PROPAGATION: Propagate by
seed or division of the
clump in the spring.

DISEASES AND INSECTS: No
special problems.

HARDINESS: Zones 5–8.

Native to Japan.   Perennial

SCIENTIFIC NAME/FAMILY: *Pelargonium graveolens*   Geraniaceae

(pel-är-gō'ni-um gra-vē'o-lenz)

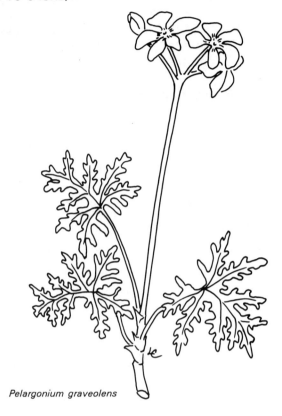

COMMON NAME: Rose Geranium, Sweet-Scented Geranium

LEAVES: Opposite leaves, long-petioled, nearly heart shaped, deeply lobed into 3–5 lobes, which are further lobed and round-toothed. The 2"–4" wide leaves are softly pubescent and very fragrant.

FLOWER: Small pink flowers are borne in umbels composed of 2–7 flowers. The corolla is ½" long and composed of 5 petals with the 2 upper petals being larger.

HABIT: Bushy plant, 12"–24" tall and 24" wide.

SEASON OF BLOOM: Summer.

CULTURE: Rose geranium is a tender perennial that is treated as an annual and usually grown in containers. Container soil mix needs to be well-drained. Water deeply during dry periods but avoid overwatering. Stems should be pinched to promote a bushy habit. Scented geranium has a tendency to become leggy.

Pelargonium graveolens

UTILIZATION: Rose geranium can be used to flavor tea, jelly, and sugar. Leaves can be added to apple jelly to create a distinguished scent. Dried leaves of rose geranium can be added to sachets and potpourris. As ornamentals, scented geraniums make excellent house and garden plants. Indoors or outside, these geraniums provide a pleasing fragrance, and many have striking foliage of different shapes and colors. Container plants should be placed in areas where the foliage can be touched or brushed against to release the fragrance.

PROPAGATION: Propagation is generally by softwood cuttings in spring or summer. Cuttings should be taken just below a node.

DISEASES AND INSECTS: Under optimal conditions, there are few serious problems. Under poor growing conditions, scented geranium is susceptible to bacterial wilt, botrytis, and whiteflies.

HARDINESS: Zone 10.

RELATED SPECIES:
It is nearly impossible to list or describe the many scented geraniums that may be placed in the herb garden for their fragrance and foliage. The following are just a few that are interesting to me because of their foliage shapes and textures.
Lemon—'Mabel Grey'—Intense lemon-scented foliage.
Nutmeg (*P.* × *fragrans*) (frā'granz)—Small gray leaves, ¾" wide and white flowers ⅜"–½" wide. Spicy nutmeg fragrance.

Peppermint (*P. tomentosum*) (tō-men-to'sum)—Large, silver grey, pubescent leaves, strong peppermint fragrance, 3"–4" wide, 3–5 lobes.

Pungent peppermint—Strong peppermint scent, 5–7 lobes, with serrated segments, 3"–4" wide.

Silver Edge Rose—Notched grey-green leaves with white edges.

'Snowflake'—Large leaves, 4"–5" wide, have white to cream-colored variegation, lemon-rose scent.

Native to South Africa   Tender perennial

P. × *fragrans—Nutmeg Geranium*

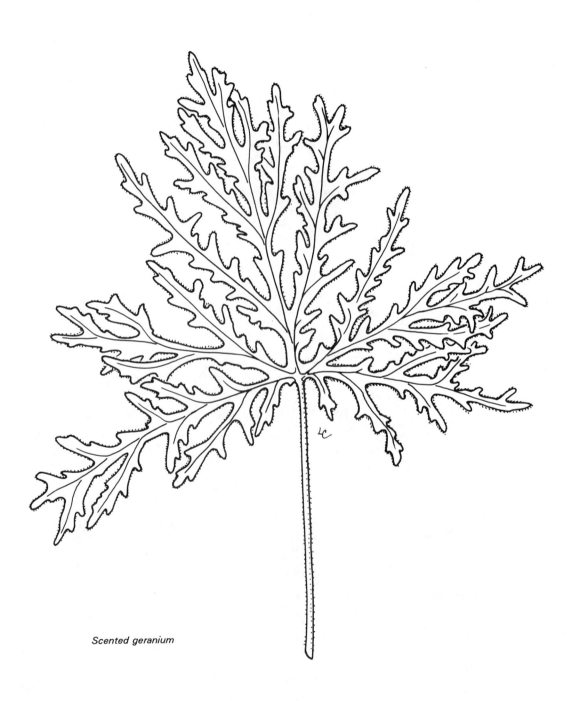

Scented geranium

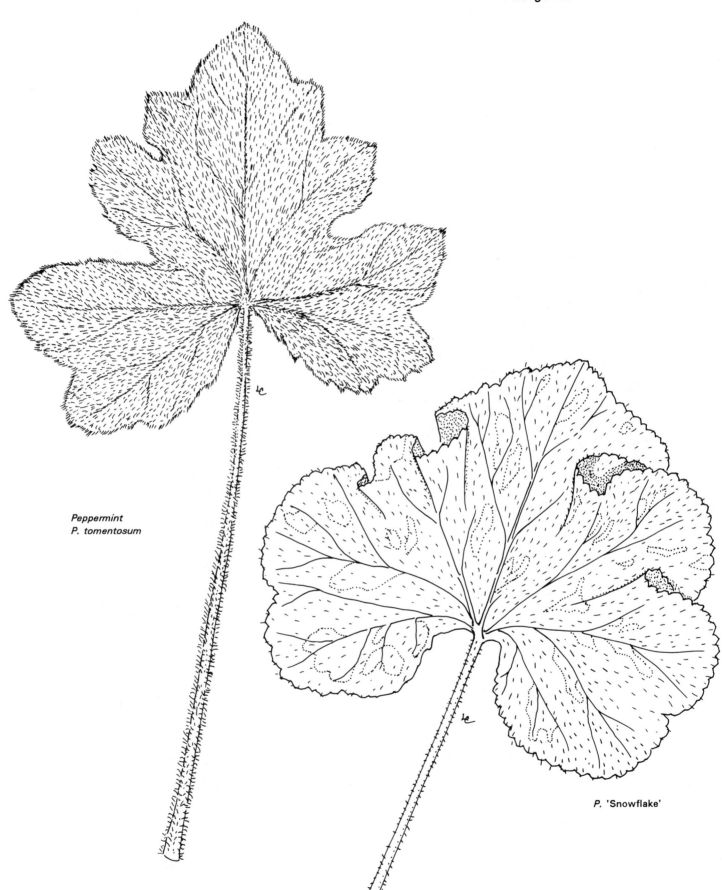

Peppermint
P. tomentosum

P. 'Snowflake'

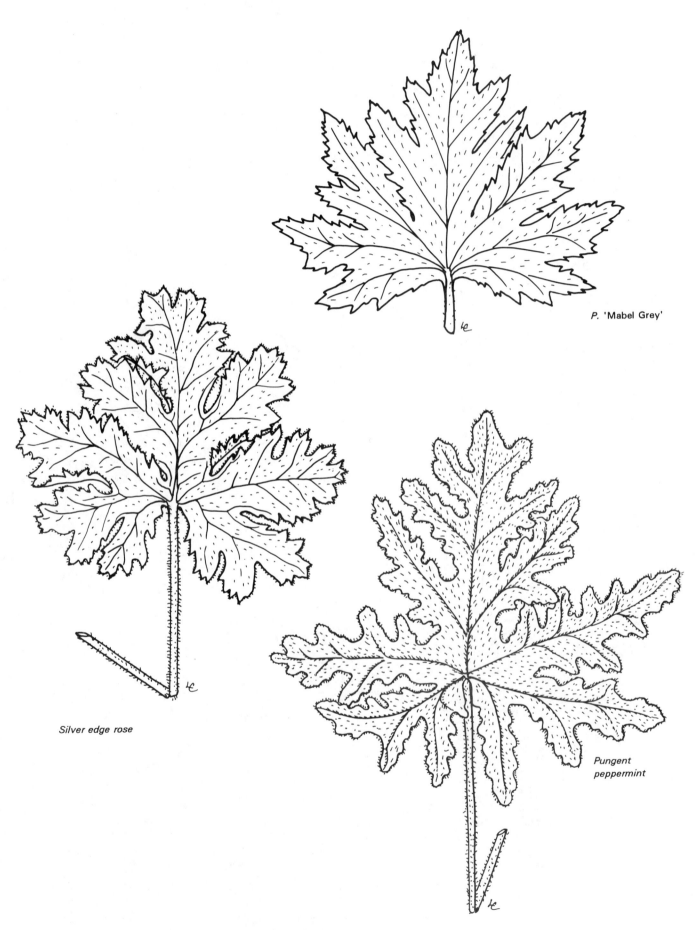

P. 'Mabel Grey'

Silver edge rose

Pungent
peppermint

SCIENTIFIC NAME/FAMILY: *Pelargonium* × *hortorum*   Geraniaceae

(pel-är-gō'ni-um hôr-tôr'um)

COMMON NAME: Geranium, Zonal Geranium, Bedding Geranium

LEAVES: Mostly opposite, leaves round to reniform, 3"–5" across, cordate, leaf margin scalloped, and crenate-toothed; leaves often zoned or variegated; heavy odor to bruised foliage.

FLOWER: Umbel, densely flowered, calyx spur elongate, petals nearly equal; red, pink, salmon, white, usually uniform in color but sometimes variegated. Flowers may be single, semi-double or double and 2" to 3" wide.

HABIT: 12" to 20", round habit.

SEASON OF BLOOM: All summer.

CULTURE: Full sun, moist, well-drained soil with a cool root zone.

UTILIZATION: Border, bedding, containers, hanging baskets.

PROPAGATION: Propagated by seed or stem cuttings. Homeowners usually purchase established plants grown from seed. Best germination occurs in 3 weeks with a constant soil temperature of 70°–75°F.

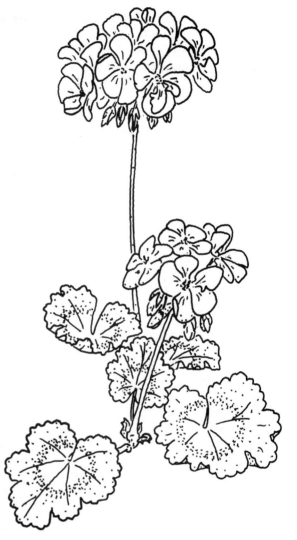

DISEASES AND INSECTS: Bacterial leaf spot, black leg, *Botrytis* blight, root and stem rots, rust, mealybugs, various caterpillars, and mites.

CULTIVARS: The cultivar selection is large. Available flower colors are red, salmon, pink/rose, white, bicolor, and violet. The following are a few of the available cultivar series.

'Elite' Series—Early flowering type with compact growth, 10"–12" tall. Available in 6 colors and a mix. Good selection for selling in packs in the spring.

'Freckles'—Pink flowers with dark rose centers, compact grower. 1991 All American Selection winner.

'Orange Appeal'—True orange flowers on a free-flowering compact plant. It is a 1991 Fleuroselect medal winner.

'Orbit' Series—This popular cultivar is compact, early flowering, and has excellent zonation. The color choice is wide, with 17 colors from which to choose.

'Pinto' Series—Good flowering plant with multiple flower heads that is usually grown for pot sales. 12"–14" tall.

'Ringo' Series—This series contains 8 colors. It is a good selection to use for plug production because of a high germination rate and consistency.

'Sprinter' Series—This cultivar is one of the standards in the industry with uniform early bloom and long bloom season. Plants are 14"–16" tall.

RELATED SPECIES:

Pelargonium peltatum (pel-tā'-tum) — Ivy-leaved Geranium. Vinelike in habit and popular for use in hanging baskets and window boxes. It has smooth leathery leaves.

'Breakaway' — Good symmetrical branching from the base; one plant will fill an 8″ basket. Plants flower profusely even in hot weather. Available in red or salmon.

'Summer Showers' — This seed-grown selection is a good alternative to cutting-grown material because it is faster growing, is more vigorous, and is very floriferous. There is less disease and more basal branching with 'Summer Showers'.

ADDITIONAL NOTES: *Pelargonium* is derived from the Greek, *pelargos,* a stork, which refers to the shape of the fruit, which slightly resembles the beak of a stork.

Hybrid origin.   Annual

SCIENTIFIC NAME/FAMILY: *Pennisetum alopecuroides*

(pen-i-sē'tum a-lō-pek-ū-roi'-dēz)

Poaceae
(Gramineae)

COMMON NAME: Chinese Pennisetum, Perennial Fountain Grass

LEAVES: The leaves are ¼" wide and 2' to 3' long. The culms are slender and grow to 4 feet. The foliage is bright green during the summer and turns to a golden brown in the fall.

FLOWER: The single flower spike is 5" to 7" long. The bristles are long and prominent with a scabrous texture. The flower spikes resemble bottle brushes. Mature flowers are reddish brown.

HABIT: The leaves are strongly arching, which creates a mounded habit, 3' to 4' tall and 3'–4' wide.

SEASON OF BLOOM: Midsummer.

CULTURE: Full sun in a well-drained, moist soil is ideal. In arid areas, supplemental moisture is required. Fountain grass will tolerate light shade but does not thrive if there is insufficient light. If there is dense shade, flowering will not occur. Reseeding can occur especially in soils that are moist. Plants will need a 3 to 4 foot space at maturity.

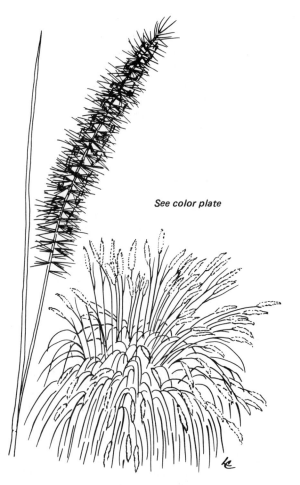

See color plate

UTILIZATION: Fountain grass is an excellent plant for mass plantings, groupings, or as a specimen plant. It is at home in the border or near water and is tolerant of the wind and water of coastal areas. The flowers are attractive during the summer and fall. During the summer the flowers can be used in fresh flower arrangements. They shatter in early winter, which makes them unsuitable as a winter feature that is found with other grasses such as those in the *Miscanthus* genus. Although the flower heads shatter, the growth form of *Pennisetum* is good during the winter. Perennial fountain grass is an excellent complement to *Sedum* 'Autumn Joy', *Pervoskia atriplicifolia,* and members of the *Rudbeckia* genus.

PROPAGATION: Division and seed. Clump division should be completed in the spring. All cultivars should be propagated by clump division.

DISEASES AND INSECTS: None serious.

HARDINESS: Zones 5–9.

CULTIVARS:

'Cassian'—Newer dwarf selection with 12″ tall foliage and flower stems to 24″ tall. It has a bright golden fall color. Kurt Bluemel, Baldwin, Maryland, introduced this cultivar.

'Hameln'—'Hameln' is smaller than the species with finer-textured foliage and smaller whitish flower heads. Plant size is 24″ tall with an 18″–24″ width. This cultivar and 'Cassian' are good for gardens where the species is too large.

'Little Bunny'—Very short *Pennisetum* that is suitable for the rock garden.

'Moudry'—Dark brown, almost black, foxtail seed heads highlight this cultivar. It is later flowering than the species and stands 2 to 3 feet tall. Gardeners should be aware that this cultivar is noted for its ability to reseed in most gardens.

'Weserbergland'—This cultivar is similar to 'Hameln' but is taller with a more spreading habit.

RELATED SPECIES:

P. caudatum (kà-da′-tum)—White Flowering Fountain Grass. This species differs from *P. alopecuroides* due to the whitish flowers which bloom earlier. The flower heads are narrower and fade to tan at maturity. Plants are 4 to 5 feet tall. Landscape uses include planting in masses, groups, or as an accent plant. Plants are hardy in zones 6–9.

P. incomptum (in-comp′-tum)—Meadow Fountain Grass. Most of the *Pennisetum* species are clump formers but meadow fountain grass is an aggressive spreader that can quickly take over an area. It is valuable when used as a mass in large areas to create a meadow effect. Plants are 3′–4′ tall and perform best in full sun to partial shade in moist, well-drained soil. Zones 6–9.

P. orientale (or-i-en-ta′-lē)—Oriental Fountain Grass. The pink inflorescences of this species have a cottony appearance. Many "grassophiles" consider this species to be the most attractive of the *Pennisetum*. Unfortunately for the northern gardener, it is only hardy to zone 7, perhaps to zone 6. Oriental fountain grass is 2 to 3 feet tall. It should be sited so that the pinkish flowers are lit by early morning or late afternoon sun. This *Pennisetum* starts flowering early and continues until late fall. It is an excellent specimen for Southern California gardens.

ADDITIONAL NOTES: *Pennisetum* is derived from *penna,* a feather, and *seta,* a bristle, and refers to the feathery bristles (awns).

Native to China.   Perennial

SCIENTIFIC NAME/FAMILY: *Pennisetum setaceum* (P. ruppelii)   Poaceae
(Gramineae)

(pen-i-sē'tum se-tā'sē-um)

COMMON NAME: Annual Fountain Grass

LEAVES: Leaf blades are long and narrow, scabrous, sheaths long, ciliate at the ligule.

FLOWER: Inflorescence to 12" long, nodding, loose, pink or purple, awns plumose toward the base.

HABIT: 2' to 4' with a mound to upright arching habit.

SEASON OF BLOOM: Summer to frost.

CULTURE: Full sun or partial shade; prefers moist, well-drained soil.

UTILIZATION: Annual fountain grass can be used in the border, as a background or specimen plant, or in fresh flower arrangements. The flowers shatter too easily for this species to be used in dried arrangements.

See color plate

PROPAGATION: Seeds will germinate in 3 to 4 weeks when held at 70°–80°F. In warm climates, zones 9 and 10, *Pennisetum setaceum* can be an invasive spreader due to its seeding nature. This species will quickly spread into native populations, a characteristic that should be considered in placement of this species.

DISEASES AND INSECTS: None serious.

HARDINESS: Zones 8–10. In northern areas, including the northern portion of zone 8, a hard frost will kill this grass.

CULTIVARS:
'Rubrum' (also listed as 'Cupreum') — The purple-leaved fountain grass has become a popular annual species for providing an accent to the herbaceous border. The burgundy foliage and reddish-purple plumes are a highlight in the border or in fresh flower arrangements. It is hardy to zones 9 and 10. In northern areas the clumps can be dug in the fall, overwintered in a greenhouse, and divided in the spring for replanting. Plant height is 3'-4' tall. 'Rubrum Dwarf' is a compact form with a height of 30"-36".

RELATED SPECIES:

P. villosum (vil-lō'-sum)—Feathertop Fountain Grass. This annual fountain grass has fluffy foxtail flower plumes that look like white feather dusters. In zones 9 and 10 it can be an aggressive perennial grass. In colder areas it performs as an annual and can be used for mass plantings on slopes. The white flowers are especially useful in fresh or dried arrangements.

P. 'Burgundy Giant'—'Burgundy Giant' fountain grass looks like a purple-leaved corn plant. The leaves are 1" wide and are carried on stems that rise to 5 feet. The nodding foxtail plumes are purple, 1"–2" wide and 8" to 12" long. This selection makes a stunning accent in the border. It is only hardy in zones 9 and 10 and must be lifted in northern climates before frost.

Native to Ethiopia.   Annual

SCIENTIFIC NAME/FAMILY: *Penstemon barbatus*   Scrophulariaceae

(pen-stē'mon bar-bā'tus)

COMMON NAME: Penstemon, Beardtongue

LEAVES: Opposite, lanceolate to ovate-lanceo-late, 2"–4" long, entire, sometimes dentate.

FLOWER: The 2-lipped, tubular flowers are borne in terminal racemes. They are 1"–2" long and scarlet-pink in color. There are 5 sta-mens, four of them fertile, the 5th is sterile. The sterile stamen is often bearded, which gives rise to the common name beardtongue.

HABIT: Cultivars vary in height from 18" to 36", round habit.

SEASON OF BLOOM: Late spring to mid-summer.

CULTURE: *Penstemon* should be grown in a well-drained soil. Drainage is very important because it will rot in wet soils. The soil can be of average fertil-ity. An exposure in full sun is best. A light mulch in the winter is beneficial.

UTILIZATION: Perennial border, naturaliz-ing and cutting flowers.

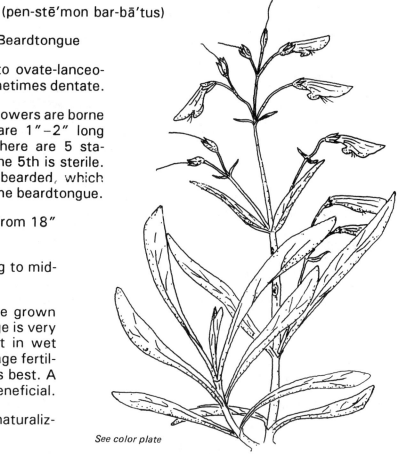

See color plate

PROPAGATION: Sowing seeds in late summer is a common propagation technique. Seeds planted indoors should be germinated at 60°–65°F for 2 weeks. Cuttings can be made in midsummer, but must be protected during the winter. Division should be done in the spring.

DISEASES AND INSECTS: Leaf spots and rusts occur, but are rarely serious enough to warrant control measures.

HARDINESS: Zones 3–8.

CULTIVARS:
    'Alba'—White flowers.
    'Bashful'—Orange flowers, 12" tall.
    'Elfin Pink'—Clear pink flowers 12" tall.
    'Hyacinth Mix'—Seed-propagated selection with mixed colors of scarlet, rose, pink, violet, and dark blue.
    'Nana Rondo'—Mixture of various flower-colored flowers on compact plants, 12"–14" tall.
    'Prairie Dusk'—Rose-purple flowers on 24" tall stems. This cultivar and 'Prairie Fire' were introduced by the North Platte Experiment Station, University of Nebraska. The late Dr. Glenn Viehmeyer was responsible for these cultivars.
    'Prairie Fire'—Scarlet flowers on 24" tall stems.
    'Rose Elf'—Rose flowers, 18" tall plants.

RELATED SPECIES:
    P. digitalis (dij-i-tāl'-iss) 'Husker Red'. This recent introduction from the University of Nebraska has maroon-red foliage and white flowers with a tinge of pink. Plant height is 30"–36". It flowers in early to mid-summer.

P. × *gloxinoides* (glok-sin-oi'-dez). This hybrid of *P. hartwegii* and *P. cobaea* has large flowers that are 2" wide. These are very showy penstemons; unfortunately they only perform as perennials in Zones 9 and 10. In other areas they function as annuals in the garden.
'Firebird'—Scarlet flowers, 24" tall.
'Sour Grapes'—Indigo-blue flowers.

P. hirsutus (hir-sut'-us). Native plant of eastern North America with lanceolate to oblong leaves to 4½" long. Short panicles of bluish lavender flowers are carried on mounds of foliage 12"–18" tall and 18" wide. 'Pygmaeus' is 6" tall. Zones 4–8.

P. pinifolius (pin-i-fōl'ē-us). This species has fine green needle-like foliage. The mounded habit is 8" tall and 18" wide. In moist, well-drained soil, small, scarlet, trumpet-shaped flowers cover the plant. 'Mersea Yellow' has pure yellow flowers. Zones 4–8.

There is a large number of hybrids of uncertain origin. These cultivars require excellent drainage and need to be mulched in winter and summer. These cultivars are seen more often in England than in North America. In September 1992, I saw a beautiful collection of penstemon at the Pershore Horticulture College in England.

'Alice Hindley'—Pink flowers with white throats, 24" tall.
'Evelyn'—Pale pink flowers, 18" tall. It seems to be hardier than other selections.
'Garnet'—Wine-red flowers. It is a beautiful specimen but is only marginally hardy in most areas of North America.
'Scarlet Queen'—Bright red flowers with white throats, 3' tall.

ADDITIONAL NOTES: *Penstemon* is derived from *pente,* five, and *stemon,* stamen, meaning five stamens.

Native to Mexico.   Perennial

SCIENTIFIC NAME/FAMILY: *Perovskia atriplicifolia*   Lamiaceae
(Labiatae)

(pe-rof'ski-à at-rip-lis-ē-fō'-lē-à)

COMMON NAME: Russian Sage, Azure Sage

LEAVES: The stems are gray-white and the leaves are gray-white beneath. Both are aromatic. The oppositely arranged leaves are strongly dissected and 1½" long.

FLOWER: *Perovskia* is in the mint family; consequently, the small flowers are 2-lipped. The lavender-blue flowers are arranged in an interrupted spire that extends above the foliage.

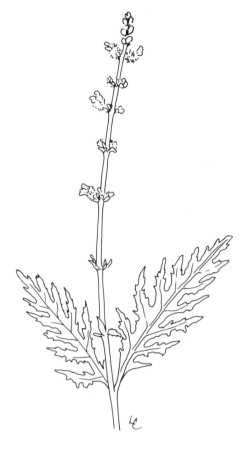

HABIT: Upright growing, fine-textured plant, 3' to 4' tall and 3'–4' wide.

SEASON OF BLOOM: Summer.

CULTURE: Russian sage performs well in full sun sites in well-drained soil. The base of the plant is woody. To promote good growth and flowers, *Perovskia* should be cut back to within several inches of the ground in the spring.

UTILIZATION: The combination of gray-white foliage and lavender-blue flowers is very nice. The gray stems are attractive in the winter. It is an excellent plant for a filler in the border.

PROPAGATION: Tip cuttings can be taken during the summer. Humidity should be maintained with a plastic tent rather than a mist system to prevent rotting of the cuttings from excessive moisture. The species can also be propagated by seed. Germination is often irregular and occurs over a long period. Chilling at 35–40°F will enhance the germination percentage.

DISEASES AND INSECTS: No serious problems.

HARDINESS: Zones 5–9.

CULTIVARS:
   'Blue Haze'—Pale blue flowers and leaves that are nearly entire.
   'Blue Spire'—Finely dissected leaves and deep violet flowers.
   'Longin'—This selection is narrower and more upright than the species. However, the leaves are not as dissected as the species. 'Longin' is a hybrid of unknown origin.

See color plate

RELATED SPECIES:

   P. abrotanoides (a-bro-ta-noi′-dēz). This species is more branched and larger growing than Russian sage. The leaves are gray-green and deeply incised. It is not as available as Russian sage although the cultivars previously listed may be hybrids of *P. abrotanoides* × *P. atriplicifolia.*

Native from Afghanistan to Tibet.   Perennial

SCIENTIFIC NAME/FAMILY: *Persicaria virginiana* 'Variegata'   Polygonaceae
(Tovara virginiana)

(per-si-car'-i-a vẽr-jin-i-ā'nȧ)

COMMON NAME: Tovara

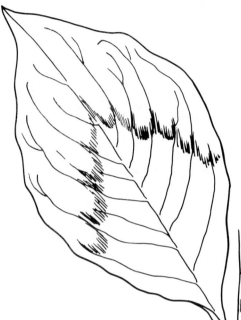

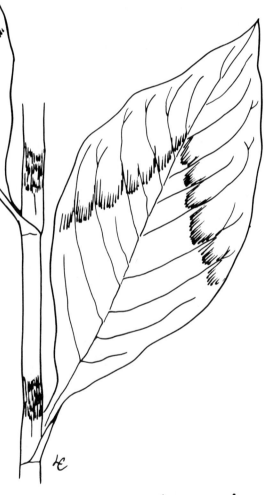

LEAVES: Alternate leaves are simple, ovate shaped and entire, and 4"–6" long. The dark green leaves are irregularly marbled with ivory-yellow variegation. The stems are jointed on this species. The leaves of *Persicaria virginiana* var. *filiformis*, 'Painter's Palette,' have a distinct brick red V-sign that runs across the center of the leaf. The red fades to a blackish bronze color as the leaf matures.

FLOWER: Small brownish flowers are borne in thin spikes. Tovara is grown for its foliage effect and the flowers are not ornamentally important.

HABIT: Rounded clump of broad leaves, 24" tall and 24" wide.

SEASON OF BLOOM: Not grown for flower effect. Foliage is attractive all summer.

CULTURE: Tovara should be placed in a partial shade area in soils that are fertile and moist. It should be protected from the wind because the delicate leaves are damaged in windy areas.

See color plate

UTILIZATION: Plants of this species are used for tall ground covers, massing, or edging in shaded borders. In optimum conditions, such as moist soils, tovara can be an aggressive grower.

PROPAGATION: Division in fall or spring.

DISEASES AND INSECTS: No serious problems.

HARDINESS: Zones 4–7.

CULTIVARS:
   var. *filiformis* (fil'i-form-is) 'Painter's Palette'—As mentioned above, this cultivar is easily identified by the reddish V-sign that runs across the center of the leaf. The new leaves are creamy white with areas of light green and pink. This is a very noticeable cultivar.

Native to eastern United States, eastern Canada, and Japan.   Perennial

SCIENTIFIC NAME/FAMILY: *Petasites japonicus*   Asteraceae (Compositae)

(pet-a-sī'tes ja-pon'-i-cus)

COMMON NAME: Japanese Butterbur, Sweet Coltsfoot, Fuki

LEAVES: Basal leaves with long petioles; reniform to orbicular shaped, 16" wide; leaf margins are lightly toothed, upper surfaces pubescent and lower surfaces tomentose. The leaf petioles are channeled and winged.

FLOWER: White daisy flowers borne on a 6" long scape, green bracts to 2½", upper bracts forming an involucre beneath the inflorescence. The flowers appear before the leaves in very early spring.

HABIT: 36" tall with overlapping mounds of foliage. In wet summers, the foliage can get 3½' tall; drier seasons will create smaller leaves and a lower height.

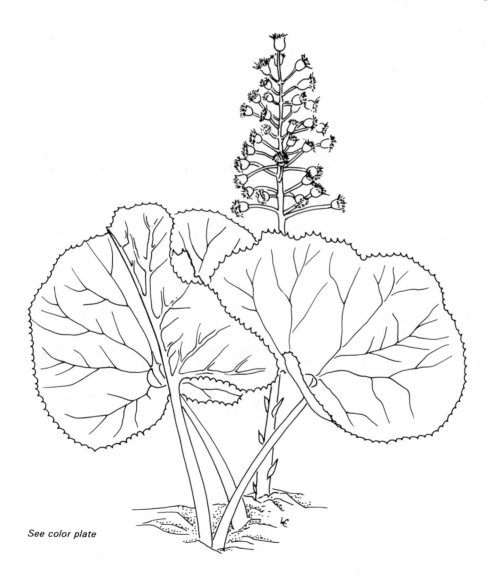

See color plate

SEASON OF BLOOM: Early spring (early March in Ohio).

CULTURE: Best performance occurs in moist soils and shaded areas. During a dry season, *Petasites* will wilt during the day but revive in the evening, much like the selections of *Ligularia.* Janet Oberliesen, Worthington, Ohio, has grown this species for 15 years and found that it has tolerated all types of weather conditions and has persevered.

UTILIZATION: Butterbur is found along streams in woods of Japan and China and a similar siting would be ideal for this species. The overall sculptured quality of the leaves in a mass planting is excellent. Butterbur can increase readily by rhizomes. This characteristic needs to be given careful consideration. Some gardeners report easy removal of unwanted sections, while others feel it can be difficult to eradicate. In small gardens, *Petasites* can be contained by planting in sunken tubs. Plants should be spaced at 2 feet.

PROPAGATION: *Petasites* can be propagated by seeds or division. Two-inch rhizome sections can be used to start new plants.

DISEASES AND INSECTS: Slugs can disfigure the foliage. Mechanical damage such as holes from hail also occur. However, these problems are not serious enough to detract from the overall foliage affect.

HARDINESS: Zones 5–9.

CULTIVARS:
   var. *giganteus* (ji-gan-tē'-us)—Giant Butterbur. This selection has 3'–4' wide leaves borne on 6' long petioles. It is too large for the small garden due to its size and spreading tendency.

RELATED SPECIES:
   P. fragrans (frā'granz)—Winter Heliotrope. 1' tall with 8" wide leaves. Leaves appear at the same time as the flowers. Flowers are pinkish-white and have an almond or vanilla scent.

ADDITIONAL NOTES: The stems have a sweet fragrance when cut and work well as cut specimens if they are hardened properly. The National Herb Garden includes *Petasites* in the Oriental Garden. Flower buds are used as a spice with soups and fish. Leafstalks and rhizomes are eaten as a vegetable by the Japanese. *Petasites* is from the Greek *petasos*, meaning a broad-brimmed hat, in reference to the large leaves.

Native to Japan, China.   Perennial

SCIENTIFIC NAME/FAMILY: *Petrorhagia saxifraga* (Tunica saxifraga)   Caryophyllaceae

(pe-tro-rāg'-i-á saks-e-frā'-ga)

COMMON NAME: Saxifrage Tunicflower, Coat Flower

LEAVES: Opposite leaves are linear and narrow, ¼" to ½" long, acute, with a setose-serration.

FLOWER: Pale pink flowers, ⅛" wide, similar to baby's-breath flowers.

HABIT: Low mound, 8"–10" tall and 12"–18" wide.

SEASON OF BLOOM: Summer.

CULTURE: Full sun and a moist, well-drained soil.

UTILIZATION: Front of the border or rock garden. In my experience, *Petrorhagia* prefers the drainage of a rock garden to that found in a border.

PROPAGATION: Seeds or cuttings. Vegetative propagation is needed to insure true-to-type cultivars.

DISEASES AND INSECTS: No serious problems.

HARDINESS: Zones 4–8.

CULTIVARS:
    'Alba'—White flowers.
    'Alba Plena'—Double white flowers, 8" tall.
    'Rosette'—Pink, double flowers, 8" tall.

Native to central Europe.   Perennial

SCIENTIFIC NAME/FAMILY: *Petroselinum crispum*   Apiaceae (Umbelliferae)

(pe-trō-se-lī'num kris'pum)

COMMON NAME: Parsley

LEAVES: Leaves are pinnately divided into fine-textured sections; stems are grooved. Leaves of some varieties lay flat like celery leaves while other varieties have crinkled, frilled leaves.

FLOWER: Tiny, greenish-yellow flowers are borne in compound umbels. Flowers are not important for culinary or ornamental uses.

HABIT: Fine-textured branches form a dense mound 6″ to 12″ tall and 12″–15″ wide. Space plants about 8″ apart in the garden.

SEASON OF BLOOM: Early summer. Flowers are not important.

CULTURE: Parsley is easily grown in a moist, well-drained soil with a full sun or partial shade exposure. Mature plants will produce new growth after shearing for culinary purposes. Parsley is started new each year.

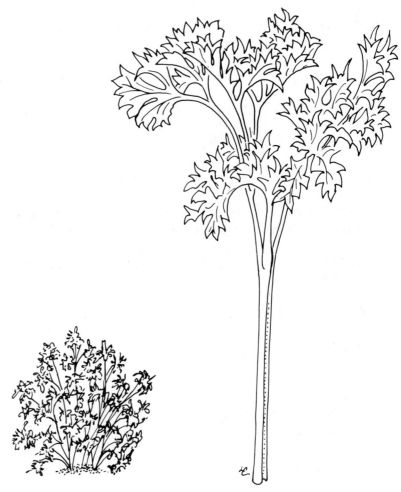

See color plate

UTILIZATION: Most people recognize parsley as the decorative herb found on the entrée at a restaurant. However, it is very edible and has many culinary uses. Parsley is also used as an edging plant or massed in the border front. The bright green leaves and compact habit work well in herb or ornamental beds. Parsley can also be used in mixed container plantings or hanging baskets.

PROPAGATION: Seeds should be covered and germinated at 65°–70°F. Soaking seeds in 34°F water for 24 hours may enhance germination. Home gardeners often buy plants rather than starting from seeds.

DISEASES AND INSECTS: There are no major pests. Swallowtail Butterfly larvae will feed on parsley but major damage is usually not seen.

CULTIVARS:

var. *neopolitanum* (nē-ō-pol-i-tā'num)—Broad-leaf Italian Parsley. Flat leaves have a stronger flavor and dry better than the curly leaf form.

var. *tuberosum* (tu-be-rō'sum)—Turnip-rooted Parsley. This selection forms an 8″–10″ long root. Also called Hamburg Parsley.

Seed catalogs carry several different forms of the curled parsley.

Native to north and central Europe.   Biennial (used as an annual)

SCIENTIFIC NAME/FAMILY: *Petunia* × *hybrida*   Solanaceae

(pē-tū'ni-á hīb'ri-da)

COMMON NAME: Petunia

LEAVES: Alternate, sometimes opposite on upper leaves, broad-ovate to cordate shaped, 1½" to 3" long, simple, entire margin, surfaces of leaves and stems covered with a viscid-pubescence.

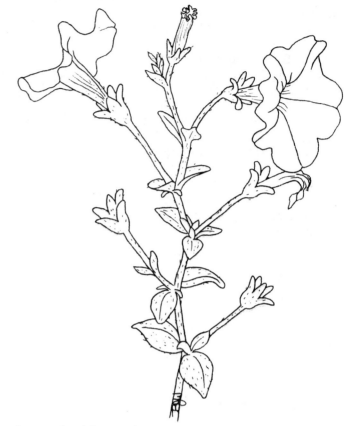

FLOWER: Flower 2"–4" long; has funnel-shaped corolla tube with a very broad limb. Various cultivars have flowers varying in size, form, and color, often deeply fringed or fully double. Many colors available from white to deep purple with various striped or starlike markings. The flower has a very sweet fragrance.

HABIT: 8" to 15", round or trailing habit.

SEASON OF BLOOM: All summer.

CULTURE: Sun to partial shade; light, well-drained soils. Petunias will grow in heavy shade but they will not bloom satisfactorily. Deadheading is required for optimum performance.

UTILIZATION: Grandiflora and multiflora singles are used in beds and borders; doubles are used in flower boxes, containers. Doubles have a tendency to lodge in the garden.

PROPAGATION: Seeds germinate in one week at 72°–75°F.

DISEASES AND INSECTS: *Botrytis,* tobacco mosaic, stem rot, aphids, and flea beetle. Tobacco mosaic, which is transmitted by aphids, is the principle problem.

CULTIVARS:
4 categories:
1. Single grandiflora—huge blossoms, sometimes 5" across, with ruffled or fringed petals.
2. Single multiflora—great number of 2"–3" blossoms.
3. Double grandiflora—fewer but large double blossoms.
4. Double multiflora— great number of doubles about 2" across.

The types of petunias are quite varied and the list of cultivars seems to be endless. It is difficult to list some without leaving out some very good forms. Furthermore, the list is added to yearly. The best way to keep abreast of petunia cultivars is to visit gardens, garden centers, and read current articles and seed catalogs.

ADDITIONAL NOTES: No other bedding plant even approaches the petunia for universal dependability, garden value, and long season of bloom. Add to this the diversity of color, flower forms, and growth habits and you have the answer to why it stays atop the popularity list. Petunia is derived from *Petun,* a colloquial name for tobacco, to which petunia is related.

Native to South America.   Annual

SCIENTIFIC NAME/FAMILY: *Phalaris arundinaceae* var. *picta*   Poaceae
(Gramineae)

(fal'ar-iss à-run-di-nā'sē-ē pik'tà)

COMMON NAME: Ribbon Grass, Gardener's-Garters

LEAVES: The leaves are flat, 6" to 12" long, 2/3" wide, and grow away from the stem in an arching fashion. The leaves are striped longitudinally in alternating stripes of green and white. One side of the leaf is usually predominantly white and the other predominantly green. The proportion of green to white is nearly equal.

FLOWER: The flowers are whitish to pale pink and are arranged in a panicle that is loose at the base and denser in the upper portion. The flowers are not especially attractive and are usually not considered an asset.

HABIT: 24" to 36" tall rapidly spreading ground cover.

SEASON OF BLOOM: Early summer.

CULTURE: Ribbon grass is quite tolerant of light, sandy soils and dry locations; or it can be used effectively in wet areas along stream banks. It is suitable in sun or partial shade. Peak ornamental effect is in early spring through midsummer. The foliage becomes brown and unattractive by late summer. Mowing the foliage off will promote fresh new growth.

See color plate

UTILIZATION: This species is very invasive. If it is placed in a border, the plant should be planted inside a bottomless container to control its spread. The invasive feature can be an advantage if one has a large area to cover and a weed-free ground cover is desired. Ribbon grass is very useful in wet areas, such as along stream banks, where it is able to compete with other invasive species.

PROPAGATION: Division in spring. It can become invasive; consequently, division will be required to maintain a tidy plant. The outer sections of the plant should be used for the new planting.

DISEASES AND INSECTS: None serious.

HARDINESS: Zones 4–9.

CULTIVARS:
'Dwarf Garters'—This is a dwarf sport of var. *picta* which has narrower leaves and a height of 24". The white leaves are also brighter. It is not as invasive as *picta*.
'Feesey' (listed as 'Feesey Form' and 'Feesey Variety')—The new growth is white with green stripes with a bright pink blush. The pink color will bleach out by the summer.
'Luteo-Picto'—This selection has pale gold-yellow variegation rather than the white variegated leaves of the species. It is also an aggressive spreader.

ADDITIONAL NOTES: *Phalaris* is derived from the Greek word *phalaros,* shining, referring to the polished seeds of this genus. Ribbon grass was mentioned in early herbals and it is probably the first of the variegated grasses to be brought into the garden.

Native to North America and Europe.   Perennial

SCIENTIFIC NAME/FAMILY: *Phlomis russeliana*   Lamiaceae
                                                               (Labiatae)

(flō'mis ru-sē'li-a-na or ru-sel'-i-ā-na)

See color plate

COMMON NAME: Greek Jeru-
   salem Sage, Sticky Jerusalem Sage.

LEAVES: The opposite leaves
   are arranged on a square
   stem, both stems and lower leaf surfaces pubescent.
   The leaves are ovate, with
   a truncate to subcordate
   leaf base, and a crenate
   margin. The leaf blade has
   a wrinkled appearance.

FLOWER: The stout flower
   stems bear several whorls
   of yellow hooded flowers.
   The seed heads that follow
   the flowers are attractive
   when green or brown.

HABIT: Upright habit, with a
   large mound of dark green
   leaves about 12" tall and
   stout flower stems as tall
   as 3'. Plants are 3' wide.

SEASON OF BLOOM: Early to
   midsummer.

CULTURE: *Phlomis* should be grown in full sun in a well-drained, sandy loam soil that is
   low in fertility. Plants grown in rich soil will often have weak stems, making the plant
   more susceptible to lodging.

UTILIZATION: *Phlomis* is an interesting species for the perennial border. The whorls of
   yellow flowers are handsome and certainly unique. The yellow flowers are a nice
   combination with the blue-flowered geraniums.

PROPAGATION: Division in the fall or spring and seed propagation are suitable methods.
   Stratifying the seeds usually enhances germination.

DISEASES AND INSECTS: This species is usually trouble-free.

HARDINESS: Zones 4–8.

ADDITIONAL NOTES: *Phlomis* is derived from *phlomos,* Greek for mullein, and is in
   reference to the woolly character of the leaves, which was thought to resemble mullein
   species.

Native to Asia.   Perennial

SCIENTIFIC NAME/FAMILY: *Phlox divaricata*   Polemoniaceae

(floks di-vār-i-kā'tȧ)

COMMON NAME: Wild Sweet William, Blue Phlox,
   Woodland Phlox

LEAVES: Opposite leaves are sessile, elliptic or
   lanceolate, ½" to ¾" wide, and 2" long. The
   stems and leaves are viscid-pubescent.

FLOWER: The blue flowers are slightly fragrant, very
   symmetrical, and composed of 5 petals, which
   are convolute in bud. The tips of the petals are
   usually notched or irregularly jagged.

HABIT: A 12"–15" tall perennial with basal stems
   and upright flowering stems. Plant spread is
   12".

SEASON OF BLOOM: Late spring to early summer.

CULTURE: A partial shade to full shade site in a
   moist, humus soil is ideal. In more sun and/or dry
   soil, this plant will become partially dormant,
   causing leaf drop. The root system is shallow, so
   mulching will aid moisture retention. Faded
   flowers should be removed to stimulate branching and to encourage new foliage.

See color plate

UTILIZATION: Front of the border, wild flower garden, or as a woodland ground cover.

PROPAGATION: Tip cuttings in summer or spring division are easy propagation methods.

DISEASES AND INSECTS: Powdery mildew can be a problem in hot and humid areas.
   Mildew is most prevalent in early spring and during the summer. Cutting back the stems
   to initiate new growth is an effective treatment. An additional pest, one that is not an
   insect or disease, but probably a worse offender, is the rabbit. It seems that the wild
   Sweet William is one of its favorites.

HARDINESS: Zones 4–9.

CULTIVARS:
   'Chattahoochee'—Lavender-blue flowers with dark purple centers, long bloom period,
      12" tall. This selection is a hybrid of *P. divaricata* var. *laphamii* and *P. pilosa*.
   'Dirigo Ice' (Dirgo Ice)—Pale lavender flowers, 8"–12" tall.
   'Fuller's White'—Creamy-white flowers, notched petals, 8"–12" tall. This may be the
      best cultivar. It is a very prolific bloomer.
   var. laphamii—Deep blue flowers, 8"–10" tall.

RELATED SPECIES:
   P. stolonifera (stō-lōn-if'-er-a)—Creeping Phlox. Native woodland ground cover with low
      mats of foliage. It produces flowering and sterile stems. The leaves of the sterile
      shoots are elliptic and 1"–3" long. Leaves of the erect flowering stems are oval and
      less than 1" long. The flowers are purple to violet, 1" wide, and borne in an open
      cyme with usually 2–3 flowers. Creeping phlox increases by rooting at the nodes

and production of stolons. Moist, humus-enriched soil in partial shade is the ideal site. In cool climates, creeping phlox will tolerate a sunnier location.

'Blue Ridge'—Blue flowers with overlapping petals, 12" tall flowering stems.

'Bruce's White' ('Ariane')—White flowers with very conspicuous yellow eyes, 6" tall.

'Pink Ridge'—This is a pink-flowered form of 'Blue Ridge'.

'Home Fires'—Deep pink flowers.

'Sherwood Purple'—Purplish-blue fragrant flowers, 6" tall. This is a popular cultivar that makes an excellent ground cover.

Native to eastern United States.   Perennial

SCIENTIFIC NAME/FAMILY: *Phlox drummondi*   Polemoniaceae

(floks drum'und-ī)

COMMON NAME: Annual Phlox, Drummond Phlox, Texas Pride

LEAVES: Lowermost leaves opposite, others alternate, broad-ovate to oblong and lanceolate, 1"–3" long. The leaf apex is acute and mucronate; base is narrow or clasping.

FLOWER: Flowers showy, about 1" across, in copious close cymose clusters. Five round-tipped or star-shaped petals may be white, pink, salmon, purple, yellow, and bi-colored.

HABIT: Low-spreading mound, 6"–8" tall and 12" wide.

SEASON OF BLOOM: Summer to frost.

CULTURE: Sun to partial shade in well-drained, moist soil.

UTILIZATION: Edging, bedding (mass the colors), rock garden, and window boxes.

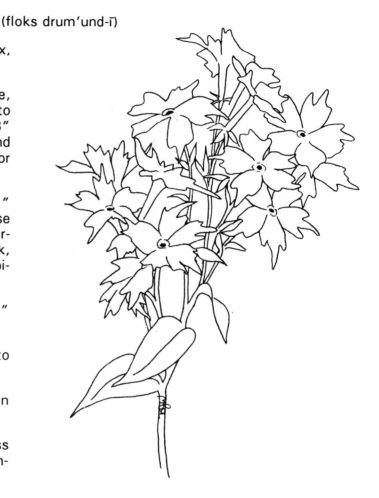

PROPAGATION: Phlox should be germinated in the dark at 55°–60°F. Germination occurs in 2 weeks. Too much moisture will cause damping off.

DISEASES AND INSECTS: Leaf spot, powdery mildew, potato flea beetle, and mites are occasional problems. They can be controlled with normal pesticides.

CULTIVARS:
'Dwarf Early Mix'—Wide color range, compact and early flowering.
'Cecily'—Compact plants, 8" tall, with mixed colors. Flowers are large with well-defined eyes.
'Globe Mixture'—8", rounded compact plant, very uniform growth habit, mixed colors.
'Palona' Series—Very compact and floriferous selection with earlier flowers, 6"–8" tall. Nine colors and a mix are available.
'Petticoat Mix'—This selection offers a good mix of colors on compact plants 6" tall. It is reported to be more heat and drought tolerant than other selections of annual phlox.
'Twinkle'—8", smaller star-shaped flower with pointed petals; blooms early and continues well into the summer, mixed colors.

ADDITIONAL NOTES: Annual phlox is a very colorful and desirable bedding plant when at its best. However, many cultivars reach peak bloom in early summer, decline, and then present a fairly good color display again in late fall. The name *phlox* means flame, and refers to the brilliant coloring of the flowers.

Native to Texas.   Annual

SCIENTIFIC NAME/FAMILY: *Phlox paniculata* (P. decussata)   Polemoniaceae

(floks pan-ik-ū-lā'tȧ)

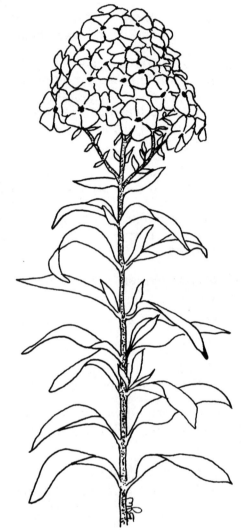

COMMON NAME: Summer Phlox, Garden Phlox, Fall Phlox, Perennial Phlox

LEAVES: Opposite, leaves thin, veiny, oblong-lanceolate to ovate-lanceolate, 3"–5" long, pointed, tapering to the bases; the upper ones partially clasping, the margins minutely bristly-ciliate.

FLOWER: White, pink, red, blue, and purple. Huge clusters (10"–12") of disk-shaped flowers (1" across) arranged in large panicles.

HABIT: 2' to 4' clump-forming plant with stiff, erect stems.

SEASON OF BLOOM: Summer and early fall.

CULTURE: Summer phlox grows best in a fertile, moist soil in sun or partial shade. It should be protected from wind and provided a mulch during the winter. Phlox needs abundant fertilizer and water for optimum growth and flowering in the summer. Summer phlox is a widely grown perennial but it is not a low-maintenance plant. It is susceptible to powdery mildew. If a gardener is prepared to spray every 2 weeks for powdery mildew, summer phlox is unequaled for its showy bloom over a long season. Faded flower clusters should be removed to prolong the blooming period and to prevent self-seeding. This practice will prevent seedlings of inferior color, which will crowd out preferred cultivars.

See color plate

UTILIZATION: Border

PROPAGATION: For the home gardener, division is the easiest method for multiplication. Commercially, the clumps should be dug in the fall, and the large roots should be removed to within 2" of the crown, which is replanted. The root pieces are cut into 2" lengths and placed in flats of sandy soil and covered 1/2". These cuttings can be transplanted in the spring and often will flower during the summer. Summer phlox can also be germinated from seed that has been prechilled at 32°–40°F for 2 weeks.

DISEASES AND INSECTS: Powdery mildew, root rot, phlox plant bug, and two-spotted mite. Powdery mildew is the most serious problem. Garden phlox should be watered at the base with a garden hose or a soaker hose. Overhead watering promotes the incidence of powdery mildew as do afternoon and evening rains.

HARDINESS: Zones 4–8.

CULTIVARS: A wide selection of summer phlox is available to the gardener. A few selections are included here:

'B. Symons-Jeune'—Rose-pink florets with crimson eye, 4' tall.

'Blue Boy'—Dark lavender blue, 24".

'Bright Eyes'—Pale pink petals with a crimson eye, 24".

'David'—White flowers, shows good mildew resistance.

'Dodo Hanbury Forbes'—Very large panicles of light pink flowers, 36" tall.

'Dresden China'—Pastel pink flowers with crimson eye.

'Fairest One'—Pale salmon petals with a white eye, 20".

'Franz Schubert'—Lilac-blue petals with crimson eye, 36" tall.

'Kirchenfurst'—White flowers with a red eye, 4' tall.

'Mt. Fujiyama' ('Mt. Fuji')— Large white flower heads to 15" long. One of the best whites.

'Norah Leigh'—Leaves have a white marbled edge and green midrib. It is noted more for its variegated foliage than for the lavender flowers. Performs better with shade in the afternoon.

'Orange Perfection'—Salmon-orange flowers, 24".

'Pinafore Pink'—Small plants, 6"–12" tall, with bright pink flowers.

'Sir John Falstaff'—Salmon-pink, 30".

'Starfire'—Crimson-red flowers, one of the reddest, 30".

'White Admiral'—Pure white flowers, 2'–3' tall.

RELATED SPECIES:

P. maculata (mak-ū-lā'-ta)—Wild Sweet William. The dark green leaves are linear to lanceolate, 3"–4" long. The flower heads are conical rather than round as found with *P. paniculata*. The major difference between these two species is that *P. maculata* has better powdery mildew resistance. Plants are 2'–3' tall and 2' wide.

'Alpha'—Rose-pink flowers with a dark eye, 3' tall.

'Miss Lingard'—Large, pure white flowers make this an excellent garden selection. It is sometimes listed as a cultivar of *Phlox carolina*.

'Omega'—White flowers with light pink eyes, 30" tall.

'Rosalinde'—Purple-pink flowers, 3'–4' tall.

Native to southeastern United States.   Perennial

SCIENTIFIC NAME/FAMILY: *Phlox subulata* (P. setacea)   Polemoniaceae

(floks sub-ū-lā′tȧ)

COMMON NAME: Moss Pink, Moss Phlox, Mountain Phlox, Ground Pink, Flowering Moss

LEAVES: Opposite leaves are linear to subulate, up to 1″ long.

FLOWER: The flowers are borne in small terminal cymes or panicles atop short, flowering branches. Flower color ranges from red-purple to violet-purple, pink, or white. Individual flowers are approximately ½″ across and the corolla lobes are shallowly notched.

HABIT: 3″–6″ prostrate, dense mound to 2′ wide.

SEASON OF BLOOM: Early to mid-spring.

CULTURE: A very effective ground cover is created when this plant is grown in a sunny site on a well-drained soil, particularly gritty soils, which may be slightly alkaline. Shearing the plants back halfway following flowering will promote dense foliage and some rebloom.

UTILIZATION: The mass of bright flowers is a very welcome sight in the spring after a long winter. The carpetlike mat is useful for edging, walls, and as a ground cover on a sunny slope.

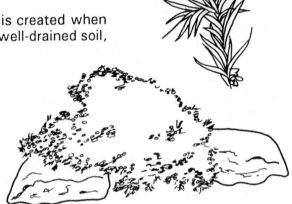

See color plate

PROPAGATION: Propagation is by layering or division after flowering or late fall cuttings rooted in a sandy medium in the greenhouse or cold frame. The root system is shallow and sparse; consequently, the foliage should be cut back before the divisions are replanted.

DISEASES AND INSECTS: Spider mites are a problem during hot weather, especially if the plants are not watered. Rust is sometimes noted, but it is usually not serious enough to warrant control measures.

HARDINESS: Zones 3–9.

CULTIVARS:
　　'Crimson Beauty'—Bright red flowers.
　　'Emerald Cushion'—Pink flowers.
　　'Millstream Coral Eye'—White with a crimson eye.
　　'Millstream Daphne'—Clear pink with a darker eye.
　　'Millstream Jupiter'—Dark blue flowers.
　　'Oakington Blue'—Sky blue flowers.
　　'Red Wings'—Deep crimson with dark red eye.
　　'Scarlet Flame'—Rose red flowers with darker eyes.
　　'White Delight'—Large white flowers.

Native to eastern United States.   Perennial

SCIENTIFIC NAME/FAMILY: *Phygelius capensis*   Scrophulariaceae

(fī-jē'li-us kȧ-pen'sis)

COMMON NAME: Cape Fuchsia, Cape Figwort

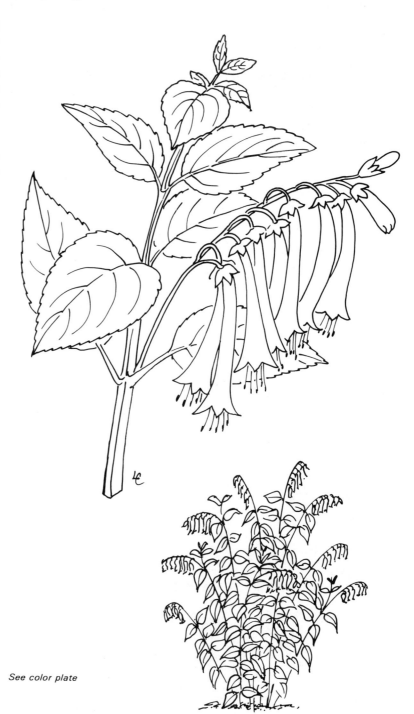

LEAVES: The 2"–5" leaves are opposite and broadly ovate with crenate margins. Leaves higher on the stem are smaller (see drawing). Stems are 4-angled or slightly winged.

FLOWER: The tubular flowers are borne in open panicles that can be 12"–18" long. Individual flowers are red with a yellow throat and are 2" long. The common name of the cape fuchsia is misleading, as this species is more closely related to penstemon and snapdragon than fuchsia.

HABIT: Cape fuchsia is a 4'–5' upright shrubby plant that can grow to 8' on a wall. It is 2' wide.

SEASON OF BLOOM: Summer and early autumn.

CULTURE: This species is native to South Africa. It is evergreen in warm climates but will need more protection in northern areas. In a northern site (Zone 6) place this plant against a south-facing wall. In the fall, cut back the stem and mulch heavily. Soils should be well-drained and moist during the growing season. Pruning will help keep the plants compact. It is a subshrub in southern zones.

See color plate

UTILIZATION: Good selection to plant among massing of other sun-loving plants such as *Perovskia.* It can also be used as a wall plant.

PROPAGATION: Propagation is by seed, division, or cuttings. Seed should be germinated at warm temperatures (75°F) in high humidity. Cuttings or division of the plant can be done in the spring.

DISEASES AND INSECTS: There are no serious problems.

HARDINESS: Zones 6–10.

CULTIVARS:
  'Coccineus'—Darker red corolla with a more pronounced yellow throat.

RELATED SPECIES:
  P. aequalis (ē'-kwol-is)—This species has shorter flowers, denser flower panicles, and salmon-colored flowers. It is 3' tall and 18" wide. 'Yellow Trumpet' ('Cream Trumpet') has creamy, butter-colored flowers. Species and cultivar are hardy to Zones 7–10.

Native to South Africa.   Perennial

SCIENTIFIC NAME/FAMILY: *Phyllitis scolopendrium* (Asplenium scolopendrium)
Polypodiaceae

(fi-lī'tis scō-lō-pend'ri-um)

COMMON NAME: Hart's Tongue Fern

FRONDS: The evergreen fronds are oblong, 12" to 18" long and 1" to 2"
wide, and have a leathery texture.
They are undivided with an auriculate
to heart-shaped leaf base. The leaf
margins are entire or slightly undulating. The stalk is chaffy.

SORI: The sori are linear and are arranged
in rows on each side of the midrib.

HABIT: The strap-shaped fronds are 12"
to 18" tall and are arranged in a circular tuft of 20 or more fronds.

CULTURE: Hart's tongue fern grows best
in full shade and a constantly moist,
well-drained soil. It is intolerant of
drought. Best performance occurs in
calcareous-based soils.

UTILIZATION: This species provides a
nice contrast to most any vegetation.
It makes a good complement to fine-
textured ferns or the bold leaves of
hosta.

PROPAGATION: Hart's tongue fern can
be propagated by division and spores.

DISEASES AND INSECTS: None serious.

HARDINESS: Zones 3 to 8.

ADDITIONAL NOTES: Hart's tongue fern
is a relatively rare fern that is found in
isolated areas of Tennessee, New
York, and Ontario. It is more widely
available in England. There are a number of variations of Hart's tongue fern
that are commercially available.

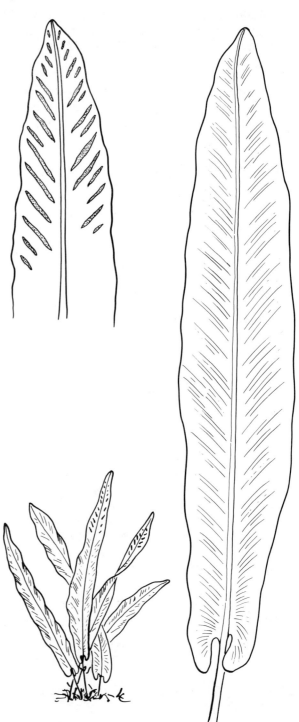

Perennial

SCIENTIFIC NAME/FAMILY: *Physalis alkekengi* (P. franchetii)   Solanaceae

(fī′sȧ-lis al-ke-ken′jē)

COMMON NAME: Chinese Lantern Plant, Alke-kengi, Winter Cherry, Japanese Lantern Strawberry Tomato, Bladder Cherry, Strawberry Ground Cherry.

LEAVES: Alternate, ovate to ovate-rhombic, with a wide base, 2″–3″ long, short acuminate, angular, entire or undulate margin, petiole widening at the top.

FLOWER: White, borne in axillary positions, usually not showy. The large, inflated red calyx is the ornamental feature of the plant.

HABIT: 18″ to 24″, round habit.

SEASON OF BLOOM: The spring flower is insignificant. The showy orange-red calyx, which resembles a Chinese lantern, is present in late summer.

CULTURE: Full sun and well-drained soil. Less success is possible if planted in shaded or poorly drained sites.

UTILIZATION: The fruiting stems of Chinese lantern are useful in dried floral arrangements in autumn and winter. Plants in the perennial border will add a bright color in the fall, but they can quickly become invasive because of their ability to spread by underground stems. A gardener should think long and hard before placing this species in the border, because of its invasive tendency.

See color plate

PROPAGATION: The easiest method of propagation is to dig and separate the plants into rooted pieces in the spring and replant.

DISEASES AND INSECTS: The striped cucumber beetle and flea beetle can quickly devour the foliage.

HARDINESS: Zones 3–9.

CULTIVARS:
'Gigantea'—This selection is 4′ tall with large orange fruits that can be up to 8″ wide.
'Pygmea'—Dwarf form, 12″–15″ tall.

ADDITIONAL NOTES: *Physalis* is derived from *physa,* which means bladder, and refers to the large calyx.

Native from southeastern Europe to Japan.   Perennial

SCIENTIFIC NAME/FAMILY: *Physostegia virginiana*

(fī-so-stē'ji-ȧ vĕr-jin-i-ā'nȧ)

Lamiaceae
(Labiatae)

COMMON NAME: False Dragonhead, Obedient
Plant, Stay-in-Place, Lions-heart

LEAVES: Opposite, oblong to lanceolate, 3"–5"
long, serrate, acuminate; floral leaves bract-
like, lanceolate; square stems.

FLOWER: Spikes closely flowered, usually panicled, corolla showy, to 1¼" long, rose
purple or white; flowers are arranged in 4
widely spaced vertical rows.

HABIT: 2' to 4' erect plant with a 3' width.

SEASON OF BLOOM: Late summer and fall.

CULTURE: Obedient plant grows well in sun or
partial shade in most soils although low pH
soils are ideal. This species will usually
require staking especially when grown in
high fertility soils. It is an aggressive spreader which will require frequent lifting and
rogueing of plants.

UTILIZATION: Cut flowers, backgrounds, naturalization in semi-wild areas or informal wild
flower garden. Use in perennial borders only
if it can be easily kept in bounds.

See color plate

PROPAGATION: Seeds will germinate in 2 to 3 weeks at 70°–75°F. Division every two
years in spring will prevent the plant from becoming invasive.

DISEASES AND INSECTS: Rust is an occasional problem.

HARDINESS: Zones 3–9.

CULTIVARS:
var. *alba*—Pure white flowers on spikes 18"–24" tall.
'Bouquet Rose'—3'–3½', rose-pink flowers.
'Summer Snow'—2½', white flowers, less invasive but will still need frequent division.
'Variegata'—Green and white variegated leaves, pink flowers, 3' tall.
'Vivid'—Rosy-pink flowers, compact, but just as invasive, 20".

ADDITIONAL NOTES: The two common names have an interesting derivation. False
dragonhead refers to the early confusion of this genus with *Dracocephalum* (Dragonhead). Obedient plant refers to the ability of individual flowers to be twisted on the
stem and remain as they are arranged. The genus name is a derivation from the Greek
words, *physa,* bladder; *stege,* roof covering, and refers to the fruit which are covered
by an inflated calyx.

Native to eastern North America.

Perennial

SCIENTIFIC NAME/FAMILY: *Platycodon grandiflorus* (P. glaucus)   Campanulaceae

(plat-i-kō'don gran-di-flō'rus)

COMMON NAME: Balloon Flower, Japanese Bell-flower, Chinese Bellflower

LEAVES: The leaves are ovate to ovate-lanceolate, 1"–3" long, short-petioled and acute. The leaf margins are sharply dentate. The alternate leaves are glabrous with glaucous-blue lower surfaces.

FLOWER: Usually blue, but white and pink are also available. Flowers are saucer-shaped 2"–3" across. Buds are balloon-shaped and pop when squeezed. Flowers are terminated on long branches or peduncles.

HABIT: 24" to 36". The species is often erect but smaller cultivars have a round habit.

SEASON OF BLOOM: Summer.

CULTURE: Balloon flower is an adaptable perennial that grows well in sun or partial shade in a well-drained soil that is slightly acid. It does not tolerate wet soil. *Platycodon* is slow to emerge in the spring so care is needed to prevent cutting the crown off during early cultivation.

UTILIZATION: Cutting, rock garden, border. Keeps very well (1 week) as a cut flower if the ends of the stems are seared with a flame before they are placed in water.

See color plate

PROPAGATION: Seed or division. *Platycodon* is easily grown from seed and will flower the second year. Germination occurs in 2 to 3 weeks at 65°–70°F. Division is more difficult but not impossible. The roots are very coarse, like stringy carrot roots, and one must dig deeply to aid transplant success. Division is usually best in the spring, especially in northern areas.

DISEASES AND INSECTS: Pest and disease free.

HARDINESS: Zones 3–8. Excellent plant for northern and southern gardens.

CULTIVARS:
    var. *album*—White-flowered form of the species.
    'Apoyama'—Violet-blue flowers on stems 10" tall. Flowers almost all summer.
    'Double Blue'—Double blue flowers, 18"–24" tall.
    'Fuji'—This is a seed-grown series available in blue, white or pink colors. It is often used for cut flowers.
    'Hakone Blue'—Double blue flowers, 20" tall.
    var. *mariesii*—Compact, 18" tall, bright blue flowers.

'Sentimental' Series—Compact selection, 6″–8″ tall and 12″–15″ wide. Available in blue or white.

'Shell Pink'—Soft shell-pink flowers, coloring best in semishade, 18″–24″ tall.

ADDITIONAL NOTES: *Platycodon* is Greek for "broad bell," referring to the shape of the flowers. The common name of balloon flower describes the inflated balloon-like buds.

Native to eastern Asia.   Perennial

SCIENTIFIC NAME/FAMILY: *Podophyllum peltatum*   Berberidaceae

(pō-dō-fil'um pel-tā'tum)

COMMON NAME: Mayapple, Mandrake, Ground Lemon

LEAVES: Two pale green leaves are borne at the top of the flowering stem. The leaf may measure 12" in diameter and has 5–9 palmately arranged lobes. The lobes are oblong and usually 2-cleft and dentate at the apex.

FLOWER: The ill-smelling, white flowers are solitary and nodding and are borne on the fork between the two leaves. Flowers usually have 6 petals. A yellow ovoid-shaped berry, 1"–2" long, follows the flower.

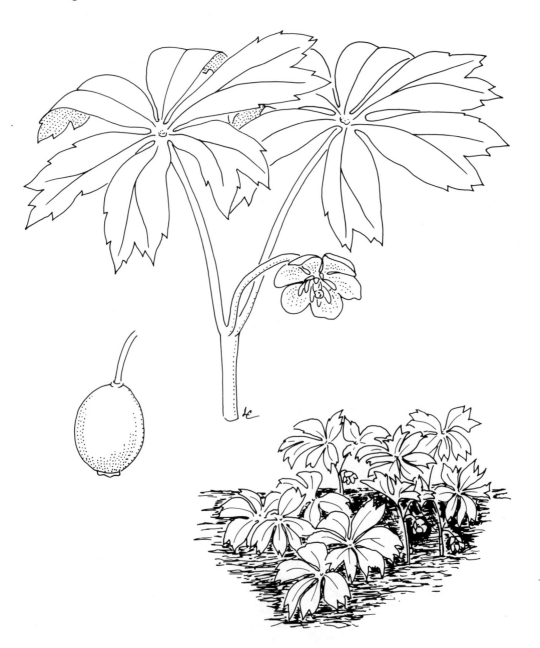

HABIT: Individual plants with one stem colonize to create a ground cover effect. Plants are 12"–18" tall and 12" wide.

SEASON OF BLOOM: Early to mid spring.

CULTURE: Best growth occurs in partial shade in a moist soil with an acid pH (5–6). After establishment, mayapple is a vigorous colonizer. In small gardens it should be contained in a buried pot.

UTILIZATION: Mayapple can be used to create a carpet of green beneath deciduous trees in a moist, woodland setting. The bold leaf texture can be a nice contrast to the fine texture of native ferns. Since the nodding flowers are hidden from above by the large leaves, the plants are best located on slopes above a walk, where the flowers will be more visible. Due to its spreading tendencies, mayapple is not for the small garden.

PROPAGATION: Division of the rhizomes in late summer or spring is the easiest method. Seeds can be used but germination is slow even following stratification. It is best to collect the fruit and sow fresh seeds.

DISEASES AND INSECTS: None serious.

HARDINESS: Zones 4–8.

Native to eastern North America   Perennial

SCIENTIFIC NAME/FAMILY: *Polemonium caeruleum* (P. sibiricum)   Polemoniaceae

(pol-e-mō'ni-um se-rū'lē-um)

COMMON NAME: Jacob's Ladder, Greek Valerian, Charity

LEAVES: Alternate, basal leaves form dense mounds, odd-pinnate, 3"– 5" long, 11–21 leaflets, lanceolate and acuminate, 1" long; stem leaves are smaller and nearly sessile.

FLOWER: Blue, pink, or white cup-shaped flowers borne in loose panicled clusters, 4" to 6" long.

HABIT: 18"–24" erect plant with a large clump of basal foliage.

SEASON OF BLOOM: Late spring to early summer.

CULTURE: Full sun or partial shade in soil of average fertility and good drainage. Jacob's ladder does poorly in sites that are extremely hot and sunny; in these locations, the foliage becomes unsightly.

UTILIZATION: Rock garden and the perennial border. The neat, compound foliage adds interest to the garden, and the blue flowers appear at a time when there are few blues in the garden.

PROPAGATION: Seed, cutting, and division. It takes 3–4 weeks to germinate the seed at 70°. Stem cuttings of the selected cultivars should be taken in midsummer. Larger clumps can be divided in late summer.

See color plate

DISEASES AND INSECTS: Leaf spots, powdery mildew, rusts, and wilt have been reported as pests; but none are usually serious enough to warrant control.

HARDINESS: Zones 3–7.

CULTIVARS:
var. *album*—White flower form of the species.

RELATED SPECIES:

    P. foliosissimum (fō-lē-ō-sis'-si-mum). A vigorous growing species which is a stronger grower than *P. caeruleum.* This species is a good choice for the garden but it is seldom available in North America even though it is native to western United States. Plants are 24"–30" tall and 24" wide.

ADDITIONAL NOTES: The leaves are arranged in a ladderlike formation, hence the common name Jacob's ladder.

Native to North America.   Perennial

SCIENTIFIC NAME/FAMILY: *Polemonium reptans* (P. humile)   Polemoniaceae

(pol-e-mō'ni-um rep'-tanz)

COMMON NAME: Creeping Jacob's Ladder, Creeping Polemonium

LEAVES: Alternate, pinnately compound leaves, 8" long with 7–19 leaflets. Leaflets are lanceolate to oblong, 1" long, and entire.

FLOWER: Blue, bell-shaped flowers are ¾" long, borne in a loose corymb-type inflorescence.

HABIT: 12"–15" mounded perennial, which may sprawl due to weak stems, but it does not creep as the name might suggest.

SEASON OF BLOOM: Mid spring to early summer.

CULTURE: A moist, well-drained soil in partial shade is the optimum placement. Plants grown in drier sites will incur scorch on the leaf tips.

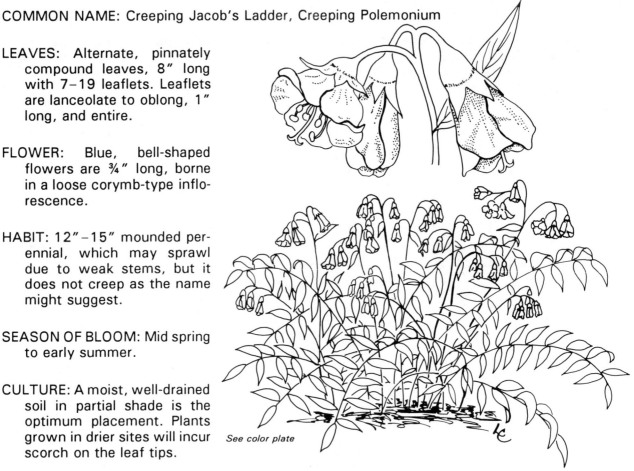

See color plate

UTILIZATION: Good in naturalized settings or in the partially shaded rock garden.

PROPAGATION: Division in spring or fall, summer tip cuttings, or seed are all suitable propagation methods.

DISEASES AND INSECTS: No serious problems.

HARDINESS: Zones 3–8.

CULTIVARS:
   var. *alba*—White flowers.
   'Blue Pearl'—Medium blue flowers on 12" tall stems.

Native to United States.   Perennial

SCIENTIFIC NAME/FAMILY: *Polygonatum biflorum*   Liliaceae

(pō-lig-ō-nā'tum or po-li-gō-nā'-tum bī-flōr'um)

COMMON NAME: Small Solomon's Seal

LEAVES: Alternate, sessile, ovate-lanceolate to ovate, up to 4" long, 1"–2" wide, pale and pubescent lower leaf surface, upper side is glabrous. Foliage turns a nice brownish yellow in the fall.

FLOWER: Yellowish green to greenish white, ½" to 1" long, on 1 to 3 flowered peduncles. Flowers are borne on the lower side of the upper parts of the leafy stem. The flowers are followed by bluish black fruit in the fall.

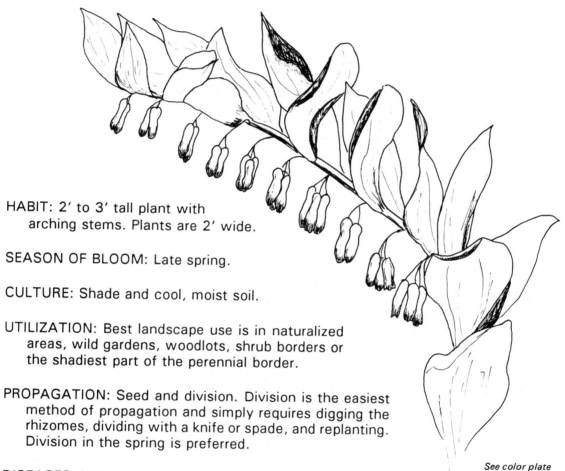

HABIT: 2' to 3' tall plant with arching stems. Plants are 2' wide.

SEASON OF BLOOM: Late spring.

CULTURE: Shade and cool, moist soil.

UTILIZATION: Best landscape use is in naturalized areas, wild gardens, woodlots, shrub borders or the shadiest part of the perennial border.

PROPAGATION: Seed and division. Division is the easiest method of propagation and simply requires digging the rhizomes, dividing with a knife or spade, and replanting. Division in the spring is preferred.

See color plate

DISEASES AND INSECTS: There are no serious insect or disease problems.

HARDINESS: Zones 3–9. Solomon's seal is a native plant of North America and is at home in various climatic zones.

RELATED SPECIES:

P. commutatum (kom-mu-tā'-tum)—Great Solomon's Seal. This is the giant of the *Polygonatum* genus. It is normally 3'–5' tall but can grow to 7 feet. The late spring flowers are greenish-white with 3–8 flowers at each axil. Plants will form large groupings, so it is not ideal for the small garden. It is more favored when used at the edge of a woodland. Culture requirements include partial shade and moist soil.

P. odoratum (ō-dō-rā'-tum) 'Variegatum'—Variegated Solomon's Seal. The leaf margins and tips are edged with white. This cultivar is an excellent choice for the garden especially in the shade area where the variegated leaves make a statement. The leaves can also be cut and used in floral arrangements. It is 2' to 3' tall and is hardy in Zones 3–9.

Native to North America.   Perennial

SCIENTIFIC NAME/FAMILY: *Polygonum affine* (*Persicaria affinis*)   Polygonaceae
(pō-lig′ō-num af-fin′-e)

COMMON NAME: Himalayan Fleeceflower

LEAVES: Basal leaves, oblanceolate or spatulate in shape, with the leaf base tapering into a petiole. Leaves are 3″ to 4″ long, dark green with a prominent white midvein, and the margins are finely serrated.

FLOWER: The bright rose flowers are small but very numerous. They are packed tightly in a spike 2″ to 3″ long, which terminates in a 6″ tall, red peduncle.

HABIT: Mat-forming ground cover, 9″ tall with a spread of 12″.

SEASON OF BLOOM: Mid to late summer.

CULTURE: This species should be grown in a sunny location with a moist soil. Moist soil is particularly important if a dense planting is desired.

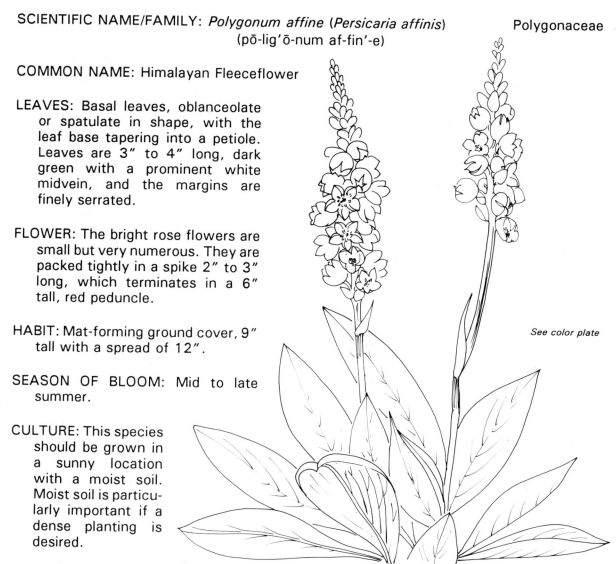

See color plate

UTILIZATION: The neat tufted habit is perfect for the border front, the rock garden, or the edge of a pool or slow moving stream.

PROPAGATION: Division in the spring or fall is the easiest propagation method. Tip cuttings and seed propagation can also be used.

DISEASES AND INSECTS: None serious.

HARDINESS: Zones 3–7.

CULTIVARS:
'Darjeeling Red'—Dark pink flowers which mature to a crimson color. It is 9″ tall and vigorous.
'Dimity'—This Alan Bloom introduction is more compact with denser foliage. It makes a nice carpet perennial.
'Donald Lowndes'—Double salmon-pink flowers, 8″–10″ tall.
'Superba'—(also listed as 'Superbum')—Profuse blooming selection with good vigor and rose-pink flowers that mature to crimson.

Native to Himalayas.

Perennial

SCIENTIFIC NAME/FAMILY: *Polygonum bistorta* (*Persicaria bistorta*)   Polygonaceae

(pō-lig′ō-num bis-tōr′ta)

COMMON NAME: European Bistort

LEAVES: The basal leaves are large and resemble large paddles. They are 8″–10″ long and 3″ to 5″ wide. The blade narrows to a petiole, which is sometimes winged. The leaves are dark green with a prominent, white midrib. The foliage resembles the common garden or field weed, *Rumex* or dock.

FLOWER: Clear pink flowers are tightly clustered in a spike held atop a long, slender, usually leafless peduncle. This arrangement gives an appearance of a long pink poker or pink bottle brush.

HABIT: Large clump-forming plant with flower spikes 24″ to 30″ tall and a width of 24″.

SEASON OF BLOOM: Late spring to midsummer.

CULTURE: Full sun or partial shade with constantly moist soil is ideal. It can tolerate wet soil but must be given more shade where soil conditions are drier and the summers hotter.

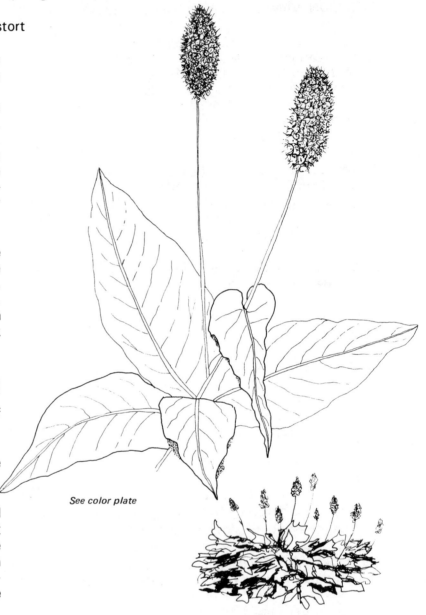

See color plate

UTILIZATION: Useful plant for the border, and in areas of moist to wet soils such as the edges of ponds, pools, and streams.

PROPAGATION: Division in the spring or fall or seed propagation.

DISEASES AND INSECTS: No serious problems.

HARDINESS: Zones 3–8.

CULTIVARS:
  'Superbum'—This cultivar is slightly taller, with larger flowers and flower spikes. It is the favored selection.

RELATED SPECIES:

P. amplexicaule (am-plek-si-kâl'-e) — Mountain Fleece. 3' tall. Leaves are ovate to lanceolate, 6" long; the upper leaves clasp the stem. Flowers are rose red. 'Atrosanguineum' has darker red flowers and 'Firetail' has large spikes of bright red flowers, 3' to 4'. Mountain fleece flowers from early summer to fall. A new introduction from Bloom's of Bressingham is 'Taurus.' This cultivar is compact with large leaves and bright scarlet flowers. 30" tall.

P. milettii (mil-et'-ē-ī) — This species is similar to European bistort, but the leaves are narrower and the growth habit is stiff. The flowers are crimson, and the spikes are smaller than *P. bistorta* 'Superbum'. 18"–24" tall.

Native to northern Europe.   Perennial

SCIENTIFIC NAME/FAMILY: *Polygonum capitatum* 'Magic Carpet'   Polygonaceae
(*Persicaria capitatum*)
(pō-lig'ō-num kap-i-tā'tum)

COMMON NAME: Magic Carpet Polygonum, Pinkhead Knotweed

LEAVES: Alternate, leaves elliptic to 1½" long, variegated, bronze-red foliage.

FLOWER: Flowers pink in dense heads ¾" across.

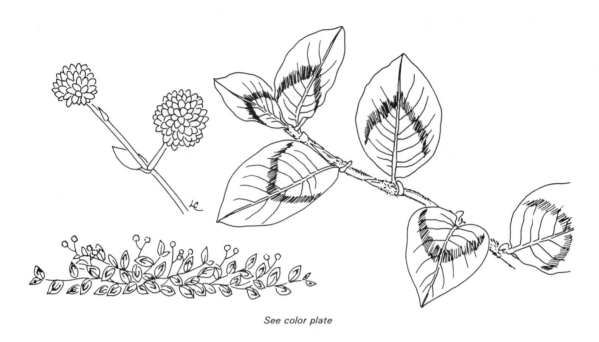

See color plate

HABIT: Low, dense masses of bronzy-red foliage, 2"–3" tall.

SEASON OF BLOOM: Mid-summer.

CULTURE: Full sun or partial shade; tolerates wet areas. Pinkhead knotweed is an easily
grown annual. It can be placed in full sun or partial shade and is tolerant to heat. Plants
do well in a wide variety of soils including dry, infertile soils or wet soils.

UTILIZATION: Ground cover, rock garden, hanging baskets, planters.

PROPAGATION: Seed germinates easily at 70°–80°F after 3 weeks.

DISEASES AND INSECTS: None serious.

CULTIVARS:
'Magic Carpet' is one of the best annual ground covers we have, but is also useful in
hanging baskets, planters, and rock gardens. A strong grower, yet not weedy.

ADDITIONAL NOTES: *Polygonum* is taken from the Greek, *poly,* many, and *gony,* a knee
joint, and refers to the swollen-jointed stems.

Native to Asia, Australia.   Annual

SCIENTIFIC NAME/FAMILY: *Polygonum cuspidatum*   Polygonaceae

(pō-lig'ō-num kus-pi-dā'-tum)

COMMON NAME: Japanese Knotweed, Mexican-bamboo

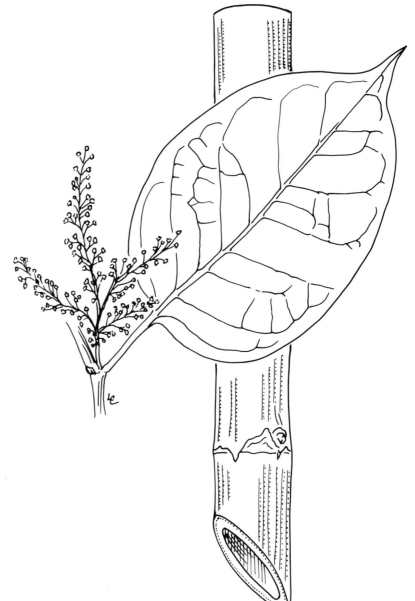

LEAVES: Alternate leaves, 4"–5" long, ovate shape, abruptly acuminate, leaf base rounded to truncate; 1" long petiole. The hollow main stem is ¾" in diameter, resembling the jointed stems of bamboo. The common name Mexican bamboo reflects this resemblance.

FLOWER: The greenish-white flowers are very small. They are borne in loose, axillary panicled racemes. The inflorescences are usually shorter than the leaves. Flowers are not important as an ornamental feature.

HABIT: Upright growing specimen, similar to bamboo; 8' tall with a 4' spread.

SEASON OF BLOOM: Mid to late summer.

CULTURE: Full sun to partial shade, moist to wet soils.

UTILIZATION: Japanese knotweed should only be placed in very large gardens or in wild gardens. This species will quickly colonize due to rhizomes that spread and send up the stout stems. In some areas it can be used as a specimen group in a grassed area where the spread can be controlled by frequent mowing. In large areas, it has great landscape beauty but it is not a plant for the small, refined garden.

PROPAGATION: Easily propagated by division in spring or fall.

DISEASES AND INSECTS: No serious problems. In areas where the plant has become a weedy pest, the gardener may wish for an insect or disease problem.

HARDINESS: Zones 5–9.

RELATED SPECIES:

Polygonum sachalinense (sak-al-in-en'-se) — Giant Knotweed. This species resembles a Japanese knotweed on steroids. The leaves are 12″ long and the stems rise 10–12 feet high. It is more vigorous in growth than Japanese knotweed. A very large area, perhaps along a stream, is required for this potential garden thug.

Native to Japan.   Perennial

SCIENTIFIC NAME/FAMILY: *Polygonum cuspidatum* var. *compactum*   Polygonaceae
(P. reynoutria)

(pō-lig'ō-num kus-pi-dā'tum kom-pak'tum)

COMMON NAME: Reynoutria Fleeceflower

LEAVES: Leaves alternate, short-oval to orbicular-ovate, abruptly pointed, petiole to 1"
long, sheaths short, deciduous; stems are jointed.

FLOWER: Pink flowers borne in panicled racemes.

HABIT: 12" to 18", spreading growth habit.

SEASON OF BLOOM: Midsummer to frost.

CULTURE: Best site is one with full sun and semi-dry soil conditions. *Polygonum* is
adaptable to a wide variety of exposures and soils. It spreads by rhizomes and can
become very invasive.

UTILIZATION: Ground cover. Quite useful for large areas or banks in full sun where other
ground covers, such as *Pachysandra,* are not effective. It spreads by rhizomes and can
become very invasive.

PROPAGATION: Reproduction is easiest with spring division.

DISEASES AND INSECTS: There are no serious diseases or insects.

HARDINESS: Zones 5-9. Fleeceflower grows well in the south.

RELATED SPECIES:
P. aubertii (â-ber'-tē-ī), Silver Fleece Vine. Twining perennial vine to 20', white flowers
in July and August, rapid grower.

ADDITIONAL NOTES: *Polygonum* is derived from Greek *poly*, many, and *gony,* knee joint,
and is in reference to the swollen-jointed stems. Light green foliage turns to crimson in
the fall.

Native to Japan.

Perennial

SCIENTIFIC NAME/FAMILY: *Polystichum acrostichoides*   Aspleniaceae

(pō-lis'ti-kum ak-rōs'tik-oy'dez)

COMMON NAME: Christmas Fern

FRONDS: The evergreen fronds are lance-shaped, once-pinnate. Pinnae are narrowly lance-shaped and bristly serrated. The stipe and rachis are quite chaffy. The fertile and sterile fronds are quite different. The sterile fronds are shorter and usually broader, while the fertile fronds are longer, slender and contracted near the apex.

SORI: The tan sori nearly cover the lower surface of the fertile pinnae.

HABIT: Two-foot-tall leaves, rising from the crown, create a bushy habit which is 24" wide.

CULTURE: Partial shade in moist, well-drained soil is the optimum site for Christmas fern.

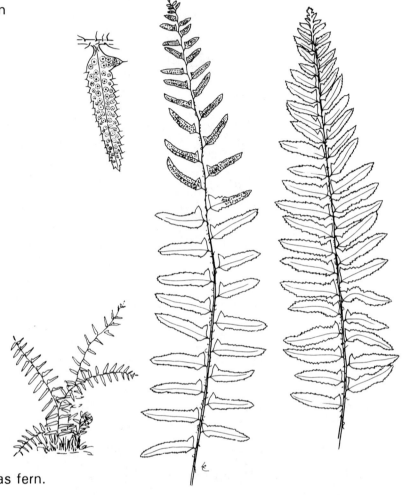

UTILIZATION: Christmas fern is useful as a border plant. The dark green foliage provides a good backdrop for smaller plants. The dark green leathery fronds are often cut and used in floral decorations and wreaths.

PROPAGATION: Propagation is by dividing the crowns in the spring or growing the plants from spores.

DISEASES AND INSECTS: No problems.

HARDINESS: Zones 3 to 9.

ADDITIONAL NOTES: Christmas fern is native from New Brunswick to Florida and east of the Mississippi River.

Perennial

SCIENTIFIC NAME/FAMILY: *Polystichum braunii*   Aspleniaceae

(pō-lis′ti-kum brawn′ē-ī)

COMMON NAME: Braun's Holly Fern, Shield Fern, Tassel Fern

FRONDS: The fronds are thick, twice-pinnate, 18″ to 30″ tall, 6″ to 8″ wide. The pinnules are profusely covered with hairs and scales. The rachis and stipe (stalk below the blade) are covered with golden-brown chaff. The chaff is very noticeable and ornamental.

SORI: The sori are clustered along the midveins of the pinnules.

HABIT: Dense, upright fern with a lacy foliage, 2′ tall.

CULTURE: Best grown in cool woodland soil that has good moisture retention.

UTILIZATION: Large fern for the shaded border or woodland garden.

PROPAGATION: Crown division is the fastest but spore propagation also works well.

DISEASES AND INSECTS: No serious insects or diseases.

HARDINESS: Zones 3-8.

ADDITIONAL NOTES: Braun's holly fern is native to deep woods of the northeastern United States.

Perennial

SCIENTIFIC NAME/FAMILY: *Portulaca grandiflora*   Portulacaceae

(pōr-tū-lā′kȧ gran-di-flō′ra)

See color plate

COMMON NAME: Rose Moss, Moss Rose, Portulaca, Sun Plant

LEAVES: Prostrate or ascending, with loose hairs at the joints and among the flowers, leaves scattered, terete, 1″ or less long, mostly long and prominent beneath the flowers, very succulent.

FLOWER: Flowers 1″ and more across, in bright colors, rose, red, yellow, white, striped; sepals broad, short acute; petals obovate, more or less notched at the end. There are singles and doubles. Flowers close in mid-afternoon.

HABIT: 6″ to 8″ spreading plant.

SEASON OF BLOOM: Early summer to frost.

CULTURE: Sun, hot and dry—where many flowers will not grow.

UTILIZATION: Rock garden, ground cover, edging. It is good for direct seeding in areas where perennials will die down to leave a void.

PROPAGATION: Seed germinates best at a constant 70°F. Seeds can also be sown directly where the plant is to grow.

DISEASES AND INSECTS: Usually none serious.

CULTIVARS:
   'Afternoon Delight'—This sun loving cultivar has flowers that stay open all day long. The mixture contains many bright colors.
   'Cabaret Mix'—Double flowers, wide color range. This F_2 hybrid is compact and flowers early.
   'Calypso Mixture'—Flowers nearly 100% double, wide range of colors, F_2 hybrid.
   'Double Mixture'—Double flowers (85%–90%), brilliant assortment of colors, F_2 hybrid.

'Minilaca Mixture'—Dwarf, non-trailing plant. The flowers are double and come in colors of scarlet, rose, pink, yellow, and cream. This is an open-pollinated selection.

'Sundance Mix'—This F_2 mixture has semidouble flowers that stay open most of the day. Colors include red, orange, yellow, cream, and white.

'Sundial' Series—This F_1 hybrid has large flowers which open early in the morning and stay open longer. Available in 7 colors and a mixture.

'Sunglo'—Excellent improvement over open-pollinated types, double flowers, longer flowering season, vigorous grower, 10 colors available.

ADDITIONAL NOTES: A succulent with narrow, fleshy leaves. *Portulaca* is derived from the Latin words *porto,* to carry, and *lac,* milk, and refers to the milky sap of some species.

Native to Brazil.   Annual

SCIENTIFIC NAME/FAMILY: *Potentilla nepalensis*   Rosaceae

(pō-ten-til'á ne-pal-en'-sis)

COMMON NAME: Nepal Cinquefoil

LEAVES: The palmately compound leaves have 5
    leaflets. Leaflets are 1″ to 2½″ long, obovate to
    oblanceolate, and coarsely dentate.

FLOWER: The branching stems bear flower heads
    that have 1″ pubescent, cup-shaped blossoms.
    The species has 5 petals, cultivars may be semi-
    double or double. The flowers are deep rose in
    color.

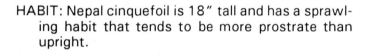

HABIT: Nepal cinquefoil is 18″ tall and has a sprawl-
    ing habit that tends to be more prostrate than
    upright.

SEASON OF BLOOM: Late spring to summer.

CULTURE: Nepal cinquefoil performs best in full sun
    and a well-drained soil. Optimum growth will oc-
    cur in climatic regions which have moderate
    summers and winters. This species does not
    grow well in extremes of heat or cold.

See color plate

UTILIZATION: This species and its cultivars are suited for the rock garden where the
    sprawling habit can spread over the stone work. If it is placed in the border, it should
    be massed so the weak stems can support one another.

PROPAGATION: Cinquefoil can be propagated by seed. It is easy to germinate with con-
    stant moisture and a temperature of 70°F. Division in fall or spring is also a good meth-
    od.

DISEASES AND INSECTS: No serious problems.

HARDINESS: Zones 5-8.

CULTIVARS:
    'Miss Willmott'—Cherry pink flowers, 12″ tall. This and the next cultivar come true
        from seed.
    'Roxana'—Bright rosy-orange flowers, 15″ tall.

RELATED SPECIES:

P. atrosanguinea (at-rō-san-gwin'-ē-à), Himalayan Cinquefoil, Ruby Cinquefoil. This species also has 5-fingered foliage and a sprawling habit. The leaflets are silvery beneath. Zones 5–8. It has hybridized with *P. argyrophylla* and *P. nepalensis* to give rise to the following cultivars:

'Fire Dance'—Flower has a scarlet center with a wide, yellow border, 15″ tall.
'Gibson's Scarlet'—Red, single flowers, 15″ tall.
'William Rollison'—Deep orange and yellow flowers, semidouble, 18″ tall.
'Yellow Queen'—Bright, clear yellow flowers, 12″ tall.

Native to Nepal.   Perennial

SCIENTIFIC NAME/FAMILY: *Potentilla tridentata*   Rosaceae

(pō-ten-til'å tri-den-tā'tå)

COMMON NAME: Wineleaf Cinquefoil, Three-Toothed Cinquefoil

LEAVES: Palmately compound, 3 leaflets. Leaflets leathery, evergreen, cuneate-oblong, 3 to 5 notches at tip, usually glabrous. The foliage is shiny-green.

FLOWER: White flowers, ¼" wide, borne in a sparsely branched cyme.

HABIT: Prostrate spreader, 2" to 6" tall.

SEASON OF BLOOM: Late spring to midsummer.

CULTURE: Full sun in a well-drained soil, preferably a slightly acid, sandy loam.

UTILIZATION: Rock gardens, dry slopes, and ground cover.

See color plate

PROPAGATION: Division in spring or fall is an easy method.

DISEASES AND INSECTS: No serious problems.

HARDINESS: Zones 2–8.

CULTIVARS:
    'Minima'—Low growing selection, 3" tall. This form makes a nice "carpet" over the soil.

Native to northeastern North America.   Perennial

SCIENTIFIC NAME/FAMILY: *Potentilla verna* (tabernaemontani)   Rosaceae

(pō-ten-til'a ver'na)

COMMON NAME: Spring Cinquefoil

LEAVES: The stems of this potentilla are prostrate. The leaves are palmately compound with 5 leaflets, sometimes 3. The leaflets are cuneate at the base and have 3–7 teeth on each side. The leaflets are 1/2" to 3/4" long and are pilose on both surfaces.

FLOWER: The golden-yellow flowers are 3/8" to 1/2" wide and borne in a few flowered, loose cymes. Individual flowers have 5 petals, which are obovate.

HABIT: Very prostrate, 2"–3" tall, with stems trailing to 20".

SEASON OF BLOOM: Mid to late spring.

CULTURE: Full sun and a well-drained soil is the best combination.

UTILIZATION: A useful plant for dry walls or sites which need a prostrate, deciduous ground cover. This species is a vigorous grower and will spread through a border planting unless the creeping stems are cut back.

PROPAGATION: Division in spring or fall is easy. The stems tend to root forming a mat so it is easy to dig clumps of this plant.

DISEASES AND INSECTS: I have not seen any insect or disease check the growth of this plant.

HARDINESS: Zones 4–8.

CULTIVARS:
    'Nana'—Yellow flowers are slightly larger than the species, 4" tall.

Native to Europe.   Perennial

SCIENTIFIC NAME/FAMILY: *Primula* × *polyantha*   Primulaceae

(prim'ū-là pol-i-an'thà)

COMMON NAME: Polyanthus Primrose

LEAVES: Basal leaves, obovate, tapering to a winged petiole, wrinkled leaves.

FLOWER: Flowers are available in a
wide range of colors; flowers may
be solitary or in many-flowered umbels on scapes
longer than the leaves.

HABIT: 6" to 12" erect flower
stems with basal leaves.

SEASON OF BLOOM: Spring.
Primula is derived from the
Latin *primus,* meaning first,
and is apparently so named
because of the early flowering.

CULTURE: Partial shade is imperative along with a cool
and moist soil containing
abundant organic matter. A summer mulch and deep watering during dry periods are
essential. Cold winters and hot summers are not desirable for *Primula.*

UTILIZATION: Shaded areas in the perennial border and naturalized along shaded streams.

PROPAGATION: Seed and division. Seeds germinate in 3–6 weeks at 68°F. Collecting and
sowing seeds as soon as they ripen is ideal. Clumps can be divided after flowering.

DISEASES AND INSECTS: Spider mites and slugs are the major problems with polyanthus
primrose.

HARDINESS: Zones 3–8.

CULTIVARS: There are unnamed polyanthus primroses with mixed or separate colors in
addition to several named cultivars.
'Barnhaven Hybrids'—Bright-colored flowers on compact plants, heat tolerant and free
flowering.
'Crescendo'—Good garden strain with large flowers, 12" tall.
'Pacific Giants'—Free-flowering cultivar with large flowers, over 2" wide, and an
extensive range of colors.

RELATED SPECIES:

P. denticulata (den-tik-u-lā'-ta), Himalayan Primrose. Lilac flowers in a round floral head to 2" across and 12" tall. Blooms in midspring. This species needs moist to boggy soil.

P. japonica (jȧ-pon'i-ka), Japanese Primrose. Red, white, pink, or crimson colored flowers, starting in late spring. Plant has many umbels superimposed in tiers. This 2' tall species also requires moist to wet soils.

P. vulgaris (vul-gā'ris), *(P. acaulis),* Common Primrose. Fragrant, early flowering primrose. Flowers are available in various colors.

Hybrid origin.   Perennial

SCIENTIFIC NAME/FAMILY: *Prunella grandiflora*   Lamiaceae
                                                                  (Labiatae)

(pru-nel'a grand-di-flō'ra)

COMMON NAME: Bigflower Selfheal

LEAVES: Opposite leaves, lanceolate to ovate, 2"–3" long, entire or slightly toothed. The stems and leaves are sparsely pilose.

FLOWER: The hooded, violet-blue flowers are carried in a tight-clustered spike at the top of the stem. The upper lip is 2-lobed, the lower is 3-lobed. Flowers have 4 stamens.

HABIT: Low, broad clump, 12" tall and 12" wide.

SEASON OF BLOOM: Early summer.

CULTURE: In cooler zones, *Prunella* can be grown in full sun or in an ordinary well-drained soil. In warmer zones, *Prunella* should be placed in partial shade in a fertile, moist soil. The seed spikes need to be removed before maturity. *Prunella* will self-seed, and flowering seedlings will be different colors.

UTILIZATION: Good plant for a frontal position in the border.

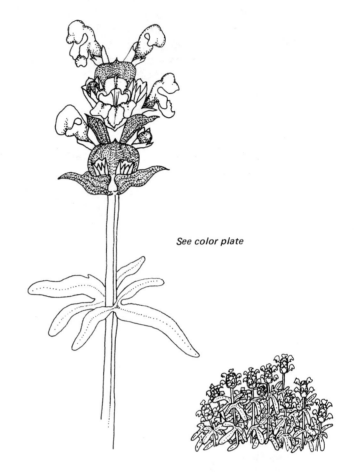

See color plate

PROPAGATION: Spring or fall division are suitable methods for propagation. Seed is also an option, but with cultivars the plants are usually not true to type.

DISEASES AND INSECTS: None serious.

HARDINESS: Zones 4–8.

CULTIVARS:
   'Little Red Riding Hood'—Red flowers; also known as 'Rotkappchen'; 6" tall.
   'Loveliness'—Pale violet flowers.
   'Pink Loveliness'—Clear bright pink flowers.
   'White Loveliness'—White flowers, very excellent cultivar.
   The above cultivars are probably hybrids of *P. grandiflora* × *P. hastifolia*. Some catalogs list the cultivars under *P.* × *webbiana*.

Native to Europe.   Perennial

SCIENTIFIC NAME/FAMILY: *Pulmonaria angustifolia* (P. azurea)   Boraginaceae

(pul-mo-nā'ri-á an-gus-ti-fō'li-a)

COMMON NAME: Blue Lungwort, Cowslip Lungwort

LEAVES: Alternate, leaves simple, basal leaves linear-lanceolate to oblong-lanceolate, stem leaves linear-lanceolate to lanceolate-elliptic, 6". Leaves have a bristly pubescence.

FLOWER: Blue, ½" long trumpet-shaped flowers are in drooping clusters on stems about 12" tall.

HABIT: 8" to 12" tall clump-forming perennial that will spread 18"–24".

SEASON OF BLOOM: Early spring.

CULTURE: Shade to partial shade in moist and cool soil of average fertility. Lungwort may eke out an existence in full sun, but the foliage will look poor by midsummer.

See color plate

UTILIZATION: Single specimen or massed to create a ground cover effect. The low height, early flowers, and an attractive foliage that lasts until fall are desirable features.

PROPAGATION: Division. Since they start growth early in the spring, the best time to divide *Pulmonaria* is in the fall. If planted in the fall, frequent watering will be necessary so the root system will develop well before the onset of cold weather.

DISEASES AND INSECTS: None serious.

HARDINESS: Zones 3–8.

CULTIVARS:
'Azurea'—Sky-blue flowers.
'Blaues Meer'—Large blue flowers, 10" tall.
'Johnson's Blue'—Blue flowers and compact growth habit, 8" tall.
'Mawson's Blue'—Violet-blue flowers, similar to 'Munstead Blue'.
'Munstead Blue'—Deep blue flowers, vigorous grower, 12" tall.

RELATED SPECIES:

P. rubra (ru'-bra)—Red Lungwort. The pale green leaves are oblong and narrowed abruptly, making them nearly sessile to the stem. Each leaf has a velvety texture which is created by long soft hairs. Bright red flowers form very early in spring before the leaves develop. Plants are 12"–24" tall and have a 24" width. Plants grow best in moist soils in partial shade. Zones 4–7.

'Bowle's Red'—Dark red flowers.

'Redstart'—Salmon-red flowers, faint spotting of leaves in the fall. This is often promoted as the best cultivar.

'Salmon Glow'—Salmon colored flowers, 10" tall.

ADDITIONAL NOTES: *Pulmonaria* is derived from *pulmo,* a lung, and refers to the reported value of the leaves in treatment of lung diseases. In the past, leaves were even boiled in beer to treat afflicted horses.

Native to Europe.   Perennial

SCIENTIFIC NAME/FAMILY: *Pulmonaria longifolia*   Boraginaceae

(pul-mo-nā'ri-á long-i-fo'lē-a)

COMMON NAME: Long-leafed Lungwort, Joseph and Mary, Spotted Dog

LEAVES: Alternate; basal leaves are narrow and acutely pointed, 1"–1½" wide and 9"–12" long. Stem leaves are shorter and narrower. They are dark green and have conspicuous white spots. The leaves of this species are much narrower than those of *Pulmonaria saccharata.*

FLOWER: Vivid blue flowers are borne in tight, terminal cymes. The flower inflorescences do not elongate on this species as they do on *P. saccharata.* Flowers either open before the foliage emerges or at the same time.

HABIT: Clump forming perennial, 12" tall and 18"–24" wide. The leaves are more erect than on other *Pulmonaria* species.

SEASON OF BLOOM: Mid to late spring.

See color plate

CULTURE: Full to partial shade in moist and cool soil of average fertility. It is important to have sufficient moisture. Wilted and ragged leaves are often the result of dry conditions.

UTILIZATION: This is a good species for the front of the border or as a ground cover in shaded areas. The distinctively spotted leaves make this plant valuable even after the flowers are gone.

PROPAGATION: The easiest method of propagation is by division of the clumps in the fall. Some have suggested that root cuttings can also be used.

DISEASES AND INSECTS: No serious problems.

HARDINESS: Zones 3–8.

CULTIVARS:
   'Bertram Anderson'—Violet-blue flowers, dark green leaves with silvery spots.
   'Roy Davidson'—This cultivar is very similar to 'Bertram Anderson'. It seems that the leaves are darker green and about twice as wide as those of 'Bertram Anderson'. They are similar enough that both serve the same function in the landscape.

Native to western Europe.   Perennial

SCIENTIFIC NAME/FAMILY: *Pulmonaria saccharata*   Boraginaceae

(pul-mo-nā'ri-ȧ sak-ȧ-rā'tȧ)

COMMON NAME: Bethlehem Sage

LEAVES: Alternate, basal leaves are elliptic, acuminate at both ends; cauline leaves are linear-lanceolate, petioled or subsessile, 6". The dark green leaves are covered with a bristly pubescence and are conspicuously flecked with white spots.

FLOWER: Funnel-shaped flowers are borne in terminal, branched cymes on 12"–18" tall stems. The flower color is initially pinkish but turns to blue as the flowers mature.

HABIT: 12"–18" compact, clump-forming perennial that spreads to 24".

SEASON OF BLOOM: Early to mid-spring.

See color plate

CULTURE: Full to partial shade in moist and cool soil of average fertility. Bethlehem sage may be grown in full sun, but the foliage suffers in midsummer.

UTILIZATION: Single specimen or massed to create a ground cover effect. The distinctive spots on the leaves make this plant valuable even after flowering.

PROPAGATION: Division and seed. Bethlehem sage starts growth early in the spring; consequently, the best time to divide the plant is in the fall. If planted in the fall, frequent watering will be necessary so the root system will develop well before the onset of cold weather. Seeds can be sown in early spring and will flower the second year. Cultivars are reproduced by division or tissue culture.

DISEASES AND INSECTS: None serious.

HARDINESS: Zones 3–8.

CULTIVARS:
   'Alba'—9", marbled leaves and white flowers.
   'Argentea'—Blue flowers and silver-frosted leaves.
   'British Sterling'—A newer introduction with silvery leaves with narrow green margins and midribs. It should be a winner!
   'Excalibur'—The leaves of this 1993 introduction are silver with green outlines. They are arched and have a long, tapered point. It is an introduction of Terra-Nova Nursery, Portland, Oregon.

'Highdown'—Taller-growing than the species. It has deep blue flowers which appear earlier than the species.

'Janet Fisk'—This cultivar has a great amount of marbling that tends to coalesce, creating a whitish leaf. This selection can really lighten a dark area of the garden.

'Mrs. Moon'—Pink flowers that turn blue as the flowers mature. The foliage is attractively spotted with silver-white spots. This cultivar has been the industry standard.

'Margery Fish'—The spots are larger on this cultivar than they are on 'Mrs. Moon'. It is a vigorous grower.

'Pink Dawn'—9"–12", rose-pink flowers and spotted leaves.

'Sissinghurst White'—White flowers add an excellent touch to the attractively spotted foliage.

Native to Europe.   Perennial

SCIENTIFIC NAME/FAMILY: *Pulsatilla vulgaris* (Anemone pulsatilla)   Ranunculaceae

(pul-sa-til'a vul-gā'ris)

COMMON NAME: Pasque Flower

LEAVES: Soft pubescent foliage, basal leaves to 6" long, thrice pinnate into linear segments. Leaves appear after the flowers. The silken hairs on the leaves create a glistening appearance to the foliage.

FLOWER: Blue to reddish purple, solitary, 6 sepals; flowers are 2½" across. The seed heads, which resemble those of the clematis, are as attractive as the purplish flowers.

HABIT: 10" to 12" tall with basal foliage and erect flower stems. Width is 12".

SEASON OF BLOOM: Early to mid spring.

CULTURE: Pasque flower can be grown in full sun and is fairly drought tolerant in cool climates. In warmer areas it will benefit from additional water and partial shade. Poorly drained soil can be detrimental.

UTILIZATION: Rock garden, border.

PROPAGATION: Seed, division, or root cuttings. Fresh seeds should be used and will germinate in 5 to 6 weeks at 70°F. Division of older plants can be done in the spring. Root cuttings can be taken in the spring by soaking the soil around the plant and then carefully digging around the root so a root piece can be broken off, taken up, and replanted.

DISEASES AND INSECTS: No serious problems.

HARDINESS: Zones 5–8.

CULTIVARS:
   'Alba'—6"–10", white flowers.
   'Barton's Pink'—6"–10", pink flowers.
   'Rubra'—6"–10" burgundy-red flowers.

ADDITIONAL NOTES: *Anemone* is derived from the Greek, anemos, which means wind, and apparently refers to the open and windy areas some species inhabit.

Native to Europe.   Perennial

SCIENTIFIC NAME/FAMILY: *Puschkinia scilloides*   Liliaceae

(pösh-kin′ē-a sil-oi′dēz)

COMMON NAME: Striped Squill

LEAVES: The glossy basal foliage is composed of 2 to 4 linear-strap-shaped leaves, 1/2″ wide and 6″ long.

FLOWER: Pale blue flowers, 1/2″ long, are borne in a terminal raceme at the end of the flowering stalk. Individual flowers are bell-shaped and have a dark blue stripe running down the center of the petal.

HABIT: Small bulb with an erect flower stalk, 4″–6″ tall and 4″ wide.

SEASON OF BLOOM: Early spring.

CULTURE: In the fall, plant the bulb about 3″ deep in a moist but well-drained soil in full sun or partial shade. Space the bulbs every 4″–6″. Bulbs can be left undisturbed for several years.

See color plate

UTILIZATION: This bulb should be planted in large masses. The flower is not as showy as other spring bulbs and it will take hundreds to develop a visible display. Smaller numbers could be used in a rock garden. *Puschkinia* will self-seed, so a naturalistic planting would also be a good use. It can also be used in a container. However, it should be scheduled to flower close to the natural flowering period. It does not respond well to hard forcing used with other bulbs.

PROPAGATION: New plants can be propagated from offsets taken from the bulbs and planted in a nursery row. It usually takes one season to develop flowering size bulbs from the larger offsets. Seed can also be collected and sown outside in the spring or germinated at alternating 70° and 40°F temperatures. It takes a minimum of 2 years for the seedlings to reach flowering size.

DISEASES AND INSECTS: No serious problems.

HARDINESS: Zones 4–9.

ADDITIONAL NOTES: The genera *Scilla, Chionodoxa,* and *Puschkinia* are closely related. The botanical difference that separates *Puschkinia* from the other genera is that the flower filaments are united into a cuplike crown or corona. *Puschkinia* is named for the Russian Count Apollos Apollosvich Mussin-Puschkin. The specific epithet, *scilloides,* is from *Scilla,* indicating "like Scilla."

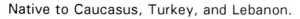

Native to Caucasus, Turkey, and Lebanon.   Bulb

SCIENTIFIC NAME/FAMILY: *Ranunculus repens* 'Flore Pleno'   Ranunculaceae

(ra-nun'kū-lus rē'penz)

COMMON NAME: Double-flowered Creeping Buttercup

LEAVES: The alternate leaves are triangular-ovate in shape, ternately compound, and 3"–4" wide. Each of the three lobes is again cut into 3-toothed segments. Leaf margins are closely crenate to dentate. The leaves are long petioled.

FLOWER: The flowers are bright yellow with a waxy sheen, fully double, and approximately ¾" in diameter. They are borne in sparsely branched peduncles on stems 18" tall.

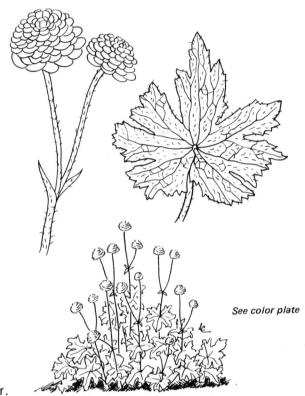

See color plate

HABIT: Stoloniferous perennial growing 18" tall.

SEASON OF BLOOM: Mid to late summer.

CULTURE: Creeping buttercup performs best in a moist, sunny location. It will also tolerate partial shade. Left unchecked, creeping buttercup will spread rapidly in moist soils. It spreads by stolons that will root at the nodes. If the stolons are pinched off as the plant develops, the spread of the plant is easily controlled.

UTILIZATION: Creeping buttercup is attractive in the border if the creeping stolons are removed. It is also useful in highly informal or native sites where the possible rampant spread would not be detrimental.

PROPAGATION: The stoloniferous habit allows for easy division in spring or fall.

DISEASES AND INSECTS: None serious.

HARDINESS: Zones 3–8.

RELATED SPECIES:
   R. acris (ak'ris) 'Flore Pleno'—This species has similar flowers, grows to 3 feet, and is not invasive like *R. repens*. Plants sold as *R. acris* are often *R. repens*. A quick check of the height listed will indicate which species one will likely receive. Zones 3–7.

ADDITIONAL NOTES: The species *R. repens* has 5-petaled flowers and is not considered as valuable as 'Flore Pleno'. Some references list 'Flore Pleno' as 'Pleniflorus'. *Ranunculus* is a derivative of the Latin name *rana*. Rana means "little frog" and was given by Pliny because many of the *Ranunculus* are found in damp areas.

Native to Europe.   Perennial

SCIENTIFIC NAME/FAMILY: *Ratibida columnifera*

Asteraceae
(Compositae)

(ra-tib'-i-da ka-lum-nif'-er-a)

COMMON NAME: Prairie Coneflower, Mexican Hat, Long-head Coneflower

LEAVES: Alternate leaves to 5″ long, pinnately lobed into lanceolate, coarsely toothed segments. Leaves are covered with stiff, adpressed hairs.

FLOWER: Bright yellow flower heads are borne on long peduncles. The disk is cylindrical or columnar, 1/2″ to 1″ long cone which is equal to or longer than the ray flowers. Prairie coneflower is recognized for its drooping ray flowers.

HABIT: Erect and finely branched perennial 2′–3′ tall and 18″ wide.

SEASON OF BLOOM: Summer.

CULTURE: Prairie coneflower is found as a native plant in dry prairies. Consequently, optimum conditions will include full sun and a well-drained soil.

UTILIZATION: This species can be placed in a sunny border or a meadow planting.

PROPAGATION: Seed and division. Cover seed very lightly and germinate at 70°F. Division should be done in the spring.

DISEASES AND INSECTS: There are no serious problems.

HARDINESS: Zones 4–9.

RELATED SPECIES:
   R. pinnata (pin-nā'tà)—This species is taller than *R. columnifera,* 3′–5′, with larger leaves and flowers.

ADDITIONAL NOTES: The common name Mexican hat is due to the resemblance to a sombrero because of the long cone (disk) flowers with drooping ray flowers.

Native to southwestern Canada to northern Mexico.   Perennial

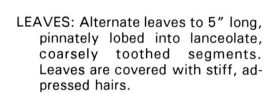

SCIENTIFIC NAME/FAMILY: *Rehmannia elata*   Scrophulariaceae

(rā-man'i-á ē-lā'ta)

COMMON NAME: Rehmannia

LEAVES: Leaves are of two types: basal and stem. The stem leaves are alternate. Leaf blades are ovate to elliptic with a wedge-shaped base. Leaves can have 2 to 6 entire or toothed lobes. Leaves and stems are hairy.

FLOWER: The pink flowers with yellow throats are borne in the leaf axils or in terminal racemes. The 2" long tubular flowers have a large 3-lobed lip. Flowers have a similarity to a hybrid between *Digitalis* and *Salpiglossis*.

HABIT: Erect perennial with branched stems, 2' tall and 1' wide.

SEASON OF BLOOM: Early summer. In mild climates, *Rehmannia* has a longer bloom time.

CULTURE: This species can be grown in sun or partial shade in a well-drained, fertile soil. It does not have good winter hardiness especially if the soils are wet during the winter. It is usually treated as a biennial and overwintered in a cool greenhouse.

See color plate

UTILIZATION: Good flower effect for the herbaceous border.

PROPAGATION: Seed is the normal method but it may take 12 months to produce a flowering plant. Seed germinates best at warm temperatures (75°F). The 1st year plants will usually need to be placed in a cool greenhouse for the winter with the 2nd year plants planted in the garden in the spring. For northern zones this seems like a lot of work to obtain a flowering plant for the border.

DISEASES AND INSECTS: No serious problems.

HARDINESS: Zones 8–10

RELATED SPECIES:
This genus appears to need some taxonomic work. In most references, *R. angulata* is listed as a separate species. In other instances, there is some thought that plants once grown as *R. angulata* are actually *R. elata*. *Rehmannia angulata* should have red flowers while *R. elata* should be rosy-purple to pink. The family even offers confusion. In some texts it is listed as *Scrophulariaceae* and in another, it is found as the family *Gesneriaceae*.

Native to China.   Biennial

SCIENTIFIC NAME/FAMILY: *Rheum palmatum*   Polygonaceae

(rē'um pal-mā'tum)

COMMON NAME: Ornamental Rhubarb

LEAVES: The large basal leaves, 2'–3' wide, are dark green, cordate, and deeply and sharply palmately lobed. The nearly round leaves have 3–5 ribs. Stem and leaf can reach 6'.

FLOWER: Tiny pinkish to red flowers are arranged in 2' long panicles that terminate 7' tall stems.

HABIT: Tall flowering stems rise above the mounded basal leaves. Six to eight feet tall and 6' wide.

SEASON OF BLOOM: Early summer.

CULTURE: This species is harder to grow than the edible rhubarb (*R. rhabarbarum*). Ornamental rhubarb requires a well-drained soil that remains moist, abundant fertilizer in the spring, and of course, plenty of room to grow. Mulching would help conserve soil moisture. Best growth will occur in partial shade. This plant will persist for many years after establishment.

UTILIZATION: The texture of this plant makes it a natural for a bold display in a border, as an accent, or along the edge of water.

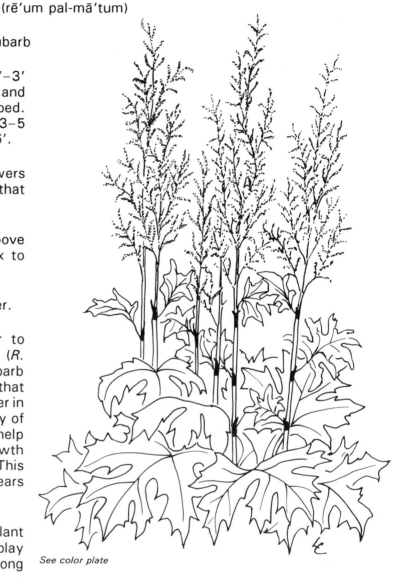

See color plate

PROPAGATION: Ornamental rhubarb is usually propagated by division. The key thing in this process is to insure that each piece contains a dormant eye (crown bud).

DISEASES AND INSECTS: No serious problems.

HARDINESS: Zones 4–7.

CULTIVARS:
'Atrosanguineum'—This selection has dark purple leaves which are reddish maroon upon emergence in the spring with the purplish color remaining on the lower surface until flowering. The flowers are a deep crimson followed by reddish fruit. I first became acquainted with this cultivar in the Red Border at Hidcote Manor, near Gloucestershire, England. In this famous double border, it is combined with red poppies, redleaf Japanese barberry, and purple leaf sage. What a striking combination!
'Bowles' Variety'—Similar to the above with rose-red flowers.

var. *tanguticum* (tan-gū'ti-kum)—Leaves of this selection are less deeply cut but have a stronger purplish tint on both surfaces of the leaf. Flowers may be white, pink, or crimson. This cultivar is often produced from seed, so there is considerable variation in flower color. Flowers appear on side shoots and the overall appearance is not as striking as the species or other cultivars.

Native to China.   Perennial

SCIENTIFIC NAME/FAMILY: *Ricinus communis*   Euphorbiaceae

(ris'i-nus kom-mū'nis)

COMMON NAME: Castor Bean, Castor-Oil-Plant, Palma Christi, Wonder Tree

LEAVES: Alternate, to 3' across, parted beyond the middle into ovate-oblong or lanceolate acuminate lobes, palmately 5–11 lobed, lobes serrate. Leaves come in many colors: green, red, bluish-gray, maroon, purplish, or variegated.

FLOWER: The unattractive flowers, which have no petals, are borne in erect panicles, 1'–2' long, which flower from the base. The fruit are more obvious but not necessarily ornamental. They are ½"–1" long and may be smooth or covered with dark brown soft spines.

HABIT: 5' to 10' in cultivation but will reach 40' in its native habitat, erect to round growth habit.

SEASON OF BLOOM: Summer, not important.

CULTURE: Open sun and rich fertile soil. Castor bean grows best with abundant water and fertilizer.

UTILIZATION: Large scale plant that can be used as a specimen or "annual shrub" for quick screening or temporary landscaping. Staking is often required in exposed areas. The plant is so big and bold that it fills a huge area very nicely.

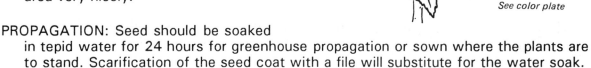

See color plate

PROPAGATION: Seed should be soaked in tepid water for 24 hours for greenhouse propagation or sown where the plants are to stand. Scarification of the seed coat with a file will substitute for the water soak.

DISEASES AND INSECTS: Bacterial leaf spot, bacterial wilt, charcoal rot, gray mold, blight, and southern armyworm occur largely on plants grown commercially for oil. Some of these are occasionally problems on plants grown as ornamentals.

CULTIVARS:
'Gibsonii'—More compact, 4'–5', dark red foliage.
'Red Spire'—Red stems and bronze-green foliage.
'Sanguineus'—Stems and leaves are blood-red.
'Zanzibarensis'—Bright green, white-veined leaves.

ADDITIONAL NOTES: Seeds are poisonous; *do not plant* where children may play. The seeds yield an oil which is extensively used medicinally and in the manufacture of soap, paints, and varnishes. *Ricinus* is derived from *ricinus,* a tick, because the seeds somewhat resemble a tick. Castor bean can be grown over a wide range. Plants I have seen in Georgia were equal to those observed in Illinois or Kansas.

Native to tropics.   Annual—perennial in tropics

SCIENTIFIC NAME/FAMILY: *Rodgersia pinnata*   Saxifragaceae

(rod-jĕr'si-a pin-nā'tà)

COMMON NAME: Featherleaf Rodgersflower

LEAVES: Alternate leaves, pinnately compound with 5 to 7 leaflets. Leaflets are oblanceolate to 8" long and have a finely serrated margin. The leaf can be 12" to 18" wide.

FLOWER: The flowers are creamy pink, very small, but many are arranged in large terminal panicles which are 6" to 10" long.

HABIT: 3' to 4' tall, bold, rounded specimen that can grow to 4' wide.

SEASON OF BLOOM: Late spring to midsummer.

CULTURE: This species requires a permanently moist soil. If this requirement is not met, the leaves scorch and the leaf margins become brown. If the soil is moist, the plant can be grown in full sun as well as partial shade.

See color plate

UTILIZATION: *Rodgersia* has attractive foliage as well as an ornamental flower. It is an excellent plant for the waterside or for the partially shaded, moist border.

PROPAGATION: *Rodgersia* can be divided for propagation but it will seldom need division.

DISEASES AND INSECTS: None serious.

HARDINESS: Zones 5–7.

CULTIVARS:
   'Elegans'—Creamy white flowers.
   'Superba'—Pink flowers and a bronzish-green foliage. The foliage contrasts nicely with blue-leaf hostas.

RELATED SPECIES:
   R. aesculifolia (es-kū-lif-o'-lē-a)—Fingerleaf Rodgersia. The leaves are palmately compound and resemble the leaves of the horse-chestnut, *Aesculus*; consequently, the use of *aesculifolia* as the specific epithet. The creamy-white flowers are borne in large panicles that are 18"–24" long. Plants are 3'–5' tall and 4'–5' wide. Moist soil is required for optimum growth.

R. podophylla (pod-o-fil'-la) — Bronzeleaf Rodgersia. This species also has palmately compound leaves. Each leaflet is broadly ovate and toothed at the tip, somewhat shaped like a duck's foot. In the summer, the leaves turn a bronzy color. The flowers are creamy-white. The following three cultivars were introduced by Pagels Nursery in Germany.

'Pagode' ('Pagoda') — Large inflorescences of white flowers.

'Rotlaub' — The foliage colors to a bronze-red during the summer.

'Smaragd' — Creamy-white flowers.

Native to China.

Perennial

SCIENTIFIC NAME/FAMILY: *Rodgersia tabularis* (Astilboides tabularis)   Saxifragaceae

(rod-jĕr'si-a tab-ū-lah'ris)

COMMON NAME: Shieldleaf Roger's Flower

LEAVES: The leaves arise from thick rhizomes on petioles 2'–3' long. Leaves are peltate, meaning the petiole attaches to the center of the leaf. Unlike other *Rodgersia*, this species has round, shield-like leaves rather than compound leaves. Each leaf can be up to 3' wide and it has an undulating lobing pattern with numerous small teeth on the margin. The leaf surface has a texture like very fine sandpaper.

FLOWER: Numerous small white flowers are borne in a slightly nodding panicle that rises well above the leaves. The flowers are similar to those of astilbe.

HABIT: The large leaves create a bold, massive clump that is 3'–4' tall and 4' wide. Space plants 3' to 4' apart.

SEASON OF BLOOM: Late spring to early summer.

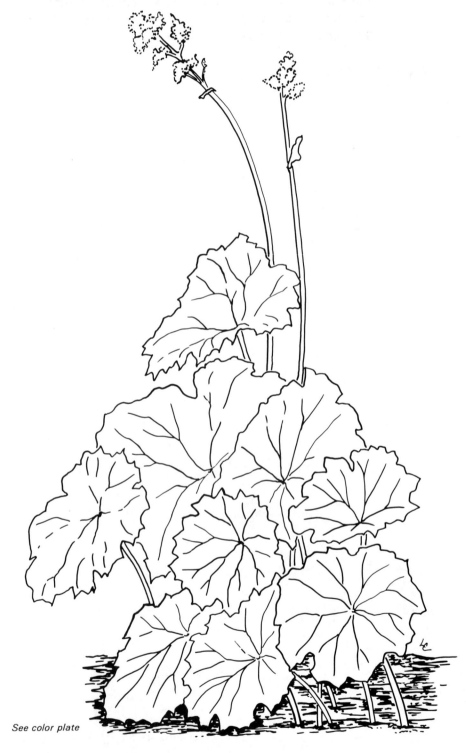

See color plate

CULTURE: Best performance will be in a moist, humus enriched soil in partial shade.

UTILIZATION: *Rodgersia tabularis* is an excellent foliage plant for the waterside or in damp soils.

PROPAGATION: Division or seed.

DISEASES AND INSECTS: None serious.

HARDINESS: Zones 5–7.

ADDITIONAL NOTES: *Rodgersia tabularis* is the only member of this genus with flowers containing petals.

Native to China.

SCIENTIFIC NAME/FAMILY: *Rosmarinus officinalis*   Lamiaceae (Labiatae)

(ros-mà-rī'nus o-fis-i-nā'lis)

COMMON NAME: Rosemary

LEAVES: Rosemary has leathery leaves which are very closely spaced on the stem. Leaves are linear, ⅛" wide and ¾"–1¼" long. The lower leaf surface is white tomentose. A prominent vein runs down the middle of the leaf and the leaf margins turn downward.

FLOWER: Pale blue flowers are borne in axillary clusters nestled among the leaves. The corolla is two lipped, the upper lip is two lobed; the lower lip has three lobes. Corolla is ¼" to ½" long—3 times longer than the calyx.

HABIT: Rosemary is an evergreen shrub with a many-branched, dense, erect habit, 3' to 8' tall. Space rosemary 3–5 feet apart.

SEASON OF BLOOM: Early to mid summer

CULTURE: Rosemary is grown outside in the soil or in containers which can be brought indoors during the winter. Minimum winter temperature will dictate this choice. In areas where temperatures do not go below −10°F, there are several cultivars which can remain outside. Rosemary performs best in full sun but will achieve acceptable growth if provided 4 hours of midday sun. In heavier soils, soil amendments of peat moss or compost should be added. Rosemary is tolerant to a wide pH range. Container plants should also be placed in full sun. Water and fertilize as needed. When the plant is brought inside in the winter, it should be placed in a cool spot where it will receive as much direct sunlight as possible. The soil should be moist and should never be allowed to dry completely. Drying out usually means "instant death" for rosemary.

UTILIZATION: Rosemary is an important culinary herb. Its leaves are used to flavor vegetables and meats. Rosemary oil is used to add a pine scent to soaps, creams, and perfumes. Sachets of rosemary can be added to clothes drawers. As an ornamental, rosemary is as much at home in the garden border as it is in the herb garden. Rosemary in containers can provide accents on patios or decks. The prostrate selections are nice for trailing over walls.

PROPAGATION: Rosemary can be propagated by seed or cuttings. Propagation by stem cuttings is the preferred commercial practice. Three-inch cuttings should be taken in spring. The lower ⅓ of the leaves should be stripped and a rooting hormone should be applied. Rooting will occur in 2–3 weeks. Propagation by seed is a second choice. Rosemary seed lacks vigor and plants are often not true to type.

DISEASES AND INSECTS: Plants moved indoors can become infected with aphids, mealybugs, and spider mites. Plants grown outdoors generally do not have these pests. In cool and moist situations, rosemary is susceptible to powdery mildew and botrytis.

HARDINESS: Zones 8–10.

CULTIVARS:
   'Arp'—Gray-green leaves, sprawling habit, wider than tall. This cultivar is reported as being the hardiest and should be tried in northern areas. It is reported in one publication as being hardy to -10°F; however, some gardeners question this. Give it a try; it just might work in your cold climate.
   'Benenden Blue'—Narrow leaves much like a pine tree; upright growth habit. Used in potpourri rather than in cooking. Hardy to 20°F with protection. 5' tall.

'Blue Boy'—Compact grower with a mild fragrance. Good as a container plant. Hardy to 15°F. 4' tall.

'Marjorca Pink'—Amethyst-violet flowers are borne in large clusters at the stem tip. Has a fruity fragrance. Hardy to 15°F. 5' tall.

'Prostratus'—Arching, procumbent habit to 3 feet tall. Excellent as a ground cover or as a trailing wall plant. Hardy to 20°F.

'Severn Sea'—Light blue flowers cover the trailing stems, 2 feet tall. Hardy to 0°F.

'Tuscan Blue'—This cultivar has short, glossy leaves on erect stems, which creates a unique character. It can be trained into a standard. Grows 10'–12' tall. Hardy to 5°F.

ADDITIONAL NOTES: Rosemary is known as a symbol of remembrance, friendship, and love.

Native to Mediterranean region, Portugal, and Spain.   Tender perennial

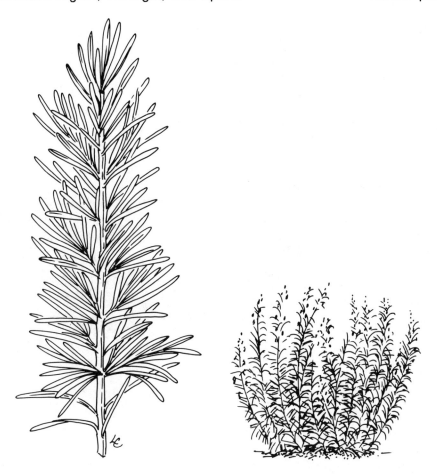

Rosmarinus officinalis 'Severn Sea'
stem × 1   habit × 1/6

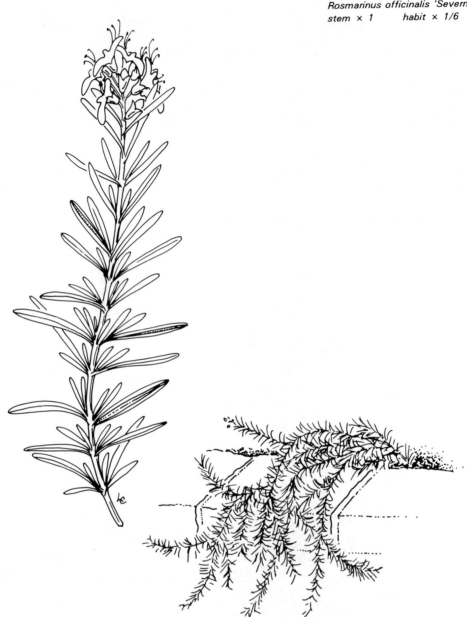

SCIENTIFIC NAME/FAMILY: *Rudbeckia hirta* var. *pulcherrima*
(R. flava)

Asteraceae
(Compositae)

(rud-bek'i-à hẽr'tà pul-ker'ri-ma)

COMMON NAME: Black-eyed Susan, Yellow Oxeye Daisy, English Bulls-eye, Gloriosa Daisy

LEAVES: Leaves alternate, coarsely hairy, simple, lower leaves petioled, upper leaves sessile, oblong to lanceolate, 2"–5" long.

FLOWER: Flowers with golden-yellow rays and often deeply colored toward the base of the rays, 1"–2" long, disk flowers are dull brown to nearly black.

HABIT: 2' to 3' erect to round growth habit.

SEASON OF BLOOM: Summer and fall.

CULTURE: Full sun or light shade in ordinary soil. Hot, dry summers do not bother the gloriosa daisy.

UTILIZATION: Cutting, background, borders and bedding.

See color plate

PROPAGATION: Annual that is seed propagated that will reseed naturally each year. Perennial types are propagated by division. Gloriosa daisy requires a soil temperature of at least 70°F for best germination.

DISEASES AND INSECTS: Downy mildew, rust, powdery mildew (quite common), ambrosia aphid, and sawfly, which can quickly defoliate gloriosa daisy.

CULTIVARS:
'Becky Mix'—Compact plants, 8"–10" tall, with golden-yellow flowers with bronze centers.
'Gloriosa, Single Daisy'—36", golden yellow ray flowers, brown disk flowers.
'Gloriosa, Double Daisy'—36", double and semidouble flowers, golden-yellow, tetraploid.
'Goldilocks'—This Fleuroselect winner is compact, 10" to 15" tall, with 2½" to 3½" diameter double or semidouble golden yellow flowers.
'Irish Eyes'—30", golden flowers, 5" across with green centers.
'Marmalade'—22", shorter than other selections with golden-orange flowers, which are freely produced.
'Rustic Colors'—18"–22", similar to 'Marmalade' but with mixed colors of orange, bronze, brown, bicolors, intershades, and solid colors.
'Sputnik'—Bright yellow flowers with very dark brown centers. Excellent plant for cut flowers.

RELATED SPECIES:

R. fulgida. (ful-ji'-da)—Orange Coneflower. This perennial species is one of the very best perennials for garden or meadow use. In midsummer to fall, it lights up the border with bright yellow blooms. It is similar to *Rudbeckia hirta* var. *pulcherrima* except the leaves are darker green and glabrous. When planted side by side, *R. fulgida* is free of powdery mildew, while *hirta* is covered with the characteristic "white film." Plants are 18"–30" tall and 24" wide.

var. *deamii.* (dē-am'-ē-i) This variety has broader, coarser-toothed foliage and is more floriferous than the species. Plants are 24" tall.

var. *speciosa.* (spē-si-ō'-sa) The basal leaves of this variety are entire or shallowly lobed while the stem leaves are coarsely toothed. Flowers have orange petals.

var. *sullivantii.* (sul-i-van'-tē-ī) This variety is similar to *deamii* but the stem leaves become smaller until the uppermost leaves tend to be bract-like. 'Goldsturm' is the famous cultivar of this variety. It has dark green foliage and 3"–4" diameter bright yellow flowers. 'Goldsturm' is a compact form, 24" tall.

ADDITIONAL NOTES: One can rely on black-eyed Susan for bold splashes of color. These first year blooming perennials of medium height require no support or special care. Always vigorous, well-flowered, and showy. *Rudbeckia* honors Olaf Rudbeck and his son, both Swedish botanists of the 18th century.

Native to the United States.   Short-lived perennial grown as an annual

SCIENTIFIC NAME/FAMILY: *Rudbeckia nitida*
                               Asteraceae
                   (rud-bek'i-á nit'i-da)   (Compositae)

See color plate

COMMON NAME: Coneflower

LEAVES: The bright green leaves are entire or slightly toothed and arranged alternately. Basal leaves are ovate to lanceolate-oblong and petioled. The upper leaves are oblong to lanceolate and sessile. Leaves are 3 to 6 inches long.

FLOWER: The yellow flower heads are 3" to 4" wide and have drooping ray flowers. The heads are on long peduncles that terminate the stems and branches.

HABIT: Tall upright perennial. The species is 2' to 4' and some cultivars are 7 feet tall.

SEASON OF BLOOM: Mid to late summer.

CULTURE: It can be grown easily in well-drained soil in full sun.

UTILIZATION: Rear of the border or middle of an island bed.

PROPAGATION: Clump division in spring or fall.

DISEASES AND INSECTS: The cultivars of *R. nitida* have few problems.

HARDINESS: Zones 4–10.

CULTIVARS:
'Herbstsonne'—Large single yellow flowers, with green ray flowers. It is 7 feet tall and may require staking. The catalog of Valleybrook Gardens Ltd., Abbotsford, British Columbia, calls this selection the "Godzilla of Coneflowers." It is a fine selection for the fall perennial border. It attracts butterflies, especially monarchs, and is very good for cut flowers.

RELATED SPECIES:
R. laciniata (lå-sin-i-å'tå)—Cutleaf Coneflower. This species is closely related to *R. nitida.* A main difference is the leaves of the cutleaf coneflower, which are 3–5 lobed on the lower leaves and usually 3 lobed on the upper leaves. The foliage of *R. nitida* is only slightly toothed. Cutleaf coneflower requires moist soil and full sun to partial shade for optimum growth.

'Golden Glow'—This cultivar was introduced as 'Hortensis' and was listed by Bailey as early as 1894. 'Golden Glow' is a double-flowered selection with 3" diameter yellow flowers borne on 4' to 5' tall plants. It can be invasive. 'Goldquelle' is a better selection for the small garden.

'Goldquelle'—Double yellow flowers, late summer bloom, 2'–3' tall. Staking is not needed unless lush growth is forced by placing this cultivar in highly fertile soil.

R. maxima (maks'-im-a)—Great Coneflower. This species is another native of North America. It is valued for its basal bluish-grey leaves which are 12"–18" long and look like paddles. The large yellow flowers are borne atop stems that are 5'–6' tall. It is an attractive but coarse perennial that is best situated in a native site in full sun and a moist, well-drained soil.

R. triloba (tri-lo'ba)—Three-lobed Coneflower. A United States native which flowers over a longer period of time than 'Goldsturm'. The basal leaves are 3-lobed, which leads one to the significance of the specific epithet, *triloba.* Plants are 2'–3' tall and 18" wide. It is not a common nursery plant but several native plant nurseries are starting to offer it in their catalogs.

Native to North America.   Perennial

SCIENTIFIC NAME/FAMILY: *Ruta graveolens*   Rutaceae

(ru'-ta gra-vē ō'-lenz)

COMMON NAME: Common Rue, Herb-of-Grace

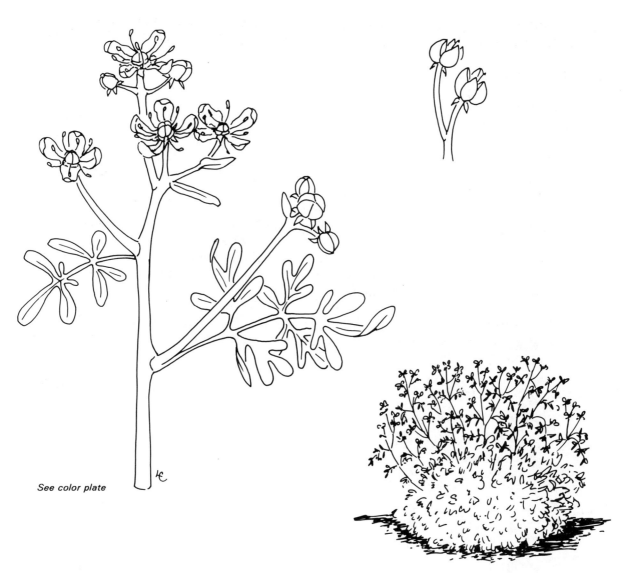

See color plate

LEAVES: Leaves are alternate, 2 to 3 pinnately dissected. Leaf segments are oblong or spatulate. The foliage is blue-green and aromatic when bruised. Some would describe the odor as pungent.

FLOWER: Flowers are yellow, not particularly showy, and are borne in terminal corymbs. Individual flowers, ½"–¾" wide, have 4 petals and 4 sepals. The petals are concave with a notch at the tip.

HABIT: Round habit, 2' to 3' tall and 24"–30" wide.

SEASON OF BLOOM: Midsummer.

CULTURE: *Ruta* grows best in full sun and a well-drained soil. It is a subshrub or woody herbaceous that needs to be pruned back to the old wood in the spring. This will help maintain a dense form. In northern winters, it should be heavily mulched.

UTILIZATION: *Ruta* is primarily grown for its unique blue-green foliage and is often found in herb gardens. It can be useful in areas where a low edging plant is desired. Useful in the front of the border or as a soft contrast to the bright, summer-colored perennials.

PROPAGATION: Seed or cuttings. Seed should be exposed to light and germinated at 70°F. Germination will take about 14 days. Terminal cuttings can be taken in spring or fall.

DISEASES AND INSECTS: No serious problems.

HARDINESS: Zones 4–9.

CULTIVARS:
'Blue Beauty'—18″ tall, mounded plant with very glaucous, blue-green leaves. This selection and 'Blue Mound' are most similar.
'Blue Mound'—18″–24″ tall, steel blue leaves.
'Jackman's Blue'—Excellent blue-green foliage, 18″–24″ tall. This selection appears to be the more popular selection, especially in Europe.
'Variegata'—The leaves are splashed with white, which is most noticeable on young foliage. Pruning to force new growth will enhance the variegation. The foliage is sometimes used in floral arrangements. 18″ tall.

ADDITIONAL NOTES: Rue will cause dermatitis in some individuals particularly under hot, sunny conditions. One needs to exercise caution when first handling this plant to make sure he or she is not allergic.

Perennial

Native to southern Europe.

SCIENTIFIC NAME/FAMILY: *Sagina subulata*   Caryophyllaceae

(så-ji'na sub-ū-lā'ta)

COMMON NAME: Corsican Pearlwort

LEAVES: The opposite leaves are awl-shaped, less than ¼" long, with a bristle tip. The foliage looks like a glossy mat. Pearlwort is a very fine-textured plant.

FLOWER: Most of the white flowers are solitary, have 5 petals, and are ¼" wide. They are borne on pedicels about 1" long.

HABIT: Low mat, 2" to 4" high with a 12" spread.

SEASON OF BLOOM: Early to midsummer.

CULTURE: Sun or partial shade in a well-drained soil. The soil should not be dry.

UTILIZATION: Ground cover, rock garden, and planting among stepping stones.

PROPAGATION: Division and seed are easy methods. It spreads easily from plugs planted among paving stones.

DISEASES AND INSECTS: No serious problems.

HARDINESS: Zones 4–7.

CULTIVARS:
    'Aurea'—Yellow-green leaves and white flowers.

Native to Europe.   Perennial

See color plate

SCIENTIFIC NAME/FAMILY: *Salpiglossis sinuata*   Solanaceae

(sal-pi-glos'is sin-ū-ā'tá)

COMMON NAME: Painted Tongue

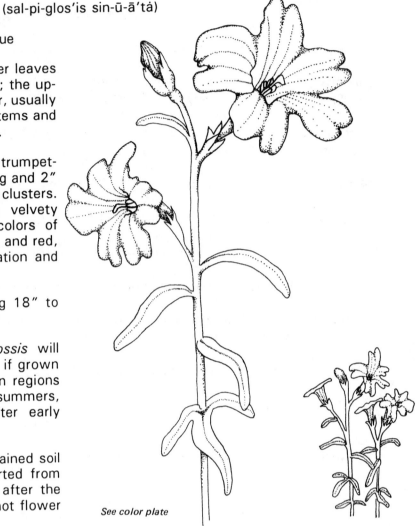

See color plate

LEAVES: Leaves alternate, lower leaves elliptic, toothed or pinnatifid; the upper leaves lanceolate to linear, usually entire, 3" to 4" long. The stems and leaves have a sticky texture.

FLOWER: The wide-throated, trumpet-shaped flowers are 2½" long and 2" wide, borne in loose terminal clusters. Individual flowers have a velvety appearance and come in colors of gold, primrose, yellow, blue, and red, with great variation in venation and color patterns.

HABIT: Upright, open branching 18" to 24" tall and 12" wide.

SEASON OF BLOOM: *Salpiglossis* will bloom through the summer if grown in cool summer climates. In regions with hot and/or humid summers, flowering will diminish after early summer.

CULTURE: Full sun in a well-drained soil is ideal. Plants can be started from seeds and planted outside after the frost free date. Plants will not flower well in hot weather.

UTILIZATION: Painted tongue is an unusual and colorful plant for the border area. It tends to be leggy and staking may be required if it is grown in an exposed area. The flowers can also be used for cut flowers.

PROPAGATION: Seed propagation. Sow the seeds indoors in late winter at a temperature of 65°F.

DISEASES AND INSECTS: This species is usually pest free. Two wilts have been reported and some nematode problems, but these situations are not widespread.

CULTIVARS:
'Bolero'—This F_2 mixture has flower colors of gold, rose, red, crimson, and blue. 18"–24".
'Casino'—This selection has basal branching which results in a more compact growth habit. Colors include blue, orange, purple, red, and yellow. Plants are 15" tall and 12" wide.
'Dwarf Friendship Mixture'—Compact, long flowering, and more heat resistant.
'Splash'—F_1 hybrid of various colors. This cultivar is common in cultivation. It has a more compact branching habit, profuse blooms, and tends to be more durable than the species.

Native to Chile.   Annual

SCIENTIFIC NAME/FAMILY: *Salvia coccinea*   Lamiaceae (Labiatae)

(sal'vi-à kok-sin'-ē-a)

COMMON NAME: Texas Salvia, Scarlet Salvia

LEAVES: Opposite leaves, ovate to triangular, 1″ to 2″ long, crenate margin, long
petiole. Leaves have pubescent surfaces.

FLOWER: Bright red flowers, ¾″–1″ long,
borne on a raceme inflorescence.

HABIT: Upright, 2′–3′ tall, space 12″ apart.

SEASON OF BLOOM: Summer.

CULTURE: Full sun and well-drained soil.

UTILIZATION: Excellent annual for the mixed
border. It is an underused annual which
should be considered by more gardeners.
It is probably a better choice for an infor-
mal-appearing border than the more formal appearance of *Salvia splendens.*

PROPAGATION: Seed will germinate in 10–
14 days at a temperature of 70°–80°F.

DISEASES AND INSECTS: None serious.

CULTIVARS:
    'Starry-Eyed Mixed'—Mixture containing
      white, salmon, and brilliant red flow-
      ers, 36″ tall.

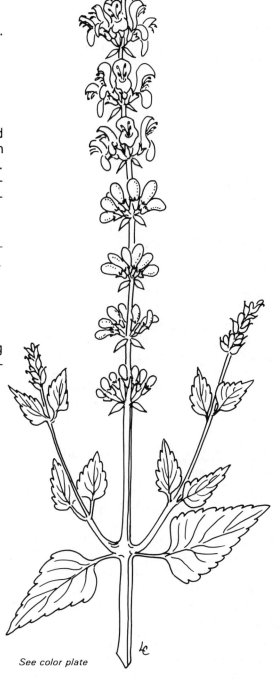

See color plate

Native to southern United States and South America.   Annual

SCIENTIFIC NAME/FAMILY: *Salvia elegans*   Lamiaceae (Labiatae)

(sal'vi-à el'e-ganz)

COMMON NAME: Pineapple Sage

LEAVES: Opposite leaves, 2"–4" long, ovate to lanceolate shaped, apex is acuminate. Margins are serrate. The square stems and leaves are pubescent to hairy. The crushed foliage has a distinct pineapple fragrance.

FLOWER: The ruby red flowers are arranged in 4-flowered whorls on a terminal spike-like inflorescence. The corolla is 1½" long with a reflexed lower lip.

HABIT: 3'–4' tall plant with a similar spread.

SEASON OF BLOOM: Late summer until frost.

CULTURE: This half-hardy perennial is grown in full sun and well-drained soils. In northern climates, flowering barely starts before the first frost. In these areas, the plants can be cut back in late summer, potted, and taken indoors for flowering in fall and early winter.

UTILIZATION: This species is valued for its vivid red flowers in late summer. It is used in the border or as a tub plant. As a culinary herb, pineapple sage is used for drinks, jams, and jellies. The bright red flowers attract hummingbirds to the garden.

PROPAGATION: Easily propagated from tip cuttings taken in the spring.

DISEASES AND INSECTS: None serious.

HARDINESS: Zones 7–8. Salvia elegans is usually grown as an annual. Plants can be carried through the winter and placed outside in the spring.

Native to Mexico.

Tender perennial

SCIENTIFIC NAME/FAMILY: *Salvia farinacea*   Lamiaceae
                                                             (Labiatae)

(sal'vi-à fãr-i-nā'sē-à)

COMMON NAME: Mealycup Sage

LEAVES: Leaves opposite to whorled, minutely
    pubescent, leaves ovate-lanceolate to ovate,
    1½"–3" long, acute at apex, coarsely and
    irregularly serrate, uppermost leaves linear-
    lanceolate, square stems.

FLOWER: Flowers are borne on an interrupted
    spike, corolla ½" long, violet blue or white
    flowers, bracts small, green, early deciduous,
    calyx densely white to purplish tomentose.

HABIT: 2' to 3' erect plant.

SEASON OF BLOOM: Midsummer to frost.

CULTURE: Sun—prefers well-drained, moist soil.

UTILIZATION: Cutting flowers, middle of bor-
    ders, and bedding.

PROPAGATION: Seeds germinate in 2 weeks at
    70°F. Softwood cuttings 3"–4" long root
    readily. The plant can also be divided, but
    recovers slowly.

DISEASES AND INSECTS: Damping-off in seed
    beds, downy and powdery mildews.

HARDINESS: Zone 7. Mealycup sage is an excel-
    lent choice for southern gardens. In Zone 9 it
    is an evergreen perennial.

See color plate

CULTIVARS:
    'Argent'—Flowers are silvery-white.
    'Blue Bedder'—24", compact, blue flowers.
    'Catima'—24", dark blue flowers, uniform, bushy habit.
    'Regal Purple'—24", deep violet-blue flowers.
    'Rhea'—Violet-blue flowers on compact stems. 'Rhea' is 12" to 14" tall and it is
        shorter than 'Victoria'.
    'Silvery White'—Silver-white flowers, 18"–20" tall. It can be used in combination with
        'Victoria'.
    'Victoria'—18", dwarf, uniform with basal branching. 14" spread, intense violet-blue
        flowers. 'Victoria' is a Fleuroselect winner.

ADDITIONAL NOTES: For sheer dependability year in and year out, mealycup sage is unsur-
    passed. It is a strong grower in extreme heat, attractive, and certainly excellent for
    bedding purposes, also good for cutting. *Salvia* is derived from *salveo,* "save," and
    refers to the medicinal value ascribed to the plant.

Native to Texas.   Perennial treated as an annual in northern areas

SCIENTIFIC NAME/FAMILY: *Salvia officinalis*   Lamiaceae
                                                               (Labiatae)

(sal'vi-à o-fis-i-nā'lis)

COMMON NAME: Garden Sage, Common Sage

See color plate

LEAVES: Leaves 3" to 4" long, half of the length being the petiole, 1/2"–3/4" wide. Margins are finely crenate to entire. Both surfaces are softly pubescent, upper surface resembling the pebbly surface of a basketball. The leaves of dwarf sage are 1"–2" long and 1/4" wide. Stems are square with opposite arranged leaves.

FLOWER: Lilac-blue flowers are arranged in whorls that are widely separated on an erect raceme. Individual flowers are 2-lipped, with the upper lip being straight or arched; a hairy ring is found inside each corolla.

HABIT: Garden sage is a subshrub (woody-like stems), with an erect to round growth habit, 18"–24" tall. Spacing 18".

SEASON OF BLOOM: Early to midsummer.

CULTURE: Sage grows best in full sun in a well-drained soil. Root rot can be a problem in wetter soils.

UTILIZATION: Garden sage is another herb that is usually a permanent fixture of the herb garden. As a culinary item sage is used in sausage, stuffings, salads, and soups. In the ornamental garden, the variegated forms of this subshrub create a nice background for front of the border annuals and perennials. The variegated foliage can be a nice accent.

PROPAGATION: The species is propagated by seed. Seeds are covered and germinated at 70°F. Germination will take 10–14 days. Cultivars with colored or variegated foliage are propagated by tip or basal cuttings, 3"–4" long. Rooting is enhanced with 1000 ppm K-IBA. Plants may be divided but divisions are often slow to recover.

DISEASES AND INSECTS: Root rot can occur with poorly drained soils.

HARDINESS: Zones 4–8.

CULTIVARS:
'Icterina' (Aurea)—Variegated gold and green foliage, 18" tall. Good culinary selection. Tender perennial.
'Purpurascens'—Purple foliage, 24" tall. Good culinary selection. Tender perennial.
'Tricolor'—White and purple marbled leaves have pink margins, 18". Tender perennial.
var. *nana*, Dwarf sage—12" tall, compact habit makes this selection valuable for edging.

Native to Mediterranean region.   Perennial

Dwarf Sage

Salvia officinalis 'Icterina'

SCIENTIFIC NAME/FAMILY: *Salvia splendens*   Lamiaceae
                                                              (Labiatae)

(sal'vi-à splen'denz)

COMMON NAME: Scarlet Sage, Red Salvia

LEAVES: Opposite, petioled, 2"–4" long, acuminate; dentate margin, square stems.

FLOWER: Terminal raceme, bracts red, deciduous; calyx campanulate, scarlet; corolla to 1½" long, scarlet, lower lip much reduced. There are many cultivars, the flowers varying in color from scarlet to purple, pink, lavender, or white.

HABIT: 8" to 30" erect to round growth habit.

SEASON OF BLOOM: Summer to frost. Dwarf cultivars flower first, taller ones flower later in the season.

CULTURE: Red salvia performs best in full sun in a well-drained moist soil. In southern or southwestern zones, it will do better in partially shaded sites. The gardener should remove faded inflorescences to encourage continual flowering.

UTILIZATION: Bedding, border, cut flowers.

PROPAGATION: Tender perennial grown as an annual. Germinate at 70°F; then grow at 55°F night temperature. Seeds should not be covered.

DISEASES AND INSECTS: Damping-off in seed beds, downy and powdery mildews.

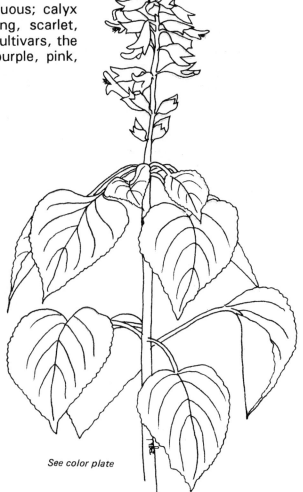

See color plate

CULTIVARS:

Dwarf Selections

'Carabiniere' Series—Early flowering, 10"–12" tall, with deep glossy green foliage. Available in white, purple, rose, and scarlet.

'Empire' Series—Excellent compact grower with good garden performance, 10"–12" tall, compact habit, 6 colors.

'Fireball'—Scarlet flowers, early flowering, 12".

'Firecracker' Series—Excellent compact grower with good garden performance, 10"–12" tall and 12" wide. Available in 10 colors and two mixes.

'Fuego'—Scarlet flowers, earliest to flower, 8"–10".

'Hotline'—This series blooms 6 weeks after sowing and is very compact with a height of 8"–10" and a spread of 10 inches. Colors include red, white, violet, salmon, and a mix.

'Hot Stuff'—Bright red, 10".

'Melba'—Early flowering, compact plants, 8" tall with salmon-colored flowers with lighter-colored tips.

'Red Hussar'—10"–12", scarlet spikes, deep green leaves, flowers later than other dwarf types.

'St. John's Fire'—12", scarlet-red flowers, blooms early.

Medium Selections
'America'—18"–20", red flowers, starts blooming midseason.
'Flare'—Scarlet red spikes, 18" tall, free-flowering selection.
'Red Pillar'—14", fiery-red flowers.
'Red Pompei'—Red flowers, 16".

Tall Selections
'Bonfire'—26", scarlet spikes, very even growth.
'Early Bonfire'—24", flowers 10 days earlier than 'Bonfire', red flowers.
'Splendens Tall'—30", late-flowering red flowers.

ADDITIONAL NOTES: Garden value and popularity of *Salvia* are excellent. Brilliant reds will overpower softer colors. Mass of red against evergreen foliage is an effective use; also useful with white flowers.

Native to Brazil.   Annual

SCIENTIFIC NAME/FAMILY: *Salvia × superba* (S. nemorosa)

(sal'vi-à sū-pĕr'bà)

COMMON NAME: Perennial Salvia

LEAVES: Opposite, lanceolate to oblong, crenate, obtuse or acute, rugose above and
slightly pubescent beneath, basal leaves have
short petioles, stem leaves sessile or often
clasping, 3" to 6".

FLOWER: Violet-blue, long spikelike racemes,
densely flowered, 4"–8" long; corolla is
violet or purple, while the calyx is reddish
purple.

HABIT: 2' to 3' tall, round growth habit with a
24" width.

SEASON OF BLOOM: Summer.

CULTURE: Optimum performance is promoted by
planting in full sun and in a moist, well-
drained soil. Cool evenings enhance the
length of bloom and the intensity of the
violet-blue color. Perennial salvia is tolerant
to drought conditions.

See color plate

UTILIZATION: Perennial border, particularly the
all-blue garden.

PROPAGATION: Stem cuttings and division. Stem cuttings, 3"–4" long, root readily when
placed under mist. Clump division is done in the spring, but reestablishment is slow because of a long, stringy root system.

DISEASES AND INSECTS: There are a few leaf spots and rusts but none are generally serious. Scale and white fly are the principle insect pests.

HARDINESS: Zones 3–8.

CULTIVARS: *Salvia × superba* is a probable hybrid of *S. nemorosa × S. villicaulis.* It is
often listed in trade catalogs as *Salvia nemorosa.*
'Blauhugel' ('Blue Mound')—Pure blue flowers on 20" tall stems. This is an introduction
from Germany by the Pagel Nursery.
'Blaukonigin' ('Blue Queen')—This selection is a seed-propagated form with blue-violet
flowers on stems 18"–24" tall. It is noted as being heat and drought tolerant.
'Lubeca'—Violet-blue flowers, 30" tall. The bloom period is several weeks longer than
'East Friesland.'
'Mainacht' ('May Night')—The famous German horticulturist, Karl Foerster, introduced
this cultivar in 1956. This selection has indigo-blue flowers and is 18" tall.
'Negrito'—Blue flowers, 16"–18" tall.
'Ostfriesland' ('East Friesland')—A much-branched plant which does not require staking
due to its compact habit, 18" tall. It has a dark violet flower color.
'Primevere'—Blue-violet flowers, 18" tall.
'Rose Queen'—Rose-pink flowers, 20"–24" tall.

'Viola Klose'—This 1975 introduction from the Klose Nursery, Lohfelden, Germany, has dark blue flowers and is 16"–18" tall.

'Wesuwe'—Violet flowers, 18" tall.

RELATED SPECIES:

S. argentea (ar-jen'-te-a). This species has beautiful woolly-white leaves up to 8" long. During the summer, flowering stems grow to 30" tall and bear white or pink-tinted flowers. It is a short-lived perennial which is often treated as an annual.

S. azurea (az-ū-rē'-a), Azure Salvia. 4'–5', blue flowers in later summer and fall. It tolerates heat and humid conditions.

S. a. var. *grandiflora* (gran-di-flō'-ra). Pitcher's Salvia (often listed as *S. pitcheri* (pitch'-er-ī)). 3'–4', deep blue flowers.

S. haematodes (hē-mat'-ō-dez). 3', lavender-blue flowers in large panicles in late spring; often acts as a biennial.

S. haematodes 'Indigo'. This cultivar has indigo blue flowers, 3' tall.

S. patens (pa'-tens). This zone 9 species has gentian-blue flowers in summer and early fall.

Hybrid origin.   Perennial

SCIENTIFIC NAME/FAMILY: *Salvia viridis (Salvia horminum)*   Lamiaceae (Labiatae)

(sal'vi-à vir'i-dis)

COMMON NAME: Painted Sage

LEAVES: Opposite leaves, oblong to ovate, 1"–2" long. Margins may have very small teeth or may be entire.

FLOWER: White and blue flowers are complemented by pink to purple bracts. Bracts are usually more noticeable than the flowers. The terminal bracts are leaflike and form tuftlike crowns. Flowers and bracts are borne in loose spikes.

HABIT: 18" tall, erect plant. Space 12" apart.

SEASON OF BLOOM: Summer. It will flower until frost if old flowers are removed.

CULTURE: Full sun and well-drained soil.

See color plate

UTILIZATION: Painted sage is a flashy plant suitable for the mixed border. It is also excellent for cutting and can be dried as an everlasting.

PROPAGATION: Seed should be uncovered and germinated at 70°F; 14 days to germination.

DISEASES AND INSECTS: None serious.

CULTIVARS:
'Claryssa'—This strain is listed as being more compact with wider and bolder bracts.

Native to southern Europe.   Annual

SCIENTIFIC NAME/FAMILY: *Sanguisorba canadensis* (Poterium canadense)   Rosaceae

(sang-gwi-sôr'bå kan-a-den'sis)

COMMON NAME: Canadian Burnet

LEAVES: The compound leaves are odd-pinnate with the lower leaves 12"–18" long. There are 7–15 leaflets which are ovate to oblong and sharply toothed on the margin. The margin looks as if it were cut with pinking shears. Individual leaflets are 2"–3" long.

FLOWER: White flowers are borne in terminal spikes. The cylinder-shaped spike has exerted stamens which gives the flower the appearance of a 3"–8" long white bottlebrush. All flowers are apetalous.

HABIT: Canadian burnet has a distinct upright habit, 4'–5' tall with a 2'–3' spread.

SEASON OF BLOOM: Late summer.

CULTURE: This North American native thrives in moist to wet conditions in full sun. In southern zones it will perform best in partial shade with a mulch added to retain soil moisture. It will tolerate most conditions, but the soil should not dry out. Canadian burnet can be invasive so it should be located in areas where spread is not a problem.

UTILIZATION: Use in the border or native garden. The flowers are handsome and enhance the garden in late summer.

PROPAGATION: Fresh seed should germinate in 3–4 weeks at 70°F. Cold stratification for 4 weeks is beneficial for older seeds. Division is done in the spring.

DISEASES AND INSECTS: Plants are usually vigorous with no major pest problems.

HARDINESS: Zones 4–8.

RELATED SPECIES:
S. obtusa (ob-tūs'-a) Japanese Burnet—This species has grey-green foliage which creates a nice backdrop for the reddish pink flowers. The leaves are 18" long with 5–17 leaflets. The flowers have extremely long stamens resulting in fluffy appearing flowers, which are 4" long. Japanese burnet is 3'–4' tall and 2'–3' wide. This species is not as vigorous as Canadian burnet. Cultural conditions are the same. Alan Bloom, in his book, *Hardy Perennials*, writes that *S. stipulata* (stip-ū-la'-ta) (sitchensis) is taller and more graceful than *S. obtusa*. Zones 4–9.

Native from Newfoundland to Michigan and south to Georgia.   Perennial

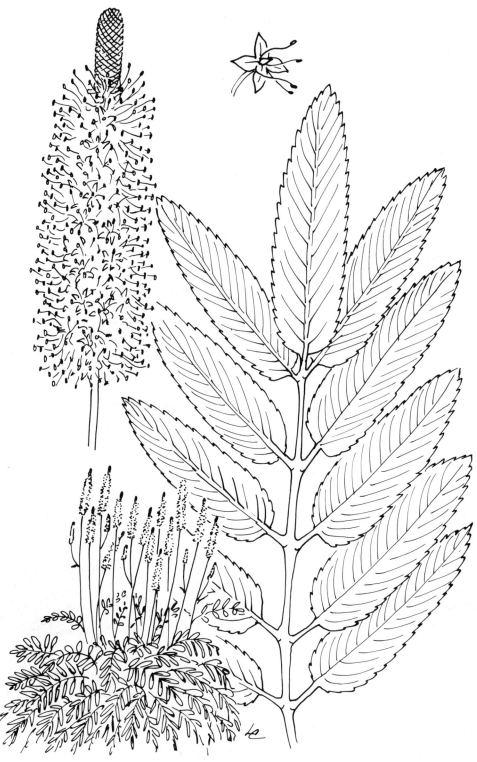

See color plate

SCIENTIFIC NAME/FAMILY: *Sanguisorba minor (Poterium sanguisorba)*   Rosaceae

(san-gwi-sôr′ba mī′nor)

COMMON NAME: Salad Burnet

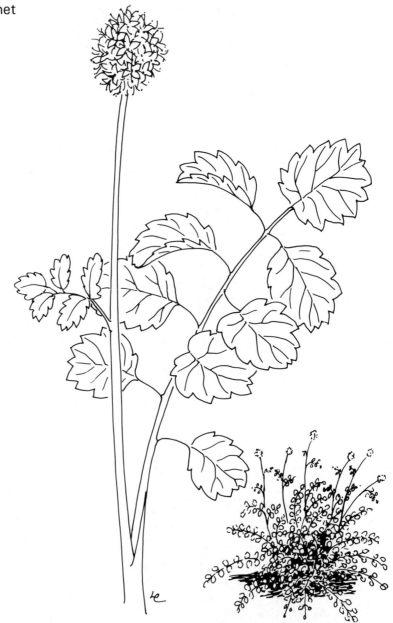

LEAVES: Basal leaves are odd-pinnate with 9–21 leaflets. Individual leaflets are round to elliptic and sharply serrated. Leaf blades are ¾″–1″ long and ¾″–1″ wide. There are few stem leaves.

FLOWER: Pink flowers are borne in ½″ diameter, round heads. Lower flowers in the head are staminate, middle flowers are bisexual and upper flowers are pistillate.

HABIT: Basal clump of foliage is 12″ tall; flower stalks rise to 2½′. Space plants 12″–15″ apart.

SEASON OF BLOOM: Early to midsummer.

CULTURE: Salad burnet can be grown in full sun or partial shade in a well-drained soil. New leaf growth is prompted by removal of the flower stalks. Highly fertile and moist soils will cause the rosette to rot in the winter.

UTILIZATION: Young leaves of salad burnet are added to green salads to contribute a cucumber flavor. Trimmings of the stems and leaves are used for burnet vinegar. Salad burnet can be used as an attractive edging in the herb garden. The unique foliage is also valuable in the flower border.

PROPAGATION: Seed and division. Germinate lightly covered seed at 70°F. Division of established clumps should be done in the spring.

DISEASES AND INSECTS: None serious.

HARDINESS: Zones 3–8.

ADDITIONAL NOTES: Salad burnet is one of the forgotten herbs that was more popular in colonial times.

Native to Europe and western Asia.   Perennial

SCIENTIFIC NAME/FAMILY: *Santolina chamaecyparissus* (S. incana)   Asteraceae
(Compositae)

(san-tō-lĭ'nȧ kam-e-sip'ȧ-ris-sus, kam-e-sip-ar-iss'-sus)

COMMON NAME: Lavender Cotton

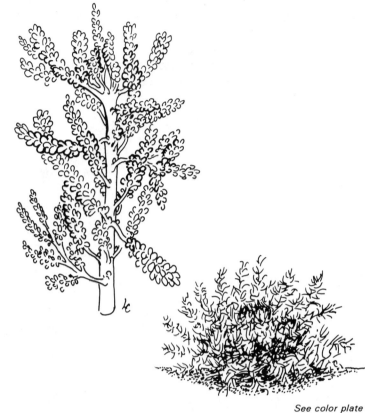

See color plate

LEAVES: Foliage silver-gray and pubescent, ½"–1½" long, pinnately divided into very small ovate-oblong segments. The foliage has a musty fragrance.

FLOWER: Bright yellow flowers borne in round, buttonlike heads, ½"–¾" wide.

HABIT: 18" to 24" broad spreading clump. Space 18"–24" on center.

SEASON OF BLOOM: The buttonlike flowers occur in late summer but are rarely seen because the plant is often kept tightly sheared.

CULTURE: Full sun and ordinary, well-drained soil. A dry site is much preferred to a wet one. *Santolina* is hardy to zone 6 and may need to be overwintered in cold frames in northern regions. A winter mulch will be of benefit in other areas.

UTILIZATION: Rock garden, low hedge, and carpet bedding. Lavender cotton is also a favorite for knot gardens. *Santolina* is usually trimmed to maintain the compact habit.

PROPAGATION: Propagated from cuttings taken in the spring from plants overwintered in a cold frame or from cuttings in the fall that can be rooted in a cold frame or in the greenhouse. Cuttings also root easily during the growing season. Seed germination is often erratic. Placing the seed in a cooler at 35°–40°F for 3–4 weeks may improve germination.

DISEASES AND INSECTS: None serious.

HARDINESS: Zones 6–8. In southern areas, lavender cotton survives, but it is not really vigorous. The high humidity in southern zones is the probable culprit.

CULTIVARS:
ssp. *nana*—Dwarf form to 10", yellow flowers.

RELATED SPECIES:

S. virens (vī'renz) *(S. viridis)* Green Lavender Cotton. Leaves are green and glabrous, and the culture is identical with that of lavender cotton. This species also has yellow flowers and is 18" to 24" tall. Hardy to zone 6.

S. rosmarinifolia (ros-mar-in-i-fo'-lē-a)—Dark green leaves, yellow flowers, 24" tall. In Europe, this species is used in lieu of *S. virens.* In the United States, taxonomists keep the two species separate. The difference between these two species is related to the foliage and flowers. *Santolina rosmarinifolia* has leaves which have a checkered upper surface created by crowded flattened segments.

S. neapolitana (nē-a-pol-i-ta'-na)—Silver-gray leaves and bright yellow flowers. The leaves are longer and more feathery than *Santolina chamaecyparissus.* 2½ feet tall. This excellent species is rarer than *S. chamaecyparissus.*

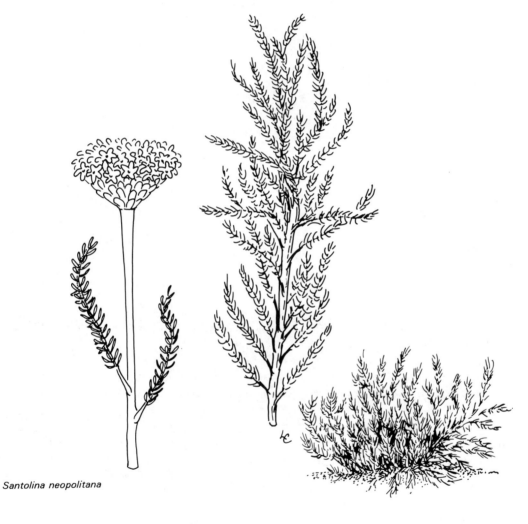

Santolina neopolitana

Native to Mediterranean region.   Perennial

SCIENTIFIC NAME/FAMILY: *Sanvitalia procumbens*   Asteraceae
                                                                   (Compositae)

(san-vi-tā'li-á prō-kum'benz)

COMMON NAME: Creeping Zinnia, Trailing Sanvitalia

LEAVES: Leaves opposite, ovate, ½"–1" long, petiolate, strigose pubescence, entire
    margins; branches are procumbent.

FLOWER: Solitary heads, about ¾" across, closely subtended by a pair of leafy bracts;
    rays yellow, disk flowers dark purple. Heads may be single or double. The flowers
    resemble small zinnias.

HABIT: 6" stems tend to trail
    along the ground. Plants will
    spread 18".

SEASON OF BLOOM: Early sum-
    mer to frost.

CULTURE: *Sanvitalia* grows best
    in full sun and a loose, well-
    drained soil. It is very tolerant
    of heat, drought, and humi-
    dity.

See color plate

UTILIZATION: Edging along bor-
    ders or paths, rock garden,
    and as a ground cover.

PROPAGATION: Seeds germinate
    in one week with a minimum
    temperature of 70°F.

DISEASES AND INSECTS: None serious.

CULTIVARS:
    'Gold Braid'—Double golden-yellow flowers with purple centers, 6" tall.
    'Mandarin Orange'—This 1987 All American Selection winner is the first orange-
        flowering *Sanvitalia*. The flowers are 1" wide and are semidouble. It has a spread
        of 16" to 18".

ADDITIONAL NOTES: The genus was named for Frederico Sanvitali, an 18th century
    professor in Italy.

Native to Mexico.   Annual

SCIENTIFIC NAME/FAMILY: *Saponaria ocymoides*   Caryophyllaceae

(sap-ō-nā′ri-á ō-kē-moi′dēz)

COMMON NAME: Rock Soapwort

LEAVES: Opposite, spatulate, or elliptic to ovate-lanceolate in shape, to 1″ long; lower leaves are short-petioled, and the upper leaves are sessile. Individual leaves are simple and entire with an acute apex. The stems are reddish with many branches.

FLOWER: The deep pink, 5-petaled flowers are borne in a broad, loose cyme. The calyx is cylindrical, 5-toothed, glandular-hairy, and up to ½″ long. Some cultivars have double flowers.

HABIT: 4″–10″ trailing plant which forms a broad mound.

SEASON OF BLOOM: Late spring is the peak period but sporadic flowering will occur until fall.

See color plate

CULTURE: Full sun and a well-drained site are needed for best performance. *Saponaria* will tolerate poor soils, but it is unable to survive in a wet site during the winter. Cutting the plant back after flowering helps keep the plant compact; otherwise, it develops into a large sprawling mass.

UTILIZATION: Rock soapwort has been successfully used in the rock garden, perennial border, or on dry stone walls. Although the individual pink flowers are small, the clusters of these flowers are quite effective in June.

PROPAGATION: Division, seed, and cuttings. Division is best done in the spring, while cuttings root more easily in midsummer. Seeds started indoors will germinate in 2 weeks when maintained at 60°–65°F in the dark.

DISEASES AND INSECTS: None serious.

HARDINESS: Zones 3–7.

CULTIVARS:
'Alba'—Pure white flowers.
'Rosea'—Bright rose flowers.
'Rubra Compacta'—Dark pink flowers, prostrate mat, 3" tall and 12" wide.
'Splendens'—Deep rose flowers which are larger than the species.

RELATED SPECIES:
S. officinalis (ō-fis-i-nā'lis)—Bouncing Bet. This southern European native has naturalized over much of the eastern United States. It is composed of strong, upright, unbranched stems which carry pale pink flowers held in terminal or axillary clusters. Plants are 12"–24" tall and 18" wide. Full sun and a well-drained soil are minimal requirements. This species can quickly spread by underground stolons. The double flowering cultivar, 'Rosea Plena', is a better choice as it is not as vigorous.

ADDITIONAL NOTES: *Saponaria* is derived from the Latin word *sapo,* "soap," and refers to the fact that several species of *Saponaria* have sap in the roots that creates a lather when mixed with water. Supposedly, the roots of *S. officinalis,* Bouncing Bet, were once used as a substitute for soap.

Native to southern and central Europe, especially in the Alps of Switzerland.   Perennial

SCIENTIFIC NAME/FAMILY: *Satureja montana*   Lamiaceae
                                                               (Labiatae)

(sat-ū-rē'ya mon-tā'-na)

COMMON NAME: Winter Savory

LEAVES: Leaves opposite, narrow
   linear to linear-lanceolate, entire
   margins, leaf surfaces dotted with
   small pits, 1/2″ to 3/4″ long and
   1/8″ wide. Stems and leaves have
   a hispid pubescence.

FLOWER: Flowers are white or lilac,
   3/8″ long; calyx and corolla are
   resinous-dotted, calyx is bristly.
   The flowers are borne in whorls in
   open, racemose-paniculate stems.

HABIT: Compact, semi-evergreen perennial, 12″ tall. Space plants 12″
   apart.

SEASON OF BLOOM: Mid to late
   summer.

CULTURE: Winter savory grows best
   in a well-drained soil located in full
   sun. Well-drained soil is particularly important during the winter so
   winterkill does not occur.

UTILIZATION: As an ornamental, winter savory can be used as an
   edging or border plant. Its compact habit makes winter savory a
   candidate for the rock garden. In
the culinary area, winter savory has a strong pine flavor and is used with strong-
flavored game meats and pâtés. Summer savory (*S. hortensis*) has a milder taste and
is used in a wider variety of foods.

PROPAGATION: Winter savory is propagated by seeds or cuttings. Seed germination is
   slow and erratic. Seeds should be uncovered and germinated at 70°F. From seed to
   garden, transplants will require about 7 weeks. Take stem cuttings in the summer.

DISEASES AND INSECTS: None serious.

HARDINESS: Zones 5–8.

RELATED SPECIES:
   S. hortensis (hôr-ten'sis), Summer Savory. White or pale pink flowers, glabrous leaves,
      1″ long. Summer savory is an annual with a more delicate flavor than winter
      savory. It is easy to grow.

Native to Mediterranean region.   Perennial

SCIENTIFIC NAME/FAMILY: *Saxifraga* × *arendsii*   Saxifragaceae

(saks-if'rȧ-gȧ a-ren'si-i)

COMMON NAME: Mossy Saxifrage

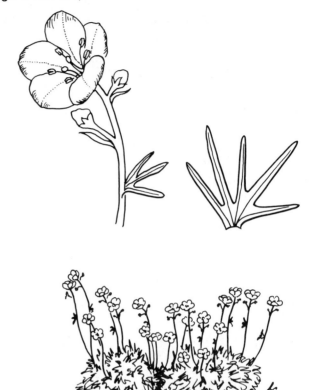

LEAVES: Leaves are borne in dense tufts. Each leaf is palmately dissected, usually 3 to 4 lobes, and colored a bright green.

FLOWER: Five-petaled, rose to blood-red flowers are arranged in 4 to 5 flowered, terminal racemes. Individual flowers are ¾" wide.

HABIT: The total height of this tufted perennial is 4" to 6". The tufted leaves are usually 2" high with 4" tall flower stems which resemble colorful pins sticking out of a pincushion.

SEASON OF BLOOM: Mid to late spring.

CULTURE: Mossy saxifrage should be planted in partial shade with a preference for morning sun. The soil needs to be well-drained but should not dry out. It is not a plant for hot, dry areas. In warm, high-humidity areas, it has a tendency to "melt out" in the center of the clump.

UTILIZATION: Excellent plant for the partially shaded rock garden or in wall gardens.

PROPAGATION: Easily propagated by division, cutting, or seed. Seeds should be propagated at 65° to 75°F. Cuttings can be obtained by removing small rosettes which can be taken after flowering. In areas of potential frost heaving, division should be done in the spring.

DISEASES AND INSECTS: No serious problems.

HARDINESS: Zones 4–7.

CULTIVARS:
    'Carpet' Series—This series contains a number of cultivars of differing flower colors. Plants are 4"–8" tall. 'Blood Carpet' has dark red flowers; 'Purple Carpet'—purple-carmine flowers; 'Snow Carpet'—white flowers; 'Flower Carpet'—pink, free-flowering cultivar.
    'Sulfur Flower' ('Schwefelblute')—Pale sulfur-yellow flowers, vigorous grower with a compact mound of foliage.
    'Triumph'—This is a common cultivar with dark red flowers on 6"–8" tall stems.

There are 300 species of saxifrage found in the subarctic and temperate zones. Most of them are grown by collectors or specialists; however, a few are worthy of general garden culture. *Saxifraga* species are grouped into sections to illustrate relationships and for identification. For example, Hortus III lists 15 different classifications. Nurseries will often segregate the species, but the number of divisions is much smaller. One nursery lists the following groups:

<u>Encrusted Saxifrage</u>. This division includes those selections that secrete lime, which creates a lime-encrusted leaf margin. Species in this group require full sun and a well-drained soil with an alkaline pH.

<u>Mossy Saxifrage</u>. Selections in this group do well in more shade and richer soil. *Saxifraga* × *arendsii* is a member of the Mossy Saxifrage group.

ADDITIONAL NOTES: *S.* × *arendsii* is a hybrid of mixed parentage, which probably includes *S. exarata* and *S. rosacea.*

Hybrid origin.   Perennial

SCIENTIFIC NAME/FAMILY: *Saxifraga paniculata* (S. aizoon)   Saxifragaceae

(saks-if'rá-gá pan-ik-ū-lā'tá)

COMMON NAME: Aizoon Saxifrage

LEAVES: Leaves are arranged in dense basal rosettes, leaves obovate-oblong to narrow-spatulate, to 1½" long. The leaf apex has encrusted white teeth.

FLOWER: Flowers are creamy-white, marked with purple, ½" across and arranged in panicles.

HABIT: 3"–12" tall clump of many rosettes.

SEASON OF BLOOM: Late spring to early summer.

CULTURE: *Saxifraga* does best in moist, well-drained soil located in partial shade. This plant is a poor choice for hot, dry areas. At Ohio State University, we have had very poor success in growing this perennial.

UTILIZATION: *Saxifraga* is favored as a rock garden species. In fact, *Saxifraga* means "rock breaking" in Latin.

PROPAGATION: This species can be propagated by taking a small cutting (single rosette) after flowering. Division is also possible in the spring or summer.

DISEASES AND INSECTS: Aphids and rust are sometimes problems.

HARDINESS: Zones 3–6.

CULTIVARS:
    var. *baldensis*—White flowers, 2"–3" tall.
    var. *lutea*—Yellow flowers, 6"–10" tall.
    'Paradoxa'—White flowers, blue leaves.
    var. *rosea*—Bright pink flowers.

ADDITIONAL NOTES: *Saxifraga* is derived from the Latin words *saxum,* rock, and *frango,* to break. This species of plant, when grown in a rock crevice, was supposed to be capable of breaking rocks.

Native to Europe, Asia, and Canada.   Perennial

SCIENTIFIC NAME/FAMILY: *Scabiosa atropurpurea*   Dipsacaceae

(skā-bi-ō'så at-rō-pĕr-pū'rē-à)

COMMON NAME: Pincushion Flower, Sweet Scabious, Mourning-Bride

LEAVES: Opposite, basal leaves oblong-spatulate, undivided or lyrate, coarsely dentate; stem leaves pinnately parted, the oblong lobes dentate or cut. Leaves 2″ to 4″ long.

FLOWER: Flowers in long-peduncled heads to 2″ across, stamens appear as pins in a cushion. Flower colors are lavender, pink, purple, maroon, red, yellow, or white.

HABIT: Rosette leaves with a stem 1′ to 3′ tall, erect habit.

SEASON OF BLOOM: Early summer to frost.

CULTURE: Full sun, fertile, well-drained soil.

UTILIZATION: Bouquets, bedding, cut flowers which keep for several days.

PROPAGATION: Seeds germinate in 2 weeks at 65°–70°F.

DISEASES AND INSECTS: No serious problems.

CULTIVARS:
'Dwarf Double Mixed'—18″, mixed colors, plants compact enough for bedding, but flower stems are still long enough for cut flowers.
'Giant Imperial Mixed'—30″–36″, double flowers, 3″–4″ across, mixed colors.

ADDITIONAL NOTES: Anyone's poll would show scabiosas to be very low in popularity. Nevertheless, they are reasonably reliable garden annuals. The name scabiosa is derived from *scabies,* meaning "itch," and refers to the plant's supposed properties for curing irritations of the skin.

Native to southern Europe.   Annual

SCIENTIFIC NAME/FAMILY: *Scabiosa caucasica*   Dipsacaceae

(skā-bi-ō'sȧ kâ-kas'i-kȧ)

COMMON NAME: Pincushion Flower, Caucasian Scabious

LEAVES: Opposite, basal leaves lanceolate-linear and glaucous; stem leaves are divided into linear segments.

FLOWER: Light blue flowers are borne in flattened 3″ diameter involucrate heads, which are borne on long stems. The calyx is cup-shaped and has an involucre that is covered with dense matted gray hairs. An outer ring of flat petals surrounds a tufted central cushion from which dark gray stamens protrude.

HABIT: 18″–24″ rounded plant with long flowering stems. Plants are 18″ wide.

SEASON OF BLOOM: Summer.

CULTURE: Full sun and a well-drained fertile soil with a pH near neutral. Organic matter in the soil and a mulch during the summer will aid in plant maintenance because this plant prefers cool, humid climates. Remove faded flowers to promote additional flowering.

UTILIZATION: Pincushion flower is very effective in the border when planted in groups of at least 3. It is also excellent as a long-lasting cut flower.

PROPAGATION: Seeds can be sown outside in the spring or summer. If started indoors, germinate at 60°–65°F for 2 weeks. Division in the spring is a reliable but slow method.

See color plate

DISEASES AND INSECTS: Diseases and insects are generally not serious. However, slugs have been reported as a problem in some areas.

HARDINESS: Zones 3–7.

CULTIVARS:
'Blauer Atlas'—Deep blue flowers carried on stiff stems. Good selection for a cut flower.
'Blue Perfection'—Lavender-blue flowers, 24″.
'Bressingham White'—This 3′ tall white cultivar was selected by Alan Bloom from a group of seedlings. It is very similar to 'Miss Willmott'.
'Butterfly Blue'—A newer introduction with lavender-blue flowers on stems 20″–24″ tall. It flowers continuously from early summer to frost.

'Clive Greaves'—Lavender-blue flowers. This is a reliable cultivar that was introduced in 1929.

'Fama'—Deep blue flowers on 18″ stems. It is an excellent long-lasting cut flower.

'Isaac House Hybrids' (sometimes listed in catalogs as 'House Mixture' or 'House Hybrids'). These names refer to their place of origin at Isaac House, Bristol, England. The mixture is basically shades of lavender-blue.

'Kompliment'—Dark lavender flowers, 24″.

'Miss Willmott'—Creamy-white flowers.

'Moerheim Blue'—Lavender-blue flowers.

'Perfecta'—Large pale lilac flowers.

'Perfecta Alba'—Large white flowers.

'Prachtkerl' ('Great Guy')—Bright blue flowers.

Native to Caucasus Mountains.   Perennial

SCIENTIFIC NAME/FAMILY: *Scilla sibirica*   Liliaceae

(sil'à sī-ber'i-kà)

COMMON NAME: Siberian Squill, Blue Squill

LEAVES: Leaves 2 to 5, strap-shaped, to
  6" long, ½" wide, blunt or acute
  tipped and bright green.

FLOWER: Blue, wheel, or star-shaped
  flowers borne in groups of 3 to 5 on
  a pendulous raceme; 1 to 6 scapes
  per plant. Individual flowers are ½"
  wide.

HABIT: 6" erect plant.

SEASON OF BLOOM: Early spring.

CULTURE: Partial shade to full sun, in a
  well-drained soil. Several species
  thrive in partial shade as they are
  native to woodland areas. Plant bulbs
  3" deep and 4"–6" apart.

UTILIZATION: Siberian squill is valued for
  its early bright blue flowers. Useful in
  grassed areas, rock gardens, naturalized woodlands, and in massed drifts
  around shrubs and trees.

PROPAGATION: *Scilla* is easily multiplied
  by lifting the clumps after the foliage
  has died in late summer and dividing the bulbs. This procedure can be done every 4 to
  5 years.

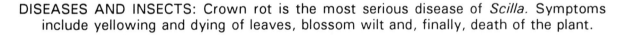

DISEASES AND INSECTS: Crown rot is the most serious disease of *Scilla.* Symptoms
  include yellowing and dying of leaves, blossom wilt and, finally, death of the plant.

HARDINESS: Zones 2–8.

CULTIVARS:
  alba—White flowers.
  'Spring Beauty'—4"–6", large blue flowers, readily self-sows. The flower spikes are
    taller than those of the species.

RELATED SPECIES:
  S. bifolia (bī-fō'lē-a)—Two-leaved Squill. This is an early spring flowering bulb with blue
    flowers. There are usually 2 leaves but sometimes as many as 4 leaves. Plants are
    3"–6" tall and are excellent for naturalizing. The var. *rosea* has rose-colored
    flowers. Hardy to zones 4–8.

Endymion hispanicus (en-dē'-mē-on his-pan'-ik-us) (Scilla hispanica), Spanish Bluebell. 12"–24", 12–15 blue flowers per stem in May, much larger specimen than Siberian Squill. This species likes deep shade and is utilized for cut flowers.
'Blue Queen'—Blue flowers.
'Rosabella'—Dark pink flowers.
'White Triumphator'—Large white flowers.

ADDITIONAL NOTES: *Scilla* is a Greek word used by Hippocrates meaning "to wound" or "harm," and refers to the poisonous properties of some species.

Native to Russia and southwestern Asia.   Perennial—hardy bulb

SCIENTIFIC NAME/FAMILY: *Sedum kamtschaticum*   Crassulaceae
(sē'dum kam-chat'i-kum)
COMMON NAME: Kamschatka Stonecrop, Orange Stonecrop

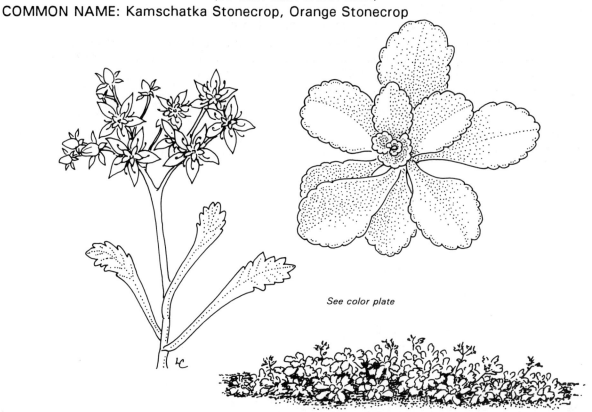

See color plate

LEAVES: Alternate leaves; leaf shapes vary from broad spatulate to linear-oblanceolate to
linear. Leaves are 1½″ long and toothed above the middle.

FLOWER: Yellow star-shaped flowers, ½″–¾″ wide, are borne in a 6–10 flower cyme;
stamens are as long as the petals. The barren shoots give rise to flat, terminal
inflorescences.

HABIT: Open, spreading habit; the foliage is about 4″ tall with flowering stems to 9″. This
sedum spreads 15″–18″ wide.

SEASON OF BLOOM: Summer.

CULTURE: Full sun and a well-drained soil. Poor drainage can be fatal.

UTILIZATION: Kamschatka stonecrop can be used in planting pockets on stone walls, on
hillsides, steep banks, and borders. The habit is too open to be an effective ground
cover mat, which is often associated with sedum.

PROPAGATION: Tip cuttings, 1″–2″ long, taken in spring and summer, root easily.

DISEASES AND INSECTS: None serious.

HARDINESS: Zones 3–8.

CULTIVARS:
'Variegatum'—leaves have white margins which are flushed with pink. Flowers are a
deeper yellow than the species.

RELATED SPECIES:

S. ellacombianum (el-la-ko-me-a'-num) — This species is often listed as a variety of *Sedum kamtschaticum*. However, it has fleshier leaves, arching stems, and pale, yellowish green leaves. Flowers are yellowish green. 6" tall.

S. floriferum (flō-rif'-er-um) — This species is also found in listings as a variety of *Sedum kamtschaticum*. Flowers are greenish-yellow, sepals are linear rather than broad. The gold-yellow flowering cultivar 'Weihenstephaner Gold' is quite attractive and is the preferred choice in this species.

Native to Japan and Kamchatka.   Perennial

SCIENTIFIC NAME/FAMILY: *Sedum spectabile*   Crassulaceae

(sē'dum spek-tab'i-le)

COMMON NAME: Showy Stonecrop Sedum,
    Live-Forever

LEAVES: Opposite or ternate, about 3" long,
    obovate, fleshy, and somewhat toothed.

FLOWER: Flowers ½" across, in large dense
    corymbose cymes 3"–6" across. Flower
    colors are pink, red, or white. Butterflies
    are often attracted to the flowers to
    gather nectar.

HABIT: 18" to 24", round growth habit.

SEASON OF BLOOM: Late summer to late
    fall (August to frost).

CULTURE: Sun or light shade, any soil that is
    well-drained.

UTILIZATION: Rock garden, border; display
    as single specimen or in groups of three
    or more.

PROPAGATION: Stem cuttings in summer.
    Clump divisions in spring, but it may not
    be necessary for years.

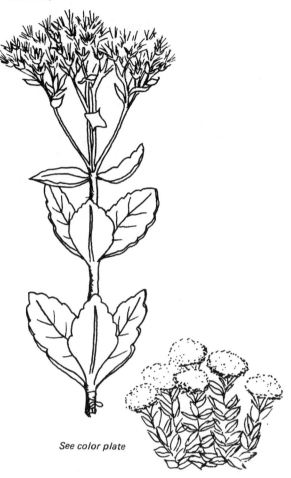

See color plate

DISEASES AND INSECTS: This sedum is very easy to grow and has no serious pests.

HARDINESS: Zones 3–10. *Sedum spectabile* grows very well in the south.

CULTIVARS:
    var. *atropurpurea*—Red leaf form of the species.
    'Brilliant'—Carmine flowers, 18".
    'Carmen'—Rose-pink flowers with light grey-green foliage, 18".
    'Meteor'—Large wine-red flowers, 18".
    'Star Dust'—Ivory-white flowers with blue-green leaves, 18".
    'Variegatum'—Foliage is variegated with yellow, bright pink flowers.

RELATED SPECIES:
    S. aizoon (aī-zō'-on)—This strong growing sedum is 12"–18" tall, has leathery stems,
        bright green leaves, and is covered with yellow flowers in the spring. It is a very
        easy sedum to grow. 'Aurantiacum' is a dark yellow flowered cultivar with red-
        tinged stems and seed heads.
    S. 'Autumn Joy,' (also called 'Herbstfreude')—This hybrid is probably a cross of
        S. spectabile and *S. telephium.* 'Autumn Joy' is one of the best perennials available
        to the gardener. It seems to be attractive year round. In early spring gray-green
        buds emerge. By midsummer, leaves and flower buds create an attractive mound
        that resembles a broccoli head. Later in the summer, the buds turn a pale pink and
        mature to a rosy red. After frost the plant stays intact in a rusty color. Unless heavy

snows smash the stems, the dried inflorescences and stems last until spring. I have observed beautiful plantings of 'Autumn Joy' in the snow during March in Columbus, Ohio. The cultivar 'Indian Chief' is considered to be the same as 'Autumn Joy'.

S. *maximum* (maks'-e-mum) 'Atropurpureum'—This 18" to 24" tall selection has maroon colored foliage with dull pink flowers. It has a tendency to sprawl.

S. 'Ruby Glow'—This selection has purple-grey foliage with deep ruby red flowers. The flowers that appear in the fall are attractive to butterflies. It is 6" to 8" tall. This cultivar is also known as 'Rosy Glow'.

ADDITIONAL NOTES: The plant is indestructible but not invasive. Plants need not be disturbed unless an increase is desired. *Sedum* is from *sedo,* to sit, which refers to the manner in which the plants affix themselves to rocks or walls. The common name, stonecrop, refers to the ability of many species to flourish on stoney ledges.

Native to Japan.   Perennial

SCIENTIFIC NAME/FAMILY: *Sedum spurium*   Crassulaceae

(sē'dum spū'ri-um)

COMMON NAME: Two Row Stonecrop

LEAVES: Leaves opposite, ½" – 1" long, obovate with a wedge-shaped base, crenate-toothed on upper third of leaf. The leaf margins are reddish with leaves near the apex turning a deeper red in the fall. Many of the leaves are deciduous, but those near the shoot tip are evergreen and turn red in the winter.

FLOWER: Pinkish red flowers, ½" – ¾" wide are borne in dense, 4-branched inflorescences.

HABIT: Ground cover sedum which roots at the nodes, 2"–6" tall and 18" wide.

SEASON OF BLOOM: Midsummer.

CULTURE: Full sun and well-drained soil. Two row stonecrop is a more vigorous grower in northern gardens than in southern gardens.

UTILIZATION: *Sedum spurium* is a durable stonecrop for rock garden, stone wall, or ground cover use. Numerous stems arise from branches which root at the nodes. This creates a rapidly spreading habit that can become invasive in a formal design.

PROPAGATION: Propagation by cuttings or division can be done at any time during the growing season.

DISEASES AND INSECTS: None serious.

HARDINESS: Zones 3–8.

CULTIVARS:
  'Bronze Carpet'—Reddish bronze leaves, usually most prominent in the early season. Green stem reversion will sometimes occur. Pink flowers.
  'Coccineum'—Scarlet flowers.
  'Dragon's Blood'—This selection is popular because the foliage has a strong reddish bronze color. Flowers are scarlet. It is also listed as 'Schorbuser Blut.'
  'Fuldaglut'—Deep red foliage and scarlet flowers. Some consider this as an improved 'Dragon's Blood'.
  'Red Carpet'—Red flowers and bronze foliage.
  'Variegatum'—Leaves have creamy pink margins.

Native to Caucasus.   Perennial

SCIENTIFIC NAME/FAMILY: *Sempervivum tectorum*   Crassulaceae

(sem-pẽr-vī'vum tek-tō'rum)

COMMON NAME: Hen-and-Chickens, Old-Man-and-Woman, Houseleeks

LEAVES: Open rosette, flat, 3"–4" wide, 50–60 cuneate-obovate cuspidate leaves 1½"–3" long, glabrous.

FLOWER: Purple-red flowers, ¾"–1" wide, on secund curving branches; flower stems are 6"–15" high and are densely pubescent.

HABIT: Foliage is 3"–4" tall with a flower stem to 15". *Sempervivum* is characterized by flat, crowded rosettes.

SEASON OF BLOOM: The plants flower in midsummer but are more valued for the foliage effect and compact, neat habit.

See color plate

CULTURE: Full sun and good drainage are the only requirements. The plants do best in poor, rocky soil.

UTILIZATION: Rock garden, dry wall, edging, front of the perennial border, carpet bedding and potted into containers such as strawberry jars.

PROPAGATION: Propagation is easily done by separating the small outer rosettes from the "mother" rosette.

DISEASES AND INSECTS: Rust and crown rot are the principal diseases.

HARDINESS: Zones 3–8.

RELATED SPECIES:
   S. t. var. *calcareum*—Glaucous leaves tipped with reddish-brown. Also listed as *S. calcareum.*
   S. arachnoideum (ar-ak-noi'-de-um), Cobweb Hen-and-Chickens. Leaf tips are connected by cobwebby strands; bright red flowers in July.
   S. a. var. *tomentosum*—Habit is similar to *S. arachnoideum* but the flowers are yellow.

ADDITIONAL NOTES: *Sempervivum* is derived from *semper,* forever, and *vivo,* to live, meaning live forever, perfectly characterizing this species. *Sempervivum* can be seen on tiled roofs of European country districts. The superstition is that houseleek on the roof repels lightning and prevents fires. *Sempervivums* hybridize easily and there are many variants. One nursery catalog lists 80 selections. Consequently, this species has been distributed under a great number of names, a vast number of which are not correct.

Native to Europe.   Perennial

SCIENTIFIC NAME/FAMILY: *Senecio cineraria* (Cineraria maritima)   Asteraceae
(Compositae)

(se-nē'shi-ō sin-e-rā'ri-à)

COMMON NAME: Dusty Miller

LEAVES: Stiff, white-woolly leaves pinnately cut into blunt oblong segments, branching from the base. The leaves sometimes become green on the upper surface. The silver-white film is quite ornamental and is most conspicuous when the leaves are dry. Leaves 2″ to 6″ long.

FLOWER: The flowers are daisylike, single, and about ½″ in diameter. They may be yellow or cream in color and are borne in corymb-like groups of 10–12. However, if the plants are grown for the foliage effect, the flowers should be removed.

See color plate

HABIT: 8″ to 15″ round habit.

SEASON OF BLOOM: Late summer.

CULTURE: Full sun, does well in dry soil but does prefer good organic matter content.

UTILIZATION: Edging, foliage plant. Useful for edging, specimen in mixed border or for the foliage effect in combination pots.

PROPAGATION: Seed and stem cuttings. Stem cuttings can be made from soft or slightly mature growth in September and placed in the greenhouses or cold frame; however, seed propagation is the normal method. Seeds should be uncovered and germinated at a constant 75°F. 'Silver Lace' is an exception to this with best germination at 62°–65°F. Dusty miller should be seeded thinly and transplanted quickly to deter damping off.

DISEASES AND INSECTS: Root rot, stem rot, and nematodes.

CULTIVARS:
'Cirrus'—6″–8″, compact rounded leaves, strong silver color.
'Diamond'—10″, compact and even grower, very white foliage.
'Hoar Frost'—12″, similar to 'Silver Dust' but the leaves are not as finely cut or white.
'New Look'—The leaves of this selection are oak-leaf shaped and very white. The plants are 9″ tall and 15″ wide.
'Silver Dust'—8″, a nice dwarf plant with finely cut and silvery foliage.
'Silver Lace'—6″–8″, compact, delicate lacy foliage. 'Silver Lace' has the most laciniated foliage of all selections of dusty miller.
'Snow Crystals'—This selection is listed as an improved 'Silver Dust'. It is earlier and has a better silver color.
'Snow Storm'—10″, broad straplike leaves are arranged on dense basal branching plants. It has been sold as 'Silver Cloud'.

ADDITIONAL NOTES: In a mild climate, with winter temperatures never below 32°F, dusty miller can be left outside and will become shrublike. *Cineraria* in Latin means ash, from the ashy color of the foliage. *Senecio* is from the Latin word *senex,* old, and alludes to the grey and hoary seed pappus.

Native to Mediterranean region.   Annual

SCIENTIFIC NAME/FAMILY: *Setcreasea pallida* 'Purple Heart'   Commelinaceae

(set-crē′se-a pal′lid-à)

COMMON NAME: Purple Heart

LEAVES: Alternate leaves are fleshy, lanceolate to oblong, with soft hairs on both surfaces. There are cobwebby hairs near the base of the leaf that forms a sheath around the stem. Individual leaves are trough-shaped and up to 7″ long. The foliage has an intense purple color which is darkest on the lower leaf surface.

FLOWER: Flowers are borne at a branch terminal or sometimes in the branch axil. Individual flowers are small, 3-petaled, and borne on 2 large, leaflike bracts. Flower color is violet-purple.

HABIT: Purple heart has a sprawling habit with ascending stems. It grows 12″ tall with an 18″ spread.

SEASON OF BLOOM: This species is a strong bloomer from spring to the fall. It flowers very well in warm weather.

CULTURE: *Setcreasea* grows best in a well-drained soil in full sun. Excess moisture will cause rotting.

UTILIZATION: It is used as a bedding plant or ground cover in southern zones 9–10. Northern gardeners may grow it indoors or use it as a container plant during the summer. The intense purple leaf color can be difficult to use in the garden. It works well when combined with grey or silver-foliage plants.

PROPAGATION: It is easily propagated from tip cuttings.

DISEASES AND INSECTS: No serious pests.

HARDINESS: Zone 9–10.

Native to Mexico.   Tender perennial

SCIENTIFIC NAME/FAMILY: *Shortia galacifolia*   Diapensiaceae

(shôr′ti-á gā-las-i-fō′li-á)

COMMON NAME: Oconee Bells, Shortia, One Flowered Coltsfoot

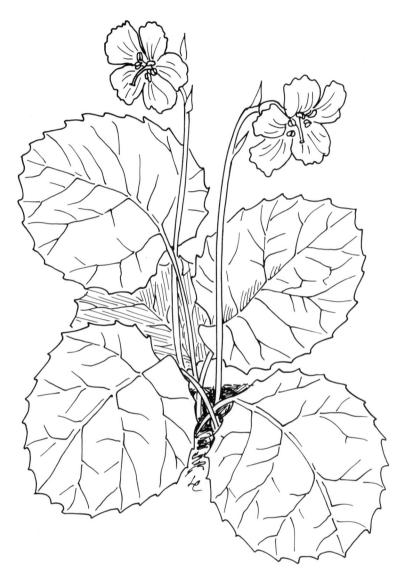

LEAVES: Evergreen leaves are glossy, orbicular to oval-shaped, with crenate-serrate margins, 2″–3″ wide. The teeth on the margin are often spiny-tipped. Foliage turns to reddish bronze in the winter.

FLOWER: White solitary flowers, 1″ wide, hang from erect, leafless stems. Individual flowers have 5 irregularly toothed lobes. Flowers can occasionally be tinged with pink.

HABIT: Low, compact habit, 8″ tall and 12″ wide.

SEASON OF BLOOM: Spring.

CULTURE: The soil conditions are quite exacting for oconee bells. It should be planted in partial shade to shade areas in soils that are abundantly amended with sand and humus. The soil should be well drained and have a pH of 4.5–6.0. Oconee bells is difficult to establish and will spread slowly. After establishment, this species may go undisturbed for many years.

UTILIZATION: Charming plant suitable for use as a ground cover for woodland sites and rock gardens in shaded areas. It is often found in association with rhododendrons and azaleas due the acid soil conditions required for these woody species. It is typically not considered the plant that would first be grown by the novice gardener. The conditions listed in the culture section must be adhered to for success with this woodland species.

PROPAGATION: Division in early spring is usually the method of propagation. Seed can be used, but germination can be erratic and plants slow to develop. Fresh seed may enhance germination success.

DISEASES AND INSECTS: No major problems.

HARDINESS: Zones 4–8.

ADDITIONAL NOTES: This species is rare and many states within its native range list it as an endangered species. It was first discovered in 1788 in the Carolina mountains. Interestingly, it was not found again in the wild until 1877.

Native to mountains of Georgia, North Carolina, and South Carolina.   Perennial

SCIENTIFIC NAME/FAMILY: *Sidalcea malviflora*   **Malvaceae**

(sī-dal'shē-à mal-vi-flōr'-à)

COMMON NAME: Sidalcea, Checkermallow, Checkerbloom

LEAVES: The alternate leaves are of two types. The basal leaves are glossy green and round or they may be shallowly 7 to 9 lobed. The stem leaves are deeply lobed with narrow segments.

FLOWER: The pink-rose or watermelon pink flowers are borne in a terminal raceme. Individual flowers are 2" to 3" wide, and have shallow bowl shapes.

HABIT: 2' to 4' erect perennial. The foliage, flowers, and plant habit resemble the hollyhock.

SEASON OF BLOOM: Summer.

CULTURE: *Sidalcea* can be grown in sun or partial shade in a moist, well-drained soil. Optimum growth will occur in moist and cool climates. It has been my experience in Ohio that *Sidalcea* browns and looks quite inferior when subjected to hot and dry situations. The key with this species is adequate moisture. Deadheading or cutting back the stems will promote a longer blooming period.

UTILIZATION: The erect habit of this species makes it a good addition for the middle to background areas of the border or island bed.

PROPAGATION: The species can be seed-propagated but cultivars do not come true from seed. Division is an easy alternative.

DISEASES AND INSECTS: No serious problems except in areas of Japanese beetles. These insects tend to be attracted to members of the Malvaceae.

HARDINESS: Zones 5–7.

CULTIVARS:
'Elsie Heugh'—Light pink flowers, fringed petals, 2' to 2½' tall.
'Loveliness'—Shell-pink flowers, 30" tall.
'Mrs. Alderson'—Large rose-pink flowers, 3'–4' tall.

See color plate

'Oberon'—Soft rose-pink flowers on 30″ tall stems.
'Puck'—Dwarf cultivar, 2′ tall with clear pink flowers.
'Rose Queen'—Rose-pink flowers, 4′ tall.
'Stark's Hybrid'—Rose-red flowers, 4′ tall.
'Sussex Beauty'—Satiny pink flowers, 3′–4′ tall.
'William Smith'—Salmon-pink flowers, profuse bloomer, 3′ tall.

ADDITIONAL NOTES: This species is also listed as *Sidalcea* × *hybrida.*

Native to western United States.   Perennial

SCIENTIFIC NAME/FAMILY: *Silene dioica*   Caryophyllaceae

(si-lē'nē dī-ō-ī'ka)

COMMON NAME: Red Campion

LEAVES: Basal leaves are obovate, stem leaves opposite, ovate to ovate-lanceolate. Stem leaves are up to 4" long and short-petioled to sessile. Stems and leaves have soft, straight hairs.

FLOWER: Flowers are reddish-purple and borne in an open cyme inflorescence. The five-petaled flower has an emarginate tip.

HABIT: Upright to rounded habit, 2'–3' tall and 2' wide.

SEASON OF BLOOM: Summer.

CULTURE: Plant in full sun in a well-drained soil. *Silene* usually does well in hot and dry areas.

UTILIZATION: Selections of *Silene* are valuable for the border because of the bright color and late flowering.

PROPAGATION: Propagate by seed, division, or tip cuttings. Seed should be covered lightly, kept moist, and germinated at 70°F. Division can occur in spring or fall.

DISEASES AND INSECTS: No serious problems.

HARDINESS: Zones 5–8.

CULTIVARS:
'Flore Plena'—Old fashioned garden perennial with carmine-pink flowers. Double flowers resemble those of *Matthiola*.

RELATED SPECIES:
S. schafta (shaf'-ta)—Schafta Campion. This species is used more than the above. It is 3"–6" tall and spreads to 12". Flowers are magenta-pink and the petals are notched. Unlike the above species, the calyx of *S. schafta* is not inflated. This is a valuable plant for the sunny rock garden.
S. schafta 'Robusta'—This cultivar found its way to the Bloom Nursery, England, by way of a plant-hunting expedition to Turkey. It has a bright deep pink flower in late summer. Plant height is 6".

Native to Europe.   Perennial

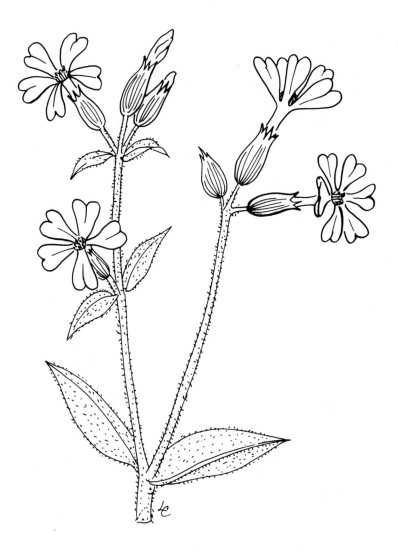

See color plate

SCIENTIFIC NAME/FAMILY: *Sisyrinchium striatum*   Iridaceae

(sis-i-rin′ki-um strī-ā′-tum)

COMMON NAME: Blue-eyed Grass

LEAVES: Gray green, iris-like leaves are 18″ long and 3/4 to 1″ wide. The foliage is similar to iris and can be misidentified if the plant is not in flower.

FLOWER: Cream-colored flowers, 1/2″–3/4″ wide, are clustered on a spike on the upper half of a narrowly winged stem. Individual flowers are darker in the middle with purplish stripes on the back of the flowers.

HABIT: Erect clump 12″–24″ tall and 12″ wide.

SEASON OF BLOOM: Early summer.

CULTURE: Full sun and well-drained, moist soil are the best growing conditions. The flower stem will cause the death of the leaf-shoot on which it is produced. To prevent this natural yellowing, the clump should receive additional nutrition. If the leaves do yellow, they should be cut back to 6 inches.

UTILIZATION: Useful for the sunny border or in a large rock garden.   *See color plate*

PROPAGATION: Seed and division. The seeds should be lightly covered and germinated at 70–75°F in high humidity conditions. Division may be needed every 2 to 3 years and can be done in the spring.

DISEASES AND INSECTS: No problems.

HARDINESS: Zones 4–8.

CULTIVARS:
'Variegatum' ('Aunt May')—Leaves have creamy colored margins.

RELATED SPECIES:
S. angustifolium (an-gus-ti-fō′li-um)—Leaves are narrow (grass-like), 10″–12″ tall. Flowers are blue with a yellow throat. This species has a clump habit of growth and is an excellent choice to fill small areas such as in rock gardens or as an edging plant. Zones 3–8.

Native to Argentina and Chile.   Perennial

SCIENTIFIC NAME/FAMILY: *Smilacina racemosa*   Convallariaceae
(Liliaceae)

(smī-lā-sī'nā ra-se-mō'sa)

COMMON NAME: False Solomon's Seal

LEAVES: Leaves alternate, short-petioled to sessile, elliptic to lanceolate ovate to 6″ long and 3″ wide. The strongly ribbed leaves are arranged on a slightly zigzagged stem.

FLOWER: Creamy-white flowers are very small and are arranged in a fluffy panicle that is about 6″ long. Red berries follow flowering during the summer.

HABIT: The upright, arching stems create a 3′ tall clump that is 3′–4′ wide.

SEASON OF BLOOM: Mid to late spring.

CULTURE: *Smilacina* is a woodland plant and performs best when planted in similar sites. A partial shade to full shade site with moisture-retentive, acid soil is best. It is not dry shade tolerant and should not be planted where it might compete with well-established shade trees. Unless propagules are desired, division is not needed.

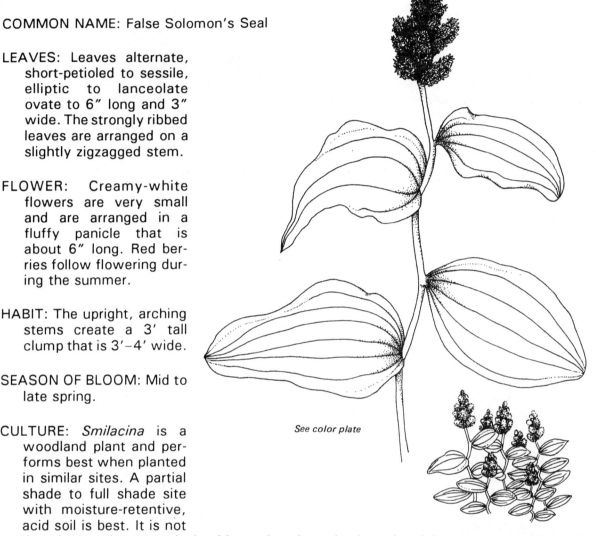

See color plate

UTILIZATION: False solomon's seal is one of the prettiest of the large native woodland plants. The fleecy flowers and, later, red fruit are attractive in the moist, woodland garden.

PROPAGATION: Spring or fall division of the horizontal root is an easy propagation method. Seed propagation is possible but the stratification process is complex.

DISEASES AND INSECTS: Insects and diseases are not serious.

HARDINESS: Zones 3–7.

ADDITIONAL NOTES: *Smilacina* is derived from *Smilax* which is a genus of woodland vines. The ribbed leaves and zigzag stems are similar to *Smilax*.

Native to North America.   Perennial

SCIENTIFIC NAME/FAMILY: *Solidago* hybrids

(sol-i-dā'gō)

Asteraceae
(Compositae)

COMMON NAME: Goldenrod

LEAVES: Alternate leaves, linear-lanceolate to elliptic-lanceolate, 2"–5" long. Leaves can be glabrous or scabrous above and often pubescent below. Margins are serrated.

FLOWER: The small yellow flower heads (1/8"–1/12") are borne in large panicles with 1-sided, recurving branches.

HABIT: The native American species *(Solidago canadensis)* can be 4'–6' tall. However, the more compact hybrids are closer to 2'–3' tall and 18" wide.

SEASON OF BLOOM: Midsummer to late fall.

CULTURE: Goldenrod grows well in full sun or partial shade in a well-drained soil of average fertility. Abundant nutrition will promote rampant growth. Division will be necessary every 2–3 years.

UTILIZATION: Goldenrod can be used to add needed color to the fall border. Mix goldenrod with asters and ornamental grasses. It can also be used as a cut flower.

PROPAGATION: Division and tip cuttings should be used to propagate the hybrid selections. The species can be propagated by seed germinated in humid conditions at 70–75°F.

DISEASES AND INSECTS: Leaf rust can be a problem.

See color plate

HARDINESS: Zones 2–8.

CULTIVARS: There are numerous cultivars of unknown parentage. Many of the hybrids were developed by Walkden of Cheshire, England, in the 1940s. Most are shorter than the native species and more appropriate for small garden use.

'Cloth of Gold'—Dense, deep yellow flowers, 18"–24" tall.

'Crown of Rays' (Strahlenkrone)—Bright yellow flowers, stiff columnar clump, 24" tall.

'Golden Baby'— Golden yellow plumes, 24" tall.

'Golden Fleece'—This cultivar is listed as a selection of *Solidago sphacelata*. It grows less than 18" tall and has a spreading profile. In late summer and early fall, the much-branched plant is covered with bright yellow flowers. It is a recent introduction from the Mt. Cuba Center for the Study of Piedmont Flora, Greenville, Delaware.

'Goldenmosa'—Large yellow flower heads, early bloomer, 30" tall.

'Golden Shower'—Clear yellow flowers borne in horizontal to drooping panicles, 36"–48" tall.

'Golden Thumb'—Clear yellow, fluffy flower inflorescence, 12" tall. This is a very good cultivar for the small garden.

'Golden Wings'—Deep yellow flowers, similar to the species at 5'–6' tall.

'Goldstrahl' ('Peter Pan')—Canary-yellow flowers, late flowering, 24"–36" tall.

'Lemore'—Primrose-yellow flowers, 30"–36" tall. This cultivar is listed as a cultivar of × *Solidaster luteus*.

ADDITIONAL NOTES: *Solidago* has been wrongly accused of causing hay fever. Actually ragweed, *Ambrosia*, is the real culprit.

Native to North America.   Perennial

SCIENTIFIC NAME/FAMILY: *Sorghastrum nutans*   Poaceae
                                                                (Gramineae)

(sōr-gas'trum, sōr-has'-trum nū'tanz)

COMMON NAME: Indian Grass

LEAVES: Leaf blades 1/4" to 3/8"
    wide, 18" long, all leaf surfaces
    are scabrous, and the blades have
    attenuate tips.

FLOWER: The inflorescence is a nar-
    row panicle, somewhat loose, 10"
    to 12" long. The spikelets are
    yellowish turning to a golden
    brown in late summer.

HABIT: Upright-open, 3' to 5' tall.

SEASON OF BLOOM: Late summer. Flowers remain
    of interest until early winter.

CULTURE: Indian grass grows best in full sun and
    deep, fertile, moist soils, although it tolerates
    many situations.

UTILIZATION: This species is suitable for mass
    plantings and in prairie restorations. It is also
    useful in naturalized areas or in an informal
    perennial border. The flowers provide an accent
    and the foliage adds a nice effect for the winter
    garden. The fall foliage turns to an orange-red or
    purplish color. Foliage and flowers can also be
    used in fresh and dried arrangements.

PROPAGATION: Seed or division are appropriate methods. Indian grass will reseed in the
    garden.

DISEASES AND INSECTS: None serious.

HARDINESS: Zones 4–9.

Native to midwestern United States   Perennial

SCIENTIFIC NAME/FAMILY: *Spartina pectinata* (S. michauxiana)   Poaceae
(Gramineae)

(spar'ti-na pek-ti-nā'tà)

COMMON NAME: Prairie Cord Grass, Cord Grass

LEAVES: Leaf blades are 2/3" wide, 24" long, flat in section, very scabrous on the margin, with a graceful arch. Foliage is light green. The cultivar 'Aureo-margina-ta' has shiny green leaves with yellow marginal stripes. The leaf blades are a bright yellow in the fall and turn beige for an early winter interest.

FLOWER: The narrow inflorescences are borne on wiry stems that rise above the arching leaf blades. The 6"–8" long inflorescence is composed of several adpressed spikes that are held in a race-mose fashion on the stem. It is light green turning to beige at maturity.

HABIT: Upright-open to upright-arching, 4'–6' tall.

SEASON OF BLOOM: Late summer.

CULTURE: This grass is found in swamps and wet prairies of North America and will grow best in moist soil and full sun. It is a rhizomatous grass which could create spreading problems in a small garden. Plants grown in shade will lodge.

UTILIZATION: *Spartina* is a good sand binder in soils near fresh or salt water. Best used in water areas or naturalized gardens. Flowers are suitable for drying. The foliage and flowers remain ornamental until early winter.

PROPAGATION: Division in spring or fall.

DISEASES AND INSECTS: None serious.

HARDINESS: Zones 4–9.

See color plate

CULTIVARS:
'Aureo-marginata' — The margins of the leaf blades are marked with yellow bands. 5'–7' tall.

Native to North America.   Perennial

SCIENTIFIC NAME/FAMILY: *Spigelia marilandica*   Loganiaceae

(spī-jē′li-a mar-i-lan′di-ka)

COMMON NAME: Pinkroot, Indian Pink

LEAVES: The oppositely arranged leaves are ovate-lanceolate, 3″–4″ long, entire margins, and are borne sessile to the stem. The veins on the lower leaf surface are lightly pubescent.

FLOWER: Individual flowers are red and trumpet-shaped. The flower faces upward revealing a yellow throat on the interior of the 5-lobed corolla. The 2″ long flowers are arranged in one-sided cymes.

HABIT: 12″ to 18″ tall perennial, 18″ wide.

SEASON OF BLOOM: Late spring to early summer.

CULTURE: Pinkroot performs best in a slightly acid soil. In warmer climates, partial shade is required. If the summers are cool, pinkroot may be grown in full sun if the soil is moist and amended with organic matter. *Spigelia* is not competitive with surface-rooted trees, such as Norway maple.

See color plate

UTILIZATION: Effective as a front to mid border perennial in the partial shade garden. It is an excellent plant for use near a path where it can be easily viewed.

PROPAGATION: Clump division is very easy, as well as stem cuttings taken in early summer. Rooting will occur in 2 to 3 weeks.

DISEASES AND INSECTS: None serious.

HARDINESS: Zones 5–9.

ADDITIONAL NOTES: There are about 30 species of *Spigelia* but only *S. marilandica* is grown as a perennial. The name spigelia commemorates the name of Adrian van der Spigel, a Brussels-born physician who lived from 1578 to 1625.

Native to southeastern United States.   Perennial

SCIENTIFIC NAME/FAMILY: *Spodiopogon sibiricus*   Poaceae (Gramineae)

(spōd-i-o-po′gon sī-bir′i-kus)

COMMON NAME: Graybeard Grass, Frost Grass

LEAVES: Alternate leaves are narrow, linear, and arranged on the stem in a bamboo-like arrangement. Leaves are 1″ wide and 10″ long. Foliage turns reddish in the fall.

FLOWER: A 12″ long inflorescence is an ovoid panicle composed of purplish-tinged spikelets. After flowering, the panicle contracts and becomes narrower, creating a spike-like inflorescence. Later in the season the inflorescence again opens after ripening.

HABIT: Erect clump grass, 4′–5′ tall and 24″ wide.

SEASON OF BLOOM: *Spodiopogon* starts flowering in early summer with a flower interest continuing until late fall.

CULTURE: This grass grows best in moist soils although it is somewhat tolerant to drought. Best growth will occur in full sun.

UTILIZATION: *Spodiopogon* can be used as a specimen or in groupings. The flower and foliage interest will last until late fall. It has a fair dried flower effect. *Spodiopogon* does not have a good winter interest.

PROPAGATION: Propagation is by division or seed. Clumps should be divided in the spring. Seed should be kept in moist conditions and germinated at 70°F.

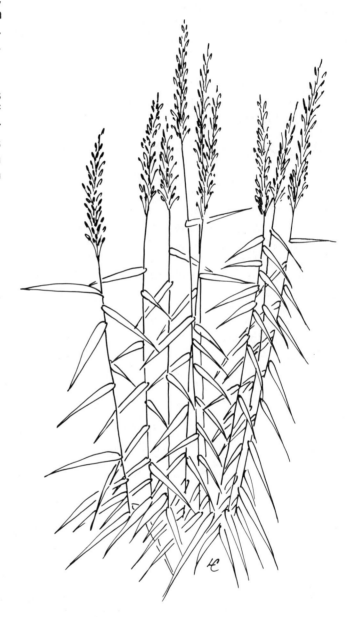

DISEASES AND INSECTS: No serious problems.

HARDINESS: Zones 5–8.

Native to northern China and Japan.   Perennial

SCIENTIFIC NAME/FAMILY: *Stachys byzantina*   Lamiaceae
                    (S. lanata, S. olympica)   (Labiatae)

(stā′kis bī-zan-tin′à)

COMMON NAME: Lamb's Ear, Woolly Betony, Woolly Woundwort

LEAVES: Stems and leaves white, tomentose, leaves petiolate, oblong-elliptic, narrowed at both ends, minutely crenate, rugose, to 4″ long; leaves have a feltlike or velvety texture. This is one of the most outstanding features and is responsible for the common name, lamb's ear.

FLOWER: Corolla purplish-pink, about ½″–1″ long, borne on 4″–6″ spikes. The flowers are not outstanding but continue opening from summer until frost. Most gardeners will probably remove the flowers to enhance the foliage effect.

HABIT: 12″ to 15″ tall with an 18″ spread.

SEASON OF BLOOM: Summer.

CULTURE: Lamb's ear should be grown in full sun in a well-drained soil. Better growth occurs in a low fertility soil. A well-drained soil is particularly important in humid regions where the excess moisture causes the gray-felted leaves to rot. If the soil conditions are optimum, lamb's ear requires little care except for an occasional division.

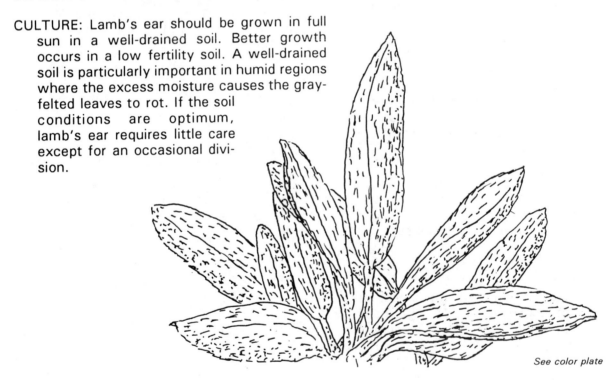

See color plate

UTILIZATION: This species can be used in the border or as a ground cover. It is especially effective in areas where the leaves can spread onto a path.

PROPAGATION: Seeds may be sown in the spring. However, clump division in the spring is the usual method.

DISEASES AND INSECTS: None serious if growing conditions are optimal. Humid and hot summer nights will cause leaf diseases.

HARDINESS: Zones 4–8.

CULTIVARS:
  'Cotton Boll' (also listed as 'Sheila McQueen')—This selection is 12″ tall and more compact than the species. Flower spikes are produced but they tend to be abortive. The leaves are a little larger and less tomentose than the species.
  'Primrose Heron'—The new foliage emerges golden in the spring but reverts to gray-green as the summer progresses. The flowers are like the species. Plant height is 18 inches.
  'Silver Carpet'—This selection is a non-flowering form, which will reduce the labor required for dead-heading.

In 1992, I saw a plant at the Floriade in Rotterdam, Netherlands, labeled as 'Big Ears'. The foliage tended to be more ovate and slightly cupped compared to the elliptic foliage of *Stachys byzantina.* I have been unable to determine if it was a new cultivar or simply a common name.

ADDITIONAL NOTES: The genus is from the Greek word *stachus,* spike, and refers to the pointed inflorescences.

Native to Iran.   Perennial

SCIENTIFIC NAME/FAMILY: *Stachys macrantha* (S. grandiflora, Betonica grandiflora)

Lamiaceae

(Labiatae)

(stā'kis má-kran'tha)

COMMON NAME: Big Betony

LEAVES: *Stachys* is a member of the mint family; consequently, the stems of this species are 4-angled. The leaves are 2½" to 3½" long. The stem leaves are similar in shape, but are smaller and sessile. The leaves and stems are hairy and the leaves have a heavy textured wrinkled appearance.

FLOWER: The violet-purple flowers are arranged in whorls equally spaced on stiff stems that are 18" tall. The individual flowers are cylindrical, up to 1" long with 2-lipped limbs. The upper lip is usually concave and 2-lobed while the lower lip is 3-lobed.

HABIT: 18" tall rosette-forming perennial with a 12" width.

SEASON OF BLOOM: Late spring to early summer.

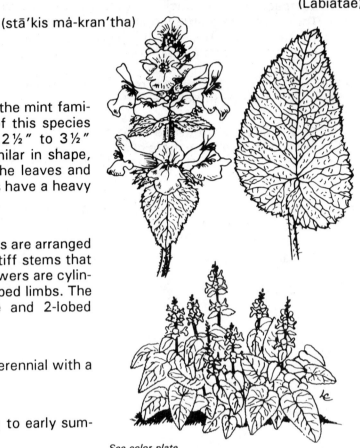

See color plate

CULTURE: Best growth occurs in full sun and ordinary soil with good drainage. Big betony will tolerate light shade. The flowers will last longer when grown in shade.

UTILIZATION: Best utilized in the border.

PROPAGATION: Betony can be increased easily by clump division or seed.

DISEASES AND INSECTS: None serious.

HARDINESS: Zones 3–8.

CULTIVARS:
'Alba'—White flowers
'Robusta'—This selection has rosy pink flowers and is considered to have the richest flower color. It is often planted in the garden.
'Rosea'—Rose-red flowers, similar to the species.
'Violacea'—Dark violet flowers. A cultivar listed as 'Superba' is very similar.

RELATED SPECIES:

> *S. officinalis* (o-fis-i-na'-lis), Common Betony, Wood Betony. This species is very similar to *Stachys macrantha.* Common betony is slightly larger in height with larger foliage. The dense mat produces a lot of stiff stems with two or three tight flower heads. 'Alba', white flowers, and 'Rosea', rose-colored flowers are the available cultivars. Flowering is in late spring and plants are hardy in zones 4–8.

ADDITIONAL NOTES: *Stachys* is from the Greek word *stachus,* meaning spike, and refers to the pointed inflorescences. There are over 200 species of *Stachys* but only a few are worth cultivating.

Native to the Caucasus Mountains.   Perennial

SCIENTIFIC NAME/FAMILY: *Stipa pennata*   Poaceae
                                                          (Gramineae)

(stī'på pen-nā'ta)

COMMON NAME: Feather Grass

LEAVES: Leaf blades are ¼" wide, 24"
    long, U-shaped in cross section, medi-
    um green, tapering to an attenuated
    point.

FLOWER: The flowers are borne in a very
    loose, open panicle. The most notable
    feature of the flower is the awn,
    which resembles a feathery streamer
    trailing out of each floret. Some awns
    can be 10"–12" long. The awn is
    sensitive to humidity and twists and
    turns as the humidity changes. Flower
    color is beige to light green.

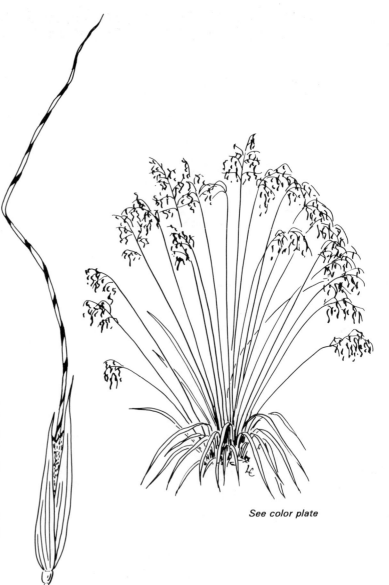

See color plate

HABIT: Narrow upright stems, with an
    open spreading crown, 2' to 3' tall.

SEASON OF BLOOM: Early to midsum-
    mer

CULTURE: Well-drained fertile soil in full
    sun is the optimum site.

UTILIZATION: Suitable for the perennial
    border and use as a dried flower. The
    long, feathery awns are quite showy
    in a dried flower arrangement. In the
    1600s, the awns were used in feather
    beds and as decoration on women's
    hats.

PROPAGATION: Division in the spring is
    the preferred method, as the seeds
    are difficult to germinate.

DISEASES AND INSECTS: No problems.

HARDINESS: Zones 5–8.

RELATED SPECIES:
    S. gigantea (ji-gan-tē'-a)—Giant Feather Grass. This 6 foot tall perennial has showy
        yellow panicles, 10"–15" long in early to midsummer. Zones 6–8.

Native to Europe.   Perennial

SCIENTIFIC NAME/FAMILY: *Stokesia laevis* (S. cyanea)   Asteraceae
(Compositae)

(stō-kē'zhi-á lē'vis)

COMMON NAME: Stokes' Aster

LEAVES: Stems are tomentose; leaves alternate, oblong-lanceolate, to 8" long,
spiny-toothed toward
the base, the
upper leaves
clasping.

FLOWER:
Lavender-
blue solitary
flower heads to
4" across.

HABIT: 12" to 24", round
growth habit and a
spread of 18 inches.

SEASON OF BLOOM:
Summer.

CULTURE: Full sun
and a well-drained
soil. Drainage is
imperative during the winter,   *See color plate*
particularly in the areas where alternate freezing and thawing is common. Plants in
Zone 5 will benefit from a winter mulch.

UTILIZATION: Best used in groups of three in the perennial border. In proper soil
requirements, it is a decorative plant and can also be used for cut flowers.

PROPAGATION: Seed, cuttings, and division. Germinate seeds at 70°–75°F for 4–6
weeks. Two-inch root cuttings and clump division may be done in the spring.

DISEASES AND INSECTS: None serious.

HARDINESS: Zones 5–9.

CULTIVARS:
'Alba'—White flowers.
'Blue Danube'—A popular cultivar with lavender-blue flowers which are up to 5" wide.
'Blue Moon'—Hyacinth-blue flowers.
'Blue Star'—Light blue flowers borne on strong stems.
'Klaus Jelitto'—Allen Bush of Holbrook Farm & Nursery named this selection for Klaus
Jelitto, a friend and perennial seed dealer from Germany. This plant has 3"–4"
diameter powder blue colored flowers and dark green, leathery leaves.
'Silver Moon'—The creamy white flowers of this cultivar are larger than those of 'Alba'.
'Wyoming'—This cultivar has the darkest blue flowers available.

ADDITIONAL NOTES: There is only one species in the *Stokesia* genus, and it is native from South Carolina to Florida and Louisiana. In earlier years, *Stokesia* was a popular plant, but present demand is relatively small. *Stokesia* was named for Dr. Jonathan Stokes, an English botanical author.

Native to southern United States.   Perennial

SCIENTIFIC NAME/FAMILY: *Stylophorum diphyllum*   Papaveraceae

(stī-lof'o-rum dif-fil'um)

COMMON NAME: Celandine Poppy, Wood Poppy

LEAVES: Basal leaves are usually grouped in twos, sometimes 1 or 3. Leaves are 9"–15" long, long petioled, pinnately lobed into 5–7 lobes with lobed margins. Leaves have an oak leaf-like appearance. Lower leaf surface is glaucous. Stems and leaves contain a bright yellow sap.

FLOWER: The bright yellow flowers are 2" wide, have 4 petals, 2 sepals, and many stamens. There are usually 2, sometimes 4, flowers found in terminal clusters.

HABIT: Upright plant, 18" tall and 12" wide.

SEASON OF BLOOM: Spring.

CULTURE: Shade and moist soils are prime requirements for this native woodland plant. If not controlled, celandine poppy will colonize large areas. In drier shade areas, the foliage dies by early summer. In moist soils, the foliage will persist into the fall with occasional rebloom occurring.

UTILIZATION: *Stylophorum* is a charming plant for the shaded

See color plate

moist woodland garden or the shaded perennial border. It is one of the more noticeable wild flowers for spring bloom.

PROPAGATION: Seed or division are both effective methods. Seed should be sown in a moist soil medium and held at 70°F. Division of the long, thick roots may be done in spring or fall.

DISEASES AND INSECTS: None serious.

HARDINESS: Zones 4–9.

ADDITIONAL NOTES: *Stylophorum* is derived from the Greek, *stulos,* a style, and *phoreo,* to bear, and may refer to the style being retained on the seed capsule. The yellow sap was used as a dye by American Indians.

Native to the woodlands of eastern North America.   Perennial

SCIENTIFIC NAME/FAMILY: *Symphytum grandiflorum*   Boraginaceae

(sim'fi-tum gran-di-flō'rum)

COMMON NAME: Ground-cover Comfrey

LEAVES: The alternate leaves are mainly basal. Leaves are ovate, up to 4" long, with a long, grooved petiole. The leaves are covered with a bristle-like pubescence and have a ciliate margin. The pubescence creates a very scabrous leaf texture.

FLOWER: The tubular, creamy yellow flower is subtended by a 5-lobed, bristly calyx. The flower is ¾" to 1" long and the corolla is 2 or 3 times longer than the calyx. Flowers are arranged in a scorpioid, racemose cyme.

HABIT: 8" to 12" tall mound with an 18"–24" spread.

SEASON OF BLOOM: Late spring to early summer.

CULTURE: *Symphytum grandiflorum* is an excellent plant for dry soils in partial shade. Many plants can tolerate shade but few are able to perform well in shade and dry soil.

See color plate

UTILIZATION: This species is a good ground cover for the dry shade border. The creamy-white flowers are a bonus in the late spring. There are few weeds that will find their way through a massed grouping of *Symphytum.*

PROPAGATION: Division in spring or fall is a very easy method.

DISEASES AND INSECTS: There are no serious problems with this species.

HARDINESS: Zones 3–8.

CULTIVARS: The following cultivars are available in Europe but are seldom seen in United States or Canada nurseries.
'Blaue Glocken'—Pure blue flowers, introduced by Ernst Pagels.
'Goldsmith'—Creamy-white flowers and yellowish leaves.
'Hidcote Blue'—Soft blue flowers which fade to white.
'Hidcote Pink'—Pink flowers fading to cream.
'Variegatum'—This selection has bold cream-edged margins. It was introduced by Eric Smith of England.

Native to Caucasus mountains.   Perennial

SCIENTIFIC NAME/FAMILY: *Symphytum × rubrum*   Boraginaceae

(sim'fi-tum rū'brum)

COMMON NAME: Comfrey

LEAVES: Alternate leaves, ovate-lanceolate to lanceolate, to 3″ long. The leaves are very hispid and have ciliate margins.

FLOWER: The crimson flowers are tubular ½″ to 1″ long and are borne in a scorpioid, racemose cyme.

HABIT: 18″ tall, mounded perennial spreading to 18 inches.

SEASON OF BLOOM: Late spring to early summer.

CULTURE: Sun or partial shade in a well-drained soil. It increases slowly and is not invasive.

UTILIZATION: Border plant in sun or part shade.

PROPAGATION: Division in spring or fall.

DISEASES AND INSECTS: No serious problems.

HARDINESS: Zones 3–8.

See color plate

RELATED SPECIES:

  S. × uplandicum (up-land'-i-kum)—Russian Comfrey. Coarse perennial, 3′ to 4′ tall and fairly vigorous. The flowers occur in the summer and are in shades of blue and purple. The cultivar 'Variegatum' is probably more widely cultivated. It is a handsome foliage plant with bold leaves having a cream colored border. *S. × uplandicum* is a hybrid of *S. asperum* and *S. officinale.* Hardy in zones 4–8.

ADDITIONAL NOTES: *S. × rubrum* is listed as a possible hybrid between the red-flowered *S. officinale* 'Coccineum' and *S. grandiflorum.*

Hybrid origin.   Perennial

SCIENTIFIC NAME/FAMILY: *Tagetes erecta*   Asteraceae
                                                                         (Compositae)

(tȧ-jē'tēz ē-rek'ta)

COMMON NAME: American Marigold, African Marigold, Big Marigold, Aztec Marigold

LEAVES: Opposite, 5"–6" long, pinnately divided into oblong or lanceolate serrate
   segments, ½"–2" long, all with a few large glands near the margin and some tipped
   with a long, weak awn. Foliage is highly aromatic.

FLOWER: Heads solitary, yellow to orange, 2"–5" across, ray flowers long clawed,
   peduncle swollen just below the head.

HABIT: Tall: 30" to 36". Medium: 15" to 20". Dwarf:
   10" to 14". Habit varies from erect to rounded.

SEASON OF BLOOM: Early summer to frost.

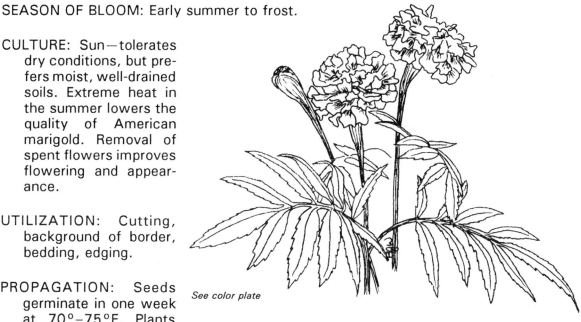

CULTURE: Sun—tolerates
   dry conditions, but prefers moist, well-drained
   soils. Extreme heat in
   the summer lowers the
   quality of American
   marigold. Removal of
   spent flowers improves
   flowering and appear-
   ance.

UTILIZATION: Cutting,
   background of border,
   bedding, edging.

PROPAGATION: Seeds   *See color plate*
   germinate in one week
   at 70°–75°F. Plants
   can be started in the greenhouse or sown in place.

DISEASES AND INSECTS: Marigolds are seldom bothered by insects or diseases. Slugs,
   spider mites, and Japanese beetles are occasional problems. Aster yellows, a virus
   disease that is transmitted by leafhoppers, can sometimes occur.

CULTIVARS:
   Dwarf Types
   'Crush' Series—10"–12" tall plants, 4" wide, double blooms, early bloom, 3 colors
      plus a mixture.
   'Discovery' Series—10"–12" tall, 3" wide blooms, very early bloom; orange, yellow,
      and a mix.
   'Space Age' Series—14", very early flower, 3" double blooms, 'Apollo' (orange), and
      'Moonshot' (yellow) are cultivars.
   Medium Types
   'Galore' Series—16"–18", large double flowers.
   'Inca' Series—18", compact plants, double flowers, with an early bloom, 3 bright
      colors plus a mixture. This series is an excellent choice for bedding purposes.
   'Jubilee' Series—18"–20", 3" flowers, sturdy plants resist wind and rain.

'Lady' Series—15"–18", double carnation type flowers, on compact, uniform plants, 4 colors plus a mixture.

'Voyager' Series—14"–16" tall, 3"–3½" wide blooms, early bloom, good disease tolerance; available in yellow and gold.

Tall Types

'Gold Coin' Series—30"–36", double flowers, 3"–4" across, one of the best tall types, 3 colors plus a mixture.

'Crackerjack Mixture'—30"–36", double flowers in orange, yellow, and gold shades.

Native to Mexico.   Annual

SCIENTIFIC NAME/FAMILY: *Tagetes patula*   Asteraceae
(tȧ-jē'tēz pat'ū-lȧ)   (Compositae)

COMMON NAME: Dwarf French Marigold

LEAVES: Opposite, pinnately divided into about 12 lanceolate or oblong serrate segments ½"–1" long, these or their teeth are tipped with a weak awn, each tooth usually with a large gland at base.

FLOWER: Heads to 2" across, solitary, peduncles long, slightly enlarged upward, ray flowers few to many. Flower colors are yellow, orange, or red-brown. Many are marked with crimson and maroon. Heads can be single or double.

HABIT: 6" to 18", round habit.

SEASON OF BLOOM: Early summer to frost.

CULTURE: Sun—tolerates dry soil but prefers moist well-drained soil.

UTILIZATION: Edging, bedding, cut flowers.

PROPAGATION: Seeds germinate in one week at 70°–75°F.

DISEASES AND INSECTS: Leafhoppers, slugs, and spider mites.

See color plate

CULTIVARS: The following are just a few of the numerous cultivars available to the home gardener.
'Bolero'—14", mahogany-red and gold bicolor flowers.
'Bonanza' Series—Compact habit, 8"–10" tall and 12"–14" spread, early bloom; available in 7 colors and a mixture.
'Boy' Series—8"–10", double blooms, early flowering, 5 colors and a mixture.
'Burgundy Ripple'—12"–14", single flowers with maroon petals edged with golden yellow.
'Cinnabar'—12"–14", single flowers with velvety maroon petals and orange centers.
'Hero' Series—This selection is early and compact and similar to 'Bonanza'. It also is available in 7 colors and a mix.
'Honeycomb'—14", deep red petals edged with orange.
'Janie' Series—8"–10" with 2" diameter blooms. Flowers show well above the foliage. Available in 6 colors.
'Lemon Drop'—8", yellow double flowers.
'Sophia' Series—This series features plants with large, broad-petaled, double flowers on plants 12"–14" tall. 'Queen Sophia' is one selection with red petals edged with bronzy-orange.

<u>Triploid Types</u>. Marigolds often show heat stall in the summer. The use of triploid hybrids (*T. patula* × *T. erecta*) which do not set seeds will provide plants that flower even in the hottest part of the summer. The following triploid selections can be used:

'Laguna' Series—This group has large double, anemone flowered blossoms. They are 12" tall and available in yellow, gold, and orange.

'Nugget' Series—This series has large double flowers on plants 12"–15" tall and 18"–24" wide. Colors include gold, orange, red, yellow, and a mix.

RELATED SPECIES:

T. tenuifolia (ten-u-i-fo'li-a), Signet Marigold. Tiny single flowers cover compact mounds of fernlike foliage. It is more petite than other marigolds. Plants are 6–9 inches tall. 'Lemon Gem' and 'Golden Gem' are common cultivars.

ADDITIONAL NOTES: Marigolds are among the most popular bedding plants because they are easily grown and reward the gardener with great quantities of bright color. *Tagetes* is named for Tages, an Etruscan deity, who is said to have sprung from the earth as it was being plowed and to have taught the Etruscans the art of divination.

Native to Mexico.   Annual

SCIENTIFIC NAME/FAMILY: *Tanacetum coccineum*   Asteraceae
                            (Pyrethrum roseum or   (Compositae)
                            Chrysanthemum coccineum)

(tan-a-sē'tum kok-sin'ē-um)

COMMON NAME: Painted Daisy, Pyrethrum, Persian Insect Flower

LEAVES: Alternate, 1 to 2 pinnatifid; foliage has a thin, fern-like appearance.

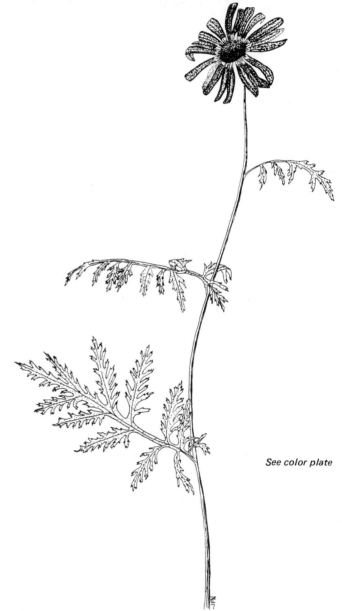

FLOWER: The radiate flower head is 2" to 4" wide, usually single, and is borne solitary on sparsely branched stems. The ray flowers can be white, pink, lilac, crimson, and dark red.

HABIT: 2' to 3' erect plant; stems are usually unbranched. The spread is 12".

SEASON OF BLOOM: Late spring to early summer with sporadic flowering later in the season. Cutting plants back after flowering will often promote this later bloom.

CULTURE: Full sun in well-drained soil works best with this species. Poor drainage in winter is detrimental. A winter mulch is also advisable to prevent frost heaving during alternating periods of freezing and thawing. Staking may be required for this species. It is not heat tolerant and plants in southern zones should be located to receive afternoon shade.

See color plate

UTILIZATION: Painted daisy is a popular summer flowering perennial that looks best when planted in masses or as a combination with other perennials. This is the first "mum" to flower, and it is desired for providing cut flowers.

PROPAGATION: Propagation is by seed or division in spring or late summer. Seeds germinate in 3–4 weeks at 70°F. Clumps should be divided every 3 to 4 years.

DISEASES AND INSECTS: None serious.

HARDINESS: Zones 3–7.

CULTIVARS:

'Atrosanguineum'—Dark red flowers, single.
'Brenda'—Bright red, single.
'Eileen May Robinson'—Salmon-pink, single, 2½'.
'Evenglow'—Salmon-red flowers, single.
'Helen'—Soft, light-pink flowers, double, 2½'.
'James Kelway'—Rich scarlet flowers, single.
'Pink Bouquet'—Pink with silver centers, double.
'Robinson's Pink'—Pink flowers, 2'.
'Robinson's Red'—Red flowers, 2'.

Native to Asia and Europe.   Perennial

SCIENTIFIC NAME/FAMILY: *Tanacetum parthenium*   Asteraceae (Compositae)
(Chrysanthemum parthenium)

(tan-à-sē'tum par-thē'ni-um)

COMMON NAME: Feverfew, Matricaria

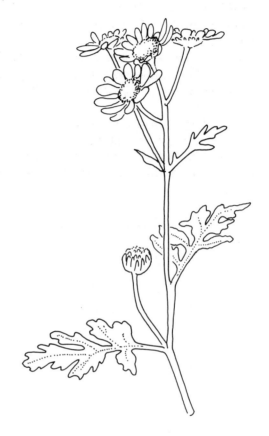

LEAVES: The alternate, pinnately lobed leaves are 2"–3" long, oblong to broadly ovate, and are strongly scented. The leaves are glabrous above, hairy beneath, and conspicuously toothed. The foliage is fernlike and releases the pungent scent when the leaves are bruised.

FLOWER: The species has buttonlike composite flowers which cover the plant with white flowers and yellow centers. Each head is 3/4" in diameter.

HABIT: Bushy, many-branched perennial with an oval to rounded outline, 1–3 feet tall. The height is determined by cultivar selection. Space at 2 feet.

SEASON OF BLOOM: Mid to late summer.

CULTURE: Feverfew is easily grown in most soils as long as it is placed in full sun. In southern zones, the dwarf selections do not perform well, often succumbing to the heat and humidity. In northern areas, a winter mulch is important for overwintering success. Feverfew self-seeds freely.

UTILIZATION: The large selections can be used in the border while the smaller cultivars are suited for edging purposes. Of course, a major use will remain as a cut flower.

PROPAGATION: Feverfew can be propagated by division in spring or fall, from cuttings taken from vegetative shoots in spring or summer, or from seed.

HARDINESS: Zones 5–8

CULTIVARS:
'Aureum'—This cultivar is known as Golden Feather. It has yellow foliage, single white flowers and is 8"–12" tall. Often used as an annual for bedding purposes.

'Flore Pleno'—Double white flowers, 2'–3' tall.

'Golden Ball'—Double yellow flowers, 18" tall.

'Santana'—Creamy white flowers, 10"–12" tall.

'Snowball'—Double white flowers, 2'–3' tall.

'Ultra Double White'—Double white flowers, 2' tall.

'White Bonnet'—Double white flowering cultivar with compact button-flowers surrounded by wide ray-petals, 2' tall.

ADDITIONAL NOTES: One needs a score card to keep up with the name changes with this species. At one time it was placed in the genus, *Matricaria,* which is still found in many catalogs. From there it moved to *Chrysanthemum* and now the taxonomists tell us it fits better in the genus *Tanacetum.* It will take years to get all plant catalogs in agreement.

Native to Caucasus and England.   Perennial

SCIENTIFIC NAME/FAMILY: *Tanacetum vulgare*   Asteraceae (Compositae)

(tan-à-sē'tum vul-gā'-re)

COMMON NAME: Tansy, Golden Buttons

LEAVES: Alternate leaves, pinnately divided into 12–16 finely dissected leaflets. The fernlike leaves are 6"–8" long. In the variety *crispum* (see drawing), the leaf divisions are larger and more finely cut. The foliage of the species has a pine odor, the variety less so.

FLOWER: Golden yellow flowers tightly packed into flower heads ¼"–½" wide. The numerous heads are carried in a dense, flat-topped cyme inflorescence.

HABIT: Upright growing, 3'–4' tall. Tansy should be spaced at 2–3 feet because of its quick spread.

SEASON OF BLOOM: Mid to late summer.

CULTURE: Tansy does extremely well in a wide variety of soils and light conditions. It is equally at home in sun or partial shade. Fertile soils promote lush growth and a quick-spreading plant.

UTILIZATION: Tansy has little use as a culinary or medicinal herb. In fact, any medicinal use is presently low key due to questions of safety. Cut branches of tansy have been used to repel ants from kitchen cabinets. An old time practice included planting tansy near the door to discourage flies from entering the house. The tropical look of the foliage enhances the border. Some gardeners like to plant tansy in a container along the walk where passersby will brush the leaves and release the pine fragrance. Bear in mind that tansy can become invasive. It took quite a while for Chadwick Arboretum volunteers at Ohio State University to remove a rapidly spreading clump of tansy. I am sure that those individuals will be cautious in their use of tansy.

PROPAGATION: Tansy is propagated by seed or division.

DISEASES AND INSECTS: None serious.

HARDINESS: Zones 3–9.

CULTIVARS:
var. *crispum*—Curly Tansy. This selection with very finely cut foliage is less invasive than the species. Curly tansy would be the choice for the border or herb garden.

ADDITIONAL NOTES: *Tanacetum* is from the Greek *athanatos* for long lasting. Gerard, the 16th century herbalist, noted that "long lasting" referred to tansy flowers, which do not wilt easily.

Native to Europe and naturalized over much of North America.   Perennial

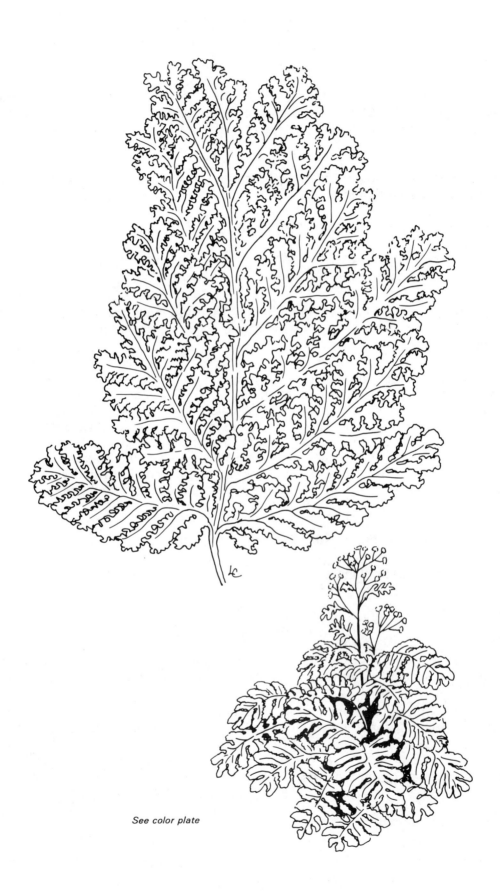

See color plate

SCIENTIFIC NAME/FAMILY: *Tellima grandiflora*   Saxifragaceae

(te-lī'mȧ gran-di-flō'ra)

COMMON NAME: Fringecup, Alaska Fringecup, False Alum Root

LEAVES: The 3"–4" wide basal leaves are lobed, cordate to reniform-shaped with toothed margins. The long petioles (up to 6") are hirsute. This is an evergreen species.

FLOWER: Small (1/4") creamy-white flowers are borne in racemes on thin, wiry stems that rise above the basal foliage. The flowers have 5 reflexed, fringed petals which age to a pinkish color. The racemes can sometimes carry up to 30 flowers.

HABIT: Ground cover plant with basal foliage and thin flower stems which are 12"–18" high. Plant width is 12"–18".

SEASON OF BLOOM: Late spring to early summer.

CULTURE: This species should be grown in shaded areas in a moist, organic amended soil. Additions of peat moss and other organic materials aid in moisture retention.

UTILIZATION: Fringecup is a vigorous grower that can be used as a ground cover or in the shade border.

PROPAGATION: Seed and division. Seed should be sowed on the surface or lightly covered and germinated at 70°F.

DISEASES AND INSECTS: There are no major problems.

HARDINESS: Zones 4–7.

CULTIVARS:
  'Purpurea' ('Rubra')—A selection with reddish foliage that turns nearly maroon in the winter. Yellow flowers. 12"–18" tall.

See color plate

Native to western North America from Alaska to California.   Perennial

SCIENTIFIC NAME/FAMILY: *Teucrium chamaedrys*   Lamiaceae
                                                                (Labiatae)

(tū'kri-um kam'á-drīz)

COMMON NAME: Germander, Wall Germander

LEAVES: Evergreen, opposite, short-petioled, ovate
  oblong, ½" – ¾" long,
  often a serrate or
  crenate margin,
  cuneate at
  the base.

FLOWER: Pale to
  deep purple flowers
  borne in a loose raceme, calyx tubular or
  campanulate, ¼" long, corolla ⅝" long,
  lower lip large and upper lip small and
  deeply cleft. Usually grown for foliage
  effect.

HABIT: 12" tall, clump-forming plant that is
  12"–24" wide.

SEASON OF BLOOM: Early to midsummer.

CULTURE: Full sun and a well-
  drained soil. In areas where
  the foliage will persist during
  the winter, plants should be
  covered with evergreen
  boughs to prevent winter
  damage from cold, drying
  winds. Cutting back after
  flowering promotes a tighter
  plant.

UTILIZATION: Edging, rock gardens, and as formal or informal
  hedges. The foliage can be
  easily trimmed and the plants
  maintained at 6"–8" for many
  years.

PROPAGATION: Cuttings can be   *See color plate*
  easily rooted in summer.
  Spring is the best time to
  divide established clumps.

DISEASES AND INSECTS: Although downy mildew, powdery mildew, leaf spots, rusts,
  and mites have been reported as pests of germander, usually none are serious.

HARDINESS: Zones 4–9.

CULTIVARS:
  'Nanum' (also listed as 'Prostratum')—Rose-pink flowers, 6"–10" tall.

RELATED SPECIES:

T. canadense, (kan-a-denz')—Wild Germander. This clump-forming species, native to North America, is 18"–36" tall. It bears purple or cream colored flowers in loose terminal clusters. Wild germander grows best in moist soils. It can be found growing in coastal areas where it is tolerant to salt spray.

ADDITIONAL NOTES: *Teucrium* spreads by rhizomes and is semiwoody. *Teucrium* was named after Teucher, a Trojan prince who first used one of the species in medicine.

Native to Europe and southwestern Asia.   Perennial

SCIENTIFIC NAME/FAMILY: *Teucrium fruticans*   Lamiaceae (Labiatae)

(tū′kri-um frū′ti-cans)

COMMON NAME: Tree Germander

LEAVES: Leaves opposite, ovate shape, obtuse tip, entire margin; ¾″ to 1¼″ long. Stems and leaves are covered with a soft pubescence. Upper leaf surface is a dull green, lower surface is silver, which creates a silver appearance.

FLOWER: Pale blue flowers are borne 1 or 2 in each whorl; corolla 1″ long, stamens and style are exserted.

HABIT: Evergreen sub-shrub with an erect to rounded shrub, 3′–4′ tall. It can spread 4′–6′ wide.

SEASON OF BLOOM: Tree germander will flower during the winter in mild climates or if the potted plant is brought inside in northern winters.

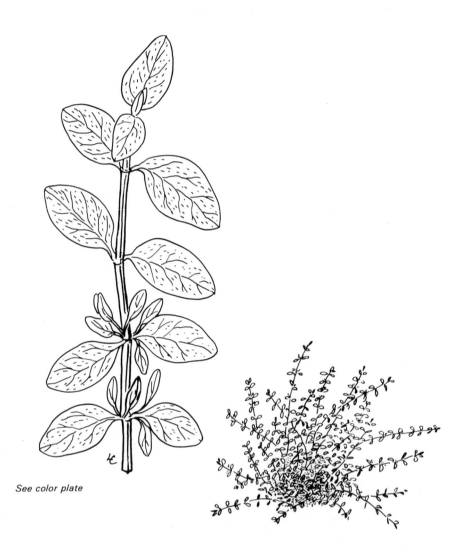

See color plate

CULTURE: Tree germander is a tender perennial that must be placed indoors in cold climates. It performs well in full sun and a well-drained soil. Tree germander will require pruning to encourage branching.

UTILIZATION: Tree germander is a striking plant when used in a gray and silver garden. It can be grown as a containerized patio plant which can be moved indoors in the winter.

PROPAGATION: Tip cuttings taken in the spring is the optimum choice for propagation.

DISEASES AND INSECTS: None serious.

HARDINESS: Zone 9.

ADDITIONAL NOTES: This species has a mild fruity scent, hence a common name of tutti-frutti.

Native to Mediterranean.   Tender perennial

SCIENTIFIC NAME/FAMILY: *Thalictrum aquilegifolium*   Ranunculaceae

(thà-lik'trum ak-wil-e-jif-ō'-le-um)

COMMON NAME: Columbine Meadow Rue

LEAVES: The alternate leaves are bipin-
nately or ternately compound. The
leaflets are suborbicular to short-
oblong; entire on the lower margins
and base. The terminal of each leaflet
usually has 3 broad teeth. The foliage
color is gray-green and resembles that
of columbine. The specific epithet
aquilegifolium means *Aquilegia* or
columbine leaf.

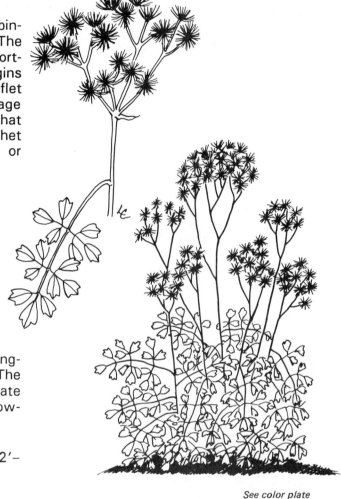

FLOWER: The flowers of this
species are dioecious. The
male selections are generally showier. The inflorescence is composed of
staminate flowers with numerous mauve erect
stamens. The pistillate
flowers are less showy
with only a few stalked
pistils which mature into large, hanging 3-winged inflated achenes. The
overall appearance of the staminate
flowers is a wide head of fluffy flowers.

HABIT: Erect perennial, 2'–3' tall and 2'–
3' wide.

See color plate

SEASON OF BLOOM: Late spring to early summer.

CULTURE: *Thalictrum* is a woodland plant, thus it is accustomed to partial shade and a
moist, well-drained soil. If the soil is moist and the summers are cool, columbine
meadow rue can be planted in full sun. Space at least 2' from other plants. If this is
done, plants will not need division for about 4 years.

UTILIZATION: The plant should be valued for its light, airy, glaucous foliage and delicate
powder puff flowers. Place it in the perennial border, in the wildflower garden, or in a
naturalized area. *Thalictrum* can be placed next to *Iris, Echinacea,* or *Echinops* to add
a softness and daintiness to the planting.

PROPAGATION: Division is best accomplished in the spring. Fall division is suitable if mulch
is provided for winter protection. Seed is a very suitable method for the species and
varieties.

DISEASES AND INSECTS: None serious.

HARDINESS: Zones 5–8.

CULTIVARS:
'Album'—White flowers on plants 3'–4' tall. This selection is a very notable occupant of the white garden at Sissinghurst Gardens, Kent, England.
'Atropurpureum' ('Purpureum')—Lilac-rose flowers and dark purple stems and stamens.
'Purple Cloud'—Rosy purple flowers.
'Thundercloud'—Deep purple flowers are borne in flower heads larger than the species.

Native to eastern Europe.   Perennial

SCIENTIFIC NAME/FAMILY: *Thalictrum minus*   Ranunculaceae

(thȧ-lik'trum mī'-nus)

COMMON NAME: Low Meadow Rue

LEAVES: Alternate leaves are bi- or tripinnate, leaflets are rounded or wedge shaped at the base and slightly notched with 3 lobes at the apex. The foliage color can be green or glaucous. The dainty texture of the foliage is similar to the maidenhair fern.

FLOWER: The flowers are bisexual, but the greenish yellow stamens tend to dominate. The fine-textured panicle branches above the middle of the flowering stems. The small flowers are not as noticeable on this species as they are on other meadow rues.

HABIT: 12"–24" tall, dense clump that is 12"–18" wide. Plant height is variable.

SEASON OF BLOOM: Late spring to early summer.

CULTURE: Best growth will occur in partial shade in a moist, well-drained soil. In cool summer climates, it can be grown in full sun. Transplanting is best done in the spring.

UTILIZATION: This meadow rue can be used near the front or middle of the border. It is grown more for the attractive foliage rather than the insignificant flowers.

PROPAGATION: Division is best accomplished in the spring. Fall division is suitable if mulch is provided for winter protection.

DISEASES AND INSECTS: None serious.

HARDINESS: Zones 3–7.

ADDITIONAL NOTES: *T. minus* is a very variable species. The selection described above is just one type that can arise from this species. A taller growing selection is *T. minus* var. *adiantifolium* (ad-ē-an-tif-o'-lē-um) (sometimes listed as a species) which grows 2' to 3' tall. The taller-growing selections tend to be more invasive.

Native to Europe.   Perennial

SCIENTIFIC NAME/FAMILY: *Thalictrum rochebrunianum*   Ranunculaceae

(thȧ-lik'trum rok-brun-i-ā'num)

COMMON NAME: Lavender Mist Meadow Rue

LEAVES: Alternate, pinnately compound, leaflets obtuse, entire, or the terminal leaflets 3-lobed. Leaves create a fine texture somewhat similar to the maidenhair fern.

FLOWER: Lavender-violet flowers with primrose-yellow stamens. The flowers have no true petals, only petal-like sepals and many colored stamens. This unusual characteristic draws attention to this plant.

HABIT: 4' to 6' erect plant.

SEASON OF BLOOM: Late summer.

CULTURE: The native habitat of lavender mist is woodland areas; consequently, plants do best in partial shade. However, full sun is no problem if the soil has a good organic matter content and is moist.

UTILIZATION: Due to their tall nature, some meadow rues are often used as background plants. These plants will need to be staked, or they can be grown among bushy plants on which they can lean.

PROPAGATION: Seed and division. Seeds will germinate in 4 to 6 weeks at 70°F and may be seeded in the greenhouse or outside in the fall. Individual plants can be divided in spring or fall, with preference toward spring; if they are divided in the fall, winter protection should be provided.

DISEASES AND INSECTS: Powdery mildew, rust, and smut are occasional problems, but none is serious enough to require specific control methods.

HARDINESS: Zones 3–7.

RELATED SPECIES:

     T. delavayi (del-a-va'-i)—Yunnan Meadow Rue. 5', lavender flowers with yellow stamens appear in summer. This species was discovered by the great plant explorer, Ernest H. Wilson, during his travels in western China. Stems of this species are very thin and staking will be required to keep the stems erect. 'Album' has white sepals but is not as vigorous as the species. 'Hewitt's Double' has double lavender flowers. It is an excellent garden selection. Hardy to Zones 4–7. *Thalictrum dipterocarpum* (dip'-ter-ō-kar''-pum) is very similar to *T. delavayi*. It is possible that plants sold as *T. dipterocarpum* are likely *T. delavayi* and vice-versa. They can be distinguished by comparing fruiting structures but it is probably not worth the effort. The performance and culture of each are the same.

     T. speciosissimum (spē-si-ō-sis'i'mum)—Dusty Meadow Rue. 4'–6', blue-green leaves, dense clusters of creamy yellow flowers in summer. This species has good heat tolerance.

ADDITIONAL NOTES: *Thalictrum* is derived from the Greek word *thaliktron*. Dioscorides used *thaliktron* to describe a plant with compound leaves.

Native to Japan.   Perennial

See color plate

SCIENTIFIC NAME/FAMILY: *Thermopsis caroliniana*   Fabaceae
                                                                  (Leguminosae)

(ther-mop'sis ka-ro-lin-i-ā'na)

COMMON NAME: Carolina Thermopsis, Carolina Lupine

LEAVES: The alternate leaves are palmately compound with 3 leaflets. Leaflets are ovate or obovate, 2" to 3" long, pubescent and glaucous on the lower leaf surface.

FLOWER: The yellow pealike flowers are borne in dense, terminal racemes, which are 8" to 12" long. The flowers look like a yellow lupine, hence the common name, Carolina lupine.

HABIT: Erect, sparsely branched, 3' to 5' tall and 3' wide.

SEASON OF BLOOM: Late spring to early summer.

CULTURE: Full sun and a deep, well-drained soil is the best situation. Since *Thermopsis* is in the legume family, it has the capability of growing well in low-fertility soils. If grown in a deep soil, it is fairly drought tolerant. This species has a tap root and division is difficult. Plant in a site where a quick move will not be necessary.

UTILIZATION: Carolina lupine is useful as background plant or as a cut flower. The flowers should be cut just as the basal florets start to open. It can be combined with peonies and bellflowers.

See color plate

PROPAGATION: Seed is the usual method, division is more difficult due to the taproot system. *Thermopsis* has a hard seed coat and scarification is required. Fresh seed is usually more reliable than older seed.

DISEASES AND INSECTS: No serious problems.

HARDINESS: Zones 3–8.

RELATED SPECIES:
 T. lupinoides (lu-pin-oi'-d ēz) — Lanceleaf Thermopsis. The silver-pubescent leaves of this plant distinguishes it from other species. Plants are 12″ tall and 18″ wide and are not as invasive as other *Thermopsis.* Hardy to zones 2–7.
 T. montana (mon-tā'-na) — Mountain Thermopsis. This species is shorter than *T. caroliniana,* earlier flowering, and spreads more rapidly. Plants are 12″–24″ tall. Hardy to zones 3–7.

ADDITIONAL NOTES: *Thermopsis* is derived from *thermos,* a lupin, and *opsis,* a resemblance, referring to the similarity of the flower of *Lupinus* and *Thermopsis.*

Native to southeastern United States.   Perennial

SCIENTIFIC NAME/FAMILY: *Thunbergia alata*   Acanthaceae

(thun-bĕr'ji-á á-lā'tá)

COMMON NAME: Black-eyed Susan Vine, Clock Vine

LEAVES: Opposite, triangular-ovate, to 3" long, base cordate or hastate, apex usually apiculate, margins toothed, pubescent on both surfaces; petioles are winged.

FLOWER: Solitary flowers on long axillary peduncles, the funnel-shaped corolla is cream-colored with a black eye. Each flower has 5 rounded segments and the corolla can vary in color from cream to white to yellow to orange.

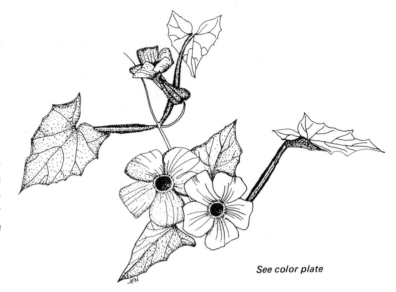

See color plate

HABIT: 3' to 6' twining climber.

SEASON OF BLOOM: Summer.

CULTURE: Partial shade to full sun in a moist, fertile soil. A light shade may be best because *Thunbergia* does not like excess heat. The best flower displays are usually in late summer or early fall when cooler conditions occur.

UTILIZATION: *Thunbergia* is a flowering vine that has uses as a trailing plant for containers such as window boxes, urns, and hanging baskets. It also serves well as a screen when allowed to twine on a trellis or fence. The plant is a dense grower, literally covering supports with foliage and flowers.

PROPAGATION: The seeds can be sown directly or started in the greenhouse 6–8 weeks before transplanting. Seeds germinate in 2 weeks when temperature is maintained at 70°–75°F.

DISEASES AND INSECTS: None serious.

CULTIVARS: *Thunbergia* is available in the 'Susie' Series which provides 3 distinct colors, with or without dark eyes. Colors are orange, white, and yellow.

ADDITIONAL NOTES: *Thunbergia* was named for Carl Peter Thunberg, a 12th century Swedish botanist.

Native to South Africa.   Perennial treated as an annual

SCIENTIFIC NAME/FAMILY: *Thymus praecox* ssp. *arcticus* 'Lanuginosus'   Lamiaceae
(*T. pseudolanuginosus*)   (Labiatae)

(thī'mus prē'koks ark-ti'-cus la-nū-ji-nō'sus)

COMMON NAME: Woolly Thyme

See color plate

LEAVES: Small leaves, elliptic or obovate, 1/6″–1/8″ long, densely pubescent, margin has long-ciliate hairs.

FLOWER: Rose-purple flowers, 3/16″ long, are borne in the leaf axils.

HABIT: Woolly thyme has a very prostrate habit, 1/2″ tall, and an 18″ wide spread.

SEASON OF BLOOM: Late spring to early summer.

CULTURE: Full sun and a well-drained soil.

UTILIZATION: Woolly thyme can be planted in flagstone paths and terrace areas. It is also suitable on stone walls or in the rock garden.

PROPAGATION: Tip cuttings during the growing season and division in the spring. Propagation is similar to garden thyme.

DISEASES AND INSECTS: Fungal diseases and root rots can be problems in poorly drained soils.

HARDINESS: Zones 5–7.

CULTIVARS:
'Hall's Variety'—Rose purple flowers and pubescent leaves. Woolly thyme is very grey whereas Hall's variety tends to be greener.

Nativeness is not known.   Perennial

SCIENTIFIC NAME/FAMILY: *Thymus serpyllum* (T. angustifolius)   Lamiaceae
(Labiatae)

(thī'mus ser-fil'-um)

COMMON NAME: Mother-of-Thyme, Creeping Thyme

LEAVES: Opposite, elliptic to oblong, ¼"–⅓" long, resin-dotted nearly sessile, entire. Leaves have a strong mint-like odor.

FLOWER: Purple, inflorescence is a small spike about ¼" long; flowers are fragrant.

HABIT: 3" to 6" tall, mat-forming perennial.

SEASON OF BLOOM: Late spring.

CULTURE: Full sun in a loose, well-drained soil. Thyme will thrive in poor, dry soil and is less vigorous in shade.

UTILIZATION: Rock garden, herb garden, stone walls and planted among paving stones as it can withstand some traffic.

See color plate

PROPAGATION: Seed and division. Seed will germinate under light in 1–2 weeks at 55°–60°F. Clump division is possible during the spring.

HARDINESS: Zones 3–8

CULTIVARS:
'Albus'—White flowers.
'Coccineus'—Bright red flowers, evergreen foliage turns bronze in the fall.
'Elfin'—A neat, small alpine plant. It is 2" tall and will slowly spread to 5".
'Pink Chintz'—Clear pink flowers.

ADDITIONAL NOTES: Confusion seems to exist concerning nomenclature in trade and botanical listings. Numerous variations are encountered in *T. serpyllum. Thymus* is the ancient Greek name for aromatic herbs.

Native to Europe.   Perennial

SCIENTIFIC NAME/FAMILY: *Thymus vulgaris*   Lamiaceae
                                                                                  (Labiatae)

(thī'mus vul-gā'ris)

COMMON NAME: Garden Thyme, Common Thyme

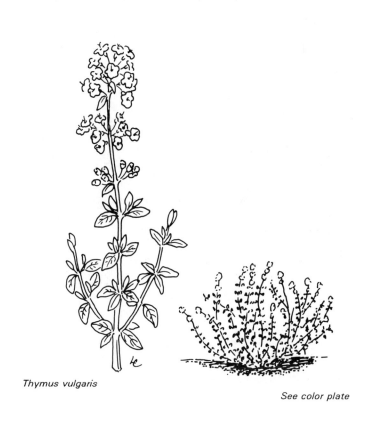

Thymus vulgaris

See color plate

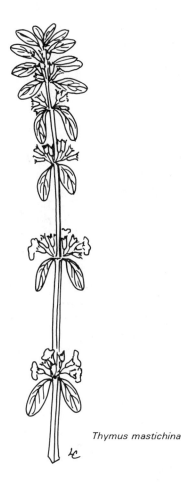

Thymus mastichina

LEAVES: Opposite leaves, linear to elliptic, 1/4″ long, slightly tomentose. The edges of the leaves are rolled under (revolute). Lower leaf surface is paler than the upper surface. All plant parts are highly aromatic.

FLOWER: Lilac to pink tubular flowers are borne in dense terminal clusters. Individual flowers are 3/16″ long.

HABIT: Dense, mound, 12″ tall and 12″ wide.

SEASON OF BLOOM: Summer.

CULTURE: Full sun in a loose, well-drained soil. Thyme will perform very well in poor, dry soil and is less vigorous in partial shade. Poorly drained soil will likely lead to fungal diseases. This culinary species may need to be replaced about every 3 years because it will become woody and open in its habit. In cold climates, the upper stems are often damaged during the winter, leaving only a few basal, evergreen shoots. These plants must be cut back to new growth in the spring.

UTILIZATION: Garden thyme is a universal herb that is so widely used for culinary purposes that it prompted the writers of the *Grass Roots Herb Society Newsletter* to offer the following to cooks—"When in doubt, use thyme." Indeed it is a favorite of cooks and used with all types of meats and vegetables. The leaves and flowering stems are used in sachets, and the dried flowers have been used to preserve linens from insects.

Thyme is also reported to be a benefit as a companion planting to eggplant, potatoes, and tomatoes. Bees are attracted in great numbers to thyme when it is in flower. Gardeners who do not wish to welcome this insect should cut the blossoms off before they begin to open. The oil of "Thymol" is used in pharmaceuticals.

PROPAGATION: Seed, cuttings, and division. Seeds will germinate in 3–4 weeks at 60°–65°F. Cuttings should be made from 3" tip cuttings of new growth. Rooting will take about 2 weeks. Division should be done in the spring.

DISEASES AND INSECTS: Fungal diseases and root rot can be problems in poorly drained soils.

HARDINESS: Zones 5–8.

CULTIVARS:
'Bittersweet'—This cultivar is very rare and seldom found in commerce. Morphologically, it is indistinguishable from 'Narrow-leaf French'. It has an acrid, tarlike odor which is much different than the sweet, spicy fragrance of 'Narrow-leaf French'.
'Fragrantissimus'—Foliage has the odor of rose geranium. It is not known to be in cultivation. In the trade, the cultivar name is sometimes applied to any form of *T. vulgaris* that does not have the typical odor of the culinary herb.
'Miniature'—Mr. Cyrus Hyde, Well-Sweep Herb Farm, Port Murray, NJ, selected this dwarf seedling from a collection of 'Narrow-leaf French'. The essential oil of 'Miniature' is the same as 'Narrow-leaf French'. The smaller size, about 6" tall, is the difference between the two selections.
'Narrow-leaf French', French Thyme—This cultivar is the most common in cultivation as it is the source for the culinary thyme. The cultivar includes a number of variants. Some plants are gray, others are green, and some are intermediate between the two. Individual plants may be erect while others have a spreading habit.
'Orange Balsam'—Foliage has a strong, bitter orange, turpentine-like odor. It is sometimes found in cultivation.

RELATED SPECIES:
T. × citriodorus (sit-rē-ō-dōr'-us), Lemon Thyme—The lemon odor is very pronounced with this hybrid. It is usually grown for its fragrant and culinary uses. Listed as a hybrid of *T. vulgaris* and *T. pulegioides*. 'Aureus' is a yellow variegated form of lemon thyme. It can be unstable and green leaves will develop. The propagator must be careful in the selection process.
T. mastichina (mas-ti-chi'-na), Mastic Thyme—Plants can be erect to sprawling in habit, gray to green in color, with a eucalyptus-like odor. The flower calyx has long teeth, which creates a fine-textured, plumose appearance that is unlike other selections of thyme. It is available in the trade but not common. Its winter hardiness is suspect.
Thymus 'Broad-leaf English', English Thyme—This selection is commonly grown as a culinary herb. It differs from common thyme because it has flat leaf margins and not revolute margins as in common thyme. English thyme could be a hybrid of *T. vulgaris* and *T. serpyllum*.
Thymus 'Doone Valley'—This prostrate to low mound plant has a lemon odor. The foliage is yellow variegated in the spring and fall but the leaves are green during the majority of the growing season.

ADDITIONAL NOTES: The nomenclature of the genus *Thymus* can be quite confusing. I recommend that the student or nursery person review the PhD thesis of Harriet Ballard Flannery. Ms. Flannery, as a student at Cornell University wrote a most informative thesis entitled "A Study of the Taxa of Thymus L. (Labiatae) Cultivated in the United States." It is available from University Microfilms International, Ann Arbor, MI.

Native to western Mediterranean to southeastern Italy.   Perennial

SCIENTIFIC NAME/FAMILY: *Tiarella cordifolia*   Saxifragaceae

(tī-à-rel'à kôr-di-fōl'i-à)

COMMON NAME: Foam Flower, Allegheny Foam Flower, False Mitrewort

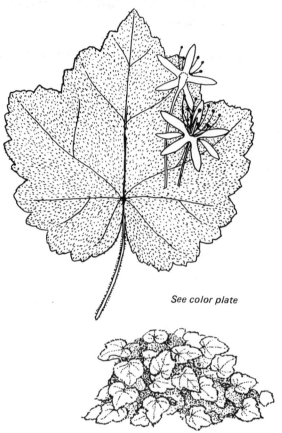

See color plate

LEAVES: Leaves basal, broadly ovate-cordate to 4" long; leaves are dentately toothed, 3–7 lobed, with a scattered pubescence on both surfaces. Leaves are borne on hirsute petioles. The leaves of *Tiarella* are similar to those of *Heuchera sanguinea* except they are more sharply toothed than those of *Heuchera.*

FLOWER: White flowers, about ¼" across, are borne on 6"–9" long racemes. Individual flowers have 5 petals and 10 stamens, the latter being conspicuously exserted. The inflorescence is similar to that of *Astilbe.*

HABIT: 6"–12" compact plant, suitable as a ground cover. This species can have a spread of 12"–24".

SEASON OF BLOOM: Midspring.

CULTURE: Best growth will occur when the plant is placed in a cool, moist site with soil high in organic matter. Although I have seen *Tiarella* growing in full sun, the preferred site would be in partial to full shade.

UTILIZATION: *Tiarella* is an excellent plant for placement in shaded areas, to include borders, rock gardens, and woodland sites. For best display, arrange the plant in masses. *Tiarella* spreads by underground stems, which help create the compact mat that makes it suitable as a ground cover.

PROPAGATION: Clump division is easily done in the spring. Seeds sown in a cold frame in early spring will also work.

DISEASES AND INSECTS: None serious.

HARDINESS: Zones 3–8.

CULTIVARS:
'Moorgrun'—White flowers, smaller leaves than the species.
'Purpurea'—The foliage of this cultivar is purple-tinged with maroon petioles and the flowers are pale pink to rose.

RELATED SPECIES:

T. wherryi (wher'-rē-i) (*T. cordifolia* var. *collina*)—Wherry's Foamflower. This species is similar in appearance to *T. cordifolia* except it is a clump former and not stoloniferous like *T. cordifolia.* The flowers are pinkish to creamy white. Plants are 6"–10" tall. For southern conditions, Sam Jones, Piccadilly Farm, Bishop, Georgia, reports that *Tiarella wherryi* outperforms *T. cordifolia* when planted in a side-by-side comparison.

ADDITIONAL NOTES: *Tiarella* is derived from the Greek word *tiara,* a small crown, and refers to the shape of the fruit.

Native to eastern North America from southeastern Canada to Alabama.   Perennial

SCIENTIFIC NAME/FAMILY: *Tigridia pavonia*   Iridaceae

(ti-grid'i-á pá-vō'ni-á)

COMMON NAME: Tiger Flower, Mexican Shell Flower, Peacock Tiger Flower

LEAVES: The sword-like leaves are borne in a basal fan usually composed of 3–6 leaves. Individual leaves are ribbed and rigid.

FLOWER: Very colorful flowers are a highlight of this species. Flowers range in size from 2"–4" wide and come in colors of red, orange, yellow, and white with blotches of purple, red, or yellow in the centers of the flowers. Individual flowers are composed of 6 segments. Three large segments create a triangle and 3 smaller perianth segments form a cup in the center of the flower. Each flower only lasts for a day but numerous buds create a long bloom season (2–4 weeks).

HABIT: Erect habit, similar to bearded iris, 18"–24" tall.

See color plate

SEASON OF BLOOM: Mid to late summer.

CULTURE: Plant the corm in full sun in a well-drained soil. *Tigridia* is a tender corm and must be lifted in the fall as is done with other tender corms such as gladiolus. Plant the corm in the spring after threat of frost is past. If one wishes to replant the corms, they should be dug in early fall after the foliage dies down. In climates with winter lows around 20°F, corms can be left in the ground if the area is mulched. Typically, the corms are not expensive and it is easier to start with new corms in the spring.

UTILIZATION: The bright warm flowers are welcome in any sunny border. It is advisable to plant tiger flower in among other plants so the sparse foliage and stems are not as obvious.

PROPAGATION: Tiger flower can be produced from seed but the process will take 2–3 years to develop a flowering-sized corm. The very small seed should be exposed to light and germinated at 70°F. Bulbils that are obtained during lifting in the fall can also be lined out. However, most gardeners will find that it is probably easier to treat this species as an annual and plant new corms each spring.

DISEASES AND INSECTS: There are no special problems.

HARDINESS: Zones 7–10. Flower production is sparse even though the plant survives in Zones 7 and 8.

Native to Mexico.   Tender corm

SCIENTIFIC NAME/FAMILY: *Tithonia rotundifolia* (T. speciosa)   Asteraceae
(Compositae)

(ti-thō′ni-à rō-tun-di-fō′li-à)

COMMON NAME: Mexican Sun-
flower, Tithonia

LEAVES: Alternate, leaves ovate
to triangular-ovate, 3″–10″
long, cordate leaf base, narrowed to a petiole 5″ long,
undivided to 3-lobed, serrate
to crenate. Leaf surface has a
velvet texture.

FLOWER: Heads to 3″ across
with orange-scarlet ray flowers
and orange-yellow disk flowers.

HABIT: 4′ to 6′, coarse-textured,
erect plant.

SEASON OF BLOOM: Summer.

CULTURE: Full sun—withstands
intense heat and dry conditions and continues to flower.
The first frost kills this plant.

UTILIZATION: Cutting, background, screen.

PROPAGATION: Seeds germinate
in 2 to 3 weeks at 70°F.
Seeds should not be covered.

DISEASES AND INSECTS: No
serious problems.

CULTIVARS:
'Goldfinger'—Dwarf cultivar, 2′–3′, orange-scarlet flowers, 3″ diameter.
'Torch'—3′–4′, orange-scarlet flowers, which are 4″ wide.
'Yellow Torch'—3′–4′, yellow flowers, 3″ wide.

ADDITIONAL NOTES: Hollow stems must be seared to increase keeping quality of cut
flowers. In the very limited list of tall growing annuals, *Tithonia* isn't too bad a choice.
It has a uniform growth habit and showy orange-scarlet flowers of good size. However,
the foliage masses are rather coarse, and plants sometimes break over from midseason
on. *Tithonia* is named for Tithonus, a young man much loved by Aurora, the dawn
goddess.

Native to Central America.   Annual

SCIENTIFIC NAME/FAMILY: *Torenia fournieri*   Scrophulariaceae

(tō-rē'ni-a̍, tor-e'-ne-a fōr-nē-er'-ī, four-ne-air'-i)

COMMON NAME: Wishbone Flower, Torenia, Bluewings

LEAVES: Opposite, ovate or ovate-cordate, serrate, 1½"–2" long, petiole more than half as long as blade.

FLOWER: Calyx 5-winged; corolla tube pale violet, yellow on the back, upper lip pale blue, lower lip with 3 purplish-blue lobes and a yellow blotch at the base of the middle lobe.

HABIT: 12", round habit.

SEASON OF BLOOM: Summer to frost.

CULTURE: Shade and moist soil; plants like humidity and have a tendency to fade in a dry atmosphere. Best growth occurs in cool areas.

UTILIZATION: Garden borders, pots, hanging baskets. Dig plants before frost for winter indoor use.

PROPAGATION: For best germination, do not cover seed and keep soil temperature at least 70°F. Germination takes 2 weeks.

DISEASES AND INSECTS: Usually none serious.

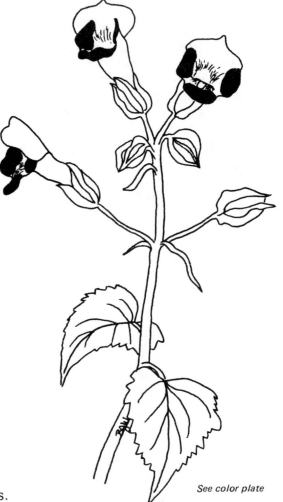

See color plate

CULTIVARS:
'Clown' Series—This 1989 All American Selection has colors of blue, blue and white, burgundy, rose, violet, and a mixture. A strong attribute of this series is the continuous flowering during the summer.
'Compacta Blue'—8" tall, blue flowers with a violet and yellow blotch on the lip.
'Panda' Series— Blue or pink colors are available on plants that are 8"–10" tall.

ADDITIONAL NOTES: The throat of the *Torenia* flower has a pair of yellow stamens positioned in the shape of a chicken wishbone, hence the common name. Torenia is a minor bedding plant, but may be useful for shaded areas. It is nice when massed. It almost gives a feeling of a bed of miniature pansies due to the different-colored petals on each flower, but it is shaped more like a sweet pea or snapdragon. *Torenia* is named for the Reverend Olof Toren, an 18th century chaplain in India and China.

Native to China.   Annual

SCIENTIFIC NAME/FAMILY: *Tradescantia* × *andersoniana*   Commelinaceae

(trad-es-kan'shi-á an-der-sōn'-i-a'ná)

COMMON NAME: Virginia Spiderwort, Widow's-Tears

LEAVES: Alternate, linear-lanceolate, to 15" long, 1" wide, straplike leaves.

FLOWER: Flowers borne in terminal umbels, subtended by linear-lanceolate bracts; flowers violet-purple, sometimes white, pink, or red, sepals bright green, somewhat turgid and inflated, 3 pubescent petals.

HABIT: 18" to 24" tall with a 24" width.

SEASON OF BLOOM: Late spring to midsummer.

CULTURE: *Tradescantia* is an easily grown perennial. It can be grown in sun or partial shade and in soils that are moist to boggy. The flowers last one day but do not require deadheading like the daylily. The three petals of spiderwort dissolve cleanly, leaving none of the fleshy remains found with plants like daylily. In midsummer, the foliage becomes unkempt and should be cut back to the ground. New foliage will develop, and flowers will return in the fall.

UTILIZATION: Border planting, naturalized shade areas, and wild gardens.

PROPAGATION: Plants grown from seeds will flower the second year. Divide clumps every 3–4 years to prevent excessive spreading. Cultivars should be produced by division in spring or fall.

DISEASES AND INSECTS: *Botrytis* blight, leaf tier, leaf cutter, and orange tortix caterpillar, although none are considered serious.

HARDINESS: Zone 3–9.

See color plate

CULTIVARS:
    'Blue Stone'—Solid blue, 18".
    'Carmine Glow' ('Karminglut')—Carmine
        to magenta flowers, 16".
    'Innocence'—Pure white flowers.
    'Iris Pritchard'—White flowers flushed
        with blue.
    'Isis'—Deep blue, 18".
    'J. C. Weguelin'—Sky blue flowers.
    'Osprey'—Large white flowers with blue
        feathery stamens.
    'Pauline'—Orchid pink flowers
    'Purple Dome'—Rosy purple flowers.
    'Red Cloud'—Rosy red flowers, 15" tall.
    'Snowcap'—Pure white flowers, 18" tall.
    'Valor'—Crimson-purple flowers, 18"–24" tall.
    'Zwanenburg Blue'—Rich blue flowers, 18"–24".

ADDITIONAL NOTES: *T.* × *andersoniana* is a hybrid of *T. virginiana* and other species. *Tradescantia virginiana* is native over most of the eastern United States. The species offered by wildflower nurseries is usually *T. virginiana. Tradescantia* is named for the plant collector, John Tradescant, who on a plant collection trip to the United States, sent this genus back to England in the 17th century.

Native to central United States.   **Perennial**

SCIENTIFIC NAME/FAMILY: *Tricyrtis hirta*   Convallariaceae
                                                            (Liliaceae)

(trī-sēr'tis hēr'tà)

COMMON NAME: Hairy Toad Lily

LEAVES: The leaves are alternate, 3" to 4" long, and ovate to ovate-lanceolate. Leaves have parallel venation and clasp the stem. The stems and leaves are softly pubescent.

FLOWER: There are 6 perianth segments; the outer 3 have a bulbous nectary at the base. Flowers are pale lilac, liberally covered with dark purple spots. Six stamens and 3 styles form a central crown that stands above the bell-shaped perianth. The flower structure is one of the most unique in the perennial world.

HABIT: Upright, arching stems from 2' to 3' tall. Plant width is 2 feet.

SEASON OF BLOOM: Late summer to early fall.

CULTURE: Toad lily performs best in partial shade in moist soils rich in organic matter. In these favorable sites, toad lily is closer to 3 feet. If the soils are drier, growth will be nearer to 2 feet.

See color plate

UTILIZATION: Nice plant for the lightly shaded border. Although the flowers are unusual, they are not showy when viewed from a distance. Plant toad lily where it can be closely observed.

PROPAGATION: *Tricyrtis* can be propagated by division in the spring or by seed. The seed will need a cold stratification period for dependable germination.

DISEASES AND INSECTS: None serious.

HARDINESS: Zones 4–8.

CULTIVARS:
  var. *alba*—White flowers and pink stamens.
  'Miyazaki'—This suspected hybrid of *T. hirta* and *T. formosana* has 2' tall arching stems with purple-blotched flowers found in axillary positions on the stem.
  'Variegata'—The leaves are narrowly edged creamy-yellow.
  'White Towers'—Ivory-white flowers.

RELATED SPECIES:
  T. formosana (for-mo'sā-na)—Formosa Toad Lily. This species has oval-shaped leaves which are pubescent below. Plants are 2 feet tall and 18 inches wide. The terminal flowers are pale pink, heavily spotted with reddish-purple, and have yellow throats.
    var. *amethystina* (a-me-this'-ti-na)—Purplish blue flowers with white throats spotted with red. Cold hardiness in northern zones has not been established. It is presently listed as zone 6 hardiness.
    var. *stolonifera* (stō-lōn-if'ēr-a)—This variety grows taller than the species and spreads more rapidly. Plants are 36"–42" tall with pale lilac flowers with fewer spots than the species.

Native to Japan.   Perennial

SCIENTIFIC NAME/FAMILY: *Trillium grandiflorum*   Trilliaceae (Liliaceae)

(tril'i-um gran-di-flō'rum)

See color plate

COMMON NAME: White Wake-Robin, Snow Trillium, Great White Trillium

LEAVES: Three leaves are carried atop a solitary, unbranched stem. Leaves are rhombic-ovate to rhombic-oval and have a cuneate base which is sessile to the stem. Leaves are 3"–6" long.

FLOWER: Single flowers are borne on pedicels above the leaves. Each flower has 3 pure white petals 2"–3" long and 3 greenish sepals that are up to 1½" long. The petals fade to a pinkish blush with age or after pollination.

HABIT: Mounded woodland plant 1½'–2' tall and 2' wide.

SEASON OF BLOOM: Early spring.

CULTURE: *Trillium grandiflorum* grows best in a moist, well-drained soil with a neutral or slightly acid pH. Additions of organic matter, such as leaf compost and peat moss, will greatly enhance the vigor and size of snow trillium. It should be grown in shaded conditions and will tolerate all shade situations except shade created by low-branched evergreens. Uniform moisture is required and supplemental watering should occur during dry periods. Space new plants 12" apart.

UTILIZATION: Snow trillium is a majestic plant when displayed in a mass planting. Interplanting *Trillium* with other woodland plants like native ferns, wild geranium, bloodroot, and wild ginger sets the stage for a delightful wildflower spring bloom.

PROPAGATION: Seed and bulblet production are used to produce new plants. *Trillium* seed may mature before the white berry starts to split. The propagator needs to start regular inspections 5–6 weeks after flowering. The berry should be opened to check the seed color. Dark seeds indicate that they should be collected and sown immediately. Dry seed may take years to germinate. Sow seed in a moist medium and overwinter outside to break the dormancy. Flowering can occur in 3 years but it is more likely to occur at 4–5 years.

The second propagation method includes exposing the rhizome and cutting a V-shaped groove along the length of the rhizome. Fungicide is dusted on the wound to prevent disease. Bulblets will form at the wound site and can be removed after one year.

DISEASES AND INSECTS: None serious.

HARDINESS: Zones 4–9.

CULTIVARS:

var. *roseum*—Clear rose-pink flowers. Some taxonomists feel that this color is simply a variation of the natural flower color and they do not treat it as a separate variety.

'Flore-pleno'—Double flower type.

ADDITIONAL NOTES: *Trillium* has been a target of plant collectors, both amateur and nursery, and frequently does not transplant well. It is a shame that this practice has occurred and many natural populations have been depleted. Fortunately, some commercial nurseries are starting to propagate *Trillium*. Gardeners should buy from nurseries that propagate *Trillium*.

Native to eastern United States.   Perennial

SCIENTIFIC NAME/FAMILY: *Trollius europaeus*   Ranunculaceae

(trol'i-us ū-rō-pē'us)

COMMON NAME: Globeflower, Common Globeflower, European Globeflower

LEAVES: Leaves are dark green above and paler
below. Basal leaves are petioled and palmately 3-
to 5-lobed, while the stem leaves are sessile and
3-lobed. The margins are toothed.

FLOWER: The lemon yellow flowers are globular, 1" to 2"
across, and are borne solitary or in twos on terminal stems.
The showy part of the flower is actually the petaloid sepals,
which are ovate and incurved. The 5 or more petals are
generally small and spatulate.

HABIT: 18" to 24" erect-growing perennial with a 2' width.

SEASON OF BLOOM: Late spring with sporadic flowering to
midsummer.

CULTURE: Sun or partial shade. Best growth occurs in a soil
that is continuously moist. In lighter soils, organic matter is
essential. Water must be added during drought periods.
Plants that are grown in dry soils will be a disappointment
to the gardener.

UTILIZATION: Globeflower is an attractive plant for a damp
area. It is an excellent plant for the very moist rock garden,
border of wildflower garden, or along a stream or around a
pond. The cut flowers make excellent long-lasting flower
arrangements.

See color plate

PROPAGATION: Division can be done in late fall or early spring, but it will usually not be
necessary for 5 years or more. Freshly harvested seed will germinate in about 3 weeks,
although percentages will probably not be high. Old seeds may require over a year for
germination. An alternative to try with old seed is to plant the seeds in an outdoor
seedbed and allow nature to provide the scarification and stratification to enhance
germination.

DISEASES AND INSECTS: Powdery mildew can be an occasional problem.

HARDINESS: Zones 3–7.

CULTIVARS:
'Superbus'—Bright lemon-yellow flowers, 24" tall.

RELATED SPECIES:
T. chinensis (chi-nen'-sis) (previously listed as (*ledebourii*). This species is taller and
later flowering than *T. europaeus* or *T. × cultorum*. The formation of the flower is
distinctly different than the other two species. The outer petals have the familiar
globe shape but the inner portion of the flower has narrow petaloid-stamens.
'Golden Queen' has deep orange flowers in early summer.

T. × cultorum (kul-tōr'-um)—Hybrid Globeflower. This hybrid is a result of crosses of *T. europaeus × T. asiaticus × T. chinensis*. The waxy, globe-shaped flowers resemble large double buttercups. Cultivars are included in the following list.

'Alabaster'—Ivory-tinted flowers, 2' tall, Georg Arends introduction.

'Bressingham Sunshine'—Bright yellow flowers, vigorous grower.

'Canary Bird'—Pale canary-yellow flowers with a tinge of green.

'Commander-in-Chief'—Bright orange flowers.

'Earliest of All'—Early flowering selection with orange-yellow flowers.

'Etna'—Dark orange flowers, vigorous grower, 3' tall.

'Fire Globe' ('Feuertroll')—Orange-red flowers.

'Goldquelle'—Long-lasting pure yellow flowers suited for cut flowers.

'May Gold' ('Maigold')—Early flowering, golden-yellow flowers.

'Orange Princess'—Deep orange flowers, 2' tall, very good cultivar for cut flowers.

'Prichard's Giant'—3' tall, medium yellow flowers. Excellent as a cutflower.

'Salamander'—Orange flowers, 30" tall.

ADDITIONAL NOTES: *Trollius* is from the Swiss-German name *Trollblume,* "something round," in reference to the shape of the flower.

Native to damp areas of northern Europe.   Perennial

SCIENTIFIC NAME/FAMILY: *Tropaeolum majus*   Tropaeolaceae

(trō-pē'ō-lum mā'jus)

COMMON NAME: Nasturtium (nȧ-stĕr'shum), Indian Cress

LEAVES: Alternate, long-petioled, orbicular or somewhat reniform, 2"–7" across, peltate, with about 9 main veins radiating from the petiole, margins usually entire.

FLOWER: Flowers orange, yellow, red, white, scarlet, bicolored; 1"–2½" across, with a spur 1"–1½" long, straight or curved; petals mostly rounded, but some are toothed or short pointed. There are also spurless cultivars.

HABIT: The habit of nasturtium can be dwarf and bushy, 1' tall and 2' wide or a climbing vine reaching 6' to 8'.

SEASON OF BLOOM: Summer to frost.

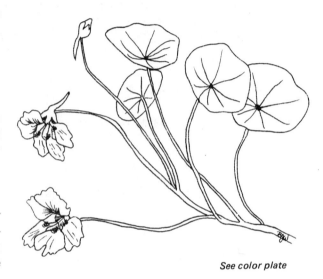

See color plate

CULTURE: Full sun, will grow in poor soils such as gravelly banks. Highly fertile soil produces abundant foliage but very few flowers. Nasturtium will stop flowering when subjected to prolonged heat.

UTILIZATION: Cut flowers, vines to cover trellises, etc. Foliage tends to hide flowers. Nasturtium is good for direct seeding where perennials have died down. The nectar in the spur attracts hummingbirds.

PROPAGATION: Direct seeding in the garden is often best. Seeds germinate in 1 to 2 weeks at 65°–70°F but are difficult to transplant. For best germination, cover seed with about ¼" of soil.

DISEASES AND INSECTS: Leaf spot, wilt, aphid, cabbage looper, thrips, and two-spotted mite. The most serious pest is the aphid. Organic gardeners often plant nasturtium near vegetable gardens to serve as trap plants to lure the aphids away from the vegetables.

CULTIVARS:
'Jewel Mixed'—Dwarf compact plants, double flowers borne above the foliage, free-flowering, wide array of colors.
'Peach Melba'—Orange-pink flowers on a compact plant.
'Tip Top Apricot'—Yellow-orange flowers on dwarf plants, 6" tall.
'Whirlybird'—This cultivar is spurless, which causes the flower to face upward, presenting a more colorful effect.

RELATED SPECIES:
T. polyphyllum (pol-i-fil'-um)—Wreath Nasturtium. This species is a perennial vine in warm climates. Yellow flowers are displayed in late spring on vines that are 3'–4' long. It performs best in warm sunny sites in well-drained soils. It makes a nice display when allowed to trail over a wall or rocky bank.

T. speciosum (spē-si-o'-sum) — Scotch Flame Flower, Vermilion Flower. The tiny, scarlet flowers of this perennial vine are present for many weeks during the summer. The optimum location is on a north-facing wall in an organic enriched soil that is kept cool and moist. It is a tender vine that may grow in climates such as the Pacific Northwest. It is a common vine in England where the garlands of scarlet can be found climbing on walls and draping over shrubs.

ADDITIONAL NOTES: Nasturtiums contain mustard oil, so the flower buds and young fruits are sometimes used for seasoning and pickling. The leaves may also be used in green salads. Nasturtium (Latin for cress) is derived from the biting, pungent flavor of the leaves, which resembles the flavor of watercress *(Nasturtium officinale).* Everything but the root is edible. My wife, Carolyn, even has a cookbook with a recipe for pickled nasturtium seeds. *Tropaeolum* is from *tropaion,* a trophy, from the resemblance of the leaves to a buckler and the flowers to a helmet.

Native to South America.   Annual

SCIENTIFIC NAME/FAMILY: *Tulipa* (hybrids and species)   Liliaceae

(tū'li-pà)

COMMON NAME: Tulip

LEAVES: Leaves are generally radical, stems are sometimes branched, leaves are broad and thick, glabrous and glaucous, ovate-lanceolate, 6"–10" long.

FLOWER: Flower color and shape vary with type and cultivar of the tulip. Most flowers are erect, bell or saucer shaped with 6 perianth segments. Flowers are available in solid or mixed colors.

Lily

Darwin

Double

Parrot

See color plate

HABIT: 6″ to 36″. The shorter types tend to have a clumplike habit, while the taller ones are erect.

SEASON OF BLOOM: Early to late spring.

CULTURE: Tulips are some of the most easily grown bulbs. They do best in full sun and seem to prefer a heavier soil than other bulbs. For tulips, the soil should be dug at least 12″ deep and amended with peat or leaf compost. Tulips are planted in the fall, 5″–6″ deep. Some cultivars are planted deeper, while others are placed nearer the surface. Tulips have a tendency to decline in flower vigor when the bulbs are exposed to temperatures above 70°F. Plant as late as possible and store bulbs in a cool area.

UTILIZATION: Tulips can offer a wide selection of flower sizes, colors and shapes during the spring. If possible, tulips should be massed. A dozen can be as effective as a large border massing. There are several sizes for every use from rock gardens to perennial borders. Their clear colors and variety of forms lend interest to mixed spring bouquets. In addition, they are popular as potted plants available from florists from late winter through the spring.

PROPAGATION: Propagation is easiest by division and multiplication of the bulbs.

DISEASES AND INSECTS: The most common problem is gray mold. Basal rot and stem rot are occasional problems. Tulip break (virus) causes flowers to "break" color, which produces white or green streaks in the petals.

HARDINESS: Zone 5. It is normally too hot in the south for good tulip culture.

ADDITIONAL NOTES: The genus name *Tulipa* is derived from the Persian word *toliban,* "turban," and refers to the inverted flower of some species, which resembles a turban. There are literally hundreds of tulip introductions that have originated from extensive breeding and selection work. In addition to these hybrids, there are several groups called species or botanical tulips that are used in rock gardens for early spring bloom.

The following is one scheme for the classification of cultivated tulips:
Early
  1. Single Early—April and early May flowers, 6″–8″ tall, often with fragrant flowers. Good selection for the border front or in rock gardens. 'Princess Irene' with orange and purple flowers is an example from this group.
  2. Double Early—Tulips in this group flower later than the single early tulip and are slightly taller, 10″–12″. Of course, the flowers are also double. 'Triumphator' is a rosy red.
Midseason
  3. Mendel—This group resulted from a cross of Duc von Tol (6″) and the Darwin tulip (30″). The 18″–24″ height is good in the garden and this bulb forces well. 'Apricot Beauty,' a salmon rose, is a good choice.
  4. Triumph—This tulip is a cross between single early and Darwin cultivars. It reaches 2′ and flowers in mid-May. 'Merry Widow' is a notable cultivar with deep red petals edged with silvery-white.
  5. Darwin hybrid—A cross of *T. fosteriana* and a Darwin tulip. The flowers are the largest of all classes. Bloom is late April to early May. A well-known hybrid of this class is 'Apeldoorn' which has scarlet petals with black bases.

Late flowering

6. Darwin—This class is probably the best known tulip. They are tall, 24"–32", with flowers that are generally rectangular in shape, with flat top and bottom. Darwin selections are excellent for bedding and cut flowers. 'Aristocrat' is a soft violet-rose edged with white.

7. Lily-flowered—Flowers have petals which are pointed and reflexed. The parents of this hybrid are *T. retroflexa* and the Cottage tulip. Plants are usually 24" tall. 'Queen of Sheba' is red edged with golden yellow.

8. Cottage—The flowers are large with a basic shape of an egg. Heights vary from 12" up to 30". The name "Cottage" was given this group as they were found in the cottage gardens of France and England. 'Mrs. John T. Scheepers' is a good golden yellow.

9. Rembrandt—These tulips are "broken," which refers to the colors that are striped or blotched. They were depicted in many of the paintings of the Old Masters. The main use of these unusual tulips is as cut flowers.

10. Parrot—The flowers have fringed petals, often finely shredded, scalloped or undulating. Individual flowers are large in proportion to the stem and are best placed in a protected site away from the wind. 'Black Parrot' is a dark, maroon-purple.

11. Double late—This group is also known as peony flowered because the double rows of petals resemble the flowers of the peony. Plant height is 16"–24" tall. Flowering occurs in late May. 'Bonanza' is a deep red with gold edged petals.

Species

12. *kaufmanniana*—Very early blooming cultivars that are often found in rock gardens. Plant height is 4"–8". It was originally introduced as the water-lily tulip. 'Daylight' has scarlet and yellow flowers and mottled leaves.

13. *fosteriana*—Large flowers are borne in early spring over gray-green foliage that may be striped or mottled. Flower height can be as high as 18". 'Red Emperor' has bright vermilion-red petals with light yellow bases.

14. *greigii*—Cultivars in this group always have mottled or striped foliage. Flowers are present in April and reach a height of 8"–16". The brightly colored flowers often have different colors on the outside than on the inside. 'Red Riding Hood' has bright red flowers with black bases.

15. Other Species and Varieties—This is a "catchall" class containing all other species.

Native to Turkey.   Perennial—hardy bulb

SCIENTIFIC NAME/FAMILY: *Uvularia grandiflora*   Convallariaceae
(Liliaceae)

(ū-vū-lā′ri-a gran-di-flō′ra)

COMMON NAME: Bellwort, Big
Merrybells

LEAVES: The alternate leaves are
perfoliate (the leaf base completely surrounds the stem).
They are oblong to lanceolate-
ovate, 3″ to 5″ long, and pubescent on the lower leaf surface.

FLOWER: The yellow, campanulate flowers are pendulous and
are usually solitary at the end
of arching branches. Flowers
are 1½″ long. The flower petals and leaves have a slight
twist.

HABIT: 18″–24″ tall plant with arching branches. Plants
are 12″–18″ wide.

SEASON OF BLOOM: Mid to late spring.

CULTURE: The optimum environment is partial to full shade
and a soil that is fertile and moist, and slightly alkaline.
Addition of leaf compost would be an ideal soil amend-
ment for this species.

UTILIZATION: This native wildflower is useful in the shaded
border or the woodland garden.

See color plate

PROPAGATION: Division in the spring.

DISEASES AND INSECTS: There are no serious problems.

HARDINESS: Zones 4–9.

RELATED SPECIES:
U. perfoliata (per-fol-e-ā′-ta) — Wood Merrybells. This species is similar to *U. grandiflora*
but differs in the following: The lower leaf surface is glabrous, and the insides of
the flower petals are pubescent versus the smooth surfaces of *U. grandiflora.* Wood
merrybells is smaller, 15″, and flowers about 2 weeks later.
U. sessilifolia (ses-si-li-fo′-lē-a) — Little Merrybells. The leaves of this species are sessile
rather than perfoliate as found in *U. grandiflora* and *U. perfoliata.* Yellow flowers in
mid to late spring. 12″.

Native to North America.   Perennial

SCIENTIFIC NAME/FAMILY: *Vancouveria hexandra*   Berberidaceae

(van-ko-vē'ri-á heks-an'-dra)

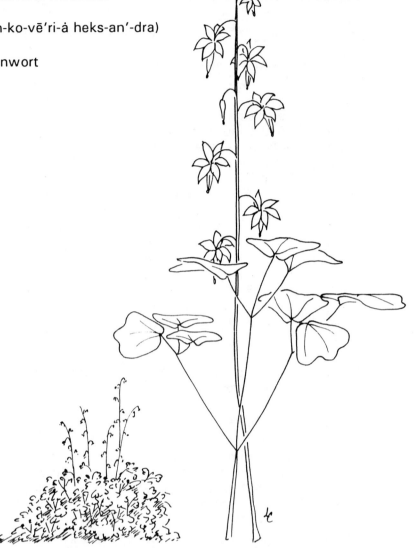

COMMON NAME: American Barrenwort

LEAVES: Basal leaves are ternate to twice ternate, 1½" long. Leaflets are cordate and 3-lobed. The pale green foliage is dainty and reminiscent of maidenhair fern.

FLOWER: Drooping white flowers, 1/2" long, are borne in loose panicles that contain 10–25 flowers. Each panicle is carried atop a leafless stem. *Vancouveria* is similar to *Epimedium* but has 6 petals compared to 4 petals found with *Epimedium.*

HABIT: Ground cover 12" tall and 12" wide.

SEASON OF BLOOM: Late spring to early summer.

CULTURE: *Vancouveria* will spread quickly if provided optimum conditions. These include partial shade and cool, moist, organic soil with an acid pH. Addition of leaf mold or humus is beneficial. Little success will be found in areas that have hot and dry summers.

UTILIZATION: Excellent plant for ground cover use in shaded areas.

PROPAGATION: Propagation is by division of the rhizome in spring or fall.

DISEASES AND INSECTS: No serious problems.

HARDINESS: Zones 5–7.

RELATED SPECIES:
   V. chrysantha (kris-an'tha). An evergreen to semi-evergreen species with golden yellow flowers, 12" tall.
   V. planipetala (plan-i-pet'-a-la). Evergreen foliage, white flowers with a lavender tinge. It is slower growing than *V. hexandra* and harder to establish.

ADDITIONAL NOTES: *Vancouveria* was named after Captain G. Vancouver, an English explorer.

Native to northwestern North America.   Perennial

SCIENTIFIC NAME/FAMILY: *Veratrum viride*

(ve-rā′trum vi′ri-dē)

Melanthiaceae
(Liliaceae)

COMMON NAME: Indian Poke, American White Hellebore

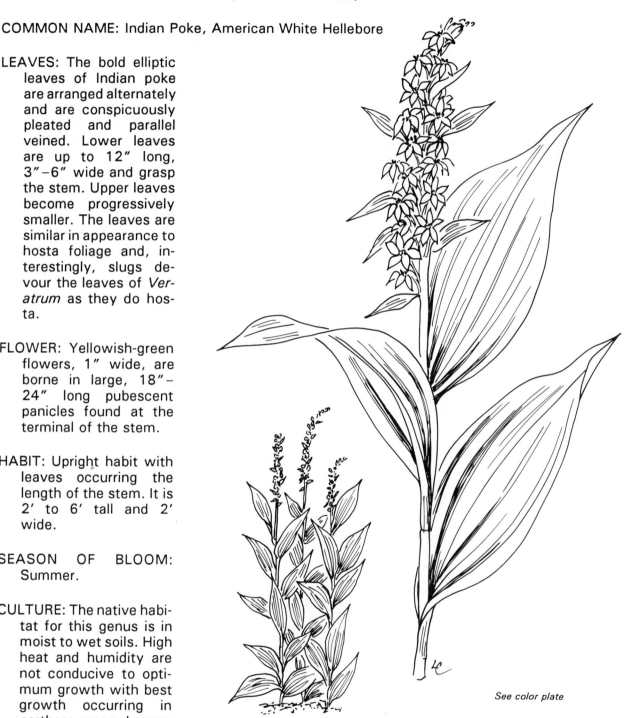

See color plate

LEAVES: The bold elliptic leaves of Indian poke are arranged alternately and are conspicuously pleated and parallel veined. Lower leaves are up to 12″ long, 3″–6″ wide and grasp the stem. Upper leaves become progressively smaller. The leaves are similar in appearance to hosta foliage and, interestingly, slugs devour the leaves of *Veratrum* as they do hosta.

FLOWER: Yellowish-green flowers, 1″ wide, are borne in large, 18″–24″ long pubescent panicles found at the terminal of the stem.

HABIT: Upright habit with leaves occurring the length of the stem. It is 2′ to 6′ tall and 2′ wide.

SEASON OF BLOOM: Summer.

CULTURE: The native habitat for this genus is in moist to wet soils. High heat and humidity are not conducive to optimum growth with best growth occurring in northern areas. Leaves will brown on the edges if the soil dries out and the plant is planted in a windy site in full sun. Partial shade or protection from afternoon sun will help prevent leaf damage. *Veratrum* can also be sited behind other plants to hide the foliage.

UTILIZATION: *Veratrum* should be used in areas where moist to wet conditions are provided. Any area where bog plants can be highlighted is ideal for placement of Indian poke. Members of this genus are more often used in English gardens than they are in North America. Indian poke will grow many years without attention but it is slow to start from seed.

PROPAGATION: Seed and division are suitable. It will take 3 years to develop a flowering specimen from seed. This species requires a warm-cold-warm stratification. This can be done in the field or cold greenhouse. Division in fall or spring is also an effective method for increasing this species.

DISEASES AND INSECTS: Slugs find this species a most tasty morsel. Slug bait needs to be applied as soon as the foliage emerges in the spring.

HARDINESS: It is cold hardy to zones 7 and 8 but heat tolerance is better in zones 4 to 6.

ADDITIONAL NOTES: There are 20 to 45 species of this genus with very few commercially available. European sources list *V. album* (whitish green flowers), *V. nigrum* (dark purple flowers), and *V. californicum* but they are seldom seen in North America. The root and foliage are poisonous.

Native to North America.   Perennial

SCIENTIFIC NAME/FAMILY: *Verbascum chaixii*   Scrophulariaceae

(vĕr-bask'kum shā-zē-i)

COMMON NAME: Chaix Mullein

LEAVES: Leaves are alternate, 6" long, and coarsely toothed. The stems and leaves are gray tomentose.

FLOWER: The flowers are borne in erect, terminal racemes atop slim stems. Individual flowers are ½" to 1" wide, yellow with purple, woolly stamens that create an "eye" in the flowers. Flower parts are in 5's.

HABIT: 3' columnar perennial that arises from large, gray basal leaves. Plants have an 18"–24" spread.

SEASON OF BLOOM: Summer.

CULTURE: Easily grown in full sun or partial shade in well-drained soil. Mullein will do poorly in wet or cold soils.

UTILIZATION: Good plant for the border due to its tall, columnar habit.   *See color plate*

PROPAGATION: Chaix mullein can be propagated by root cuttings in spring or seed. Cuttings should be utilized for propagating cultivars since the flower colors from seed are variable. Seed should be germinated at 65° to 75°F in a moist, but not wet, germination medium.

DISEASES AND INSECTS: Members of this genus are prone to spider mite damage in hot areas.

HARDINESS: Zones 5–8.

CULTIVARS:
'Album'—White flowers, 3–4 feet. The white flowers combined with the gray foliage is a very effective color combination present on one plant.

RELATED SPECIES:
V. × *hybridum* (hī'brid-um)—Members of this group were derived from crosses of species including *V. olympicum* and *V. phoeniceum*. Most are short-lived plants with hairy leaves and tall flowers spikes. Flowers appear in late spring and early summer and cutting back will induce additional inflorescences. Plant height is 3–4 feet.
'Cotswold' Hybrids—Cultivars in this group are 3'–4' tall and should be produced from root cuttings to maintain true flower colors. 'Cotswold Gem' has rosy flowers with purple centers; 'Cotswold Beauty' has yellow flowers with a lilac eye; and 'Cotswold Queen' has bronze-salmon flowers with maroon stamens.

'Gainsborough'—Sulfur-colored flowers and gray-green leaves. Normal height is 3'-4' tall but in highly fertile soils plants will be 5' tall.

'Hartleyi'—Yellow flowers with purple eyes, 4' tall.

'Mont Blanc'—Pure white flowers with woolly gray foliage, 3' tall.

'Pink Domino'—Rose-pink flowers on stems 3 to 4 feet tall.

V. olympicum (o-lim'-pik-um)—Olympic Mullein. This bold perennial has entire, white, woolly leaves that are 6"–8" long. They are arranged in a basal rosette which makes the plant attractive even when not in flower. The yellow flowers are present in the summer for 6–8 weeks. Rebloom will occur in the fall if spent blossoms are removed. Olympic mullein is a dramatic plant for the back of the border. This species is normally 4'–5' tall but if grown in rich soil it can soar to 7'–8' tall. Hardy in zones 6–8.

V. phoeniceum (fen-ĭk'-ē-um)—Purple Mullein. The basal rosettes on this species contain lobed, dark green, crinkled leaves. Plants are 3'–4' with unbranched stems bearing rose-pink to purple flowers. Zones 6–8.

Native to Europe.   Perennial

SCIENTIFIC NAME/FAMILY: *Verbena × hybrida* (*V. × hortensis*)   Verbenaceae

(vĕr-bē'nȧ hīb'ri-dȧ)

COMMON NAME: Garden Verbena

LEAVES: Opposite, oblong to oblong-ovate, 2"–4" long, broadened or truncate at base, margins obtusely dentate or slightly lobed at the base.

FLOWER: Heads flattish or convex to 2" across, long peduncled, petals have deeply notched lobes, and the flowers have distinct white or yellow centers. Flower colors are white, pink, red, blue, lavender, or purple.

HABIT: 12" tall with spread of 18"–24". There are two types of growth habit: upright or spreading.

SEASON OF BLOOM: Summer.

CULTURE: Garden verbena is easily grown in full sun and a well-drained soil. During periods of prolonged heat and drought, verbena will often cease blooming. Watering during these periods aids flowering, but it is cooler weather that promotes a return to profuse flowering.

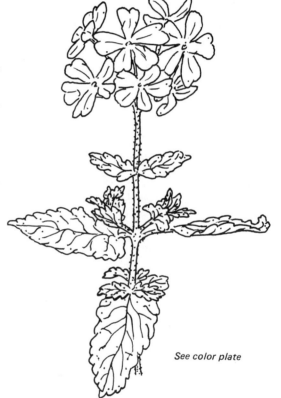

UTILIZATION: Ground cover, beds, edging, rock garden, window boxes, and hanging baskets.

PROPAGATION: Seed of garden verbena is difficult to germinate. Seed should be prechilled for 7 days before seeding. Seeds should be covered and germinated in the dark at 70°F. Seeds are sensitive to moisture. Keep the germination medium on the dry side and watch for symptoms of damping off.

See color plate

DISEASES AND INSECTS: Damping off.

CULTIVARS:
'Amethyst'—6"–9" tall spreading plant with violet-blue flowers with small white eyes.
'Amour' Series—8" tall cultivar with basal-branching available in 6 colors and a mixture. The florets form a large ball-shaped flower head atop the upright plants.
'Blaze'—Large, fiery scarlet-red flowers cover spreading plants.
'Blue Lagoon'—Excellent blue flowers cover compact plants. This selection is later flowering.
'Crystal'—Pure white flowers.
'Delight'—Coral-pink flowers.
'Imagination'—This 1993 AAS award winner has deep violet blue/magenta flowers over lacy foliage. The spread of this cultivar is 24". It is an excellent summer ground cover for sunny areas.
'Novalis' Series—An early flowering, compact cultivar which tolerates summer heat. There are 7 separate colors available.
'Peaches N' Cream'—Unique blend of pastel colors of salmon and apricot cover the top of this heat tolerant verbena. It spreads 10"–12" and grows well in full sun. It has the 1992 AAS and Fleuroselect Gold Medal award.

'Romance' Series—This group contains compact selections which have low, dense spreading habits. Five colors and a mix are available.

'Sandy' Series—Upright habit, 8"–10", early bloom, 7 color choices.

'Showtime' Series—Bright colors are displayed on plants 10" tall and 14" wide.

'Springtime Mix'—Good uniformity in color mix. Early flowering, 10"–12" tall.

'Trinidad'—Compact selection with rose-pink flowers.

ADDITIONAL NOTES: Garden verbenas are popular and attractive bedding plants that are fairly dependable. Verbenas are divided into two distinct classes. The spreading type is procumbent, while the upright type is free branching with a bushy habit. *Verbena* is the Latin name for leaves and shoots of laurel and myrtle.

Hybrid origin.   Annual

SCIENTIFIC NAME/FAMILY: *Verbena rigida (V. venosa)*   Verbenaceae

(ver-bē'na rij'i-dà)

COMMON NAME: Rigid Verbena

LEAVES: Opposite; rigid, hispid, oblong to oblong-lanceolate, 2" to 4" long. The leaf margins are strongly serrated. The leaf bases are sessile or partially clasping. The stems are four angled.

FLOWER: The purplish-blue flowers are ¼" wide and are clustered in a 1"–3" long spike that is part of a terminal panicle.

HABIT: Erect plant with rigid, branching stems, 18"–24" tall and 18" wide.

SEASON OF BLOOM: Early summer to fall.

CULTURE: Easily grown in full sun in a well-drained soil.

UTILIZATION: *Verbena rigida* is a tender perennial that can be grown in northern areas as a bedding plant. It is not well known, but should be. The flowering is continuous during the summer and it is fairly drought tolerant.

PROPAGATION: Cuttings will work in mild climate areas. However, seeds germinate quickly, and it flowers 4 months after seeding.

DISEASES AND INSECTS: No notable problems.

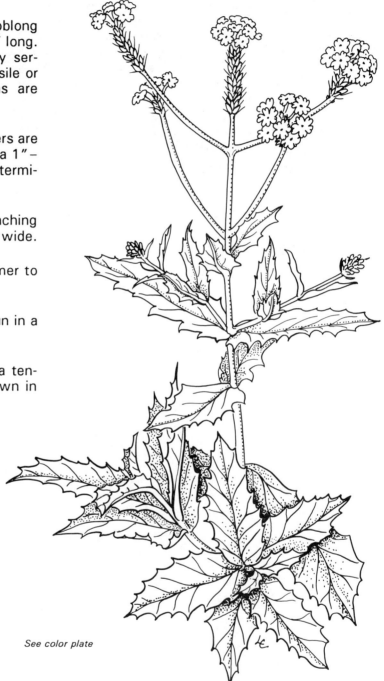

See color plate

HARDINESS: Zones 8–10. Mulching heavily in the fall may extend the hardiness to Zone 7.

CULTIVARS:
'Polaris'—12" tall, bluish-white flowers.

RELATED SPECIES:

V. bonariensis (bon-ar-ē-en'-sis) — Brazilian Verbena. This South American native looks like a giant *Verbena rigida*. Plants are 3'–4' tall and can be taller in highly fertile soils. Severe pruning will be required in these instances. The rose-violet flowers are produced throughout the summer into the fall. Powdery mildew can be a problem. Regardless of this problem, Brazilian verbena is an excellent plant for the middle border of Southern gardens. Zones 7–9.

V. canadensis (kan-a-den'-sis) — Clump Verbena. This species has pubescent stems which grow along the ground with the stem ends turned upward. The deeply lobed ovate leaves are 3"–4" long and have wedge-shaped bases. Bold clusters of rose-pink flowers are borne throughout the summer and autumn. It should be planted in well-drained soils in sunny locations. In northern areas clump verbena is used as an annual. In zones 6–10 it assumes a perennial character. Clump verbena is suited for a low plant at the front of the border or as a rock garden plant. In the wild, *Verbena canadensis* is variable in flower color and habit of growth.

'Gene Cline' — Rose flowers, 6"–9" tall. Poorly drained soils will lead to low plant vigor.

'Homestead' — Low spreading form with rich deep purple flowers all summer up until frost. The leaves are deep green and scalloped.

Native to South America.   Tender perennial, often used as an annual

SCIENTIFIC NAME/FAMILY: *Verbena tenuisecta* (V. erinoides)   Verbenaceae

(vẽr-bē'nȧ ten-ū-i-sek'ta)

COMMON NAME: Moss Verbena

LEAVES: Numerous decumbent stems have opposite leaves with triangular outlines. The 1"–1½" leaves are divided into linear segments.

FLOWER: The solitary spikes are composed of 5–15 lavender flowers which are 1/2" wide.

HABIT: 8"–12" tall spreader which carpets the ground.

SEASON OF BLOOM: Spring until frost.

CULTURE: Moss verbena is easily grown in full sun and well-drained soil. In warm climates, zones 8–10, it will reseed throughout the garden. Wet soil in winter can foster root rot. Leggy plants can be pruned with a lawnmower at 2" to promote fresh growth.

See color plate

UTILIZATION: This verbena is an excellent summer ground cover. It is a fast grower and will quickly carpet an area. If given protection, moss verbena can be hardy to zone 8. In northern areas, it could be a very good low maintenance annual.

PROPAGATION: Moss verbena is quickly propagated from 2"–3" long terminal cuttings taken at any time during the growing season.

DISEASES AND INSECTS: Spider mites can be an occasional problem.

HARDINESS: Zones 8–10.

CULTIVARS:
'Alba'—White flowers. Does not spread as quickly as the species.

Native to South America.   Perennial

SCIENTIFIC NAME/FAMILY: *Vernonia noveboracensis*   Asteraceae
(Compositae)

(vĕr-nō′ni-a no-ve-bor-a-sēn′-sis)

COMMON NAME: Ironweed

LEAVES: Alternate leaves, linear to linear-lanceolate, 4″–6″ long and 1/2″ wide, entire to serrate margins. Upper leaf surface has a scabrous texture. Leaves below the flower cluster may be opposite.

FLOWER: The terminal inflorescence is composed of several purple-violet flower heads, 1/2″ wide, arranged in a loose, corymbose cyme. In the fall the flowers are followed by purplish, rusty seed clusters.

HABIT: This native United States species has a distinct columnar habit. Ironweed is 4′–6′ tall and 2′ wide. Plants should be spaced on 3′ centers.

SEASON OF BLOOM: Late summer and fall.

CULTURE: Best growth occurs in full sun in

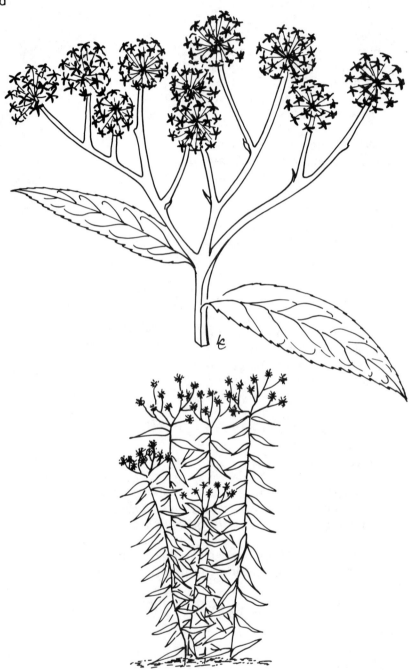

a moist soil with a slightly acid pH. If the plant is cut back to the ground when 2′ tall, it will bloom at a shorter height. This would be an important cultural practice in small gardens where a tall plant would not be in scale.

UTILIZATION: Ironweed is not a perennial in the first tier of usage. However, it does have beautiful violet-purple flowers, which makes it a welcome addition to the garden in late summer. It can be used in perennial borders as well as the meadow or native plant garden. Try this late bloomer with *Rudbeckia* or *Solidago.* It is presently used more in Europe than it is in the United States where it is native.

PROPAGATION: Seed and division in fall or spring. *Vernonia* germinates quickly at 70°F following 3 months stratification at 40°F. Selected forms can also be propagated by cuttings in early summer.

DISEASES AND INSECTS: There are no serious problems.

HARDINESS: Zones 5–9.

RELATED SPECIES:

V. crinita (kri-nī′tà) (V. arkansana)—This species is listed with a mature height of 10′ with 5′ probably more common in cultivation. The flower heads are nearly 1″ in diameter and larger than *V. noveboracensis.*

ADDITIONAL NOTES: There are 17 species of *Vernonia* native to the United States and many intercross to form fertile hybrids. There is certainly opportunity to select better forms of this species. *Vernonia* is named in honor of an early English botanist, William Vernon, who travelled in the United States.

Native to eastern United States from Massachusetts to Florida.   Perennial

SCIENTIFIC NAME/FAMILY: *Veronica austriaca* ssp. *teucrium*   Scrophulariaceae
(*V. teucrium*)

(ve-ron'i-ka as-tri'-a-ka tu'kri-um)

COMMON NAME: Hungarian Speedwell

LEAVES: The opposite leaves are short-petioled near the base and sessile higher on the stem. They are oblong or linear-lanceolate, to 1½" long, and are crenate to sparsely toothed.

FLOWER: The flowers of the species are blue, ½" wide, and are borne in loose racemes originating from the upper leaf axils. Most other ornamental speedwells have flowers in terminal racemes. Individual flowers have a 4–5 parted calyx and a corolla with a short tube and a spreading limb, usually with 4–5 lobes.

HABIT: This speedwell grows to 18" tall but tumbles informally compared to the erect stems of other speedwells. Cultivar selection allows one to choose compact forms.

SEASON OF BLOOM: Late spring to early summer.

CULTURE: Easily grown in well-drained soils in sun or partial shade. Re-bloom will often occur later in summer if this species is trimmed after flowering. The tumbling habit may require that branched twigs be inserted as the plant starts growth in the spring to provide an "internal" support.

See color plate

UTILIZATION: Border or informal naturalized planting. The flowers are very brilliantly colored, and this feature alone makes this speedwell valuable in the landscape.

PROPAGATION: Same as *V. spicata.*

DISEASES AND INSECTS: None serious.

HARDINESS: Zones 3–8.

CULTIVARS:
'Blue Fountain'—Bright blue flowers are borne in racemes which terminate stems that are up to 24" tall.
'Crater Lake Blue'—Bright blue flowers, 12"–15" tall. This is a very good selection for the front of the sunny border.
'Kapitan'—Blue flowers are carried on short spikes, 10" tall.
'Royal Blue'—Deep-blue flowers are carried on dense plants, 12"–18" tall.
'Shirley Blue'—Brilliant blue flowers, 8"–10" tall and 12" wide.
'Trehane'—Dark blue flowers, golden green foliage, 6"–8" tall. This cultivar is very striking with the blue flowers combined with the bright golden foliage.

Native to Europe.   Perennial

SCIENTIFIC NAME/FAMILY: *Veronica prostrata*   Scrophulariaceae

(ve-ron'i-ka pros-tra'ta)

COMMON NAME: Harebell Speedwell

LEAVES: Opposite, linear to ovate, to 1½" long. Margins may be entire or toothed.

FLOWER: Bright blue flowers, ⅓" across, are borne in short, dense, axillary racemes.

HABIT: Prostrate growth habit, flower stems are 8" high.

SEASON OF BLOOM: Late spring to early summer.

CULTURE: Full sun or partial shade and well-drained soil are the optimum growing conditions for this speedwell.

UTILIZATION: The prostrate habit makes this species suitable for the border front.

PROPAGATION: Propagation can be done by division in the spring or fall or by taking terminal cuttings from sterile basal branches during the summer.

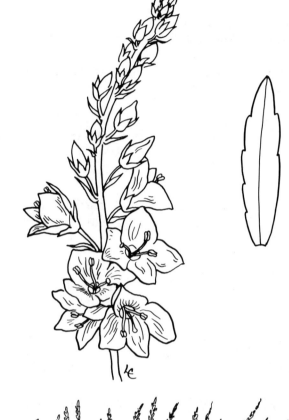

DISEASES AND INSECTS: Downy mildew and leaf spot are sometimes noted but are not serious problems.

HARDINESS: Zones 4–8.

CULTIVARS:
   'Blue Sheen'—Profuse lavender flowers on stems 4" tall.
   'Heavenly Blue'—Deep blue flowers, 4" tall.
   'Loddon Blue'—Dark blue flowers, 4".
   'Mrs. Holt'—This selection has pink flowers and grows to about 6" tall.
   'Spode Blue'—Light blue flowers, 6" tall.

Native to Europe.   Perennial

SCIENTIFIC NAME/FAMILY: *Veronica spicata* (*V. australis*)   Scrophulariaceae

(ve-ron'i-kȧ spī-kā'ta)

COMMON NAME: Spike Speedwell

LEAVES: Opposite, oblong to lanceolate, to 2" long, tapering base, crenate to serrulate margin, except entire at base and apex.

FLOWER: Blue flowers are borne in dense, terminal racemes; pedicels are shorter than the bracts and calyx.

HABIT: Spike speedwell has an upright habit with spikelike racemes. Heights range from 10" to 36" depending upon the cultivar selected. Plant spread is 18" to 24".

SEASON OF BLOOM: Late spring to midsummer. Flowers are produced for 4–8 weeks.

CULTURE: Full sun is preferred, partial shade tolerated. Soil should be moderately fertile and well-drained, particularly in the winter. Plants should be deadheaded for repeat bloom.

UTILIZATION: Quite suitable for midsummer flower in the perennial border, also as cut flowers. There are dwarf and trailing species that have uses on dry rock walls or in rock gardens.

PROPAGATION: Seed, division, and softwood cuttings. Seeds will germinate in 2 weeks from 60°–80°F, but variation in plant type will probably result. Cuttings can be rooted during the summer, while clump division is easily done in spring and fall.

DISEASES AND INSECTS: There are no significant pest problems.

HARDINESS: Zones 3–8.

CULTIVARS:
   var. *alba*—Pure white flower form of the species.
   'Blue Fox' ('Blaufuchs')—Lavender-blue flowers on 15"–20" tall stems.
   'Blue Peter'—18"–24" tall, well-branched plant, with deep blue flowers.
   'Blue Spires'—Blue flowers and glossy green leaves, 18"–24" tall.
   'Heidekind'—Rose-pink flowers on 8"–10" tall plants.
   'Icicle'—This cultivar is one of the best white flowering speedwells. It grows 18"–24" tall and flowers most of the summer. It is probably a hybrid between *V. longifolia* var. *subsessilis* and *V. spicata*.
   'Red Fox' ('Rotfuchs')— Rose-pink flowers are carried on stems 15" tall. It is an excellent flowering selection that remains in bloom for 5–6 weeks.

RELATED SPECIES:
   V. longifolia (long-i-fō'le-a)—Long-leaf Speedwell. This species is taller growing than *V. spicata*. Average height is 30" but if this speedwell is grown in moist, fertile soils, the height can be 4 feet. Plants are in flower for 6–8 weeks. Soils must be moist to maintain optimum performance.

CULTIVARS:
  var. *alba*—White flowers, 18"–24" tall.
  'Blue Giant'—Lavender-blue flowers, 36"–42" tall.
  'Foerster's Blue'—Dark blue flowers last 2 months, 24" tall.
  'Romiley Purple'—Purple flowers on stems 24" tall.
  var. *subsessilis*—Lilac flowers on 2'–3' tall stems. This selection is better branched and more compact than the species.

ADDITIONAL HYBRIDS:
  'Goodness Grows'—This long flowering hybrid is probably a hybrid of *V. alpina* 'Alba' and *V. spicata*. It is low growing, 10"–12", with blue flowers. It originated at Goodness Grows Nursery in Crawford, Georgia. It has proven to be an excellent cultivar.
  'Sunny Border Blue'—This dark blue flowering cultivar was selected from a group of seedlings from crosses of several varieties of *V. spicata* and *V. longifolia.* Robert Bennerup of Sunny Border Nurseries, Inc., of Kensington, Connecticut, made the selection from the above plants obtained from Denmark in 1947. The leaves are a luxurious dark green and wrinkled, bearing some resemblance to spinach leaves. Plants are 18"–24" tall. 'Sunny Border Blue' was the 1993 Perennial Plant of the Year.

ADDITIONAL NOTES: *Veronica* honors St. Veronica.

Native to Europe.   Perennial

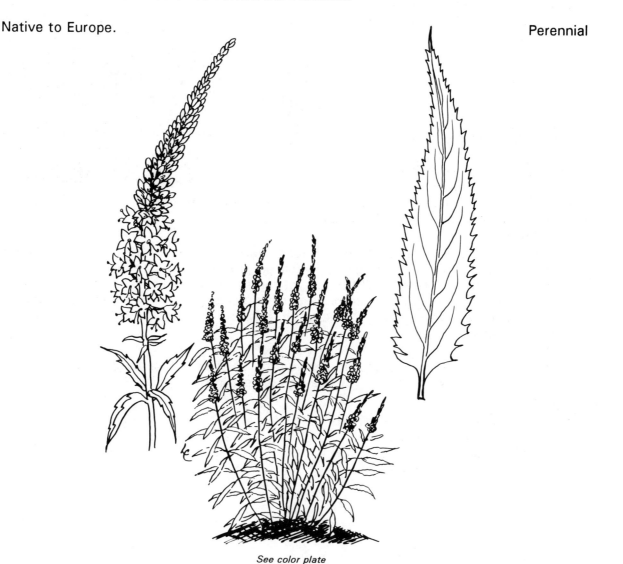

See color plate

SCIENTIFIC NAME/FAMILY: *Veronica spicata* ssp. *incana*   Scrophulariaceae

(ve-ron'i-kȧ spī-kā'ta in-kā'na)

COMMON NAME: Woolly Speedwell

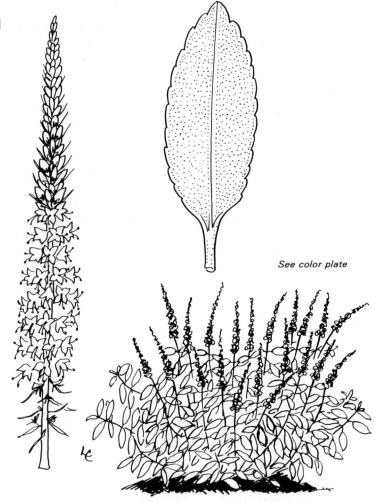

See color plate

LEAVES: The leaves are opposite and have a soft white-tomentose. The lower leaves are oblong and the upper stem leaves are lanceolate. Length varies from 2" to 4". The leaves are petioled and obtusely crenate.

FLOWER: The small (¼") blue flowers are packed tightly into 6" terminal racemes. The individual flowers have a 4- or 5-parted calyx and a rotate corolla that is 4- or 5-lobed.

HABIT: 12"–18" tall clump with ascending stems. The foliage alone is 6" tall. Plants will spread to 18".

SEASON OF BLOOM: Early summer.

CULTURE: Plants perform best in full sun to partial shade in well-drained soils. Performance is reduced in areas with high temperatures and abundant rainfall. The tomentose leaves tend to trap the moisture and diseases develop with the high heat.

UTILIZATION: Woolly speedwell is valued for its foliage, with or without flowers. Together, the blue of the flowers and the gray foliage provide contrast. Without the flowers, woolly speedwell shows well because of the silver mats of foliage. It can be used in rock garden, front of the border, or as an edging plant if the flower stems are removed. In warm climates where the foliage is evergreen, woolly speedwell can be utilized as ground cover.

PROPAGATION: Easily produced by division in fall or spring or by cuttings during the summer. Seed germination of the species is best at 65° to 75°F.

DISEASES AND INSECTS: None serious.

HARDINESS: Zones 3–7.

CULTIVARS:

'Barcarolle'—Rose-pink flowers and gray-green foliage, 12" tall. This selection is from the Blooms of Bressingham Nursery in England and it is a hybrid of *V. spicata* and *V. spicata* ssp. *incana.*

'Minuet'—Bright pink flowers and silver leaves, 12" tall. 'Minuet' has similar parentage to 'Barcarolle' although the foliage is more silver on 'Minuet'.

'Nana'—Violet-blue flowers, gray-green leaves, 8" tall.

'Saraband'—Violet-blue flowers and gray leaves, 12"–18" tall.

'Wendy'—Lavender-blue flowers, gray-green leaves, 18"–24" tall.

Native to Russia.   Perennial

SCIENTIFIC NAME/FAMILY: *Veronicastrum virginicum*   Scrophulariaceae
(*Veronica virginica*)

(ve-ron'i-kás'trum vĕr-jin'-ik-kum)

COMMON NAME: Culver's Root, Black Root, Bowman's Root

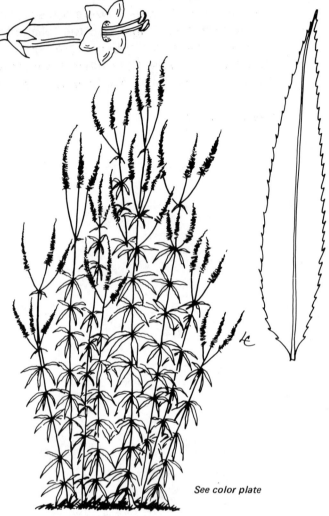

LEAVES: The leaves are whorled in groups of five. Leaves are lanceolate to oblong-lanceolate, to 6" long with toothed margins. The nodes of whorled leaves are parallel, which presents a strong horizontal effect.

FLOWER: The white flowers are borne in dense, erect racemes that can reach 9" long. Individual flowers are small (⅛") with a 4- to 5-parted calyx, a salverform corolla with the tube being much longer than the lobes. Flowers may sometimes be a pale lavender.

HABIT: Culver's root has a very distinct vertical habit, much taller than wide and is 3'–6' tall.

SEASON OF BLOOM: Late summer.

CULTURE: This native of eastern United States is easily grown in sun or partial shade in ordinary, well-drained soil. Occasional division may be needed to reduce the size of older plants.

See color plate

UTILIZATION: The strong vertical and horizontal aspects of this species allow it to be used as a strong accent in the perennial or mixed shrub border. It would also be useful as a background plant.

PROPAGATION: This species can be propagated by seed, division or cuttings. Seeds should be thinly covered and germinated at 65–70°F. Germination will usually take 3–4 weeks. Division in spring and terminal cuttings in the summer are also suitable.

DISEASES AND INSECTS: None serious.

HARDINESS: Zones 3–8.

CULTIVARS:
var. *alba*—Pure white flowers with dark green foliage. This is an attractive variety that should be used more often.
var. *rosea*—Pale-pink flowers.

ADDITIONAL NOTES: The taxonomists keep moving this species back and forth between *Veronicastrum* and *Veronica*. In the last edition, it was a Veronica. It may well change before the fifth edition is printed.

Native to eastern United States.   Perennial

SCIENTIFIC NAME/FAMILY: *Viola odorata*   Violaceae

(vī'ō-là ō-dō-rā'tà)

COMMON NAME: Sweet Violet, Garden Violet, Florist's Violet, English Violet

LEAVES: Leaves are cordate-ovate to reniform, 1″ to 2″ wide, obtusely serrated, and are often finely pubescent. The often leafy, persistent stipules are ovate-lanceolate.

FLOWER: The fragrant flowers are about ¾″ across and are deep violet, sometimes rose or white. The flowers are borne on peduncles that arise directly from the base or crown. The irregularly symmetrical flowers have 5 petals and 5 sepals. Cleistogamous flowers are often produced.

HABIT: 6″ to 8″ tall, broad, tufted clump, 12″–15″ wide.

SEASON OF BLOOM: Spring.

CULTURE: Sweet violet performs best in a cool, partially shaded site with a well-drained soil high in organic matter. Leaf mold or other compost materials should be dug into the soil. Moisture is needed frequently during the growing season.

UTILIZATION: This plant has a function in almost any garden. It can be used for edging, for limited massing, a specimen plant in the rock garden or border, or as a wildflower in a naturalized site. Although the flower stems are short, the flowers are often utilized as cut flowers. In moist, fertile sites, these stoloniferous plants will spread quickly and may become weedy. One should keep this in mind in site selection.

PROPAGATION: Sweet violet can be propagated by offsets, division, or seed. Offsets can be removed in early spring and rooted in sand. Seeds can be sown outside in the fall and will germinate in the spring. Seeds germinated indoors in the spring will produce flowering plants for the summer. Germination takes 2 to 3 weeks. Division should be carefully done in the spring.

DISEASES AND INSECTS: Anthracnose, downy mildew, leaf spots, crown rot, cutworms, and slugs.

HARDINESS: Zones 5–8.

CULTIVARS:
'Czar'—Violet flowers, early bloom.
'Duchesse de Parme'—This is one member of the Parma violets which are hybrids believed to be derived from *V. odorata* or *V. alba*. This group is characterized by fragrant, double flowers borne on long stems. 'Duchesse de Parme' has lavender-violet flowers; 'Lady Hume Campbell' has mauve flowers; 'Marie Louise' has dark violet-mauve flowers, and 'Swanley White' has pure white flowers.
'Queen Charlotte' ('Konigin Charlotte')—Dark blue flowers, 6″–8″ tall.
'Rosina'—Free-flowering selection with rose-pink flowers with maroon eyes.

RELATED SPECIES:

V. cornuta, (kor-nu'-a)—Horned Violet, Tufted Violet. The leaves are subcordate-ovate and crenately serrate. The leaves are subtended by large, triangular-shaped stipules. Horned violet is 4"–10" tall and has a peak bloom in spring with rebloom occurring if old blossoms are removed. Zones 6–9.

CULTIVARS

'Arkwright Ruby'—Maroon flowers with a darker blotch.

'Jersey Gem'—Long-stemmed purple flowers.

'Lord Nelson,'—Small violet flower with yellow eyes.

'Scottish Yellow'—Large golden yellow flowers.

'White Perfection'—White flowers, 6"–8" tall plants.

V. cucullata (ku-kū-lā'-ta) (V. obliqua)—Marsh Blue Violet. The flowers and leaves of this species arise from the roots creating a stemless plant. The leaves are ovate to heart-shaped, 3" or more across, and are borne on 3"–5" long petioles. The pale violet flowers appear in spring. The lower petal has purple veins while the laterals are bearded. Marsh blue violet can be used in moist, shaded areas. It self-sows easily and can become a nuisance. Zones 4–9.

'Freckles'—Pale blue flowers conspicuously speckled with purple spots.

'Red Giant'—Rose-red flowers, 6" to 8" tall.

'Royal Robe'—Dark violet-blue flowers, 6" tall.

'White Czar'—White flower with a yellow eye, 6" tall.

V. pedata, (pe-dā'tȧ), Bird's Foot Violet. This native violet is 2"–6" tall with 5-petaled flowers. The upper two petals are violet, and the lower three are lavender. The common name refers to the palmately dissected leaves. *Viola pedata* requires full sun or partial shade in a low-nutrient, well-drained soil. Adding sandy or gritty mix to the soil is recommended. This species needs good drainage and should be planted on a slope or surrounded by coarse sand or pea gravel. If this requirement is not met, bird's foot violet will develop crown rot. Zones 4–9.

V. tricolor, (trī'kul-er), Johnny-jump-up. This annual or short-lived perennial has ovate to lanceolate leaves which are cuneate at the bases. The leaf margins are crenate. The blossoms resemble "smiling faces" with three colors of deep violet, light blue, and gold. It is native to Europe and has naturalized in the United States.

Native to Europe, Asia, and Africa.   Perennial

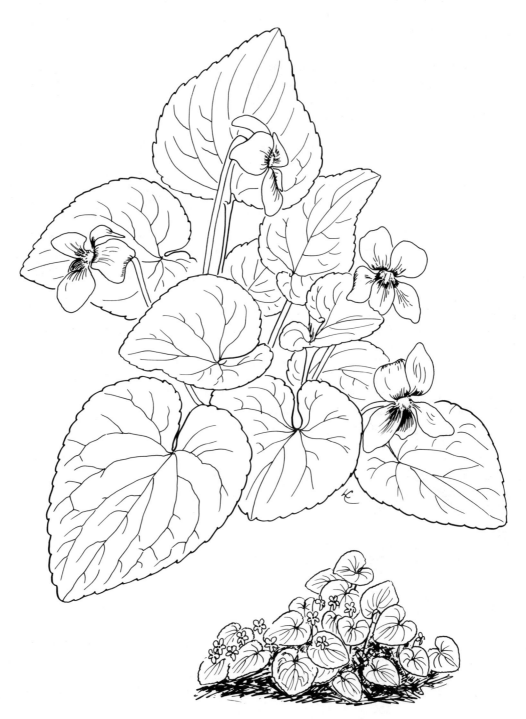

See color plate

SCIENTIFIC NAME/FAMILY: *Viola* × *wittrockiana*   Violaceae

(vī'ō-lá wit-rock-i-ā'ná)

COMMON NAME: Pansy, Ladies-Delight

LEAVES: Basal leaves round, cordate; stem leaves ovate-oblong or lanceolate, crenate-dentate, petioled, the large stipules are pinnately parted toward the base. Leaves 1½″ to 2″.

FLOWER: Flowers large, 1″–2″ across, usually having three colors, petals are nearly orbicular in shape and overlap. Pattern on flower resembles a smiling face. Flower colors are purple, white, blue, dark red, rose, sienna, apricot, brown, or yellow combinations.

HABIT: 4″–8″ tall and 12″ wide.

SEASON OF BLOOM: Spring to early summer in northern climate. Fall and spring in southern zones.

CULTURE: Sun to partial shade; soils should be cool, moist, and well-drained. Pansy is a cool-season plant, and summer heat will often reduce flowering. Keep well watered and remove faded flowers for continued bloom.

UTILIZATION: Borders, edging, window boxes, cut flowers, early bedding. Pansy is a good early bedding plant in northern areas and a fall bedding plant in warmer climates.

PROPAGATION: Best germination occurs when seeds are kept dark and grown at 65°F. After germination, grow at 50°F. The seeds should be moistened and chilled at 40°–45°F for 1 week before sowing.

DISEASES AND INSECTS: Anthracnose, crown rot, leaf spots, stem rot, and slugs.

CULTIVARS: F_1 hybrids are popular because they usually have larger flowers, are more vigorous, earlier flowering, and more heat tolerant than F_2 hybrids or non-hybrid pansies. The following is a partial listing of cultivars:
'Crown'—This selection has 4″ wide, clear blossoms with no blotches, available in 9 colors.
'Crystal Bowl'—Clear-faced hybrid with early flowering and heavy bloom. It is available in 9 colors.
'Happy Face'—Attractive blotched flowers highlight this hybrid with 2½″ wide blooms, 6 colors.
'Imperial'—This series has both clear and blotched faces available in many colors. Plants are uniform and have good heat tolerance.
'Majestic'—The cultivars of this group have flowers up to 4″ across and bloom for long periods. A large color choice is available.
'Maxim'—Strong blooming pansy with 2½″ wide, blotched flowers. Noted for good heat tolerance.

'Springtime'—A wide range of individual colors highlights this series. It has good heat tolerance and a uniform habit of growth.

'Universal'—Early flowering, multiflora type, with excellent weather tolerance for cool and warm climates. Full color range includes both blotched and clear faces.

ADDITIONAL NOTES: *Viola* is the ancient Latin name for violet.

Hybrid origin. Annual

SCIENTIFIC NAME/FAMILY: *Waldsteinia fragarioides*   Rosaceae

(wâld-stīn'i-ȧ frȧ-gā'ri-oi''dēz)

COMMON NAME: Barren Strawberry

LEAVES: Basal leaves long petioled, 3 leaflets palmately compound; leaflets wedge shaped, dentate, or crenate at the apex, sometimes incised. Leaves are similar to the true strawberry, *Fragaria × ananassa*, 1" to 3".

FLOWER: Yellow flowers in 3–8 flowered corymbs borne on scapes, which appear above the foliage. The flowers have 5 sepals and 5 petals. The small fruit are inedible.

HABIT: This tufted perennial is 4"–6" tall forming a mat that is 18"–24" wide.

SEASON OF BLOOM: Late spring to early summer.

CULTURE: Barren strawberry tolerates a wide variety of soils. I have seen this plant growing equally well in partial shade or full sun. Peak performance occurs in cool climates.

UTILIZATION: *Waldsteinia* has a nice, clean-looking foliage that can be used as a low-growing ground cover. It spreads slowly by short rhizomes and stolons; consequently, it performs well as an edging plant for the herbaceous or shrub border.

PROPAGATION: Easily propagated by division of the rhizome or terminal tip cuttings.

DISEASES AND INSECTS: None serious.

HARDINESS: Zones 4–7.

RELATED SPECIES:

Duchesnea indica (dū-kes'nē-ȧ in'di-ka)—Mock Strawberry, Indian Strawberry—The foliage features of *Duchesnea* are similar to those of *Waldsteinia.* However, these two differences can be noted: *Duchesnea* has 15 or more pistils and will produce a red fruit, while *Waldsteinia* has 2–5 pistils and smaller fruit. *Waldsteinia* is sometimes sold as *Duchesnea. Duchesnea* is a rampant spreader that can even invade turf areas. It should not be planted near smaller perennials.

W. ternata (ter-na'-ta)—Siberian Barren Strawberry. This species is similar to *W. fragarioides* except that *W. ternata* has a more compact habit.

ADDITIONAL NOTES: *Waldsteinia* was named for Count Franz Adam Waldstein-Wartenburg, an Austrian botanist (1759-1823).

Native to northeastern United States.   Perennial

SCIENTIFIC NAME/FAMILY: *Xanthisma texana*   Asteraceae
                                                             (Compositae)

(zan-thiz′má or zan-this′-ma tek-san′á)

COMMON NAME: Star-of-Texas, Sleepy
   Daisy

LEAVES: Alternate, leaves mostly sessile
   oblong to lanceolate, the lower leaves
   to 2½″ long, pinnatifid; the upper
   leaves are much smaller and entire.

FLOWER: Heads 1″–2½″ across, disk
   and ray flowers yellow; ray flowers
   close at night.

HABIT: 18″ to 30″, round habit.

SEASON OF BLOOM: Summer.

CULTURE: Star-of-Texas is native to dry,
   open prairies which makes it well-
   suited to hot, dry areas with well-
   drained soils.

UTILIZATION: Naturalized gardens or
   open areas which have stress conditions.

PROPAGATION: Seeds can be started in
   a greenhouse or sown directly in final
   location. Seeds germinate at 70°–
   75°F after 3–4 weeks.

DISEASES AND INSECTS: Usually none.

ADDITIONAL NOTES: Staking is sometimes needed if plants are in an exposed location. *Xanthisma* is derived
   from *xanthos*, yellow, which describes the flower color. Star-of-Texas
   is a little-known annual and will rarely be found for sale except through
   some seed catalogs.

Native to Texas.   Annual

SCIENTIFIC NAME/FAMILY: *Yucca filamentosa*   Agavaceae

(yuk′à fil-à-men-tō′sà)

COMMON NAME: Yucca, Adam's Needle, Needle Palm, Spanish Bayonet

LEAVES: Many leaves in a basal rosette, to 2½′ long, 1″ wide, spatulate, abruptly narrowed to a stout terminal spine, margins with long, curly threads.

FLOWER: Inflorescence is a stout scape, 3′–12′ high; a long panicle with spreading or ascending branches, flowers many, hanging, nearly white, and 1″–2″ long. The scapes of the cultivars are usually 3′ to 5′ tall.

HABIT: 2′ to 3′ tall foliage, scape is 3′–12′. Basal rosette has a round growth habit, flowering scape is erect.

SEASON OF BLOOM: Early to midsummer.

CULTURE: Full sun, light-textured soil with good drainage. The yucca is noted for its drought resistance.

UTILIZATION: Specimen plant in border or as specimens among shrubbery.

PROPAGATION: Seeds germinate slowly at 55°F and require 4–5 years to flower. Offsets growing from the base of the plant can be removed and handled as cuttings; sections of the old stems may be placed on sand in a warm greenhouse, and new side shoots that develop can be removed and planted. Vegetatively produced plants will flower more quickly.

DISEASES AND INSECTS: Yucca is subject to few diseases or insects. Leaf blight and leaf spot are occasional problems.

HARDINESS: Zones 5–10.

CULTIVARS:
'Bright Edge'—Variegated gold edge on leaf margin.
'Golden Sword'—Middle of the leaf is yellow with a green leaf margin.

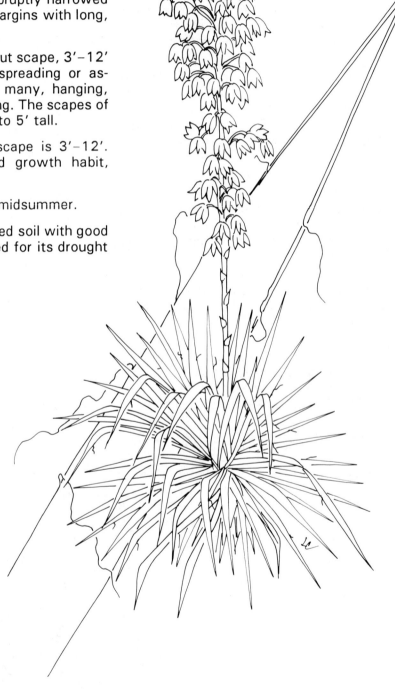

RELATED SPECIES:

Y. flaccida (flak'sid-a) 'Ivory Tower'. Leaves are less rigid than *Y. filamentosa,* and the white flowers face upright in the panicle.

Y. glauca (glā'ka), Soapweed. Soapweed is more refined than *Y. filamentosa.* The leaves are narrow (½") and quite linear to 24" long. All leaves have a white or greenish white margin with long threads. Greenish cream flowers, which are often tinged rosy brown are borne on shorter stems and flower earlier than *Y. filamentosa.* Soapweed is an excellent choice for the rock garden. It is the hardiest of the yuccas.

ADDITIONAL NOTES: The genus *Yucca* is the native name for Manihot, which belongs to the Euphorbiaceae family. However, it was erroneously applied to the members of the above genus.

Native to the warm regions of North America.   Perennial

SCIENTIFIC NAME/FAMILY: *Zantedeschia aethiopica*   Araceae

(zan-tē-des'ki-ȧ ē-thi-ō'-pi-kȧ)

COMMON NAME: Calla Lily, Arum Lily, Garden Calla, Trumpet Lily, Lily of the Nile

LEAVES: Long petioled basal leaves and flower stalks arise from thick rhizomes as this plant has no stems. The dark green leaves are sagittate (arrow-shaped), often 15"–18" long and 8"–10" wide. However, leaf size can vary.

FLOWER: The white spathe is 6"–10" with a large trumpet-shaped flare. The yellow spadix is fragrant and about 1/3 the length of the spathe. Most people are probably familiar with the flower shape and color because of its extensive use in the florist industry, particularly for funerals and weddings. The spathe is borne on a leafless stalk (scape).

HABIT: Erect clump composed of leaves and flower stalks, 24"–36" tall and 24" wide.

SEASON OF BLOOM: Late spring to early summer.

CULTURE: Calla lily is grown from a tender rhizome. In areas where the winter temperature are 20°F or lower, the rhizomes should be lifted in the fall. Plant the rhizomes 4" deep and 18" apart. Best growth will be in partial shade but it is tolerant to full sun. Calla lily is excellent for water and can be planted in bog areas or along streams. The soil should be abundantly amended with organic matter. This species will survive winter temperatures if planted in the mud below the freeze line of the water.

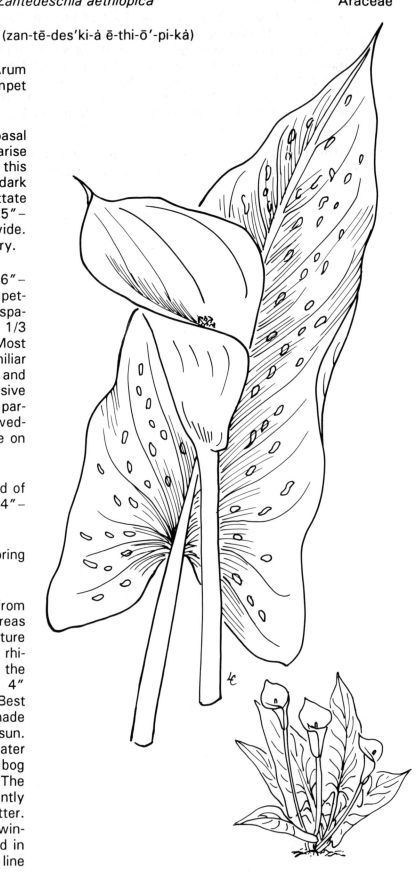

UTILIZATION: In warm climates, calla lily is found in the border. It is also used as a container plant and as a cut flower. A shallow pond or pool is an excellent site for displaying calla lilies.

PROPAGATION: Propagation is by separation of the cormels that form readily. Seed can also be collected and sown in the fall, with germination occurring in 2–3 months.

DISEASES AND INSECTS: Leaf spot fungi can appear but are usually controlled by removing any leaves showing the problem.

HARDINESS: Zones 9–10.

CULTIVARS:

var. *childsiana*—Dwarf selection with more flowers than the species. It is often the plant of choice for the greenhouse industry.

'Crowborough'—A more cold hardy type with greater tolerance to sun. It was found in Crowborough, England.

'Green Goddess'—This selection has a greenish spathe and white throat. A good plant for flower arrangers.

'Little Gem'—This 12"–18" dwarf was introduced in 1890. It has a good fragrance and is suitable for a patio container.

RELATED SPECIES:

Z. albo-maculata (albo-mak-ū-lā'ta)—The white spathes are more trumpet shaped versus the flared shape found in *Z. aethiopica.* Leaves are arrow shaped, 12"–18" long, 3"–6" wide, with white translucent spots. 2 to 3 feet tall.

Z. elliottiana (el-i-ot-i-ā'na)—This selection, introduced in 1896, has bright yellow spathes that are 6" long. The leaves are dark green with silver-white spots. It is not as hardy as *Z. aethiopica.* 2 feet tall.

Z. rehmannii (rā-man'ė-i)—Spathe color ranges from white to shades of pink to deep maroon. The leaves are lanceolate with a tapered leaf base rather than a lobed base. 12"–18" tall.

ADDITIONAL NOTES: The genus honors the Italian botanist and physician, Giovanni Zantedeschi.

Native to South Africa.   Tender rhizome

SCIENTIFIC NAME/FAMILY: *Zauschneria californica*   Onagraceae

(zȧsh-nēr'-i-a kal-if-or'-nik-a)

COMMON NAME: California False Fuchsia

LEAVES: Leaves are linear to lance-olate, sessile, and ¾"–1½" long. The lower leaves are opposite while the upper are alternate. Foliage varies from green to gray-green and it is pubescent. The leaves of *Z. californica* ssp. *latifolia* are ovate to ovate-lanceolate. The subspecies does not have pubescent foliage.

FLOWER: The fuchsia-like flowers are bright scarlet. 1"–2" long, and borne in a raceme. Each flower has 4 petals and is funnel-shaped.

HABIT: Spreading, many-branched, dense plant 12"–24" tall and 18" wide.

SEASON OF BLOOM: Late summer.

CULTURE: This drought tolerant plant performs well in a full sun to partial shade location and well-drained soil. Excess winter moisture is a particular problem.

UTILIZATION: Use in the rock garden or front of the border.

PROPAGATION: Propagate by seed or cuttings. Seed germinates best when kept in moist conditions at 75°F. Germination usually takes 2–3 weeks. Tip cuttings can be taken in early summer.

DISEASES AND INSECTS: No serious problems.

HARDINESS: Zones 7–10.

CULTIVARS:
'Dublin'—Compact version of species, 12"–18" tall.
'Glasnevin'—This cultivar of unknown parentage has been promoted by Alan Bloom. According to Mr. Bloom, he discovered this bright red flowering selection in the Glasnevin Botanic Garden near Dublin in 1958. He named it 'Glasnevin'. It is 24" tall and a vigorous grower.
ssp. *latifolia*—This selection is listed as being hardier than the species.

Native to California.   Perennial

SCIENTIFIC NAME/FAMILY: *Zinnia elegans*

Asteraceae
(Compositae)

(zin'i-à el'e-ganz)

COMMON NAME: Zinnia

LEAVES: Opposite, sessile, more or less clasping, cordate-ovate to elliptic, 1½"–4" long and 1"–2" wide, rough-hispid.

FLOWER: Heads large, to 6" across in many cultivars, receptacle scaly, ray flowers broad and showy, becoming reflexed, disk flowers in most cultivars usually absent. Flower colors are rose, apricot, red, white, violet, pale yellow, green, orange, with bi-colors. Flowers can be single or double.

HABIT: Less than 1' up to 3', often with blossoms 5"–7" diameter, round or erect growth habit.

SEASON OF BLOOM: Best from early to midsummer.

CULTURE: Sun—likes hot, dry weather; the drier the weather, the less the amount of mildew.

UTILIZATION: Borders, edging, cut flowers; all purpose annual.

PROPAGATION: Good germination occurs at temperatures of 75°–80°F.

DISEASES AND INSECTS: Powdery mildew, blight, root and stem rots, Japanese beetle, and mites. Sun, good air circulation, and dry weather help prevent mildew. A fungicide can be used as a preventative measure.

See color plate

CULTIVARS: Zinnia is a very popular bedding annual. There are many cultivars from which to choose and they are classified by height. The following cultivars are examples of this diversity.
Small
'Buttons'—12"–14" tall; flowers are 1½" diameter; available in cherry, pink, red, yellow, and a mix.
'Dasher'—10"–12" tall; double and semidouble flowers; 3" to 3½" in diameter. 'Dasher Scarlet' is a Fleuroselect Medal winner.
'Dreamland'—12" tall, dense rounded habit, double flowers available in 6 colors.
'Peter Pan'—10"–12" tall; uniform, free-flowering plants with large blossoms, 3½" to 5" wide; eight colors and a mix.
'Pulcino'—12"–15" tall; fluffy double flowers are 2½" wide; 6 colors plus a mix.
'Thumbelina'—This extra dwarf series is only 6" tall. It is a good plant for edging. Blossoms are 1" to 1½" wide.

Medium

'Lilliput'—18"–24" tall, good for cut flowers. Blossoms are double and 1½" to 2" wide.

'Sun'—18"–24" tall; double dahlia-like blossoms to 4" wide. 'Gold Sun' and 'Red Sun' are choices.

'Yellow Marvel'—15"–18" tall; bright yellow flowers, 2½" diameter.

Tall

'Big Top Mixture'—30" tall; highlighted by large cactus-flowered blossoms, which can be 6"–8" wide.

'Envy'—30"; unusual chartreuse-green colored flowers.

'Fruit Bowl'—36"; mixture of giant cactus-flowered blossoms.

'Ruffles'—24"–30" tall; 2½" diameter blooms are excellent for cutting.

'State Fair'—30"–36" tall; tetraploid hybrid; 5" to 6" diameter blooms are carried on thick, sturdy stems.

RELATED SPECIES:

Z. angustifolia (an-gus-ti-fo'li-a) (also listed as *Z. linearis*) Leaves of this member of the *Zinnia* genus are linear or linear-lanceolate, 3/4" long and 1/16" wide. Plants are 6"–12" tall with 1½" wide, orange flowers. The spreading habit of this species makes this zinnia an excellent choice as a ground cover or border plant. Plants are in flower from late spring until frost. 'Classic Golden Orange' and 'Classic White' are improved choices.

ADDITIONAL NOTES: Few kinds of bedding plants are as easily grown, enjoy as much popularity, or show such a diversity of colors and types as the zinnia. *Zinnia* is named for Johann Gottfried Zinn, an 18th century professor of botany.

Native to Mexico.   Annual